THE CENTURY PHILOSOPHY SERIES

STERLING P. LAMPRECHT, *Editor*

READINGS IN PHILOSOPHICAL
ANALYSIS

READINGS IN
PHILOSOPHICAL
ANALYSIS

SELECTED AND EDITED BY

HERBERT FEIGL AND WILFRID SELLARS

DEPARTMENT OF PHILOSOPHY

UNIVERSITY OF MINNESOTA

New York

APPLETON - CENTURY - CROFTS, INC.

PRINTED IN THE UNITED STATES OF AMERICA

PREFACE

One of the perennial complaints of philosophy teachers has concerned the dearth of readily accessible and worthwhile reading material in modern philosophical analysis. As a first step toward improving this situation we have prepared the present volume of selections. Our idea was this: In the tremendous bulk of the periodical literature of recent decades, there is a small percentage of articles definitely worthy of reproduction in an anthology. This material required only proper grouping to provide a usable text for intermediate and advanced courses or seminars.

The project in preliminary form was presented by circular letter to about ninety teachers of philosophy in this country and in England. We asked for responses to our proposed selections, that is, endorsements or rejections of titles contained in a list of about 130 items. We also asked for recommendations of valuable material that we might have overlooked. We are pleased to acknowledge with sincere gratitude the enthusiastic and most helpful reactions received from an impressive majority of our correspondents. Because of the limitations of space we had to exclude, with a heavy heart, several excellent articles by authors from whom we had already obtained permission for reprinting.

With the exception of a very few cases in which it seemed clear from the beginning that an article belonged in our collection, we have pondered our choices seriously and long. In many instances it was extremely difficult for us to make up our minds. The exclusion of any article which was either on our original list or had been recommended by our friends was painful; and here, as everywhere, to choose is to exclude. Recognizing in the end that it would be impossible to make our choices coincide with the valuations of all prospective users of this book, we can only plead that within the given aims and limitations we have selected what, after countless considerations, comparisons and consultations seemed the most suitable body of material available for reprinting.

We have been guided in our selections on the whole by the reactions and suggestions of our correspondents. Since some of our own articles met with a very favorable reaction, we felt it would not appear presumptuous to include them. Generally our tendency was not to concentrate exclusively on the work of the great and the famous thinkers, but rather to select on the basis of didactic effectiveness. Clarity, pertinence, incisiveness of presentation, intelligibility independent of too high a degree of technical knowledge, integration into the total pattern of the contents—these were the essential criteria for our choices.

The conception of philosophical analysis underlying our selections springs from two major traditions in recent thought, the Cambridge movement deriving from Moore and Russell, and the Logical Positivism of the Vienna Circle (Wittgenstein, Schlick, Carnap) together with the Scientific Empiricism of the Berlin group (led by Reichenbach). These, together with related developments in America stemming from Realism and Pragmatism, and the relatively independent contributions of the Polish logicians have increasingly merged to create an approach to philosophical problems which we frankly consider a decisive turn in the history of philosophy. Although it is realized that there are no sharp lines of demarcation between this and other contemporary schools, we could not possibly have attempted to represent them all.

Since the clearest and most helpful formulation of an idea is not always the first in order of time, or historically the most representative, we have paid relatively little attention to originality as a condition for inclusion. It was rather the penetration, the finesse, and the challenge of the work which counted most. In some instances we succeeded in grouping together divergent and mutually incompatible contributions around controversial subjects. We have tried to avoid definitely obsolete material. Certainly up-to-date-ness in any significant sense is not a mere function of date of publication. Frege, one of whose contributions we included, and Peirce, whose work is not represented because it is so amply available, have more to say to us than many who are writing today.

It did not seem required to add our own comments to the material published. The skillful instructor will find many ways in which to use this book to full advantage. We have, however, provided a bibliography of further readings, books as well as articles. If space had permitted, a good deal of this material, or excerpts therefrom, would have been included. It is to a large extent our original list together with items suggested by our correspondents.

Courses and seminars in Principles of Philosophy, Contemporary Philosophy, Philosophical Analysis, Theory of Knowledge, Logical Theory, Philosophy of Language, etc., should find ample material for reading and discussion in this anthology. Although some basic articles in Philosophy of Science, Modern Logic, and Theoretical Ethics have been included, we can conceive of additional volumes of selections, very much needed, in these special fields. We express the hope that others will consider work on anthologies along those lines. May we assure them that such work, while arduous, is at least intrinsically rewarding.

H.F.
W.S.

ACKNOWLEDGEMENTS

We express our deep appreciation to the authors of the articles included in this anthology for their kind permission to reprint, either in full or by way of excerpt or adaptation, the material here presented. Our gratitude is also extended to the original editors and publishers of these articles for their friendly coöperation. Specific acknowledgement is made on the first page of each selection.

ACKNOWLEDGMENTS

CONTENTS

V. INDUCTION AND PROBABILITY

VI. DATA, REALITY, AND THE MIND-BODY PROBLEM

VII. PROBLEMS OF DESCRIPTION AND EXPLANATION IN THE EMPIRICAL SCIENCES

VIII. PROBLEMS OF THEORETICAL ETHICS

SUGGESTED FURTHER READINGS

INTRODUCTION

Logical Empiricism *

HERBERT FEIGL

POSITIVISM, NOT NEGATIVISM

Probably the most decisive division among philosophical attitudes is the one between the worldly and the other-worldly types of thought. Profound differences in personality and temperament express themselves in the ever changing forms these two kinds of outlook assume. Very likely there is here an irreconcilable divergence. It goes deeper than disagreement in doctrine; at bottom it is a difference in basic aim and interest. Countless frustrated discussions and controversies since antiquity testify that logical argument and empirical evidence are unable to resolve the conflict. In the last analysis this is so because the very issue of the jurisdictive power of the appeal to logic and experience (and with it the question of just what empirical evidence can establish) is at stake.

It seems likely that this situation in philosophy will continue as long as human nature in its relations to its cultural environment remains what it has been for the last three or four thousand years. The tough-minded and the tender-minded, as William James described them so brilliantly, are perennial types, perennially antagonistic. There will always be those who find this world of ours, as cruel and deplorable as it may be in some respects, an exciting, fascinating place to live in, to explore, to adjust to, and to improve. And there will always be those who look upon the universe of experience and nature as an unimportant or secondary thing in comparison with something more fundamental and more significant. This tendency of thought may express itself theologically or metaphysically. It may lead to a faith in extra-mundane existence, or it may in various attenuated fashions assert merely the supremacy of some rational or intuitive principles.

Empiricism, Skepticism, Naturalism, Positivism, and Pragmatism [1] are typical thought movements of the worldly, tough-minded variety. Respect for the facts of experience, open-mindedness, an experimental trial-and-error attitude, and the capacity for working within the frame of an incomplete, unfinished world view distinguish them from the more impatient, imaginative, and often aprioristic thinkers in the tender-minded camp. Among the latter are speculative metaphysicians, intuitionists, rationalists,

---

* Reprinted with omissions from *Twentieth Century Philosophy*, D. D. Runes, ed., Philosophical Library, New York, 1943, by kind permission of the editor and the publishers.

[1] Disregarding some of James' own tender-minded deviations.

3

and absolute idealists. An amusing anecdote concerning two celebrated contemporary philosophers has become widely known. One considers the other muddle-headed and the other thinks the one simple-minded. This fairly epitomizes the history of philosophy, that grandiose "tragicomedy of wisdom." [2] Plato and Protagoras, St. Thomas and William of Ockham, Spinoza and Hobbes, Leibniz and Locke, Kant and Hume, Hegel and Comte, Royce and James, Whitehead and Russell are in many regards, though of course not in every feature, outstanding examples of that basic difference.

Inasmuch as this divergence of attitudes establishes a continuum of positions between extremes, there is also among the tough-minded thinkers a gradation of shades from a nominalistic, pan-scientific radicalism to a more liberal, flexible form of empiricism. Typical among the radicals is the use of the phrase "nothing but." We are familiar with this expression from earlier doctrines, such as *materialism:* "Organisms are nothing but machines." "Mind is nothing but matter." "The history of ideas is only an epiphenomenon of the economic processes." We also know it from *phenomenalism:* "Matter is nothing but clusters of sensations." Or from *nominalism:* "Universals are mere words." Or from *ethical skepticism* and *relativism:* "Good and evil are no more than projections of our likes and dislikes."

One of the great merits of logical empiricism lies in the fact that it is conscious of the danger of these reductive fallacies. It may not always have been able to avoid them. A young and aggressive movement in its zeal to purge thought of confusions and superfluous entities naturally brandishes more destructive weapons than it requires for its genuinely constructive endeavor. But that is a socio-psychological accident which in time will become less important. The future of empiricism will depend on its ability to avoid both the *reductive* fallacies of a narrowminded positivism—stigmatized as *negativism*—as well as the *seductive* fallacies of metaphysics. Full maturity of thought will be attained when neither aggressive destruction nor fantastic construction, both equally infantile, characterize the philosophic intellect. The alternative left between a philosophy of the "Nothing But" and a philosophy of the "Something More" is a philosophy of the "What is What." Thus an attitude of *reconstruction* is emerging: an attitude which recognizes that analysis is vastly different from destruction or reduction to absurdity, an attitude that is favorable to the integration of our knowledge, as long as that integration is carried on in the truly scientific spirit of caution and open-mindedness. The reconstructive attitude demands that we describe the world in a way that does not impoverish it by artificial reductions, and it thus requires that we make important distinctions wherever there is an objective need for them. But, on the other hand, the empiricist will with equal decision reject wishful thinking of

[2] In a shrewd and entertaining book, *Die Tragikomoedie der Weisheit*, R. Wahle many years ago rewrote the history of philosophy from a positivistic point of view.

all sorts, the reading into experience of features which are incapable of test and the multiplication of entities beyond necessity.

It would be puerile optimism to hope that out of such revision and reform should grow a generally accepted philosophy to end all philosophies. But what may seem questionable as an historical prediction may yet be justifiable as a working attitude in a living enterprise. The spirit of enlightenment, the spirit of Galileo, of Hume, and of the French Encyclopedists is fully alive again in the contemporary encyclopedists of a unified science. These modern logical empiricists hope to have freed themselves from the naïveté and dogmatism of the various nineteenth-century materialists and monists. They are conscious of their philosophy's rôle as a turning point in the history of critical thought. Nevertheless, they do not claim originality, for they are aware that the empirical and analytic trend in philosophy is no less persistent than the speculative and intuitive approach, though it is admittedly less spectacular and popular. The tradition they now represent has centered its chief inquiries around the two humble questions, "What do you mean?" and "How do you know?" The systematic pursuit of meaning by the Socratic method and the searching scrutiny of the foundations of knowledge are thus again declared the genuine task of philosophy, a task which differs from the quest for truth as carried on by science and yet is most intimately related to it.

Neither the construction of a world view nor a vision of a way of living is the primary aim. If through the progress of knowledge and through social, political, and educational reform one or the other objective is pursued, philosophy in its critical and clarifying capacity may aid or guide such developments. But it cannot, by mere reflective analysis, *prescribe or produce* them. Quackish and dilettantish projects in both directions have always been abundant and cheap in the market of ideas. The main contribution that philosophical reconstruction can make in this regard lies in the direction of an education toward maturer ways of thinking, thinking which possesses the virtues characteristic of science: clarity and consistency, testability and adequacy, precision and objectivity. Immature attitudes are associated with attempts to explain experience in ways which lack the distinguishing marks of science. Certain of these pre-scientific modes of explanation, like the magical, the animistic, and the mythological, are nearly defunct; others, like the theological and the metaphysical, still prevail.

Throughout its history philosophy has been the particular stronghold of verbal magic. By purely verbal means it has tried to explain things which only science could explain or which cannot be explained at all. In the process it creates its own perplexities, and at its worst it attempts the "solution" of these pseudo-problems—problems arising only out of linguistic confusion—by means of pseudo-techniques—more verbal magic. Analysis teaches us that all this is altogether unnecessary. Thus, if a little levity be permitted, we may define philosophy as the disease of which it should be the cure.

THE ANALYSIS OF LANGUAGE AND THE MEANINGS OF "MEANING"

The systematic pursuit of the problem of meaning by means of a logical analysis of language distinguishes Logical Empiricism from the earlier, more psychologically oriented types of Empiricism, Positivism, and Pragmatism. The imperative need for a logic of language was impressed upon scientists and logicians most poignantly in the last few decades. Just as the seminal ideas of some nineteenth-century philosophies originated in a scientific achievement (Darwin's theory of evolution) so twentieth-century Logical Empiricism was conceived under the influence primarily of three significant developments in recent mathematics and empirical science. These are the studies in the foundations of mathematics (led by Russell, Hilbert, and Brouwer), the revision of basic concepts in physics (advanced especially by Einstein, Planck, Bohr, and Heisenberg) and the reform of psychology by the behaviorists (Pavlov, Watson, et al.). Though very different in context and subject-matter, these three developments focussed attention on the necessity for an inquiry into the limits and structure of meaningful discourse. Russell, through his discovery of logical and mathematical paradoxes, could show that traditional logic had to be revised and that certain laws, like his rule of types, had to be incorporated in logic in order to avoid inconsistencies in the very foundations of mathematics. Einstein, in his analysis of the electrodynamics of moving bodies, was led to a most revolutionary critique of such basic concepts as simultaneity, length, duration, and mass. Thus he showed that the traditional phraseology of "absolute space" and "absolute time" was in certain important respects devoid of the factual meaning it was supposed to possess. Analogous revisions of basic concepts, touching also on the principle of causality, resulted from the elaboration of the theory of quanta. Finally, by developing objective procedures for the study of mental life, the behaviorists made us aware of the fact that all of the scientific content of psychology can be formulated in the physical language [3] and that the assumption of a "something more," a surplus of factual meaning attached to mentalistic terminology, is an illusion. (Earlier reductive naïvetés were gradually eliminated here, as elsewhere.)

Whatever the future of mathematics, physics, and psychology may decide about the theoretical content of these recent ideas, we have, in any case, been awakened once for all to the need for logical analysis, and we have been witnesses to the fruitfulness of its results.

[3] I. e., the language whose undefined, primitive terms are spatiotemporal coördinates (referring to observable or measurable locations and dates) and thing-predicates (referring to observable properties of things).

Three disciplines are being developed to carry out this task of clarifying language and meaning. *Pragmatics* investigates the functions of language in its full biological, psychological, and sociological setting. Here language in its relation to behavior is the primary object of study. By two successive steps of abstraction the disciplines of *semantics* and *syntax* are arrived at. Semantics analyzes the meaning of terms and expressions. Its studies center about the relation of designation and the concept of truth. While pragmatics is interested predominantly in the expression and appeal function of language, semantics explores the symbolic or representative aspect of language. Syntax, finally, ignores even the meaning-relation and studies exclusively the connections of linguistic signs with each other. It systematizes the purely formal, structural rules for the formation of sentences and the transformation rules of logical derivation.

Granting that language as used in common life serves in a fusion or a combination of various functions, it would seem imperative that some sort of theoretical separation of functions be undertaken for the sake of greater clarity and the avoidance of confusion. The list below is the result of such an analysis. Among the dozens of meanings of "meaning" we shall enumerate only those which are of prime importance for philosophical purposes.

THE FUNCTIONS OF LANGUAGE, OR THE MEANINGS OF "MEANING"

Cognitive meanings (Informational function)	Non-cognitive meanings (Emotive expression and appeal function)
Purely formal	*Pictorial (Imaginative)*
Logico-arithmetical	*Emotional (Affective)*
Factual (= Empirical)	*Volitional-motivational (Directive)*

This table, correctly understood and properly used, is a powerful tool in the disentanglement of the traditional puzzles of philosophy. Many metaphysical "problems" and their "solutions" depend upon the erroneous presumption of the presence of factual meaning in expressions which have only emotive appeals and/or a formally correct grammatical structure. And many an epistemological question has been obscured by mistaking logico-mathematical for factual meanings. It is such confusion or erroneous pretense that is exposed to criticism on the basis of our table of meanings. No evaluation of the functions of language as such is implied. Emotive appeals are indispensable in the pursuits of practical life, in education, in propaganda (good or bad), in poetry, in literature, in religious edification and moral exhortation. Some of the highest refinements of our civilized existence depend upon the emotional overtones of spoken and written language.

However, Logical Empiricism as an approach in the theory of knowledge is primarily concerned with *cognitive* meanings. It avoids the errors of the psychologistic approach by the sharp distinction between the pictorial connotations of words, i. e., the imagery that accompanies their use, and the syntactical-semantical *rules* that govern their use. The meaning of words, then, or of signs quite generally, consists in the way in which they are used, the way they are connected with other words or related to objects of experience. The *definition* of a term, the declaration of its meaning, amounts to a statement of the rule according to which we employ or intend to employ the term. Dictionary definitions are translations of relatively less familiar into relatively more familiar expressions; the meaning of the latter is presupposed. Logical analysis, however, pushes beyond these familiar terms of common language. By stepwise procedures all terms are reduced to a comparatively small number of basic or primitive terms. Though further verbal definition is then still possible—no term can be said to be "indefinable"—to continue the process may turn out to be unenlightening and hence fruitless. At this point we must connect language with something outside of language, with experience. Thus in all full definitions of empirical terms there is a terminal ostensive step as an indispensable ingredient. In contradistinction to this, the symbols of purely logical or mathematical systems are introduced (i. e., whatever meaning they have is defined) by relating them only to each other by formal rules. In applied mathematics, as in every language with empirical reference, these purely formal or syntactical rules are supplemented by semantical rules that correlate at least some of the symbols with items of experience.

Philosophical or logical analysis, in the sense of a clarification of the meaning of language, differs from *philological* analysis in at least three important respects. First, logical analysis concentrates on terms of basic importance for the representation of knowledge. The more general these terms the greater is the danger of various confusions due either to unclarity in type of meaning or simply to vagueness or ambiguity of meaning. Hence the necessity and the value of such an analysis as a therapeutic measure. Second, the logical reconstruction is independent of the grammatical (and *a fortiori* the emotive) peculiarities of the specific language, living or dead, in question. Inasmuch as it is the cognitive meanings that we are interested in, idealized models, or in the extreme limit, an ideal language (something in the direction of Leibniz' Mathesis Universalis) may be used. The tools developed in modern symbolic logic prove of utmost value for this purpose. Third, logical analysis is usually *directed* analysis. That is to say, it is either *postulational codification* (as in the mathematical and the exact empirical sciences) or *epistemological reduction* (the reconstruction of factual terms and propositions on a basis of observational evidence).

A characteristic difference between two types of procedure in logical analysis is worth observing. Wittgenstein, very much like G. E. Moore before him, and like the English analytic school on the whole, pursues the Socratic task in a casuistic fashion; individual confusions are subjected to elucidation. It is the specific case that is treated, and the general theory of the treatment is not elaborated systematically. Carnap and his followers, on the other hand, proceeded with the development of a complete system, very much like Whitehead and Russell in *Principia Mathematica*. A whole system is set up, and the theory of the machinery fully set forth. In the course of later developments this difference in procedure became associated with another one; in their choice of a basis for logical reconstruction, Wittgenstein, followed by Schlick, Waismann, and others, remained experientialistic, whereas Neurath, Carnap, Hempel, and others became physicalistic.

THE CRITERION OF FACTUAL MEANING
AND THE CRITIQUE OF METAPHYSICS

The most important, the most widely debated, and, unfortunately, the most frequently misunderstood regulative principle used by Logical Empiricism is the criterion of factual meaningfulness. The purpose of this criterion is to delimit the type of expression which has possible reference to fact from the other types which do not have this kind of significance: the emotive, the logico-mathematical, the purely formal, and—if there should be such—the completely non-significant.

If it is the ostensive steps that connect a purely formal array of signs (e. g., words) with something outside of language, no sign or combination of signs can have factual meaning without this reference to experience. Furthermore, if a sentence is considered true when it corresponds to an existing state of affairs, a sentence is factually-meaningful only if we are in principle capable of recognizing such states of affairs as would either validate or invalidate the sentence. If we cannot possibly conceive of what would have to be the case in order to confirm or disconfirm an assertion we would not be able to distinguish between its truth and its falsity. In that case we would simply not know what we are talking about. C. S. Peirce's pragmatic maxim, formulated in his epoch-making essay, "How to Make Our Ideas Clear," [4] has essentially the same import. We may paraphrase it crudely: A difference that is to be a difference (i. e., more than merely a verbal or an emotive one) must *make* a difference. Or, a little more precisely: If and only if assertion and denial of a sentence imply a difference capable of observational (experiential, operational, or experimental) test, does the sentence have factual meaning. Another useful formulation is Ayer's: [5] "It is the mark of a genuine factual proposition

---

[4] *Popular Science Monthly*, Vol. 12, 1878. Reprinted in *Chance, Love, and Logic,* and in *Collected Papers of C. S. Peirce*, Charles Hartshorne and Paul Weiss, eds.

[5] A. J. Ayer, *Language, Truth, and Logic*, p. 26.

. . . that some experiential propositions can be deduced from it in conjunction with certain other premises without being deducible from these other premises alone." This is simply empiricism brought up to date. The psychologistic formulations, an example of which may be found in Hume (ideas must have their basis and origin in impressions), are replaced by logical ones. The most helpful exposition of these concepts for physical scientists was given by P. W. Bridgman.[6] Realizing the close relationship between knowledge and action, or as Dewey would put it, the place of meaning in the context of inquiry, he asks by what procedures we decide the validity of our assertions. Thus Bridgman maintains that concepts and assertions are meaningless if no operations can be specified that define the former and test the latter.

It was, however, a typical reductive fallacy on the part of Auguste Comte to rule out as meaningless such a question as that concerning the chemical constitution of the stars because at that time no procedure was known to answer that question. Of course we can hardly blame him for not having conceived of spectroscopy before Bunsen and Kirchhoff developed it, yet even in Comte's day it should have been clear that the impossibility of solving that problem was neither a physical nor a logical one. It was a technical-practical difficulty of the sort that may have a bearing on the fruitfulness of an inquiry but certainly not on the meaningfulness of a question. Similar reductive fallacies are inherent in the insistence of some of the more radical positivists that only *directly* and *completely* verifiable or refutable sentences are factually meaningful. Although most of these thinkers never intended as drastic a restriction of meaningful discourse as they were accused of doing in effect,[7] it seems terminologically more convenient today to classify as factually-meaningful all sentences which are in principle capable of being confirmed or disconfirmed, i. e., capable of at least indirect and incomplete test.

Thus in a general classification of sentences and expressions we distinguish today: (1) Logically true sentences, also called analytic sentences. (2) Logically false sentences, also called contradictions. These sentences are true or false, respectively, by virtue of their form. Even if descriptive empirical terms are contained in them they function only "vacuously," and their factual reference is irrelevant to the validity of the sentence. (3) Factually true and (4) factually false sentences whose validity depends upon their correspondence to observed fact. In the majority of instances this correspondence or non-correspondence is only incompletely and indirectly indicated by whatever is immediately observable. Therefore these sentences are usually not *known* to be true or false but

---

[6] In *The Logic of Modern Physics*, New York, 1927.

[7] Scientific laws, hypotheses, and theoretical assumptions, for example, were considered by them perfectly legitimate frames for the formation of empirical sentences although, by terminological decision, they were not classified as genuine propositions.

are considered to be confirmed or disconfirmed to an extent which may vary considerably with the accumulation of favorable or unfavorable evidence. (5) Emotive expressions without cognitive meaning and the emotive components of otherwise cognitive expressions. Pictorial, figurative, and metaphorical expressions, exclamations, interjections, words of praise or blame, appeals, suggestions, requests, imperatives, commands, questions, and prayers belong to this category. Even in definitions we recognize a motivational element: the resolution or invitation to use a term in a certain way.

In the light of the preceding distinctions, we may say that an expression is devoid of empirical meaning (i. e., of factual reference) or, briefly, is *factually-meaningless*, if it belongs to any one or several of the following five groups: (*a*) Expressions violating the syntactical formation-rules of a given language; (*b*) Analytic sentences; (*c*) Contradictory sentences; (*d*) Sentences containing extra-logical terms for which no experiential or operational definitions can be provided; (*e*) Sentences whose confirmability, i. e., even indirect and incomplete testability-in-principle, is logically excluded by the assumptions of the system of which they are a part.[8]

As indicated above, the positivistic critique of metaphysics is primarily an attack upon confusions of meanings and is not intended as a wholesale repudiation of what has been presented under that label. In point of fact, "metaphysics" has been used in such a wide variety of ways that here also a little logical analysis of meanings is indispensable. The customary definitions of metaphysics as the discipline concerned with "first principles" or with "reality as a whole" are not illuminating as long as the methods of procedure remain unspecified. From the point of view of method, then, we may distinguish intuitive, deductive, dialectical, transcendental, and inductive metaphysics.

To take the last-mentioned first, we may say that inductive metaphysics, in the sense of a speculative cosmology derived by extrapolation from scientific evidence and scientific theory, need not contain factually-meaningless elements at all. There is no sharp line between the inductive generalizations of common sense and science on one side and those of cosmology on the other. It scarcely needs to be mentioned that metaphysics in *this* sense, though *logically* unassailable, is open to criticism from the point of view of the criteria of adequacy and precision,

---

[8] Illustrations: ad (*a*): "Soft is the square of green." "Nor here I you neither was." Also, Hegel's famous definitions of light and heat (these suffer as well from the defect classified under *d*). ad (*b*): "Octogenarians are more than ten years old." "Birds can build nests without previous training because they have nest-building instincts." ad (*c*): "Octogenarians are sometimes more than ninety years old." Also, H. G. Wells' idea of a time-machine. ad (*d*): "Entelechies are responsible for the adaptability of organisms to their environment." "The true essence of electricity is undiscoverable." ad (*e*): The ether hypothesis; and metaphysical realism—both as discussed below.

reliability and fruitfulness. Conjectures regarding the heat-death of the universe, the origin of life, and the future of evolution may be perfectly meaningful. But anyone with even a superficial acquaintance with scientific method will realize how uncertain and vague these guesses must be. Occasionally they may be valuable as suggestions for new approaches in scientific research, but with the exception of a few notable instances like the ancient atomic hypothesis, they are apt to remain barren, if not actually misleading. Inductive metaphysics is thus merely the risky, sanguine, disreputable extreme of science.

The critique of meaning, however, applies with full force to the other approaches in metaphysics. *Deductive* metaphysics indulges in the rationalistic practice of producing factual conclusions of a relatively specific character from a few sweepingly general (and often completely vague) premises. It thus misconstrues the nature of logical derivation and is guilty of a confusion of logical with factual meaning. Similarly, dialectical metaphysics, especially the Hegelian, confuses what may—most charitably interpreted—appear as a psychological thought-movement or as a form of historical processes with the logical forms of inference. Intuitive metaphysics, convinced of the existence of a privileged shortcut to "Truth," mistakes having an experience for knowing something about it. Then, too, it is habitually insensitive to the distinction between pictorial and emotional appeals and factual meaning. Finally, transcendental metaphysics in its attempt to uncover the basic categories of both thought and reality may turn out to be nothing else than an unclear combination of epistemology and cosmology, which is then dignified with the name "ontology." It could thus be salvaged and restated in purified form. But it is precisely in ontology that we find the greatest accumulation of factually-meaningless verbalisms. Speculations concerning the "Absolute," even if not entirely devoid of empirical components, generally contain an ample measure of "absolutely" untestable pseudo-propositions. The customary excuse that further experience or reasoning will validate these ideas has no bearing on the question of meaningfulness. The most a patient empiricist can do here is to hope that doubtful promises to define empirically the terms, used so far only emotively, will sometime be fulfilled. But until that happens, the empiricist will fail to attach any glimmering of factual-meaning to the metaphysics which rotates about these terms.

To the empiricist one of the most gratifying trends in the history of science is the gradual liberation of theory from metaphysical bondage. The ideas of absolute space, time, and substance, of numbers as real entities, of the cause-effect relation as an intrinsic necessity, of vital forces and entelechies, and of all manner of obscure faculties and mythical powers have gradually disappeared from respectable science as it was seen that they were either ad hoc explanations or samples of verbal legerdemain or both. One incident in this process of growing epistemological sophistication must suffice for illustration. When after many experiments (Fizeau, Michelson-Morley, de Sitter, Trouton-Noble) physicists realized that it was hopeless to look for effects of the universal ether upon moving bodies, some of them were nevertheless not ready to give up the ether hypothesis. H. A. Lorentz, certainly one of the greatest physicists, pardoned the ether of its undiscoverability by postulating an ingenious set of assumptions, which jointly guaranteed that whatever effects might be produced by the ether, such effects would be exactly cancelled by other counter-effects. Einstein very soon afterwards realized that by this token the stationary-ether hypothesis had become not only scientifically superfluous but strictly meaningless as well. An essentially similar situation prevailed long before in the Newton-Leibniz controversy regarding absolute space and time in which Leibniz used arguments very much like those of the modern pragmatists and positivists.

A word of warning should not be amiss here. The danger of a fallaciously reductive use of the meaning-criterion is great, especially in the hands of young iconoclasts. It is only too tempting to push a very difficult problem aside and by stigmatizing it as meaningless to discourage further investigation. If, for example, some of the extremely tough-minded psychologists relegate questions such as those concerning the instincts, the unconscious, or the relative rôles of constitution and environment to the limbo of metaphysics, then they cut with Ockham's razor far into the flesh of knowledge instead of merely shaving away the metaphysical whiskers. No meaningful problem is in principle insoluble, but there is no doubt that the human race will leave a great many problems unsolved.

THE LOGICAL ANALYSIS OF EMPIRICAL KNOWLEDGE

The question "How do we know?" presupposes the question "What do we mean?", and in the pursuit of both these questions we find ourselves urged to reconstruct our knowledge and to justify its truth-claims on a basis of observational evidence. Not the origin and psychological development of knowledge but its logical structure and empirical validation are the subject of a thus reformed epistemology. The psychology of knowledge (from the experimental study of discrimination behavior on the animal level to the scarcely begun investigation of the higher creative thought processes on the human level) is, after all, only one among the sciences and, therefore, itself one of the subjects of epistemological analysis.

As we shall deal with logical and mathematical knowledge somewhat more fully in the next section, only a few words are necessary to delimit it from empirical knowledge. A pair of Kant's distinctions, though not his philosophy as it elaborates them, are most helpful here. He distinguished between analytic (i. e., true by definition) and synthetic (i. e., factual) sentences and between *a priori* (i. e., logically independent of experience) and *a posteriori* (i. e., empirical) validity. All forms of empiricism agree in repudiating the existence of synthetic *a priori* knowledge. Here the logical empiricists differ from the pre- and the post-Kantian rationalists, from Kant and the Neo-Kantians, as well as from Husserl, the phenomenologists, and the English intuitionists. Logical Empiricism, with Hume and Leibniz, places both mathematical knowledge and formal logic in the class of analytic and hence *a priori* truth. In this respect, Logical Empiricism differs from the extreme empiricism of Mill, who considered mathematics and most of logic synthetic *a posteriori*. We agree with Mill, however, in the statement that all factual knowledge depends for its validity upon confirmation by experience.

As a consequence of all this, the concept of truth is disclosed to be ambiguous. In mathematical knowledge truth amounts to accordance with the formal (syntactical) definitions, the postulates, of the system. In the factual context it means accordance with the empirical definitions, the semantical rules. Thus we call a sentence true if its terms are so applied to fact that none of the designation-rules of the language in question are violated. Error, whatever its source may be (illusion, misinterpretation of evidence, or only misspeaking), simply consists in the disrupting of the one-to-one or many-one correspondence between the terms in the sentence and their referents, i. e., the constituents of the facts described. This version of the "correspondence" view of truth has none of the psychologistic inadequacies of the earlier "copy" or "picture" versions.

Yet we are guilty here of one gross oversimplification, if not distortion, of the actual situation. We presupposed that sentences can simply be confronted with the states of affairs which they claim to represent. At best, this is the case for the sentences describing facts of direct observation, and even this has been seriously disputed by many a full-fledged empiricist. But whatever the status of these basic observational (or "protocol") sentences may be, it is obvious that most of our knowledge, and especially almost all of the more interesting and important part of it, is highly indirect. It is shot through with interpretation, construction, and inference, and consequently is dependent on very general assumptions. It is here that empiricism finds itself confronted with what is traditionally considered to be its greatest problem: the validity of inductive inference and the meaning of probability. All attempts to "justify" inductive inference on rational, empirical, intuitive, or probabilistic grounds have turned out to be utter failures. Hume's critique stands still unshaken. If all *a priori* knowledge is analytic, then we cannot deduce a synthetic assertion, like the principle of the uniformity of nature, from *a priori* premises. And if we try to validate induction on the basis of its certainly eminent success in the past, we are simply making an induction about induction and thus presuppose the very principle we set out to prove. Similarly question-begging are the intuitive and probabilistic approaches. Both must assume that the samples of the world immediately experienced or statistically observed are fair samples, thereby relying also on an implicit premise of uniformity. In the same manner, Kant's ingenious twist of a transcendental deduction depends tacitly upon the constancy of the categories as embedded in our mental organization.

Logical Empiricism cuts the Gordian knot by bluntly asking the question, "What can *'justification'* possibly mean here?" And the surprisingly simple answer is that the only clear meanings of that term in common life and science are *deductive proof* for one thing and exhibition of *inductive evidence* for another. The "great problem of induction," therefore, consisted in the impossible demand to justify the very principles of all justification. If we must have a Principle of Induction, though, it had better be formulated not as a piece of knowledge but as a rule of procedure. As such it turns out to be a tautology with an added directive appeal: If you wish to discover reliable laws, you must try, try, and try again to generalize from a maximum of past experience and as simply as feasible. Then, if there is an order in nature, not too deeply hidden or too complicated, you will find it.

In this manner we are able to avoid the skeptical and psychologistic features of Hume's animal faith doctrine. Anxious to avert metaphysical pseudo-solutions, Hume concluded with a reductive fallacy by declaring inductive inference irrational. Here even the illustrious Hume created a pseudo-problem by a misuse of terms. In ordinary language we call a person "rational" if he is capable of learning from experience. Thus "rationality" does not even predominantly mean logicality in the narrower sense of formal consistency. The procedure of induction, therefore, far from being irrational, defines the very essence of rationality. The stubborn but misguided demand to know what we really don't know (or don't know yet) is perhaps only one of the expressions of an infantile quest for certainty.

A very similar, albeit somewhat more complex, group of confusions underlies the even more hotly argued issues of *the reality of the external world* and *the existence of other minds*. Reductive and seductive tendencies have dominated the scene here as elsewhere. Phenomenalists and subjective idealists, who rightly observe that knowledge must remain within the scope of experience (but note how vague that is), arrive at the conclusion of the immanence of the world within the human mind. (Any need to emphasize how absurd that is?) And metaphysical realists on the other hand, soundly maintaining that human experience is part and parcel of nature (very vague again), define the relation of subjective experience to the objective world in such a way that our knowledge of that world becomes something of a mystery, if not an outright impossibility. This has the logical result of making statements about the world by definition incapable of test. Analogous positions are taken in regard to the existence of "other minds."

Empirical Realism, held by most logical empiricists, removes the meaningless and the absurd elements from the contending philosophies in order to arrive at a reconstruction of common sense and sanity via a clarification of the meanings of "reality." The term "real" is employed in a clear sense and usually with good reason in daily life and science to designate that which is located in space-time and is a link in the chains of causal relations. It is thus contrasted with the illusory, the fictitious, and the purely conceptual. The reality, in this sense, of rocks and trees, of stars and atoms, of radiations and forces, of human minds and social groups, of historical events and economic processes, is capable of empirical test. But many philosophers do not seem to be satisfied with this empirical concept of reality. They have not learned James' lesson, according to which "things are what they are known as" (or as we would rather more cautiously say: "The only meaningful way to speak about things is in terms of what they are know*able* as"). The metaphysicians, especially those from Descartes on, have resorted to an intuitive idea of reality, replete with pictorial and emotional appeals and so incapable of definition as to be almost ineffable. If anywhere, then certainly here, Wittgenstein's famous dictum applies: "Whereof one cannot speak thereof one must be silent." Indeed, the question as to whether anything not given within the range of immediate experience has that same quality or "raw feel" of existence as that which is given—a question which pervades the reality problem—must forever remain undecided. And this must be, not because it surpasses human powers to answer the question but because the very way the terms are used logically excludes any decision whatsoever. To seek an answer is to chase a will-o'-the-wisp.

Empirical Realism may be considered a synthesis of the valid elements in experientialism and naturalism. In asserting that the scope of the natural universe is tremendously wider than the human experience on the basis of which it is known, no illegitimate transcendence is introduced. As long as we do not forget that existential assumptions must be in principle capable of test, though most of these tests are indirect, we remain within the range of the factually-meaningful. The situation in regard to the general realistic framework of knowledge is essentially the same as that in scientific theories; no scientific assumption is testable in complete isolation. Only whole complexes of inter-related hypotheses can be put to the test. In testing one, we rely upon the others and vice versa. So in the outlook of empirical realism we assume certain broad features of the physical world simultaneously with certain hypotheses concerning the process of perception. Each reinforces the presumptive validity of the other.

In the more technical enterprise of a logical reconstruction of our empirical knowledge, certain fundamental choices must be made as to the basis and the logical forms to be employed. In the great tradition of Hume, Comte, Mill, Mach, Avenarius, and Russell, this directed form of analysis consists in a gradual retracing of the validating steps of knowledge to the data of experience. If all psychological considerations are excluded and only logical ones admitted, this results in an analysis of derived terms and sentences as logical constructions erected on primitive terms and sentences which have direct experiential reference. For certain purposes, like the analysis of scientific constructions, it may be unnecessary to push the reduction as far as all that. In order to know the evidential basis of a physical or biological theory, for example, it is usually sufficient to pursue the analysis only to the level of terms designating observable things and their properties. We may therefore distinguish between *experiential* and *physicalistic* bases of reconstruction or of epistemic reduction. Carnap, utilizing the efficient and adaptable apparatus of symbolic logic, has worked out detailed sketches of such analyses for either reduction basis.

In recent years it has become clear that the reconstruction of the physicalistic basis has some decided advantages, especially in that the feature of the objectivity—or, more precisely, the intersubjectivity—of knowledge is warranted right from the start. In addition, a number of pseudo-problems are thus more effectively forestalled. But whichever basis is chosen, the essential program of all modern empiricist epistemologies can be fulfilled.

Out of these analyses has resulted the thesis of the *unity of science*. The possibility of a reconstruction of all factual sciences on the basis of a common set of root terms, be they experiential or be they physicalistic, enables us to speak of the reducibility of all sciences to a common, unitary, inter-scientific language. Earlier formulations of this thesis according to which this reducibility was identified with complete logical translatability had to be abandoned as soon as the logical forms of only indirectly and incompletely testable statements were more closely scrutinized. Common language and to an even greater extent scientific language makes wide use of *dispositional concepts* such as "combustibility," "solubility," "conductivity," etc. Of course, other words besides those ending in "-ity" or "-ility" belong to this class. Such terms as mass, force, heat content, and electrical charge in physics; as valence and ionic concentration in chemistry; and as genotypes, instincts, needs, drives, tendencies, status, tensions, powers, in the biological and social sciences are dispositional in character also. They do not describe immediately observable traits but are, as it were, condensed expressions for regularities of events or behavior exhibited under appropriate conditions. Such terms are not *definable* explicitly on the basis of primitive definientia but are, in a technical sense, *reducible to* (or introducible by) observable thing predicates. In the light of these refinements Carnap [9] formulates the thesis of the Unity of Science as follows: "There is a *unity of language* in science, viz., a common reduction basis for the terms of all branches of science, this basis consisting of the very narrow and homogeneous class of terms of the physical thing-language." As we

[9] *International Encyclopedia of Unified Science*, Vol. 1, No. 1, p. 61.

shall point out, this "unity of science" is something much more obvious and assured than the idea or project of a *unitary science* in the sense of an all-comprehensive explanatory system.

THE LOGIC AND METHODOLOGY OF THE FORMAL AND THE FACTUAL SCIENCES

Undoubtedly, the most significant constructive contributions of the Logical Empiricists are their logical and methodological analyses of scientific procedures and scientific theories. As these contributions, however, are very numerous as well as mostly quite specific and technical, our report about them must remain hopelessly sketchy and oversimplified.

The advocates of the unity of science admit but one sharp dichotomy in the classification of the sciences. They admit and even emphasize the distinction between the formal sciences (logic and mathematics) and the factual sciences (natural and social). To begin with logic, we may say that the main progress toward its fuller understanding has depended on two developments: the elaboration of the symbolic machinery of mathematical logic and the semantical and syntactical analyses of its meaning and structure. Although many important questions are still controversial, there is virtually no disagreement with the thesis that logic, in the sense of the science of the forms of valid deduction, differs radically from the factual sciences in that it does not provide any information concerning matters of fact. The rules of deduction belong to the internal regulative mechanism of a consistent language. They merely enable us to express in one form precisely what we have already said in another. Logical rules thus guide us in the transition from premises to conclusions. The appearance of genuine novelty in deductive inference is only psychological, because it is due to our incapacity to comprehend in one flash of insight the implications of more complicated sets of premises.

The theorems or laws of logic are analytic sentences—true by virtue of presupposed agreements concerning the meaning of the terms employed. The law of non-contradiction, for example, is inescapably and infallibly true as long as we agree to mean by a "sentence" an expression which is either true or false and as long as we mean by "denial" the conversion of the value "true" into the value "false" and vice versa. This view of the nature of logical laws has been criticized as conventionalistic. It is said to assert that logical laws are a matter of arbitrary decree concerning the use of symbols. Obviously enough, from a purely formal (syntactical) point of view a system of logic is just one calculus among an indefinite number of others. And yet we cannot speak of alternative *logics* in exactly the same sense in which we speak of alternative geometries. The uniqueness of logic seems to depend upon its purpose in the use of language; as long as we wish our language to use unambiguous and consistent designation-rules, we simply must have rules which regulate that definiteness of meaning. Whatever calculus—two-valued, three-valued, or many-valued —we may find adequate for this or that scientific purpose, our determination to employ symbols with constant meanings necessitates the retention of a yes-or-no logic somewhere as, so to speak, the ultimate court of appeal.

On the technical side logic has been developed not only by further extensions and applications of symbolic logic proper, but also by the introduction of meta-languages, i. e., languages about language, for the purpose of syntax and semantics. An earlier, somewhat dogmatic opinion of Wittgenstein's according to which the relation of language to fact can only be "shown" but not linguistically represented was repudiated and the error corrected by the introduction of a well-defined hierarchy of languages. Here, as so often in the progress of science, the invention of a technical device proved most fruitful; by utilizing the so-called arithmetization of syntax (an idea due to Kurt Gödel), it became possible to attack syntactical problems by means of a mathematical algorithm. In the pursuit of these problems Gödel made his epoch-making discovery of the existence of non-demonstrable mathematical theorems. Roughly, what he proved was the essential incompleteness and incompletability of mathematics. Within the framework of the concepts of any given postulate system, providing the system includes only ordinary arithmetic without limitation to the finite, it is always possible to formulate problems which cannot be solved within the framework. This discovery implies an essential modification of outlook upon the earlier positions of the formalistic, logistic, and intuitionistic schools regarding the foundations of mathematics.

In spite of Gödel's revolutionary theorem, some of the earlier rapprochements among these three schools, e. g., as envisaged by Carnap, remain unquestioned. The logistic school is right in its claim that mathematical concepts can be defined in a stepwise manner on the basis of purely logical primitive concepts. The formalistic school is justified in its claim that all mathematical systems, inasmuch as questions of deductive derivation are concerned, can be most fruitfully dealt with as purely formal symbolic games. And the intuitionist school correctly emphasizes that arithmetic as we usually understand it and use it is neither a purely formal game nor an empirical science but most intimately related to certain fundamental meanings of common language. Intuitionism, however, seems somewhat arbitrary in its limiting of "legitimate" types of mathematical proof to constructive procedures only. In any event, a great deal of work remains to be done in the foundations of mathematics. The fruitfulness and the fascination of the new methods at our disposal are evident in the steadily increasing volume of contributions to this most intricate field.

Clearly distinguished from the studies of pure mathematics are those in the analysis of mathematics as applied in the empirical sciences. While syntactical methods suffice for the investigation of the formal aspects of mathematical systems, semantical methods must be used for the reconstruction of empirically interpreted calculi. The essential ideas have been clear since Einstein, if not since Gauss and Riemann. The question whether a given mathematical system is applicable to the facts of experience acquires definite meaning only if the semantical definitions (rules of designation, "Zuordnungsregeln") which correlate symbols in the calculus with observable or measurable magnitudes are explicitly stated. Careful analyses by Reichenbach and others have applied these critical procedures most fruitfully to the problems of physical geometry as they appear, for example, in the theory of relativity. One result is the insight that not every concept of the formal system need be interpreted in terms of observables. As the advances of recent physics especially indicate, a great many of the theoretical concepts are simply efficient and parsimonious symbolic superstructures designed to connect the observables in a systematic way in order to make them more easily predictable. Therefore, the representation of a theory as a postulate system (i. e., hypothetico-deductive system) becomes an important device in the clarification of the relation between the assumptions of the theory and the observational data. By setting up a theory as a system of independent (i. e., non-overlapping and non-redundant) postulates, it becomes possible to recognize exactly which part of the theory corresponds to which facts of experience. If, then, due to further observations, the theory has to be modified, it will be clear which part of the theory will be affected. Such talk as indulged in by some speculative scientists, that their theories are "monolithic," in the sense that they can be accepted or rejected only in their totality can thereby be unmasked as prejudice.[10]

The modern empirical outlook also provides an answer in the longstanding controversy concerning the aims and achievements of theoretical science. There is a good meaning of the term "explanation" over against "mere description." Not only *how* things behave and events occur, but also *why* they do so, can be found out by science. If we only avoid the seductive fallacy of confusing scientific empirical explanation with "ultimate," "absolute," "metaphysical" explanation (which turns out to be verbal magic and therefore pseudo-explanation), we realize that the legitimate scientific procedure of that name consists in the deductive derivation of more specific descriptive conclusions from more general assumptions. These assumptions (empirical laws, or on higher levels, theoretical postulates) are considered valid only until further notice. The locus of the "necessity" in the light of which the facts appear when explained, lies neither in the laws as formulated in the assumptions nor in the specific facts described, but exclusively in the relation of logical implication be-

---

[10] This does not contradict the well-known fact that in testing any hypothesis we presuppose the validity of other hypotheses. Yet, by a process of successive confirmation (stepwise increases of scope) each hypothesis can be examined singly as to its adequacy, plausibility and simplicity within the given system.

tween premises and conclusions. This insight enables us also to avoid the reductive fallacy according to which science is nothing more than description. For description pure and simple gives merely an *account of* but does not *account for* the observed phenomena in the way just elucidated. The related dispute concerning the realistic versus the idealistic interpretation of scientific hypotheses can be resolved by realizing that all fruitful hypotheses are not merely summaries of phenomena already observed but also inductive anticipations of other phenomena yet to be discovered. This openness of the hypothetical existential constructs, as manifest, e. g. in the atomic theory, marks them off clearly from mere abbreviatory mathematical devices such as tensors and matrices.

Reductive and seductive tendencies also dominate the traditional views of causality, probability, teleology, and the mind-body relation. According to the logical empiricist analysis, causality is neither "*mere* regular sequence" nor an "intrinsic bond" but a functional relation between events or magnitudes characterized by a number of testable features such as the homogeneity of space-time, contiguity (i. e., nearby-action), continuity, simplicity, and so forth. The extent to which strictly deterministic laws are applicable is, of course, an empirical question, and the revolutionary results of quantum mechanics must therefore be taken quite seriously.[11] Statistical or probability laws are neither merely an expression of our ignorance nor preordained regularities in the equalization of chances. They are, rather, generalizations on the basis of observed stabilities of frequencies.

In biology, mechanistic interpretations are typically reductive, while vitalistic views—as it seems, highly seductive—operate with unconfirmable explanations on the basis of extra-physical agents such as entelechies and vital forces. During the long period these theories predominated, we were confronted with the sorry spectacle of two competing views, the first of which is largely false and the second factually-meaningless. Biology cannot overlook the decline of mechanism as a program of comprehensive nature explanation; neither can it, with a pious or superstitious verbalism, dismiss the possibility of a naturalistic explanation of vital processes, methodologically on a par with physics and chemistry and indebted to their continuing advances. The contemporary synthesis goes in the direction of an organismic physical theory which views organisms as intricately structured dynamic systems the parts of which interact in varying types and degrees of mutual and environmental dependence. Teleology, again, need neither be interpreted as a manifestation of a metaphysical design nor as an anthropomorphic illusion. It can be analyzed as a form of macrocausal relation typical of organized systems.

In the mind-body problem we realize today that the customary ap-

---

[11] However, the widely debated consequences for the free-will problem are precisely nil, for the simple reason that the free-will problem is a pseudo-issue arising out of confusions of meaning. Not determination but compulsion is the opposite of freedom.

proaches neither of monism nor of dualism lead anywhere. From the point
of view of an epistemological analysis, physical and psychological concept
formation do not necessarily differ in subject matter, in raw data, but only
in the languages employed (with all their differences of pictorial-emotional
connotation). The genuinely scientific work in psycho-physiology, though
still in its infancy, can only be impeded by metaphysical prejudices and
rash attempts at wholesale "solutions." Logical analysis, here as elsewhere,
merely examines possibilities and makes explicit the basic assumptions or
programs of research. It does not subscribe to the tenets of any school of
psychology, although it is in essential agreement with the methodological
outlook of behaviorism (but not necessarily with its scientific results and
certainly not with any unqualified rejection of introspective techniques).
This is simply a consequence of the acceptance of an inter-subjective criterion of factual meaning for science. The thesis of physicalism, in the
sense of the unity of the *language* of science, amounts to the same view
as that which was previously called "logical (or methodological) behaviorism."

Exactly the same kind of analysis is applied to the social sciences. There
are no other methods or aims in the social and cultural sciences than exist
in the natural sciences: observation, description, measurement, statistics,
the discovery of explanatory laws and theories—though more difficult of
achievement in the former than in the latter—are the basic procedures.
The rôle of sympathetic "understanding" or "empathy" as a practical guide
is certainly not to be minimized, but its results, if they are to be scientifically
valid, are subject to the very same objective tests as are the results of inorganic science. If history is declared both a science and an art, then the
scientific component lies as usual in the scrupulous ascertainment and interpretation of the data, and the artistic component consists in the use of
pictorially and emotionally appealing language in the representation of
facts. To what extent sociology, economics, or history are capable of discovering reliable laws on some level of concept-formation is an empirical
question and therefore cannot be decided *a priori* on logical grounds. Only
by trial and error can we determine which dimensions or variables must
be selected for the formulation of reliable dependencies.

Sharply to be distinguished from the thesis of the unity of science is the
thesis of a unitary system of explanation in the sciences. Whereas the first
thesis is relatively trivial, stating as it does only the possibility of passing
from the concepts of one science to those of any other on strictly empirical
grounds, the second thesis is as yet problematic and can be considered only
as a tentative program of research. We have witnessed a great many reductions of sciences to other sciences (astronomy, acoustics, and thermodynamics to mechanics; optics to electrodynamics) and such impressive
unifications as those of mechanics and electrodynamics as brought about
by the relativity and quantum theories. In this connection it can be safely

assumed today that chemistry is becoming reducible to atomic physics. Further unifications may be expected to emerge out of the endeavors of such borderland sciences as bio-physics, bio-chemistry, psycho-physics, psycho-physiology, social psychology, etc. As to whether these syntheses will lead to a complete reduction of the laws of the various sciences to a unitary set of basic laws, and as to whether these basic laws will be the laws of a future physics is again a matter of conjecture. Logical analysis can investigate the possibilities and the logical structure of such an extreme convergence of theories; it can dispel emotionally rooted misconceptions of or prejudices against these unifications, but it cannot afford to be dogmatic about their attainability. For the time being it seems more fruitful to analyze the different types of concepts and conceptual systems in the still relatively separate and autonomous sciences. This can be done with due attention to the already existing interconnections of the sciences and without premature attempts at complete unification.

In general, the problems in the logic of science which have been and still are being pursued by the logical empiricists are not of this grandiose, sweeping character. Some of the most intensively cultivated fields of work, aside from the results in symbolic logic, pure syntax, semantics, and the foundations of mathematics, lie in detailed analyses of the concepts and procedures of the empirical sciences. In the pursuit of these tasks and as a result of the rapid advances of the sciences, new problems are constantly opening up which require the attention of fully trained logicians and methodologists. It is here where coöperation with the scientists is the closest and the most productive.

VALUE-THEORY, ETHICS, AND OUTLOOK ON THE SOCIAL PROBLEMS

A little reflection suffices to show that the meaning of the term "ethics" is highly ambiguous and that it designates at least five different types of endeavor: (1) moral "vision," i. e., the recognition, discovery, or (alleged) demonstration of a "right" or "good" way of life or of an uppermost standard of moral evaluation; (2) moral exhortation, education, and propaganda; (3) empirical studies of actual moral evaluations, either descriptive or explanatory; (4) the technology of the "good" life—a branch of applied science concerned with the discernment and perfecting of means (instrumental values) in view of certain ends (terminal values); (5) the logical analysis of ethical terms and sentences—either by the casuistic Socratic method or by the elaboration of a hypothetico-deductive system of ethical norms. The five-fold division just outlined is itself a result of the Socratic type of approach. (Quite analogous distinctions apply to aesthetics.)

Ethical norms or imperatives as discovered or intuited in (1), proclaimed and advocated in (2), factually studied in (3), practically implemented in (4), and subjected to a meaning analysis in (5) may be reconstructed as sentences referring to a possible (usually not actualized) state of affairs and expressed with an emotional-motivational appeal. In the use of such terms as "ought," "should," "right," "good," "duty," etc. lies the irreducibly directive component of moral value-judgments. An ethical imperative like the Golden Rule simply means: "Would that everybody behaved toward his fellowmen as he expects them to behave toward him." This sentence, having its accent in the emotive appeal, could not possibly be deduced from a knowledge of facts only; it is neither true nor false. It is rather an invitation (suggestion, request, exhortation, or command) to *make* the contained factual sentence true. In traditional metaphysically or theologically oriented moral philosophies the attempt was made to validate the fundamental standards on the basis of revelation, *a priori* intuition, or logical proof. Absolute values were thus either concretely specified and dogmatically proclaimed or merely abstractly assumed and their specific content left open. From the logico-empirical point of view all of these approaches involve confusions of meaning or assumptions incapable of test. Absolute values as well as categorical imperatives can be expressed only in emotive language.

Relative values in the sense of instrumental values which are determined by needs and interests and hypothetical imperatives which state empirically confirmable means-ends relations are factually-meaningful. Here the questions of truth or falsity make sense. As long as disagreement in morals depends merely upon differences in opinion or belief regarding the efficacy of contending means, such disagreement is in principle capable of settlement by the empirical method. True enough, means and ends are often so closely related and intertwined that it would be an oversimplification to assume a clearcut hierarchy of instrumental values crowned by uppermost fixed terminal values. Dewey has taught us to drop even this last remnant of value-rationalism. Nevertheless there are leading standards, thoroughly empirical, to be sure, in the light of which we evaluate the mutual adjustment and harmonization of ends and means. These guiding principles themselves are, as a matter of fact, judged and evaluated by their correspondence to human wants and desires. The question raised (and sometimes answered negatively) by metaphysicians, "Is the satisfying of human interests morally valuable?" is therefore not a factual question at all. As long as it is not specified to *whose* interests or to *which* interests reference is being made, it is the vagueness of the question that renders it meaningless. If, however, some such specifications are made it still does not acquire factual meaning because the term "valuable" (in the non-instrumental sense) is used as a purely emotive device for the direction or redirection of attitudes. If, finally, in some moral system a definite locus has been given for the application of such terms as "valuable," "good," "right" and the like, then such a material definition renders answers to our question either analytic or contradictory, as the case may be, and thus again lacking in factual meaning. The often emphasized *indefinability* of "good" is now clarified as due to the motivational character of the term. The ever present possibility of asking the question "But is this really good?" shows that no descriptively delimited locus of valuableness forces its acceptance upon us as an ultimate criterion. We do not deny here that in the immediate experience of persons living in a given cultural context value judgments may bear the mark of intuitive self-evidence. But their very dependence upon and variability with that cultural context are a sufficient proof of their relative nature.

The quest for certainty, here in the field of morals just as elsewhere, may lead to emotionally soothing or edifying results. But the acceptance of an absolute authority or extramundane sanction for morality, like the belief in an absolute source of factual truth, manifests a not fully liberated, pre-scientific type of mind. A completely grown-up mankind will have to shoulder the responsibility for its outlook and conduct; and in the spirit of an empirical and naturalistic humanism it will acknowledge no other procedure than the experimental and no other standards than those prescribed by human nature and by our own insights into the possibilities of improving human nature.

The Scylla of metaphysical absolutism in value-theory can thus be avoided. But how about the Charybdis of an anarchical relativism of values? Historians, ethnologists, social psychologists are apt to arrive at the opinion that, with human interests and attitudes subject to so much variety (depending on epoch, climate, and socio-economic setting), each moral system is equally justified. They hold that there can be no unique system of morals binding upon all. Empiricism may often have been misled into this sort of reductive fallacy, yet a truly empirical study of human nature and social conduct discloses a considerable common denominator in at least the basic needs of all individuals living in the context of coöperation and mutual dependence. Around this nucleus as a center of orientation, all social, political, legal, economic, and educational reforms must operate if they are to achieve their aim to any degree at all. The salient evils and maladjustments of the life we call civilized can only be eliminated or mitigated if by conscious effort and planning reforms are democratically undertaken and widely supported. Human interests, and with them, human satisfaction and happiness, are flexible, educable. What originally may have had value only as a means may, through use and habituation, acquire value as an end. Even if Hobbes's pessimistic opinions concerning the utterly selfish nature of human attitudes were correct (and there *is* some evidence to the contrary) it would yet be plausible that out of the use of coöperative and reciprocal-help procedures as mere means mankind does (or will) gradually develop genuinely kind and altruistic attitudes. Ethical relativism (i. e., the assertion that evaluations depend on needs and interests, and that these needs and interests, though fairly constant in their basic aspects, are not eternally fixed or *a priori* established) does not imply moral cynicism or pessimism. The standards of justice and fairness developed in the social process have themselves become objects of greatest interest. Most civilized people are highly sensitive to them and most indignant about their violation. Yet, it should be noted that ethical relativism does not necessarily imply that the majority should rule in the determination of the good life. Breaking through older and majority-endorsed standards to a new form of morality may be envisaged at first only by a few but may nevertheless be justifiable on the basis of the expected results of the new measures for the totality of mankind. The concrete implementation of any program of action lies outside the competence of the philosopher qua logical analyst. The gap between ascertained knowledge and the knowledge required for action will always prove inhibiting to the reflective thinker. Nevertheless his contributions should not be underestimated. By removing prejudice and confusion, by spreading enlightenment through the clarification of basic ideas, he occupies an indispensable rôle as a guide on the however tortuous path of human progress.

I

LANGUAGE, MEANING, AND TRUTH

Is Existence a Predicate? *

WILLIAM KNEALE

I propose to begin by explaining how the controversy about existential propositions has arisen. I shall then try to expound the doctrine that existential propositions are a sub-division of general propositions. In my third section I shall try to apply this doctrine in the elucidation of some rather curious existential propositions. Finally I hope to show that while rejecting the view that existence is a predicate we ought also to reject certain accounts of the nature of propositions.

I

No logician wishes to deny that in ordinary speech sentences such as "tame tigers exist" can be used with perfect propriety. Some of them may be false, but it is not for the logician to determine which are and which are not. If, however, we assume that grammatical form is a sure guide to logical structure, we may be tempted to say that in these sentences the word "existence" stands for a predicate, where "predicate" has a logical sense distinct from its grammatical sense. That some philosophers have taken the word "existence" to stand for a predicate in the logical sense, i.e., for an attribute, may be seen from their use of the ontological argument to prove the existence of God.

Descartes' exposition of the argument is clearer than most others. He starts from the position, supposed to be already established, that we can know some propositions, e.g., simple theorems of mathematics, to be necessarily true. It does not matter for our purposes whether he thinks that his necessary propositions are analytic or synthetic, although we may remark in passing that the language in which he refers to them suggests that they are analytic. He wishes to say that the proposition that God exists can be proved in the same way as that in which a necessary proposition of mathematics is proved. He explicitly compares it with the proposition that the triangle has interior angles equal to two right angles. Thus he writes in the *Fifth Meditation*: "I clearly see that existence can no more be separated from the essence of God than can its having three angles equal to two right angles be separated from the essence of a rectilinear

* Reprinted by kind permission of the author and the editors from *Aristotelian Society, Supplementary Volume 15*, 1936.

triangle." [1] And in his reply to Gassendi's objections: "You are plainly in error when you say that existence is not demonstrated of God as it is demonstrated of the triangle that its three angles are equal to two right angles: for the two propositions are proved in the same way, except that the demonstration proving existence in God is much simpler and clearer." [2] And again in the *Principles of Philosophy*: "Just as the mind, perceiving that it is necessarily involved in the idea of the triangle that it should have three angles equal to two right angles, is thereby absolutely persuaded that the triangle has three angles equal to two right angles; so, from the fact that it perceives necessary and eternal existence to be comprised in the idea which it has of an absolutely perfect Being, it must obviously conclude that this absolutely perfect Being exists." [3]

This argument is based on the assumption that 'God exists' is a proposition of the same sort as a theorem of geometry. Descartes writes as though both propositions predicated something of a subject, the one being about 'God,' the other about 'the triangle.' If he did not assume this, he would not say that they can be proved in the same fashion. Gassendi was the first, I think, to criticize the argument on the ground that existence is not a property of God or of anything else. [4] His criticism drew from Descartes the interesting admission: "I do not see to what class of reality you wish to assign existence, nor do I see why it may not be said to be a property as well as omnipotence, taking the word *property* as equivalent to any attribute or anything which may be predicated of a thing." [5] No doubt Descartes and those who agree with him would say, if questioned, that they wished to make a distinction between existence and qualities such as redness. But refinements of the theory of existence as a predicate only introduce fresh difficulties. The theory is unacceptable.

Unless all true existential propositions are analytic, which no one (except perhaps Leibniz) ever maintained, some subjects of which existence is to be predicated must be conceivable apart from existence. Even of God, whose essence is said to involve existence, we establish that He may exist before we prove that He does exist. [6] That is to say, there must be some sense of "being" which is logically prior to existence and applicable to the possible as well as to the actual. The subject considered as having being in this sense is apparently a certain complex of universals. It is the addition of existence which makes it into an actual individual in the time series. For existence (with the exception of God's) is temporal, whereas

---

[1] *The Philosophical Works of Descartes*, ed. Haldane and Ross, Vol. I, p. 181. Later quotations are indicated by HR with volume number and page. I have slightly modified the translation in several places.

[2] HR, II, 229.

[3] HR, I, 224.

[4] HR, II, 185.

[5] HR, II, 228.

[6] HR, I, 224 and II, 13.

the being which is logically prior to existence is timeless. If we deny these principles, it is said that we abandon the great tradition of philosophy. Perhaps we do, but not without good cause. From the notion of a subject of predicates as a certain *nature* we should find ourselves led to the very strange conclusion that all propositions other than existential propositions must be analytic. For the nature of a thing is taken to include all its qualities. We should therefore be using a self-contradictory expression if we said of something which was red "suppose this were green." We ought rather to say "suppose there were something like this in all other respects but green instead of red." Worse consequences follow from the notion of existence as a temporal predicate. It is true, of course, that the verb "to exist" takes tenses, but in saying this we admit that if the verb symbolizes a predicate the subject of the predicate must be capable of change. It has been asserted, however, that the subject of the predicate existence is a timelessly possible somewhat, and, however little we may know about time, we know that the timeless cannot have different predicates at different times.

We must try to find a satisfactory place for existential propositions in a revised logic. But here Gassendi and Kant, who repeated Gassendi's criticism of the ontological argument, offer us no help. Indeed Kant by lending his authority to a corrupt Aristotelianism probably did something to delay the necessary revision. For example, in his definitions of analytic and synthetic propositions he assumed that every proposition must have a subject and a predicate. It was not until the end of last century that any serious attempt was made to explain the nature of existential propositions. In order to understand what modern logic can add to Gassendi's criticism we must consider the notion of logical form, the clarification of which has been the chief development of logic in the past forty years. I shall not attempt to give a definition of logical form. I am not sure that a definition is possible. But I can indicate what is meant by saying that 'this is red' has the same logical form as 'that is green' and a different logical form from either 'this is near that' or 'if Hannibal had marched on Rome, he would have taken it.' [7] Some distinctions of logical form are so obvious that they could not be entirely ignored by the older logicians. Most manuals of logic contain disconnected references to hypothetical and disjunctive propositions. What is peculiar to modern discussions is the attempt to work out a systematic account of the various possible logical forms, that is to say, the attempt to present them in a single scheme in which they are arranged according to their similarities and in which it is easy to detect the internal logical relations (i.e., entailment, etc.) which hold between them.

[7] In order to mark a distinction between a sentence and the proposition which it expresses, I use double quotation marks when I refer to the sentence and single quotation marks when I refer to the proposition.

II

We must begin with a distinction between simple and complex propositions. We may say somewhat loosely that complex propositions are about other propositions, and that simple propositions are those which are not complex, but the phrase "about other propositions" is too ambiguous to be suitable for a definition. It has been maintained that every complex proposition is a truth-function, i.e., a proposition which is about other propositions, called its arguments, in the sense that for any array of truth-values (truth or falsity) of those other propositions its own truth-value is determined. I cannot argue that question here, but I wish to assert that no complex propositions are of the subject-predicate form. Reflection will show that, although we may use sentences of the grammatical form "p is true," words which appear to stand for attributes of propositions do not in fact stand for any attributes. It is not even correct to say that all simple propositions are of the subject-predicate form, unless we extend the meaning of the word "predicate" to cover relations. For, if we refuse to admit relational propositions, we shall be driven to the monadism of Leibniz. In order to avoid the various misleading associations of the word "predicate" we may speak of the elements of simple propositions as constituents and components. We can indicate the meaning of the word "component" by saying that the component of 'this is red' is what it has in common with 'that is red' and the component of 'a is near b' what it has in common with 'c is near d.'

Let us now consider a range of propositions which differ among themselves only in respect of one element in each, e.g., 'this is red,' 'that is red,' etc. We cannot enumerate all the propositions of the range one by one, but we can indicate what range we are considering by the use of an expression such as "x is red" which stands for what is common to them all. This symbol is not the expression of a proposition, i.e., of something which can be true or false. The letter "x" is not the name of anything in particular, and it does not stand indifferently for all things which can occur in propositions of the range 'x is red,' as a real variable would. It is merely a sign to mark a place which is filled by different elements in the various propositions of the range. From consideration of such a range we can derive two general propositions, the one existential and the other universal.[8] The existential proposition, 'for some x, x is red,' is an adjunction of the propositions of the range, that is to say, its form can be exhibited in a sentence such as "a is red or b is red or c is red, etc.," where "or" has its non-adversative sense. The universal proposition, 'for all x, x is red,' is a conjunction of the same propositions.

In the example which I have selected the propositions of the range

---

[8] It should scarcely be necessary to point out that "general" is not used here as a synonym for "universal," but some critics persist in assuming that it is.

are attributive simple propositions and the elements in which they differ are constituents. But the theory of general propositions is not restricted to ranges of this kind. We must recognize that such propositions as the following are also general in the sense defined: 'for some x, x is not red,' 'for all x, x is not red or x is extended,' 'for some x, x is near this,' 'for some ϕ, this is ϕ and that is ϕ.' The ordinary expression of the last of these would be "this and that have some quality in common." It is based on a range of propositions each of which is itself a conjunction of two simple propositions with the same component and which differ among themselves only in respect of that component. The propositions in the range for generalization may even be themselves general propositions. Thus from the propositions 'for all x, x loves Jones,' 'for all x, x loves Smith,' etc., we can pass to the range 'for all x, x loves y,' and from that to the doubly-general proposition 'for some y, for all x, x loves y,' of which the ordinary expression would be "there is somebody whom everybody loves." In the technical expression of multiply-general propositions the order of the prefixes is of the utmost importance if the prefixes are of different kinds, i.e., not all existential or all universal. We must be prepared, for example, to distinguish the proposition to which we have just referred from the quite different proposition 'for all x, for some y, x loves y,' of which the ordinary expression would be "everybody has somebody whom he loves." The one is an adjunction of conjunctions, the other a conjunction of adjunctions.

In respect of their logical relations to other propositions general propositions resemble other adjunctive and conjunctive truth-functions. Just as 'p' entails 'p or q,' so '$\phi(a)$' entails 'for some x, $\phi(x)$.' And just as 'p and q' entails 'p,' so 'for all x, $\phi(x)$' entails '$\phi(a)$.' [9] Adjunction and conjunction can each be defined in terms of the other and negation. So too 'for some x, $\phi(x)$' is strictly equivalent to 'it is not the case that for all x, not-$\phi(x)$' and 'for all x, $\phi(x)$' strictly equivalent to 'it is not the case that for some x, not-$\phi(x)$.'

In order to safeguard ourselves from misunderstanding we must make clear that this account of general propositions is not intended to explain away the peculiarity in virtue of which they have been called general. It is true that "for all x, x is red" is equivalent to "a is red and b is red and c is red, etc.," but no expression in the conjunctive form without "etcetera"

[9] Professor Moore has asserted that '$\phi(a)$' is not entailed by 'for all x, $\phi(x)$,' but only by the conjunction of that and 'a exists' (Arist. Soc. Sup. Vol. vii, p. 204). Is "a" supposed to be a logically proper name? Then what does he mean by "a exists"? Is "a" a description of the form "the ψ thing"? Then "$\phi(a)$" is equivalent to "for some x, $\phi(x)$, and $\psi(x)$"; but no one wishes to maintain that 'for all x, $\phi(x)$' by itself entails 'for some x, $\phi(x)$ and $\psi(x)$.' Of course, I cannot deduce '$\phi(a)$' from any other proposition unless I can entertain '$\phi(a)$.' Perhaps this is the point which Professor Moore wishes to make. But is it necessarily absurd to say that a proposition which I entertain may entail a proposition which I cannot entertain?

would be an exhaustive analysis of the meaning of the original expression, because, as everyone agrees, there is some sense of the word "about" in which a general proposition may be about things of which we have never heard and for which we have no names. Since "etcetera" means the same as "and so on for all the propositions of the range," its use here is an admission that we are not able to resolve a general proposition into one which is complex but not general. If, then, we say that general propositions are adjunctive and conjunctive truth-functions and occasionally use an expression ending with "etcetera" in order to make the point clearer, we are only explaining in what sense general propositions may rightly be said to be complex. For a proposition to be a truth-function of a certain kind it is not essential that it should be expressible in a sentence consisting of a finite number of sentences linked by "and" or "or," but rather that its truth-conditions should be of a certain kind. An existential proposition is about the propositions of its range in the sense that it is entailed by each of them and cannot be true unless one of them is true, and a universal proposition is about the propositions of its range in the sense that it entails each of them and cannot be false unless one of them is false. The words "each" and "one" which occur in these definitions are marks of generality, and their presence shows that we have not explained away the peculiarity of general propositions. But it is important to realize that general propositions are complex in the sense defined, since it is only by considering them as truth-functions that we can understand their place in the logical scheme of forms, the nature of the distinctions between multiply-general propositions which are expressed by the ordering of prefixes, and the logical relations of general propositions to the propositions of their ranges.

What distinguishes general propositions from other truth-functions of the same types is the fact that by means of them, or rather, by means of the sentences which express them, we are able to talk about propositions which we are unable to entertain, although only in the sense of "about" which I have tried to define. General propositions are complex but not completely exponible.[10] I admit that this is a difficult notion, but I do not think that we can give up the claim to be able to talk about all the propositions of a range. Such attempts as I have seen to explain away the need for the claim seem to me obviously unsatisfactory. It has been suggested, for example, that the structure of the proposition 'for some x, x is red' is shown most clearly in the expression "redness has application." But we ought surely to deny that the proposition is of the subject-predicate form, especially when we find that we are required to talk of a predicate called "having-application," supposed to be itself applicable to universals. In order to make sense of the phrase "has application" we must add "to something," but then we have only a wordy paraphrase of "something is red." And in any case the suggestion takes no account of such general

[10] I owe the suggestion of this convenient medieval word to Mr. Ryle.

propositions as 'this and that have some quality in common.' It may perhaps be argued with some plausibility that it is impossible to entertain a proposition without knowing what would make it true or false, and that therefore a general proposition cannot be a truth-function of unentertained propositions. But the argument assumes too much. Anyone who entertains a general proposition has at least a criterion by which to determine whether any proposition which he may come to entertain does or does not belong to the range of his generalization and, possessing this criterion, he is in a position to verify or falsify the general proposition when suitable evidence offers itself. I cannot see that more than this is required for the entertainment of a proposition. I may add that it is obviously possible for a man to verify or falsify a general proposition in some situation which he could not envisage at the time of first entertaining the proposition, and that any acceptable theory of general propositions must allow for this possibility.

Of all the variety of general propositions which can be and have been entertained traditional logic recognizes only four forms, distinguished as A, E, I and O. The A form (with existential import) is 'for all x, if $\phi(x)$ then $\psi(x)$, and for some x, $\phi(x)$.' The I form is 'for some x, $\phi(x)$ and $\psi(x)$.' No doubt these forms have been recognized because they are of special interest in science. The A and E forms are the forms of easily stated laws, and the O and I forms are the contradictories of the A and E forms. Propositions of the form 'for some x, $\phi(x)$,' where ϕ is an unanalyzable characteristic, may have been ignored because we rarely trouble to assert them in ordinary discourse. We know that all such propositions are true. But it is interesting to notice that the reason why they must be true belongs to epistemology rather than to logic. We could not entertain any proposition about ϕ if we had not been able at some time to assert a proposition of the form '$\phi(a)$,' but any such proposition would entail 'for some x, $\phi(x)$.' Unfortunately, the traditional logicians while recognizing certain general propositions have tried to assimilate them in form to simple propositions such as 'this is red,' calling them all categorical. It is their obsession with the subject-predicate form which makes them reject out of hand all attempts to reduce mathematics to logic. I do not wish to assert here that any of the attempts is successful, but I do wish to maintain that no one who thinks that Aristotle exhausted formal logic can possibly hope to understand any of the attempts which have been made. As a preliminary to understanding we must first be prepared to recognize general propositions of such forms as 'for all x, y and z, if x is ρ to y, and y is ρ to z, then x is ρ to z,' which cannot be fitted into the traditional scheme of propositions. It is the same obsession which produces the fallacious ontological argument.

If the logical theories which I have summarized are correct, we can now answer the question implicit in Descartes' remark: "I do not see to what class of reality you wish to assign existence." Our answer must be that, if when Descartes talks of a class of reality he means substances or attributes or relations, existence belongs to no class of reality. The word "existence" is not a symbol for anything which can be either a constituent or a component of a simple proposition. It is only a logical auxiliary symbol. The sentence "tame tigers exist" is just one way of expressing the proposition 'for some x, x is tame and x is a tiger.' Other ways of expressing the same proposition are "there are tame tigers," "some tigers are tame," "something is a tame tiger." The sentence "tame tigers exist" may mislead philosophers into thinking that existence is a predicate, because it is grammatically similar to such sentences as "tame tigers growl" and "Rajah growls." Descartes fell into this confusion when he assumed that the proposition 'God exists' has the same form as a theorem of geometry. It is true that according to the usages of our language each of the propositions can be expressed in a sentence of the same grammatical form as those used to express attributive simple propositions, and that for most purposes such expression would be unobjectionable. But the logical forms of the two propositions are exhibited more clearly in the sentences "something is divine" and "if anything is a triangle, it has interior angles equal to two right angles." And no one who started with the new sentences would ever dream of an ontological argument. In short, the argument is merely a play on grammatical form.

III

I wish now to consider certain rather curious existential statements which are rarely if ever uttered by plain men.

(a) "*This exists*." After an account of existential propositions from which my own is in large part derived, Mr. Russell tells us that the words "*a* exists" can have no meaning if "*a*" is not a description but a logically proper name.[11] He allows that "*a* exists" may have meaning when "*a*" is a grammatically proper name. If I say "Mr. Russell exists" I may mean 'there is one and only one man who wrote *An Introduction to Mathematical Philosophy*, etc., and is called Mr. Russell.' "Mr. Russell" is then, as used by me, a unique description, i.e., a phrase connoting a complex of characters which belong all together to nothing but Mr. Russell. It would only be a logically proper name if I could use it without connotation to refer directly to something with which I was acquainted. The fundamental distinction here is between direct and indirect reference. When we think that we are making an indirect reference we may in fact be referring to nothing at all. That, I suppose, was the situation of Greeks who, believing their own mythology, said "the goddess of wisdom befriended Ulysses." But what of the sentence "this exists"? Common sense

---

[11] *Introduction to Mathematical Philosophy*, p. 178.

insists that the words have a meaning, and yet "this" does not look like a description.

It is true that if "*a*" were a logically proper name the words "*a* exists" could have no meaning such as we discover in the sentence "the President of the United States exists." If there were any meaning it could only be 'for some *x*, *x* is identical with *a*.' But in ordinary language there are no logically proper names. Symbols have sense because they are used according to habitual rules, and it is impossible that any symbol should be habitually associated with a particular which is a fleeting event. That we are able nevertheless to indicate to each other the particulars to which we wish to refer is due to the peculiarity of our habitual rules for the use of certain words such as "this," "here," "now" and "I." Each token of a demonstrative type may denote a different thing, but each token denotes whatever it does denote by locating that thing as in a certain relation to itself which anything denoted by a token of that type must have to the token denoting it. If anyone else understands my use of a demonstrative word, he does so by apprehending the particular sound which I utter and considering what thing can be in a certain relation to that particular sound. The rules for the use of tenses in verbs must be explained in a similar fashion. From these considerations it follows that even according to Mr. Russell's account of existential propositions the sentence "this exists" may have a perfectly good meaning, namely, 'there is something to which my token "this" has the deictic relation.'

(*b*) "*There are universals*." In view of the criticisms which are sometimes brought against recent developments of logic, it is important to show that we can find a sense in which this statement is undoubtedly true.

A universal is either a quality or a relation. Let us begin by considering the statement "redness is a quality." We may be tempted to think that it ascribes a predicate, namely, being-a-quality, to a thing. If, however, we try to take it in that sense, we shall certainly end in confusion, puzzling ourselves about unreal questions, such as how the things called qualities are related to the things called particulars. We must recognize that 'redness is a quality' is not a simple proposition. It seems rather to be about the rôle of redness as a component in simple propositions. I suggest that the least misleading expression of it is "for some x, x is red." If this analysis is correct, 'redness is a quality' is a general proposition. The proposition 'there are qualities' must in consequence be doubly-general. It can be expressed in the form "for some ϕ, for some x, $\phi(x)$." By a similar argument we can show that 'there are relations' can be expressed in the form "for some ρ, for some x, for some y, $\rho(x, y)$." "There are universals" is therefore equivalent to "for some ϕ, for some x, $\phi(x)$, or for some ρ, for some x, for some y, $\rho(x, y)$."

If we try to clarify the meaning of the statement "there are particulars," we find ourselves led to adopt an expression which differs from that just given in nothing but the order of the prefixes. But the order of the prefixes makes no difference to the sense of the whole expression when the prefixes are of the same kind. It follows that the two sentences, "there are universals" and "there are particulars," have the same meaning. At first sight this is a very startling conclusion, for it seems to suggest that the words "universal" and "particular" have the same meaning, which we cannot admit. But the false suggestion is the product of our own confusion. We have forgotten for the moment that the proposition which the two sentences express is multiply-general. The moral (and surely a very respectable moral) is that we cannot talk of universals without also talking of particulars and vice versa. Universals are components for constituents, and particulars are constituents for components. To say either "there are universals" or "there are particulars" is only to assert that something is somewhat or somehow to something, i.e., that there are simple facts. Universals and particulars are distinguished by their different rôles in simple facts. A universal or component is that element in a fact which determines its internal multiplicity. This we show by the way in which we use the symbols for components. We do not say "this is red that" or "this is greater than."

(c) *"There may be three-termed relations."* It has been suggested that jealousy, owing, and betweenness are three-termed relations. I agree that the words occur in sentences containing three nouns, but I do not think that those sentences ever express simple propositions. That I owe twenty pounds to my bookseller is certainly not a simple proposition. Betweenness is the most plausible of the suggested examples, but examination shows that sentences containing the word "between" are about the logical properties of two-termed relations. If I say that b is between a and c, I mean that there is some aliorelative transitive relation by which a is related to b and b to c. For my own part I cannot discover any genuine three-termed relation. This is the situation in which some logicians say "there may be three-termed relations." They wish to vindicate for pure logic the right to consider three-termed relationship as a possible form for simple propositions. Any logician who is not prepared to confine himself to consideration of propositional forms of which he can give examples must sooner or later defend himself in this fashion. For who can instance a simple fact of which the component is a thirty-seven-termed relation?

Now the sentence "there may be three-termed relations" seems to mean that it is not self-contradictory to say that there are three-termed relations. I am therefore required to understand the meaning of the statement "there are three-termed relations" while admitting that I cannot give an example and do not know whether the statement is true. It is easy, of course, to write out a set of marks analogous to that used in considering two-termed relations. It will be "for some ρ, x, y and z, $\rho(x, y, z)$." But when I wrote "for some ρ, x and y, $\rho(x, y)$" I knew the logical form which I symbolized by writing "$\rho(x, y)$." If my new set of marks is really the expression of a quadruply-general proposition, it is about a four-fold array of propositions all sharing the same form. In order to refer to those propositions I must at least know their form. And the whole difficulty in the present case is that I do not know any example of a form for which "$\rho(x, y, z)$" would by analogy be an appropriate symbol. I suggest that when logicians say "there may be three-termed relations" they are thinking only of the possibility of an extension of the rules according to which they manipulate marks like ρ and x. The only relational *symbols* to which the extended rules can be applied are incomplete symbols in Mr. Russell's sense, i.e., such words as "owing," which do not stand for elements of simple propositions.

(*d*) "*There is a natural number which. . . .*" It may be difficult to explain the meaning of such statements as "$7 + 5 = 12$." I have nothing to say about that problem except that numerals are neither proper names nor symbols for qualities. If, however, we can explain such statements, we should find no special difficulty in existential statements of the form "there is a natural number which. . . ." The fact that mathematicians sometimes make repeated trials in order to establish an existential proposition of this kind shows that the proposition is of the form 'one satisfies the conditions or two satisfies the conditions or three satisfies the conditions, etc.' But it has been suggested recently that such existential propositions are very mysterious and even that the principle of excluded middle does not apply to them. I think that the difficulty may perhaps have arisen from a failure to distinguish propositions which are contraries from propositions which are contradictories.

Let us consider a universal proposition to the effect that no number satisfies certain conditions. We may symbolize it by the letter N. The contradictory of this is the existential proposition that some number satisfies the conditions, which we may symbolize by the letter S. Now S might perhaps be established by repeated trial, i.e., we might find a number satisfying the conditions after a finite number of trials. But N can never be established in that way, since we cannot make trial of all numbers. When mathematicians establish a universal proposition they do so by demonstrating for what they call the general case or by mathematical induction (which is quite different from complete enumeration). They establish not simply N but the proposition that N is necessarily true, which we may symbolize by $! N$. N and $! N$ must be distinguished, for the contradictory of $! N$ is not S, but the proposition that S is possible, which we may symbolize by $*S$. The logical relations between the four propositions can be seen most clearly if they are arranged in a square of opposition as follows:

$$! N \qquad S$$

$$N \qquad *S$$

Each higher proposition entails that below it. Those at the opposite ends of a diagonal cannot both be true and cannot both be false. Those in the upper row cannot both be true but may both be false. Those in the lower row cannot both be false but may both be true. Since S is sufficient to refute $! N$, mathematicians, who are interested especially in $! N$, may sometimes assume that S is the contradictory of $! N$. If they do so, they will later find themselves led to the strange conclusion that the principle of excluded middle does not hold in mathematics. For $! N$ and S, being contraries, admit a *tertium*, namely, the conjunction of N and $*S$. The conjunction of N and $*S$ seems to be a very queer proposition, but I would rather recognize it as a genuine *tertium* between contraries than deny the principles of logic. What consequences would follow in the philosophy of mathematics from its recognition I do not know.

IV

The fundamental thesis of those who believe existence to be a predi-·cate is that there is a sense of "being" logically prior to existence and applicable to the possible as well as to the actual. When we have rejected the theory that existence is a predicate we must be prepared to meet the doctrine of prior possibility in another form. Some logicians who accept the analysis of existential propositions which I have outlined argue as follows: "Logic is concerned with the forms of propositions. Propositions must be distinguished both from sentences and from facts. For different sentences may express the same proposition, as any one admits who says, for example, that the speakers at an international conference are all discussing the same proposition although they speak in different languages. And not all our thinking is the knowing of facts: we often suppose that a were ϕ when we know that a is not ϕ. Now we must find a place somewhere for propositions, and it seems most reasonable to say that they are possibilities. For all facts are possibilities, but not all possibilities are facts." This theory can be stated without the use of the word "existence," but it is in effect a modern version of the doctrine which underlay the treatment of existence as a predicate by older philosophers. Here instead of existence as a predicate of possible things we have factuality as a predicate of possible states of affairs. Sometimes, indeed, the word "existence" is used in the statement of the theory. Mr. Wittgenstein, for example, seems to have held some such view when he wrote: "The existence of atomic facts [*Sachverhalten*, i.e., states of affairs] we also call a positive fact [*Tatsache*], their non-existence a negative fact."

We must admit that in its application to simple propositions this theory is free from the defects which we discovered in the doctrine of subsistent possible things. It need not involve us in any strange heresies about particulars and universals or about time. For it allows us to suppose that some particular were otherwise than in fact it is, and it does not require us to say that factuality or existence belongs to timeless possibles at certain times. We can go further and admit that whatever we think must in some sense be a possibility. But I think that we ought nevertheless to reject this form of the doctrine of prior possibility if it is offered as a finally satisfactory account of the nature of propositions.

What can we mean by the phrase "contemplating a possibility"? Some philosophers prefer to speak of knowing an analytic fact of the form 'p is possible.'[12] If this language is intended to provide an explanation of the nature of propositions, it assumes what it should explain, for the p of 'p is possible' is presumably a proposition which we must entertain in order to know that it is possible. Other philosophers who use the word "possibility" in their account of propositions apparently treat it as a synonym for "what is possible." According to them we are acquainted with a host of *possibilia* as objectives in their own right. But the word "possible" cannot stand alone as a description of anything. In order to give it a sense we must say that it is short for "possible fact." I suspect, however, that we sometimes talk of possible facts as though they were facts of some peculiar kind, which is obviously absurd. Let us then substitute for "possible fact" the less dangerous phrase "what might be the case." There is no doubt that at times we can use this phrase intelligibly, but I refuse to admit that the words ever describe an objective with which I am acquainted. To admit that they do would be to say that I know something which has the remarkable status of being ready to be a fact. Insistence that the objective is logically prior to what is the case and conceivable apart from all actuality only adds to the absurdity.

These considerations need not lead us to give up speaking of propositions, or even of possibilities, but they do suggest that we must treat propositions as logical constructions, i.e., that we must be prepared to translate sentences about propositions into sentences in which the word "proposition" and its synonyms do not occur. There is a common view (once defended by Mr. Russell in his polyadic relation theory of supposal) according to which thinking is doing something with elements abstracted from facts. But it seems clear that the elements of facts cannot be separated in such a way that a man may be acquainted with a constituent or a component when he is not knowing a fact in which it is constituent or component. That the elements of facts cannot be separated is the truth of the theory of *universale in re*. Nor is it enough to say that entertaining a proposition is imagining a as ϕ. For in its looser usage "imagining" is merely a synonym for "supposing," and in its stricter usage it means apparently having an image which is numerically distinct from a and only characterized by ϕ in some Pickwickian sense. Images may play some rôle in the situation which we call entertaining a proposition, but I think that the puzzle is to be solved only by consideration of the way in which

[12] Lewis and Langford, *Symbolic Logic*, ch. xiii.

we use symbols. The doctrine of subsistent propositions, or prior possibilities, arises from the assumption that when sentences are not used to
state facts they have meaning in precisely the same sense as when they
are. In each case, it is supposed, symbols are used only to express something of which we think without the help of symbols. I doubt whether
there is any thinking, as distinct from knowing, without the use of symbols. I wish to suggest, on the contrary, that thinking in the restricted
sense is a certain use of symbols, and that propositions are logical constructions out of sentences. The detailed development of this theory
would take too much time. I can only draw attention to some points of
the development which are especially important.

We must begin by considering the habitual use of symbols in sentences which state facts. For it is only by reference in the last resort to
this situation that any symbolism can be explained. We must then give
definitions of entailment and equivalence for primary sentences, i.e., for
sentences which are used to state facts. In this connexion we shall find
that primary sentences do not all state facts in the same sense of "state."
We have next to define the equivalence of secondary sentences, i.e., of
sentences which have been constructed out of old symbols according to
the rules of combination which those symbols obeyed when previously
used to state facts. Here we shall require the notion of analogous substitution. With these definitions we must go on to explain how various
statements about propositions can be transformed into statements about
sentences which are equivalent in either the primary or the secondary
sense. In particular we must explain what we mean when we say that a
sentence expresses a proposition, that a proposition has elements, that one
proposition entails another. We shall find that for a proposition to be
complex it is not necessary that the sentences which are said to express
it should contain other sentences as parts of themselves. Finally we must
explain in what sense it is true to say that a man always understands a
secondary sentence with which he thinks although he is not aware of anything which it represents. I think it will appear that the understanding
of a secondary sentence is for the most part not knowing anything, but
rather freedom from bewilderment, ability to detect its relations of entailment to other sentences, and readiness to determine in suitable circumstances whether the sentence does or does not state a fact according to
the old rules of usage.

It will be realized that if this account of propositions is correct the
fundamental problem in all logical analysis is the determination of the
way in which symbols are used in sentences which state facts. I have remarked that not all true sentences state facts in the same sense of "state."
This can be illustrated by consideration of existential sentences, with
which we are especially concerned. We may say, if we like, that the
sentence "something is red" states an existential fact, but it is obvious that

what we call an existential fact is not a fact of the same level as other facts. For I cannot know that something is red without knowing that a name-able particular is red. And, since the knowledge which justifies my asser-tion that something is red would also justify my assertion that the name-able particular is red, it seems better to say that the existential sentence states incompletely the same fact which the other sentence would state completely.[13] Obviously, the existential sentence states the fact incom-pletely because it is adapted to state any one of many different facts for the complete statement of which many different definite sentences would be required. And yet it is impossible to give a list of all the definite sen-tences for which the existential sentence might incompletely deputize. We can see why it is impossible, if we remember that the meaning of any symbol is determined by its rules of usage. The adjective "red" means what it does because it is habitually used in the statement of facts which have redness for their component. The word "some" does not stand for any element of facts, but its employment is governed by an habitual rule, namely, that a sentence containing the word "some" may be used to state a fact incompletely whenever a sentence of a certain sort (determined by the other words of the "some" sentence) can be used to state a fact more completely. Since we are not omniscient, we cannot hope to foresee all the cases which may be brought under such a rule. This is the explanation and justification of the doctrine that an existential proposition is an in-exponible adjunctive truth-function of the propositions of a range.

[13] Cf. J. Wisdom in *Mind*, Vol. XLII, p. 192.

Designation and Existence * [1]

W. V. QUINE

Statements of the form "There is such a thing as so-and-so" I shall call *singular existence statements;* e.g., "There is such a thing as Pegasus," "There is such a thing as Bucephalus," "There is such a thing as appendicitis." The expression following the word "as," here *purports* to designate some one specific entity—perhaps an individual, as in the case of "Pegasus" and "Bucephalus," or perhaps a property or other abstract entity, as in the case of "appendicitis"; and the statement is true just in case there *is* such a thing as this alleged designated entity, in other words just in case the expression really does designate.

The four-dimensional spatio-temporal view of nature is a device for facilitating logical analysis by rendering verbs tenseless. Let us adopt this device before proceeding farther. Bucephalus, then, is a certain four-dimensional body stretching through part of the fourth century B. C. and having horse-shaped cross-sections. Now the tensed statement "There is now no such thing as Bucephalus" is translatable into tenseless idiom roughly thus: "The temporally forward end of Bucephalus lies behind 1939." In the tenseless sense of "is," to which I shall adhere, there *is* such a thing as Bucephalus; namely, a spatio-temporally remote spatio-temporal body. Again, we will perhaps agree for the moment that there is such a thing as appendicitis; though this is not a spatio-temporal body, but another and a more abstract sort of entity. On the other hand there is no such thing as Pegasus; this word purports to designate a certain spatio-temporal body which in fact does not turn up anywhere in space-time, near or remote.

Now we must distinguish between these singular existence statements, "There is such a thing as so-and-so," and *general* existence statements: "There is such a thing as *a* so-and-so," or briefly "There is a so-and-so," "There are so-and-sos." A general existence statement, e.g., "There are unicorns," "There are horses," "There are prime numbers between 5 and

* Reprinted by kind permission of the author and the editors from *The Journal of Philosophy*, 36, 1939.

Acknowledgment is due Mr. H. Nelson Goodman and Dr. Arnold Isenberg for helpful criticism.

[1] This constitutes the bulk of a paper which was read at the Fifth International Congress for the Unity of Science, Cambridge, Mass., September 9, 1939, under the title "A Logistical Approach to the Ontological Problem."

11," says that there is at least one entity satisfying a certain condition. In logical symbols, the whole appears as an existential quantification:

$$(\exists x) \ (x \text{ is a unicorn}),$$
$$(\exists x) \ (x \text{ is a horse}),$$
$$(\exists x) \ (x \text{ is a prime number} \cdot 5 < x < 11).$$

In words:

There is *something which* is a unicorn.
There is *something which* is a horse.
There is *something which* is a prime number
and *which* is between 5 and 11.

Whereas the singular existence statement calls the alleged existent by name, e.g., "Pegasus," the general existence statement does not; the reference is made rather by a variable "*x*," the logistical analogue of a pronoun "which," "something which."

Note that a general term, such as "horse" or "unicorn," is capable also of turning up in a singular existence statement. Just as the word "appendicitis" designates a specific disease (which is abstract), and the word "Bucephalus" designates a specific horse (which is concrete), so we may regard the word "horse" as designating a specific property, an abstract combination of characteristics. Then the singular existence statement "There is such a thing as *horse*" (not "*a* horse") will mean, not that there are horses, but that there is the abstract property in question. The same holds for the word "unicorn"; and we may thus be inclined to affirm the singular existence statement "There is such a thing as unicorn" though denying the general existence statement "There is such a thing as *a* unicorn," "There are unicorns."

The distinction between singular and general existence statements thus does not correspond to the distinction between the concrete and the abstract; the entity whose existence is affirmed by a singular existence statement may be concrete (e.g., Bucephalus) or abstract (e.g., horse), and the entity or entities whose existence is affirmed by a general existence statement may likewise be concrete (e.g., horses) or abstract (e.g., prime numbers).

Now a curious problem is raised by the denial of a singular existence statement; e.g., "There is no such thing as Pegasus." If the word "Pegasus" designates something then there *is* such a thing as Pegasus, whereas if the word does not designate anything then the statement would appear to lack subject-matter and thus to fall into meaninglessness. Actually, this problem rests only on failure to observe that a noun can be meaningful in the absence of a designatum. The noun "Pegasus" *is* meaningful. If asked its meaning, we could reply with a translation into other words: "the winged horse captured by Bellerophon." The word "Pegasus" can be regarded as an abbreviation of this phrase; and the statement that there is no such thing as Pegasus then becomes, according to Russell's theory of descriptions, a statement to the effect that if Bellerophon captured any winged horses at all he captured two or more. Many words form essential parts of intelligible statements—truths and falsehoods—without being *names of* anything; such is the status of prepositions and conjunctions and adverbs, we will perhaps all agree, and it is the status likewise of many nouns, notably "Pegasus." Grammar and lexicography tell us, independently of questions of existence, that the word "Pegasus" is a noun and that it is equivalent to the phrase "the winged horse captured by Bellerophon"; it is left to history and zoölogy to tell us further that the word "Pegasus" is not a *name* in the semantic sense, i.e., that it has no designatum.

The understanding of a term thus does not imply a designatum; it precedes knowledge of whether or not the term has a designatum. If I say, e.g., that there is no such thing as hyperendemic fever, you will not agree; you will not understand. You will still refrain from asking me what hyperendemic fever *is*, for I have warned you that there is no such thing; but at least you will ask me to explain my terms. Questioned, I perhaps explain that I intend the words "hyperendemic fever" merely as an abbreviation for the phrase "the disease which killed or maimed four-fifths of the population of Winnipeg in 1903." Now that you know what I mean, an inquiry into Winnipeg history will lead you to agree that there is no such thing as hyperendemic fever.

The latter example shows incidentally that factual considerations can entail the repudiation not only of an alleged individual, e.g., Pegasus, but also of an alleged abstract entity. In contrast to these factually grounded cases, consider next the doctrine that there is no such thing as *up*. In repudiating an entity *"up"* we do not change our views as to the truth or falsehood of any ordinary factual statements containing the word "up." But we do claim that nothing, neither a spatio-temporal body nor even a property or other abstract entity, is *designated* by the word "up"; the word is meaningful, it forms an essential part of various statements, but it is not a noun, much less a name of anything.

Now the nominalist goes further than "up" in his repudiation of abstract entities. He would say, in the same spirit in which we have repudiated *up*, that there is no such thing as appendicitis. At the common-sense level from which we considered hyperendemic fever, one would rush to the defense of appendicitis; hyperendemic fever does not exist, but appendicitis certainly does. Still, just how does the nominalist err in treating appendicitis as we have treated *up?* He agrees that many people are appendicitic, and that the word "appendicitis" is meaningful and useful in context; yet he can maintain that the word is not a *name* of any *entity* in its own right, and that it is a noun at all only because of a regrettable strain of realism which pervades our own particular language. On the same grounds, the nominalist will go back and do a more ruthless job than we have done in the matter of unicorns; he will say that there is not merely no such thing as a unicorn but also no such thing as *unicorn*—no abstract entity, so-called property, such as this word has been said to designate. He keeps the word "unicorn" merely as a contextually meaningful word like "up" —a syncategorematic expression which *names* nothing, abstract or concrete. The general term "horse" will fare no better; there are many denoted entities in this case, indeed—many horses—but no *named* or designated entity, no abstract property *horse* according to the nominalist.

But now the whole question of existence is beginning to appear gratuitous. If the nominalist who renounces such abstract entities as horse, unicorn, and appendicitis does not thereby foreswear any of the ordinary uses of these words, nor take issue on any factual questions of zoölogy and medicine, then what does his renunciation amount to? Any appeal to nature, such as was involved in the case of Pegasus and hyperendemic fever, seems now to have become irrelevant. What is left but a bandying of empty honorifics and pejoratives—"existent" and "non-existent," "real" and "unreal"?

We are tempted at this point to dismiss the whole issue between nominalism and realism as a metaphysical pseudoproblem. But in thus cutting the Gordian knot we cut too deep into the level of common sense. We are all inclined, I suppose, to regard the word "up" or the suffix "ness" or the signs of punctuation as syncategorematic expressions, meaningful in context but *naming* nothing. The mere capacity to turn up in a sentence does not make a string of marks a name. Now if we allow ourselves this much freedom in repudiating designata, on what grounds can we take issue with the nominalist? On what grounds, indeed, can we take issue with someone who even outdoes the nominalist and repudiates *everything*, the concrete as well as the abstract, by construing all words indiscriminately as syncategorematic expressions designating nothing? We seem to have a continuum of possible ontologies here, ranging from a radical realism at the one extreme, where even a left-hand parenthesis or the dot of an "i" has some weird abstract entity as designatum, to a complete nihilism at the other extreme. Singular existence statements "There is such a thing as so-and-so," together with their trivial variants such as "So-and-so designates," begin to assume the air of a logically isolated class of statements—logically independent of the rest of discourse, verifiable or falsifiable at caprice, and thus void of meaning. If we are to avert this consequence, we must find some relationship of logical dependence between the singular existence statement and the rest of discourse.

Let us return to the singular existence statement "There is such a thing as appendicitis." This can indeed be affirmed or denied without affecting our attitude toward the usual statements containing the word "appendicitis"—for example, "Appendicitis is dreaded." Continuing to affirm the latter statement, the nominalist can yet maintain that the word "appendicitis" figures syncategorematically therein, like "is" or "pend," and that there is no designated object "appendicitis." The singular existence statement does not affect the truth value of the statement "Appendicitis is dreaded." However, it does prove to have other effects. If the word "appendicitis" designates an entity, then the statement "Appendicitis is dreaded" is a statement *about* that entity. It affirms the dreadedness thereof, and implies the consequence that *something* is dreaded:

$$(\exists x) \ (x \text{ is dreaded}).$$

If on the other hand the word "appendicitis" is syncategorematic and designates nothing, then the statement "Appendicitis is dreaded" is not about an entity "appendicitis," any more than it is about an entity *"pend"* or *"is"*; it does *not* have the consequence:

$$(\exists x) \ (x \text{ is dreaded}).$$

The singular existence statement "There is such a thing as appendicitis" does, therefore, have an effect on general existence statements. If we affirm the singular existence statement, we must regard any general existence statement "$(\exists x) \ (. \ . \ .x. \ . \ .)$" as following from the corresponding statement ". . .appendicitis. . ." which contains "appendicitis" in place of "x." If we deny the singular existence statement "There is such a thing as appendicitis," on the other hand, we do not countenance such inference. Let us refer to this form of inference—putting "x" for "appendicitis" in a statement and prefixing "$(\exists x)$"—as the operation of *existentially generalizing* with respect to the word "appendicitis." To say that there is such a thing as appendicitis, or that "appendicitis" designates something, is to say that the operation of existentially generalizing with respect to "appendicitis" is *valid;* i.e., that it leads from truths only to truths.

This conclusion would seem to hold in general. A word W *designates* if and only if existential generalization with respect to W is a valid form of inference. The word "appendicitis" used in the foregoing example happens to be of an abstract sort, but this is not essential. Consider again the word "Pegasus," construed as an abbreviation of the phrase "the winged horse captured by Bellerophon." If Pegasus does not exist, in other words, if it is not true that one and only one winged horse was captured by Bellerophon, then according to Russell's theory of descriptions there will be various true statements which can be turned into falsehoods by existentially generalizing with respect to the word "Pegasus." For example, the statement:

Nothing is identical with Pegasus

is true whereas the result of existential generalization:

$$(\exists x) \text{ (nothing is identical with } x)$$

is false.

Our earlier apprehension, namely, that all singular existence statements might prove logically isolated and thus affirmable or deniable at caprice, is thus overcome. Perhaps we can reach no absolute decision as to which words have designata and which have none, but at least we can say whether or not a given pattern of linguistic behavior *construes* a word W as having a designatum. This is decided by judging whether existential generalization with respect to W is accepted as a valid form of inference. A *name*—not in the sense of a mere noun, but in the semantic sense of an expression designating something—becomes describable as an expression with respect to which existential generalization is valid.

Under the usual formulation of logic there are two basic forms of inference which interchange names with variables. One is existential generalization, whereby a name is replaced by a variable "x" and an existential prefix "$(\exists x)$" is attached:

$$\ldots \text{Paris} \ldots$$

$$\therefore (\exists x) (\ldots x \ldots)$$

The other, which may be called *specification,* is the form of inference whereby a variable is replaced by a name and a *universal* prefix is dropped; it leads from a *universal quantification:*

$$(x) (\ldots x \ldots),$$

that is:

$$\text{For all choices of } x, \ldots x \ldots$$

to:

$$\ldots \text{Paris} \ldots$$

Now if existential generalization is valid with respect to a given term, say "Paris," then specification is likewise valid with respect to that term. For, suppose "$\ldots$Paris$\ldots$" is false. Then its denial:

$$\sim (\ldots \text{Paris} \ldots)$$

is true. From this, by existential generalization, we get:

$$(\exists x) \sim (\ldots x \ldots),$$

i.e.:

$$\sim (x) (\ldots x \ldots),$$

thus concluding that "$(x) (\ldots x \ldots)$" is false. The falsehood of "$\ldots$Paris$\ldots$" is thus seen to entail that of "$(x) (\ldots x \ldots)$". Therefore the truth of "$(x) (\ldots x \ldots)$" entails that of "$\ldots$Paris$\ldots$".

Hence, instead of describing names as expressions with respect to which existential generalization is valid, we might equivalently omit express mention of existential generalization and describe names simply as those constant expressions which replace variables and are replaced by variables according to the usual logical laws of quantification.

Contexts of quantification, "(x) $(. . .x. . .)$" and "$(\exists x)$ $(. . .x. . .)$," do not indeed exhaust the ways in which a variable "x" may turn up in discourse; the variable is also essential to the idioms "the object x such that . . . ," "the class of all objects x such that . . . ," and others. However, the quantificational use of variables *is* exhaustive in the sense that all use of variables is *reducible* to this sort of use. Every statement containing a variable can be translated, by known rules, into an equivalent statement in which the variable has only the quantificational use. All other uses of variables can be explained as abbreviations of contexts in which the variables figure solely as variables of quantification. And *names*, we found, are describable simply as the constant expressions which replace these variables and are replaced by these variables according to the usual laws. In short, names are the constant *substituends* of variables.

A variable "x" is ordinarily thought of as associated with a realm of entities, the so-called *range of values* of the variable. The range of values is not to be confused with the range of *substituends*. The names are substituends; the named entities are values. Numerals, names of numbers, are substituends for the variables of arithmetic; the values of these variables, on the other hand, are numbers. Variables can be thought of roughly as ambiguous names of their values. This notion of ambiguous name is not as mysterious as it at first appears, for it is essentially the notion of a pronoun; the variable "x" is a relative pronoun used in connection with a quantifier, "(x)" or "$(\exists x)$."

Here, then, are five ways of saying the same thing: "There is such a thing as appendicitis"; "The word 'appendicitis' designates"; "The word 'appendicitis' is a name"; "The word 'appendicitis' is a substituend for a variable"; "The disease appendicitis is a value of a variable." The universe of entities is the range of values of variables. To be is to be the value of a variable.

Supposing that we know where to draw the line between the *concrete* or individual and the *abstract*, we can now make some sense of the distinction between a *nominalistic* and a *realistic* language. Words of the abstract or general sort, say "appendicitis" or "horse," can turn up in nominalistic as well as realistic languages; but the difference is that in realistic languages such words are substituends for variables—they can replace and be replaced by variables according to the usual laws of quantification—whereas in nominalistic languages this is not the case. In realistic languages, variables admit abstract entities as values; in nominalistic languages they do not.

As a thesis in the philosophy of science, nominalism can be formulated thus: it is possible to set up a nominalistic language in which all of natural science can be expressed. The nominalist, so interpreted, claims that a language adequate to all scientific purposes can be framed in such a way that its variables admit only concrete objects, individuals, as values—hence only proper names of concrete objects as substituends. Abstract terms will retain the status of syncategorematic expressions, designating nothing, so long as no corresponding variables are used.

Indeed, the nominalist need not even forego the convenience of variables having abstract entities as values, or abstract terms as substituends, provided that he can explain this usage away as a mere manner of speaking. Quantification involving a new sort of variables, which ostensibly admit a new sort of entities as values, can often be introduced by a contextual definition—a mere convention of notational abbreviation. Elsewhere I have cited, by way of example, a convention of notational abbreviation introducing quantification upon variables which have statements as their substituenda. When such an abbreviation is adopted we are able to talk *as if* statements were names having certain abstract entities—so-called propositions—as designata. In so doing we do not commit ourselves to *belief* in such entities; for we can excuse our new form of quantification as a mere abridged manner of speaking, translatable at will back into an idiom which uses no statement variables and hence presupposes no propositions, no designata of statements. Under such a procedure propositions become explicitly *fictions*, in this sense: there are no such things, from the standpoint of our unabbreviated official language, but we talk as if there were by dint of an eliminable shorthand.

Similarly, if the nominalist can devise contextual definitions explaining quantification with respect to any other alleged entities of an abstract kind,[2] he becomes justified in speaking *as if* there were such entities without really forsaking his nominalism. The entities remain fictions for him; his reference to such entities remains a mere manner of speaking, in the sense that he can expand this sort of quantification at will into an official idiom which uses only variables having proper names of individuals as substituends. But if the nominalist can not supply the relevant contextual definitions, then his nominalism forbids his use of variables having abstract entities as values. He will perhaps still plead that his apparent abstract entities are merely convenient fictions; but this plea is no more than an incantation, a crossing of the fingers, so long as the required contextual definitions are not forthcoming.

[2] For work in this direction see my "Theory of Classes Presupposing No Canons of Type," *Proc. Nat. Acad. Sci.*, Vol. 22 (1936), pp. 320-326.

The Semantic Conception of Truth
AND THE FOUNDATIONS OF SEMANTICS *

ALFRED TARSKI

This paper consists of two parts; the first has an expository character, and the second is rather polemical.

In the first part I want to summarize in an informal way the main results of my investigations concerning the definition of truth and the more general problem of the foundations of semantics. These results have been embodied in a work which appeared in print several years ago.[1] Although my investigations concern concepts dealt with in classical philosophy, they happen to be comparatively little known in philosophical circles, perhaps because of their strictly technical character. For this reason I hope I shall be excused for taking up the matter once again.[2]

Since my work was published, various objections, of unequal value, have been raised to my investigations; some of these appeared in print, and others were made in public and private discussions in which I took part.[3] In the second part of the paper I should like to express my views regarding these objections. I hope that the remarks which will be made in this context will not be considered as purely polemical in character, but will be found to contain some constructive contributions to the subject.

In the second part of the paper I have made extensive use of material graciously put at my disposal by Dr. Marja Kokoszyńska (University of Lwów). I am especially indebted and grateful to Professors Ernest Nagel (Columbia University) and David Rynin (University of California, Berkeley) for their help in preparing the final text and for various critical remarks.

I. EXPOSITION

1. The Main Problem—A Satisfactory Definition of Truth. Our discussion will be centered around the notion [4] of *truth*. The main problem is that of giving a *satisfactory definition* of this notion, i.e., a definition which is *materially adequate* and *formally correct*. But such a formulation of the problem, because of its generality, cannot be considered unequivocal, and requires some further comments.

In order to avoid any ambiguity, we must first specify the conditions

* Reprinted by kind permission of the author and the editors from "Symposium on Meaning and Truth", *Philosophy and Phenomenological Research*, Vol. IV, 1944.
Footnote references will be found at the end of this selection.

under which the definition of truth will be considered adequate from the material point of view. The desired definition does not aim to specify the meaning of a familiar word used to denote a novel notion; on the contrary, it aims to catch hold of the actual meaning of an old notion. We must then characterize this notion precisely enough to enable anyone to determine whether the definition actually fulfills its task.

Secondly, we must determine on what the formal correctness of the definition depends. Thus, we must specify the words or concepts which we wish to use in defining the notion of truth; and we must also give the formal rules to which the definition should conform. Speaking more generally, we must describe the formal structure of the language in which the definition will be given.

The discussion of these points will occupy a considerable portion of the first part of the paper.

2. *The Extension of the Term "True."* We begin with some remarks regarding the extension of the concept of truth which we have in mind here.

The predicate *"true"* is sometimes used to refer to psychological phenomena such as judgments or beliefs, sometimes to certain physical objects, namely, linguistic expressions and specifically sentences, and sometimes to certain ideal entities called "propositions." By "sentence" we understand here what is usually meant in grammar by "declarative sentence"; as regards the term "proposition," its meaning is notoriously a subject of lengthy disputations by various philosophers and logicians, and it seems never to have been made quite clear and unambiguous. For several reasons it appears most convenient to *apply the term "true" to sentences,* and we shall follow this course.[5]

Consequently, we must always relate the notion of truth, like that of a sentence, to a specific language; for it is obvious that the same expression which is a true sentence in one language can be false or meaningless in another.

Of course, the fact that we are interested here primarily in the notion of truth for sentences does not exclude the possibility of a subsequent extension of this notion to other kinds of objects.

3. *The Meaning of the Term "True."* Much more serious difficulties are connected with the problem of the meaning (or the intension) of the concept of truth.

The word *"true,"* like other words from our everyday language, is certainly not unambiguous. And it does not seem to me that the philosophers who have discussed this concept have helped to diminish its ambiguity. In works and discussions of philosophers we meet many different conceptions of truth and falsity, and we must indicate which conception will be the basis of our discussion.

We should like our definition to do justice to the intuitions which adhere to the *classical Aristotelian conception of truth*—intuitions which find their expression in the well-known words of Aristotle's *Metaphysics:*

To say of what is that it is not, or of what is not that it is, is false, while to say of what is that it is, or of what is not that it is not, is true.

If we wished to adapt ourselves to modern philosophical terminology, we could perhaps express this conception by means of the familiar formula:

The truth of a sentence consists in its agreement with (or correspondence to) reality.

(For a theory of truth which is to be based upon the latter formulation the term "correspondence theory" has been suggested.)

If, on the other hand, we should decide to extend the popular usage of the term "*designate*" by applying it not only to names, but also to sentences, and if we agreed to speak of the designata of sentences as "states of affairs," we could possibly use for the same purpose the following phrase:

A sentence is true if it designates an existing state of affairs.[6]

However, all these formulations can lead to various misunderstandings, for none of them is sufficiently precise and clear (though this applies much less to the original Aristotelian formulation than to either of the others); at any rate, none of them can be considered a satisfactory definition of truth. It is up to us to look for a more precise expression of our intuitions.

4. A Criterion for the Material Adequacy of the Definition.[7] Let us start with a concrete example. Consider the sentence "*snow is white.*" We ask the question under what conditions this sentence is true or false. It seems clear that if we base ourselves on the classical conception of truth, we shall say that the sentence is true if snow is white, and that it is false if snow is not white. Thus, if the definition of truth is to conform to our conception, it must imply the following equivalence:

The sentence "snow is white" is true if, and only if, snow is white.

Let me point out that the phrase "*snow is white*" occurs on the left side of this equivalence in quotation marks, and on the right without quotation marks. On the right side we have the sentence itself, and on the left the name of the sentence. Employing the medieval logical terminology we could also say that on the right side the words "*snow is white*" occur in *suppositio formalis*, and on the left in *suppositio materialis*. It is hardly necessary to explain why we must have the name of the sentence, and not the sentence itself, on the left side of the equivalence. For, in the first place, from the point of view of the grammar of our language, an expression of the form "*X is true*" will not become a meaningful sentence if we replace in it 'X' by a sentence or by anything other than a name—since the subject of a sentence may be only a noun or an expression functioning like a noun.

And, in the second place, the fundamental conventions regarding the use of any language require that in any utterance we make about an object it is the name of the object which must be employed, and not the object itself. In consequence, if we wish to say something about a sentence, for example, that it is true, we must use the name of this sentence, and not the sentence itself.[8]

It may be added that enclosing a sentence in quotation marks is by no means the only way of forming its name. For instance, by assuming the usual order of letters in our alphabet, we can use the following expression as the name (the description) of the sentence *"snow is white"*:

the sentence constituted by three words, the first of which consists of the 19th, 14th, 15th, and 23rd letters, the second of the 9th and 19th letters, and the third of the 23rd, 8th, 9th, 20th, and 5th letters of the English alphabet.

We shall now generalize the procedure which we have applied above. Let us consider an arbitrary sentence; we shall replace it by the letter '*p*.' We form the name of this sentence and we replace it by another letter, say '*X*.' We ask now what is the logical relation between the two sentences "*X is true*" and '*p*.' It is clear that from the point of view of our basic conception of truth these sentences are equivalent. In other words, the following equivalence holds:

(T)   *X is true if, and only if, p.*

We shall call any such equivalence (with '*p*' replaced by any sentence of the language to which the word "*true*" refers, and '*X*' replaced by a name of this sentence) an "*equivalence of the form* (T)."

Now at last we are able to put into a precise form the conditions under which we will consider the usage and the definition of the term "*true*" as adequate from the material point of view: we wish to use the term "*true*" in such a way that all equivalences of the form (T) can be asserted, and *we shall call a definition of truth "adequate" if all these equivalences follow from it.*

It should be emphasized that neither the expression (T) itself (which is not a sentence, but only a schema of a sentence) nor any particular instance of the form (T) can be regarded as a definition of truth. We can only say that every equivalence of the form (T) obtained by replacing '*p*' by a particular sentence, and '*X*' by a name of this sentence, may be considered a partial definition of truth, which explains wherein the truth of this one individual sentence consists. The general definition has to be, in a certain sense, a logical conjunction of all these partial definitions.

(The last remark calls for some comments. A language may admit the construction of infinitely many sentences; and thus the number of partial definitions of truth referring to sentences of such a language will also be infinite. Hence to give our remark a precise sense we should have to explain what is meant by a "logical conjunction of infinitely many sentences"; but this would lead us too far into technical problems of modern logic.)

5. *Truth as a Semantic Concept.* I should like to propose the name *"the semantic conception of truth"* for the conception of truth which has just been discussed.

Semantics is a discipline which, speaking loosely, *deals with certain relations between expressions of a language and the objects* (or "states of affairs") *"referred to" by those expressions.* As typical examples of semantic concepts we may mention the concepts of *designation, satisfaction,* and *definition* as these occur in the following examples:

> *the expression "the father of his country" designates (denotes) George Washington;*

> *snow satisfies the sentential function (the condition) "x is white";*

> *the equation "2·x = 1" defines (uniquely determines) the number* 1/2.

While the words *"designates," "satisfies,"* and *"defines"* express relations (between certain expressions and the objects "referred to" by these expressions), the word *"true"* is of a different logical nature: it expresses a property (or denotes a class) of certain expressions, viz., of sentences. However, it is easily seen that all the formulations which were given earlier and which aimed to explain the meaning of this word (cf. Sections 3 and 4) referred not only to sentences themselves, but also to objects "talked about" by these sentences, or possibly to "states of affairs" described by them. And, moreover, it turns out that the simplest and the most natural way of obtaining an exact definition of truth is one which involves the use of other semantic notions, e.g., the notion of satisfaction. It is for these reasons that we count the concept of truth which is discussed here among the concepts of semantics, and the problem of defining truth proves to be closely related to the more general problem of setting up the foundations of theoretical semantics.

It is perhaps worth while saying that semantics as it is conceived in this paper (and in former papers of the author) is a sober and modest discipline which has no pretentions of being a universal patent-medicine for all the ills and diseases of mankind, whether imaginary or real. You will not find in semantics any remedy for decayed teeth or illusions of grandeur or class conflicts. Nor is semantics a device for establishing that everyone except the speaker and his friends is speaking nonsense.

From antiquity to the present day the concepts of semantics have played an important rôle in the discussions of philosophers, logicians, and philologists. Nevertheless, these concepts have been treated for a long time with a certain amount of suspicion. From a historical standpoint, this suspicion is to be regarded as completely justified. For although the meaning of semantic concepts as they are used in everyday language seems to be rather clear and understandable, still all attempts to characterize this meaning in a general and exact way miscarried. And what is worse, various arguments in which these concepts were involved, and which seemed otherwise quite correct and based upon apparently obvious premises, led frequently to paradoxes and antinomies. It is sufficient to mention here the *antinomy of the liar*, Richard's *antinomy of definability* (by means of a finite number of words), and Grelling-Nelson's *antinomy of heterological terms*.[9]

I believe that the method which is outlined in this paper helps to overcome these difficulties and assures the possibility of a consistent use of semantic concepts.

6. *Languages with a Specified Structure.* Because of the possible occurrence of antinomies, the problem of specifying the formal structure and the vocabulary of a language in which definitions of semantic concepts are to be given becomes especially acute; and we turn now to this problem.

There are certain general conditions under which the structure of a language is regarded as *exactly specified*. Thus, to specify the structure of a language, we must characterize unambiguously the class of those words and expressions which are to be considered *meaningful*. In particular, we must indicate all words which we decide to use without defining them, and which are called "*undefined* (or *primitive*) *terms*"; and we must give the so-called *rules of definition* for introducing new or *defined terms*. Furthermore, we must set up criteria for distinguishing within the class of expressions those which we call "*sentences*." Finally, we must formulate the conditions under which a sentence of the language can be *asserted*. In particular, we must indicate all *axioms* (or *primitive sentences*), i.e., those sentences which we decide to assert without proof; and we must give the so-called *rules of inference* (or *rules of proof*) by means of which we can deduce new asserted sentences from other sentences which have been previously asserted. Axioms, as well as sentences deduced from them by means of rules of inference, are referred to as "*theorems*" or "*provable sentences*."

If in specifying the structure of a language we refer exclusively to the form of the expressions involved, the language is said to be *formalized*. In such a language theorems are the only sentences which can be asserted.

At the present time the only languages with a specified structure are the formalized languages of various systems of deductive logic, possibly enriched by the introduction of certain non-logical terms. However, the field of application of these languages is rather comprehensive; we are able, theoretically, to develop in them various branches of science, for instance, mathematics and theoretical physics.

(On the other hand, we can imagine the construction of languages which have an exactly specified structure without being formalized. In such a language the assertability of sentences, for instance, may depend not always on their form, but sometimes on other, non-linguistic factors. It would be interesting and important actually to construct a language of this type, and specifically one which would prove to be sufficient for the development of a comprehensive branch of empirical science; for this would justify the hope that languages with specified structure could finally replace every-day language in scientific discourse.)

The problem of the definition of truth obtains a precise meaning and can be solved in a rigorous way only for those languages whose structure has been exactly specified. For other languages—thus, for all natural, "spoken" languages—the meaning of the problem is more or less vague, and its solution can have only an approximate character. Roughly speaking, the approximation consists in replacing a natural language (or a portion of it in which we are interested) by one whose structure is exactly specified, and which diverges from the given language "as little as possible."

7. *The Antinomy of the Liar.* In order to discover some of the more specific conditions which must be satisfied by languages in which (or for which) the definition of truth is to be given, it will be advisable to begin with a discussion of that antinomy which directly involves the notion of truth, namely, the antinomy of the liar.

To obtain this antinomy in a perspicuous form,[10] consider the following sentence:

The sentence printed in this paper on p. 58, l. 19, is not true.

For brevity we shall replace the sentence just stated by the letter '*s*.'

According to our convention concerning the adequate usage of the term "*true*," we assert the following equivalence of the form (T):

(1) '*s*' *is true if, and only if, the sentence printed in this paper on p. 58, l. 19, is not true.*

On the other hand, keeping in mind the meaning of the symbol '*s*,' we establish empirically the following fact:

(2) '*s*' *is identical with the sentence printed in this paper on p. 58, l. 19.*

Now, by a familiar law from the theory of identity (Leibniz's law), it follows from (2) that we may replace in (1) the expression "*the sentence printed in this paper on p. 58, l. 19*" by the symbol " '*s*.' " We thus obtain what follows:

(3)   '*s*' *is true if, and only if, '*s*' is not true.*

In this way we have arrived at an obvious contradiction.

In my judgment, it would be quite wrong and dangerous from the standpoint of scientific progress to depreciate the importance of this and other antinomies, and to treat them as jokes or sophistries. It is a fact that we are here in the presence of an absurdity, that we have been compelled to assert a false sentence (since (3), as an equivalence between two contradictory sentences, is necessarily false). If we take our work seriously, we cannot be reconciled with this fact. We must discover its cause, that is to say, we must analyze premises upon which the antinomy is based; we must then reject at least one of these premises, and we must investigate the consequences which this has for the whole domain of our research.

It should be emphasized that antinomies have played a preëminent rôle in establishing the foundations of modern deductive sciences. And just as class-theoretical antinomies, and in particular Russell's antinomy (of the class of all classes that are not members of themselves), were the starting point for the successful attempts at a consistent formalization of logic and mathematics, so the antinomy of the liar and other semantic antinomies give rise to the construction of theoretical semantics.

8. *The Inconsistency of Semantically Closed Languages.*[7] If we now analyze the assumptions which lead to the antinomy of the liar, we notice the following:

(I) We have implicitly assumed that the language in which the antinomy is constructed contains, in addition to its expressions, also the names of these expressions, as well as semantic terms such as the term "*true*" referring to sentences of this language; we have also assumed that all sentences which determine the adequate usage of this term can be asserted in the language. A language with these properties will be called "*semantically closed.*"

(II) We have assumed that in this language the ordinary laws of logic hold.

(III) We have assumed that we can formulate and assert in our language an empirical premise such as the statement (2) which has occurred in our argument.

It turns out that the assumption (III) is not essential, for it is possible to reconstruct the antinomy of the liar without its help.[11] But the assumptions (I) and (II) prove essential. Since every language which satisfies both of these assumptions is inconsistent, we must reject at least one of them.

It would be superfluous to stress here the consequences of rejecting the assumption (II), that is, of changing our logic (supposing this were possible) even in its more elementary and fundamental parts. We thus consider only the possibility of rejecting the assumption (I). Accordingly, we decide *not to use any language which is semantically closed* in the sense given.

This restriction would of course be unacceptable for those who, for reasons which are not clear to me, believe that there is only one "genuine" language (or, at least, that all "genuine" languages are mutually translatable). However, this restriction does not affect the needs or interests of science in any essential way. The languages (either the formalized languages or—what is more frequently the case—the portions of everyday language) which are used in scientific discourse do not have to be semantically closed. This is obvious in case linguistic phenomena and, in particular, semantic notions do not enter in any way into the subject-matter of a science; for in such a case the language of this science does not have to be provided with any semantic terms at all. However, we shall see in the next section how semantically closed languages can be dispensed with even in those scientific discussions in which semantic notions are essentially involved.

The problem arises as to the position of everyday language with regard to this point. At first blush it would seem that this language satisfies both assumptions (I) and (II), and that therefore it must be inconsistent. But actually the case is not so simple. Our everyday language is certainly not one with an exactly specified structure. We do not know precisely which expressions are sentences, and we know even to a smaller degree which sentences are to be taken as assertible. Thus the problem of consistency has no exact meaning with respect to this language. We may at best only risk the guess that a language whose structure has been exactly specified and which resembles our everyday language as closely as possible would be inconsistent.

9. *Object-Language and Meta-Language.* Since we have agreed not to employ semantically closed languages, we have to use two different languages in discussing the problem of the definition of truth and, more generally, any problems in the field of semantics. The first of these languages is the language which is "talked about" and which is the subject-matter of the whole discussion; the definition of truth which we are seeking applies to the sentences of this language. The second is the language in which we "talk about" the first language, and in terms of which we wish, in particular, to construct the definition of truth for the first language. We shall refer to the first language as *"the object-language,"* and to the second as *"the meta-language."*

It should be noticed that these terms "object-language" and "meta-language" have only a relative sense. If, for instance, we become interested in the notion of truth applying to sentences, not of our original object-language, but of its meta-language, the latter becomes automatically the object-language of our discussion; and in order to define truth for this language, we have to go to a new meta-language—so to speak, to a meta-language of a higher level. In this way we arrive at a whole hierarchy of languages.

The vocabulary of the meta-language is to a large extent determined by previously stated conditions under which a definition of truth will be considered materially adequate. This definition, as we recall, has to imply all equivalences of the form (T):

(T)   *X is true if, and only if, p.*

The definition itself and all the equivalences implied by it are to be formulated in the meta-language. On the other hand, the symbol 'p' in (T) stands for an arbitrary sentence of our object-language. Hence it follows that every sentence which occurs in the object-language must also occur in the meta-language; in other words, the meta-language must contain the object-language as a part. This is at any rate necessary for the proof of the adequacy of the definition—even though the definition itself can sometimes be formulated in a less comprehensive meta-language which does not satisfy this requirement.

(The requirement in question can be somewhat modified, for it suffices to assume that the object-language can be translated into the meta-language; this necessitates a certain change in the interpretation of the symbol 'p' in (T). In all that follows we shall ignore the possibility of this modification.)

Furthermore, the symbol 'X' in (T) represents the name of the sentence which 'p' stands for. We see therefore that the meta-language must be rich enough to provide possibilities of constructing a name for every sentence of the object-language.

In addition, the meta-language must obviously contain terms of a general logical character, such as the expression "if, and only if." [12]

It is desirable for the meta-language not to contain any undefined terms except such as are involved explicitly or implicitly in the remarks above, i.e.: terms of the object-language; terms referring to the form of the expressions of the object-language, and used in building names for these expressions; and terms of logic. In particular, we desire *semantic terms* (referring to the object-language) *to be introduced into the meta-language only by definition*. For, if this postulate is satisfied, the definition of truth, or of any other semantic concept, will fulfill what we intuitively expect from every definition; that is, it will explain the meaning of the term being defined in terms whose meaning appears to be completely clear and unequivocal. And, moreover, we have then a kind of guarantee that the use of semantic concepts will not involve us in any contradictions.

We have no further requirements as to the formal structure of the object-language and the meta-language; we assume that it is similar to that of other formalized languages known at the present time. In particular, we assume that the usual formal rules of definition are observed in the meta-language.

10. Conditions for a Positive Solution of the Main Problem. Now, we have already a clear idea both of the conditions of material adequacy to which the definition of truth is subjected, and of the formal structure of the language in which this definition is to be constructed. Under these circumstances the problem of the definition of truth acquires the character of a definite problem of a purely deductive nature.

The solution of the problem, however, is by no means obvious, and I would not attempt to give it in detail without using the whole machinery of contemporary logic. Here I shall confine myself to a rough outline of the solution and to the discussion of certain points of a more general interest which are involved in it.

The solution turns out to be sometimes positive, sometimes negative. This depends upon some formal relations between the object-language and its meta-language; or, more specifically, upon the fact whether the meta-language in its logical part is *"essentially richer"* than the object-language or not. It is not easy to give a general and precise definition of this notion of "essential richness." If we restrict ourselves to languages based on the logical theory of types, the condition for the meta-language to be "essentially richer" than the object-language is that it contain variables of a higher logical type than those of the object-language.

If the condition of "essential richness" is not satisfied, it can usually be shown that an interpretation of the meta-language in the object-language is possible; that is to say, with any given term of the meta-language a well-determined term of the object-language can be correlated in such a way that the assertible sentences of the one language turn out to be correlated with assertible sentences of the other. As a result of this interpretation, the hypothesis that a satisfactory definition of truth has been formulated in the meta-language turns out to imply the possibility of reconstructing in that language the antinomy of the liar; and this in turn forces us to reject the hypothesis in question.

(The fact that the meta-language, in its non-logical part, is ordinarily more comprehensive than the object-language does not affect the possibility of interpreting the former in the latter. For example, the names of expressions of the object-language occur in the meta-language, though for the most part they do not occur in the object-language itself; but, nevertheless, it may be possible to interpret these names in terms of the object-language.)

Thus we see that the condition of "essential richness" is necessary for the possibility of a satisfactory definition of truth in the meta-language. If we want to develop the theory of truth in a meta-language which does not satisfy this condition, we must give up the idea of defining truth with the exclusive help of those terms which were indicated above (in Section 8). We have then to include the term *"true,"* or some other semantic term, in the list of undefined terms of the meta-language, and to express fundamental properties of the notion of truth in a series of axioms. There is nothing essentially wrong in such an axiomatic procedure, and it may prove useful for various purposes.[18]

It turns out, however, that this procedure can be avoided. For *the condition of the "essential richness" of the meta-language proves to be, not only necessary, but also sufficient for the construction of a satisfactory definition of truth;* i.e., if the meta-language satisfies this condition, the notion of truth can be defined in it. We shall now indicate in general terms how this construction can be carried through.

11. The Construction (in Outline) of the Definition.[14] A definition of truth can be obtained in a very simple way from that of another semantic notion, namely, of the notion of *satisfaction*.

Satisfaction is a relation between arbitrary objects and certain expressions called "*sentential functions.*" These are expressions like "*x is white,*" "*x is greater than y,*" etc. Their formal structure is analogous to that of sentences; however, they may contain the so-called free variables (like '*x*' and '*y*' in "*x is greater than y*"), which cannot occur in sentences.

In defining the notion of a sentential function in formalized languages, we usually apply what is called a "recursive procedure"; i.e., we first describe sentential functions of the simplest structure (which ordinarily presents no difficulty), and then we indicate the operations by means of which compound functions can be constructed from simpler ones. Such an operation may consist, for instance, in forming the logical disjunction or conjunction of two given functions, i.e., by combining them by the word "*or*" or "*and.*" A sentence can now be defined simply as a sentential function which contains no free variables.

As regards the notion of satisfaction, we might try to define it by saying that given objects satisfy a given function if the latter becomes a true sentence when we replace in it free variables by names of given objects. In this sense, for example, snow satisfies the sentential function "*x is white*" since the sentence "*snow is white*" is true. However, apart from other difficulties, this method is not available to us, for we want to use the notion of satisfaction in defining truth.

To obtain a definition of satisfaction we have rather to apply again a recursive procedure. We indicate which objects satisfy the simplest sentential functions; and then we state the conditions under which given objects satisfy a compound function—assuming that we know which objects satisfy the simpler functions from which the compound one has been constructed. Thus, for instance, we say that given numbers satisfy the logical disjunction "*x is greater than y or x is equal to y*" if they satisfy at least one of the functions "*x is greater than y*" or "*x is equal to y.*"

Once the general definition of satisfaction is obtained, we notice that it applies automatically also to those special sentential functions which contain no free variables, i.e., to sentences. It turns out that for a sentence only two cases are possible: a sentence is either satisfied by all objects, or by no objects. Hence we arrive at a definition of truth and falsehood simply by saying that *a sentence is true if it is satisfied by all objects, and false otherwise.*[15]

(It may seem strange that we have chosen a roundabout way of defining the truth of a sentence, instead of trying to apply, for instance, a direct recursive procedure. The reason is that compound sentences are constructed from simpler sentential functions, but not always from simpler sentences; hence no general recursive method is known which applies specifically to sentences.)

From this rough outline it is not clear where and how the assumption of the "essential richness" of the meta-language is involved in the discussion; this becomes clear only when the construction is carried through in a detailed and formal way.[16]

12. Consequences of the Definition. The definition of truth which was outlined above has many interesting consequences.

In the first place, the definition proves to be not only formally correct, but also materially adequate (in the sense established in Section 4); in other words, it implies all equivalences of the form (T). In this connection it is important to notice that the conditions for the material adequacy of the definition determine uniquely the extension of the term "*true*." Therefore, every definition of truth which is materially adequate would necessarily be equivalent to that actually constructed. The semantic conception of truth gives us, so to speak, no possibility of choice between various non-equivalent definitions of this notion.

Moreover, we can deduce from our definition various laws of a general nature. In particular, we can prove with its help the *laws of contradiction and of excluded middle,* which are so characteristic of the Aristotelian conception of truth; i.e., we can show that one and only one of any two contradictory sentences is true. These semantic laws should not be identified with the related logical laws of contradiction and excluded middle; the latter belong to the sentential calculus, i.e., to the most elementary part of logic, and do not involve the term "*true*" at all.

Further important results can be obtained by applying the theory of truth to formalized languages of a certain very comprehensive class of mathematical disciplines; only disciplines of an elementary character and a very elementary logical structure are excluded from this class. It turns out that for a discipline of this class *the notion of truth never coincides with that of provability;* for all provable sentences are true, but there are true sentences which are not provable.[17] Hence it follows further that every such discipline is consistent, but incomplete; that is to say, of any two contradictory sentences at most one is provable, and—what is more—there exists a pair of contradictory sentences neither of which is provable.[18]

13. Extension of the Results to Other Semantic Notions. Most of the results at which we arrived in the preceding sections in discussing the notion of truth can be extended with appropriate changes to other semantic notions, for instance, to the notion of satisfaction (involved in our previous discussion), and to those of *designation* and *definition.*

Each of these notions can be analyzed along the lines followed in the analysis of truth. Thus, criteria for an adequate usage of these notions can be established; it can be shown that each of these notions, when used in a semantically closed language according to those criteria, leads necessarily to a contradiction;[19] a distinction between the object-language and the meta-language becomes again indispensable; and the "essential richness" of the meta-language proves in each case to be a necessary and sufficient condition for a satisfactory definition of the notion involved. Hence the results obtained in discussing one particular semantic notion apply to the general problem of the foundations of theoretical semantics.

Within theoretical semantics we can define and study some further notions, whose intuitive content is more involved and whose semantic origin is less obvious; we have in mind, for instance, the important notions of *consequence*, *synonymity*, and *meaning*.[20]

We have concerned ourselves here with the theory of semantic notions related to an individual object-language (although no specific properties of this language have been involved in our arguments). However, we could also consider the problem of developing *general semantics* which applies to a comprehensive class of object-languages. A considerable part of our previous remarks can be extended to this general problem; however, certain new difficulties arise in this connection, which will not be discussed here. I shall merely observe that the axiomatic method (mentioned in Section 10) may prove the most appropriate for the treatment of the problem.[21]

II. POLEMICAL REMARKS

14. Is the Semantic Conception of Truth the "Right" One? I should like to begin the polemical part of the paper with some general remarks.

I hope nothing which is said here will be interpreted as a claim that the semantic conception of truth is the "right" or indeed the "only possible" one. I do not have the slightest intention to contribute in any way to those endless, often violent discussions on the subject "What is the right conception of truth?"[22] I must confess I do not understand what is at stake in such disputes; for the problem itself is so vague that no definite solution is possible. In fact, it seems to me that the sense in which the phrase "the right conception" is used has never been made clear. In most cases one gets the impression that the phrase is used in an almost mystical sense based upon the belief that every word has only one "real" meaning (a kind of Platonic or Aristotelian idea), and that all the competing conceptions really attempt to catch hold of this one meaning; since, however, they contradict each other, only one attempt can be successful, and hence only one conception is the "right" one.

Disputes of this type are by no means restricted to the notion of truth. They occur in all domains where—instead of an exact, scientific terminology—common language with its vagueness and ambiguity is used; and they are always meaningless, and therefore in vain.

It seems to me obvious that the only rational approach to such problems would be the following: We should reconcile ourselves with the fact that we are confronted, not with one concept, but with several different concepts which are denoted by one word; we should try to make these concepts as clear as possible (by means of definition, or of an axiomatic procedure, or in some other way); to avoid further confusions, we should agree to use different terms for different concepts; and then we may proceed to a quiet and systematic study of all concepts involved, which will exhibit their main properties and mutual relations.

Referring specifically to the notion of truth, it is undoubtedly the case that in philosophical discussions—and perhaps also in everyday usage—some incipient conceptions of this notion can be found that differ essentially from the classical one (of which the semantic conception is but a modernized form). In fact, various conceptions of this sort have been discussed in the literature, for instance, the pragmatic conception, the coherence theory, etc.[6]

It seems to me that none of these conceptions have been put so far in an intelligible and unequivocal form. This may change, however; a time may come when we find ourselves confronted with several incompatible, but equally clear and precise, conceptions of truth. It will then become necessary to abandon the ambiguous usage of the word *"true,"* and to introduce several terms instead, each to denote a different notion. Personally, I should not feel hurt if a future world congress of the "theoreticians of truth" should decide—by a majority of votes—to reserve the word *"true"* for one of the non-classical conceptions, and should suggest another word, say, *"frue,"* for the conception considered here. But I cannot imagine that anybody could present cogent arguments to the effect that the semantic conception is "wrong" and should be entirely abandoned.

15. Formal Correctness of the Suggested Definition of Truth. The specific objections which have been raised to my investigations can be divided into several groups; each of these will be discussed separately.

I think that practically all these objections apply, not to the special definition I have given, but to the semantic conception of truth in general. Even those which were leveled against the definition actually constructed could be related to any other definition which conforms to this conception.

This holds, in particular, for those objections which concern the formal correctness of the definition. I have heard a few objections of this kind; however, I doubt very much whether any one of them can be treated seriously.

As a typical example let me quote in substance such an objection.[23] In formulating the definition we use necessarily sentential connectives, i.e., expressions like *"if . . . , then," "or,"* etc. They occur in the definiens; and one of them, namely, the phrase *"if, and only if"* is usually employed to combine the definiendum with the definiens. However, it is well known that the meaning of sentential connectives is explained in logic with the help of the words *"true"* and *"false";* for instance, we say that an equivalence, i.e., a sentence of the form *"p if, and only if, q,"* is true if either both of its members, i.e., the sentences represented by 'p' and 'q,' are true or both are false. Hence the definition of truth involves a vicious circle.

If this objection were valid, no formally correct definition of truth would be possible; for we are unable to formulate any compound sentence without using sentential connectives, or other logical terms defined with their help. Fortunately, the situation is not so bad.

It is undoubtedly the case that a strictly deductive development of logic is often preceded by certain statements explaining the conditions under which sentences of the form "*if p, then q*," etc., are considered true or false. (Such explanations are often given schematically, by means of the so-called truth-tables.) However, these statements are outside of the system of logic, and should not be regarded as definitions of the terms involved. They are not formulated in the language of the system, but constitute rather special consequences of the definition of truth given in the meta-language. Moreover, these statements do not influence the deductive development of logic in any way. For in such a development we do not discuss the question whether a given sentence is true, we are only interested in the problem whether it is provable.[24]

On the other hand, the moment we find ourselves within the deductive system of logic—or of any discipline based upon logic, e.g., of semantics— we either treat sentential connectives as undefined terms, or else we define them by means of other sentential connectives, but never by means of semantic terms like "*true*" or "*false*." For instance, if we agree to regard the expressions "*not*" and "*if . . . , then*" (and possibly also "*if, and only if*") as undefined terms, we can define the term "*or*" by stating that a sentence of the form "*p or q*" is equivalent to the corresponding sentence of the form "*if not p, then q*." The definition can be formulated, e.g., in the following way:

$$(p \text{ or } q) \text{ if, and only if, } (if \text{ not } p, \text{ then } q).$$

This definition obviously contains no semantic terms.

However, a vicious circle in definition arises only when the definiens contains either the term to be defined itself, or other terms defined with its help. Thus we clearly see that the use of sentential connectives in defining the semantic term "*true*" does not involve any circle.

I should like to mention a further objection which I have found in the literature and which seems also to concern the formal correctness, if not of the definition of truth itself, then at least of the arguments which lead to this definition.[25]

The author of this objection mistakenly regards scheme (T) (from Section 4) as a definition of truth. He charges this alleged definition with "inadmissible brevity, i.e., incompleteness," which "does not give us the means of deciding whether by 'equivalence' is meant a logical-formal, or a nonlogical and also structurally non-describable relation." To remove this "defect" he suggests supplementing (T) in one of the two following ways:

(T')   *X is true if, and only if, p is true,*

or

(T") *X is true if, and only if, p is the case (i.e., if what p states is the case).*

Then he discusses these two new "definitions," which are supposedly free from the old, formal "defect," but which turn out to be unsatisfactory for other, non-formal reasons.

This new objection seems to arise from a misunderstanding concerning the nature of sentential connectives (and thus to be somehow related to that previously discussed). The author of the objection does not seem to realize that the phrase *"if, and only if"* (in opposition to such phrases as *"are equivalent"* or *"is equivalent to"*) expresses no relation between sentences at all since it does not combine names of sentences.

In general, the whole argument is based upon an obvious confusion between sentences and their names. It suffices to point out that—in contradistinction to (T)—schemata (T') and (T") do not give any meaningful expressions if we replace in them '*p*' by a sentence; for the phrases *"p is true"* and *"p is the case"* (i.e., *"what p states is the case"*) become meaningless if '*p*' is replaced by a sentence, and not by the name of a sentence (cf. Section 4).[26]

While the author of the objection considers schema (T) "inadmissibly brief," I am inclined, on my part, to regard schemata (T') and (T") as "inadmissibly long." And I think even that I can rigorously prove this statement on the basis of the following definition: An expression is said to be "inadmissibly long" if (i) it is meaningless, and (ii) it has been obtained from a meaningful expression by inserting superfluous words.

16. Redundancy of Semantic Terms—Their Possible Elimination. The objection I am going to discuss now no longer concerns the formal correctness of the definition, but is still concerned with certain formal features of the semantic conception of truth.

We have seen that this conception essentially consists in regarding the sentence "X is true" as equivalent to the sentence denoted by 'X' (where 'X' stands for a name of a sentence of the object-language). Consequently, the term *"true"* when occurring in a simple sentence of the form "X is true" can easily be eliminated, and the sentence itself, which belongs to the metalanguage, can be replaced by an equivalent sentence of the object-language; and the same applies to compound sentences provided the term *"true"* occurs in them exclusively as a part of the expressions of the form "X is true."

Some people have therefore urged that the term *"true"* in the semantic sense can always be eliminated, and that for this reason the semantic conception of truth is altogether sterile and useless. And since the same considerations apply to other semantic notions, the conclusion has been drawn that semantics as a whole is a purely verbal game and at best only a harmless hobby.

But the matter is not quite so simple.[27] The sort of elimination here discussed cannot always be made. It cannot be done in the case of universal statements which express the fact that all sentences of a certain type are true, or that all true sentences have a certain property. For instance, we can prove in the theory of truth the following statement:

All consequences of true sentences are true.

However, we cannot get rid here of the word *"true"* in the simple manner contemplated.

Again, even in the case of particular sentences having the form "X *is true"* such a simple elimination cannot always be made. In fact, the elimination is possible only in those cases in which the name of the sentence which is said to be true occurs in a form that enables us to reconstruct the sentence itself. For example, our present historical knowledge does not give us any possibility of eliminating the word *"true"* from the following sentence:

The first sentence written by Plato is true.

Of course, since we have a definition for truth and since every definition enables us to replace the definiendum by its definiens, an elimination of the term *"true"* in its semantic sense is always theoretically possible. But this would not be the kind of simple elimination discussed above, and it would not result in the replacement of a sentence in the meta-language by a sentence in the object-language.

If, however, anyone continues to urge that—because of the theoretical possibility of eliminating the word *"true"* on the basis of its definition— the concept of truth is sterile, he must accept the further conclusion that all defined notions are sterile. But this outcome is so absurd and so unsound historically that any comment on it is unnecessary. In fact, I am rather inclined to agree with those who maintain that the moments of greatest creative advancement in science frequently coincide with the introduction of new notions by means of definition.

17. Conformity of the Semantic Conception of Truth with Philosophical and Common-sense Usage. The question has been raised whether the semantic conception of truth can indeed be regarded as a precise form of the old, classical conception of this notion.

Various formulations of the classical conception were quoted in the early part of this paper (Section 3). I must repeat that in my judgment none of them is quite precise and clear. Accordingly, the only sure way of settling the question would be to confront the authors of those statements with our new formulation, and to ask them whether it agrees with their intentions. Unfortunately, this method is impractical since they died quite some time ago.

As far as my own opinion is concerned, I do not have any doubts that our formulation does conform to the intuitive content of that of Aristotle.

I am less certain regarding the later formulations of the classical conception, for they are very vague indeed.[28]

Furthermore, some doubts have been expressed whether the semantic conception does reflect the notion of truth in its common-sense and everyday usage. I clearly realize (as I already indicated) that the common meaning of the word "*true*"—as that of any other word of everyday language—is to some extent vague, and that its usage more or less fluctuates. Hence the problem of assigning to this word a fixed and exact meaning is relatively unspecified, and every solution of this problem implies necessarily a certain deviation from the practice of everyday language.

In spite of all this, I happen to believe that the semantic conception does conform to a very considerable extent with the common-sense usage—although I readily admit I may be mistaken. What is more to the point, however, I believe that the issue raised can be settled scientifically, though of course not by a deductive procedure, but with the help of the statistical questionnaire method. As a matter of fact, such research has been carried on, and some of the results have been reported at congresses and in part published.[29]

I should like to emphasize that in my opinion such investigations must be conducted with the utmost care. Thus, if we ask a highschool boy, or even an adult intelligent man having no special philosophical training, whether he regards a sentence to be true if it agrees with reality, or if it designates an existing state of affairs, it may simply turn out that he does not understand the question; in consequence his response, whatever it may be, will be of no value for us. But his answer to the question whether he would admit that the sentence "*it is snowing*" could be true although it is not snowing, or could be false although it is snowing, would naturally be very significant for our problem.

Therefore, I was by no means surprised to learn (in a discussion devoted to these problems) that in a group of people who were questioned only 15% agreed that "*true*" means for them "*agreeing with reality*," while 90% agreed that a sentence such as "*it is snowing*" is true if, and only if, it is snowing. Thus, a great majority of these people seemed to reject the classical conception of truth in its "philosophical" formulation, while accepting the same conception when formulated in plain words (waiving the question whether the use of the phrase "the same conception" is here justified).

18. The Definition in Its Relation to "The Philosophical Problem of Truth" and to Various Epistemological Trends. I have heard it remarked that the formal definition of truth has nothing to do with "the philosophical problem of truth." [30] However, nobody has ever pointed out to me in an intelligible way just what this problem is. I have been informed in this connection that my definition, though it states necessary and sufficient conditions for a sentence to be true, does not really grasp the "essence" of this concept. Since I have never been able to understand what the "essence" of a concept is, I must be excused from discussing this point any longer.

In general, I do not believe that there is such a thing as "the philosophical problem of truth." I do believe that there are various intelligible and interesting (but not necessarily philosophical) problems concerning the notion of truth, but I also believe that they can be exactly formulated and possibly solved only on the basis of a precise conception of this notion.

While on the one hand the definition of truth has been blamed for not being philosophical enough, on the other a series of objections have been raised charging this definition with serious philosophical implications, always of a very undesirable nature. I shall discuss now one special objection of this type; another group of such objections will be dealt with in the next section.

It has been claimed that—due to the fact that a sentence like "snow is white" is taken to be semantically true if snow is *in fact* white (italics by the critic)—logic finds itself involved in a most uncritical realism.[31]

If there were an opportunity to discuss the objection with its author, I should raise two points. First, I should ask him to drop the words *"in fact,"* which do not occur in the original formulation and which are misleading, even if they do not affect the content. For these words convey the impression that the semantic conception of truth is intended to establish the conditions under which we are warranted in asserting any given sentence, and in particular any empirical sentence. However, a moment's reflection shows that this impression is merely an illusion; and I think that the author of the objection falls victim to the illusion which he himself created.

In fact, the semantic definition of truth implies nothing regarding the conditions under which a sentence like (1):

(1)   *snow is white*

can be asserted. It implies only that, whenever we assert or reject this sentence, we must be ready to assert or reject the correlated sentence (2):

(2)   *the sentence "snow is white" is true.*

Thus, we may accept the semantic conception of truth without giving up any epistemological attitude we may have had; we may remain naïve realists, critical realists or idealists, empiricists or metaphysicians—whatever we were before. The semantic conception is completely neutral toward all these issues.

In the second place, I should try to get some information regarding the conception of truth which (in the opinion of the author of the objection) does not involve logic in a most naïve realism. I would gather that this conception must be incompatible with the semantic one. Thus, there must be sentences which are true in one of these conceptions without being true in the other. Assume, e.g., the sentence (1) to be of this kind. The truth of this sentence in the semantic conception is determined by an equivalence of the form (T):

The sentence "snow is white" is true if, and only if, snow is white.

Hence in the new conception we must reject this equivalence, and consequently we must assume its denial:

The sentence "snow is white" is true if, and only if, snow is not white (or perhaps: *snow, in fact, is not white*).

This sounds somewhat paradoxical. I do not regard such a consequence of the new conception as absurd; but I am a little fearful that someone in the future may charge this conception with involving logic in a "most sophisticated kind of irrealism." At any rate, it seems to me important to realize that every conception of truth which is incompatible with the semantic one carries with it consequences of this type.

I have dwelt a little on this whole question, not because the objection discussed seems to me very significant, but because certain points which have arisen in the discussion should be taken into account by all those who for various epistemological reasons are inclined to reject the semantic conception of truth.

19. Alleged Metaphysical Elements in Semantics. The semantic conception of truth has been charged several times with involving certain metaphysical elements. Objections of this sort have been made to apply not only to the theory of truth, but to the whole domain of theoretical semantics.[32]

I do not intend to discuss the general problem whether the introduction of a metaphysical element into a science is at all objectionable. The only point which will interest me here is whether and in what sense metaphysics is involved in the subject of our present discussion.

The whole question obviously depends upon what one understands by "metaphysics." Unfortunately, this notion is extremely vague and equivocal. When listening to discussions in this subject, sometimes one gets the impression that the term "metaphysical" has lost any objective meaning, and is merely used as a kind of professional philosophical invective.

For some people metaphysics is a general theory of objects (ontology) —a discipline which is to be developed in a purely empirical way, and which differs from other empirical sciences only by its generality. I do not know whether such a discipline actually exists (some cynics claim that it is customary in philosophy to baptize unborn children); but I think that in any case metaphysics in this conception is not objectionable to anybody, and has hardly any connections with semantics.

For the most part, however, the term "metaphysical" is used as directly opposed—in one sense or another—to the term "empirical"; at any rate, it is used in this way by those people who are distressed by the thought that any metaphysical elements might have managed to creep into science.

This general conception of metaphysics assumes several more specific forms.

Thus, some people take it to be symptomatic of a metaphysical element in a science when methods of inquiry are employed which are neither deductive nor empirical. However, no trace of this symptom can be found in the development of semantics (unless some metaphysical elements are involved in the object-language to which the semantic notions refer). In particular, the semantics of formalized languages is constructed in a purely deductive way.

Others maintain that the metaphysical character of a science depends mainly on its vocabulary and, more specifically, on its primitive terms. Thus, a term is said to be metaphysical if it is neither logical nor mathematical, and if it is not associated with an empirical procedure which enables us to decide whether a thing is denoted by this term or not. With respect to such a view of metaphysics it is sufficient to recall that a meta-language includes only three kinds of undefined terms: (i) terms taken from logic, (ii) terms of the corresponding object-language, and (iii) names of expressions in the object-language. It is thus obvious that no metaphysical undefined terms occur in the meta-language (again, unless such terms appear in the object-language itself).

There are, however, some who believe that, even if no metaphysical terms occur among the primitive terms of a language, they may be introduced by definitions; namely, by those definitions which fail to provide us with general criteria for deciding whether an object falls under the defined concept. It is argued that the term *"true"* is of this kind, since no universal criterion of truth follows immediately from the definition of this term, and since it is generally believed (and in a certain sense can even be proved) that such a criterion will never be found. This comment on the actual character of the notion of truth seems to be perfectly just. However, it should be noticed that the notion of truth does not differ in this respect from many notions in logic, mathematics, and theoretical parts of various empirical sciences, e.g., in theoretical physics.

In general, it must be said that if the term "metaphysical" is employed in so wide a sense as to embrace certain notions (or methods) of logic, mathematics, or empirical sciences, it will apply *a fortiori* to those of semantics. In fact, as we know from Part I of the paper, in developing the semantics of a language we use all the notions of this language, and we apply even a stronger logical apparatus than that which is used in the language itself. On the other hand, however, I can summarize the arguments given above by stating that in no interpretation of the term "metaphysical" which is familiar and more or less intelligible to me does semantics involve any metaphysical elements peculiar to itself.

I should like to make one final remark in connection with this group of objections. The history of science shows many instances of concepts which were judged metaphysical (in a loose, but in any case derogatory sense of this term) before their meaning was made precise; however, once they received a rigorous, formal definition, the distrust in them evaporated. As typical examples we may mention the concepts of negative and imaginary numbers in mathematics. I hope a similar fate awaits the concept of truth and other semantic concepts; and it seems to me, therefore, that those who have distrusted them because of their alleged metaphysical implications should welcome the fact that precise definitions of these concepts are now available. If in consequence semantic concepts lose philosophical interest, they will only share the fate of many other concepts of science, and this need give rise to no regret.

20. *Applicability of Semantics to Special Empirical Sciences.* We come to the last and perhaps the most important group of objections. Some strong doubts have been expressed whether semantic notions find or can find applications in various domains of intellectual activity. For the most part such doubts have concerned the applicability of semantics to the field of empirical science—either to special sciences or to the general methodology of this field; although similar skepticism has been expressed regarding possible applications of semantics to mathematical sciences and their methodology.

I believe that it is possible to allay these doubts to a certain extent, and that some optimism with respect to the potential value of semantics for various domains of thought is not without ground.

To justify this optimism, it suffices I think to stress two rather obvious points. First, the development of a theory which formulates a precise definition of a notion and establishes its general properties provides *eo ipso* a firmer basis for all discussions in which this notion is involved; and, therefore, it cannot be irrelevant for anyone who uses this notion, and desires to do so in a conscious and consistent way. Secondly, semantic notions are actually involved in various branches of science, and in particular of empirical science.

The fact that in empirical research we are concerned only with natural languages and that theoretical semantics applies to these languages only with certain approximation, does not affect the problem essentially. However, it has undoubtedly this effect that progress in semantics will have but a delayed and somewhat limited influence in this field. The situation with which we are confronted here does not differ essentially from that which arises when we apply laws of logic to arguments in everyday life —or, generally, when we attempt to apply a theoretical science to empirical problems.

Semantic notions are undoubtedly involved, to a larger or smaller degree, in psychology, sociology, and in practically all the humanities. Thus, a psychologist defines the so-called intelligence quotient in terms of the numbers of *true* (right) and *false* (wrong) answers given by a person to certain questions; for a historian of culture the range of objects for which a human race in successive stages of its development possesses adequate *designations* may be a topic of great significance; a student of literature may be strongly interested in the problem whether a given author always uses two given words with the same *meaning*. Examples of this kind can be multiplied indefinitely.

The most natural and promising domain for the applications of theoretical semantics is clearly linguistics—the empirical study of natural languages. Certain parts of this science are even referred to as "semantics," sometimes with an additional qualification. Thus, this name is occasionally given to that portion of grammar which attempts to classify all words of a language into parts of speech, according to what the words mean or designate. The study of the evolution of meanings in the historical development of a language is sometimes called "historical semantics." In general, the totality of investigations on semantic relations which occur in a natural language is referred to as "descriptive semantics." The relation between theoretical and descriptive semantics is analogous to that between pure and applied mathematics, or perhaps to that between theoretical and empirical physics; the rôle of formalized languages in semantics can be roughly compared to that of isolated systems in physics.

It is perhaps unnecessary to say that semantics cannot find any direct applications in natural sciences such as physics, biology, etc.; for in none of these sciences are we concerned with linguistic phenomena, and even less with semantic relations between linguistic expressions and objects to which these expressions refer. We shall see, however, in the next section that semantics may have a kind of indirect influence even on those sciences in which semantic notions are not directly involved.

21. Applicability of Semantics to the Methodology of Empirical Science. Besides linguistics, another important domain for possible applications of semantics is the methodology of science; this term is used here in a broad sense so as to embrace the theory of science in general. Independent of whether a science is conceived merely as a system of statements or as a totality of certain statements and human activities, the study of scientific language constitutes an essential part of the methodological discussion of a science. And it seems to me clear that any tendency to eliminate semantic notions (like those of truth and designation) from this discussion would make it fragmentary and inadequate.[33] Moreover, there is no reason for such a tendency today, once the main difficulties in using semantic terms have been overcome. The semantics of scientific language should be simply included as a part in the methodology of science.

I am by no means inclined to charge methodology and, in particular, semantics—whether theoretical or descriptive—with the task of clarifying the meanings of all scientific terms. This task is left to those sciences in which the terms are used, and is actually fulfilled by them (in the same way in which, e.g., the task of clarifying the meaning of the term *"true"* is left to, and fulfilled by, semantics). There may be, however, certain special problems of this sort in which a methodological approach is desirable or indeed necessary (perhaps, the problem of the notion of causality is a good example here); and in a methodological discussion of such problems semantic notions may play an essential rôle. Thus, semantics may have some bearing on any science whatsoever.

The question arises whether semantics can be helpful in solving general and, so to speak, classical problems of methodology. I should like to discuss here with some detail a special, though very important, aspect of this question.

One of the main problems of the methodology of empirical science consists in establishing conditions under which an empirical theory or hypothesis should be regarded as acceptable. This notion of acceptability must be relativized to a given stage of the development of a science (or to a given amount of presupposed knowledge). In other words, we may consider it as provided with a time coefficient; for a theory which is acceptable today may become untenable tomorrow as a result of new scientific discoveries.

It seems *a priori* very plausible that the acceptability of a theory somehow depends on the truth of its sentences, and that consequently a methodologist in his (so far rather unsuccessful) attempts at making the notion of acceptability precise, can expect some help from the semantic theory of truth. Hence we ask the question: Are there any postulates which can be reasonably imposed on acceptable theories and which involve the notion of truth? And, in particular, we ask whether the following postulate is a reasonable one:

An acceptable theory cannot contain (or imply) any false sentences.

The answer to the last question is clearly negative. For, first of all, we are practically sure, on the basis of our historical experience, that every empirical theory which is accepted today will sooner or later be rejected and replaced by another theory. It is also very probable that the new theory will be incompatible with the old one; i.e., will imply a sentence which is contradictory to one of the sentences contained in the old theory. Hence, at least one of the two theories must include false sentences, in spite of the fact that each of them is accepted at a certain time. Secondly, the postulate in question could hardly ever be satisfied in practice; for we do not know, and are very unlikely to find, any criteria of truth which enable us to show that no sentence of an empirical theory is false.

The postulate in question could be at most regarded as the expression of an ideal limit for successively more adequate theories in a given field of research; but this hardly can be given any precise meaning.

Nevertheless, it seems to me that there is an important postulate which can be reasonably imposed on acceptable empirical theories and which involves the notion of truth. It is closely related to the one just discussed, but is essentially weaker. Remembering that the notion of acceptability is provided with a time coefficient, we can give this postulate the following form:

As soon as we succeed in showing that an empirical theory contains (or implies) false sentences, it cannot be any longer considered acceptable.

In support of this postulate, I should like to make the following remarks.

I believe everybody agrees that one of the reasons which may compel us to reject an empirical theory is the proof of its inconsistency: a theory becomes untenable if we succeed in deriving from it two contradictory sentences. Now we can ask what are the usual motives for rejecting a theory on such grounds. Persons who are acquainted with modern logic are inclined to answer this question in the following way: A well-known logical law shows that a theory which enables us to derive two contradictory sentences enables us also to derive every sentence; therefore, such a theory is trivial and deprived of any scientific interest.

I have some doubts whether this answer contains an adequate analysis of the situation. I think that people who do not know modern logic are as little inclined to accept an inconsistent theory as those who are thoroughly familiar with it; and probably this applies even to those who regard (as some still do) the logical law on which the argument is based as a highly controversial issue, and almost as a paradox. I do not think that our attitude toward an inconsistent theory would change even if we decided for some reasons to weaken our system of logic so as to deprive ourselves of the possibility of deriving every sentence from any two contradictory sentences.

It seems to me that the real reason of our attitude is a different one: We know (if only intuitively) that an inconsistent theory must contain false sentences; and we are not inclined to regard as acceptable any theory which has been shown to contain such sentences.

There are various methods of showing that a given theory includes false sentences. Some of them are based upon purely logical properties of the theory involved; the method just discussed (i.e., the proof of inconsistency) is not the sole method of this type, but is the simplest one, and the one which is most frequently applied in practice. With the help of certain assumptions regarding the truth of empirical sentences, we can obtain methods to the same effect which are no longer of a purely logical nature. If we decide to accept the general postulate suggested above, then a successful application of any such method will make the theory untenable.

22. *Applications of Semantics to Deductive Science.* As regards the applicability of semantics to mathematical sciences and their methodology, i.e., to meta-mathematics, we are in a much more favorable position than in the case of empirical sciences. For, instead of advancing reasons which justify some hopes for the future (and thus making a kind of pro-semantics propaganda), we are able to point out concrete results already achieved.

Doubts continue to be expressed whether the notion of a true sentence —as distinct from that of a provable sentence—can have any significance for mathematical disciplines and play any part in a methodological discussion of mathematics. It seems to me, however, that just this notion of a true sentence constitutes a most valuable contribution to meta-mathematics by semantics. We already possess a series of interesting meta-mathematical results gained with the help of the theory of truth. These results concern the mutual relations between the notion of truth and that of provability; establish new properties of the latter notion (which, as well known, is one of the basic notions of meta-mathematics); and throw some light on the fundamental problems of consistency and completeness. The most significant among these results have been briefly discussed in Section 12.[34]

Furthermore, by applying the method of semantics we can adequately define several important meta-mathematical notions which have been used so far only in an intuitive way—such as, e.g., the notion of definability or that of a model of an axiom system; and thus we can undertake a systematic study of these notions. In particular, the investigations on definability have already brought some interesting results, and promise even more in the future.[35]

We have discussed the applications of semantics only to meta-mathematics, and not to mathematics proper. However, this distinction between mathematics and meta-mathematics is rather unimportant. For meta-mathematics is itself a deductive discipline and hence, from a certain point of view, a part of mathematics; and it is well known that—due to the formal character of deductive method—the results obtained in one deductive discipline can be automatically extended to any other discipline in which the given one finds an interpretation. Thus, for example, all meta-mathematical results can be interpreted as results of number theory. Also from a practical point of view there is no clear-cut line between meta-mathematics and mathematics proper; for instance, the investigations on definability could be included in either of these domains.

23. Final Remarks. I should like to conclude this discussion with some general and rather loose remarks concerning the whole question of the evaluation of scientific achievements in terms of their applicability. I must confess I have various doubts in this connection.

Being a mathematician (as well as a logician, and perhaps a philosopher of a sort), I have had the opportunity to attend many discussions between specialists in mathematics, where the problem of applications is especially acute, and I have noticed on several occasions the following phenomenon: If a mathematician wishes to disparage the work of one of his colleagues, say, *A*, the most effective method he finds for doing this is to ask where the results can be applied. The hard-pressed man, with his back against the wall, finally unearths the researches of another mathematician *B* as the locus of the application of his own results. If next *B* is plagued with a similar question, he will refer to another mathematician *C*. After a few steps of this kind we find ourselves referred back to the researches of *A*, and in this way the chain closes.

Speaking more seriously, I do not wish to deny that the value of a man's work may be increased by its implications for the research of others and for practice. But I believe, nevertheless, that it is inimical to the progress of science to measure the importance of any research exclusively or chiefly in terms of its usefulness and applicability. We know from the history of science that many important results and discoveries have had to wait centuries before they were applied in any field. And, in my opinion, there are also other important factors which cannot be disregarded in determining the value of a scientific work. It seems to me that there is a special domain of very profound and strong human needs related to scientific research, which are similar in many ways to aesthetic and perhaps religious needs. And it also seems to me that the satisfaction of these needs should be considered an important task of research. Hence, I believe, the question of the value of any research cannot be adequately answered without taking into account the intellectual satisfaction which the results of that research bring to those who understand it and care for it. It may be unpopular and out-of-date to say—but I do not think that a scientific result which gives us a better understanding of the world and makes it more harmonious in our eyes should be held in lower esteem than, say, an invention which reduces the cost of paving roads, or improves household plumbing.

It is clear that the remarks just made become pointless if the word "application" is used in a very wide and liberal sense. It is perhaps not less obvious that nothing follows from these general remarks concerning the specific topics which have been discussed in this paper; and I really do not know whether research in semantics stands to gain or lose by introducing the standard of value I have suggested.

NOTES

[1] Compare Tarski [2] (see bibliography at the end of the paper). This work may be consulted for a more detailed and formal presentation of the subject of the paper, especially of the material included in Sections 6 and 9–13. It contains also references to my earlier publications on the problems of semantics (a communication in Polish, 1930; the article Tarski [1] in French, 1931; a communication in German, 1932; and a book in Polish, 1933). The expository part of the present paper is related in its character to Tarski [3]. My investigations on the notion of truth and on theoretical seman-

tics have been reviewed or discussed in Hofstadter [1], Juhos [1], Kokoszyńska [1] and [2], Kotarbiński [2], Scholz [1], Weinberg [1], et al.

[2] It may be hoped that the interest in theoretical semantics will now increase, as a result of the recent publication of the important work Carnap [2].

[3] This applies, in particular, to public discussions during the I. International Congress for the Unity of Science (Paris, 1935) and the Conference of International Congresses for the Unity of Science (Paris, 1937); cf., e.g., Neurath [1] and Gonseth [1].

[4] The words "notion" and "concept" are used in this paper with all of the vagueness and ambiguity with which they occur in philosophical literature. Thus, sometimes they refer simply to a term, sometimes to what is meant by a term, and in other cases to what is denoted by a term. Sometimes it is irrelevant which of these interpretations is meant; and in certain cases perhaps none of them applies adequately. While on principle I share the tendency to avoid these words in any exact discussion, I did not consider it necessary to do so in this informal presentation.

[5] For our present purposes it is somewhat more convenient to understand by "expressions," "sentences," etc., not individual inscriptions, but classes of inscriptions of similar form (thus, not individual physical things, but classes of such things).

[6] For the Aristotelian formulation see Article [1], Γ, 7, 27. The other two formulations are very common in the literature, but I do not know with whom they originate. A critical discussion of various conceptions of truth can be found, e.g., in Kotarbiński [1] (so far available only in Polish), pp. 123 ff., and Russell [1], pp. 362 ff.

[7] For most of the remarks contained in Sections 4 and 8, I am indebted to the late S. Leśniewski who developed them in his unpublished lectures in the University of Warsaw (in 1919 and later). However, Leśniewski did not anticipate the possibility of a rigorous development of the theory of truth, and still less of a definition of this notion; hence, while indicating equivalences of the form (T) as premisses in the antinomy of the liar, he did not conceive them as any sufficient conditions for an adequate usage (or definition) of the notion of truth. Also the remarks in Section 8 regarding the occurrence of an empirical premiss in the antinomy of the liar, and the possibility of eliminating this premiss, do not originate with him.

[8] In connection with various logical and methodological problems involved in this paper the reader may consult Tarski [6].

[9] The antinomy of the liar (ascribed to Eubulides or Epimenides) is discussed here in Sections 7 and 8. For the antinomy of definability (due to J. Richard) see e.g.. Hilbert-Bernays [1], Vol. 2, pp. 263 ff.; for the antinomy of heterological terms see Grelling-Nelson [1], p. 307.

[10] Due to Professor J. Łukasiewicz (University of Warsaw).

[11] This can roughly be done in the following way. Let S be any sentence beginning with the words "*Every sentence.*" We correlate with S a new sentence S^* by subjecting S to the following two modifications: we replace in S the first word, "*Every,*" by "*The*"; and we insert after the second word, "*sentence,*" the whole sentence S enclosed in quotation marks. Let us agree to call the sentence S "(self-)applicable" or "non-(self-)applicable" dependent on whether the correlated sentence S^* is true or false. Now consider the following sentence:

Every sentence is non-applicable.

It can easily be shown that the sentence just stated must be both applicable and non-applicable; hence a contradiction. It may not be quite clear in what sense this formulation of the antinomy does not involve an empirical premiss; however, I shall not elaborate on this point.

[12] The terms "logic" and "logical" are used in this paper in a broad sense, which has become almost traditional in the last decades; logic is assumed here to comprehend the whole theory of classes and relations (i.e., the mathematical theory of sets). For many different reasons I am personally inclined to use the term "logic" in a much narrower sense, so as to apply it only to what is sometimes called "elementary logic," i.e., to the sentential calculus and the (restricted) predicate calculus.

[13] Cf. here, however, Tarski [3], pp. 5 f.

[14] The method of construction we are going to outline can be applied—with appro-

priate changes—to all formalized languages that are known at the present time; although it does not follow that a language could not be constructed to which this method would not apply.

15 In carrying through this idea a certain technical difficulty arises. A sentential function may contain an arbitrary number of free variables; and the logical nature of the notion of satisfaction varies with this number. Thus, the notion in question when applied to functions with one variable is a binary relation between these functions and single objects; when applied to functions with two variables it becomes a ternary relation between functions and couples of objects; and so on. Hence, strictly speaking, we are confronted, not with one notion of satisfaction, but with infinitely many notions; and it turns out that these notions cannot be defined independently of each other, but must all be introduced simultaneously.

To overcome this difficulty, we employ the mathematical notion of an infinite sequence (or, possibly, of a finite sequence with an arbitrary number of terms). We agree to regard satisfaction, not as a many-termed relation between sentential functions and an indefinite number of objects, but as a binary relation between functions and sequences of objects. Under this assumption the formulation of a general and precise definition of satisfaction no longer presents any difficulty; and a true sentence can now be defined as one which is satisfied by every sequence.

16 To define recursively the notion of satisfaction, we have to apply a certain form of recursive definition which is not admitted in the object-language. Hence the "essential richness" of the meta-language may simply consist in admitting this type of definition. On the other hand, a general method is known which makes it possible to eliminate all recursive definitions and to replace them by normal, explicit ones. If we try to apply this method to the definition of satisfaction, we see that we have either to introduce into the meta-language variables of a higher logical type than those which occur in the object-language; or else to assume axiomatically in the meta-language the existence of classes that are more comprehensive than all those whose existence can be established in the object-language. See here Tarski [2], pp. 393 ff., and Tarski [5], p. 7.

17 Due to the development of modern logic, the notion of mathematical proof has undergone a far-reaching simplification. A sentence of a given formalized discipline is provable if it can be obtained from the axioms of this discipline by applying certain simple and purely formal rules of inference, such as those of detachment and substitution. Hence to show that all provable sentences are true, it suffices to prove that all the sentences accepted as axioms are true, and that the rules of inference when applied to true sentences yield new true sentences; and this usually presents no difficulty.

On the other hand, in view of the elementary nature of the notion of provability, a precise definition of this notion requires only rather simple logical devices. In most cases, those logical devices which are available in the formalized discipline itself (to which the notion of provability is related) are more than sufficient for this purpose. We know, however, that as regards the definition of truth just the opposite holds. Hence, as a rule, the notions of truth and provability cannot coincide; and since every provable sentence is true, there must be true sentences which are not provable.

18 Thus the theory of truth provides us with a general method for consistency proofs for formalized mathematical disciplines. It can be easily realized, however, that a consistency proof obtained by this method may possess some intuitive value— i.e., may convince us, or strengthen our belief, that the discipline under consideration is actually consistent—only in case we succeed in defining truth in terms of a meta-language which does not contain the object-language as a part (cf. here a remark in Section 9). For only in this case the deductive assumptions of the meta-language may be intuitively simpler and more obvious than those of the object-language— even though the condition of "essential richness" will be formally satisfied. Cf. here also Tarski [3], p. 7.

The incompleteness of a comprehensive class of formalized disciplines constitutes the essential content of a fundamental theorem of K. Gödel; cf. Gödel [1], pp. 187 ff. The explanation of the fact that the theory of truth leads so directly to Gödel's theorem is rather simple. In deriving Gödel's result from the theory of truth we make an essential use of the fact that the definition of truth cannot be given in a meta-language which is only as "rich" as the object-language (cf. note 17); however, in establishing this fact, a method of reasoning has been applied which is very closely related to that used (for the first time) by Gödel. It may be added that Gödel was clearly guided in his proof by certain intuitive considerations regarding the notion of truth, although this notion does not occur in the proof explicitly; cf. Gödel [1], pp. 174 f.

19 The notions of designation and definition lead respectively to the antinomies of Grelling-Nelson and Richard (cf. note 9). To obtain an antinomy for the notion of satisfaction, we construct the following expression:

The sentential function X does not satisfy X.

A contradiction arises when we consider the question whether this expression, which is clearly a sentential function, satisfies itself or not.

20 All notions mentioned in this section can be defined in terms of satisfaction. We can say, e.g., that a given term designates a given object if this object satisfies the sentential function "*x is identical with T*" where '*T*' stands for the given term. Similarly, a sentential function is said to define a given object if the latter is the only object which satisfies this function. For a definition of consequence see Tarski [4], and for that of synonymity—Carnap [2].

21 General semantics is the subject of Carnap [2]. Cf. here also remarks in Tarski [2], pp. 388 f.

22 Cf. various quotations in Ness [1], pp. 13 f.

23 The names of persons who have raised objections will not be quoted here, unless their objections have appeared in print.

24 It should be emphasized, however, that as regards the question of an alleged vicious circle the situation would not change even if we took a different point of view, represented, e.g., in Carnap [2]; i.e., if we regarded the specification of conditions under which sentences of a language are true as an essential part of the description of this language. On the other hand, it may be noticed that the point of view repre-sented in the text does not exclude the possibility of using truth-tables in a deductive development of logic. However, these tables are to be regarded then merely as a formal instrument for checking the provability of certain sentences; and the symbols '*T*' and '*F*' which occur in them and which are usually considered abbreviations of "*true*" and "*false*" should not be interpreted in any intuitive way.

25 Cf. Juhos [1]. I must admit that I do not clearly understand von Juhos' objec-tions and do not know how to classify them; therefore, I confine myself here to cer-tain points of a formal character. Von Juhos does not seem to know my definition of truth; he refers only to an informal presentation in Tarski [3] where the definition has not been given at all. If he knew the actual definition, he would have to change his argument. However, I have no doubt that he would discover in this definition some "defects" as well. For he believes he has proved that "on ground of principle it is impossible to give such a definition at all."

26 The phrases "*p is true*" and "*p is the case*" (or better "*it is true that p*" and "*it is the case that p*") are sometimes used in informal discussions, mainly for stylistic reasons; but they are considered then as synonymous with the sentence represented by '*p*'. On the other hand, as far as I understand the situation, the phrases in question cannot be used by von Juhos synonymously with '*p*'; for otherwise the replacement of (T) by (T') or (T″) would not constitute any "improvement."

27 Cf. the discussion of this problem in Kokoszyńska [1], pp. 161 ff.

28 Most authors who have discussed my work on the notion of truth are of the opinion that my definition does conform with the classical conception of this notion; see, e.g., Kotarbiński [2] and Scholz [1].

29 Cf. Ness [1]. Unfortunately, the results of that part of Ness' research which is especially relevant for our problem are not discussed in his book; compare p. 148, footnote 1.

30 Though I have heard this opinion several times, I have seen it in print only once and, curiously enough, in a work which does not have a philosophical character—in

fact, in Hilbert-Bernays [1], Vol. II, p. 269 (where, by the way, it is not expressed as any kind of objection). On the other hand, I have not found any remark to this effect in discussions of my work by professional philosophers (cf. note 1).

31 Cf. Gonseth [1], pp. 187 f.

32 See Nagel [1], and Nagel [2], pp. 471 f. A remark which goes, perhaps, in the same direction is also to be found in Weinberg [1], p. 77; cf., however, his earlier remarks, pp. 75 f.

33 Such a tendency was evident in earlier works of Carnap (see, e.g., Carnap [1], especially Part V) and in writings of other members of The Vienna Circle. Cf. here Kokoszyńska [1] and Weinberg [1].

34 For other results obtained with the help of the theory of truth see Gödel [2]; Tarski [2], pp. 401 ff.; and Tarski [5], pp. 111 f.

35 An object—e.g., a number or a set of numbers—is said to be definable (in a given formalism) if there is a sentential function which defines it; cf. note 20. Thus, the term "definable," though of a meta-mathematical (semantic) origin, is purely mathematical as to its extension, for it expresses a property (denotes a class) of mathematical objects. In consequence, the notion of definability can be re-defined in purely mathematical terms, though not within the formalized discipline to which this notion refers; however, the fundamental idea of the definition remains unchanged. Cf. here—also for further bibliographic references—Tarski [1]; various other results concerning definability can also be found in the literature, e.g., in Hilbert-Bernays [1] Vol. I, pp. 354 ff., 369 ff., 456 ff., etc., and in Lindenbaum-Tarski [1]. It may be noticed that the term "definable" is sometimes used in another, meta-mathematical (but not semantic), sense; this occurs, for instance, when we say that a term is definable in other terms (on the basis of a given axiom system). For a definition of a model of an axiom system see Tarski [4].

BIBLIOGRAPHY

Only the books and articles actually referred to in the paper will be listed here.

Aristotle [1]. *Metaphysica* (*Works*, Vol. VIII). English translation by W. D. Ross, Oxford, 1908.

Carnap, R. [1]. *Logical Syntax of Language*, London and New York, 1937.

Carnap, R. [2]. *Introduction to Semantics*, Cambridge, 1942.

Gödel, K. [1]. "Über formal unentscheidbare Sätze der *Principia Mathematica* und verwandter Systeme, I", *Monatshefte für Mathematik und Physik*, Vol. XXXVIII, 1931, pp. 173–198.

Gödel, K. [2]. "Über die Länge von Beweisen", *Ergebnisse eines mathematischen Kolloquiums*, Vol. VII, 1936, pp. 23–24.

Gonseth, F. [1]. "Le Congrès Descartes. Questions de Philosophie scientifique", *Revue thomiste*, Vol. XLIV, 1938, pp. 183–193.

Grelling, K., and Nelson, L. [1]. "Bemerkungen zu den Paradoxien von Russell und Burali-Forti", *Abhandlungen der Fries'schen Schule*, Vol. II (new series), 1908, pp. 301–334.

Hofstadter, A. [1]. "On Semantic Problems", *The Journal of Philosophy*, Vol. XXXV, 1938, pp. 225–232.

Hilbert, D., and Bernays, P. [1]. *Grundlagen der Mathematik*, 2 vols., Berlin, 1934–1939.

Juhos, B. von. [1]. "The Truth of Empirical Statements", *Analysis*, Vol. IV, 1937, pp. 65–70.

Kokoszyńska, M. [1]. "Über den absoluten Wahrheitsbegriff und einige andere semantische Begriffe", *Erkenntnis*, 6, 1936, pp. 143–165.

Kokoszyńska, M. [2]. "Syntax, Semantik und Wissenschaftslogik," *Actes du Congrès International de Philosophie Scientifique*, Vol. III, Paris, 1936, pp. 9–14.

Kotarbiński, T. [1]. *Elementy teorji poznania, logiki formalnej i metodologji nauk* (*Elements of Epistemology, Formal Logic, and the Methodology of Sciences*, in Polish), Lwów, 1929.

Kotarbiński, T. [2]. "W sprawie pojęcia prawdy" ("*Concerning the Concept of Truth,*" in Polish), *Przegląd filozoficzny*, Vol. XXXVII, pp. 85–91.

Lindenbaum, A., and Tarski, A. [1]. "Über die Beschränktheit der Ausdrucksmittel deduktiver Theorien", *Ergebnisse eines mathematischen Kolloquiums*, Vol. VII, 1936, pp. 15–23.

Nagel, E. [1]. Review of Hofstadter [1], *The Journal of Symbolic Logic*, Vol. III, 1938, p. 90.

Nagel, E. [2]. Review of Carnap [2], *The Journal of Philosophy*, Vol. XXXIX, 1942, pp. 468–473.

Ness, A. [1]. " 'Truth' As Conceived by Those Who Are Not Professional Philosophers", *Skrifter utgitt av Det Norske Videnskaps-Akademi i Oslo, II. Hist.-Filos. Klasse*, Vol. IV, Oslo, 1938.

Neurath, O. [1]. "Erster Internationaler Kongress für Einheit der Wissenschaft in Paris 1935", *Erkenntnis*, 5, 1935, pp. 377–406.

Russell, B. [1]. *An Inquiry Into Meaning and Truth*, New York, 1940.

Scholz, H. [1]. Review of *Studia philosophica*, Vol. I, *Deutsche Literaturzeitung*, vol. LVIII, 1937, pp. 1914–1917.

Tarski, A. [1]. "Sur les ensembles définissables de nombres réels. I." *Fundamenta mathematicae*, Vol. XVII, 1931, pp. 210–239.

Tarski, A. [2]. "Der Wahrheitsbegriff in den formalisierten Sprachen" (German translation of a book in Polish, 1933), *Studia philosophica*, Vol. I, 1935, pp. 261–405.

Tarski, A. [3]. "Grundlegung der wissenschaftlichen Semantik", *Actes du Congrès International de Philosophie Scientifique*, Vol. III, Paris, 1936, pp. 1–8.

Tarski, A. [4]. "Über den Begriff der logischen Folgerung", *Actes du Congrès International de Philosophie Scientifique*, Vol. VII, Paris, 1937, pp. 1–11.

Tarski, A. [5]. "On Undecidable Statements in Enlarged Systems of Logic and the Concept of Truth", *The Journal of Symbolic Logic*, Vol. IV, 1939, pp. 105–112.

Tarski, A. [6]. *Introduction to Logic*, New York, 1941.

Weinberg, J. [1]. Review of *Studia philosophica*, Vol. I, *The Philosophical Review*, Vol. XLVII, pp. 70–77.

On Sense and Nominatum *

GOTTLOB FREGE

The idea of Sameness [1] challenges reflection. It raises questions which are not quite easily answered. Is Sameness a relation? A relation between objects? Or between names or signs of objects? I assumed the latter alternative in my *Begriffsschrift*. The reasons that speak in its favor are the following: "a = a" and "a = b" are sentences of obviously different cognitive significance: "a = a" is valid *a priori* and according to Kant is to be called analytic, whereas sentences of the form "a = b" often contain very valuable extensions of our knowledge and cannot always be justified in an *a priori* manner. The discovery that it is not a different and novel sun which rises every morning, but that it is the very same, certainly was one of the most consequential ones in astronomy. Even nowadays the re-cognition (identification) of a planetoid or a comet is not always a matter of self-evidence. If we wished to view identity as a relation between the objects designated by the names 'a' and 'b' then "a = b" and "a = a" would not seem different if "a = b" is true. This would express a relation of a thing to itself, namely, a relation such that it holds between every thing and itself but never between one thing and another. What one wishes to express with "a = b" seems to be that the signs or names 'a' and 'b' name the same thing; and in that case we would be dealing with those signs: a relation between them would be asserted. But this relation could hold only inasmuch as they name or designate something. The relation, as it were, is mediated through the connection of each sign with the same nominatum. This connection, however, is arbitrary. You cannot forbid the use of an arbitrarily produced process or object as a sign for something else. Hence, a sentence like "a = b" would no longer refer to a matter of fact but rather to our manner of designation; no genuine knowledge would be expressed by it. But this is just what we do want to express in many cases. If the sign 'a' differs from the sign 'b' only as an object (here by its shape) but not by its rôle as a sign, that is to say, not in the manner in which it designates anything, then the cognitive significance of "a = a" would be essentially the same as that of

---

* Translated by H.F. from the article "Ueber Sinn und Bedeutung", *Zeitschr. f. Philos. und Philos. Kritik;* 100, 1892. The terminology adopted is largely that used by R. Carnap in *Meaning and Necessity*, Univ. of Chicago Press, 1947.

[1] I use this word in the sense of identity and understand "a = b" in the sense of "a is the same as b" or "a and b coincide".

"a = b", if "a = b" is true. A difference could arise only if the difference of the signs corresponds to a difference in the way in which the designated objects are given. Let a, b, c be straight lines which connect the corners of a triangle with the midpoints of the opposite sides. The point of intersection of a and b is then the same as that of b and c. Thus we have different designations of the same point and these names ('intersection of a and b', 'intersection of b and c') indicate also the manner in which these points are presented. Therefore the sentence expresses a genuine cognition.

Now it is plausible to connect with a sign (name, word combination, expression) not only the designated object, which may be called the nominatum of the sign, but also the sense (connotation, meaning) of the sign in which is contained the manner and context of presentation. Accordingly, in our examples the *nominata* of the expressions 'the point of intersection of a and b' and 'the point of intersection of b and c' would be the same;—not their senses. The nominata of 'evening star' and 'morning star' are the same but not their senses.

From what has been said it is clear that I here understand by 'sign' or 'name' any expression which functions as a proper name, whose nominatum accordingly is a definite object (in the widest sense of this word). But no concept or relation is under consideration here. These matters are to be dealt with in another essay. The designation of a single object may consist of several words or various signs. For brevity's sake, any such designation will be considered as a proper name.

The sense of a proper name is grasped by everyone who knows the language or the totality of designations of which the proper name is a part; [2] this, however, illuminates the nominatum, if there is any, in a very one-sided fashion. A complete knowledge of the nominatum would require that we could tell immediately in the case of any given sense whether it belongs to the nominatum. This we shall never be able to do.

The regular connection between a sign, its sense and its nominatum is such that there corresponds a definite sense to the sign and to this sense there corresponds again a definite nominatum; whereas not one sign only belongs to one nominatum (object). In different languages, and even in one language, the same sense is represented by different expressions. It is true, there are exceptions to this rule. Certainly there should be a definite sense to each expression in a complete configuration of signs, but the natural languages in many ways fall short of this requirement. We must be satisfied if the same word, at least in the same context, has the same

[2] In the case of genuinely proper names like 'Aristotle' opinions as regards their sense may diverge. As such may, e. g., be suggested: Plato's disciple and the teacher of Alexander the Great. Whoever accepts this sense will interpret the meaning of the statement "Aristotle was born in Stagira" differently from one who interpreted the sense of 'Aristotle' as the Stagirite teacher of Alexander the Great. As long as the nominatum remains the same, these fluctuations in sense are tolerable. But they should be avoided in the system of a demonstrative science and should not appear in a perfect language.

sense. It can perhaps be granted that an expression has a sense if it is formed in a grammatically correct manner and stands for a proper name. But as to whether there is a denotation corresponding to the connotation is hereby not decided. The words 'the heavenly body which has the greatest distance from the earth' have a sense; but it is very doubtful as to whether they have a nominatum. The expression 'the series with the least convergence' has a sense; but it can be proved that it has no nominatum, since for any given convergent series, one can find another one that is less convergent. Therefore the grasping of a sense does not with certainty warrant a corresponding nominatum.

When words are used in the customary manner then what is talked about are their nominata. But it may happen that one wishes to speak about the words themselves or about their senses. The first case occurs when one quotes someone else's words in direct (ordinary) discourse. In this case one's own words immediately name (denote) the words of the other person and only the latter words have the usual nominata. We thus have signs of signs. In writing we make use of quotes enclosing the word-icons. A word-icon in quotes must therefore not be taken in the customary manner.

If we wish to speak of the sense of an expression 'A' we can do this simply through the locution 'the sense of the expression 'A' '. In indirect (oblique) discourse we speak of the sense, e. g., of the words of someone else. From this it becomes clear that also in indirect discourse words do not have their customary nominata; they here name what customarily would be their sense. In order to formulate this succinctly we shall say: words in indirect discourse are used *indirectly*, or have *indirect* nominata. Thus we distinguish the *customary* from the *indirect* nominatum of a word; and similarly, its *customary* sense from its *indirect* sense. The indirect nominatum of a word is therefore its customary sense. Such exceptions must be kept in mind if one wishes correctly to comprehend the manner of connection between signs, senses and nominata in any given case.

Both the nominatum and the sense of a sign must be distinguished from the associated image. If the nominatum of a sign is an object of sense perception, my image of the latter is an inner picture [3] arisen from memories of sense impressions and activities of mine, internal or external. Frequently this image is suffused with feelings; the definiteness of its various parts may vary and fluctuate. Even with the same person the same sense is not always accompanied by the same image. The image is subjective; the image of one person is not that of another. Hence, the

[3] With the images we can align also the percepts in which the sense impressions and activities themselves take the place of those traces left in the mind. For our purposes the difference is unimportant, especially since besides sensations and activities recollections of such help in completing the intuitive presentation. 'Percept' may also be understood as the object, inasmuch as it is spatial or capable of sensory apprehension.

various differences between the images connected with one and the same sense. A painter, a rider, a zoölogist probably connect very different images with the name 'Bucephalus'. The image thereby differs essentially from the connotation of a sign, which latter may well be common property of many and is therefore not a part or mode of the single person's mind; for it cannot well be denied that mankind possesses a common treasure of thoughts which is transmitted from generation to generation.[4]

While, accordingly, there is no objection to speak without qualification of the sense in regard to images, we must, to be precise, add *whose* images they are and at what time they occur. One might say: just as words are connected with different images in two different persons, the same holds of the senses also. Yet this difference would consist merely in the manner of association. It does not prevent both from apprehending the same sense, but they cannot have the same image. *Si duo idem faciunt, non est idem.* When two persons imagine the same thing, each still has his own image. It is true, occasionally we can detect differences in the images or even in the sensations of different persons. But an accurate comparison is impossible because these images cannot be had together in one consciousness.

The nominatum of a proper name is the object itself which is designated thereby; the image which we may have along with it is quite subjective; the sense lies in between, not subjective as is the image, but not the object either. The following simile may help in elucidating these relationships. Someone observes the moon through a telescope. The moon is comparable with the nominatum; it is the object of the observation which is mediated through the real image projected by the object lens into the interior of the telescope, and through the retinal image of the observer. The first may be compared with the sense, the second with the presentation (or image in the psychological sense). The real image inside the telescope, however, is relative; it depends upon the standpoint; yet, it is objective in that it can serve several observers. Arrangements could be made such that several observers could utilize it. But every one of them would have only his own retinal image. Because of the different structures of the eyes not even geometrical congruence could be attained; a real coincidence would in any case be impossible. One could elaborate the simile by assuming that the retinal image of *A* could be made visible to *B;* or *A* could see his own retinal image in a mirror. In this manner one could possibly show how a presentation itself can be made into an object; but even so, it would never be to the (outside) observer what it is to the one who possesses the image. However, these lines of thought lead too far afield.

We can now recognize three levels of differences of words, expressions

---

[4] It is therefore inexpedient to designate fundamentally different things by the one word 'image' (or 'idea').

and complete sentences. The difference may concern at most the imagery, or else the sense but not the nominatum, or finally also the nominatum. In regard to the first level, we must note that, owing to the uncertain correlation of images with words, a difference may exist for one person that another does not discover. The difference of a translation from the original should properly not go beyond the first level. Among the differences possible in this connection we mention the shadings and colorings which poetry seeks to impart to the senses. These shadings and colorings are not objective. Every listener or reader has to add them in accordance with the hints of the poet or speaker. Surely, art would be impossible without some kinship among human imageries; but just how far the intentions of the poet are realized can never be exactly ascertained.

We shall henceforth no longer refer to the images and picturizations; they were discussed only lest the image evoked by a word be confused with its sense or its nominatum.

In order to facilitate brief and precise expression we may lay down the following formulations:

A proper name (word, sign, sign-compound, expression) expresses its sense, and designates or signifies its nominatum. We let a *sign express* its sense and *designate* its nominatum.

Perhaps the following objection, coming from idealistic or skeptical quarters, has been kept in abeyance for some time: "You have been speaking without hesitation of the moon as an object; but how do you know that the name 'the moon' has in fact a nominatum? How do you know that anything at all has a nominatum?" I reply that it is not our intention to speak of the image of the moon, nor would we be satisfied with the sense when we say 'the moon'; instead, we presuppose a nominatum here. We should miss the meaning altogether if we assumed we had reference to images in the sentence "the moon is smaller than the earth". Were this intended we would use some such locution as 'my image of the moon'. Of course, we may be in error as regards that assumption, and such errors have occurred on occasion. However, the question whether we could possibly always be mistaken in this respect may here remain unanswered; it will suffice for the moment to refer to our intention in speaking and thinking in order to justify our reference to the nominatum of a sign; even if we have to make the proviso: if there is such a nominatum.

Thus far we have considered sense and nominatum only of such expressions, words and signs which we called proper names. We are now going to inquire into the sense and the nominatum of a whole declarative sentence. Such a sentence contains a proposition.[5] Is this thought to be regarded as the sense or the nominatum of the sentence? Let us for the

[5] By 'proposition' I do not refer to the subjective activity of thinking but rather to its objective content which is capable of being the common property of many.

moment assume that the sentence has a nominatum! If we then substitute a word in it by another word with the same nominatum but with a different sense, then this substitution cannot affect the nominatum of the sentence. But we realize that in such cases the proposition is changed; e. g.. the proposition of the sentence "the morning star is a body illuminated by the sun" is different from that of "the evening star is a body illuminated by the sun". Someone who did not know that the evening star is the same as the morning star could consider the one proposition true and the other false. The proposition can therefore not be the nominatum of the sentence; it will instead have to be regarded as its sense. But what about the nominatum? Can we even ask this question? A sentence as a whole has perhaps only sense and no nominatum? It may in any case be expected that there are such sentences, just as there are constituents of sentences which do have sense but no nominatum. Certainly, sentences containing proper names without nominata must be of this type. The sentence "Odysseus deeply asleep was disembarked at Ithaca" obviously has a sense. But since it is doubtful as to whether the name 'Odysseus' occurring in this sentence has a nominatum, so it is also doubtful that the whole sentence has one. However, it is certain that whoever seriously regards the sentence either as true or as false also attributes to the name 'Odysseus' a nominatum, not only a sense; for it is obviously the nominatum of this name to which the predicate is either ascribed or denied. He who does not acknowledge the nominatum cannot ascribe or deny a predicate to it. It might be urged that the consideration of the nominatum of the name is going farther than is necessary; one could be satisfied with the sense, if one stayed with the proposition. If all that mattered were only the sense of the sentence (i. e., the proposition) then it would be unnecessary to be concerned with the nominata of the sentence-components, for only the sense of the components can be relevant for the sense of the sentence. The proposition remains the same, no matter whether or not the name 'Odysseus' has a nominatum. The fact that we are at all concerned about the nominatum of a sentence-component indicates that we generally acknowledge or postulate a nominatum for the sentence itself. The proposition loses in interest as soon as we recognize that one of its parts is lacking a nominatum. We may therefore be justified to ask for a nominatum of a sentence, in addition to its sense. But why do we wish that every proper name have not only a sense but also a nominatum? Why is the proposition alone not sufficient? We answer: because what matters to us is the truth-value. This, however, is not always the case. In listening to an epic, for example, we are fascinated by the euphony of the language and also by the sense of the sentences and by the images and emotions evoked. In turning to the question of truth we disregard the artistic appreciation and pursue scientific considerations. Whether the name 'Odysseus' has a nominatum is therefore immaterial to us as long as we accept the poem as a work of art.[6] Thus, it is the striving for truth which urges us to penetrate beyond the sense to the nominatum.

We have realized that we are to look for the nominatum of a sentence whenever the nominata of the sentence-components are the thing that matters; and that is the case whenever and only when we ask for the truth value.

Thus we find ourselves persuaded to accept the *truth-value* of a sentence as its nominatum. By the truth-value of a sentence I mean the circumstance of its being true or false. There are no other truth-values. For brevity's sake I shall call the one the True and the other the False. Every declarative sentence, in which what matters are the nominata of the words, is therefore to be considered as a proper name; and its nominatum, if there is any, is either the True or the False. These two objects are recognized, even if only tacitly, by everyone who at all makes judgments, holds anything as true, thus even by the skeptic. To designate truth-values as objects may thus far appear as a capricious idea or as a mere play on words, from which no important conclusion should be drawn. What I call an object can be discussed only in connection with the nature of concepts and relations. That I will reserve for another essay. But this might be clear even here: in every judgment [7]—no matter how obvious—a step is made from the level of propositions to the level of the nominata (the objective facts).

It may be tempting to regard the relation of a proposition to the True not as that of sense to nominatum but as that of the subject to the predicate. One could virtually say: "the proposition that 5 is a prime number is true". But on closer examination one notices that this does not say any more than is said in the simple sentence "5 is a prime number". This makes clear that the relation of a proposition to the True must not be compared with the relation of subject and predicate. Subject and predicate (interpreted logically) are, after all, components of a proposition; they are on the same level as regards cognition. By joining subject and predicate we always arrive only at a proposition; in this way we never move from a sense to a nominatum or from a proposition to its truth-value. We remain on the same level and never proceed from it to the next one. Just as the sun cannot be part of a proposition, so the truth-value, because it is not the sense, but an object, cannot be either.

If our conjecture (that the nominatum of a sentence is its truth value) is correct, then the truth-value must remain unchanged if a sentence-component is replaced by an expression with the same nominatum but

[6] It would be desirable to have an expression for signs which have sense only. If we call them 'icons' then the words of an actor on the stage would be icons; even the actor himself would be an icon.

[7] A judgment is not merely the apprehension of a thought or proposition but the acknowledgment of its truth.

with a different sense. Indeed, Leibnitz declares: *"Eadem sunt, quae sibi mutuo substitui possunt, salva veritate"*. What else, except the truth-value, could be found, which quite generally belongs to every sentence and regarding which the nominata of the components are relevant and which would remain invariant for substitutions of the type indicated?

Now if the truth-value of a sentence is its nominatum, then all true sentences have the same nominatum, and likewise all false ones. This implies that all detail has been blurred in the nominatum of a sentence. What interests us can therefore never be merely the nominatum; but the proposition alone does not give knowledge; only the proposition together with its nominatum, i. e., its truth-value, does. Judging may be viewed as a movement from a proposition to its nominatum, i. e., its truth-value. Of course this is not intended as a definition. Judging is indeed something peculiar and unique. One might say that judging consists in the discerning of parts within the truth-value. This discernment occurs through recourse to the proposition. Every sense that belongs to a truth-value would correspond in its own manner to the analysis. I have, however, used the word 'part' in a particular manner here: I have transferred the relation of whole and part from the sentence to its nominatum. This I did by viewing the nominatum of a word as part of the nominatum of a sentence, when the word itself is part of the sentence. True enough, this way of putting things is objectionable since as regards the nominatum the whole and one part of it does not determine the other part; and also because the word 'part' in reference to bodies has a difference customary usage. A special expression should be coined for what has been suggested above.

We shall now further examine the conjecture that the truth-value of a sentence is its nominatum. We have found that the truth-value of a sentence remains unaltered if an expression within the sentence is replaced by a synonymous one. But we have as yet not considered the case in which the expression-to-be-replaced is itself a sentence. If our view is correct, then the truth-value of a sentence, which contains another sentence as a part, must remain unaltered when we substitute for the part another of the same truth-value. Exceptions are to be expected if the whole or the part are either in direct or indirect discourse; for as we have seen, in that case the nominata of the words are not the usual ones. A sentence in direct discourse nominates again a sentence but in indirect discourse it nominates a proposition.

Our attention is thus directed to subordinate sentences (i. e., dependent clauses). These present themselves of course as parts of a sentence-structure which from a logical point of view appears also as a sentence, and indeed as if it were a main clause. But here we face the question whether in the case of dependent clauses it also holds that their nominata are truth-values. We know already that this is not the case with sentences in indirect discourse. The grammarians view clauses as representatives of sentence-parts and divide them accordingly into subjective, relative, and adverbial clauses. This might suggest that the nominatum of a clause is not a truth-value but rather that it is of similar nature as that of a noun or of an adjective or of an adverb; in short, of a sentence-part whose sense is not a proposition but only part thereof. Only a thorough investigation can provide clarity in this matter. We shall herein not follow strictly along grammatical lines, but rather group together what is logically of comparable type. Let us first seek out such instances in which, as we just surmised, the sense of a clause is not a self-sufficient proposition.

Among the abstract clauses beginning with 'that' there is also the indirect discourse, of which we have seen that in it the words have their indirect (oblique) nominata which coincide with what are ordinarily their senses. In this case then the clause has as its nominatum a proposition, not a truth-value; its sense is not a proposition but it is the sense of the words 'the proposition that . . .', which is only a part of the proposition corresponding to the total sentence-structure. This occurs in connection with 'to say', 'to hear', 'to opine', 'to be convinced', 'to infer' and similar words.[8] The situation is different, and rather complicated in connection with such words as 'to recognize', 'to know', 'to believe', a matter to be considered later.

One can see that in these cases the nominatum of the clause indeed consists in the proposition, because whether that proposition is true or false is immaterial for the truth of the whole sentence. Compare, e. g., the following two sentences: "Copernicus believed that the planetary orbits are circles" and "Copernicus believed that the appearance of the sun's motion is produced by the real motion of the earth". Here the one clause can be substituted for the other without affecting the truth. The sense of the principal sentence together with the clause is the single proposition; and the truth of the whole implies neither the truth nor the falsity of the clause. In cases of this type it is not permissible to replace in the clause one expression by another of the same nominatum. Such replacement may be made only by expressions of the same indirect nominatum, i. e., of the same customary sense. If one were to infer: the nominatum of a sentence is not its truth-value ("because then a sentence could always be replaced by another with the same truth-value"), he would prove too much; one could just as well maintain that the nominatum of the word 'morning star' is not Venus, for one cannot always substitute 'Venus' for 'morning star'. The only correct conclusion is that the nominatum of a sentence is *not always* its truth-value, and that 'morning star' does not always nominate the planet Venus; for this is indeed not the case when the word is used with its indirect nominatum. Such an exceptional case is before us in the clauses just considered, whose nominatum is a proposition.

[8] In "*A* lied, that he had seen *B*" the clause denotes a proposition of which it is said, firstly, that *A* asserted it as true, and, secondly, that *A* was convinced of its falsity.

When we say "it seems that . . ." then we mean to say "it seems to me that . . ." or "I opine that . . .". This is the same case over again. Similarly with expressions such as: 'to be glad', 'to regret', 'to approve', 'to disapprove', 'to hope', 'to fear'. When Wellington, toward the end of the battle of Belle-Alliance was glad that the Prussians were coming, the ground of his rejoicing was a conviction. Had he actually been deceived, he would not have been less glad, as long as his belief persisted; and before he arrived at the conviction that the Prussians were coming he could not have been glad about it, even if in fact they were already approaching.

Just as a conviction or a belief may be the ground of a sentiment, so it can also be the ground of another conviction such as in inference. In the sentence "Columbus inferred from the roundness of the earth that he could, traveling westward, reach India" we have, as nominata of its parts two propositions: that the earth is round, and that Columbus traveling westward could reach India. What matters here is only that Columbus was convinced of the one as well as of the other and that the one conviction furnishes the ground for the other. It is irrelevant for the truth of our sentence whether the earth is really round and whether Columbus could have reached India in the manner he fancied. But it is not irrelevant whether for 'the earth' we substitute 'the planet accompanied by one satellite whose diameter is larger than one-fourth of its own diameter'. Here also we deal with the indirect nominata of the words.

Adverbial clauses of purpose with 'so that', likewise belong here; obviously the purpose is a proposition; therefore: indirect nominata of the words, expressed in subjunctive form.

The clause with 'that' after 'to command', 'to request', 'to forbid' would appear in imperative form in direct discourse. Imperatives have no nominata; they have only sense. It is true, commands or requests are not propositions, but they are of the same type as propositions. Therefore the words in the dependent clauses after 'to command', 'to request', etc. have indirect nominata. The nominatum of such a sentence is thus not a truth-value but a command, a request, and the like.

We meet a similar situation in the case of dependent questions in phrases like 'to doubt if', 'not to know what'. It is easy to see that the words, here too, have to be interpreted in terms of their indirect nominata. The dependent interrogatory clauses containing 'who', 'what', 'where', 'when', 'how', 'whereby', etc. often apparently approximate closely adverbial clauses in which the words have their ordinary nominata. These cases are linguistically distinguished through the mode of the verb. In the subjunctive we have a dependent question and the indirect nominata of the words, so that a proper name cannot generally be replaced by another of the same object.

In the instances thus far considered the words in the clause had indirect nominata; this made it intelligible that the nominatum of the clause itself is indirect, i. e., not a truth-value, but a proposition, a command, a request, a question. The clause could be taken as a noun; one might even say, as a proper name of that proposition, command, etc., in whose rôle it functions in the context of the sentence-structure.

We are now going to consider clauses of another type, in which the words do have their customary nominata although there does not appear a proposition as the sense or a truth-value as the nominatum. How this is possible will best be elucidated by examples.

"He who discovered the elliptical shape of the planetary orbits, died in misery".

If, in this example, the sense of the clause were a proposition, it would have to be expressible also in a principal sentence. But this cannot be done because the grammatical subject 'he who' has no independent sense. It merely mediates the relations to the second part of the sentence: 'died in misery'. Therefore the sense of the clause is not a complete proposition and its nominatum is not a truth-value, but Kepler. It might be objected that the sense of the whole does include a proposition as its part; namely, that there was someone who first recognized the elliptical shape of the planetary orbits; for if we accept the whole as true we cannot deny this part. Indubitably so; but only because otherwise the clause "he who discovered the elliptical shape, etc." would have no nominatum. Whenever something is asserted then the presupposition taken for granted is that the employed proper names, simple or compound, have nominata. Thus, if we assert "Kepler died in misery" it is presupposed that the name 'Kepler' designates something. However, the proposition that the name 'Kepler' designates something is, the foregoing notwithstanding, not contained in the sense of the sentence "Kepler died in misery". If that were the case the denial would not read "Kepler did not die in misery" but "Kepler did not die in misery, or the name 'Kepler' is without nominatum". That the name 'Kepler' designates something is rather the presupposition of the assertion "Kepler died in misery" as well as of its denial. Now, it is a defect of languages that expressions are possible within them, which, in their grammatical form, seemingly determined to designate an object, nevertheless do not fulfill this condition in special cases; because this depends on the truth of the sentence. Thus it depends upon the truth of the sentence "there was someone who discovered the ellipticity of the orbits" whether the clause 'he who discovered the ellipticity of the orbits' really designates an object, or else merely evokes the appearance thereof, while indeed being without nominatum. Thus it may seem as if our clause, as part of its sense, contained the proposition that there existed someone who discovered the ellipticity of the orbits. If this were so, then the denial would have to read "he who first recognized the ellipticity of the orbits did not die in misery, or there was no one who discovered the ellipticity of the orbits." This, it is obvious, hinges upon an imperfection of language of which, by the way, even the symbolic language of analysis is not entirely free; there, also, sign compounds may occur which appear as if they designated something, but which at least hitherto are without nominatum, e. g., divergent infinite series. This can be avoided, e. g., through the special convention that the nominatum of divergent infinite series be the number o. It is to be demanded that in a logically perfect language (logical symbolism) every expression constructed as a proper name in a grammatically correct manner out of already introduced symbols, in fact designate an object; and that no symbol be introduced as a proper name without assurance that it have a nominatum. It is customary in logic texts to warn against the ambiguity of expressions as a source of fallacies. I deem it at least as appropriate to issue a warning against apparent proper names that have no nominata. The history of mathematics has many a tale to tell of errors which originated from this source. The demagogic misuse is close (perhaps closer) at hand as in the case of ambiguous expressions. 'The will of the people' may serve as an example in this regard; for it is easily established that there is no generally accepted nominatum of that expression. Thus it is obviously not without importance to obstruct once for all the source of these errors, at least as regards their occurrence in science. Then such objections as the one discussed above will become impossible, for then it will be seen that whether a proper name has a nominatum can never depend upon the truth of a proposition.

Our considerations may be extended from these subjective clauses to the logically related relative and adverbial clauses.

Relative clauses, too, are employed in the formation of compound proper names—even if, in contradistinction to subjective clauses, they are not sufficient by themselves for this purpose. These relative clauses may be regarded as equivalent to appositions. Instead of 'the square root of 4 which is smaller than o' we can also say 'the negative square root of 4'. We have here a case in which out of a conceptual expression a compound proper name is formed, with the help of the definite article in the singular. This is at any rate permissible when one and only one object is comprised by the concept.[9] Conceptual expression can be formed in such a fashion that their characteristics are indicated through relative clauses as in our example through the clause 'which is smaller than o'. Obviously, such relative clauses, just as the subjective clauses above, do not refer to a proposition as their sense nor to a truth-value as their nominatum. Their sense is only a part of a proposition, which in many cases, can be expressed by a simple apposition. As in the subjective clauses an independent sub-

---

[9] According to our previous remarks such an expression should always be assured of a nominatum, e. g., through the special convention that the nominatum be the number o if there is no object or more than one object denoted by the expression.

ject is missing and it is therefore impossible to represent the sense of the clause in an independent principal sentence.

Places, dates and time-intervals are objects from a logical point of view; the linguistic symbol of a definite place, moment or span of time must therefore be viewed as a proper name. Adverbial clauses of space or time can then be used in the formation of such proper names in a fashion analogous to the one we have just remarked in the case of subjective and relative clauses. Similarly, expressions for concepts which comprise places, etc., can be formed. Here too, it is to be remarked, the sense of the subordinate clauses cannot be rendered in a principal clause, because an essential constituent, namely the determination of place and time, is missing and only alluded to by a relative pronoun or a conjunction.[10]

In conditional clauses also, there is, just as we have realized in the case of subjective, relative and adverbial clauses, a constituent with indeterminate indication corresponding to which there is a similar one in the concluding clause. In referring to one another the two clauses combine into a whole which expresses, as a rule, only one proposition. In the sentence "if a number is smaller than 1 and greater than 0, then its square also is smaller than 1 and greater than 0" this constituent in the conditional clause is 'a number' and in the concluding clause it is 'its'. Just through this indeterminacy the sense acquires the universal character which one expects of a law. But it is in this way also that it comes about that the conditional clause alone does not possess a complete proposition as its sense, and that together with the concluding clause it expresses a single proposition whose parts are no longer propositions. It is not generally the case that a hypothetical judgment correlates two judgments. Putting it in that (or a similar) manner would amount to using the word 'judgment' in the same sense that I have attributed to the word 'proposition'. In that case I would have to say: in a hypothetical proposition two propositions are re-

---

[10] Regarding these sentences, however, several interpretations are easily conceivable. The sense of the sentence "after Schleswig-Holstein was torn away from Denmark, Prussia and Austria fell out with one another" could also be rendered by "after the separation of Schl.-H. from Denmark, Prussia and Austria fell out with one another" In this formulation it is sufficiently clear that we should not regard it as part of this sense that Schleswig-Holstein once was separated from Denmark; but rather that this is the necessary presupposition for the very existence of a nominatum of the expression 'after the separation of Schl.-H. from D.' Yet, our sentence could also be interpreted to the effect that Schl.-H. was once separated from D. This case will be considered later. In order to grasp the difference more clearly, let us identify ourselves with the mind of a Chinese who, with his trifling knowledge of European history, regards it as false that Schl.-H. ever was separated from D. This Chinese will regard as neither true nor false the sentence as interpreted in the first manner. He would deny to it any nominatum because the dependent clause would be lacking a nominatum. The dependent clause would only apparently indicate a temporal determination. But if the Chinese interprets our sentence in the second manner, then he will find it expressing a proposition which he would consider false, in addition to a component which, for him, would be without nominatum.

lated to each other. But this could be the case only if an indeterminately denoting constituent were absent; [11] but then universality would also be missing.

If a time point is to be indeterminately indicated in a conditional and a concluding clause, then this is not infrequently effected by *tempus praesens* of the verb, which in this case does not connote the present time. It is this grammatical form which takes the place of the indeterminately indicating constituent in the main and the dependent clause. "When the sun is at the Tropic of Cancer, the northern hemisphere has its longest day" is an example. Here, too, it is impossible to express the sense of the dependent clause in a main clause. For this sense is not a complete proposition; if we said: "the sun is at the Tropic of Cancer" we would be referring to the present time and thereby alter the sense. Similarly, the sense of the main clause is not a proposition either, only the whole consisting of main and dependent clause contains a proposition. Further, it may occur that several constituents common to conditional and concluding clause are indeterminately indicated.

It is obvious that subjective clauses containing 'who', 'what', and adverbial clauses with 'where', 'when', 'wherever', 'whenever' are frequently to be interpreted, inasmuch as their sense is concerned, as conditional sentences; e. g., "He who touches pitch soils himself".

Conditional clauses can also be replaced by relative clauses. The sense of the previously mentioned sentence can also be rendered by "the square of a number which is smaller than 1 and larger than 0, is smaller than 1 and larger than 0."

Quite different is the case in which the common constituent of main and dependent clause is represented by a proper name. In the sentence: "Napoleon who recognized the danger to his right flank, personally led his troops against the enemy's position" there are expressed two propositions:

1. Napoleon recognized the danger to his right flank.
2. Napoleon personally led his troops against the enemy's position.

When and where this happened can indeed be known only from the context, but is to be viewed as thereby determined. If we pronounce our whole sentence as an assertion we thereby assert simultaneously its two component sentences. If one of the components is false the whole is false. Here we have a case in which the dependent clause by itself has a sense in a complete proposition (if supplemented by temporal and spatial indications). The nominatum of such a clause is therefore a truth-value. We may therefore expect that we can replace it by a sentence of the same truth value without altering the truth of the whole. This is indeed the case;

[11] Occasionally there is no explicit linguistic indication and the interpretation has to depend upon the total context.

but it must be kept in mind that for a purely grammatical reason, its subject must be 'Napoleon'; because only then can the sentence be rendered in the form of a relative clause attaching to 'Napoleon'. If the demand to render it in this form and if the conjunction with 'and' is admitted, then this limitation falls away.

Likewise, in dependent clauses with 'although' complete propositions are expressed. This conjunction really has no sense and does not affect the sense of the sentence; rather, it illuminates it in a peculiar fashion.[12] Without affecting the truth of the whole the implicate may be replaced by one of the same truth value; but the illumination might then easily appear inappropriate, just as if one were to sing a song of sad content in a cheerful manner.

In these last instances the truth of the whole implied the truth of the component sentences. The situation is different if a conditional sentence expresses a complete proposition; namely, when in doing so it contains instead of a merely indicating constituent a proper name or something deemed equivalent to a proper name. In the sentence: "if the sun has already risen by now, the sky is heavily overcast", the tense is the present —therefore determinate. The place also is to be considered determinate. Here we can say that a relation is posited such that the case does not arise in which the antecedent sentence nominates the True and the consequent sentence nominates the False. Accordingly, the given (whole) sentence is true if the sun has not as yet risen (no matter whether or no the sky be heavily overcast), and also if the sun has risen and the sky is heavily overcast. Since all that matters are only the truth-values, each of the component sentences can be replaced by another one of the same truth-value, without altering the truth-value of the whole sentence. In this case also, the illumination would usually seem inappropriate; the proposition could easily appear absurd; but this has nothing to do with the truth-value of the sentence. It must always be remembered that associated thoughts are evoked on the side; but these are not really expressed and must therefore not be taken account of; their truth-values cannot be relevant.[13]

We may hope we have considered the simple types of sentences. Let us now review what we have found out!

The sense of a subordinate clause is usually not a proposition but only part of one. Its nominatum is therefore not a truth-value. The reason for this is *either:* that the words in the subordinate clause have only indirect nominata, so that the nominatum, not the sense, of the clause is a proposition, *or,* that the clause, because of a contained indeterminately indicating constituent, is incomplete, such that only together with the principal

[12] Similarly in the cases of 'but', 'yet'.

[13] The proposition of the sentence could also be formulated thus: "either the sun has not as yet risen or the sky is heavily overcast". This shows how to interpret this type of compound sentence.

clause does it express a proposition. However, there are also instances in which the sense of the dependent clause is a complete proposition, and in this case it can be replaced by another clause of the same truth-value without altering the truth-value of the whole; that is, inasmuch as there are no grammatical obstacles in the way.

In a survey of the various occurrent clauses one will readily encounter some which will not properly fit within any of the considered divisions. As far as I can see, the reason for that is that these clauses do not have quite so simple a sense. It seems that almost always we connect associated propositions with the main proposition which we express; these associated propositions, even if unexpressed, are associated with our words according to psychological laws also by the listener. And because they appear as associated automatically with our words (as in the case of the main proposition) we seem to wish, after all, to express such associated propositions along with the main propositions. The sense of the sentence thereby becomes richer and it may well happen that we may have more simple propositions than sentences. In some cases the sentence may be interpreted in this way, in others, it may be doubtful whether the associated proposition belongs to the sense of the sentence or whether it merely accompanies it.[14] One might find that in the sentence: "Napoleon, who recognized the danger to his right flank, personally led his troops against the enemy's position" there are not only the previously specified two propositions, but also the proposition that the recognition of the danger was the reason why he led his troops against the enemy. One may indeed wonder whether this proposition is merely lightly suggested or actually expressed. Consider the question whether our sentence would be false if Napoleon's resolution had been formed before the recognition of the danger. If our sentence were true even despite this, then the associated proposition should not be regarded as part of the sense of the sentence. In the alternative case the situation is rather complicated: we should then have more simple propositions than sentences. Now if we replaced the sentence: "Napoleon recognized the danger for his right flank" by another sentence of the same truth-value, e. g., by: "Napoleon was over 45 years old" this would change not only our first but also our third proposition; and this might thereby change also the truth-value of the third proposition —namely, if his age was not the reason for his resolution to lead the troops against the enemy. Hence, it is clear that in such instances sentences of the same truth-value cannot always be substituted for one another. The sentence merely by virtue of its connection with another expresses something more than it would by itself alone.

Let us now consider cases in which this occurs regularly. In the sentence: "Bebel imagines that France's desire for vengeance could be assuaged

---

[14] This may be of importance in the question as to whether a given assertion be a lie, an oath or a perjury.

by the restitution of Alsace-Lorraine" there are expressed two propositions, which, however, do not correspond to the main and the dependent clause—namely:

1. Bebel believes that France's desire for vengeance could be assuaged by the restitution of Alsace-Lorraine;
2. France's desire for vengeance cannot be assuaged by the restitution of Alsace-Lorraine.

In the expression of the first proposition the words of the dependent clause have indirect nominata; while the same words, in the expression of the second proposition, have their usual nominata. Hence, we see that the dependent clause of our original sentence really is to be interpreted in a twofold way; i. e., with different nominata, one of which is a proposition and the other a truth-value. An analogous situation prevails with expressions like 'to know', 'to recognize', 'it is known'.

A condition clause and its related main clause express several propositions which, however, do not correspond one-to-one to the clauses. The sentence: "Since ice is specifically lighter than water, it floats on water" asserts:

1. Ice is specifically lighter than water.
2. If something is specifically lighter than water, it floats on water.
3. Ice floats on water.

The third proposition, being implied by the first two, would perhaps not have to be mentioned expressly. However, neither the first and the third, nor the second and the third together would completely render the sense of our sentence. Thus we see that the dependent clause 'since ice is specifically lighter than water' expresses both our first proposition and part of the second. Hence, our clause cannot be replaced by another of the same truth-value; for thereby we are apt to alter our second proposition and could easily affect its truth-value.

A similar situation holds in the case of the sentence: "If iron were lighter than water it would float on water". Here we have the two propositions that iron is not lighter than water and that whatever is lighter than water floats on water. The clause again expresses the one proposition and part of the other. If we interpret the previously discussed sentence: "After Schleswig-Holstein was separated from Denmark, Prussia and Austria fell out with one another" as containing the proposition that Schleswig-Holstein once was separated from Denmark, then we have: firstly, this proposition, secondly, the proposition that, at a time more precisely determined by the dependent clause, Prussia and Austria fell out with one another. Here, too, the dependent clause expresses not only one proposition but also part of another. Therefore, it may not generally be replaced by another clause of the same truth-value.

It is difficult to exhaust all possibilities that present themselves in language; but I hope, in essence at least, to have disclosed the reasons why, in view of the invariance of the truth of a whole sentence, a clause cannot always be replaced by another of the same truth-value. These reasons are:

1. that the clause does not denote a truth-value in that it expresses only a part of a proposition;
2. that the clause, while it does denote a truth-value, is not restricted to this function in that its sense comprises, beside one proposition, also a part of another.

The first case holds

a. with the indirect nominata of the words;
b. if a part of the sentence indicates only indirectly without being a proper name.

In the second case the clause is to be interpreted in a twofold manner; namely, once with its usual nominatum; the other time with its indirect nominatum; or else, the sense of a part of the clause may simultaneously be a constituent of another proposition which, together with the sense expressed in the dependent clause, amounts to the total sense of the main and the dependent clause.

This makes it sufficiently plausible that instances in which a clause is not replaceable by another of the same truth-value do not disprove our view that the nominatum of a sentence is its truth-value and its sense a proposition.

Let us return to our point of departure now.

When we discerned generally a difference in cognitive significance between "a = a" and "a = b" then this is now explained by the fact that for the cognitive significance of a sentence the sense (the proposition expressed) is no less relevant than its nominatum (the truth-value). If a = b, then the nominatum of 'a' and of 'b' is indeed the same and therefore also the truth-value of "a = b" is the same as that of "a = a". Nevertheless, the sense of 'b' may differ from the sense of 'a'; and therefore the proposition expressed by "a = b" may differ from the proposition expressed by "a = a"; in that case the two sentences do not have the same cognitive significance. Thus, if, as above, we mean by 'judgment' the transition from a proposition to its truth-value, then we can also say that the judgments differ from one another.

On Denoting *

BERTRAND RUSSELL

By a "denoting phrase" I mean a phrase such as any one of the follow-ing: a man, some man, any man, every man, all men, the present King of England, the present King of France, the centre of mass of the Solar System at the first instant of the twentieth century, the revolution of the earth round the sun, the revolution of the sun round the earth. Thus a phrase is denoting solely in virtue of its *form*. We may distinguish three cases: (1) A phrase may be denoting, and yet not denote anything; e.g., "the present King of France". (2) A phrase may denote one definite object; e.g., "the present King of England" denotes a certain man. (3) A phrase may denote ambiguously; e.g., "a man" denotes not many men, but an ambigu-ous man. The interpretation of such phrases is a matter of considerable difficulty; indeed, it is very hard to frame any theory not susceptible of formal refutation. All the difficulties with which I am acquainted are met, so far as I can discover, by the theory which I am about to explain.

The subject of denoting is of very great importance not only in logic and mathematics, but also in theory of knowledge. For example, we know that the centre of mass of the Solar System at a definite instant is some definite point, and we can affirm a number of propositions about it; but we have no immediate *acquaintance* with this point, which is only known to us by description. The distinction between *acquaintance* and *knowledge about* is the distinction between the things we have presentations of, and the things we only reach by means of denoting phrases. It often happens that we know that a certain phrase denotes unambiguously, although we have no acquaintance with what it denotes; this occurs in the above case of the centre of mass. In perception we have acquaintance with the objects of perception, and in thought we have acquaintance with objects of a more abstract logical character but we do not necessarily have acquaint-ance with the objects denoted by phrases composed of words with whose meanings we are acquainted. To take a very important instance: There seems no reason to believe that we are ever acquainted with other people's minds, seeing that these are not directly perceived; hence what we know about them is obtained through denoting. All thinking has to start from acquaintance; but it succeeds in thinking *about* many things with which we have no acquaintance.

The course of my argument will be as follows. I shall begin by stating

* Reprinted from *Mind*, 14, 1905, by kind permission of the author and the editors.

the theory I intend to advocate; [1] I shall then discuss the theories of Frege and Meinong, showing why neither of them satisfies me; then I shall give the grounds in favour of my theory; and finally I shall briefly indicate the philosophical consequences of my theory.

My theory, briefly, is as follows. I take the notion of the *variable* as fundamental; I use "C (x)" to mean a proposition [2] in which x is a constituent, where x, the variable, is essentially and wholly undetermined. Then we can consider the two notions "C (x) is always true" and "C (x) is sometimes true".[3] Then *everything* and *nothing* and *something* (which are the most primitive of denoting phrases) are to be interpreted as follows:

C (everything) means "C (x) is always true";
C (nothing) means " 'C (x) is false' is always true";
C (something) means "It is false that 'C (x) is false' is always true".[4]

Here the notion "C (x) is always true" is taken as ultimate and indefinable, and the others are defined by means of it. *Everything, nothing*, and *something*, are not assumed to have any meaning in isolation, but a meaning is assigned to *every* proposition in which they occur. This is the principle of the theory of denoting I wish to advocate: that denoting phrases never have any meaning in themselves, but that every proposition in whose verbal expression they occur has a meaning. The difficulties concerning denoting are, I believe, all the result of a wrong analysis of propositions whose verbal expressions contain denoting phrases. The proper analysis, if I am not mistaken, may be further set forth as follows.

Suppose now we wish to interpret the proposition, "I met a man". If this is true, I met some definite man; but that is not what I affirm. What I affirm is, according to the theory I advocate:

" 'I met x, and x is human' is not always false".

Generally, defining the class of men as the class of objects having the predicate *human*, we say that:

"C (a man)" means " 'C (x) and x is human' is not always false".

This leaves "a man," by itself, wholly destitute of meaning, but gives a meaning to every proposition in whose verbal expression "a man" occurs.

Consider next the proposition "all men are mortal". This proposition [5]

[1] I have discussed this subject in *Principles of Mathematics*, ch. v, and § 476. The theory there advocated is very nearly the same as Frege's, and is quite different from the theory to be advocated in what follows.

[2] More exactly, a propositional function.

[3] The second of these can be defined by means of the first, if we take it to mean, "It is not true that 'C (x) is false' is always true".

[4] I shall sometimes use, instead of this complicated phrase, the phrase "C (x) is not always false," or "C (x) is sometimes true," supposed *defined* to mean the same as the complicated phrase.

[5] As has been ably argued in Mr. Bradley's *Logic*, Book I, ch. ii.

is really hypothetical and states that *if* anything is a man, it is mortal. That is, it states that if x is a man, x is mortal, whatever x may be. Hence, substituting 'x is human' for 'x is a man,' we find:

"All men are mortal" means " 'If x is human, x is mortal' is always true".

This is what is expressed in symbolic logic by saying that "all men are mortal" means " 'x is human' implies 'x is mortal' for all values of x". More generally, we say:

"C (all men)" means " 'If x is human, then C (x) is true' is always true".

Similarly

"C (no men)" means " 'If x is human, then C (x) is false' is always true".

"C (some men)" will mean the same as "C (a man)," [6] and

"C (a man)" means "It is false that 'C (x) and x is human' is always false".

"C (every man)" will mean the same as "C (all men)".

It remains to interpret phrases containing *the*. These are by far the most interesting and difficult of denoting phrases. Take as an instance "the father of Charles II was executed". This asserts that there was an x who was the father of Charles II and was executed. Now *the*, when it is strictly used, involves uniqueness; we do, it is true, speak of "*the* son of So-and-so" even when So-and-so has several sons, but it would be more correct to say "*a* son of So-and-so". Thus for our purposes we take *the* as involving uniqueness. Thus when we say "x was *the* father of Charles II" we not only assert that x had a certain relation to Charles II, but also that nothing else had this relation. The relation in question, without the assumption of uniqueness, and without any denoting phrases, is expressed by "x *begat Charles II*". To get an equivalent of "x was the father of Charles II," we must add, "If y is other than x, y did not beget Charles II," or, what is equivalent, "If y begat Charles II, y is identical with x". Hence "x is the father of Charles II" becomes "x begat Charles II; and 'if y begat Charles II, y is identical with x' is always true of y".

Thus "the father of Charles II was executed" becomes:

"It is not always false of x that x begat Charles II and that x was executed and that 'if y begat Charles II, y is identical with x' is always true of y".

This may seem a somewhat incredible interpretation; but I am not at present giving reasons, I am merely *stating* the theory.

[6] Psychologically "C (a man)" has a suggestion of *only one*, and "C (some men)" has a suggestion of *more than one*; but we may neglect these suggestions in a preliminary sketch.

To interpret "C (the father of Charles II)," where C stands for any statement about him, we have only to substitute C (x) for "x was executed" in the above. Observe that, according to the above interpretation, whatever statement C may be, "C (the father of Charles II)" implies:

"It is not always false of x that 'if y begat Charles II, y is identical with x' is always true of y,"

which is what is expressed in common language by "Charles II had one father and no more". Consequently if this condition fails, *every* proposition of the form "C (the father of Charles II)" is false. Thus, e.g., every proposition of the form "C (the present King of France)" is false. This is a great advantage in the present theory. I shall show later that it is not contrary to the law of contradiction, as might be at first supposed.

The above gives a reduction of all propositions in which denoting phrases occur to forms in which no such phrases occur. Why it is imperative to effect such a reduction, the subsequent discussion will endeavour to show.

The evidence for the above theory is derived from the difficulties which seem unavoidable if we regard denoting phrases as standing for genuine constituents of the propositions in whose verbal expressions they occur. Of the possible theories which admit such constituents the simplest is that of Meinong.[7] This theory regards any grammatically correct denoting phrase as standing for an *object*. Thus "the present King of France," "the round square," etc., are supposed to be genuine objects. It is admitted that such objects do not *subsist*, but nevertheless they are supposed to be objects. This is in itself a difficult view; but the chief objection is that such objects, admittedly, are apt to infringe the law of contradiction. It is contended, for example, that the existent present King of France exists, and also does not exist; that the round square is round, and also not round; etc. But this is intolerable; and if any theory can be found to avoid this result, it is surely to be preferred.

The above breach of the law of contradiction is avoided by Frege's theory. He distinguishes, in a denoting phrase, two elements, which we may call the *meaning* and the *denotation*.[8] Thus "the centre of mass of the Solar System at the beginning of the twentieth century" is highly complex in *meaning*, but its *denotation* is a certain point, which is simple. The Solar System, the twentieth century, etc., are constituents of the *meaning*; but the *denotation* has no constituents at all.[9] One advantage of this dis-

---

[7] See *Untersuchungen zur Gegenstandstheorie und Psychologie*, Leipzig, 1904, the first three articles (by Meinong, Ameseder and Mally respectively).

[8] See his "On Sense and Nominatum," in this volume.

[9] Frege distinguishes the two elements of meaning and denotation everywhere, and not only in complex denoting phrases. Thus it is the *meanings* of the constituents of a denoting complex that enter into its *meaning*, not their *denotation*. In the proposition "Mont Blanc is over 1,000 metres high," it is, according to him, the *meaning* of "Mont Blanc," not the actual mountain, that is a constituent of the *meaning* of the proposition

tinction is that it shows why it is often worth while to assert identity. If we say "Scott is the author of *Waverley*," we assert an identity of denotation with a difference of meaning. I shall, however, not repeat the grounds in favour of this theory, as I have urged its claims elsewhere (*loc. cit.*), and am now concerned to dispute those claims.

One of the first difficulties that confront us, when we adopt the view that denoting phrases *express* a meaning and *denote* a denotation,[10] concerns the cases in which the denotation appears to be absent. If we say "the King of England is bald," that is, it would seem, not a statement about the complex *meaning* "the King of England," but about the actual man denoted by the meaning. But now consider "the King of France is bald". By parity of form, this also ought to be about the denotation of the phrase "the King of France". But this phrase, though it has a *meaning* provided "the King of England" has a meaning, has certainly no denotation, at least in any obvious sense. Hence one would suppose that "the King of France is bald" ought to be nonsense; but it is not nonsense, since it is plainly false. Or again consider such a proposition as the following: "If *u* is a class which has only one member, then that one member is a member of *u*," or, as we may state it, "If *u* is a unit class, *the u* is a *u*". This proposition ought to be *always* true, since the conclusion is true whenever the hypothesis is true. But "the *u*" is a denoting phrase, and it is the denotation, not the meaning, that is said to be a *u*. Now if *u* is *not* a unit class, "the *u*" seems to denote nothing; hence our proposition would seem to become nonsense as soon as *u* is not a unit class.

Now it is plain that such propositions do *not* become nonsense merely because their hypotheses are false. The King in "The Tempest" might say, "If Ferdinand is not drowned, Ferdinand is my only son". Now "my only son" is a denoting phrase, which, on the face of it, has a denotation when, and only when, I have exactly one son. But the above statement would nevertheless have remained true if Ferdinand had been in fact drowned. Thus we must either provide a denotation in cases in which it is at first sight absent, or we must abandon the view that the denotation is what is concerned in propositions which contain denoting phrases. The latter is the course that I advocate. The former course may be taken, as by Meinong, by admitting objects which do not subsist, and denying that they obey the law of contradiction; this, however, is to be avoided if possible. Another way of taking the same course (so far as our present alternative is concerned) is adopted by Frege, who provides by definition some purely conventional denotation for the cases in which otherwise there would be none. Thus "the King of France," is to denote the null-class; "the only son of Mr. So-and-so" (who has a fine family of ten), is

[10] In this theory, we shall say that the denoting phrase *expresses* a meaning; and we shall say both of the phrase and of the meaning that they *denote* a denotation. In the other theory, which I advocate, there is no *meaning*, and only sometimes a *denotation*.

to denote the class of all his sons; and so on. But this procedure, though it may not lead to actual logical error, is plainly artificial, and does not give an exact analysis of the matter. Thus if we allow that denoting phrases, in general, have the two sides of meaning and denotation, the cases where there seems to be no denotation cause difficulties both on the assumption that there really is a denotation and on the assumption that there really is none.

A logical theory may be tested by its capacity for dealing with puzzles, and it is a wholesome plan, in thinking about logic, to stock the mind with as many puzzles as possible, since these serve much the same purpose as is served by experiments in physical science. I shall therefore state three puzzles which a theory as to denoting ought to be able to solve; and I shall show later that my theory solves them.

1. If *a* is identical with *b*, whatever is true of the one is true of the other, and either may be substituted for the other in any proposition without altering the truth or falsehood of that proposition. Now George IV wished to know whether Scott was the author of *Waverley;* and in fact Scott *was* the author of *Waverley.* Hence we may substitute *Scott* for *the author of "Waverley,"* and thereby prove that George IV wished to know whether Scott was Scott. Yet an interest in the law of identity can hardly be attributed to the first gentleman of Europe.

2. By the law of excluded middle, either "A is B" or "A is not B" must be true. Hence either "the present King of France is bald" or "the present King of France is not bald" must be true. Yet if we enumerated the things that are bald, and then the things that are not bald, we should not find the present King of France in either list. Hegelians, who love a synthesis, will probably conclude that he wears a wig.

3. Consider the proposition "A differs from B". If this is true, there is a difference between A and B, which fact may be expressed in the form "the difference between A and B subsists". But if it is false that A differs from B, then there is no difference between A and B, which fact may be expressed in the form "the difference between A and B does not subsist". But how can a non-entity be the subject of a proposition? "I think, therefore I am" is no more evident than "I am the subject of a proposition, therefore I am," provided "I am" is taken to assert subsistence or being,[11] not existence. Hence, it would appear, it must always be self-contradictory to deny the being of anything; but we have seen, in connexion with Meinong, that to admit being also sometimes leads to contradictions. Thus if A and B do not differ, to suppose either that there is, or that there is not, such an object as "the difference between A and B" seems equally impossible.

The relation of the meaning to the denotation involves certain rather curious difficulties, which seem in themselves sufficient to prove that the theory which leads to such difficulties must be wrong.

[11] I use these as synonyms.

When we wish to speak about the *meaning* of a denoting phrase, as opposed to its *denotation*, the natural mode of doing so is by inverted commas. Thus we say:

> The centre of mass of the Solar System is a point, not a denoting complex;
> "The centre of mass of the Solar System" is a denoting complex, not a point.

Or again,

> The first line of Gray's *Elegy* states a proposition.
> "The first line of Gray's *Elegy*" does not state a proposition.

Thus taking any denoting phrase, say C, we wish to consider the relation between C and "C", where the difference of the two is of the kind exemplified in the above two instances.

We say, to begin with, that when C occurs it is the *denotation* that we are speaking about; but when "C" occurs, it is the *meaning*. Now the relation of meaning and denotation is not merely linguistic through the phrase: there must be a logical relation involved, which we express by saying that the meaning denotes the denotation. But the difficulty which confronts us is that we cannot succeed in *both* preserving the connexion of meaning and denotation *and* preventing them from being one and the same; also that the meaning cannot be got at except by means of denoting phrases. This happens as follows.

The one phrase C was to have both meaning and denotation. But if we speak of "the meaning of C", that gives us the meaning (if any) of the denotation. "The meaning of the first line of Gray's *Elegy*" is the same as "The meaning of 'The curfew tolls the knell of parting day'," and is not the same as "The meaning of 'the first line of Gray's *Elegy*' ". Thus in order to get the meaning we want, we must speak not of "the meaning of C", but of "the meaning of 'C'," which is the same as "C" by itself. Similarly "the denotation of C" does not mean the denotation we want, but means something which, if it denotes at all, denotes what is denoted by the denotation we want. For example, let "C" be "the denoting complex occurring in the second of the above instances". Then C = "the first line of Gray's *Elegy*", and the denotation of C = The curfew tolls the knell of parting day. But what we *meant* to have as the denotation was "the first line of Gray's *Elegy*". Thus we have failed to get what we wanted.

The difficulty in speaking of the meaning of a denoting complex may be stated thus: The moment we put the complex in a proposition, the proposition is about the denotation; and if we make a proposition in which the subject is "the meaning of C", then the subject is the meaning (if any) of the denotation, which was not intended. This leads us to say that, when we distinguish meaning and denotation, we must be dealing with the meaning: the meaning has denotation and is a complex, and there is not something other than the meaning, which can be called the complex, and be said to *have* both meaning and denotation. The right phrase, on the view in question, is that some meanings have denotations.

But this only makes our difficulty in speaking of meanings more evident. For suppose C is our complex; then we are to say that C *is* the meaning of the complex. Nevertheless, whenever C occurs without inverted commas, what is said is not true of the meaning, but only of the denotation, as when we say: The centre of mass of the Solar System is a point. Thus to speak of C itself, i.e., to make a proposition about the meaning, our subject must not be C, but something which denotes C. Thus "C", which is what we use when we want to speak of the meaning, must be not the meaning, but something which denotes the meaning. And C must not be a constituent of this complex (as it is of "the meaning of C"); for if C occurs in the complex, it will be its denotation, not its meaning, that will occur, and there is no backward road from denotations to meanings, because every object can be denoted by an infinite number of different denoting phrases.

Thus it would seem that "C" and C are different entities, such that "C" denotes C; but this cannot be an explanation, because the relation of "C" to C remains wholly mysterious; and where are we to find the denoting complex "C" which is to denote C? Moreover, when C occurs in a proposition, it is not *only* the denotation that occurs (as we shall see in the next paragraph); yet, on the view in question, C is only the denotation, the meaning being wholly relegated to "C". This is an inextricable tangle, and seems to prove that the whole distinction of meaning and denotation has been wrongly conceived.

That the meaning is relevant when a denoting phrase occurs in a proposition is formally proved by the puzzle about the author of *Waverley*. The proposition "Scott was the author of *Waverley*" has a property not possessed by "Scott was Scott," namely the property that George IV wished to know whether it was true. Thus the two are not identical propositions; hence the meaning of "the author of *Waverley*" must be relevant as well as the denotation, if we adhere to the point of view to which this distinction belongs. Yet, as we have just seen, so long as we adhere to this point of view, we are compelled to hold that only the denotation can be relevant. Thus the point of view in question must be abandoned.

It remains to show how all the puzzles we have been considering are solved by the theory explained at the beginning of this article.

According to the view which I advocate, a denoting phrase is essentially *part* of a sentence, and does not, like most single words, have any significance on its own account. If I say "Scott was a man," that is a statement of the form "*x* was a man," and it has "Scott" for its subject. But if I say "the author of *Waverley* was a man," that is not a statement of the form "*x* was a man," and does not have "the author of *Waverley*" for its subject. Abbreviating the statement made at the beginning of this article, we may put, in place of "the author of *Waverley* was a man," the following: "One and only one entity wrote *Waverley*, and that one was a man". (This is not so strictly what is meant as what was said earlier; but it is easier to follow.) And speaking generally, suppose we wish to say that the author of *Waverley* had the property φ, what we wish to say is equivalent to "One and only one entity wrote *Waverley*, and that one had the property φ".

The explanation of *denotation* is now as follows. Every proposition in which "the author of *Waverley*" occurs being explained as above, the proposition "Scott was the author of *Waverley*" (i.e., "Scott was identical with the author of *Waverley*") becomes "One and only one entity wrote *Waverley*, and Scott was identical with that one"; or, reverting to the wholly explicit form: "It is not always false of *x* that *x* wrote *Waverley*, that it is always true of *y* that if *y* wrote *Waverley* *y* is identical with *x*, and that Scott is identical with *x*". Thus if "C" is a denoting phrase, it may happen that there is one entity *x* (there cannot be more than one) for which the proposition "*x* is identical with C" is true, this proposition being interpreted as above. We may then say that the entity *x* is the denotation of the phrase "C". Thus Scott is the denotation of "the author of *Waverley*". The "C" in inverted commas will be merely the *phrase*, not anything that can be called the *meaning*. The phrase *per se* has no meaning, because in any proposition in which it occurs the proposition, fully expressed, does not contain the phrase, which has been broken up.

The puzzle about George IV's curiosity is now seen to have a very simple solution. The proposition "Scott was the author of *Waverley*," which was written out in its unabbreviated form in the preceding paragraph, does not contain any constituent "the author of *Waverley*" for which we could substitute "Scott". This does not interfere with the truth of inferences resulting from making what is *verbally* the substitution of "Scott" for "the author of *Waverley*," so long as "the author of *Waverley*" has what I call a *primary* occurrence in the proposition considered. The difference of primary and secondary occurrences of denoting phrases is as follows:

When we say: "George IV wished to know whether so-and-so," or when we say "So-and-so is surprising" or "So-and-so is true," etc., the "so-and-so" must be a proposition. Suppose now that "so-and-so" contains a denoting phrase. We may either eliminate this denoting phrase from the subordinate proposition "so-and-so," or from the whole proposition in which "so-and-so" is a mere constituent. Different propositions result according to which we do. I have heard of a touchy owner of a yacht to whom a guest, on first seeing it, remarked, "I thought your yacht was larger than it is"; and the owner replied, "No, my yacht is not larger than it is". What the guest meant was, "The size that I thought your yacht was is greater than the size your yacht is"; the meaning attributed to him is, "I thought the size of your yacht was greater than the size of your yacht". To return to George IV and *Waverley*, when we say, "George IV wished to know whether Scott was the author of *Waverley*," we normally mean "George IV wished to know whether one and only one man wrote *Waverley* and Scott was that man"; but we *may* also mean: "One and only one man wrote *Waverley*, and George IV wished to know whether Scott was that man". In the latter, "the author of *Waverley*" has a *primary* occurrence; in the former, a *secondary*. The latter might be expressed by "George IV wished to know, concerning the man who in fact wrote *Waverley*, whether he was Scott". This would be true, for example, if George IV had seen Scott at a distance, and had asked "Is that Scott?" A *secondary* occurrence of a denoting phrase may be defined as one in which the phrase occurs in a proposition *p* which is a mere constituent of the proposition we are considering, and the substitution for the denoting phrase is to be effected in *p*, not in the whole proposition concerned. The ambiguity as between primary and secondary occurrences is hard to avoid in language; but it does no harm if we are on our guard against it. In symbolic logic it is of course easily avoided.

The distinction of primary and secondary occurrences also enables us to deal with the question whether the present King of France is bald or not bald, and generally with the logical status of denoting phrases that denote nothing. If "C" is a denoting phrase, say "the term having the property F," then

"C has the property ϕ" means "one and only one term has the property F, and that one has the property ϕ".[12]

If now the property F belongs to no terms, or to several, it follows that "C has the property ϕ" is false for *all* values of ϕ. Thus "the present King of France is bald" is certainly false; and "the present King of France is not bald" is false if it means

"There is an entity which is now King of France and is not bald,"

but is true if it means

"It is false that there is an entity which is now King of France and is bald".

That is, "the King of France is not bald" is false if the occurrence of "the King of France" is *primary*, and true if it is *secondary*. Thus all propositions in which "the King of France" has a primary occurrence are false; the denials of such propositions are true, but in them "the King of France"

---

[12] This is the abbreviated, not the stricter, interpretation.

has a secondary occurrence. Thus we escape the conclusion that the King of France has a wig.

We can now see also how to deny that there is such an object as the difference between A and B in the case when A and B do not differ. If A and B do differ, there is one and only one entity x such that "x is the difference between A and B" is a true proposition; if A and B do not differ, there is no such entity x. Thus according to the meaning of denotation lately explained, "the difference between A and B" has a denotation when A and B differ, but not otherwise. This difference applies to true and false propositions generally. If "a R b" stands for "a has the relation R to b", then when a R b is true, there is such an entity as the relation R between a and b; when a R b is false, there is no such entity. Thus out of any proposition we can make a denoting phrase, which denotes an entity if the proposition is true, but does not denote an entity if the proposition is false. E.g., it is true (at least we will suppose so) that the earth revolves round the sun, and false that the sun revolves round the earth; hence "the revolution of the earth round the sun" denotes an entity, while "the revolution of the sun round the earth" does not denote an entity.[13]

The whole realm of non-entities, such as "the round square," "the even prime other than 2," "Apollo," "Hamlet," etc., can now be satisfactorily dealt with. All these are denoting phrases which do not denote anything. A proposition about Apollo means what we get by substituting what the classical dictionary tells us is meant by Apollo, say "the sun-god". All propositions in which Apollo occurs are to be interpreted by the above rules for denoting phrases. If "Apollo" has a primary occurrence, the proposition containing the occurrence is false; if the occurrence is secondary, the proposition may be true. So again "the round square is round" means "there is one and only one entity x which is round and square, and that entity is round," which is a false proposition, not, as Meinong maintains, a true one. "The most perfect Being has all perfections; existence is a perfection; therefore the most perfect Being exists" becomes:

"There is one and only one entity x which is most perfect; that one has all perfections; existence is a perfection; therefore that one exists". As a proof, this fails for want of a proof of the premiss "there is one and only one entity x which is most perfect".[14]

Mr. MacColl (*Mind*, N.S., No. 54, and again No. 55, p. 401) regards individuals as of two sorts, real and unreal; hence he defines the null-class

[13] The propositions from which such entities are derived are not identical either with these entities or with the propositions that these entities have being.

[14] The argument can be made to prove validly that all members of the class of most perfect Beings exist; it can also be proved formally that this class cannot have *more* than one member; but, taking the definition of perfection as posssession of all positive predicates, it can be proved almost equally formally that the class does not have even one member.

as the class consisting of all unreal individuals. This assumes that such phrases as "the present King of France," which do not denote a real individual, do, nevertheless, denote an individual, but an unreal one. This is essentially Meinong's theory, which we have seen reason to reject because it conflicts with the law of contradiction. With our theory of denoting, we are able to hold that there are no unreal individuals; so that the null-class is the class containing no members, not the class containing as members all unreal individuals.

It is important to observe the effect of our theory on the interpretation of definitions which proceed by means of denoting phrases. Most mathematical definitions are of this sort: for example, "$m - n$ means the number which, added to n, gives m". Thus $m - n$ is defined as meaning the same as a certain denoting phrase; but we agreed that denoting phrases have no meaning in isolation. Thus what the definition really ought to be is: "Any proposition containing $m - n$ is to mean the proposition which results from substituting for '$m - n$' 'the number which, added to n, gives m' ". The resulting proposition is interpreted according to the rules already given for interpreting propositions whose verbal expression contains a denoting phrase. In the case where m and n are such that there is one and only one number x which, added to n, gives m, there is a number x which can be substituted for $m - n$ in any proposition containing $m - n$ without altering the truth or falsehood of the proposition. But in other cases, all propositions in which "$m - n$" has a primary occurrence are false.

The usefulness of *identity* is explained by the above theory. No one outside a logic-book ever wishes to say "x is x," and yet assertions of identity are often made in such forms as "Scott was the author of *Waverley*" or "thou art the man". The meaning of such propositions cannot be stated without the notion of identity, although they are not simply statements that Scott is identical with another term, the author of *Waverley*, or that thou art identical with another term, the man. The shortest statement of "Scott is the author of *Waverley*" seems to be: "Scott wrote *Waverley;* and it is always true of y that if y wrote *Waverley*, y is identical with Scott". It is in this way that identity enters into "Scott is the author of *Waverley*"; and it is owing to such uses that identity is worth affirming.

One interesting result of the above theory of denoting is this: when there is anything with which we do not have immediate acquaintance, but only definition by denoting phrases, then the propositions in which this thing is introduced by means of a denoting phrase do not really contain this thing as a constituent, but contain instead the constituents expressed by the several words of the denoting phrase. Thus in every proposition that we can apprehend (i.e., not only in those whose truth or falsehood we can judge of, but in all that we can think about), all the constituents are really entities with which we have immediate acquaintance. Now such things as matter (in the sense in which matter occurs in physics) and the minds of other people are known to us only by denoting phrases, i.e., we are not *acquainted* with them, but we know them as what has such and such properties. Hence, although we can form propositional functions $C(x)$ which must hold of such and such a material particle, or of So-and-so's mind, yet we are not acquainted with the propositions which affirm these things that we know must be true, because we cannot apprehend the actual entities concerned. What we know is "So-and-so has a mind which has such and such properties" but we do not know "A has such and such properties," where A *is* the mind in question. In such a case, we know the properties of a thing without having acquaintance with the thing itself, and without, consequently, knowing any single proposition of which the thing itself is a constituent.

Of the many other consequences of the view I have been advocating, I will say nothing. I will only beg the reader not to make up his mind against the view—as he might be tempted to do, on account of its apparently excessive complication—until he has attempted to construct a theory of his own on the subject of denotation. This attempt, I believe, will convince him that, whatever the true theory may be, it cannot have such a simplicity as one might have expected beforehand.

II

MEANINGFULNESS AND CONFIRMATION

Truth and Confirmation *

RUDOLF CARNAP

The difference between the two concepts 'true' and 'confirmed' ('verified', 'scientifically accepted') is important and yet frequently not sufficiently recognized. 'True' in its customary meaning is a time-independent term; i. e., it is employed without a temporal specification. For example, one cannot say "such and such a statement is true today (was true yesterday; will be true tomorrow)" but only "the statement is true." 'Confirmed', however, is time-dependent. When we say "such and such a statement is confirmed to a high degree by observations" then we must add: "at such and such a time." This is the pragmatical concept of degree of confirmation. The semantical concept of the degree of confirmation of a statement *with respect to other statements* which formulate the evidence is again independent of the temporal aspect; in using this concept we are merely asserting an analytic or logical truth which is a sheer consequence of the definition of 'degree of confirmation' (weight, strength of evidence) presupposed.

As is well known, the concept of truth, when used without restrictions (as in conversational language), leads to contradictions (the so-called antinomies). For this reason some logicians in recent times have been rather diffident in regard to this concept and have tried to avoid it. At times it was considered altogether impossible to establish an exact and consistent definition of truth (in its customary meaning); this has brought it about that the term 'true' was used in the sense of the entirely different concept 'confirmed'. But this leads to considerable deviations from the common usage of language. Thus one would find it necessary to abandon, e. g., the principle of the excluded middle. This principle maintains for every statement that either it or its negation is true. But as to the vast majority of statements, neither they nor their negations are confirmed or scientifically accepted. Tarski,[1] however, succeeded in establishing an unobjectionable definition of truth which explicates adequately the meaning of this word in common language (but of course is also bound to restrict its employment, as compared with common usage, in order to eliminate the contra-

* Adapted by the author and translated by H. F. from "Wahrheit und Bewährung", *Actes du Congrès International de Philosophie Scientifique*, 1936, by kind permission of Hermann & Cie., Paris, and from "Remarks on Induction and Truth", *Philosophy and Phenomenological Research*, Vol. VI, by kind permission of the editor.

[1] Cf. Tarski's article in this collection.

dictions). Hence the term 'true' should properly no longer be used in the sense of 'confirmed'. We must not expect the definition of truth to furnish a criterion of confirmation such as is sought in epistemological analyses. On the basis of this definition the question regarding the criterion of truth can be given only a trivial answer, which consists in the statement itself. Thus, from the definition of truth we can conclude only, e. g.: The statement "Snow is white" is true if and only if snow is white. This conclusion is surely correct; which shows that the definition was adequately established. But the question of the criterion of confirmation is thereby left unanswered.

The neglect of the distinction between truth and knowledge of truth (verification, confirmation) is widespread and has led to serious confusions. Perhaps the following analysis will help towards a clarification.

Let us consider the following four sentences:

1. "The substance in this vessel is alcohol."

2. "The sentence 'the substance in this vessel is alcohol' is true."

3. "X knows (at the present moment) that the substance in this vessel is alcohol."

4. "X knows that the sentence 'the substance in this vessel is alcohol' is true."

First a remark concerning the interpretation of the term 'to know' as it occurs in (3) and (4), and generally as it is applied with respect to synthetic propositions concerning physical things. In which of the following two senses (a) and (b) should it be understood?

a. It is meant in the sense of *perfect knowledge*, that is, knowledge which cannot possibly be refuted or even weakened by any future experience.

b. It is meant in the sense of *imperfect knowledge*, that is, knowledge which has only a certain degree of assurance, not absolute certainty, and which therefore may possibly be refuted or weakened by future experience. (This is meant as a theoretical possibility; if the degree of assurance is sufficiently high we may, for all practical purposes, disregard the possibility of a future refutation.)

I am in agreement with practically everybody that sentences of the kind (3) should always be understood in the sense (b), not (a). For the following discussion I presuppose this interpretation of the sentences (3) and (4).

Now the decisive point for our whole problem is this: *the sentences (1) and (2) are logically equivalent;* in other words, they entail each other;

they are merely different formulations for the same factual content; nobody may accept the one and reject the other; if used as communications, both sentences convey the same information though in different form. The difference in form is indeed important; the two sentences belong to two quite different parts of the language. (In my terminology, (1) belongs to the object part of the language, (2) to its meta-part, and, more specifically, to its semantical part.) This difference in form, however, does not prevent their logical equivalence. The fact that this equivalence has been overlooked by many authors (e. g., C. S. Peirce and John Dewey,[2] Reichenbach,[3] and Neurath [4]) seems to be the source of many misunderstandings in current discussions on the concept of truth. It must be admitted that any statement of the logical equivalence of two sentences in English can only be made with certain qualifications, because of the ambiguity of ordinary words, here the word 'true'. The equivalence holds certainly if 'true' is understood in the sense of the semantical concept of truth.[5] I believe with Tarski that this is also the sense in which the word 'true' is mostly used both in everyday life and in science.[6] However, this is a psychological or historical question, which we need not here examine further. In this discussion, at any rate, I use the word 'true' in the semantical sense.

The sentences (1) and (3) obviously do not say the same. This leads to the important result, which is rather obvious but often overlooked, that *the sentences (2) and (3) have different contents*. (3) and (4) are logically equivalent since (1) and (2) are. It follows that (2) and (4) have different contents. It is now clear that a certain terminological possibility cannot be accepted. "If we constantly bear in mind that the acceptance of any proposition may be reversed," in other words, that we have always to use interpretation (*b*), not (*a*), "then we might instead call an accepted proposition a true proposition." This usage, however, would be quite misleading because it would blur the fundamental distinction between (2) and (3).

Felix Kaufmann [7] comes to the conclusion that my conception, although

[2] See John Dewey, *Logic: The Theory of Inquiry*, 1938, p. 345, footnote 6, with quotations from Peirce.

[3] Hans Reichenbach, *Experience and Prediction*, 1938; see §§22, 35.

[4] Otto Neurath, "Universal Jargon and Terminology," *Proceedings Aristotelian Society*, 1940–1941, pp. 127–148; see especially pp. 138 f.

[5] For this point and the subsequent discussion compare Alfred Tarski, "The Semantic Conception of Truth, and the Foundations of Semantics," in this volume, where a number of common misunderstandings are cleared up. Compare also my *Introduction to Semantics*, 1942; see p. 26: "We use the term ['true'] here in such a sense that *to assert that a sentence is true means the same as to assert the sentence itself*."

[6] Arne Ness has expressed doubts in this respect; but he has admitted that in 90% of the cases examined by him the persons questioned reacted in the sense of the equivalence. See Tarski, with reference to Ness.

[7] *Philosophy and Phenomenological Research*, Vol. II (1942), pp. 457–471; and, especially Vol. IV (1944), pp. 267–284.

in agreement with "the traditional view", "is incompatible with the principle of inquiry which rules out the invariable truth of synthetic propositions. It is impossible for an empirical procedure to confirm to any degree something which is excluded by a general (constitutive) principle of empirical procedure. *Knowledge of invariable truth of synthetic propositions (whether perfect or imperfect) is unobtainable, not because of limitations of human knowledge, but because the conception of such knowledge involves a contradiction in terms.*" This reasoning seems to me based on the wrong identification of truth with perfect knowledge, hence, in the example, the identification of (2) with (3) in interpretation (*a*). The principles of scientific procedure do indeed rule out perfect knowledge but not truth. They cannot rule out (2), because this says nothing else than sentence (1), which, I suppose, will be acknowledged by all of us as empirically meaningful. When Kaufmann declares that even imperfect knowledge of truth is unobtainable, then this means that even imperfect knowledge of (2) is unobtainable and hence that an event as described in (4), even in interpretation (*b*), cannot occur. However, as soon as the event (3) occurs (now always assuming interpretation (*b*)), which nobody regards as impossible, the event (4) thereby occurs too; for the sentences (3) and (4) describe merely in different words one and the same event, a certain state of knowledge of the person X.

Let us represent in a slightly different way the objection raised against the concept of truth, in order to examine the presupposition underlying its chief argument. The objection concerns the concept of truth in its semantical sense; Kaufmann uses here the term "invariable truth" because truth in this sense is independent of person and state of knowledge, and hence of time. (Incidentally, the word "invariable" is not quite appropriate; it would be more correct to say instead that truth is a "time-independent" or "non-temporal" concept. The volume of a body *b* may or may not change in the course of time; hence we may say that it is variable or that it is invariable. The sentence "the volume of *b* at the time *t* is *v*" is meaningful but without the phrase "at the time *t*" it would be incomplete. On the other hand, the formulation "the sentence *S* is true at the time *t*" is meaningless; when the phrase "at the time *t*" is omitted we obtain a complete statement. Therefore, to speak of change or non-change, of variability or invariability of truth, is not quite correct.) Now Kaufmann, Reichenbach,[8] Neurath,[9] and other authors are of the opinion that the

[8] Reichenbach, *op. cit.*, footnote 20, p. 188: "Thus there are left no propositions at all which can be absolutely verified. The predicate of truth-value of a proposition, therefore [!], is a mere fictive quality, its place is in an ideal world of science only, whereas actual science cannot make use of it. Actual science instead employs throughout the predicate of weight."

[9] I agree with Neurath when he rejects the possibility of absolutely certain knowledge, for example, in his criticism of Schlick, who believed that the knowledge of certain basic sentences ("Konstatierungen") was absolutely certain. See Neurath, "Radikaler Physikalismus und 'Wirkliche Welt,'" *Erkenntnis*, Vol. IV (1934), pp. 346–362.

semantical concept of truth, at least in its application to synthetic sentences concerning physical things, ought to be abandoned because it can never be decided with absolute certainty for any given sentence whether it is true or not. I agree that this can never be decided. But is the inference valid which leads from this result to the conclusion that the concept of truth is inadmissible? It seems that this inference presupposes the following major premise P: "A term (predicate) must be rejected if it is such that we can never decide with absolute certainty for any given instance whether or not the term applies." The argumentation by the authors would be valid if this principle P were presupposed, and I do not see how they reach the conclusion without this presupposition. However, I think that the authors do not actually believe in the principle P. In any case, it can easily be seen that the acceptance of P would lead to absurd consequences. For instance, we can never decide with absolute certainty whether a given substance is alcohol or not; thus, according to the principle P, the term "alcohol" would have to be rejected. And the same holds obviously for *every* term of the physical language. Thus I suppose that we all agree that instead of P the following weaker principle P* must be used; this is indeed one of the principles of empiricism or of scientific inquiry: "A term (predicate) is a legitimate scientific term (has cognitive content, is empirically meaningful) if and only if a sentence applying the term to a given instance can possibly be confirmed to at least some degree." "Possibly" means here "if certain specifiable observations occur"; "to some degree" is not meant as necessarily implying a numerical evaluation. P* is a simplified formulation of the "requirement of confirmability" [10] which, I think, is essentially in agreement with Reichenbach's "first principle of the probability theory of meaning," [11] both being liberalized versions of the older requirement of verifiability as stated by C. S. Peirce, Wittgenstein, and others.[12] Now, according to P*, 'alcohol' is a legitimate scientific term, because the sentence (1) can be confirmed to some degree if certain observations are made. But the same observations would confirm (2) to the same degree because it is logically equivalent to (1). Therefore, according to P*, 'true' is likewise a legitimate scientific term.

We shall now examine more closely the concept of confirmation. This will require that we describe the procedure of scientific testing and that we specify the conditions under which a statement, as a result of such

---

But I cannot agree with him when he proceeds from this view to the rejection of the concept of truth. In the paper mentioned earlier (in footnote 21) he says (pp. 138 f.): "In accordance with our traditional language we may say that some statements are accepted at a certain time by a certain person and not accepted by the same person at another time, but we cannot say some statements are true today but not tomorrow; 'true' and 'false' are 'absolute' terms, which we avoid."

[10] Compare my "Testability and Meaning", *Philosophy of Science*, Vol. III (1936), pp. 419-471, and Vol. IV (1937), pp. 1-40; see Vol. IV, p. 34.

[11] See Reichenbach, *op. cit.*, footnote 20, §7; he formulated this principle first in 1936.

[12] See the references in Reichenbach, *op. cit.*, footnote 20, p. 49.

testing, is considered as more or less confirmed, i. e., scientifically accepted or rejected. The description of that procedure is not a matter of logic but is itself empirically-scientific (psychological and sociological). One might call it 'methodological', especially if it is presented in the form of proposals and precepts. Only the essential features of the scientific procedure will here be schematically outlined; what matters here are not so much the details but rather a clear emphasis upon the distinction between the two most important operations of the procedure.

The statements of (empirical) science are such that they can never be definitively accepted or rejected. They can only be confirmed or disconfirmed to a certain degree. For the sake of simplicity we may distinguish two types of statements which are, however, not sharply separable (i. e., differing only by degree): the directly testable and the (only) indirectly testable statements. We shall speak of 'directly testable statement' when circumstances are conceivable in which we confidently consider the statement so strongly confirmed or else disconfirmed on the basis of one or very few observations that we would either accept or reject it outright. Examples: "There is a key on my desk". Conditions for the test: I stand near my desk, sufficient illumination is provided, etc. Condition of acceptance: I see a key on my desk; condition of rejection: I don't see a key there. Indirect testing of a statement consists in directly testing other statements which stand in specifiable logical relations to the statement in question. These other statements may be called 'test-sentences' for the given statement. Occasionally an indirectly testable statement may be confirmed by confirming statements from which it is deducible; this is the case, e. g., with existential statements. Scientific laws, however, have the form of universal statements. A universal statement (of simplest form) can be confirmed to ever higher degrees by confirming more and more statements derivable from the law and thereby accepting them (while none are rejected). There are important questions as to the logical relations between such statements which are to be tested and their respective test-sentences. We shall however not examine these any further but rather attend to the analysis of the confirmation of directly testable statements. Here we must distinguish mainly the following two operations:

1. *Confrontation of a statement with observation.* Observations are performed and a statement is formulated such that it may be recognized as confirmed on the basis of these observations. If, e. g., I see a key on my desk and I make the statement: "There is a key on my desk", I accept this statement because I acknowledge it as highly confirmed on the basis of my visual and, possibly, tactual observations. (The concept of observation is here understood in its widest sense; "I am hungry" or "I am angry" in this context are also taken as observation statements.[13] Ordi-

---

[13] It is a matter of convention as to whether these directly established statements (protocol statements) are to be taken as referring to observed things and processes

narily no definite rules are expressly stipulated as to how a statement may or must be formulated when certain observations have been made. Children learn the use of common language, and thereby the correct performance of the operation described, through practice, imitation, and usually without the benefit of rules. These rules, however, could be specified. But if no foreign language or the introduction of new terms is involved, the rules are trivial. For example: "If one is hungry, the statement 'I am hungry' may be accepted"; or: "If one sees a key one may accept the statement 'there lies a key' ". In this context the definition of the concept of truth enters into the question of confirmation; the rules we mentioned originate from this definition.

2. *Confrontation of a statement with previously accepted statements.* A statement established on the basis of the first operation is held as (sufficiently strongly) confirmed as long as in the second operation no statements are found which were previously established by confirmation but are incompatible with the statement under consideration. In the event of such an incompatibility either the new statement or at least one of the previously accepted statements must be revoked. Certain methodological rules have to be stipulated; they tell us which of the two decisions is to be made in a given case (see Popper, *loc. cit.*). This sheds light upon the relation of the two operations to one another. The first one is more important. Without it there could be nothing like confirmation. The second one is an auxiliary operation. Its function is mostly negative or regulative: it serves in the elimination of incongruous elements from the system of statements in science.

Closer attention to these two operations and their mutual relations will help to clarify a number of recently much discussed questions. There has been a good deal of dispute as to whether in the procedure of scientific testing *statements must be compared with facts* or as to whether such comparison be unnecessary, if not impossible. If 'comparison of statement with fact' means the procedure which we called the first operation then it must be admitted that this procedure is not only possible, but even indispensable for scientific testing. Yet it must be remarked that the formulation 'comparison of statement and fact' is not unobjectionable. First, the concept 'comparison' is not quite appropriate here. Two objects can be compared in regard to a property which may characterize them in various ways (e. g., in regard to color, size, or number of parts, and so on). We therefore prefer to speak of 'confrontation' rather than 'comparison'. Confrontation is understood to consist in finding out as to whether one object (the statement in this case) properly fits the other (the fact); i. e., as to whether the fact is such as it is described in the statement, or, to express it differently, as to whether the statement is true to fact. Further-

("there is on the table . . .") or to the act of perception ("I see . . ."). Cf. Carnap, "Ueber Protokollsaetze", *Erkenntnis*, 3, 1933; also K. Popper, *Logik der Forschung*.

more, the formulation in terms of 'comparison', in speaking of 'facts' or 'realities', easily tempts one into the absolutistic view according to which we are said to search for an absolute reality whose nature is assumed as fixed independently of the language chosen for its description. The answer to a question concerning reality however depends not only upon that 'reality', or upon the facts but also upon the structure (and the set of concepts) of the language used for the description. In translating one language into another the factual content of an empirical statement cannot always be preserved unchanged. Such changes are inevitable if the structures of the two languages differ in essential points. For example: while many statements of modern physics are completely translatable into statements of classical physics, this is not so or only incompletely so with other statements. The latter situation arises when the statement in question contains concepts (like, e. g., 'wave-function' or 'quantization') which simply do not occur in classical physics; the essential point being that these concepts cannot be subsequently included since they presuppose a different form of language. This becomes still more obvious if we contemplate the possibility of a language with a discontinuous spatio-temporal order which might be adopted in a future physics. Then, obviously, some statements of classical physics could not be translated into the new language, and others only incompletely. (This means not only that previously accepted statements would have to be rejected; but also that to certain statements—regardless of whether they were held true or false—there is no corresponding statement at all in the new language.)

The scruples here advanced regarding the assertion that statements are to be compared with facts (or reality) were directed not so much against its content but rather against its form. The assertion is not false—if only it is interpreted in the manner indicated—but formulated in a potentially misleading fashion. Hence, one must not, in repudiating the assertion, replace it by its denial: "Statements cannot be compared with facts (or with reality)"; for this negative formulation is as much open to objection as the original affirmative one. In repudiating the formulation one must take care not to reject the procedure which was presumably intended, viz., the confrontation with observation. Nor must the significance and indispensability of such confrontation be overshadowed by exclusive attention to the second operation. (Besides, the phrase 'Comparison of statements with each other', instead of 'confrontation', seems open to the same objections.) He who really repudiates the first operation—I do not think that anyone in scientifically oriented circles does—could not be considered an empiricist.

The result of these considerations may now be briefly summarized:

1. The question of the definition of *truth* must be clearly distinguished from the question of a criterion of *confirmation*.

2. In connection with confirmation two different operations have to be performed: the formulation of an observation and the confrontation of statements with each other; especially, we must not lose sight of the first operation.

LITERATURE

Popper, K. *Logik der Forschung*, Vienna, 1935.
Neurath, O. "Pseudo-Rationalismus der Falsifikation", *Erkenntnis*, 5, 353 ff. 1935.
Carnap, R. "Testability and Meaning", *Philosophy of Science*, Vols. III (1936) and IV (1937).

Experience and Meaning *

C. I. LEWIS

Ever since the provisional skepticism of Descartes' First Meditation the attack upon any problem of reality has always been shadowed by the question "How do you know?". The extent to which this perennial challenge has determined the course of modern philosophy requires no exposition. That on the whole the results of it have been salutary will hardly be denied; though it may be said—and has been said—that it leads, on occasion, to the confusion of methodological considerations with positive conclusions. The last thirty-five years have witnessed a growing emphasis upon another such challenge, which bids fair to prove equally potent in its directing influence. This is the question "What do you mean?" asked with intent to require an answer in terms of experience. That is, it is demanded that any concept put forward or any proposition asserted shall have a definite denotation; that it shall be intelligible not only verbally and logically but in the further sense that one can specify those empirical items which would determine the applicability of the concept or constitute the verification of the proposition. Whatever cannot satisfy this demand is to be regarded as meaningless.

For any sufficient consideration of this empirical-meaning requirement it would be essential to sketch those developments which have brought it to the fore: pragmatism and the "pragmatic test"; neo-realism, both of the American school and the similar view of Russell; the new methodology in physics which came in with relativity, especially Einstein's treatment of definition and Bridgman's operational theory of the concept; Whitehead's method of "extensive abstraction", by which certain previously refractory concepts can now be defined in terms of the actually observable and their empirical content thus made evident. Last and most particularly, one would mention the logical positivism of the Vienna Circle, whose program is based throughout upon this consideration of empirical meaning. It would likewise be desirable to consider the divergences between these different movements of thought in their interpretation of the general requirement of empirical meaning.

But before this audience it will be unnecessary to attempt any such

* Reprinted by kind permission of the author and the editors from *The Philosophical Review*, 43, 1934.

survey, either of this development in current theory or of the points of divergence with respect to it. Taking these matters for granted, the purpose of what follows will be to explore a little certain questions concerning the limitations imposed upon significant philosophic discussion by this requirement of empirical meaning; in particular certain issues which are likely to divide those who approach these problems with the thought of James and Peirce and Dewey in mind from the logical positivists. The ultimate objective of such discussion would be to assess the bearing of this limitation to what has empirical meaning upon ethics and the philosophy of values, and upon those metaphysical problems which concern the relation between values and reality. But that objective cannot be reached in the present paper, which will be concerned with prior questions. Even these cannot be set forth with any thoroughness; and I hope it will be understood that the purpose of this discussion is to locate issues rather than to dispose of them, and that criticisms ventured are not put forward in the spirit of debate.

The Vienna positivists repudiate all problems of traditional metaphysics, including the issue about the external world supposed to divide idealists from realists, and any question concerning the metaphysical character of other selves. In the authoritative statement of their position we find the following: "If anyone assert 'There is a God', 'The ground of the world is the Unconscious', 'There is an entelechy as the directing principle in the living', we do not say to him 'What you assert is false' but instead we ask him 'What do you mean by your statement?'. And it then appears that there is a sharp line of division between two kinds of propositions. To the one belong statements such as those made in the empirical sciences: their meaning can be determined by logical analysis; more specifically, it can be determined by reduction to statements of the simplest sort about the empirically given. The other class of propositions, to which those mentioned above belong, betray themselves as completely empty of meaning, if one take them in the fashion which the metaphysician intends. . . . The metaphysician and the theologian, misunderstanding themselves, suppose that their theses assert something, represent matters of fact. Analysis shows, however, that these propositions assert nothing, but only express a sort of feeling of life." [1] According to Carnap all value-theory and normative science are likewise without meaning, in the theoretical or empirical sense of that word.[2]

The expression of such feeling of life, and of our evaluative reactions, is, of course, admitted to be a legitimate and worth-while activity; but, as

[1] *Wissenschaftliche Weltauffassung des Wiener Kreises* (1929), 16. (I have translated somewhat freely.)

[2] "Auf dem Gebiet der Metaphysik (einschliesslich aller Wertphilosophie und Normwissenschaft) führt die logische Analyse zu dem negativen Ergebnis, dass die vorgeblichen Sätze dieses Gebietes gänzlich sinnlos sind." "Überwindung der Metaphysik durch logische Analyse der Sprache", *Erkenntnis*, 2 (1931) 220.

such expression, metaphysical theses are to be classed with art and poetry. Obviously there is room in such a theory for descriptive ethics, on a psychological or sociological basis, and for the determination of values by reference to a norm which is assumed or hypothetical; but traditional questions of the 'objectivity' of value are repudiated. We may meaning-fully ask "When is a character judged good?" or "What is actually ap-proved?", but not "With *what right* is this character said to be 'good'?" or "What is absolutely *worthy* of approbation?".[3]

This repudiation of metaphysics and normative science by the logical positivists cannot, I think, be regarded as an implication of the empirical-meaning requirement alone. At least an important light is thrown upon it by taking into account that "methodological solipsism" in accordance with which their program is developed. Even though they regard this procedure as advantageous rather than prescribed, still the negations or limitations which characterize it seem to underlie their theses, in whatever terms expressed.

On its constructive side this method means no more, at bottom, than a persistent attempt so to define the different classes of objects of our knowl-edge that the basis of this knowledge in direct experience will be exhibited. It is of the essence of knowledge that it is in the first person. Your mind and your experience can be nothing more, for my cognition, than a construction which I put upon certain data of my own experience. If, then, we are to have a thorough and completed account of knowledge, it is not sufficient that the constitution of objects known should be traced back to experience in the merely generic sense. So far as your observa-tions and reports enter into the construction of that reality which is known to me, they can do so only through the interpretation which I put upon certain modes of your behavior perceived by me. Actually given experi-ence is given in the first person; and reality as it is known in any case of actual knowledge can be nothing, finally, but a first-person construction from data given in the first person.

Consonantly, we have such construction of the objects of science in general as is outlined in Carnap's *Logischer Aufbau der Welt:* first, the different kinds of for-me entities (*eigenpsychische Gegenstände*) which are constructed out of elementary experiences (*Elementarerlebnisse*), at bottom, through the relation of remembered similarity (*Ähnlichkeits-erinnerung*); second, physical objects, which are constructions out of the simpler for-me things of actually given experience; third, other selves and the mental or cultural in general (*fremdpsychische und geistige Gegen-stände*), which are, for actual knowing, constructions out of certain classes and certain relationships of physical things and processes.

In this program we have a consistently maintained effort to be true to

[3] See M. Schlick. *Fragen der Ethik* (translated under the title *Problems of Ethics*), esp. I, 8, pp. 10–12.

the nature of knowledge as we find it. The egocentric predicament is taken seriously; and the "solipsistic" character ascribed to knowing is no more strange or fantastic than Kant's transcendental unity of apperception. The manner in which the *negative* side of logical positivism is related to this same method may, perhaps, be more readily appreciated by reference to cruder but somewhat parallel considerations which are suggested by Berkeley's argument against material substance. (It was Berkeley who first adduced the requirement of empirical meaning in order to prove his opponent's concepts empty and non-significant.)

As has often been noted, the significance and applicability of Berkeley's argument does not leave off at the point where he ceases to use it. By identical logic other selves and the past and future must go the same way as material substance. If you are more than one of my ideas, how can I know it? How can I consistently suppose that I even have an interest in that untouchable you outside my mind which *ipso facto* could make no difference in my experience of you? Also, at this moment, what is that past which I remember, as more than the present recollection, or the future as more than the present experience of anticipation? All must finally dissolve into the eternal now of actually given experience.

There is even one further step for this logic to take. What am I? This self as a recognizable or conceivable particularity can be no more than one of those ideas I call mine. And Wittgenstein gives indication that he accepts the parallel methodological implication: "The subject does not belong to the world but it is the limit of the world. *Where in* the world is a metaphysical subject to be noted? You say that this case is altogether like that of the eye and the field of sight. But you do *not* really see the eye. And from nothing *in the field of sight* can it be concluded that it is seen from an eye. . . . Here we see that solipsism strictly carried out coincides with pure realism. The I in solipsism shrinks to an extensionless point and there remains the reality coördinated with it." [4]

I must not convey the impression that the logical positivists use Berkeleyan arguments, or that they arrive at their conclusions by such a train of thought as the above. Nevertheless this may serve to suggest how methodological solipsism comports with a thoroughgoing empiricism; and it further suggests why this procedure is to be taken as having no metaphysical implications. Subjective idealism, consistently carried through, ends by qualifying every substantive with the prefix "idea of" or "experience of", which by being thus universal becomes meaningless. Whereas Berkeley supposes his argument to establish a subjectivist metaphysics by proving the realistic metaphysics to be empty of empirical meaning, logical positivism points out that the contrary of a meaningless assertion is likewise without meaning, and hence repudiates metaphysical theses of both

[4] *Tractatus Logico-Philosophicus*, pp. 151–153. Cf. Carnap, *Logischer Aufbau der Welt*, §65.

sorts, and the issue itself, as nonsignificant. Three points, here evident, contain, I think, the gist of the matter. First; when knowledge is envisaged, as it must be, from within the egocentric predicament, all objects known or conceived must reveal themselves as constructions, eventually, from data given in first-person experience. Also, what enters into such construction from past experience can only come in by way of present recollection. (This last is, I take it, the reason for the basic position of the relation of remembered-similarity in the program of Carnap.) Other selves and their experience, or their reports, can enter only as certain items of first-person experience upon which a peculiarly complex construction is put. Second; distinctions such as that between real and imaginary, or between that which is apprehensible to me alone and the object apprehended by us in common, must nevertheless find their genuine place and importance in such construction. The fact that we make these distinctions in practically useful ways evidences that they are not outside the egocentric predicament and metaphysical but inside it and empirical. They are determined by criteria which the subject can and does apply within his own experience. Berkeley, for example, offered the criterion of independence of my will as the basis for the distinction of real from imaginary. And in Carnap one finds such distinctions, and their empirical criteria, meticulously examined. Third; metaphysical issues concerning the external world and other selves do *not* turn upon such empirically applicable distinctions as those just referred to, which can be applied within first-person experience. Such metaphysical issues can arise only as it is attempted to give some second meaning to the concepts involved; meanings which do not answer to any empirical criteria which the subject can apply within his own experience. Throughout, a particular and critical point is that only first-person (*eigenpsychische*) data of experience are allowed, in the end, to enter into the construction of objects of knowledge or to function as the empirical content of any meaning.

There is, I think, one further question which is crucial for any theory of knowledge; namely, the question of immediacy and mediation, or transcendence. This has a connection with the preceding considerations; but with respect to this further problem I cannot satisfy myself that I elicit any complete and clear pronouncement from the literature of logical positivism. One can pose the principal issue involved by reference to a statement of Russell's: "Empirical knowledge is confined to what we actually observe." [5] This may seem to be a truism; but I think it is in fact thoroughly false, and demonstrably incompatible with the very existence of empirical knowledge. Let us impose this limitation quite rigorously, in conformity with the considerations set forth above. Knowledge is always

---

[5] *Our Knowledge of the External World*, 112. The author makes this statement quite in passing, and perhaps without having in mind the point with which we are concerned.

in the first person; whatever is known must be known to the subject in question, at the actual moment, within his own experience. The experience of others can enter only as certain items of their subject's own—their reports and behavior perceived by him. And the experience of yesterday or tomorrow can figure in this knowing only as it enters, in the form of memory or imagination, into experience here and now. Hence nothing can be known but what is verifiable in the subject's own experience at the moment when the knowing occurs.

Similarly for meaning. Suppose it maintained that no issue is meaningful unless it can be put to the test of decisive verification. And no verification can take place except in the immediately present experience of the subject. Then nothing can be meant except what is actually present in the experience in which that meaning is entertained. Whatever runs beyond this is unverifiable, and hence meaningless. The result of any such train of thought is obvious; knowledge would collapse into the useless echo of data directly given to the mind at the moment, and meaning would terminate in the immediate envisagement of what is meant.

This is a reduction to absurdity of both knowledge and meaning.[6] If nothing can be known but what is literally within the cognitive experience itself, and what is meant can be only that which is present in the experience which is the bearer of that meaning, then there is no valid knowledge and no genuinely significant meaning. Because the *intention* to refer to what transcends immediate experience is of the essence of knowledge and meaning both. Berkeley himself tacitly recognized that, in noting that one idea is "sign of" another which is to be expected; even the skeptic recognizes this intent of knowledge—he is skeptical precisely of the possibility that what is *not* immediate can be known. If that intention of transcendence is invalid, then the further characters of knowledge and of meaning are hardly worth discussing.

Neither the logical positivists nor anyone else (unless a mystic) intends this reduction to absurdity. But if it is something which has to be avoided by any theory which is compatible with the genuine validity of knowledge, that fact becomes important for the just interpretation of the requirement of empirical meaning. In particular, it becomes evident that the experience in terms of which a cognitive meaning requires to be explicated cannot be exclusively the subject's own given data at the moment of the cognition. Thus that manner of reading the implications of methodological solipsism which is suggested above would condemn that procedure to futility. If what the method requires is that objects known

---

[6] In order to avoid confusion with a quite different problem, the distinction between meaning in the sense of denotation and meaning as connotation should be in mind. It is only the former meaning of "meaning" which is in point in this discussion. In the classification of logical positivism meanings are (1) structural, as in logic and mathematics, or (2) empirical, as in natural science, or (3) emotive, as in art and poetry. It is meaning in sense (2) which is concerned here.

should be constructed or defined exclusively in terms of sense-data actually given to the subject at the moment when the knowing takes place, then that method is incompatible with the possibility of knowledge and the reality of empirical meaning.

We are here faced with a problem which runs through the whole history of post-Kantian epistemology—though it is Berkeley rather than Kant who precipitated it in its modern form. How can the knowledge-relation, or the relation of idea to the object it denotes, be valid unless what is known or meant is present to or in the experience which knows or means? But if what is meant or what is known is merely the cognitive experience itself, or something in it, then how can either knowledge or meaning be genuine?

In general there are three types of solution which have been offered. The first of these is representationalism, according to which the object never literally enters into the experience of the subject. This view recognizes, in at least one sense, the transcendence of the object known or meant; and thus avoids the reduction to absurdity which has been mentioned. The difficulty of this view is, of course, to reconcile such transcendence of the object with the possibility of knowing it. Second, there are identity-theories, both idealistic and realistic, according to which the object, or the object so far as it is known, is identical with some content of the subject's experience at the moment when the knowing takes place. The outstanding difficulty of this view is to avoid the reduction to absurdity, because it is incompatible with the supposition that anything can be known which lies beyond the immediate experience of the knower.[7] Such identity-theories are also liable to difficulty with the problem of error.

For the third type of theory—which includes both objective idealism and pragmatism—the object known is definable or specifiable in terms of experience, but the experience in terms of which the object is thus definable is not, exclusively, the experience of the subject at the moment of knowing; it transcends that experience. In rough general terms, objective idealism takes this relation between the experience in terms of which the object is specifiable and the experience which cognizes, to be the relation of something *deductively* implied to that in which it is implicit. That is, the present experience in which the knowing occurs—the idea or the given—is taken as determining implicitly the whole object in its reality, and as determining it unambiguously and with certainty, if only we could be explicitly aware of all that is implied. In equally rough terms, pragmatism may be said to take this relation as *inductive*; the given experience of the moment of knowing is the basis of a probability-judgment

---

[7] For an identity-theory of the realistic variety, the object known may transcend the knowing experience—because it is known only in part—but the object so far as it is genuinely cognized cannot.

concerning the experience (or experiences) which would verify, and in terms of which the real nature of the object is expressible.

It would probably be incorrect to take the logical positivists as holding an identity-theory of the cognitive relation.[8] But if they do not, then their conception of the object known, as constructed or 'constituted' in terms of given sense-data, requires to be interpreted so as to avoid an ambiguity which is possible. At this moment I am thinking of the wall behind my back. If I should turn around, I could verify my idea of it. But if at this moment I refer to the wall as a construction from presently given data, then the distinction between 'construction' as present concept, and 'construction' as that which this concept means to denote, is essential. Both are empirical data, if you like—but they are not the same data. The data which have their place in the concept are memories, visual and tactile images, anticipations; the data which would verify this conception would be perceptions. Not only are memories, ideas of imagination, and perceptions different events, but they are empirically distinguishable kinds of experience-content. Either, then, the wall which my idea denotes is merely the imagination-wall or recollection-wall, which is the immediate datum; or I cannot at this moment know the real wall which I mean; or—the third possibility—it is false that what I now know and mean by 'the wall' coincides with any complex of sense-data now in my mind.

It is on this point that the third type of theory is significant. For the pragmatic form of this third type knowing begins and ends in experience; but it does not end in the experience in which it begins. Hence the emphasis on the temporal nature of the knowing process, the leading character of ideas, and the function of knowledge as a guide to action. Knowing is a matter of two 'moments', the moment of assertion or entertainment and the moment of verification; both of these moments belonging to experience in the generic sense of that word. Knowledge will be true or correct only in so far as the present experience—of the entertainment of the meaning—envisages or anticipates correctly the experience or experiences which would verify it; that is, our knowledge is true if the anticipated experience is genuinely to be met with. But the entertaining experience can be truly cognitive, as against a mere enjoyment of itself, only by the fact that what would be realized in the moment of verification is distinct from the experience which entertains or anticipates it. Otherwise

[8] There could be doubt; for example, Carnap says, "Between 'concepts' and 'objects' there is only a difference in the manner of speech" (*Der Logische Aufbau der Welt*, Zusammenfassung, p. 262); and their conception of the relation between physical and mental might be taken to argue an identity-theory. But they have, I think, been principally absorbed in the problem of the *analysis* of the concept (or the object as an intellectual construction), and one should be chary of attempting to elicit from their writings any answer to the present question, which is of a quite different order. At least, I should not wish to presume to do so.

error would be impossible—one cannot be mistaken about the immediate —and hence knowledge, as the opposite of error, would likewise be impossible. I do not mean to say, of course, that at the moment when something is believed or asserted it cannot have a ground in given experience, or be 'partially verified'; but it *is* meant that there must be something more, which is believed in or asserted, than what is verified immediately, if the experience is to have the significance of a knowing as contrasted with an esthetic enjoyment.

The same point can be phrased in another way by reference to the question whether, and in what sense, the datum, by means of which any item of reality is known, is distinct in its being from the cognoscendum.[9]

I should urge that any identity-theory which denies this difference between datum and cognoscendum is incompatible with the cognitive function of the idea or datum. This cognitive function is the guidance of behavior; and in order that the cognizing experience may perform this function there must be at least an element of anticipation or implicit prediction which foreshadows what is *not* here and now present in the datum.

For certain types of realism the problem thus set is taken to be that of the relation between data as items of experience and the reality in its independent existence, which is not any item or complex of items in experience. Pragmatism, in common with idealism and with logical positivism, repudiates the problem in this form as unreal.[10] For all three of these views the relation of datum to cognoscendum is taken to be a relation within experience (in the generic sense), or between one experience and others; not a relation between something in experience and something altogether out of it. The reasons for this attitude would be different in each case, but for all three views the principal ground of this repudiation is the obvious one that a relation of experience to what cannot be brought within experience is a relation which cannot be investigated, and one the very conception of which as cognitive involves a confusion of thought.

All three of these theories would agree that the cognoscendum must be defined, or constructed, or constituted for knowledge, in terms of experience. But if we are not to fall into the opposite error of the reduction to absurdity, which comes from identifying datum and cognoscendum, it must be recognized that the experience of knowing and the experience in terms of which the object is specified cannot be simply identical

The very simple point which is pertinent to the further issues of this paper is the fact that although knowledge is subject to the here-and-now predicament—the data must be immediate—it is essential to the cognitive

[9] I borrow this formulation from the recent discussion of Strong and Lovejoy in the pages of *The Journal of Philosophy*, XXIX (1932) 673–687 and XXX (1933) 589–606.

[10] There may be doubt of this. I do not affirm it dogmatically; but this seems to express the intent of Dewey's denial of "antecedent reality", James's insistence that a thing is what it is "known as," and Peirce's pronouncement that our concept of the effects of an object, which have practical bearings, exhausts our whole concept of the object.

function of the present experience that its cognoscendum should *not* be merely here and now. If, for example, there can be knowledge of a future event in one's own life, then the datum which is the vehicle of this anticipation is not the anticipated cognoscendum. And in so far as all empirical knowing has the dimension of anticipation or implicit prediction, the thing known is not to be identified with, or phrased exclusively in terms of, here-and-now experience. What is known now, *now* has the status of being verifi*able;* but in the nature of the case it does not and cannot have the status of being verifiable-now.[11] The only thing which is literally and completely verifiable-now is that which is immediate and now-verified.

This account is, of course, hopelessly inadequate, and raises all sorts of questions which cannot be dealt with here. But the points which are directly pertinent to the further discussion are these. (1) The conception that "empirical knowledge is confined to what we actually observe" is false. To know (empirically) is to be able to anticipate correctly further possible experience. If this is not the whole significance of such knowing, at least it is an essential part of it. (2) What is anticipated, known, or meant must indeed be something envisaged in terms of experience—the requirement of empirical meaning stands. But equally it is essential that what is empirically known or meant should *not* be something which is immediately and exhaustively verified, in what I have called the moment of entertainment.

It will also be of importance to consider a little the sense, or senses, of the word 'verifiable'. Like any word ending in 'able', this connotes possibility and hence connotes conditions under which this possibility is supposed to obtain. To advance the dictum that what is empirically known, and what is meant, must be verifiable, and omit all examination of the wide range of significance which could attach to 'possible verification', would be to leave the whole conception rather obscure. But instead of attempting here some pat formulation *a priori*, let us briefly survey different modes of the 'possibility' of the verifying experiences projected by meaningful assertions.

At this moment I have a visual presentation which leads me to assert that my watch lies before me on the table. If what I assert is true, then I could touch the watch, pick it up, and I should then observe certain familiar details which are not discernible at this distance from my eye. This verifying experience is not actual; I do not touch the watch. But nothing is lacking for it except my own initiative. At least I believe that to be the case; and this belief is coördinate with the degree of my felt assurance that the watch is real and is mine. This is, perhaps, the simplest case of verifiability

—observability at will. All the conditions of the verifying experience are present except only my intent to make the verification.[12]

Next, let us consider the other side of the moon.[13] This is something believed in but never directly observed. The belief is an inference or interpretation based upon direct observation; the moon behaves like a solid object and must, therefore, have another side. But what is believed in must, in order to be real, possess characters which are left undetermined in our belief about it. For instance, there must be mountains there; or there must be none. To speak more precisely, our belief includes alternatives which are not determined; but, if the thing believed in is what it is believed to be, these alternatives must be *determined in the object*. If there were nothing more, and more specific, to the other side of the moon than what is specifically determined in our construction of it, then it would be a logical abstraction instead of a physical reality. These undetermined characters are what we should see if we could build an X-ray telescope, or what we should find about us if we could construct a spaceship to fly up there and land. What we should observe if these things could be accomplished is what we mean by the other side of the moon as a physically real thing—as something more than a logical construction put upon presently given data.

The projected verification in this case is ideal in a sense which goes quite beyond the preceding example. It is humanly possible, perhaps; men may some day build space-ships or X-ray telescopes. But the conditions of this verification—or any other direct empirical verification of the thing in question—include some which we cannot meet at will. We cannot, by any chain of planned activity, completely bridge the gap between actual conditions and the projected verification. Obviously, then, unless belief in the other side of the moon is meaningless, it is not requisite to such empirical meaning that the verifying experience should even be possible at present, in any narrow interpretation of that word 'possible'. To analyse the conception of 'verifiable' which would extend to such cases would be a large order. I shall only suggest what I think might be some of the critical points. (1) As this example serves to illustrate, any reality must, in order to satisfy our empirical concept of it, transcend the concept itself. A construction imposed upon given data cannot be identical with a real object; the thing itself must be more specific, and in comparison with it the construction remains abstract. In making any verification we expect

---

[12] Such a single experience would not be a theoretically complete verification of my assertion about the watch. As I have elsewhere indicated, no verification of the kind of knowledge commonly stated in propositions is ever absolutely complete and final. However, an *expected experience* of the watch can be completely verified—or falsified.

[13] It will be obvious that there are modes of verifiability which would fall between the preceding illustration and this one. For example, the verifying experience might be such as could be reached, from actual present conditions, by a more or less complicated chain of circumstances, but a chain every link of which is supposedly related to the preceding one in the manner of the first example.

something which we cannot anticipate. This is a paradox in language; but it is, or should be, a commonplace of the distinction between ideas and objects. (2) In making 'verifiability' a criterion of empirical meaningfulness, the primary reference is to a supposed character of what is conceived rather than to any supposed approximation of the conditions of verification to the actual. (3) The requirement of 'verifiability' for *knowledge* is a stricter one, because knowing requires, in addition to meaningfulness, some ground of the assurance of truth. But, as this example makes clear, even the 'possible verification' which is requisite to empirical knowing cannot be confined to the practicalities, or by detailed comprehension of the procedure of such verification. We do not command the means for making any direct verification of our belief in the other side of the moon; but what this signifies is that, with all the means in the world, we do not *know how* to. If it be said that it is required for empirical meaning—or even for knowledge—that we should lay down a rule of operation for the process of verification, it should be observed that sometimes this rule of operation will have to be rather sketchy. This difficulty—if it is a difficulty —will be found to affect not only such extreme cases as the other side of the moon but quite commonplace items of knowledge as well.

I join with you in feeling that such considerations smack of triviality; but certainly a theory which could be overturned by such trivial facts would not be worth holding. Just what we can sensibly mean by 'empirically verifiable' is really a bit obscure. Perhaps the chief requirement ought to be that we should be able to analyse the supposed connection between the projected verifying experience and what is actually given (the 'rule of operation') in such wise that this procedure of verification can be envisaged *in analogy with* operations which can actually be carried out. The degree to which such analogy could be made complete would, I think, justly affect the significance of our supposed knowledge.

As a third example let us take the case of the electron. The existence of electrons is inferred from the behavior of oil-droplets between charged plates, tracks registered on photographs of the discharge from cathodes, and other such actually observed phenomena. But what is it that is inferred; or is anything really inferred? Some physicists, for example Bridgman, would say that our concept of the electron comprehends nothing more than these observable phenomena, systematically connected by mathematical equations in verifiable ways. The layman, however, and probably most physicists, would not be satisfied to think of "electron" as merely a name for such observable phenomena. But what more may they suppose themselves to be believing in? An electron is too small to be seen through any microscope which ever can be made, and it would not stay put if a beam of light were directed upon it. It is equally beyond the reach of the other senses. But is the phrase "too small to be directly perceived" meaningful or is it not? And how direct must a "direct verification" be?

Suppose it to be urged that no one can set a limit to scientific inventiveness, or anticipate the surprises which investigation of the subatomic will quite surely present; and that if or when such developments take place, definitely localized phenomena may perhaps be observed within the space to which the mass of the electron is assigned.

Whether this is or is not a question about the real nature of the electron, and what limitations should be imposed on useful conceptions in physics, are matters concerning which I could not have a competent opinion. But there is a general point here which all of us can judge. A hypothetical conception of an empirical reality cannot be definitely ruled out unless we can say categorically that the conditions of its verification could never be realized. Between those conceptions for the verification of which we can definitely specify a rule of operation, and those which we can definitely eliminate as theoretically impossible, there is an enormous gap. And any conception which falls in this middle ground is an hypothesis about empirical reality which possesses at least some degree of meaningfulness. If those who believe in the electron as a sort of ultramicroscopic bullet cannot envisage this object of their belief in such wise that they would be able to recognize certain empirical eventualities as the verification of it, in case the conditions of such verification *could* be met, then they deceive themselves and are talking nonsense. But if they can thus envisage what they believe in, then the fact that such verifying experience is highly improbable, and even that the detail of it must be left somewhat indefinite, is no bar to its meaningfulness. Any other decision would be a doctrinaire attempt to erect our ignorance as a limitation of reality.

The requirement of empirical meaning is at bottom nothing more than the obvious one that the terms we use should possess denotation. As this requirement is interpreted by pragmatists and positivists and others who share the tendencies of thought which have been mentioned, no concept has any denotation at all unless eventually in terms of sensuous data or imagery. It is only in such terms that a thing meant, or what a proposition asserts, could be recognized if presented to us. But, as the preceding considerations are intended to make clear, the envisagement of what would thus exhibit the denotation or verify the assertion—which is all that meaning requires—has little or nothing to do with the question whether the conditions under which the requisite presentations could be realized can be met or not. Whether such verifying experience is mine or is yours or is nobody's; whether it happens now or in the future or never; whether it is practically possible or humanly problematic or clearly beyond our capacity to bring about—all this is beside the point when the only question is that of theoretical meaningfulness.

One may be tempted, in protest against various forms of transcendentalism and verbalism, to announce the unqualified dictum that only what is verifiable can be known, and only what is knowable can be the subject of a meaningful hypothesis. But such flat statement, while true in general, may nevertheless be misleading on account of an ambiguity in the word 'verifiable'. On the one hand this connotes a certain character of the content of one's assertion or hypothesis. This must be envisaged in sensuous terms; it must be the case that we could recognize certain empirical eventualities as verifying it, supposing that the conditions of such verifying experience could be satisfied. Verifiability in this sense requires an empirical *content* of the hypothesis, but has nothing to do with the practical or even the theoretical difficulties of verification. Whatever further restrictions may be appropriate in physics or any other natural science, the only general requirement of empirical meaning—which alone is pertinent to those hypotheses about reality which philosophy must consider—is this limitation to what can be expressed in terms which genuinely possess denotation.

On the other hand, 'verifiable' connotes the possibility of actually satisfying the conditions of verification. Or, to put it otherwise, verifiability may be taken to require 'possible experience' *as conditioned by the actual;* we must be able to find our way, step by step, from where we actually stand to this verifying experience. Hence practical or theoretical difficulties are limitations of verifiability in this second sense. These limitations may be genuinely pertinent to knowledge, because *knowledge* requires the *assurance of truth;* and whatever would prevent actual verification may prevent such assurance. But verifiability in this second sense has no relevance to meaning, because the assurance of truth is, obviously, not a condition of meaningfulness.

It is of importance to avoid confusing these two senses of 'verifiable' in assessing the significance of those considerations which methodological solipsism makes prominent. If it could be said that actual knowing must rest upon verification which, in the end, must be first-person and must be here and now when the knowing occurs, at least it would be an absurdity to translate this into the negation of meaning to whatever cannot be expressed in terms of first-person experience and of experience here and now. I impute this absurdity to no one; I would merely urge the necessity of avoiding it.

It is likewise important, in the same connection, to bear in mind what have been called the two moments of cognition. It is a fact that past experience is a given datum only in the form of memory; the future, only in the form of imagination. And the reports of others are data for the knower only in that form in which they lie within the egocentric predicament. Hence any idea which can occur with cognitive significance must be a construction by the knower, ultimately in terms of first-person present data. These predicaments, however, are limitations of the moment of entertainment. If one should conclude that because the cognizing experience must take place within the boundaries of the first-person and the immediate, therefore the object of that knowledge, so far as it is genuinely known or meant, must also lie within those limits, one would be overlooking the distinction between the experience which entertains and the projected experience which would verify what is thus entertained. The distinction of these two is of the essence of cognition as contrasted with esthetic enjoyment of the immediate. To identify them would be to reduce knowledge and meaning to absurdity. Again, I do not impute to anyone this identification of the idea, in terms of immediate data, with the object, specifiable in terms of possible experience or experience which is anticipated. I would only urge the desirability of avoiding this fallacy.

In the time which remains it is a bit absurd even to suggest any bearings which the above may be supposed to have upon metaphysical problems. But with your indulgence I shall barely mention three such issues.

One traditional problem of metaphysics is immortality. The hypothesis of immortality is unverifiable in an obvious sense. Yet it is an hypothesis about our own future experience. And our understanding of what would verify it has no lack of clarity. It may well be that, apart from a supposed connection with more exigent and mundane problems such as those of ethics, this hypothesis is not a fruitful topic of philosophic consideration. But if it be maintained that only what is scientifically verifiable has meaning, then this conception is a case in point. It could hardly be verified by science; and there is no observation or experiment which science could make, the negative result of which would disprove it. That consideration, however, has nothing to do with its meaningfulness as an hypothesis about reality. To deny that this conception has an empirical content would be as little justified as to deny empirical content to the belief that these hills will still be here when we are gone.

Next let us consider that question about the external world, supposedly at issue between idealists and realists. One suspects that the real animus of debate between these two parties is, and always has been, a concern with the question of an essential relationship between cosmic processes and human values; and that if, historically, idealists have sought to capture their conclusion on this point by arguments derived from a Berkeleyan or similar analysis of knowledge, at least such attempt has been abandoned in current discussion. So that this question about the external world, in any easily statable form, is probably not pertinent to present controversy. But there is one formulation which, if it is too naïve to be thus pertinent, at least poses an intelligible question about the nature of reality. Let us phrase this as a realistic hypothesis: If all minds should disappear from the universe, the stars would still go on in their courses.

This hypothesis is humanly unverifiable. That, however, is merely a predicament, which prevents assurance of truth but does not affect meaning. We can only express or envisage this hypothesis by means of imagination, and hence in terms of what any mind like ours *would* experience if, contrary to hypothesis, any mind *should* be there. But we do not need to commit the Berkeleyan naïveté of arguing that it is impossible to imagine a tree on a desert island which nobody is thinking of—because we are thinking of it ourselves. It is entirely meaningful, for example, to think of those inventions which nobody has ever thought of, or those numbers which no one will ever count; we can even frame the concept of those concepts which no one will ever frame. Those who would deny this on logical grounds exhibit a sense of paradox of language which is stronger than their sense of fact. Furthermore, *imagination* is sufficient for empirical meaning, though it requires *perception* for verification. I can imagine that future time which I shall never perceive; and humans can meaningfully think of that future when humanity may have run its cosmic course and all consciousness will have disappeared. It may be that the hypothesis of a reality with no sentience to be affected by it is not a particularly significant issue; though the idealist might have an interest in it for the sake of the light which decision about it would throw upon the nature which reality has now. In any case, the fact that it is unverifiable has no bearing upon its meaningfulness. Whether this hypothesis is true, is a genuine question about the nature of reality.

Finally, we may turn to the conception of other selves. The importance which this topic has for ethics will be obvious. Descartes conceived that the lower animals are a kind of automata; and the monstrous supposition that other humans are merely robots would have meaning if there should ever be a consistent solipsist to make it. The logical positivist does not deny that other humans have feelings; he circumvents the issue by a behavioristic interpretation of "having feelings". He points out that your toothache is a verifiable object of my knowledge; it is a construction put upon certain empirical items which are data for me—your tooth and your behavior. My own toothache is equally a construction. Until there are such prior constructions as the physical concept "teeth", from given sense-data, neither your toothache nor mine is a possible object of knowledge. And, similarly, until there is a construction involving such prior constructions as human bodies, there is no own-self or yourself as particular objects of knowledge. As knowable things, myself and yourself are equally constructions; and though as constructed objects they are fundamentally different in kind, the constructions are coördinate. That experience which is the original datum of *all* such constructions is, in Carnap's phrase, "without a subject." [14] Nevertheless it has that quality or status, characteristic of all given experience, which is indicated by the adjective "first-person".

With the general manner of this account of our knowledge of ourselves and others I think we should agree. But it does not touch the point at issue. Suppose I fear that I may have a toothache tomorrow. I entertain a conception involving various constructions from present data; my body,

[14] See *Der Logische Aufbau der Welt*, § 65.

teeth, etc. But my present experience, by which I know or anticipate this future toothache, is not an experience of an *ache*. There is here that difference which has been noted between the experience which entertains and the experience which would verify, to which it implicitly refers. A robot could have a toothache, in the sense of having a swollen jaw and exhibiting all the appropriate behavior; but there would be no pain connected with it. The question of metaphysical solipsism is the question whether there is any pain connected with your observed behavior indicating toothache. The logical positivist claims that this issue has no meaning, because there is no empirical content which could verify the non-solipsistic assertion—that is, no content unless, following his procedure, I identify your pain with observable items such as the behavior which exhibits it; in which case it is verifiable in the first person. To make this identification, however, is to beg precisely the point at issue.

Let us compare the two cases of your toothache now and my toothache tomorrow. I cannot verify your toothache, as distinct from your observable behavior, because of the egocentric predicament. But neither can I verify my own future toothache—because of the now-predicament. My tomorrow's pain, however, may genuinely be an object of knowledge for me now, because a pain may be cognized by an experience in which that pain is not a given ingredient. (The imagination of a pain may be painful; but it is not the pain anticipated. If it were, all future events which we anticipate would be happening already.) *Your* pain I can *never* verify. But when I assert that you are not an automaton, I can envisage what I mean —and what makes the difference between the truth and falsity of my assertion—because I can imagine your pain, as distinct from all I can literally experience of you, just as I can imagine my own future pain, as distinct from the experience in which I now imagine it.

In the nature of the case I cannot verify you as another center of experience distinct from myself. Any verification which I might suppose myself to make would violate the hypothesis by being first-person experience. But there is nothing to which I can give more explicit empirical content than the supposition of a consciousness like mine connected with a body like my own. Whether there is any such would be a terribly important question about reality if anybody entertained a doubt about the answer. Whether you are another mind or only a sleep-walking body is a question of fact. And it cannot be exorcized by definitions—by defining 'meaningful' so as to limit it to the verifiable, and 'verifiable' by reference to the egocentric predicament.

This conception of other selves as metaphysical ultimates exemplifies the philosophic importance which may attach to a supposition which is nevertheless unverifiable on account of the limitations of knowing. Though empirical meaning is requisite to theoretical significance—and that consideration is of first importance in guarding against verbal nonsense in philosophy—still the sense in which a supposition is meaningful often outruns that in which the assurance of truth, by verification, can genuinely be hoped for. In limiting cases like this last question it may even outrun the possibility of verification altogether.

Meaning and Verification *

MORITZ SCHLICK

I

Philosophical questions, as compared with ordinary scientific problems, are always strangely paradoxical. But it seems to be an especially strange paradox that the question concerning the meaning of a proposition should constitute a serious philosophical difficulty. For is it not the very nature and purpose of every proposition to express its own meaning? In fact, when we are confronted with a proposition (in a language familiar to us) we usually know its meaning immediately. If we do not, we can have it explained to us, but the explanation will consist of a new proposition; and if the new one is capable of expressing the meaning, why should not the original one be capable of it? So that a snippy person when asked what he meant by a certain statement might be perfectly justified in saying, 'I meant exactly what I said!'.

It is logically legitimate and actually the normal way in ordinary life and even in science to answer a question concerning the meaning of a proposition by simply repeating it either more distinctly or in slightly different words. Under what circumstances, then, can there be any sense in asking for the meaning of a statement which is well before our eyes or ears?

Evidently the only possibility is that we have not *understood* it. And in this case what is actually before our eyes or ears is nothing but a series of words which we are unable to handle; we do not know how to use it, how to 'apply it to reality'. Such a series of words is for us simply a complex of signs 'without meaning', a mere sequel of sounds or a mere row of marks on paper, and we have no right to call it 'a proposition' at all; we may perhaps speak of it as 'a sentence'.

If we adopt this terminology we can now easily get rid of our paradox by saying that we cannot inquire after the meaning of a proposition, but can ask about the meaning of a sentence, and that this amounts to asking, 'What proposition does the sentence stand for?' And this question is answered either by a proposition in a language with which we are already perfectly familiar; or by indicating the logical rules which will make a

* Reprinted by kind permission of Mrs. Schlick and the editors from *The Philosophical Review*, 45, 1936.

proposition out of the sentence, i.e., will tell us exactly in what circumstances the sentence is to be *used*. These two methods do not actually differ in principle; both of them give meaning to the sentence (transform it into a proposition) by locating it, as it were, within the system of a definite language; the first method making use of a language which is already in our possession, the second one building it up for us. The first method represents the simplest kind of ordinary 'translation'; the second one affords a deeper insight into the nature of meaning, and will have to be used in order to overcome philosophical difficulties connected with the understanding of sentences.

The source of these difficulties is to be found in the fact that very often we do not know how to handle our own words; we speak or write without having first agreed upon a definite logical grammar which will constitute the signification of our terms. We commit the mistake of thinking that we know the meaning of a sentence (i.e., understand it as a proposition) if we are familiar with all the words occurring in it. But this is not sufficient. It will not lead to confusion or error as long as we remain in the domain of everyday life by which our words have been formed and to which they are adapted, but it will become fatal the moment we try to think about abstract problems by means of the same terms without carefully fixing their signification for the new purpose. For every word has a definite signification only within a definite context into which it has been fitted; in any other context it will have no meaning unless we provide new rules for the use of the word in the new case, and this may be done, at least in principle, quite arbitrarily.

Let us consider an example. If a friend should say to me, 'Take me to a country where the sky is three times as blue as in England!' I should not know how to fulfill his wish; his phrase would appear nonsensical to me, because the word 'blue' is used in a way which is not provided for by the rules of our language. The combination of a numeral and the name of a color does not occur in it; therefore my friend's sentence has no meaning, although its exterior linguistic form is that of a command or a wish. But he can, of course, give it a meaning. If I ask him, 'What do you mean by "three times as blue"?', he can arbitrarily indicate certain definite physical circumstances concerning the serenity of the sky which he wants his phrase to be the description of. And then, perhaps, I shall be able to follow his directions; his wish will have become meaningful for me.

Thus, whenever we ask about a sentence, 'What does it mean?', what we expect is instruction as to the circumstances in which the sentence is to be used; we want a description of the conditions under which the sentence will form a *true* proposition, and of those which will make it *false*. The meaning of a word or a combination of words is, in this way, determined by a set of rules which regulate their use and which, following

Wittgenstein, we may call the rules of their *grammar*, taking this word in its widest sense.

(If the preceding remarks about meaning are as correct as I am convinced they are, this will, to a large measure, be due to conversations with Wittgenstein which have greatly influenced my own views about these matters. I can hardly exaggerate my indebtedness to this philosopher. I do not wish to impute to him any responsibility for the contents of this article, but I have reason to hope that he will agree with the main substance of it.)

Stating the meaning of a sentence amounts to stating the rules according to which the sentence is to be used, and this is the same as stating the way in which it can be verified (or falsified). The meaning of a proposition is the method of its verification.

The 'grammatical' rules will partly consist of ordinary definitions, i.e., explanations of words by means of other words, partly of what are called 'ostensive' definitions, i.e., explanations by means of a procedure which puts the words to actual use. The simplest form of an ostensive definition is a pointing gesture combined with the pronouncing of the word, as when we teach a child the signification of the sound 'blue' by showing a blue object. But in most cases the ostensive definition is of a more complicated form; we cannot point to an object corresponding to words like 'because' 'immediate', 'chance', 'again', etc. In these cases we require the presence of certain complex situations, and the meaning of the words is defined by the way we use them in these different situations.

It is clear that in order to understand a verbal definition we must know the signification of the explaining words beforehand, and that the only explanation which can work without any previous knowledge is the ostensive definition. We conclude that there is no way of understanding any meaning without ultimate reference to ostensive definitions, and this means, in an obvious sense, reference to 'experience' or 'possibility of verification'.

This is the situation, and nothing seems to me simpler or less questionable. It is this situation and nothing else that we describe when we affirm that the meaning of a proposition can be given only by giving the rules of its verification in experience. (The addition, 'in experience', is really superfluous, as no other kind of verification has been defined.)

This view has been called the "experimental theory of meaning"; but it certainly is no theory at all, for the term 'theory' is used for a set of hypotheses about a certain subject-matter, and there are no hypotheses involved in our view, which proposes to be nothing but a simple statement of the way in which meaning is *actually* assigned to propositions, both in everyday life and in science. There has never been any other way, and it would be a grave error to suppose that we believe we have discovered a new conception of meaning which is contrary to common opinion and which we want to introduce into philosophy. On the contrary, our conception is not only entirely in agreement with, but even derived from, common sense and scientific procedure. Although our criterion of meaning has always been employed in practice, it has very rarely been formulated in the past, and this is perhaps the only excuse for the attempts of so many philosophers to deny its feasibility.

The most famous case of an explicit formulation of our criterion is Einstein's answer to the question, What do we mean when we speak of two events at distant places happening simultaneously? This answer consisted in a description of an experimental method by which the simultaneity of such events was actually ascertained. Einstein's philosophical opponents maintained—and some of them still maintain—that they knew the meaning of the above question independently of any method of verification. All I am trying to do is to stick consistently to Einstein's position and to admit no exceptions from it. (Professor Bridgman's book on *The Logic of Modern Physics* is an admirable attempt to carry out this program for all concepts of physics.) I am not writing for those who think that Einstein's philosophical opponents were right.

II

Professor C. I. Lewis, in a remarkable address on "Experience and Meaning" (published in *The Philosophical Review*, March 1934 [1]), has justly stated that the view developed above (he speaks of it as the "empirical-meaning requirement") forms the basis of the whole philosophy of what has been called the "logical positivism of the Viennese Circle". He criticizes this basis as inadequate chiefly on the ground that its acceptance would impose certain limitations upon "significant philosophic discussion" which, at some points, would make such discussion altogether impossible and, at other points, restrict it to an intolerable extent.

Feeling responsible as I do for certain features of the Viennese philosophy (which I should prefer to call Consistent Empiricism), and being of the opinion that it really does not impose any restrictions upon significant philosophizing at all, I shall try to examine Professor Lewis' chief arguments and point out why I think that they do not endanger our position —at least as far as I can answer for it myself. All of my own arguments will be derived from the statements made in section I.

Professor Lewis describes the empirical-meaning requirement as demanding "that any concept put forward or any proposition asserted shall have a definite denotation; that it shall be intelligible not only verbally and logically but in the further sense that one can specify those empirical items which would determine the applicability of the concept or constitute the verification of the proposition" (*loc. cit.*, 125 [2]). Here it

[1] [Reprinted in this collection.]
[2] [P. 128 of this volume.]

seems to me that there is no justification for the words "but in the *further* sense . . .", i.e., for the distinction of two (or three?) senses of intelligibility. The remarks in section I show that, according to our opinion, 'verbal and logical' understanding *consists in* knowing how the proposition in question could be verified. For, unless we mean by 'verbal understanding' that we know how the words are actually used, the term could hardly mean anything but a shadowy feeling of being acquainted with the words, and in a philosophical discussion it does not seem advisable to call such a feeling 'understanding'. Similarly, I should not advise that we speak of a sentence as being 'logically intelligible' when we just feel convinced that its exterior form is that of a proper proposition (if, e.g. it has the form, substantive—copula—adjective, and therefore appears to predicate a property of a thing). For it seems to me that by such a phrase we want to say much *more*, namely, that we are completely aware of the whole grammar of the sentence, i.e., that we know exactly the circumstances to which it is fitted. Thus knowledge of how a proposition is verified is not anything over and above its verbal and logical understanding, but is identical with it. It seems to me, therefore, that when we demand that a proposition be verifiable we are not adding a new requirement but are simply formulating the conditions which have actually always been acknowledged as necessary for meaning and intelligibility.

The mere statement that no sentence has meaning unless we are able to indicate a way of testing its truth or falsity is not very useful if we do not explain very carefully the signification of the phrases 'method of testing' and 'verifiability'. Professor Lewis is quite right when he asks for such an explanation. He himself suggests some ways in which it might be given, and I am glad to say that his suggestions appear to me to be in perfect agreement with my own views and those of my philosophical friends. It will be easy to show that there is no serious divergence between the point of view of the pragmatist as Professor Lewis conceives it and that of the Viennese Empiricist. And if in some special questions they arrive at different conclusions, it may be hoped that a careful examination will bridge the difference.

How do we define verifiability?

In the first place I should like to point out that when we say that "a proposition has meaning only if it is verifiable" we are not saying ". . . if it is *verified*." This simple remark does away with one of the chief objections; the "here and now predicament," as Professor Lewis calls it, does not exist any more. We fall into the snares of this predicament only if we regard verification itself as the criterion of meaning, instead of 'possibility of verification' (= verifiability); this would indeed lead to a "reduction to absurdity of meaning." Obviously the predicament arises through some fallacy by which these two notions are confounded. I do not know if Russell's statement, "Empirical knowledge is confined to what we actually observe" (quoted by Professor Lewis, *loc. cit.*, 130 [3]), must be interpreted as containing this fallacy, but it would certainly be worth while to discover its genesis.

Let us consider the following argument which Professor Lewis discusses (131 [4]), but which he does not want to impute to anyone:

Suppose it maintained that no issue is meaningful unless it can be put to the test of decisive verification. And no verification can take place except in the immediately present experience of the subject. Then nothing can be meant except what is actually present in the experience in which that meaning is entertained.

This argument has the form of a conclusion drawn from two premisses. Let us for the moment assume the second premiss to be meaningful and true. You will observe that even then the conclusion does *not* follow. For the first premiss assures us that the issue has meaning if it *can* be verified; the verification does not have to take place, and therefore it is quite irrelevant whether it can take place in the future or in the present only. Apart from this, the second premiss is, of course, nonsensical; for what fact could possibly be described by the sentence 'verification can take place only in present experience'? Is not verifying an act or process like hearing or feeling bored? Might we not just as well say that I can hear or feel bored only in the present moment? And what could I mean by this? The particular nonsense involved in such phrases will become clearer when we speak of the 'egocentric predicament' later on; at present we are content to know that our empirical-meaning postulate has nothing whatever to do with the now-predicament. 'Verifiable' does not even mean 'verifiable here now'; much less does it mean 'being verified now'.

Perhaps it will be thought that the only way of making sure of the verifiability of a proposition would consist in its actual verification. But we shall soon see that this is not the case.

There seems to be a great temptation to connect meaning and the 'immediately given' in the wrong way; and some of the Viennese positivists may have yielded to this temptation, thereby getting dangerously near to the fallacy we have just been describing. Parts of Carnap's *Der Logische Aufbau der Welt*, for instance, might be interpreted as implying that a proposition about future events did not really refer to the future at all but asserted only the present existence of certain expectations (and, similarly, speaking about the past would really mean speaking about present memories). But it is certain that the author of that book does not hold such a view now, and that it cannot be regarded as a teaching of the new positivism. On the contrary, we have pointed out from the beginning that our definition of meaning does not imply such absurd consequences, and when someone asked, "But how can you verify a proposition about

[3] [P. 132 of this volume.]
[4] [P. 133 of this volume.]

a future event?", we replied, "Why, for instance, by waiting for it to happen! 'Waiting' is a perfectly legitimate method of verification."

*   *   *

Thus I think that everybody—including the Consistent Empiricist—agrees that it would be nonsense to say, 'We can mean nothing but the immediately given'. If in this sentence we replace the word 'mean' by the word 'know' we arrive at a statement similar to Bertrand Russell's mentioned above. The temptation to formulate phrases of this sort arises, I believe, from a certain ambiguity of the verb 'to know' which is the source of many metaphysical troubles and to which, therefore, I have often had to call attention on other occasions (see, e.g., *Allgemeine Erkenntnislehre* 2nd ed. 1925, § 12). In the first place the word may stand simply for 'being aware of a datum', i.e., for the mere presence of a feeling, a color, a sound, etc.; and if the word 'knowledge' is taken in this sense the assertion 'Empirical knowledge is confined to what we actually observe' does not say anything at all, but is a mere tautology. (This case, I think, would correspond to what Professor Lewis calls "identity-theories" of the "knowledge-relation." Such theories, resting on a tautology of this kind, would be empty verbiage without significance.)

In the second place the word 'knowledge' may be used in one of the significant meanings which it has in science and ordinary life; and in this case Russell's assertion would obviously (as Professor Lewis remarked) be false. Russell himself, as is well known, distinguishes between 'knowledge by acquaintance' and 'knowledge by description', but perhaps it should be noted that this distinction does not entirely coincide with the one we have been insisting upon just now.

*   *   *

III

Verifiability means possibility of verification. Professor Lewis justly remarks that to "omit all examination of the wide range of significance which could attach to 'possible verification', would be to leave the whole conception rather obscure" (*loc. cit.*, 137). For our purpose it suffices to distinguish between two of the many ways in which the word 'possibility' is used. We shall call them 'empirical possibility' and 'logical possibility'. Professor Lewis describes two meanings of 'verifiability' which correspond exactly to this difference; he is fully aware of it, and there is hardly anything left for me to do but carefully to work out the distinction and show its bearing upon our issue.

I propose to call 'empirically possible' anything that does not contradict the laws of nature. This is, I think, the largest sense in which we may speak of empirical possibility; we do not restrict the term to happenings which are not only in accordance with the laws of nature but also with the actual state of the universe (where 'actual' might refer to the present moment of our own lives, or to the condition of human beings on this planet, and so forth). If we chose the latter definition (which seems to have been in Professor Lewis' mind when he spoke of "possible experience as conditioned by the actual", *loc. cit.*, 141 [5]) we should not get the sharp boundaries we need for our present purpose. So 'empirical possibility' is to mean 'compatibility with natural laws'.

Now, since we cannot boast of a complete and sure knowledge of nature's laws, it is evident that we can never assert with certainty the empirical possibility of any fact, and here we may be permitted to speak of *degrees* of possibility. Is it possible for me to lift this book? Surely!— This table? I think so!—This billiard table? I don't think so!—This automobile? Certainly not!—It is clear that in these cases the answer is given by *experience*, as the result of experiments performed in the past. Any judgment about empirical possibility is based on experience and will often be rather uncertain; there will be no sharp boundary between possibility and impossibility.

Is the possibility of verification which we insist upon of this empirical sort? In that case there would be different degrees of verifiability, the question of meaning would be a matter of more or less, not a matter of yes or no. In many disputes concerning our issue it is the empirical possibility of verification which is discussed; the various examples of verifiability given by Professor Lewis, e.g., are instances of different empirical circumstances in which the verification is carried out or prevented from being carried out. Many of those who refuse to accept our criterion of meaning seem to imagine that the procedure of its application in a special case is somewhat like this: A proposition is presented to us ready made, and in order to discover its meaning we have to try various methods of verifying or falsifying it, and if one of these methods works we have found the meaning of the proposition; but if not, we say it has no meaning. If we really had to proceed in this way, it is clear that the determination of meaning would be entirely a matter of experience, and that in many cases no sharp and ultimate decision could be obtained. How could we ever know that we had tried long enough, if none of our methods were successful? Might not future efforts disclose a meaning which we were unable to find before?

This whole conception is, of course, entirely erroneous. It speaks of meaning as if it were a kind of entity inherent in a sentence and hidden in it like a nut in its shell, so that the philosopher would have to crack the shell or sentence in order to reveal the nut or meaning. We know from our considerations in section I that a proposition cannot be given 'ready made'; that meaning does not inhere in a sentence where it might be discovered, but that it must be bestowed upon it. And this is done by applying

[5] [P. 141 of this volume.]

to the sentence the rules of the logical grammar of our language, as explained in section I. These rules are not facts of nature which could be 'discovered', but they are prescriptions stipulated by acts of definition. And these definitions have to be known to those who pronounce the sentence in question and to those who hear or read it. Otherwise they are not confronted with any proposition at all, and there is nothing they could try to verify, because you can't verify or falsify a mere row of words. You cannot even start verifying before you know the meaning, i.e., before you have established the possibility of verification.

In other words, the possibility of verification which is relevant to meaning cannot be of the empirical sort; it cannot be established *post festum*. You have to be sure of it before you can consider the empirical circumstances and investigate whether or no or under what conditions they will permit of verification. The empirical circumstances are all-important when you want to know if a proposition is *true* (which is the concern of the scientist), but they can have no influence on the *meaning* of the proposition (which is the concern of the philosopher). Professor Lewis has seen and expressed this very clearly (*loc. cit.*, 142, first six lines [6]), and our Vienna positivism, as far as I can answer for it, is in complete agreement with him on this point. It must be emphasized that when we speak of verifiability we mean *logical* possibility of verification, and nothing but this.

* * *

I call a fact or a process 'logically possible' if it can be *described*, i.e., if the sentence which is supposed to describe it obeys the rules of grammar we have stipulated for our language. (I am expressing myself rather incorrectly. A fact which could not be described would, of course, not be any fact at all; *any* fact is logically possible. But I think my meaning will be understood.) Take some examples. The sentences, 'My friend died the day after tomorrow'; 'The lady wore a dark red dress which was bright green'; 'The campanile is 100 feet and 150 feet high'; 'The child was naked, but wore a long white nightgown', obviously violate the rules which, in ordinary English, govern the use of the words occurring in the sentences. They do not describe any facts at all; they are meaningless, because they represent *logical* impossibilities.

It is of the greatest importance (not only for our present issue but for philosophical problems in general) to see that whenever we speak of logical impossibility we are referring to a discrepancy between the definitions of our terms and the way in which we use them. We must avoid the severe mistake committed by some of the former Empiricists like Mill and Spencer, who regarded logical principles (e.g., the Law of Contradiction) as laws of nature governing the psychological process of think-

[6] [P. 141, ll. 20–25, of this volume.]

ing. The nonsensical statements alluded to above do not correspond to thoughts which, by a sort of psychological experiment, we find ourselves unable to think; they do not correspond to any thoughts at all. When we hear the words, 'A tower which is both 100 feet and 150 feet high', the image of two towers of different heights may be in our mind, and we may find it psychologically (empirically) impossible to combine the two pictures into one image, but it is not this fact which is denoted by the words 'logical impossibility'. The height of a tower cannot be 100 feet and 150 feet at the same time; a child cannot be naked and dressed at the same time—not because we are unable to imagine it, but because our definitions of 'height', of the numerals, of the terms 'naked' and 'dressed', are not compatible with the particular combinations of those words in our examples. 'They are not compatible with such combinations' means that the rules of our language have not provided any use for such combinations; they do not describe any fact. We could change these rules, of course, and thereby arrange a meaning for the terms 'both red and green', 'both naked and dressed'; but if we decide to stick to the ordinary definitions (which reveal themselves in the way we actually use our words) we have decided to regard those combined terms as meaningless, i.e., not to use them as the description of *any* fact. Whatever fact we may or may not imagine, if the word 'naked' (or 'red') occurs in its description we have decided that the word 'dressed' (or 'green') cannot be put in its place in the same description. If we do not follow this rule it means that we want to introduce a new definition of the words, or that we don't mind using words without meaning and like to indulge in nonsense. (I am far from condemning this attitude under all circumstances; on certain occasions— as in *Alice in Wonderland*—it may be the only sensible attitude and far more delightful than any treatise on Logic. But in such a treatise we have a right to expect a different attitude.)

The result of our considerations is this: Verifiability, which is the sufficient and necessary condition of meaning, is a possibility of the logical order; it is created by constructing the sentence in accordance with the rules by which its terms are defined. The only case in which verification is (logically) impossible is the case where you have *made* it impossible by not setting any rules for its verification. Grammatical rules are not found anywhere in nature, but are made by man and are, in principle, arbitrary; so you cannot give meaning to a sentence by *discovering* a method of verifying it, but only by *stipulating* how it *shall* be done. Thus logical possibility or impossibility of verification is always *self-imposed*. If we utter a sentence without meaning it is always *our own fault*.

The tremendous philosophic importance of this last remark will be realized when we consider that what we said about the meaning of *assertions* applies also to the meaning of *questions*. There are, of course, many questions which can never be answered by human beings. But the impossibility of finding the answer may be of two different kinds. If it is merely empirical in the sense defined, if it is due to the chance circumstances to which our human existence is confined, there may be reason to lament our fate and the weakness of our physical and mental powers, but the problem could never be said to be absolutely insoluble, and there would always be some hope, at least for future generations. For the empirical circumstances may alter, human facilities may develop, and even the laws of nature may change (perhaps even suddenly and in such a way that the universe would be thrown open to much more extended investigation). A problem of this kind might be called practically unanswerable or technically unanswerable, and might cause the scientist great trouble, but the philosopher, who is concerned with general principles only, would not feel terribly excited about it.

But what about those questions for which it is *logically* impossible to find an answer? Such problems would remain insoluble under all imaginable circumstances; they would confront us with a definite hopeless *Ignorabimus;* and it is of the greatest importance for the philosopher to know whether there are any such issues. Now it is easy to see from what has been said before that this calamity could happen only if the question itself had no meaning. It would not be a genuine question at all, but a mere row of words with a question-mark at the end. We must say that a question is meaningful, if we can *understand* it, i.e., if we are able to decide for any given proposition whether, if true, it would be an answer to our question. And if this is so, the actual decision could only be prevented by empirical circumstances, which means that it would not be *logically* impossible. Hence no meaningful problem can be insoluble in *principle*. If in any case we find an answer to be logically impossible we know that we really have not been asking anything, that what sounded like a question was actually a nonsensical combination of words. A genuine question is one for which an answer is logically possible. This is one of the most characteristic results of our empiricism. It means that in principle there are no limits to our knowledge. The boundaries which must be acknowledged are of an empirical nature and, therefore, never ultimate; they can be pushed back further and further; there is no unfathomable mystery in the world.

*   *   *

The dividing line between logical possibility and impossibility of verification is absolutely sharp and distinct; there is no gradual transition between meaning and nonsense. For either you have given the grammatical rules for verification, or you have not; *tertium non datur*.

Empirical possibility is determined by the laws of nature, but meaning and verifiability are entirely independent of them. Everything that I can describe or define is logically possible—and definitions are in no way bound up with natural laws. The proposition 'Rivers flow uphill' is meaningful, but happens to be false because the fact it describes is *physically* impossible. It will not deprive a proposition of its meaning if the conditions which I stipulate for its verification are incompatible with the laws of nature; I may prescribe conditions, for instance, which could be fulfilled only if the velocity of light were greater than it actually is, or if the Law of Conservation of Energy did not hold, and so forth.

An opponent of our view might find a dangerous paradox or even a contradiction in the preceding explanations, because on the one hand we insisted so strongly on what has been called the "*empirical*-meaning requirement", and on the other hand we assert most emphatically that meaning and verifiability do not depend on any empirical conditions whatever, but are determined by purely logical possibilities. The opponent will object: if meaning is a matter of experience, how can it be a matter of definition and logic?

In reality there is no contradiction or difficulty. The word 'experience' is ambiguous. Firstly, it may be a name for any so-called 'immediate data' —which is a comparatively modern use of the word—and secondly we can use it in the sense in which we speak, e.g., of an 'experienced traveler', meaning a man who has not only seen a great deal but also knows how to profit from it for his actions. It is in this second sense (by the way, the sense the word has in Hume's and Kant's philosophy) that verifiability must be declared to be independent of experience. The possibility of verification does not rest on any 'experiential truth', on a law of nature or any other true general proposition, but is determined solely by our definitions, by the rules which have been fixed for our language, or which we can fix arbitrarily at any moment. All of these rules ultimately point to ostensive definitions, as we have explained, and through them verifiability is linked to *experience* in the *first* sense of the word. No rule of expression presupposes any law or regularity in the world (which is the condition of 'experience' as Hume and Kant use the word), but it does presuppose data and situations, to which names can be attached. The rules of language are rules of the application of language; so there must be something to which it can be applied. Expressibility and verifiability are one and the same thing. There is no antagonism between logic and experience. Not only can the logician be an empiricist at the same time; he *must* be one if he wants to understand what he himself is doing.

* * *

IV

Let us glance at some examples in order to illustrate the consequences of our attitude in regard to certain issues of traditional philosophy. Take the famous case of the reality of the other side of the moon (which is also one of Professor Lewis' examples). None of us, I think, would be willing to accept a view according to which it would be nonsense to speak of the averted face of our satellite. Can there be the slightest doubt that, according to our explanations, the conditions of meaning are amply satisfied in this case?

I think there can be no doubt. For the question, 'What is the other side of the moon like?' could be answered, for instance, by a description of what would be seen or touched by a person located somewhere behind the moon. The question whether it be physically possible for a human being—or indeed any other living being—to travel around the moon does not even have to be raised here; it is entirely irrelevant. Even if it could be shown that a journey to another celestial body were absolutely incompatible with the known laws of nature, a proposition about the other side of the moon would still be meaningful. Since our sentence speaks of certain places in space as being filled with matter (for that is what the words 'side of the moon' stand for), it will have meaning if we indicate under what circumstances a proposition of the form, 'this place is filled with matter', shall be called true or false. The concept 'physical substance at a certain place' is defined by our language in physics and geometry. Geometry itself is the grammar of our propositions about 'spatial' relations, and it is not very difficult to see how assertions about physical properties and spatial relations are connected with 'sense-data' by ostensive definitions. This connection, by the way, is *not* such as to entitle us to say that physical substance is 'a mere construction put upon sense-data', or that a physical body is 'a complex of sense-data'—unless we interpret these phrases as rather inadequate abbreviations of the assertion that all propositions containing the term 'physical body' require for their verification the presence of sense-data. And this is certainly an exceedingly trivial statement.

In the case of the moon we might perhaps say that the meaning-requirement is fulfilled if we are able to 'imagine' (picture mentally) situations which would verify our proposition. But if we should say in general that verifiability of an assertion implies possibility of 'imagining' the asserted fact, this would be true only in a restricted sense. It would not be true in so far as the possibility is of the empirical kind, i.e., implying specific human capacities. I do not think, for instance, that we can be accused of talking nonsense if we speak of a universe of ten dimensions, or of beings possessing sense-organs and having perceptions entirely different from ours; and yet it does not seem right to say that we are able to 'imagine' such beings and such perceptions, or a ten-dimensional world. But we *must* be able to say under what *observable* circumstances we should assert the existence of the beings or sense-organs just referred to. It is clear that I can speak meaningfully of the sound of a friend's voice without being able actually to recall it in my imagination. This is not the place to discuss the logical grammar of the word 'to imagine'; these few re-marks may caution us against accepting too readily a *psychological* ex-planation of verifiability.

We must not identify meaning with any of the psychological data which form the material of a mental sentence (or 'thought') in the same sense in which articulated sounds form the material of a spoken sentence, or black marks on paper the material of a written sentence. When you are do-ing a calculation in arithmetic it is quite irrelevant whether you have before your mind the images of black numbers or of red numbers, or no visual picture at all. And even if it were empirically impossible for you to do any calculation without imagining black numbers at the same time, the mental pictures of those black marks could, of course, in no way be considered as constituting the meaning, or part of the meaning, of the calculation.

Carnap is right in putting great stress upon the fact (always emphasized by the critics of 'psychologism') that the question of meaning has noth-ing to do with the psychological question as to the mental processes of which an act of thought may consist. But I am not sure that he has seen with equal clarity that reference to ostensive definitions (which we postu-late for meaning) does *not* involve the error of a confusion of the two questions. In order to understand a sentence containing, e.g., the words 'red flag', it is indispensable that I should be able to indicate a situation where I could point to an object which I should call a 'flag', and whose color I could recognize as 'red' as distinguished from other colors. But in order to do this it is *not* necessary that I should actually call up the image of a red flag. It is of the utmost importance to see that these two things have nothing in common. At this moment I am trying in vain to imagine the shape of a capital G in German print; nevertheless I can speak about it without talking nonsense, and I know I should recognize it if I saw the letter. Imagining a red patch is utterly different from referring to an ostensive definition of 'red'. Verifiability has nothing to do with any images that may be associated with the words of the sentence in question.

*   *   *

No more difficulty than in the case of the other side of the moon will be found in discussing, as another significant example, the question of 'immortality', which Professor Lewis calls, and which is usually called, a *metaphysical* problem. I take it for granted that 'immortality' is not sup-posed to signify never-ending life (for that might possibly be meaningless on account of infinity being involved), but that we are concerned with the question of survival after 'death'. I think we may agree with Pro-fessor Lewis when he says about this hypothesis: "Our understanding of what would verify it has no lack of clarity." In fact, I can easily imagine, e.g., witnessing the funeral of my own body and continuing to exist with-out a body, for nothing is easier than to describe a world which differs from our ordinary world only in the complete absence of all data which I would call parts of my own body.

We must conclude that immortality, in the sense defined, should not be regarded as a 'metaphysical problem', but is an empirical hypothesis, because it possesses logical verifiability. It could be verified by following the prescription: 'Wait until you die!' Professor Lewis seems to hold that this method is not satisfactory from the point of view of science. He says (143 [7]):

> The hypothesis of immortality is unverifiable in an obvious sense . . . if it be maintained that only what is scientifically verifiable has meaning, then this conception is a case in point. It could hardly be verified by science; and there is no observation or experiment which science could make, the negative result of which would disprove it.

I fancy that in these sentences the private method of verification is rejected as being unscientific because it would apply only to the individual case of the experiencing person himself, whereas a scientific statement should be capable of a *general* proof, open to any careful observer. But I see no reason why even this should be declared to be impossible. On the contrary, it is easy to describe experiences such that the hypothesis of an invisible existence of human beings after their bodily death would be the most acceptable explanation of the phenomena observed. These phenomena, it is true, would have to be of a much more convincing nature than the ridiculous happenings alleged to have occurred in meetings of the occultists—but I think there cannot be the slightest doubt as to the possibility (in the logical sense) of phenomena which would form a scientific justification of the hypothesis of survival after death, and would permit an investigation by scientific methods of that form of life. To be sure, the hypothesis could never be established as absolutely true, but it shares this fate with all hypotheses. If it should be urged that the souls of the deceased might inhabit some supercelestial space where they would not be accessible to our perception, and that therefore the truth or falsity of the assertion could never be tested, the reply would be that if the words 'supercelestial space' are to have any meaning at all, that space must be defined in such a way that the impossibility of reaching it or of perceiving anything in it would be merely empirical, so that some means of overcoming the difficulties could at least be described, although it might be beyond human power to put them into use.

Thus our conclusion stands. The hypothesis of immortality is an empirical statement which owes its meaning to its verifiability, and it has no meaning beyond the possibility of verification. If it must be admitted that science could make no experiment the negative result of which would disprove it, this is true only in the same sense in which it is true for many other hypotheses of similar structure—especially those that have sprung

[7] [P. 142 of this volume.]

up from other motives than the knowledge of a great many facts of experience which must be regarded as giving a high probability to the hypothesis.

*   *   *

The question about the 'existence of the external world' will be discussed in the next section.

V

Let us now turn to a point of fundamental importance and the deepest philosophic interest. Professor Lewis refers to it as the "egocentric predicament", and he describes as one of the most characteristic features of logical positivism its attempt to take this predicament seriously. It seems to be formulated in the sentence (128 [8]), "Actually given experience is given in the first person", and its importance for the doctrine of logical positivism seems to be evident from the fact that Carnap, in his *Der logische Aufbau der Welt*, states that the method of this book may be called "methodological solipsism". Professor Lewis thinks, rightly, that the egocentric or solipsistic principle is not implied by our general principle of verifiability, and so he regards it as a second principle which, together with that of verifiability, leads, in his opinion, to the main results of the Viennese philosophy.

If I may be permitted to make a few general remarks here I should like to say that one of the greatest advantages and attractions of true positivism seems to me to be the antisolipsistic attitude which characterizes it from the very beginning. There is as little danger of solipsism in it as in any 'realism', and it seems to me to be the chief point of difference between idealism and positivism that the latter keeps entirely clear of the egocentric predicament. I think it is the greatest misunderstanding of the positivist idea (often even committed by thinkers who called themselves positivists) to see in it a tendency towards solipsism or a kinship to subjective idealism. We may regard Vaihinger's *Philosophy of As If* as a typical example of this mistake (he calls his book a "System of Idealistic Positivism"), and perhaps the philosophy of Mach and Avenarius as one of the most consistent attempts to avoid it. It is rather unfortunate that Carnap has advocated what he calls "methodological solipsism", and that in his construction of all concepts out of elementary data the "eigenpsychische Gegenstände" (for-me entities) come first and form the basis for the construction of physical objects, which finally lead to the concept of other selves; but if there is any mistake here it is chiefly in the terminology, not in the thought. "Methodological solipsism" is *not* a kind of solipsism, but a *method* of building up concepts. And it must be borne in mind that the order of construction which Carnap recommends—begin-

[8] [P. 130 of this volume.]

ning with "for-me entities"—is not asserted to be the only possible one. It would have been better to have chosen a different order, but in principle Carnap was well aware of the fact that original experience is "without a subject" (see Lewis, *loc. cit.*, 145 [9]).

The strongest emphasis should be laid on the fact that primitive experience is absolutely neutral or, as Wittgenstein has occasionally put it, that immediate data "have no owner". Since the genuine positivist denies (with Mach, etc.) that original experience "has that quality or status, characteristic of all given experience, which is indicated by the adjective 'first person' " (*loc. cit.*, 145 [10]), he cannot possibly take the 'egocentric predicament' seriously; for him this predicament does not exist. To see that primitive experience is *not* first-person experience seems to me to be one of the most important steps which philosophy must take towards the clarification of its deepest problems.

The unique position of the 'self' is not a basic property of all experience, but is itself a fact (among other facts) of experience. Idealism (as represented by Berkeley's "*esse = percipi*" or by Schopenhauer's "Die Welt ist meine Vorstellung") and other doctrines with egocentric tendencies commit the great error of mistaking the unique position of the ego, which is an empirical fact, for a logical, *a priori* truth, or, rather, substituting the one for the other. It is worth while to investigate this matter and analyse the sentence which seems to express the egocentric predicament. This will not be a digression, for without the clarification of this point it will be impossible to understand the basic position of our empiricism.

How does the idealist or the solipsist arrive at the statement that the world, as far as I know it, is 'my own idea', that ultimately I know nothing but the 'content of my own consciousness'?

Experience teaches that all immediate data depend in some way or other upon those data that constitute what I call 'my body'. All visual data disappear when the eyes of this body are closed; all sounds cease when its ears are stuffed up; and so on. This body is distinguished from the 'bodies of other beings' by the fact that it always appears in a peculiar perspective (its back or its eyes, for instance, never appear except in a looking glass); but this is not nearly so significant as the other fact that the quality of *all* data is conditioned by the state of the organs of this particular body. Obviously these two facts—and perhaps originally the first one—form the only reason why this body is called 'my' body. The possessive pronoun singles it out from among other bodies; it is an adjective which denotes the uniqueness described.

The fact that all data are dependent upon 'my' body (particularly those parts of it which are called 'sense-organs') induces us to form the concept of 'perception'. We do not find this concept in the language of unsophis-

[9] [P. 143 of this volume.]
[10] [P. 143 of this volume.]

ticated, primitive people; they do not say, 'I perceive a tree', but simply, 'there is a tree'. 'Perception' implies the distinction between a subject which perceives and an object which is perceived. Originally the perceiver is the sense-organ or the body to which it belongs, but since the body itself—including the nervous system—is also one of the perceived things, the original view is soon 'corrected' by substituting for the perceiver a new subject, which is called 'ego' or 'mind' or 'consciousness'. It is usually thought of as somehow residing *in* the body, because the sense-organs are on the surface of the body. The mistake of locating consciousness or mind inside the body ('in the head'), which has been called "introjection" by R. Avenarius, is the main source of the difficulties of the so-called 'mind-body problem'. By avoiding the error of introjection we avoid at the same time the idealistic fallacy which leads to solipsism. It is easy to show that introjection *is* an error. When I see a green meadow the 'green' is declared to be a content of my consciousness, but it certainly is not inside my head. Inside my skull there is nothing but my brain; and if there should happen to be a green spot in my brain, it would obviously not be the green of the meadow, but the green of the brain.

But for our purpose it is not necessary to follow this train of thought; it is sufficient to restate the facts clearly.

It is a fact of experience that all data depend in some way or other upon the state of a certain body which has the peculiarity that its eyes and its back are never seen (except by means of a mirror). It is usually called 'my' body; but here, in order to avoid mistakes, I shall take the liberty of calling it the body 'M'. A particular case of the dependence just mentioned is expressed by the sentence, 'I do not perceive anything unless the sense-organs of the body M are affected'. Or, taking a still more special case, I may make the following statement:

'I feel pain only when the body M is hurt.' (P)

I shall refer to this statement as 'proposition P'.

Now let us consider another proposition (Q):

'I can feel only my pain.' (Q)

The sentence Q may be interpreted in various ways. *Firstly*, it may be regarded as equivalent to P, so that P and Q would just be two different ways of expressing one and the same empirical fact. The word 'can' occurring in Q would denote what we have called 'empirical possibility', and the words 'I' and 'my' would refer to the body M. It is of the utmost importance to realize that in this first interpretation Q is the description of a fact of experience, i.e., a fact which we could very well imagine to be different.

We could easily imagine (here I am closely following ideas expressed by Mr. Wittgenstein) that I experience a pain every time the body of my friend is hurt, that I am gay when his face bears a joyful expression, that I feel tired after he has taken a long walk, or even that I do not see anything when his eyes are closed, and so forth. Proposition Q (if interpreted as being equivalent to P) denies that these things ever happen; but if they did happen, Q would be falsified. Thus we indicate the meaning of Q (or P) by describing facts which make Q true and other facts that would make it false. If facts of the latter kind occurred our world would be rather different from the one in which we are actually living; the properties of the 'data' would depend on other human bodies (or perhaps only one of them) as well as upon the body M.

This fictitious world may be empirically impossible, because incompatible with the actual laws of nature—though we cannot at all be sure of this—but it is logically possible, because we were able to give a description of it. Now let us for a moment suppose this fictitious world to be real. How would our language adapt itself to it? It might be done in two different ways which are of interest for our problem.

Proposition P would be false. As regards Q, there would be two possibilities. The first is to maintain that its meaning is still to be the same as that of P. In this case Q would be false and could be replaced by the true proposition,

'I can feel somebody else's pain as well as my own.'   (R)

R would state the empirical fact (which for the moment we suppose to be true) that the datum 'pain' occurs not only when M is hurt, but also when some injury is inflicted upon some other body, say, the body 'O'.

If we express the supposed state of affairs by the proposition R, there will evidently be no temptation and no pretext to make any 'solipsistic' statement. My body—which in this case could mean nothing but 'body M'—would still be unique in that it would always appear in a particular perspective (with invisible back, etc.), but it would no longer be unique as being the only body upon whose state depended the properties of all other data. And it was only this latter characteristic which gave rise to the egocentric view. The philosophic doubt concerning the 'reality of the external world' arose from the consideration that I had no knowledge of that world except by perception, i.e., by means of the sensitive organs of my body. If this is no longer true, if the data depend also on other bodies O (which differ from M in certain empirical respects, but not in principle), then there will be no more justification in calling the data 'my own'; other individuals O will have the same right to be regarded as owners or proprietors of the data. The sceptic was afraid that other bodies O might be nothing but images owned by the 'mind' belonging to the body M, because everything seemed to depend on the state of the latter; but under the circumstances described there exists perfect symmetry between O and M; the egocentric predicament has disappeared.

You will perhaps call my attention to the fact that the circumstances we have been describing are fictitious, that they do not occur in our real world, so that in this world, unfortunately, the egocentric predicament holds its sway. I answer that I wish to base my argument only on the fact that the difference between the two words is merely empirical, i.e., proposition P just happens to be true in the actual world as far as our experience goes. Its denial does not even seem to be incompatible with the known laws of nature; the probability which these laws give to the falsity of P is not zero.

Now if we still agree that proposition Q is to be regarded as identical with P (which means that 'my' is to be defined as referring to M), the word 'can' in Q will still indicate *empirical* possibility. Consequently, if a philosopher tried to use Q as the basis of a kind of solipsism, he would have to be prepared to see his whole construction falsified by some future experience. But this is exactly what the true solipsist *refuses* to do. He contends that no experience whatever could possibly contradict him, because it would always necessarily have the peculiar for-me character, which may be described by the 'egocentric predicament'. In other words, he is well aware that solipsism cannot be based on Q as long as Q is, by definition, nothing but another way of expressing P. As a matter of fact, the solipsist who makes the statement Q attaches a different meaning to the same words; he does not wish merely to assert P, but he intends to say something entirely different. The difference lies in the word 'my'. He does not want to define the personal pronoun by reference to the body M, but uses it in a much more general way. This leads us to ask: What meaning does he give to the sentence Q?

Let us examine this *second* interpretation which may be given to Q.

The idealist or solipsist who says, 'I can feel only my own pain', or, more generally, 'I can be aware only of the data of my own consciousness', believes that he is uttering a necessary, self-evident truth which no possible experience can force him to sacrifice. He will have to admit the possibility of circumstances such as those we described for our fictitious world; but, he will say, even if I feel pain every time when another body O is hurt, I shall never say, 'I feel O's pain', but always, 'My pain is in O's body'.

We cannot declare this statement of the idealist to be *false;* it is just a different way of adapting our language to the imagined new circumstances, and the rules of language are, in principle, arbitrary. But, of course, some uses of our words may recommend themselves as practical and well adapted; others may be condemned as misleading. Let us examine the idealist's attitude from this point of view.

He rejects our proposition R and replaces it by the other one:

'I can feel pain in other bodies as well as in my own.'   (S)

He wants to insist that any pain I feel must be called *my* pain, no matter where it is felt, and in order to assert this he says:

'I *can* feel only *my* pain.'   (T)

Sentence T is, as far as the words are concerned, the same as Q. I have used slightly different signs by having the words 'can' and 'my' printed in italics, in order to indicate that, when used by the solipsist, these two words have a signification which is different from the signification they had in Q when we interpreted Q as meaning the same as P. In T 'my pain' no longer means 'pain in body M', because, according to the solipsist's explanation, 'my pain' may also be in another body O; so we must ask: what does the pronoun 'my' signify here?

It is easy to see that it does not signify *anything;* it is a superfluous word which may just as well be omitted. 'I feel pain' and 'I feel my pain' are, according to the solipsist's definition, to have identical meaning; the word 'my', therefore, has no function in the sentence. If he says, 'The pain which I feel is my pain', he is uttering a mere tautology, because he has declared that whatever the empirical circumstances may be, he will never allow the pronouns 'your' or 'his' to be used in connection with 'I feel pain', but always the pronoun 'my'. This stipulation, being independent of empirical facts, is a logical rule, and if it is followed, T becomes a tautology; the word 'can' in T (together with 'only') does not denote empirical impossibility, but *logical* impossibility. In other words it would not be false, it would be *nonsense* (grammatically forbidden) to say 'I can feel somebody else's pain'. A tautology, being the negation of nonsense, is itself devoid of meaning in the sense that it does not assert anything, but merely indicates a rule concerning the use of words.

We infer that T, which is the second interpretation of Q, adopted by the solipsist and forming the basis of his argument, is strictly meaningless. It does not say anything at all, does not express any interpretation of the world or view about the world; it just introduces a strange way of speaking, a clumsy kind of language, which attaches the index 'my' (or 'content of my consciousness') to everything without exception. Solipsism is nonsense, because its starting-point, the egocentric predicament, is meaningless.

The words 'I' and 'my', if we use them according to the solipsist's prescription, are absolutely empty, mere adornments of speech. There would be no difference of meaning between the three expressions, 'I feel my pain'; 'I feel pain'; and 'there is pain'. Lichtenberg, the wonderful eighteenth-century physicist and philosopher, declared that Descartes had no right to start his philosophy with the proposition 'I think', instead of saying 'it thinks'. Just as there would be no sense in speaking of a white horse unless it were logically possible that a horse might *not* be white, so no sentence containing the words 'I' or 'my' would be meaningful unless we could replace them by 'he' or 'his' without speaking nonsense. But such a substitution is impossible in a sentence that would seem to express the egocentric predicament or the solipsistic philosophy.

R and S are not different explanations or interpretations of a certain state of affairs which we have described, but simply verbally different formulations of this description. It is of fundamental importance to see that R and S are not two propositions, but one and the same proposition in two different languages. The solipsist, by rejecting the language of R and insisting upon the language of S, has adopted a terminology which makes Q tautological, transforms it into T. Thus he has made it impossible to verify or falsify his own statements; he himself has deprived them of meaning. By refusing to avail himself of the opportunities (which we showed him) to make the statement 'I can feel somebody else's pain' meaningful, he has at the same time lost the opportunity of giving meaning to the sentence 'I can feel only my own pain'.

The pronoun 'my' indicates *possession;* we cannot speak of the 'owner' of a pain—or any other datum—except in cases where the word 'my' can be used meaningfully, i.e., where by substituting 'his' or 'your' we would get the description of a possible state of affairs. This condition is fulfilled if 'my' is defined as referring to the body M, and it would also be fulfilled if I agree to call 'my body' any body in which I can feel pain. In our actual world these two definitions apply to one and the same body, but that is an empirical fact which might be different. If the two definitions did not coincide and if we adopted the second one we should need a new word to distinguish the body M from other bodies in which I might have sensations; the word 'my' would have meaning in a sentence of the form 'A is one of my bodies, but B is not', but it would be meaningless in the statement 'I can feel pain only in my bodies', for this would be a mere tautology.

The grammar of the word 'owner' is similar to that of the word 'my': it makes sense only where it is logically possible for a thing to *change* its owner, i.e., where the relation between the owner and the owned object is empirical, not logical ('external', not 'internal'). Thus one could say 'Body M is the owner of this pain', or 'that pain is owned by the bodies M and O'. The second proposition can, perhaps, never be truthfully asserted in our actual world (although I cannot see that it would be incompatible with the laws of nature), but both of them would make sense. Their meaning would be to express certain relations of dependence between the pain and the state of certain bodies, and the existence of such a relation could easily be tested.

The solipsist refuses to use the word 'owner' in this sensible way. He knows that many properties of the data do not depend at all upon any states of human bodies, viz., all those regularities of their behavior that can be expressed by 'physical laws'; he knows, therefore, that it would be wrong to say 'my body is the owner of everything', and so he speaks of a 'self', or 'ego', or 'consciousness', and declares this to be the owner of everything. (The idealist, by the way, makes the same mistake when he asserts that we know nothing but 'appearances'.) This is nonsense because the word 'owner', when used in this way, has lost its meaning. The solipsistic assertion cannot be verified or falsified, it will be true by definition, whatever the facts may be; it simply consists in the verbal prescription to add the phrase 'owned by Me' to the names of all objects, etc.

Thus we see that unless we choose to call our body the owner or bearer of the data—which seems to be a rather misleading expression—we have to say that the data *have no owner* or bearer. This neutrality of experience —as against the subjectivity claimed for it by the idealist—is one of the most fundamental points of true positivism. The sentence 'All experience is first-person experience' will either mean the simple empirical fact that all data are in certain respects dependent on the state of the nervous system of my body M, or it will be meaningless. Before this physiological fact is discovered, experience is not 'my' experience at all, it is self-sufficient and does not 'belong' to anybody. The proposition 'The ego is the centre of the world' may be regarded as an expression of the same fact, and has meaning only if it refers to the body. The concept of 'ego' is a construction put upon the same fact, and we could easily imagine a world in which this concept would not have been formed, where there would be no idea of an insurmountable barrier between what is inside the Me and what is outside of it. It would be a world in which occurrences like those corresponding to proposition R and similar ones were the rule, and in which the facts of 'memory' were not so pronounced as they are in our actual world. Under those circumstances we should not be tempted to fall into the 'egocentric predicament', but the sentence which tries to express such a predicament would be meaningless under *any* circumstances.

*   *   *

After our last remarks it will be easy to deal with the so-called problem concerning the existence of the external world. If, with Professor Lewis (143 [11]), we formulate the 'realistic' hypothesis by asserting, "If all minds should disappear from the universe, the stars would still go on in their courses", we must admit the impossibility of verifying it, but the impossibility is merely *empirical*. And the empirical circumstances are such that we have every reason to believe the hypothesis to be true. We are as sure of it as of the best founded physical laws that science has discovered.

As a matter of fact, we have already pointed out that there are certain regularities in the world which experience shows to be entirely independent of what happens to human beings on the earth. The laws of motion of the celestial bodies are formulated entirely without reference

[11] [P. 142 of this volume.]

to any human bodies, and *this is the reason* why we are justified in maintaining that they will go on in their courses after mankind has vanished from the earth. Experience shows no connection between the two kinds of events. We observe that the course of the stars is no more changed by the death of human beings than, say, by the eruption of a volcano, or by a change of government in China. Why should we suppose that there would be any difference if all living beings on our planet, or indeed everywhere in the universe, were extinguished? There can be no doubt that on the strength of empirical evidence the existence of living beings is no necessary condition for the existence of the rest of the world.

The question 'Will the world go on existing after I am dead?' has no meaning unless it is interpreted as asking 'Does the existence of the stars etc. depend upon the life or death of a human being?', and this question is answered in the negative by experience. The mistake of the solipsist or idealist consists in rejecting this empirical interpretation and looking for some metaphysical issue behind it; but all their efforts to construct a new sense of the question end only in depriving it of its old one.

It will be noticed that I have taken the liberty of substituting the phrase 'if all living beings disappeared from the universe' for the phrase 'if all *minds* disappeared from the universe'. I hope it will not be thought that I have changed the meaning of the issue by this substitution. I have avoided the word 'mind' because I take it to signify the same as the words 'ego' or 'consciousness', which we have found to be so dark and dangerous. By living beings I meant beings capable of perception, and the concept of perception had been defined only by reference to living *bodies*, to physical organs. Thus I was justified in substituting 'death of living beings' for 'disappearance of minds'. But the arguments hold for any empirical definition one may choose to give for 'mind'. I need only point out that, according to experience, the motion of the stars, etc., is quite independent of all 'mental' phenomena such as feeling joy or sorrow, meditating, dreaming, etc.; and we may infer that the course of the stars would not be affected if those phenomena should cease to exist.

But is it true that this inference could be verified by experience? Empirically it seems to be impossible, but we know that only logical possibility of verification is required. And verification without a 'mind' is logically possible on account of the 'neutral', impersonal character of experience on which we have insisted. Primitive experience, mere existence of ordered data, does not presuppose a 'subject', or 'ego', or 'Me', or 'mind'; it can take place without any of the facts which lead to the formation of those concepts; it is not an experience of anybody. It is not difficult to imagine a universe without plants and animals and human bodies (including the body M), and without the mental phenomena just referred to: it would certainly be a 'world without minds' (for what else could deserve this name?), but the laws of nature might be exactly the same as in our actual world. We could describe this universe in terms of our actual experience (we would only have to leave out all terms referring to human bodies and emotions); and that is sufficient to speak of it as a world of possible experience.

The last considerations may serve as an example of one of the main theses of true positivism: that the naïve representation of the world, as the man in the street sees it, is perfectly correct; and that the solution of the great philosophical issues consists in returning to this original world-view, after having shown that the troublesome problems arose only from an inadequate description of the world by means of a faulty language.

* * *

Messrs. Schlick and Ayer on Immortality *

VIRGIL C. ALDRICH

These remarks do not aim at the final solution of a problem, but rather at a clear formulation of a problem. They are designed to stimulate a discussion which may throw light on a methodological issue which is still in the dark. Furthermore, though there may seem to be an air of impertinence about them, considering the recent tragic death of Mr. Schlick, they are intended, quite to the contrary, as a diffident reminder of the important work of that great man. . . .

Ayer writes: "The questions with which philosophy is concerned are purely logical questions; and although people do in fact dispute about logical questions, such disputes are always unwarranted. . . . In all such cases we may be sure that one party to the dispute has been guilty of a miscalculation which a sufficiently close scrutiny of the reasoning will enable us to detect" (*Language, Truth and Logic*, 209, 210).

We are all familiar with the dispute among the logical analysts themselves concerning the sort of verification to which "protocol" statements are subject, the 'leftists' or Carnapians—Ayer is one of them—holding that they are corrigible, and the 'rightists' or Wittgensteinians—of which group Schlick is a member—holding that such statements are unquestionably true. But not all of us are aware that this difference of opinion appears, in another quarter of the general theory of logical positivism, as a disagreement as to what "sentences" make empirical sense. The leftist contention that *every* significant sentence is modified at least in part by the logical syntax of the language (or by definition in a special sense) and the rightist belief that the meaning and truth of some sentences are ascertained by purely empirical considerations, result in an interesting civil war within the positivists' camp. Fortunately, Schlick and Ayer have both investigated statements concerning immortality. Let us take this as a test-case and review their conflicting treatments of it, to substantiate our suspicion of too much flexibility in their theory of meaning. Perhaps we can, in the spirit of Ayer's statement quoted above, comment on the issue in a manner which will help us to decide who has been "guilty of a miscalculation".

* Reprinted by kind permission of the author and the editors from *The Philosophical Review*, 47, 1938.

We begin with some quotations from Schlick: "I can easily imagine, e.g., witnessing the funeral of my own body, for nothing is easier than to describe a world which differs from our ordinary world only in the complete absence of all data which I would call parts of my own body. We must conclude that immortality [as simply survival, not eternal life, after death] should not be regarded as a metaphysical problem, but as an empirical hypothesis, because it possesses logical verifiability [is verifiable *in principle*]" (*Philosophical Review*, July 1936, p. 356 [1]). Continuing: "There cannot be the slightest doubt as to the possibility (in the logical sense) of phenomena which would form a scientific justification of the hypothesis of survival after death, and would permit an investigation by scientific methods of that form of life" (*op. cit.*, 357 [2]).

In flat opposition to all this, Ayer says: "It is self-contradictory to speak of a man as surviving the annihilation of his body. For that which is supposed to survive . . . is not the empirical self [which is inconceivable apart from the body] but a metaphysical entity—the soul. And this metaphysical entity, concerning which no genuine hypothesis can be formulated, has no logical connection whatsoever with the self" (*op. cit.*, 198). Ayer achieves this result by giving a *definition* of the self and personal identity which involves a reference to somatic sense-contents (194) and, since definitions are analytic or tautologous and therefore incontrovertible, it is a contradiction in terms to speak of a bodiless self.

Now Schlick also, in his analysis of solipsism (*op. cit.*, 358–367 [3]), asserts a connection between the conscious self and its body, but *only as an empirical fact*. He does not *define* consciousness with its sensory elements in terms which link it logically, *i.e.*, necessarily, with a body. Thus he can, with empirical significance, assert the sentence, "Consciousness sometimes survives bodily annihilation", since he can *imagine* such a state of affairs. Such a circumstance is therefore logically possible, not logically self-contradictory.

Presumably, Ayer would challenge Schlick to make empirically intelligible his concept of a bodiless self. Schlick need only reiterate that his conscious self or his field of consciousness as bodiless would have the same sensory components it now has, with the exception of only the bodily sensa. And it is easy to imagine such a self, as in the case of witnessing the funeral of his own body or even the complete annihilation of his own body. Schlick might point out, furthermore, that just as Ayer has made empirical sense of the assertion that a material thing exists independently of any conscious self or mind (p. 234 of *Language, Truth and Logic*), so, by allowing for *possible* sense contents and hypothetical constructions of them, the assertion of immortality is a significant empirical hypothesis,

---

[1] [Pp. 159 f. of this volume.]
[2] [P. 160 of this volume.]
[3] [Pp. 161 ff. of this volume.]

even if it be actually false. In short, it is a proposition, not a pseudo-proposition.

We do not care to assume the embarrassing rôle of judge of this dispute between two logical analysts, both of whom are by profession specialists in arbitration. We shall adopt the more prudent procedure of indicating what we consider to be some of the steps to be taken toward the solution of the difficulty.

First, Ayer must make good his contention that the above dispute is purely logical, to be settled by a more careful "calculation" on the part of Schlick. When he has done this, Ayer must further show that his "definition" of the empirical self and personal identity in terms involving bodily sensa is the only one compatible with the linguistic conventions of English-speaking people or the only one making empirical sense in that reference-frame. (Ayer shows at every turn that he is very anxious to entertain only such definitions as are compatible with actual linguistic usage. For example, he rejects a naturalistic ethics on the ground that a reduction of obligation-statements to factual statements violates the ordinary meaning of 'ought'. See op. cit., 154.) This step would get him to where it becomes necessary to define "convention" and describe in detail its operation upon or through the "creative activity" (217) of the defining agent. The need for a syntactical analysis—or empirical description—of the symbol "convention" and what it stands for is widely felt among the appraisers of the new positivism. (See Miss Stebbing's review of Ayer's book in Mind, July 1936, p. 364. Also Nagel: "Impressions and Appraisals of Analytic Philosophy in Europe", The Journal of Philosophy, Jan. 16, 1936, p. 45. Also Von Juhos: "Empiricism and Physicalism", in Analysis, June 1935, where the issue is raised from the Schlick-group's point of view.)

Second, Schlick must find some evidence for the fact that his powers of imagination are not supernormal, and then get Ayer to agree that what is imaginable is verifiable in principle, hence perhaps factually significant. (It appears that Ayer considers the question, 'What is imaginable?' as a psychological, not a logical question; since he raises it nowhere in his book. And he may be right.) Moreover, if Schlick can successfully reprimand Ayer for having fixed the nature of the body-mind relation by definition rather than by empirical observation, they will both be on the way to an understanding. Ayer at present believes that all answers to any question of the form, 'What is the nature of x?' are conventional, tautologous and in that sense "necessary" definitions (65), such that, indirectly if not directly, the solution of the dispute about immortality depends simply on how "self" is defined. Schlick, with his different estimate of the hypothesis of immortality, must show either that the nature of the connection between mind and body is incorrectly defined by Ayer or that it is not to be determined by definition at all—instead, by empirical observation.

This survey has been made in the sympathetic belief that the neo-positivistic principle, "No meaningful problem can be insoluble in principle", is sound. And it results in the impression that the neo-positivists themselves are laboring with a too flexible or inarticulate theory of meaning and experience. On the one hand, they disagree as to what is empirically significant; and on the other as to what is experienceable. Since empirical significance is determined at least in part by what can in principle be experienced, the two above considerations are really one. According to Schlick, simple sense-data are not the only objects of direct "ostensive" definitions but also certain "complex situations", denoted ostensively by such symbols as "immediate", "chance", "again", etc. (*op. cit.*, 342–343 [4]). But Ayer allows only "sense-contents" the status of objects of ostensive experience, all else being logical constructions. In short, Schlick can "experience", in a genuine though attenuated sense, being immortal; Ayer cannot. What are they going to do about it?

As to who is "guilty of a miscalculation" we have not ascertained. Our guess is that Schlick's broader conception of what can be experienced is more in accord with actual linguistic usage or convention, but that this stand of his is an unconsciously camouflaged departure from the *positivistic* principle of empirical verifiability and meaning. On the other hand, Ayer's narrower conception of the empirical, truer though it be to radical phenomenalism and radical conventionalism, and more rigorously formulated than Schlick's, makes nonsense of much of what is *imaginable* in the ordinary sense. And since what can be imagined is very commonly recognized as empirically *significant* though not always *true*, Ayer should either (1) give us better proof that we cannot really imagine such states of affairs as being immortal, or (2) prove that imagination is not sufficient for empirical meaning contrary to general belief, or (3) show that some imaginable states of affairs are empirically significant and others, such as immortality, not.

Any honest philosopher wants, when he puts pen to paper, or opens his mouth, to make theoretical sense. The Logical Analysts have awakened in him the wholesome but dreadful suspicion that maybe he is writing or saying nothing. This paralyzes him intellectually. And the paralysis will linger until some definite and commonly acceptable criterion of sense and nonsense is uncovered. Naturally, he depends on logical analysts—the specialists in theory of meaning—for the discovery. The whole of current philosophy is feeling and will feel the shock of the failure of the Logical Positivists themselves to settle this issue in their own camp.

[4] [P. 148 of this volume.]

Pictorial Meaning and Picture Thinking *

VIRGIL C. ALDRICH

I

Professor Charles W. Morris, in his essay "Empiricism, Religion, and Democracy," writes:

Imagine a community of men living on a cell in the blood stream of one of us, but so small that we have no evidence, direct or indirect, of their existence. Imagine further that they themselves are provided with scientific instruments of the type we use, and possess a method of science and a body of scientific knowledge comparable to ours. One of the bolder of these thinkers proposes that the universe they inhabit is a Great Man. Is this hypothesis admissible on scientific grounds or is it to be laughed down by the Minute Empiricists on the ground that it is "metaphysical"? We Macroscopic Empiricists would at least seem to have to favor the hypothesis! But then why at our own level cannot a similar hypothesis be raised: namely, that *we* are parts of a Great Man, the whole of our known universe being perhaps but a portion of the Great Blood Stream? . . . The liberal empiricist I have championed would side with the Minute Empiricists in asserting that the hypothesis is empirically meaningful since the properties ascribed to the Great Man would be properties drawn from objects that had been observed; he would merely say that in terms of evidence available to them this hypothesis was too poorly confirmed to have a place in their system of scientific knowledge.[1]

I have quoted Morris at length, because the excerpt highlights the point to the examination of which this essay is given, namely, the concept of "empirically significant possibilities" and a way of treating it which persists despite recent refinements in the general theory of meaning—a way I take to be inadequate. If as competent a specialist in the theory of signs as Morris (and C. I. Lewis) can go wrong on this count, it is little wonder that the mistake is such a common one among those who have given the matter less systematic attention. The matter concerns a kind of meaning, or a way of using language, that has not been isolated with sufficient rigor from other kinds, the result being a tendency to accommodate it under the general category of cognitive sense, to the detriment of both kinds, as we shall see. The ill-advised mixture converts both into renegades that frequently lead inquiry and discussion into an impasse.

* Reprinted by kind permission of the author and the editors from *The Kenyon Review*, 5, 1943.
[1] *Conference on Science, Philosophy and Religion*, New York, p. 219.

Another illustration—and yet others later—will help us to detect, isolate, and tag the new kind of sense.

Suppose someone—whom we shall call Typical Tom—says there is a little blue devil in his watch. We open it and find nothing but the usual mechanism. Tom says the little devil disappears into thin air the moment the watch is opened. We then weigh the watch, when it is open and again when it is closed, noticing no difference in weight. Tom says the little blue imp, like any genuine spirit, is an immaterial and therefore imponderable substance. Then we observe that the watch keeps time accurately, which would be unlikely with a blue devil inside, getting its tail and legs caught in the gears and hairspring. Well, we can guess what Tom says to that. And so on.

To such a position as Tom's there are four usual reactions. The first, and least cautious, is the assertion that Tom's blue-devil utterance is patently false. But a plainly false expression is, by definition, one that can be disproved; and there is *no* way to disprove, there is *no* evidence against, what Tom says. The second reaction to it is the more cautious objection that he's talking nonsense—making "pure nonsense," which explains our inability to prove the falsity of his utterance. But even little children could clearly understand—and be delighted by—Tom's remark, and would clamor for its expansion into a story about the little blue devil. So evidently Tom has made himself intelligible in some sense. A third reaction might be the suggestion that Tom's utterance is indeed significant but only with motivational or emotive meaning. (In Morris' own terminology, one might say Tom's expression contains "motivators" or "expressors," but no "referors.") But Tom correctly points out that, for him, the blue-devil utterance did not express a mood or feeling, neither was it aimed at getting somebody to do something.

Suppose now we ask Tom how he *knows* that a little blue devil haunts his watch, pointing out that one can *imagine* the presence or absence of anything in it. He then concedes that his original statement, "It is *true* that there is a little blue devil in my watch," is too strong, and weakens it to read, "It is just *possible* that there is . . . etc."

This, I take it, is the position that Morris would assume, adding of course, as he did in the Blood Stream case, that the blue-devil hypothesis is "too poorly confirmed to have a place in the system of scientific knowledge." Moreover, this conclusion seems in general so harmless from any point of view—that of the scientist, artist, speculative cosmologist, theologian, moralist—that it is the one most commonly arrived at. It has, in addition, the air of being "liberal," in as much as it seems to give the speculative imagination the important place it apparently has even in the field of scientific inquiry. Such difficulties as the position has appear only after analysis of meaning has been pressed beyond the province of specific interests. For general methodology, pressing the analysis further is crucial and shows the way out of verbal predicaments even on the level of common discourse—predicaments that are simply battered down out of the way (instead of being solved) by disputants who don't understand them. So let us try to formulate—here necessarily in a rough and popular way—certain distinctions.

The main point we are going to make is that Tom's utterance, "It is possible that there is a little blue devil in the watch," is comparable to the expression, "It is possible that please go away." As the expression "please go away" does not make cognitive sense—it is neither true nor false—but motivational, so the expression "There is a little blue devil in the watch" does not make cognitive sense but (what we shall call) *pictorial* sense. Our task now is to so define pictorial meaning as to disengage it from the cognitive with which it is so readily confused, and to explain why the confusion is so prevalent. With this task we now come to grips.

Discourse frequently takes a turn that makes argument concerning its subject-matter irrelevant. But this happens in at least two quite different ways. That there is a grain of sand in the watch is arguable. That there is a neutrino in the watch is also appropriately argued. But people would naturally refuse even to argue the proposition that the mechanism of the watch consists of nothing but thirteen hydrogen atoms, because the proposition is too plainly false. They would be annoyed with anyone who would continue elaborating such a position. This is *one* way in which argument becomes irrelevant. But suppose it were said that the watch is the cosy habitat of an army of a million little archers, each armored in mother-of-pearl and bearing a bow made of a splinter of diamond, all too small ever to be observed; and when the watch is closed it is filled with a soft, iridescent radiance—the light of their world; each tick of the watch marks off a day in their lives and an hour a life-span; they are unerring marksmen, capable in that twilight of knocking the spinning electrons out of their orbits with their golden arrows . . . .

Now in this case also we would find argument irrelevant, but is it because the utterance is too plainly false, or, in Morris' words, "too poorly confirmed"? This would be an inadequate estimate, since there is *no* possible evidence against the utterance, and it may be "poorly confirmed" in the sense that "please go away" is poorly confirmed, neither expression being the sort with respect to which the demand for evidence is relevant.

But the important point is that in this case of the archer, far from being annoyed at the elaboration of such a position, we *want more*. It is as if the sense that is now being made lies in a different dimension of meaning, or differs in kind, from that of the expressions concerning the grain of sand, the neutrino, and the thirteen hydrogen atoms. We have shifted gears into a different form of discourse, which in its own way may be highly intelligible and even important (if charged also with emotive and motivational significance) without formulating an empirically significant "possibility" awaiting confirmation. We shall call such meaning "pictorial" and we call its formulation "picture thinking."

One is tempted to object that all four of the above expressions formulate empirically significant possibilities, the only difference being that the archer possibility is so much more picturesque than the others (sand, neutrino, etc.) that we naturally incline to contemplate and enjoy it for its own sake, thus ignoring the question—which nevertheless remains relevant—of its truth or falsity. In short, it formulates an empirically significant possibility.

The answer to this hinges mostly on a terminological issue: people who say that a sentence formulates an "empirically possible" state of affairs usually mean that it is true or false and that some day it *might* be confirmed or infirmed. (This, I take it, is what Morris means; it is true or false that there are little men on a blood cell in one of us, and if we had fine enough instruments and if there *are* little men on blood cells, we would detect their existence, etc.) But the archer-situation has been so couched (or could be) as not only to make proof or disproof impossible but to make the demand for either irrelevant, while retaining a very clearcut intelligibility of the pictorial sort. We conclude, therefore, that language can be used with the primary intention of expressing or evoking pictures (imagery), and in a way that differs from the sign usage that formulates empirically significant possibilities.

So far, our illustrations have involved cases where the pictorial intent is so salient as to be fairly readily distinguished from the cognitive or empirical. We don't ordinarily argue the blue devil or archer utterances because we "get," by a kind of linguistic instinct or habitual propriety, what the speaker primarily means by them. His primary intention is obvious, namely, to tease and entertain us (and himself) with pictures that, as verbally treated by him, have nothing to do even with *possibilities* for matters of fact.

II

But pictorial sense can be made of practically anything, and *this may be the only kind of sense that is being made even where the aim is to make statements about matters of fact.* It is in such cases that disputants reach an impasse, which blocks them until a distinction is made between the pictorial and the cognitive content of the expression in question. Instances of such predicaments are common. Let us examine some.

We are looking at a scarf and "observe" that, in a certain light, it is "red." Typical Tom says that maybe it isn't "really" red. We call in others to take a look, or ourselves look more closely, or even make measurements of wave-frequency, etc., getting a confirmation of our judgment. But Tom says that what he means by "red" is a visual sensation in each one of our minds and, for all we will ever know, no two of these sensations are alike. Yours may actually be blue while mine is green, though both of us have been taught to say "red" when we are aware of these color patches as data in our minds.

Now it would be a mistake to say wholesale that Tom is talking nonsense. He evidently "means" something by these remarks and, moreover, most of us "get" something at the receiver's end of the communication. What is evoked in most of us by the utterance is a set of pictures, such as two non-overlapping, translucent spheres ("minds") inside one of which we imagine a tiny blue patch and a green patch in the other, as effects of streams of light radiation reaching the spheres from a common external source. Then, if we imagine each of these spheres as hovering near the head of a human organism which says "red" when the color patch appears in its sphere, the picture is complete, and we have understood what Tom said. But his primary intention in this case is to say something that might be true of matter of fact, something that is "just possible." Has he succeeded in this? The fact that he has not said anything demonstrably *false* must not, it should be remembered, be taken by itself as a sign of his having formulated an empirically significant possibility, for reasons noted above. An examination of what Tom put across by his utterance shows that he has made himself intelligible in the dimension of pictorial meaning. But that he has made sense of any other than the blue devil kind is doubtful. And if, objecting to the picturesque turn we have given his expression, he attempts a "literal" interpretation, he will, in this quest for its empirical (cognitive) meaning, find himself looking in a dark room for a black cat that isn't there. ("Attempting a literal interpretation" means, of course, trying to get the expression coördinated with some matters of fact that serve as evidence for or against it; but it has been so worded as to preclude this possibility.) It is the function of the philosophical analyst to show Tom that, with respect to cognitive significance, he has failed to understand himself, since, in that dimension of meaning, he has either said nothing, or something so ill-defined as to be unintelligible without preliminary (and perhaps strange) linguistic conventions. But this, of course, does not militate against the intelligibility of the expression in its dimension of pictoral significance.

Current discussion of the dimensions of space provide us with another illustration of how one may make pictorial sense only, while intending to say something true about matters of fact. People say they "observe" up to three dimensions, but can't even "imagine" a fourth. Typical Tom, associating the "possible" with the "imaginable," concludes from this that the hyperspace theorists don't know what they are talking about. (Even Poincaré suggests that someday we may be able, after strenuous exercise, to "imagine a fourth dimension," whereupon non-Euclidean geometry will possibly become more "convenient" than the Euclidean.) But this is to make the mistake of supposing that when we say, "Space has n dimensions," the pictures evoked by the expression define its cognitive meaning. Strictly speaking, the cognitive sense even of the expression, "Space has three dimensions," is left untouched by what one can or can't imagine: what this expression means empirically, through operational definitions, is as "unimaginable" as the one about four or more dimensions. Or, putting it yet another way, the sense in which three dimensions *can* be "observed" or "imagined" is precisely the sense in which the fourth dimension can be observed or imagined; in both cases, something is to be observed that proves or disproves the propositions about space, and in the same general way.

The writings of Jeans and Eddington are a fertile source of illustrations of our point about pictorial meaning. "There is a mysterious world outside us to which our minds can never penetrate"; an "inscrutable absolute behind appearances," etc. The analysis of such expressions in the light of the distinction made above is obvious, so we shall not here give them special attention. Our moral is that one should be on guard against the little blue devil, since he can assume many shapes and, if undetected, bedevil discourse in a very tantalizing way.

But special attention should be given something that so far we have dealt with only implicitly. From an inspection of linguistic properties or grammatical form alone, one cannot safely tell what the primary intention of the speaker is. Typical Tom, upon looking into the watch or into a Mexican jumping bean and seeing no little blue devils, might well have admitted at once that he was wrong. This would show that he not only intended to make empirical (factual) sense, but actually did. He was construing "blue devil" in a factually significant way. On the other hand, blue-devil sense (pictorial) might readily be made even of the expression about the grain of sand in the watch. Tom might teasingly say, upon not observing one inside, that there is one there anyway, only of a peculiar invisible sort, etc. This is what we meant by saying that practically anything can be construed pictorially, in a way that does not limit or define even a *possible* state of affairs for matters of fact. Thus, pictorial sense can be made even of objects in the field of sense-perception, and the artist makes a profession of this. Morris' mistake was the initial one of supposing that his little-men hypothesis about an object of perception, namely a blood cell, formulated an empirically significant possibility. From this mistaken assumption he argued the cognitive significance of the hypothesis of our being caught in a Cosmic Blood Stream or parts of a Great Man.

Traditionally, "theory" and "cognition" (knowledge) have meant something involving contemplation and spectacle—"vision," with emphasis on picture-thinking and pictorial meaning. This essay would be properly doomed to the limbo of all dogmatisms if its thesis were either that the words "theory" and "knowledge" and "cognitive significance" *cannot* mean these things, or that pictorially significant sign-usage is unimportant.

Its thesis is, rather, that since even the traditional theorists tended to argue what they called "theories," and since pictorial meaning is intrinsically non-arguable, as we have seen after isolating it from another sort that is arguable, we had better let "theory" and "cognitive meaning" involve this latter kind of sense and preclude the former. There is nothing anti-liberal in such a proposal. Indeed, it is aimed at liberating both the intellect and the imagination each for its special task. It explains, moreover, the sense one has of "understanding" an expression before it is in any way cognitively coördinated with matters of fact—such understanding being a grasp of pictorial significance.

The popular (and half true) notion that even the task of the scientist is implemented by a lively imagination here calls for comment. It has been noted that we have not, existentially speaking, drawn a line between a "field (or realm) of imagination" and a "field of sense-perception," confining the scientist to the latter. In fact, we flout the distinction by saying that, given *any* item, whether perceived or imagined, then either pictorial or cognitive sense can be made of it, according to the way in which it is construed and articulated. That is why much of the experimental work of the great scientist can be (and usually is) of the armchair variety. Not that he is, in such moments, doing what the poet or artist does, but rather that he is articulating imagined states of affairs in empirically (factually) significant propositions. This is the crucial difference. The notion that the great theorist is necessarily half-poet is mistaken and misleading. Of course, he may also be a poet, but not with respect to theoretic acumen. Much of the published work of theorists such as Eddington, Montague, Santayana, and others, great though it is as a provocative for thought and imagination, is marred by the failure to distinguish theorizing from picture thinking.

The Scientific World-Perspective *

KASIMIR AJDUKIEWICZ

In the following, a line of thought is sketched which, though lacking rigor of formulation, is perhaps suitable as it stands for initiating a discussion of certain questions which constantly confront us as we work in our circle of problems, and which questions can be brought nearer solution by a thorough airing.

Every scientific judgment and every scientific question is composed of concepts. These concepts are linguistically pinned down, and constitute the meaning of language expressions. Now, the meanings of the expressions of a language involve certain criteria to which one must conform in accepting or rejecting sentences composed of the expressions if one is not to do violence to these meanings. We shall call these criteria meaning-rules of the language. (In this connection, see K. Ajdukiewicz, "Sprache und Sinn", *Erkenntnis*, 4, pp. 100 ff.)

A rule of this kind for the English language demands, for example, that one be ready to accept without further ado every sentence of the form "Every A is an A". Should anybody reject a sentence of this form, should he, for example, say with conviction "Not every man is a man", this would be an infallible indication that though the person in question made use of English syllables, he does not attach to them *the* meaning which belongs to them in the English language. Another meaning-rule of the English language states that anyone who has accepted as true a conditional sentence of the form "If a then b" together with the antecedent "a", and bearing this acceptance in mind rejects the consequent "b" as false, can only do this if he does not attach to the connective "if, then" its assigned English meaning. A final example: if anyone has a sharp toothache and simultaneously denies with conviction the sentence "It hurts", he can only do this if he does not attach to the sentence "It hurts" the meaning which belongs to it in English.

That there exist such meaning-rules seems to me to be perfectly evident. Furthermore we tacitly make use of these rules as premises when we note that somebody misuses words, that is, employs them otherwise than in their prescribed sense. If we suspect somebody of a misuse of a given word,

---

* Translated from the German by W. S.; reprinted by kind permission of the author and the publisher from *Erkenntnis*, 6, 1935.

we induce him to answer on certain suppositions (or even without these) a question in answering which he will use this word. If the answer to this question takes—as we see it—a turn contrary to sense, we see in this fact an infallible indication that the person in question has used words in other than the prescribed meaning.

There are three kinds of meaning-rules. To the first kind belong those which demand an unconditional readiness to accept certain sentences. This is what was done, for example, by the first of the meaning-rules we have cited. Meaning-rules of the first kind I call *axiomatic meaning-rules*, since by them are specified the sentences in a language which have the status of axioms.

Meaning-rules of the second kind demand a readiness to accept certain sentences, not unconditionally, but only on the supposition that certain other sentences are accepted. Such meaning-rules I call *deductive meaning-rules*, as by them the modes of deductive inference are determined. In the language of symbolic logic, detachment and substitution are examples of these modes of inference involved in the meaning of symbols.

The third kind of meaning-rule demands the readiness to accept certain sentences in the presence of certain data of experience. I call such rules *empirical meaning-rules*, as by them are specified sentences which can be established with certainty, in a purely empirical way.

The totality of meaning-rules of a language in conjunction with certain data of experience sets apart certain sentences of this language together with the judgments which constitute their meaning. In the first place, there are the sentences which are to be accepted according to the axiomatic meaning-rules, and which are set apart by the fact that one cannot reject them as false if one attaches to them the meaning which they possess in the language in question. In the second place, there are the sentences which are set apart by the empirical meaning-rules and the data of experience as those which cannot be rejected in the face of those data of experience, without violating the meaning which belongs to them in that language. The third class of sentences which are set apart is constituted by the totality of those sentences which are derivable in accordance with the deductive meaning-rules from the sentences thus set apart by axiomatic and empirical meaning-rules.

The totality of all sentences in a given language which are set apart in one or the other of the three ways indicated above by the meaning-rules of that language together with certain data of experience, we call the *world-perspective (corresponding to those experiential data) of that language.*

We shall call the totality of the judgments which make up the meaning of those sentences which belong to the world-perspective of a language (which world-perspective corresponds to certain data of experience) *the world-perspective (corresponding to these data) of the conceptual apparatus* out of which is built the meaning of the expressions of the language in question.

Sentences which belong to the world-perspective of a language constitute (ultimately, with certain qualifications) the indubitable component of the knowledge of anyone who makes use of that language. The sentences dictated by the axiomatic meaning-rules can under no circumstances be rejected as long as they are used in the sense prescribed by the language. The sentences dictated by the empirical meaning-rules can often be rejected without violating their meaning; this, however, only when the corresponding data of experience are not present. In the presence of such data of experience, the rejection of these sentences is possible only if one attaches to them a meaning other than assigned them in the language in question. Those sentences belonging to the world-perspective of a language at which one can arrive from the axiomatic or empirical sentences in accordance with deductive meaning-rules can also often be rejected without doing violence to their meaning. If, however, one accepts exactly those sentences which a deductive meaning-rule coördinates as premises with these sentences as conclusions, the latter cannot be rejected without doing violence to their meaning.

In a given language the world-perspective coördinated with a set of data of experience is thus made up of sentences which at least potentially constitute the unshakeable component of the knowledge which can be achieved by making use of this language or its corresponding conceptual apparatus. This knowledge, however, need not be restricted to those sentences already gained in accordance with the meaning-rules of the language; for it can also include sentences which are accepted, although, on the basis of the hitherto achieved portion of the world-perspective and the hitherto enjoyed data of experience, they are not demanded (nor forbidden) by any meaning-rule of the language. To this class of cognitions belong all sentences accepted on the basis of inductive inference. With its help, we attempt to piece together by way of anticipation the as yet unknown parts of the world-perspective.

The world-perspective is a function of two factors. On the one hand, it depends on the material of experience, which is its foundation; on the other hand, it depends on the conceptual apparatus, and the meaning-rules that are bound up with it. The first part of this assertion is obvious. The second, however, is no less clear. A change in conceptual apparatus is reflected in a change in the problems which one solves on the basis of the same data of experience. Different sciences make use of different conceptual structures which can only partially coincide. But even one and the same science changes its conceptual apparatus in the course of its historical development. This change, however, is often concealed by the fact that while the concepts are changed, the words remain the same.

As long as one makes use of a limited conceptual apparatus, which does not exclude an enrichment, one can only arrive, however completely one exploits the material of experience, at a world-perspective, and never to a complete world-picture. Thus, if anyone limits his conceptual apparatus, and rejects certain modes of enriching it, he is putting on blinkers and deliberately neglects certain portions of the world-picture; that is to say, he contents himself with the contemplation of a selected world-perspective.

Now it seems to us that science as a whole is taking this course. It chooses its conceptual apparatus along certain lines, and rejects every enlargement which runs counter to these lines. We shall give examples to back up this assertion.

The conceptual apparatus is determined by the establishment of the meaning-rules. Now, meaning-rules can be so chosen that by following them on the basis of enjoyed data of experience, or, in other cases, immanently, that is without reference to data of experience, we are led to contradiction. We can determine concepts by laying down axiomatic and deductive meaning-rules. The building of concepts in formalized deductive systems proceeds in this manner. However, a conceptual apparatus can be constructed along these lines which is associated with meaning-rules which lead to contradiction. Science rejects such a building of concepts, and seizes upon different prescriptions (for example the theory of types) in order to protect itself from such conceptual structures which lead to contradiction. This, however, is a deliberate restriction of conceptual apparatus.

The empirical portion of the scientific conceptual apparatus has arisen in a natural way out of the conceptual apparatus of everyday life. The latter has, in the course of its development, gone through phases in which its employment in relation to the actual data of experience led to contradictions which are known under the name of the illusions of sense. Once there were empirical meaning rules which assigned the sentence "This is bent" to the optical data of experience which one has when one looks at a bent stick. There was also an empirical meaning-rule which assigned the sentence "This is straight" to certain tactual data. Now the following of these rules in the case of a stick half immersed in water led to mutually incompatible sentences. The rules were therefore discarded, in that these concepts, bound up with the rules, were put aside. People, therefore, freed themselves from the illusions of sense by restricting the conceptual apparatus, as a consequence of which one part of the complete world-picture was left out of account.

The above can perhaps be generalized by saying that we have to do with so-called illusions of sense either when the following of certain empirical meaning-rules in the presence of certain data of experience leads directly to contradiction, or when such a contradiction is derivable from the sentences dictated by the data of experience with the help of axiomatic and deductive meaning-rules—often also with the help of inductive hypotheses. In the latter case, the contradiction could be avoided by the rejection of the hypothesis without the need of any narrowing of the conceptual apparatus and empirical meaning-rules. If, however, in such cases one sees no *instantia contraria* against the hypothesis, but speaks instead of "sensory illusion", this shows that in these cases one had decided for a change of empirical meaning-rules, and therefore of conceptual apparatus.

Still another lesson is to be drawn from illusions of sense. There we have to do with two sentences arrived at from the data of experience in accordance with empirical meaning-rules, which in view of other meaning-rules, and, finally, of certain hypotheses, lead to contradiction. If one removes the contradiction by annulling the authority of the empirical meaning-rules, this is usually done in such a way that after the change of meaning-rules, one of the two empirical sentences is discarded and the other retained. Which of the two is retained depends on which fits better in the totality of sentences already accepted either on the basis of meaning-rules, or as hypotheses.

This continual and continuous reciprocal accommodation of "facts to theories" has set our entire original use of language, which at first was connected in a simple and naive way to the material of experience, to fluctuating. One would soon find oneself in difficulties if he attempted to specify the empirical meaning-rules in accordance with which a certain person oriented himself in his use of language. This, however, by no means implies that a language, which in accordance with the very concept of a language must be unambiguously determined by its dictionary, its syntax and its meaning stipulations, might have no empirical meaning-rules. The impossibility of specifying the empirical meaning-rules which hold for the language used by an individual, shows merely that this language usage vacillates between different languages.

From what we have said it becomes clear, when we consider the human effort to gain knowledge, that instead of man being placed, so to speak, in front of a heap of factual material with the task of encompassing it by a theory, he is rather in the position of hunting for a conceptual apparatus, for it is this alone which can give rise to empirical sentences—and with its help he obtains only an excerpt of the entire world-picture, obtains, that is to say, a world-perspective, which is to satisfy certain conditions. We have suggested consistency and systematic order as two such conditions, to which undoubtedly many others should be added. What we have said relates as well to every-day as to scientific knowledge.

We have thus asserted that science deliberately restricts its conceptual apparatus, and among many possible conceptual structures aspires to one of a special sort, whereby science renounces a complete world-picture and aims instead at only one world-perspective besides which are many others.

Why does science seek exactly this and not another conceptual apparatus? Why does science prefer exactly this world-perspective to the others? Perhaps it does this on the ground that only those judgments which constitute the world-perspective at which it aims are true, and the judgments which belong to the other world-perspectives are to be rejected as false? To reject a judgment as false can signify one of two things: (1) that the same judgment is made with negative assertion, (2) it can mean, however, the predication of falsity of the rejected judgment. Now it seems to be clear that one can only make a judgment if one makes use of the conceptual apparatus corresponding to this judgment. From this it follows that one can only reject as false a judgment which belongs to a different conceptual apparatus by making a judgment about this judgment in which one predicates falsity of it. It is indeed very doubtful whether one can predicate falsity of a judgment if the conceptual apparatus of that judgment is foreign to us, if, that is to say, we cannot translate the sentence formulating the judgment into our own language. We cannot, however, exclude this as impossible. It may therefore be the case that one who employs conceptual apparatus B_1 can predicate falsity of judgments which belong to the world-perspective of a foreign conceptual apparatus B_2. This predication, however, occurs either at random, or else it belongs to our own world-perspective, and as such it derives its entire value and status from the value and status of our own world-perspective.

We must take into consideration, however, that in opposition to our own unfavorable judgment of the sentences of a foreign world-perspective there stands a conflicting positive judgment on the part of one who makes use of the conceptual apparatus corresponding to that world-perspective. For it can be shown that any one who employs conceptual apparatus B, provided only that the data of his experience are sufficiently rich, and that he has a sufficiently sharp deductive insight, must accept as true every judgment which belongs to the world-perspective of his conceptual apparatus and to which he takes any stand at all. For should he reject a sentence of his language the meaning of which is constituted by such a judgment, he would be running counter to meaning-rules of his language, that is to say, would be rejecting with that sentence, not the judgment in question, but rather another. In so far, however, as he accepts the judgments of his world-perspective as true, he will also, in accordance with the meanings of the words "true" and "false", reject the predication of falsity with respect to these judgments. (See in this connection K. Ajdukiewicz, "Das Weltbild und die Begriffsapparatur", *Erkenntnis*, 4, 278 ff.)

Thus there would stand over and against one another two opposed judgments of the truth of a world-perspective. Each of them is itself part of a world-perspective. Now the epistemologist takes upon himself the rôle of an impartial umpire. To which of the two world-perspectives shall he concede the advantage with respect to truth? Is, however, the epistemologist truly an impartial umpire? Is he not also imprisoned in a conceptual apparatus which dictates to him his world-perspective? Even the epistemologist cannot speak without a language, cannot think without a conceptual apparatus. He will thus make his decision as to truth in a way which corresponds to his world-perspective.

The epistemologist therefore is not suited for the rôle of an impartial umpire in the struggle between two world-perspectives for the title of truth. Consequently, he should not push forward to assume this rôle. Instead of this he should set himself another task. He should give his attention to the changes which occur in the conceptual apparatus of science and in the corresponding world-perspectives, and should seek to ascertain the motives which bring these changes about. Perhaps this sequence of world-perspectives permits of being conceived as a goal-directed process which advances as though someone consciously wished to achieve the goal by means of the sequence. The task involved in such a conception of the history of science constitutes the sound kernel of the *geisteswissenschaftlichen* (culture-theoretical) understanding of the evolution of science.

III

THE NATURE OF LOGIC AND MATHEMATICS

Logic Without Ontology *

ERNEST NAGEL

The fact that the world we inhabit exhibits periodicities and regularities has been frequently celebrated by poets, philosophers, and men of affairs. That frost will destroy a fruit crop, that a convex lens will concentrate the heat of the sun, or that populations tend to increase toward a fixed maximum, are typical of the uniformities discoverable in innumerable sectors of the physical and social environment; and however we may formulate such uniformities, no philosophy which construes them as anything else than discoveries will conform with the long experience of mankind. Every form of naturalism, to whatever extent it may emphasize the impermanence of many of these regularities or note the selective human activities involved in discovering them, will recognize them as basic features of the world; and even when it attempts to account for them, it will do so only by exhibiting a more pervasive, if more subtle, pattern in the behavior of bodies.

Nevertheless, no demonstrable ground has yet been found which can guarantee that such regularities will continue indefinitely or that the propositions asserting them are necessary. If, as many philosophers have maintained, the proper objects of scientific knowledge are principles capable of *a priori* validation, both the history of science and the analysis of its methods supply ample evidence to show that no science of nature has ever achieved what is thus proclaimed as its true objective. There are, indeed, relatively few practicing scientists today who place any credence in arguments claiming to prove that any principle about an identifiable subject matter is at once logically necessary and empirical in content.

No such general agreement can be found, even among lifelong students of the subject, concerning the status of various logical and mathematical principles constantly employed in responsible inquiries. Indeed, it is difficult to ascertain which natural structures, if any, such propositions express; and it is often no less difficult to exhibit clearly and without self-deception the grounds upon which they are acknowledged. In any event, many of the sharp divisions between professed naturalists are centered around the different interpretations which they assign to principles as

* Excerpted and reprinted from Yervant H. Krikorian, *Naturalism and the Human Spirit* (Copyright 1944 by Columbia University Press) by kind permission of the author.

familiar as the so-called "laws of thought," the basic assumptions of arithmetic or the axioms of geometry. Thus, one classical form of naturalism maintains, for example, that the principle of noncontradiction is a necessary truth which is descriptive of the limiting structure of everything both actual and possible; another form of naturalism holds this principle to be a contingent, but highly reliable, conclusion based on an empirical study of nature; and a third type of naturalism takes this principle to be void of factual content and an arbitrary specification for the construction of symbolic systems. Analogous differences among naturalists occur in their interpretation of more complicated and recondite mathematical notions.

Such disagreements among those professing naturalism is not a source of embarrassment to them, since naturalism is not a tightly integrated system of philosophy; perhaps the sole bond uniting all varieties of naturalists is that temper of mind which seeks to understand the flux of events in terms of the behaviors of identifiable bodies. Nevertheless, a naturalistic philosophy must be consistent with its own assumptions. If it professes to accept the methods employed by the various empirical sciences for obtaining knowledge about the world, it cannot with consistency claim to have *a priori* insight into the most pervasive structure of things. If it aims to give a coherent and adequate account of the various principles employed in acquiring scientific knowledge, it cannot maintain that all of them are empirical generalizations when some are not subject to experimental refutation. And if it admits that logical principles have a recognizable function in certain contexts (namely, in inquiry), it cannot consistently hold those principles to be completely arbitrary simply on the ground that they are void of factual content when considered apart from those contexts.

No one seriously doubts that logic and mathematics are used in specific contexts in identifiable ways, however difficult it may be to ascertain those ways in any detail. Does it not therefore seem reasonable to attempt to understand the significance of logico-mathematical concepts and principles in terms of the operations associated with them in those contexts and to reject interpretations of their "ultimate meaning" which appear gratuitous and irrelevant in the light of such an analysis? Such, at any rate, is the point of view of the present essay. In what follows, the difficulties and futilities of some non-operational interpretations of logical principles will first be noted; the limitations of certain naturalistic but narrowly empirical approaches to logic will then be discussed; and finally, an operational interpretation of a small number of logical and mathematical notions will be sketched. However, and this is perhaps the common fate of essays such as the present one, no more than the outline of an argument will be found in the sequel. The present essay contributes no unfamiliar analyses. Its sole objective is to make plausible the view that the rôle of the logico-mathematical disciplines in inquiry can be clarified without requiring the invention of a hypostatic subject matter for them; and to suggest that a naturalism free from speculative vagaries and committed to a thorough-going operational standpoint expresses the temper of modern mathematico-experimental science.

I

1. Among the principles which Aristotle believed "hold good for every-thing that is" and therefore belong to the science of being qua being, he counted certain axioms of logic. These principles, according to him, were to be asserted as necessary truths and were not to be maintained as hypotheses, since "a principle which every one must have who knows anything about being is not a hypothesis." One such principle is that "the same attribute cannot at the same time belong and not belong to the same subject in the same respect."

Aristotle's formulation of the principle contains the qualification "in the same respect." This qualification is important, for it makes possible the defense of the principle against all objections. For suppose one were to deny the principle on the ground that an object, a penny for example, is both sensibly circular in shape and sensibly noncircular. The standard reply to this alleged counterexample is that the penny is circular when viewed from a direction perpendicular to its face and noncircular when viewed from a direction inclined to the face, and that since the different shapes do not occur "in the same respect" the principle has not been invalidated. But if one were now to ask for an unequivocal specification, antecedent to applying the principle, of a definite "same respect" with regard to the penny, so that the principle might then be subjected to a clear-cut test, a skillful defender of the principle as an ontological truth would refuse to supply the desired stipulation. For he would recognize that if a "respect" is first specified, it is always possible to find within that respect a way of apparently violating the principle.

For example, suppose a "same respect" is specified as viewing the penny from a direction perpendicular to its face. The penny will, nevertheless, subtend an angle of thirty degrees and also an angle of sixty degrees. To this, the obvious and proper retort is: "But not at the same distance from the face of the penny." Nevertheless, the principle is saved only by a new restriction upon what is to be understood by "the same respect"; the de-fender of the principle has altered his *initial* specification of what is the *same* respect. It is, of course, possible, when an attribute is suitably speci-fied, to discover a set of conditions under which a thing does not both have and not have that attribute. The crucial point is that in specifying both the attribute and the conditions, *the principle is employed as a criterion* for deciding whether the specification of the attribute is suit-able and whether those conditions are in fact sufficiently determinate. Because of the manner in which the qualification "the same respect" is used, the principle cannot be put to a genuine test, since no proposed case for testing the principle will be judged as admissible which violates the principle to be tested. In brief, conformity to the principle is the condition for a respect being "the same respect." [1]

Analogous comments are relevant for the phrases "same attribute," "belong," and "not belong," which are contained in Aristotle's formulation of the principle. For example, how is one to tell in a disputed instance of the principle whether an attribute is "the same" or not? If someone were to maintain that a penny has a diameter of $11/16$ of an inch and also a diameter of $12/16$ of an inch, he would be told that the assertion is impossible, because even though the attributes are not "the same," in predicating the former one implicitly excludes the latter; and he would, perhaps, be asked whether the measurements were carefully made, whether the same system of units was really employed, and so forth. In short, since the assertion in effect maintains "the same attribute" to belong and also not to belong to the same subject, it is absurd. But let us press the question why, if the penny has the first of these attributes, it cannot have the other. The impossibility is not simply an empirical one, which rests on inductive arguments; for if it were, the supposition would not be absurd, contrary to the hypothesis, that an unexpected observation may one day discover the penny's diameter to have both dimensions. The impossibility arises from the fact that we use the expressions "length of $11/16$ inches" and "length of $12/16$ inches" in such a way—in part because of the manner in which they may have been defined in relation to one another—that each formulates a different outcome of measurement. We may be sure that no penny will ever turn up with a diameter having both dimensions, because what it means for the diameter to have one of the attributes of dimension is specified in terms of the absence of the other attribute. The principle of contradiction is impregnable against attack, because the "sameness" and the "difference" of attributes are specified in terms of the conformity of attributes to the principle.

Accordingly, the interpretation of the principle as an ontological truth neglects its function as a norm or regulative principle for introducing distinctions and for instituting appropriate linguistic usage. To maintain that the principle is descriptive of the structure of antecedently determinate "facts" or "attributes" is to convert the outcome of employing the principle into a condition of its employment. The Aristotelian view is thus

[1] The point at issue involves noting the difference between the following two statements: "However an attribute is selected, it is possible to find a respect such that a given attribute does not at the same time belong and not belong to a given subject in that respect," and "It is possible to find a respect such that, however an attribute is selected, the given attribute does not at the same time belong and not belong to a given subject in that respect." The hypothetical defender of the principle can successfully maintain the first, though not the second, because he undertakes to specify the "sameness" of respects only after he has selected an attribute—that is, after the principle is used to determine a respect, which will thus automatically satisfy the principle.

a gratuitous and irrelevant interpretation of one function of this logical law.

2. More recent advocates of an ontological interpretation of logical principles argue their claim in terms of the conception of logical relations as invariants of all possible worlds—a conception also sponsored by Leibnitz. "Pure logic and pure mathematics," according to an influential proponent of this view, "aim at being true in all possible worlds, not only in this higgledy-piggledy job-lot of a world in which chance has imprisoned us." Reason, according to this interpretation, is an investigation into the very heart and immutable essence of all things actual and possible: "Mathematics takes us into the region of absolute necessity, to which not only the actual world but every possible world must conform." As another version puts it, logic is the most general of all the sciences: "Rules of logic are the rules of operation or transformation according to which all possible objects, physical, psychological, neutral, or complexes can be combined. Thus, logic is an exploration of the field of most general abstract possibility." According to this view, then, logical principles are "principles of being," as well as "principles of inference"; they formulate the most general nature of things, they are universally applicable, and they express the limiting and necessary structure of all existence.

Two issues raised by these brief citations from contemporary literature require comment.

a. When logical principles are asserted to hold for "all possible worlds," what is to be understood by the adjective "possible"? The crux of the matter lies in ascertaining whether "possible worlds" can be specified without using the principles of logic as the *exclusive* means of specification. For if a "possible world" is one whose sole identifiable trait is its conformity to the principles of logic, the view under consideration asserts no more than this: the subject matter of logical principles is whatever conforms to them. In that case no "possible world" could fail to satisfy the principles of logic, since anything which failed to do so would not, by hypothesis, be a possible world.

The point involved is so fundamental that it is desirable to illustrate it in another way. Consider any abstract set of postulates E, for example, Hilbert's postulates for Euclidean geometry, containing the *uninterpreted* terms P, L, and N. It is clearly not significant to ask whether E is true as long as these terms have this character. But physical experiments become relevant for deciding the truth or falsity of E if, for example, L is used to denote the paths of light-rays, P the intersections of two such paths, and N the surfaces determined in another way by any two intersecting paths. Nevertheless, an experimental inquiry can be undertaken only if the paths of light-rays can be identified in some manner *other* than by the sole requirement that light-rays are things satisfying the formal demands contained in E. For if a different method for identifying light-rays did not exist, it would not be possible to ascertain whether a particular physical configuration is such a path without first establishing that the configuration conforms to the implicit specifications of E—that is, without first ascertaining the truth of E for that configuration. Accordingly, since by definition nothing could be a path of a light-ray which did not satisfy E, the question whether E is true of all paths of light-rays would not be a matter to be settled by experiment.[2] It is evident, therefore, that if the question of the truth of a set of principles is to be a factual or experimental issue, their subject matter must be identifiable in terms of some other characteristic than that it satisfies those principles.

Let us apply these considerations to the formula: "Not both P and non-P." If it is simply a formula in some uninterpreted symbolic system, the question whether the formula is true in "all possible worlds" cannot arise. On the other hand, if its constituent symbols are interpreted in some manner, great care must be used in deriving further conclusions from the fact that on one such interpretation the formula expresses a "necessary truth." Thus, suppose that the letter "P" is taken to denote any "proposition" and that the other expressions in the formula are assigned their usual meanings; the formula will then express the principle of noncontradiction. But either there is some way of identifying propositions other than by the criterion that anything is a proposition which satisfies the formula, or there is not. On the first alternative, the assertion that the formula holds for all propositions will be a statement strictly analogous to general hypotheses in the empirical sciences; the evidence for the assertion, considerable though it may be, will be only partially complete, and in any case there will be no reason to regard the formula as expressing a necessary truth. On the second alternative, the assertion will be an implicit definition of what a proposition is; the principle of noncontradiction will be a necessary truth, since nothing could be a proposition which does not conform to it.[3]

The view that logic is the science of all possible worlds thus suffers from a fundamental ambiguity. If the only way of identifying a "possible world" is on the basis of its conformity to the canons of logic, logic is indeed the science of all possible worlds. But the view is then no more than a mislead-

[2] Of course, the question whether *a particular physical configuration* is the path of a light-ray (that is, whether it satisfies E) would remain an experimental issue.

[3] This discussion is obviously oversimplified. Thus, if the formula is a logical consequence of some set of axioms which are used as implicit definitions for propositions, then the principle of noncontradiction will be a necessary truth even though it now falls under the first of the above two alternatives. However, the point of the discussion is not affected by the neglect of such complications. In the present essay the word "proposition" is used loosely, and is frequently employed interchangeably with the word "statement." It is, of course, important in many contexts to distinguish between a proposition and a statement, since the former is often taken to be the "meaning" of the latter. However, the issues under discussion are fairly neutral with respect to the different views which are current concerning what propositions are, so that no serious confusions need arise from the loose use of the word.

ing formulation of the fact that logical principles are employed as stipulations or postulates, which define what we understand by the consistency of discourse.

b. The second point requiring comment bears on the view that logical principles express the limiting and necessary structures of all things. If the domain of application of logical principles is identified on the basis of the actual use to which those principles are put, this view cannot be construed literally. For it is not things and their actual relations which are said to be logically consistent or inconsistent with one another, but propositions or statements about them; and it is to the latter that principles such as the principle of noncontradiction are relevant. No one will hesitate to acknowledge that "The table on which I am now writing is brown" and "The table on which I am now writing is white" are mutually inconsistent statements. But this inconsistency cannot, according to the view under discussion, be predicated of two "facts," "states of affairs," or "objects"; for if there were such facts the view would be self-refuting. Accordingly, inconsistency is something which can be located only in discourse, among statements, not among things in general. And if so much is admitted, an obvious dialectic requires that consistency be localized in a similar domain, in discourse and among statements.

But dialectic aside and bearing in mind only the identifiable functions of logical principles, there is no obvious warrant for the claim that the latter are the rules in accordance with which all possible objects can be transformed or combined. Certainly they are not rules of operation upon things in any familiar or literal sense of "transformation of things"—unless, indeed, the things said to be transformed and combined are elements of discourse, constellations of signs of varying degrees of complexity. The "pervasive traits" and "limiting structures" of all "possible worlds" which logic is alleged to formulate thus appear to be traits of discourse when it has been ordered in a certain way. The interpretation of logical principles as ontological invariants seems therefore, on closer view, to be an extraneous ornamentation upon the functions they actually exercise. But the regulative rôle of logical principles, suggested by the foregoing discussion, will be exhibited more clearly in the sequel.

II

Empirically minded naturalists, convinced that propositions concerning matters of fact must be supported by sensory observation, but convinced also that logical principles have factual content, have not had an easy time in accounting for the apparent universality and necessity of these principles. The interpretation of logical principles widely accepted by both traditional and contemporary empiricists is that they are hypotheses about traits of minds and things, based on inductive arguments from experience.

I readily admit [Mill declared] that these three general propositions [the Laws of Thought] are universally true of all phenomena. I also admit that if there are any inherent necessities of thought, these are such. . . . Whether the three so-called Fundamental Laws are laws of our thoughts by the native structure of the mind, or merely because we perceive them to be universally true of observed phenomena, I will not positively decide: but they are laws of our thoughts now, and invincibly so.

More recent writers concerned with defending an empirical philosophy, though they may reject Mill's psychological atomism and sensationalism, frequently do not differ from him on the view that logical principles are inductive truths. The following is a sufficiently forthright contemporary statement of this conception.

Logical validity is grounded on *natural* fact. . . . When we are in doubt as to the logical validity of an argument, there is only one test. If the class of such arguments gives us materially true conclusions from materially true premises, it is valid, if not, it is invalid. . . . The crucial question which this frankly empirical approach to logic must face is whether it can explain the formal characters of logical inference. The experimental hypothesis attempts the explanation by showing that those inferential procedures which have brought knowledge in the past exhibit a certain invariant *order* whose metaphysical correlate is to be sought in the *serial* characters of existence. . . . The laws of logic . . . cannot be disproved, but they may become inapplicable and meaningless. We can say nothing about the *probability* of this being so, but we can just conceive of the possibility that the so-called *a-priori* laws of logic may not enable us to organize our experience. That is why they are not formal or empty. That is why they tell us something about the *actual* world. That is why we can say that every additional application of logic to existence is an experimental verification of its invariance.

However attractive such an interpretation of logical principles may appear to a consistent empirical naturalism—to a philosophy which appreciates the limitations natural structures place upon our thought and action, but which nevertheless finds no warrant for the assertion that a priori knowledge of such structures is possible—there are insuperable difficulties involved in it. These difficulties arise in the main because those who profess such an interpretation misconceive the character of empirical or scientific method.

1. Little need be said in refutation of the view that logical principles formulate the "inherent necessities of thought" and are generalized descriptions of the operations of minds. Surely the actual occurrence in the same person of beliefs in logically incompatible propositions makes nonsense of the claim that the principle of non-contradiction expresses a universal fact of psychology. Moreover, if logical principles were true descriptions of anthropological behavior, they would be contingent truths, refutable on evidence drawn from the observation of human behavior; but in that case, the necessity which is so generally attributed to logical principles, however much this may be disguised by calling their contradictories "unbelievable," would be left unexplained.

2. The view under consideration maintains that the validity of a type of inference sanctioned by logic can be established only by presenting empirical evidence to show that an inference of that form always leads from materially true premises to materially true conclusions. It must be admitted, of course, that a valid inference is often defined as one which invariably yields true conclusions from true premises. But it by no means follows that an inference ever is or can be established as valid in the manner proposed. Suppose, for example, "A" and "If A then B" are asserted as true statements (the expression "if . . . then" being used in some one of the customary ways), so that the conclusion that "B" is true may be drawn in accordance with the familiar rule of *ponendo ponens*. Let us now imagine that as a matter of fact "B" is false and that we are therefore urged by someone to abandon the rule as a universal logical principle. Would not such a suggestion be dismissed as grotesque and as resting upon some misunderstanding? Would we not retort that in the case supposed "A" or "If A then B" must have been asserted as true mistakenly or that if this is no mistake then the assertion of the falsity of "B" must be an error? Would we not, in any event, maintain that statements of the form: "If A and (if A then B) then B" are necessarily true, since not to acknowledge them as such is to run counter to the established usage of the expressions "and" and "if . . . then"?

Proponents of the view under discussion often declare that in interpreting logical principles as empirical hypotheses they are offering a justification for logic in terms of the procedures and standards of adequacy employed in the most advanced natural sciences. It is worth noting, therefore, that not a single instance can be cited from the history of science which would support the conception that the validity of logical principles is ever established by the suggested method. Is it not significant that whenever consequences derived from premises believed to be true are in disagreement with the facts of experimental observation, it is not the logical principles in accordance with which those consequences were drawn that are rejected as experimentally unwarranted? Indeed, it is not apparent how the suggested method for establishing the validity of logical principles could operate in any typical inquiry. For the truth of most premises employed in the sciences cannot be established except on the basis of an investigation of the consequences which are drawn from them —drawn in accordance with and with the help of logical principles. For example, the principles of Newtonian mechanics, which constitute part of the premises in many physical inquiries, cannot be established as adequate to their subject matter unless it is first discovered what these principles imply. This will be even more obvious if we note that these premises employ such complex notions as differential coefficients, real numbers, and point masses; the premises cannot be construed as "descriptions" of matters of fact accessible to a direct observation, that is, as statements whose

truth or falsity may be settled prior to examining their logical consequences. The proposed method for establishing the validity of arguments
is thus clearly not a feasible one, since no experimental control can be
instituted for determining the alleged material truth of logical principles.

It follows that no "metaphysical correlate" to logical principles need be
sought in the "serial character of existence." And if logical principles
do not function as contingent hypotheses about matters of fact, if they
are not to be established inductively on the ground of their conformity
to "certain structural and functional invariants of nature," there is no
clear sense in which "every additional application of logic to existence
is an experimental verification of its invariance." Logical principles are
compatible with any order which the flux of events may exhibit; they
could not be in disagreement with anything which inquiry may disclose,
and if they should ever require revision, the grounds for such alterations
must lie elsewhere than in the subject matter of the natural sciences. To
be sure, should the cosmos become a chaos to the extent of making the
continued existence of reflective thought impossible, the use of logical
principles would thereby also become impossible. But as the above discussion indicates, the continued employment of those principles is not
contingent upon the invariance of structures other than those which sus-
tain the continuance of reflective inquiry.

3. In spite of its profession of allegiance to scientific methods as the
canonical techniques of competent inquiry, the empiricistic interpretation
of logic is based upon an inadequate conception of what is involved in those
methods. Indeed, even when, as has already been noted, those subscribing
to this interpretation explicitly reject Mill's psychological atomism, they
do not always successfully free themselves from his over-simple views on
the formation of scientific concepts. Two closely related points require
brief discussion in this connection: the narrow criterion of meaningful
discourse which is explicitly or tacitly assumed by many empirical naturalists; and the inadequate conception which they hold of the rôle of symbolic constructions in the conduct of inquiry.

a. It has often been maintained that the theoretical sciences deem to
be ultimately meaningful only the statements which either formulate directly observable relations of qualities and things or can be translated without remainder into statements that do so. According to another version of
this thesis, every meaningful statement must consist of terms which either
denote simple, directly experienceable qualities and relations or are com-
pounded out of terms denoting such simples. Even false hypotheses, so it
has been urged on occasion, are meaningful only because they formulate
the structure of some actual observable situation—a structure which happens to be wrongly attributed to a given situation. Since the familiar logical and mathematical principles seem so obviously significant, and since
in their usual formulation they are ostensibly about the relations which

properties of things bear to one another, the interpretation of these principles as empirical hypotheses is sometimes deduced as a corollary from this general view.

Little need be said to show the inadequacy of the suggested criterion of meaning. If it were applied consistently, most of the theories employed in the various positive sciences would have to be dismissed as in fact meaningless; and indeed, those who have accepted the criterion have been consistent enough to exclude almost all general statements as not expressing "genuine propositions." For in the first place, to the extent that theoretical propositions have the form of unrestricted universals, they do not formulate the explicit outcome of any actual series of direct observations. And in the second place, many theoretical statements contain terms (such as "point-particle," "light-wave," "electron," "gene," and the like) which denote nothing that can be directly observed and cannot be construed as being explicitly definable with the help of only such terms as do so. Moreover, there is surely no evidence for the claim that for every false hypothesis there is a situation for which it is true.[4] It is clear that underlying the suggested criterion of meaningful discourse is an ill-concealed reproductive psychology of abstraction and that in any case those who employ it cannot do justice to the actual procedures of the sciences.

A naturalism which is based on modern scientific methods cannot afford to propose illiberal restrictions upon inquiry. It must recognize that no formula can be constructed which will express once for all "*the* meaning" of any portion of scientific discourse. Instead of attempting to construct such formulae, it must turn seriously to the analysis of specific uses and functions of specific systems of expressions in specific contexts. It will have to note that statements in scientific discourse always occur as elements in a system of symbols and operations, and it will therefore attempt to understand the significance of statements in terms of the complicated uses to which they are subject. It will, accordingly, not assume dogmatically that the directly observed qualities and relations of the explicit subject matter of a science must constitute the sole and ultimate reference of every significant complex of its symbols. It will surely recognize that according to standard scientific procedure evidence taken from sensory observation must be relevant to propositions alleged to be about matters of fact: such propositions must entail consequences, obtained by logical operations in determinate ways, which can be experimentally tested when the appropriate circumstances occur. It will thus accept the pragmatic maxim that there is no difference between the objects of beliefs and conceptions where

---

[4] For example, within the framework of the Newtonian analysis of motion, an indefinite number of false hypotheses for gravitational attraction can be constructed, since a false theory of gravitation is obtained if the exponent "2" in Newton's formula is replaced by a different numeral. Are these different theories to be dismissed as meaningless because there do not happen to exist an infinity of situations for which these theories are true?

there is no possible difference in observable behavior. But it will not, therefore, insist that all significant statements must be descriptive of what can be directly observed. And it will remain sensitive to the possibility that even statements about the explicit subject matter of a science may involve a reference to the operations (overt and symbolic) performed in inquiries into that subject matter.

b. Nowhere is the systematic undervaluation of the constructive function of thought in inquiry more glaring than in the widespread neglect of the rôle played by symbolic manipulations in scientific procedure. The more comprehensive and integrated a theoretical system is, the more obvious does the need for such manipulations appear. For especially in the theories of modern science symbols usually occur which refer to nothing that can be directly experienced; and the significance for matters of direct experience of the conceptual constructions which enter into those theories cannot be made explicit except with the help of extensive symbolic transformations. Accordingly, no statement detached from the symbolic system to which it is integral can be evaluated for its empirical validity; and no isolated concept can be judged as warranted on the basis of the essentially irrelevant criterion of pictorial suggestiveness. But since calculation or symbolic manipulation thus acquires an indispensable though intermediary rôle in inquiry, the need for reliable techniques of constructing and expanding symbolic systems becomes progressively more pressing; the institution of an entire department of investigation devoted to the formal study of symbolic systems is the practically inevitable consequence.

It is a common and tempting assumption that in performing a chain of calculations one is at the same time tracing out the existential connections between things, so that the formal pattern of symbolic transformations reproduces in some manner the structure of the subject matter under investigation. However, the specific mode in which theories are constructed and bodies of knowledge are integrated is only partially determined by experimental findings. Various norms or ideals—such as the desire for a certain degree of precision, for intellectual economy and notational convenience, or for a certain type of comprehensiveness—also control the direction of inquiry and the articulation of theories. Many symbolic constructions and operations are therefore indices of the standards regulating the course of systematic investigations, and are not merely indications of the expected conclusions of experiment or of the intrinsic relations between phases of subject matter. A myopic concern with the sensory warrants for scientific findings—such as often characterizes traditional empiricism—easily leads to neglect of this aspect of systematic scientific formulations; the traits of discourse are then identified as traits of subject matter,[5] and principles

---

[5] An example of such a transference is found in the claim that, because the consistency of a set of formal postulates is established by exhibiting a group of related objects

whose function it is to institute a desired order into inquiry are not distinguished from statements about the explicit subject matter of inquiry. When the identification is made, the construction of symbolic systems (including the use of hypotheses) is in effect viewed as an inessential scaffolding for attaining some form of intuitive knowledge. When the distinction is not made, logical principles are in effect deprived of their identifiable functions.

III

The preceding discussion has, in the main, been negative. There remains the task of making explicit the suggestions it contains concerning an alternative interpretation of some logical and mathematical notions. Nothing like a systematic account of logic and mathematics can be attempted, and only a small number of logical principles and mathematical terms will be briefly examined. But even such an examination may exhibit the fruitfulness of an operational analysis of formal concepts and may make plausible the view that the content of the formal disciplines has a regulative function in inquiry.

Although logic is one of the oldest intellectual disciplines, considerable difference of opinion exists as to the scope of logical theory and as to which concepts and principles properly belong to logic. The present discussion will be confined to such admittedly formal principles as the so-called laws of thought and other "necessary truths" and to principles of inference such as the principle of *ponendo ponens*. The discussion will be facilitated if at the outset two senses are distinguished in which logical principles are commonly asserted: as principles which are explicitly about symbolism or language; and as necessary truths whose ostensible subject matter is usually some nonlinguistic realm.[6]

a. The three laws of thought are employed in the first sense in cases something like the following. Suppose that in a bit of reasoned discourse the term "animal" occurs several times. The argument will clearly be a cogent one only if in each of its occurrences the word retains a fixed "meaning"—that is, only if it is used as a name for the same kind of object. The requirement that in a given context a term must continue to be used in essentially the same manner, is expressed as the principle of identity.

—a so-called "concrete model"—satisfying those postulates, logical traits (such as consistency) must represent pervasive ontological or empirical invariants. In point of fact, however, not only can some postulate sets be established without recourse to empirical facts in the indicated manner; most postulate systems cannot be shown to be consistent by genuinely empirical methods. But what is perhaps more to the point, this argument for identifying logical with existential properties fails to observe that consistency is demanded of symbolic systems as part of an ideal for the organization of statements and is not a trait subsisting in nature independently of symbolic formulations.

[6] This distinction roughly corresponds to the difference noted in much current literature between "meta-logical" statements and statements in the "object-language" of a science.

Analogously, the principle of noncontradiction requires that in a given context a term must not be applied to a given thing and also denied to it; and the principle of excluded middle is formulated in a corresponding way.

When stated in this manner, these principles are obviously *prescriptive* for the use of language, and as such are not *descriptive* of actual usage. They specify minimal conditions for discourse without confusion, for they state at least some of the requirements for a precise language. Everyday language, and to some extent even the specialized languages of the sciences, are vague in some measure, so that they do not entirely conform to the requirement set by these principles.[7] Although fairly effective communication is nevertheless possible in connection with many pursuits, situations do arise in which a greater precision in the use of language is required. The laws of thought thus formulate an ideal to be achieved—an ideal which is capable of being attained at least approximately—and they indicate the direction in which the maximum of desired precision may be obtained.

Few will deny that the laws of thought as here formulated have a regulative function. Nevertheless, the admission is often qualified by the claim that if the ideal these laws formulate is a reasonable one, not an arbitrary norm, there must be an objective ground—a "structural invariant"—which lends them authority. Moreover, it is sometimes urged that this ideal must be a necessary and inescapable one, since otherwise a genuine alternative to it would be possible; however, communication would be impossible if language were so employed as to conform, for example, to the denial of the principle of identity. But this latter argument for the intrinsic necessity of these principles is surely circular. For if by "communication" is understood processes similar to those in which we are familiarly engaged when talking, writing, or carrying on research—processes which illustrate the use of symbols in at least partial conformity to the laws of thought—communication would indeed be impossible were the requirements set by these laws satisfied in no degree; but communication would not be possible simply because these laws are analytic of what is understood by the word "communication." Whatever might be the human needs which communication satisfies, the desire to communicate and the desire to enforce the ideal specified by the laws are directed toward the same end. It must, nevertheless, be acknowledged that the ideal of precision in using language is not an arbitrary one. It is not arbitrary, because communication and inquiry are directed to the achievement of certain objectives, and these objectives are best attained when language is employed in a manner approximating as closely as possible the norms expressed by the laws of thought. The assertion that this is so requires support by empirical evi-

---

[7] Thus, if the term "red" is vague, there is a class of colors concerning which it is indeterminate whether the term applies to them or not, so that the principle of excluded middle fails in this case.

dence—evidence which it is possible to produce. But the available evidence is drawn from the study of the behavior of men engaged in inquiry; it does not come from a consideration of structural invariants found in other domains.

The three laws of thought are, however, not the only principles of logic explicitly dealing with symbolism, and some consideration must now be given to that important class of principles known as rules of inference— of which the rule of *ponendo ponens* is, perhaps, the most familiar. The first point to note in connection with such principles is that it is possible to specify accurately what rules govern the valid inferences in a language, only when the "meanings" of certain terms in that language are precise— that is, when terms like "and," "or," and "if—then" are used in determinate ways. In fact, however, the ordinary usage of such terms is vague and unclear. Everyday language, in the main, is employed according to routine habits which are fixed and stable over a narrow range, but which are indeterminate in many crucial cases; accordingly, inferences are drawn and sanctioned on the basis of crude intuitive considerations as to what is "really meant" by the terms involved.[8] The explicit formulation of canons of inference serves to clarify vague intent; and what is, perhaps, less commonly recognized, such formulations help to fix usages when they have previously been unsettled: they serve as proposals for modifying old usages and instituting new ones.

The various modern systems of formal logic must, accordingly, be viewed, not as accounts of the "true nature" of an antecedently identifiable relation of "implication," but as alternative proposals for specifying usages and for performing inferences. The adoption of a system such as is found in Whitehead and Russell's *Principia Mathematica* is in effect the adoption of a set of regulative principles for developing more inclusive and determinate habits for using language than are illustrated in everyday discourse. No known recent system of formal logic is or can be just a faithful transcription of those inferential canons which are embodied in common discourse, though in the construction of these systems hints may be taken from current usage; for the entire *raison d'être* for such systems is the need for precision and inclusiveness where common discourse is vague and incomplete, even if as a consequence their adoption as regulative principles involves a modification of our inferential habits.

---

[8] For example, everyone who has an elementary knowledge of English would agree that the rule of *ponendo ponens* is a correct canon of inference. On the other hand, a person unsophisticated by training in formal logic and not committed to one of the modern logical systems, may hesitate to accept the rule that a statement of the form "Either A or B" is a consequence of "A," where "A" and "B" are any statements; and he will probably seriously doubt the correctness of the rule that "If A then (if B then C)" follows from "If A and B, then C," where "A," "B," and "C" are any statements. The hesitation and the doubt must be attributed to the fact that "or," "and," and "if— then" are frequently used ambiguously and have fairly clear and determinate meanings only in relatively few contexts.

The question naturally arises whether the conventions which explicitly formulated rules of inference institute are entirely arbitrary—whether, in other words, the adoption of one set of regulative principles for reconstructing linguistic behavior is as "justifiable" as the adoption of a different set. The issue raised does not refer to the construction of various abstract "uninterpreted" symbolic calculi, for which diverging rules of "inference" or "transformation" may be developed; for it is usually admitted that the arbitrariness of such abstract systems can be limited only by the formal requirements of symbolic construction. The issue refers to the ground upon which one system of regulative principles is to be preferred to another system, when such principles are to be employed in the conduct of scientific inquiry. But this manner of putting the question suggests its own answer. If everyday language requires completion and reorganization for the sake of attaining the ends of inquiry, the "justification" for a proposed set of regulative principles will not be arbitrary and can be given only in terms of the adequacy of the proposed changes as means or instruments for attaining the envisaged ends. Thus, if inquiry is directed toward achieving a system of physics which will be coherent, comprehensive, and economical in its use of certain types of assumption and operation, one set of canons for inference will be preferable to another if the former leads to a closer approximation to this goal than does the latter. The choice between alternative systems of regulative principles will then not be arbitrary and will have an objective basis; the choice will not, however, be grounded on the allegedly greater inherent necessity of one system of logic over another, but on the relatively greater adequacy of one of them as an instrument for achieving a certain systematization of knowledge.[9]

It is needless to dwell further on the function of rules of inference: their primary rôle is to guide the development of discourse in a certain direction, namely, in the deduction of the consequences of sets of statements; they thereby contribute to making the use of language more determinate and precise and to attaining the goals of specific inquiries. It must be admitted, however, that it is frequently difficult to exhibit adequate evidence for the superior efficacy of one type of inferential system over another, especially when the specific goals of inquiry are themselves vague and are conceived, in part at least, in aesthetic terms.[10] The point to be stressed is that however great this difficulty may be, it can be resolved only by considering the specific functions of such logical principles in

[9] Something more will be said on this point below. These remarks should not, however, be taken to mean that all habits of inference, and in particular language itself, have been instituted on the basis of a deliberate convention. How language first arose and how some of our common modes of inference actually came into being, are questions of fact about which there is in general little reliable information and concerning which everyone seems to be equally in the dark.

[10] For example, when a theory is required to be "simple" and "elegant."

determinate contexts of inquiry; it cannot be resolved by investigating the causal factors which lead men to adopt those principles or by a genetic account of inferential habits.

For example, the view has been advanced that certain simple forms of inference are generated by physiological mechanisms sharing a common character with mechanisms present in the subject matter of inquiry in which those inferences are used; and it is sometimes said that a theory of logic is "naturalistic" only if it holds that rational operations "grow out of" the more pervasive biological and physical ones. It may be safely assumed that there are causes and physical conditions for habits of inference, even when we happen to be ignorant of them. It is not evident, however, especially since habits of inference may change though the subject matter in connection with which they are employed does not, that the mechanism underlying a specific habit of inference is identical with the mechanism involved in that subject matter. And it is even less evident how, even if this were the case, the causal account would enable us to evaluate inferential principles, since the cogency of such an account is established only with the help of those principles. Suggestions for inferential canons may indeed be obtained from observations of natural processes; but the fact that a principle may have been suggested in this way does not explain its normative function. Again, the known facts about the earth's history make it most reasonable to assume that the higher and more complex activities of men did not always exist and that they have been developed out of more primitive ones; and it would certainly be a matter of great interest to learn just how this has come about. However, in the present state of our knowledge a genetic account of logical operations is at best a highly speculative and dubious one; and what is more to the point, even if a well-supported genetic account were available, it would contribute little or nothing to an understanding of the present functioning of logical principles or to the explanation of the grounds of their authority. In the absence of a detailed knowledge of the past, the reaffirmation of the historical and structural continuity of our rational behavior with the activities of other organisms is an act of piety; it does not increase the clarifying force of an experimentally orientated naturalism.[11]

b. Logical principles are also asserted as necessary truths which do not refer to linguistic subject matter. Thus, "Everything is identical with itself" and "If A then A" (where "A" is any statement) are formulations of the principle of identity; "Nothing has and also lacks a given property" and "It is not the case that A and not-A" (where "A" is any state-

---

[11] These comments should not be construed as a rejection of some form of "the principle of continuity" as a fruitful guide and norm in inquiry. Nor should they be taken as denying that the study of simpler and more basic biological behavior may provide an illuminating context and essential clews for the understanding of the "higher" functions. These remarks are included simply as a protest against frequent abuses of a useful postulate of procedure.

ment) are formulations of the principle of noncontradiction; while "If A and (if A then B), then B," and "If (if A then B) then (if not-B then not-A)" (where "A" and "B" are any statements) are examples of other principles usually regarded as necessary. These principles are ostensibly about things, their attributes and their relations, not about symbols for them; they are held to be necessary truths, because their denials are self-contradictory.

The first point to note about these logical laws is that if they are asserted as necessary truths, they are asserted to be such in some more or less precisely formulated language, whether in the crudely precise language of everyday use or in some more exact artificial symbolic system. And it is not difficult to show that although their subject matter is not the language of which they are parts, they occur in that language because of the habits of usage or the tacit or explicit rules which govern that language. For example, if the characterizations "true" and "false" are employed in the customary manner, no statement can properly (that is, without contravening that usage) be characterized as both true and false; and if the word "not" is so used in connection with acts of affirming and denying statements that a false statement is rejected as not true, the principle of noncontradiction is instituted as a necessary truth. More generally, if a precise usage is fixed for a number of expressions in a symbolic system, statements constructed out of some of these expressions will usually occur such that to deny them is to misuse those expressions. Accordingly, the laws which are regarded as necessary in a given language may be viewed as implicit definitions of the ways in which certain recurrent expressions are to be used or as consequences of other postulates for such usages. No language is so utterly flexible in its formal structure that no limits exist as to the way expressions in it can be combined and used. The necessary statements of a language help to specify what these limits are. But to the extent to which ordinary language is not precise, which statements in it are necessary cannot be determined exactly. The so-called systems of "pure logic" do not suffer from this fault; they can therefore be used as norms for instituting a more precise employment of language in situations in which such precision is essential for the task at hand. Indeed, as is well known, one result of such instituted precision is to facilitate the process of deriving consequences from premises and to supply dependable means for checking inferences.

This function of logical laws—to serve as instruments for establishing connections between statements which are usually not themselves logically necessary—is too familiar to require more than passing mention. A point worth observing, however, is that the necessary laws of logic can be reformulated so as to become principles of inference, having as their explicit subject matter the relations of expressions in a symbolic system. For it can be shown that a given language may be so reconstructed that it no longer will contain necessary truths—without thereby affecting the original possibilities for deducing statements which are not necessary—provided that corresponding to the necessary truths initially in the language appropriate rules of inference are introduced. The cost of such a reconstruction may be prohibitive in terms of the inconveniences and complexities which arise from it.[12] Nevertheless, the theoretical possibility of making it helps to show that the function of necessary truths is to regulate and control the process of deduction. It follows that the previous comments on rules of inference apply with equal force to laws expressing necessary connections.

A few final remarks concerning the grounds for accepting logical laws must be made. The main stress which is to be made in this connection is that any "justification" of such laws can be given only in terms of the adequacy of the language in which they are part to the specific tasks for which that language is employed. This point can be enforced by recalling that in the empirical sciences it is not possible to perform experiments which would subject isolated statements to a crucial test, since every experiment actually tests a vaguely delimited system of theoretical and factual assumptions involved in the experiment and the statement. Analogously, it is not feasible to "justify" a law of logic by confronting it with specific observational data; the belief that it is possible to do so is part of the heritage of traditional empiricism. On the other hand, since logical laws are implicit laws for specifying the structure of a language, and since their explicit function is to link systematically statements to which data of observation are relevant, logical laws may be evaluated on the basis of their effectiveness in yielding systems of a desired kind. Thus, it has recently been suggested that in order to develop the theory of subatomic phenomena in a manner conforming both to experimental evidence and to certain ideals of economy and elegance, a "logic" different from those normally employed may have to be instituted.[13] The suggestion is still in a speculative stage, and it is interesting only as a possibility. Nevertheless, it calls attention to the fact in a striking way that under the pressure of factual observation and norms of convenience familiar language habits

[12] For example, the necessary truth "if (if A then B), then (if not-B then not-A)" could be eliminated from our language, provided that we introduce the rule that a statement of the form "if not-B then not-A" is deducible from a statement of the form "if A then B." On the other hand, it is usually assumed that when "A," "B," "C," "D" are any statements, they may be combined to form the new statements "if A then B," "if C then D," and "if (if A then B), then (if C then D)"; accordingly, since "not-A" and "not-B" are statements, "if (if A then B), then (if not-B then not-A)" must be accepted as a statement on the basis of the stipulation just mentioned. Hence, if the occurrence of such necessary truths is to be prevented, more complicated rules must be introduced for combining statements to form new ones.

[13] See Garrett Birkhoff and John von Neumann, "The Logic of Quantum Mechanics", *Annals of Mathematics*, XXXVII (1936), 823-43. The proposed logical system involves abandoning certain rules of inference which seem truistic both to "common sense" and to those accustomed to the system of *Principia Mathematica*.

may come to be revised; and it indicates that the acceptance of logical principles as canonical need be neither on arbitrary grounds nor on grounds of their allegedly inherent authority, but on the ground that they effectively achieve certain postulated ends.

It must be emphasized, however, that this way of justifying logical principles has nothing in common with the view which construes them as descriptive of an intrinsic and pervasive structure of things. It has been argued that just as in geometry there are intrinsically different kinds of surface and each kind imposes "certain limits on the range of alternative coördinate systems which can be used to map it out," so "the objective structure of the system of fact imposes some limitation on the alternative systems of language or symbolism which are capable of representing it." The conclusion drawn from this argument by analogy is that propositions which would describe this structure "would almost inevitably take the form of propositions which formulate certain very abstract and general and widespread linguistic usages"; and since logical principles do "formulate" these usages, there can be only one genuinely valid logic, only one absolute system of necessary truths. But even if one accepts the questionable analogy which underlies the argument, elementary considerations of scientific procedure must lead one to reject the conception of "*the* objective structure of *the* system of fact" capable of being known without the mediation of any selective symbolic system. The study of scientific inquiry requires us to admit that structures cannot be known independently of activities of symbolization; that structures considered for investigation are selected on the basis of special problems; that the various structures discovered are not, according to the best evidence, all parts of one coherent pattern; and that the precise manner in which our theories are formulated is controlled by specifically human postulates no less than by experimental findings. The attempt to justify logical principles in terms of their supposed conformity to an absolute structure of facts thus completely overlooks their actual function of formulating and regulating the pursuit of human ideals. If the preceding discussion has any merit, however, the reasonable view is that the relative success of a system of logic in doing these things is the sole identifiable and objective basis for measuring its worth. . . .

The Relevance of Psychology to Logic *

FRIEDRICH WAISMANN [1]

Of the various aspects of the question included in the title I will try to throw some light upon three topics:

I. The question as to whether there is any indubitable knowledge of immediate experience;

II. The way in which mental acts like believing or doubting are relevant to logic;

III. The misunderstandings which I think are involved in any causal theory of meaning.

I

Since the time of Descartes philosophers have always been deeply interested in the question whether any of the knowledge we possess is absolutely indubitable and forms the basis of the rest of our knowledge. It is well known that philosophers, under sceptical criticism, have retreated step by step to the position that it is only momentary experience which is beyond all doubt. When I am looking at a rose, and utter the words "This is red," there seems to be no possibility of questioning its truth. Even if I am dreaming, it is true that I am having an experience of redness. Many philosophers have distinguished between propositions such as this, which they take to be indubitable, and other empirical propositions, for example, about physical objects, which can be refuted by experience in the future and which can therefore be said to be of the nature of hypotheses. Is this view tenable?

The answer to this question depends partly upon what we understand by a proposition. Many philosophers hold that what a proposition is cannot be defined, because the characteristic feature in it is a specific state of mind which we have when we make a judgment. In order to clarify this question, let us use a method which I think is helpful philosophically, namely, to invent games with words which throw light upon our actual

* Reprinted by kind permission of the author and the editors from the *Aristotelian Society, Supplementary Volume 15*, 1936.

[1] I wish to emphasize my indebtedness to Dr. Wittgenstein, to whom I owe not only a great part of the views expressed in this paper but also my whole method of dealing with philosophical questions. Although I hope that the views expressed here are in agreement with those of Dr. Wittgenstein, I do not wish to ascribe to him any responsibility for them.

language. Each of these games can be described exactly and completely, without reference to the complication of mental processes which every sentence of our language involves.

We will describe three games and draw some conclusions from their comparison.

1. A person *A* who cannot use any language has been trained to point to a red or to a green piece of material whenever he hears the words "red" or "green" respectively. He learns the game by someone showing him what he is to do until he imitates it. We take his imitating the game to be the criterion of his understanding it.

If I say "red" and he points to the green material, we say that this is wrong. But in what sense is it wrong? Is it a mistake or a slip? There can be no doubt as to the answer: it is a slip comparable to the case where someone makes a slip of the tongue, makes a slip in calculation, etc.; it is a wrong move in the game, but it is entirely different from a mistake in the sense of a mistaken belief.

2. Now we will modify the game.

There is a lamp in the room which shows red and green at irregular times. *A* is to watch the lamp and to say which colour he sees. It is assumed that he knows nothing about the use of the words "red" and "green" in our ordinary language, except in this game. He learns the game in a manner similar to that in which he learned the first one.

Supposing that the lamp shows red and *A*, looking at it, says "green" —in what sense can we speak of an error? Let us remember first that *A* has learned the use of the words "red" and "green" only in this game; he does not know the meaning of the words "true" and "false," or of such phrases as "it is correct," "it is incorrect." Therefore we, who are watching him, can only ask whether *A* has used the words correctly, that is, in a way which is in accordance with the rules of the game. We cannot ask whether he expresses with the words "red" and "green" what is true or what is false. Analogously to the first game this, too, is a case of a slip, the only difference being that he says the wrong word, instead of pointing to the wrong colour. In this game there is no occasion for mistake in the sense of mistaken belief. *A* can use the words according to the rules; if he does not do so, he does not play the game. But within the game there is no possibility of speaking of "true" or "false."

3. Now we will describe a game in which the opposition true-false does apply. Let us suppose that *A* is to guess which colour the light will be. When the lamp lights up he can say: "What I've guessed is correct" or "it is incorrect"; "it is true" or "it is false." And this can be said by those who play the game, not only by those who watch it.

The question before us now is this: Which are the features that account for the fact that we can speak of an error in the sense of a false opinion with regard to the third game, but not with regard to the first two games?

The answer to this question will throw light upon the nature of judgment.

One might say that in the second game the words "red" and "green" do not express a statement. They merely are names for the colours of the light. It is only in the third game that A wants to describe a fact with these words, and that is why his utterance can be true or false. This answer, although it points to a real distinction, is not satisfactory, for it is precisely the nature of the difference between naming and describing which we want to get clear about.

There are at first sight two answers:

a. The difference is psychological. When the speaker, by uttering the words "red" or "green," expresses an opinion or expectation, a peculiar mental process occurs. This differs from what is felt in naming something. There occurs a specific act of believing or thinking or supposing, and that is what makes the utterance a statement.

Whether or not there is such a peculiar mental act of believing we will not discuss now. But even if there is, reference to that state of mind will be of no help. Although we have not investigated the processes occurring in A's mind when he is playing the third game, still we say that he makes judgments. We do not wish to maintain that there is not an experience peculiar to judgments, but we draw attention to the fact that this experience is not the criterion for our deciding whether a given case is a judgment or not; therefore, the reference to such an experience would be superfluous.

b. In the third game, in which A had to guess, the words "red" and "green" are compared with reality, they are in accordance or in discordance with reality, and that is why they can be said to be true or false. A closer examination of this answer will show that it also is not satisfactory. In the second game as well as in the third one, the word "red" was explained by demonstrative definition, and this explanation constitutes, as is generally said, a connection between the word "red" and the perception of the red light. In applying the demonstrative definition to the game (2), A looks at the lamp and gives a name to the colour of the light—is it not correct to describe this as a comparison? We could even imagine the game (2) modified in such a way that A has a sheet of paper on which there are green and red patches of colour next to the written words "green" and "red." Whenever the coloured light appears, he compares the light with the colours on his paper till he finds the right one, then passes across to the word written next to it, and utters the word. In the game (3) where he has to guess, he utters the word before the coloured light appears and the word is subsequently compared with reality; in the game (2) the light appears first and the word is uttered afterwards. This is the only difference I can see. The words "red" and "green" have as much, or, if one prefers, as little connection with reality in the second game as in the third.

The real reason for the difference must be found in the different rules for the games. And here we can notice the following difference: In the second game it is not permissible to give the wrong name; in other words, if *A*, looking at the red light says "green," this is contrary to the convention; he violates the rules and thus ceases to play the game. In the third game, on the other hand, he remains within the rules of the game even when he guesses wrongly. There are the two possibilities of his guessing the colour and of his not guessing it, and these possibilities are distinguished within the game as "true" and "false." This is what constitutes the difference, and not any process of believing or judging which might accompany uttering the words.

We do not wish to maintain that the uttering of the word is true or false *because* it is a statement, but rather that it is a statement because it *can* be true or false, that is, because both possibilities occur within the game.

We are led by considerations such as these to the formulation of what is essential to a proposition: a proposition is what can be true or false; that is, a proposition is something which obeys certain rules of a calculus of truth-values. Thus a proposition is always to be understood as embodied in such a calculus. There are many different calculuses of truth-values; hence the concept of proposition is limited in different ways according to the calculus to which it is referred. So to have an exact concept of proposition, it is necessary to specify the calculus which defines it. Ordinary language is, of course, so blurred that we cannot derive from it a clear-cut notion of proposition.

To take an analogous case: if we are asked to define a real number, we would describe the calculus of real numbers. In the same way we would define a proposition by describing a particular propositional calculus.

Let us return to the original question as to whether we possess any indubitable knowledge. It is obvious that if I say "There is a chair in the next room," I am asserting a proposition which may be true or false. Even if it is false, my asserting it is not excluded by the rules of my language. But now let us take the example of my looking at a coloured patch in my visual field and saying "This is yellow." Suppose that what I see is in fact blue. In what sense is my utterance false? We must not forget that the colour-words "yellow," "blue," etc., are explained by demonstrative definitions and that these definitions form part of the grammar of the colour-words. Therefore, if I say, while referring to a blue patch in my visual field, "This is yellow," I am sinning against the rules of grammar. In this case, following the rules for the use of colour-words which can be codified in a list, I am compelled to choose the word "blue" and I have not freedom to choose any other colour-word. This case is therefore entirely different from that of game (3), in which the player has a free choice to choose as he wishes. In game (3) there are two choices, each of which would be in accordance with the rules of the game; in our case the choice has been predetermined by the rules of grammar previously fixed. My utterance, "This is yellow," is a falsely formed proposition, but not a false proposition.

What is the case in this example holds, I think, of every description of immediate experience. If I describe a pain, a sound, or any other experience, the only question that can be raised is whether or not I use the words correctly in accordance with the rules of language; but not whether my utterance is true or false. What, then, is the nature of the utterance? It is not a proposition, if we understand by a proposition something which can be true or false. We can say, if we like, that it is a border-line case of proposition in a rather similar way to that in which a tautology is a degenerate case. But it is perhaps clearer to say that it is not a proposition at all. It corresponds to what Schlick has called a "*Konstatierung*," a term which he used to describe the only synthetic propositions which cannot be doubted. We are now in a position to separate what is true from what is false in Schlick's view: I cannot doubt a *Konstatierung*, not because I am so sure of it that I cannot mistrust it, but because to doubt it doesn't make sense. In speaking of doubting, we must be very careful to distinguish the kind of doubt referring to the truth of the proposition from the kind of doubt referring to the correct use of words. In the case which we are considering, only "grammatical doubt" is possible.

If this analysis is correct, it shows that Mr. Russell is mistaken in thinking that "in a critical scrutiny of what passes for knowledge, the ultimate point is one where doubt is psychologically impossible." At the same time, it confirms and explains Mr. Braithwaite's view that what is in question is "something whose correction is logically impossible."

Such an account as I have given removes, I think, a good deal of the mysterious air which many philosophers have attributed to descriptions of immediate experience. My account shows that there are no such things as empirical judgments which are indubitably true. Every empirical proposition can be doubted, and what cannot be doubted is not an empirical proposition.

II

In this section I want to say a little more about the problems involved in the attitude of doubt, chiefly in order to see more clearly if it is true that the study of particular mental phenomena is important for the logician. Consider a case in which a child is instructed to look at a lamp which shows successively three different colours and then to call out the names of the three different colours. What he has learnt is only the use of the colour-words, but not the use of propositions. Is the child able to doubt? The next question is: What do we mean by the word "doubt" in such a case? Perhaps that the child hesitates, stammers or that the words are accompanied by a feeling of uncertainty? Suppose the child hesitates in uttering the word "red." Shall we say that the child doubts that he has seen a red colour? Or that he is doubtful as to whether he is using the right word? But the question leads us in a wrong direction. The child uttered the word "red" and hesitated—that's all that happened. To ask whether the child's doubt refers to the fact or to the use of the word would only be correct if he were able to ask himself questions like these: "Was the light really red?" "Is this really the right word?" that is to say, if he had learnt to think in propositions. In what does the possibility of doubting consist? It consists in the fact that a more complicated game can be played by adults than by this child.

It is obvious that a child who has only learnt to call out the names of things, but who is not familiar with the use of propositions and the difference of true and false, is not in a position to doubt. In this sense we may say that the possibility of doubting is bound up with the language, and that this possibility appears as soon as the learning of language has reached a certain stage of development.

On the other hand, there are cases in which we do speak of an animal's doubting. A horse wades through a river, testing the depth at each step. If someone is inclined to call this behaviour "doubt," we will not object; we would only point out that what is here meant by "doubt" is just *defined* by this behaviour.

In the first case doubting is not a state of mind which stands as it were *behind* the words. And this brings me to an important point. The relation between the doubt as to whether or not the light was red and the proposition which expresses this doubt is not of the same nature as the relation between a toothache and the proposition which states that I have toothache. A toothache may exist without being expressed in language; but a doubt cannot exist without such an expression. For doubting expression in some form of symbolism is essential.

It is true a person can be in a mood of uncertainty; if we wanted to describe such a state of mind with the help of the verb "to doubt," we should have to use it in an intransitive way. This use of the verb "to doubt" is similar to the intransitive use of the verbs "to be afraid" and "to yearn"; for there are certainly cases where we speak of an experience of yearning without reference to an object, and then we mean by it a certain objectless feeling: "*Ich sehne mich und weiss nicht recht nach was.*" In the same way we may speak of an intransitive fearing, if we want to describe certain bodily sensations of anxiety, e.g., a feeling of constriction in the throat. But such experiences do not constitute what in ordinary life we mean by "fearing," "longing," "doubting." In the ordinary use of these verbs it is essential that they should refer to objects, that is to say, that it does not make sense to say, "I am doubtful, but I don't know of what."

Brentano said that it is this reference to objects which is characteristic of mental states like thinking, doubting, wishing, fearing, hoping, etc. In opposition to him, I hold that the reference of a thought, a doubt, etc., to its object is determined by language. A doubt cannot exist without a language in which it is expressed; nevertheless, to doubt something is not the same as to utter the words, "I doubt whether . . ." The doubt is more than the words in which it is expressed. Let us, therefore, introduce a distinction which may be shown by the contrast of the phrases

"expression of the doubt" "description of the doubt"

and analogously

"expression of the wish" "description of the wish"
"expression of the fear" "description of the fear"
etc.

Expression of the doubt is the proposition expressing the doubt; description of the doubt is the proposition describing what occurs in the mind of a person when he is doubting.

The situation then is this: "to be doubtful of . . ." has not the same meaning as the phrase "to express a doubt." The relation between the two facts is that the expression of a doubt is part of that doubt, so that the doubt could not exist without its expression. The words expressing the doubt may be accompanied by a peculiar state of mind, say, a feeling of uncertainty, or they may be part of a characteristic form of behaviour. The description of the doubt is, therefore, composed of the expression of the doubt together with the description of certain other occurrences.

But this is by no means essential. A person may express a doubt without feeling a specific experience or without showing a characteristic form of behaviour. In such a case the words do not allude to a hidden mental state in the mind of the doubter, indeed, their utterance may be the only process which takes place.

In the case where there is a certain feeling of uncertainty behind the words, it can be said that the intensity of doubting is revealed by the modulation and timbre of the voice. That is to say, we can use the modulation of the voice to indicate the intensity of the doubt. In many cases the hesitating sound would represent the doubtful state of mind. On the other hand, this cannot be the criterion for doubt; since it is perfectly possible for a person to speak in a hesitating voice and to behave as if he were in doubt without in fact being in such a state.

In practical life we make use of various symptoms in order to diagnose whether a person merely pretends to doubt or is really doubting. But none of these symptoms can be said to be the defining criterion for doubt.

Mr. Russell in the paper of this symposium is very near to the truth when he explains that "my belief that today is Tuesday or Wednesday cannot be described without the use of such words ['or,' 'not,' etc.]." He implies that the description of the belief must contain the expression of the belief. But the way in which he develops his view is open to criticism. He writes: "If there were no such mental phenomena as doubt or hesitation, the phrase 'today is Tuesday or Wednesday' would be devoid of significance. The non-mental world can theoretically be completely described without the use of such logical words as 'or,' 'not,' 'all' and 'some'; but certain mental occurrences—e.g., my belief that today is Tuesday or Wednesday—cannot be described without the use of such words. This is one important respect in which, on my view, logic is dependent upon psychology." This whole train of thought is surely erroneous. If the word "doubt" is used to express the fact that a person is in a mood of uncertainty or that an animal behaves in a characteristic way, this feeling or this behaviour can be completely described without the use of such logical words as "or" and "not." But what Mr. Russell has in mind are, of course, other cases of doubting. He appears not to notice that, when he is describing a doubt as to whether today is Tuesday or Wednesday, he is describing an expression of the doubt and, therefore, has to use logical words. Mr. Russell is misled by the ambiguity of such words as "mental phenomenon," "mental occurrence," which are used in such a way that they designate in some cases what may be called private experiences, in other cases operations with symbols or dispositions to do such operations.

I agree with Mr. Russell that our logic is not a system unalterable to all eternity like the Platonic ideas, but that the way in which logic is embodied in our ordinary language and the direction in which we develop it when we construct a formal system is induced and guided by various occasions and conditions of our life. In this connection, I should like to say that there is a wide field of most fascinating questions as to the relation between logic and life. But it seems to me that the example chosen by Mr. Russell, with its appeal to such phenomena as belief and doubt, is unfortunate.

I have said that the rules of our logic are induced by certain experiences, so that if these experiences had been different, another system of rules would be more suitable, in the same way in which one system of geometry can fit a given system of physics better than another one. This raises questions of a peculiar and difficult kind. Let us imagine a language which contains merely the words "and" and "if," but not "or." What would be involved in saying that there are certain circumstances by which the members of such a tribe would be induced to invent the concept "or"? What would such a process be like? Shall we say that the introduction of the concept "or" would be caused by these circumstances? What would it mean to speak of causation in such a case? I will not deny that one can look at things from such an angle. But I would prefer to compare this case with the discovery of a new system in logic or mathematics. Should we say that a mathematical discovery is "caused" by the circumstances which preceded it? Certain situations may be the occasion for people to invent a concept like "or"; nevertheless, there is a gulf between these situations and the invention of the concept "or."

Therefore, the problem lies deeper than Mr. Russell seems to think. In any case, it would be an over-simplification to say that words like "or" are read off from a state of mind, e.g., from a feeling of uncertainty, as a tune is read off from the notes. Such a view would imply that the idea of "or" was pre-existent in the mind, and that all we have to do is to translate it from an amorphous form into the articulate form of language.

III

What puzzles Mr. Russell most is the relation between an object-word and its meaning. He says that if I describe what I am seeing at this moment and utter certain words, this utterance is causally produced by the situation; and that the study of such causal processes is necessary for getting a clear understanding of the function of our language. I think that this view is the result of a misunderstanding, upon which I hope to be able to throw some light.

Let us start with the idea of a transition, which may be explained by a few examples:

1. A move in the game of chess is the transition from one position of the chessmen to another according to the rules of the game.

2. Suppose someone is addressing envelopes and using a list which correlates the names of people with their addresses. In looking up the address of a person he is making a transition in this list.

3. Another example would be the use of a list of colours. If the name of a colour is called, I have to pass over from the name to the corresponding colour and to copy it.

4. In solving an algebraic equation, I have to transform it step by step. Each of these steps is a transition according to the rules of algebra.

5. Every deduction is a transition from one proposition to another in a calculus.

What then is the difference between a causal connection and such a transition? For example, what is the difference between a calculation made by a machine and that made by a person? An important difference is that a person's calculation can be justified by rules which the person can give when he is asked for; not so the calculating of a machine, where the question, "Why do these numbers appear?" can only be answered by describing the mechanism, that is to say, by describing causal connections. On the other hand, if we ask the person why he has calculated in such a way, he will appeal to the rules of arithmetic. He will not reply by describing the mode of action of a hidden mechanism in his brain.

Does this mean that we contrast the act of calculating with the working of a machine? Or, to put it more exactly, that the behaviour of the calculator does not obey causal laws? By no means. We do not deny that his behaviour is caused by the situation and by previous circumstances. He would not act as he does if he had not undergone a process of education. But this process of education, as Mr. Russell admits, is irrelevant.

Let us imagine a case in which a person has to call out the names of the colours which a lamp shows. There are two ways to consider it:

1. The colour of the lamp automatically causes the uttering of the word.

2. The case is a transition from the colour of the lamp to the word according to given rules.

From this example we can see the two ways in which we can look at language. Language may be regarded as a kind of mechanism, to explain the mode of operation of which is a task for psychology. But this is not the way in which a logician describes language. What he is interested in is the geometry of language, not its physics.

What we have said can be expressed by saying: We look upon language not as a mechanism, but as a calculus. To put it more accurately: We *compare* language to a calculus. It wouldn't be correct to say: language is *not* a mechanism, it *is* a calculus. There is no question that words produce many various affects and are in their turn caused by various processes. All we want to maintain is that the logician considers language, not as a mechanism, but as a calculus. In saying this, we are not making any statement about language, but are giving the point of view from which the logician wishes to consider language.

The calculus proceeds no matter what are the causes which determine its separate steps. If a person paints a surface red at the command "Red!" this process may be regarded as a transition in a calculus. The actual procedure may be:

1. The word "red" has been explained to him by a demonstrative definition. Before carrying out the command, he recalls the colour of the specimen.

2. The word produces his action in an automatic way.

3. The person uses a list correlating colour-words with colours. If he hears the command "Red!" he looks for the corresponding word on the list, passes across from it to the colour and copies it.

The fact that he obeys the command, i.e., that he chooses the right colour, may be causally explained by the hypothesis that there is a linking mechanism of a particular kind; but whatever the mechanism, one and the same transition is represented.

The explanation of a word can play a double rôle:—

1. The explaining is the cause of the word's being used in a particular way;

2. The explanation is the ground for this use.

We should not use the words of our mother-tongue in the way we do, unless we had learned this use. In this sense a word's having been explained to me is the cause of my understanding of the word; but this account wouldn't justify the use of the word. There is a connection between the two rôles of explanation, and it is this fact which misleads us into thinking that the meaning of a word is the way in which it functions causally. It would be more correct to say that the meaning of a word is its purpose. For purpose and causal functioning are connected in such a way that an effect which never occurs would not be said to be purposed.

If we explain a word by means of a demonstrative definition, we use a gesture to guide the eyes of the other person in a certain direction. Influences such as these play an important part in our original learning of language. In speaking of training, we lay stress upon the causal, in using the word "explanation," the normative aspect; in the latter case we *compare* the words and the gestures of a demonstrative definition with rules in the fully-developed language.

On the Nature of Mathematical Truth *

CARL G. HEMPEL

1. THE PROBLEM

It is a basic principle of scientific inquiry that no proposition and no theory is to be accepted without adequate grounds. In empirical science, which includes both the natural and the social sciences, the grounds for the acceptance of a theory consist in the agreement of predictions based on the theory with empirical evidence obtained either by experiment or by systematic observation. But what are the grounds which sanction the acceptance of mathematics? That is the question I propose to discuss in the present paper. For reasons which will become clear subsequently, I shall use the term "mathematics" here to refer to arithmetic, algebra, and analysis—to the exclusion, in particular, of geometry.[1]

2. ARE THE PROPOSITIONS OF MATHEMATICS SELF-EVIDENT TRUTHS?

One of the several answers which have been given to our problem asserts that the truths of mathematics, in contradistinction to the hypotheses of empirical science, require neither factual evidence nor any other justification because they are "self-evident." This view, however, which ultimately relegates decisions as to mathematical truth to a feeling of self-evidence, encounters various difficulties. First of all, many mathematical theorems are so hard to establish that even to the specialist in the particular field they appear as anything but self-evident. Secondly, it is well known that some of the most interesting results of mathematics—especially in such fields as abstract set theory and topology—run counter to deeply ingrained intuitions and the customary kind of feeling of self-evidence. Thirdly, the existence of mathematical conjectures such as those of Goldbach and of Fermat, which are quite elementary in content and yet undecided up to this day, certainly shows that not all mathematical truths can be self-evident. And finally, even if self-evidence were attributed only to the

* Reprinted by kind permission of the author and the editors from the *American Mathematical Monthly*, 52, 1945.

[1] A discussion of the status of geometry is given in my article, "Geometry and Empirical Science" [which is reprinted as the next article in the present collection, and which appeared originally in the] *American Mathematical Monthly*, Vol. 52, pp. 7–17, 1945.

basic postulates of mathematics, from which all other mathematical propositions can be deduced, it would be pertinent to remark that judgments as to what may be considered as self-evident are subjective; they may vary from person to person and certainly cannot constitute an adequate basis for decisions as to the objective validity of mathematical propositions.

3. IS MATHEMATICS THE MOST GENERAL EMPIRICAL SCIENCE?

According to another view, advocated especially by John Stuart Mill, mathematics is itself an empirical science which differs from the other branches such as astronomy, physics, chemistry, etc., mainly in two respects: its subject matter is more general than that of any other field of scientific research, and its propositions have been tested and confirmed to a greater extent than those of even the most firmly established sections of astronomy or physics. Indeed, according to this view, the degree to which the laws of mathematics have been borne out by the past experiences of mankind is so overwhelming that—unjustifiably—we have come to think of mathematical theorems as qualitatively different from the well-confirmed hypotheses or theories of other branches of science: we consider them as certain, while other theories are thought of as at best "very probable" or very highly confirmed.

But this view, too, is open to serious objections. From a hypothesis which is empirical in character—such as, for example, Newton's law of gravitation—it is possible to derive predictions to the effect that under certain specified conditions certain specified observable phenomena will occur. The actual occurrence of these phenomena constitutes confirming evidence, their non-occurrence disconfirming evidence for the hypothesis. It follows in particular that an empirical hypothesis is theoretically disconfirmable; i.e., it is possible to indicate what kind of evidence, if actually encountered, would disconfirm the hypothesis. In the light of this remark, consider now a simple "hypothesis" from arithmetic: $3 + 2 = 5$. If this is actually an empirical generalization of past experiences, then it must be possible to state what kind of evidence would oblige us to concede the hypothesis was not generally true after all. If any disconfirming evidence for the given proposition can be thought of, the following illustration might well be typical of it: We place some microbes on a slide, putting down first three of them and then another two. Afterwards we count all the microbes to test whether in this instance 3 and 2 actually added up to 5. Suppose now that we counted 6 microbes altogether. Would we consider this as an empirical disconfirmation of the given proposition, or at least as a proof that it does not apply to microbes? Clearly not; rather, we would assume we had made a mistake in counting or that one of the microbes had split in two between the first and the second count. But under no circumstances could the phenomenon just described invalidate the arithmetical proposition in question; for the latter asserts nothing whatever about the behavior of microbes; it merely states that any set consisting of $3 + 2$ objects may also be said to consist of 5 objects. And this is so because the symbols "$3 + 2$" and "5" denote the same number: they are synonymous by virtue of the fact that the symbols "2," "3," "5," and "$+$" are *defined* (or tacitly understood) in such a way that the above identity holds as a consequence of the meaning attached to the concepts involved in it.

4. THE ANALYTIC CHARACTER OF MATHEMATICAL PROPOSITIONS

The statement that $3 + 2 = 5$, then, is true for similar reasons as, say, the assertion that no sexagenarian is 45 years of age. Both are true simply by virtue of definitions or of similar stipulations which determine the meaning of the key terms involved. Statements of this kind share certain important characteristics: Their validation naturally requires no empirical evidence; they can be shown to be true by a mere analysis of the meaning attached to the terms which occur in them. In the language of logic, sentences of this kind are called analytic or true *a priori*, which is to indicate that their truth is logically independent of, or logically prior to, any experiential evidence.[2] And while the statements of empirical science, which are synthetic and can be validated only *a posteriori*, are constantly subject to revision in the light of new evidence, the truth of an analytic statement can be established definitely, once and for all. However, this characteristic "theoretical certainty" of analytic propositions has to be paid for at a high price: An analytic statement conveys no factual information. Our statement about sexagenarians, for example, asserts nothing that could possibly conflict with any factual evidence: it has no factual implications, no empirical content; and it is precisely for this reason that the statement can be validated without recourse to empirical evidence.

Let us illustrate this view of the nature of mathematical propositions by reference to another, frequently cited, example of a mathematical—or rather logical—truth, namely the proposition that whenever $a = b$ and $b = c$ then $a = c$. On what grounds can this so-called "transitivity of identity" be asserted? Is it of an empirical nature and hence at least theoretically disconfirmable by empirical evidence? Suppose, for example, that a, b, c, are certain shades of green, and that as far as we can see, $a = b$ and $b = c$,

---

[2] The objection is sometimes raised that without certain types of experience, such as encountering several objects of the same kind, the integers and the arithmetical operations with them would never have been invented, and that therefore the propositions of arithmetic do have an empirical basis. This type of argument, however, involves a confusion of the logical and the psychological meaning of the term "basis." It may very well be the case that certain experiences occasion psychologically the formation of arithmetical ideas and in this sense form an empirical "basis" for them; but this point is entirely irrelevant for the logical questions as to the *grounds* on which the propositions of arithmetic may be accepted as true. The point made above is that no empirical "basis" or evidence whatever is needed to establish the truth of the propositions of arithmetic.

but clearly $a \neq c$. This phenomenon actually occurs under certain conditions; do we consider it as disconfirming evidence for the proposition under consideration? Undoubtedly not; we would argue that if $a \neq c$, it is impossible that $a = b$ and also $b = c$; between the terms of at least one of these latter pairs, there must obtain a difference, though perhaps only a subliminal one. And we would dismiss the possibility of empirical disconfirmation, and indeed the idea that an empirical test should be relevant here, on the grounds that identity is a transitive relation by virtue of its definition or by virtue of the basic postulates governing it.[3] Hence, the principle in question is true *a priori*.

5. MATHEMATICS AS AN AXIOMATIZED DEDUCTIVE SYSTEM

I have argued so far that the validity of mathematics rests neither on its alleged self-evidential character nor on any empirical basis, but derives from the stipulations which determine the meaning of the mathematical concepts, and that the propositions of mathematics are therefore essentially "true by definition." This latter statement, however, is obviously oversimplified and needs restatement and a more careful justification.

For the rigorous development of a mathematical theory proceeds not simply from a set of definitions but rather from a set of non-definitional propositions which are not proved within the theory; these are the postulates or axioms of the theory.[4] They are formulated in terms of certain basic or primitive concepts for which no definitions are provided within the theory. It is sometimes asserted that the postulates themselves represent "implicit definitions" of the primitive terms. Such a characterization of the postulates, however, is misleading. For while the postulates do limit, in a specific sense, the meanings that can possibly be ascribed to the primitives, any self-consistent postulate system admits, nevertheless, many different interpretations of the primitive terms (this will soon be illustrated), whereas a set of definitions in the strict sense of the word determines the meanings of the definienda in a unique fashion.

Once the primitive terms and the postulates have been laid down, the entire theory is completely determined; it is derivable from its postulational basis in the following sense: Every term of the theory is definable in terms of the primitives, and every proposition of the theory is logically deducible from the postulates. To be entirely precise, it is necessary also to specify the principles of logic which are to be used in the proof of the propositions, i.e., in their deduction from the postulates. These principles can be stated quite explicitly. They fall into two groups: Primitive sentences, or postulates, of logic (such as: If p and q is the case, then p is the

---

[3] A precise account of the definition and the essential characteristics of the identity relation may be found in A. Tarski, *Introduction to Logic*, New York, 1941, ch. III.

[4] For a lucid and concise account of the axiomatic method, see A. Tarski, *loc. cit.*, ch. VI.

case), and rules of deduction or inference (including, for example, the familiar *modus ponens* rule and the rules of substitution which make it possible to infer, from a general proposition, any one of its substitution instances). A more detailed discussion of the structure and content of logic would, however, lead too far afield in the context of this article.

6. PEANO'S AXIOM SYSTEM AS A BASIS FOR MATHEMATICS

Let us now consider a postulate system from which the entire arithmetic of the natural numbers can be derived. This system was devised by the Italian mathematician and logician G. Peano (1858–1932). The primitives of this system are the terms "o," "number," and "successor." While, of course, no definition of these terms is given within the theory, the symbol "o" is intended to designate the number o in its usual meaning, while the term "number" is meant to refer to the natural numbers o, 1, 2, 3 . . . exclusively. By the successor of a natural number n, which will sometimes briefly be called n', is meant the natural number immediately following n in the natural order. Peano's system contains the following 5 postulates:

P1. o is a number
P2. The successor of any number is a number
P3. No two numbers have the same successor
P4. o is not the successor of any number
P5. If P is a property such that (a) o has the property P, and (b) whenever a number n has the property P, then the successor of n also has the property P, then every number has the property P.

The last postulate embodies the principle of mathematical induction and illustrates in a very obvious manner the enforcement of a mathematical "truth" by stipulation. The construction of elementary arithmetic on this basis begins with the definition of the various natural numbers. 1 is defined as the successor of o, or briefly as o'; 2 as $1'$, 3 as $2'$, and so on. By virtue of P2, this process can be continued indefinitely; because of P3 (in combination with P5), it never leads back to one of the numbers previously defined, and in view of P4, it does not lead back to o either.

As the next step, we can set up a definition of addition which expresses in a precise form the idea that the addition of any natural number to some given number may be considered as a repeated addition of 1; the latter operation is readily expressible by means of the successor relation. This definition of addition runs as follows:

D1.   (a) $n + o = n;$ (b) $n + k' = (n + k)'.$

The two stipulations of this recursive definition completely determine the sum of any two integers. Consider, for example, the sum $3 + 2$. According to the definitions of the numbers 2 and 1, we have $3 + 2 = 3 + 1' =$

$3 + (o')'$; by D1 (b), $3 + (o')' = (3 + o')' = ((3 + o)')'$; but by D1 (a), and by the definitions of the numbers 4 and 5, $((3 + o)')' = (3')' = 4' = 5$. This proof also renders more explicit and precise the comments made earlier in this paper on the truth of the proposition that $3 + 2 = 5$: Within the Peano system of arithmetic, its truth flows not merely from the definition of the concepts involved, but also from the postulates that govern these various concepts. (In our specific example, the postulates P1 and P2 are presupposed to guarantee that 1, 2, 3, 4, 5 are numbers in Peano's system; the general proof that D1 determines the sum of any two numbers also makes use of P5.) If we call the postulates and definitions of an axiomatized theory the "stipulations" concerning the concepts of that theory, then we may say now that the propositions of the arithmetic of the natural numbers are true by virtue of the stipulations which have been laid down initially for the arithmetical concepts. (Note, incidentally, that our proof of the formula "$3 + 2 = 5$" repeatedly made use of the transitivity of identity; the latter is accepted here as one of the rules of logic which may be used in the proof of any arithmetical theorem; it is, therefore, included among Peano's postulates no more than any other principle of logic.)

Now, the multiplication of natural numbers may be defined by means of the following recursive definition, which expresses in a rigorous form the idea that a product nk of two integers may be considered as the sum of k terms each of which equals n.

D2.   (a) $n \cdot o = o$;   (b) $n \cdot k' = n \cdot k + n$.

It now is possible to prove the familiar general laws governing addition and multiplication, such as the commutative, associative, and distributive laws ($n + k = k + n$; $n \cdot k = k \cdot n$; $n + (k + l) = (n + k) + l$; $n \cdot (k \cdot l) = (n \cdot k) \cdot l$; $n \cdot (k + l) = (n \cdot k) + (n \cdot l)$). In terms of addition and multiplication, the inverse operations of subtraction and division can then be defined. But it turns out that these "cannot always be performed"; i.e., in contradistinction to the sum and the product, the difference and the quotient are not defined for every couple of numbers; for example, $7 - 10$ and $7 \div 10$ are undefined. This situation suggests an enlargement of the number system by the introduction of negative and of rational numbers.

It is sometimes held that in order to effect this enlargement, we have to "assume" or else to "postulate" the existence of the desired additional kinds of numbers with properties that make them fit to fill the gaps of subtraction and division. This method of simply postulating what we want has its advantages; but, as Bertrand Russell [5] puts it, they are the same as the advantages of theft over honest toil; and it is a remarkable fact that the negative as well as the rational numbers can be obtained from Peano's

[5] Bertrand Russell, *Introduction to Mathematical Philosophy*, New York and London. 1919, p. 71.

primitives by the honest toil of constructing explicit definitions for them, without the introduction of any new postulates or assumptions whatsoever. Every positive and negative integer (in contradistinction to a natural number which has no sign) is definable as a certain set of ordered couples of natural numbers; thus, the integer $+ 2$ is definable as the set of all ordered couples (m, n) of natural numbers where $m = n + 2$; the integer $- 2$ is the set of all ordered couples (m, n) of natural numbers with $n = m + 2$. (Similarly, rational numbers are defined as classes of ordered couples of integers.) The various arithmetical operations can then be defined with reference to these new types of numbers, and the validity of all the arithmetical laws governing these operations can be proved by virtue of nothing more than Peano's postulates and the definitions of the various arithmetical concepts involved.

The much broader system thus obtained is still incomplete in the sense that not every number in it has a square root, and more generally, not every algebraic equation whose coefficients are all numbers of the system has a solution in the system. This suggests further expansions of the number system by the introduction of real and finally of complex numbers. Again, this enormous extension can be effected by mere definition, without the introduction of a single new postulate.[6] On the basis thus obtained, the various arithmetical and algebraic operations can be defined for the numbers of the new system, the concepts of function, of limit, of derivative and integral can be introduced, and the familiar theorems pertaining to these concepts can be proved, so that finally the huge system of mathematics as here delimited rests on the narrow basis of Peano's system: Every concept of mathematics can be defined by means of Peano's three primitives, and every proposition of mathematics can be deduced from the five postulates enriched by the definitions of the non-primitive terms.[6a]. These deductions can be carried out, in most cases, by means of

[6] For a more detailed account of the construction of the number system on Peano's basis, cf. Bertrand Russell, *loc. cit.*, esp. chs. I and VII. A rigorous and concise presentation of that construction, beginning, however, with the set of all integers rather than that of the natural numbers, may be found in G. Birkhoff and S. MacLane, *A Survey of Modern Algebra*, New York, 1941, chs. I, II, III, V. For a general survey of the construction of the number system, cf. also J. W. Young, *Lectures on the Fundamental Concepts of Algebra and Geometry*, New York, 1911, esp. lectures X, XI, XII.

[6a] As a result of very deep-reaching investigations carried out by K. Gödel it is known that arithmetic, and *a fortiori* mathematics, is an incomplete theory in the following sense: While all those propositions which belong to the classical systems of arithmetic, algebra, and analysis can indeed be derived, in the sense characterized above, from the Peano postulates, there exist nevertheless other propositions which can be expressed in purely arithmetical terms, and which are true, but which cannot be derived from the Peano system. And more generally: For any postulate system of arithmetic (or of mathematics for that matter) which is not self-contradictory, there exist propositions which are true, and which can be stated in purely arithmetical terms, but which cannot be derived from that postulate system. In other words, it is impossible to construct a postulate system which is not self-contradictory, and which contains

nothing more than the principles of formal logic; the proof of some theorems concerning real numbers, however, requires one assumption which is not usually included among the latter. This is the so-called axiom of choice. It asserts that given a class of mutually exclusive classes, none of which is empty, there exists at least one class which has exactly one element in common with each of the given classes. By virtue of this principle and the rules of formal logic, the content of all of mathematics can thus be derived from Peano's modest system—a remarkable achievement in systematizing the content of mathematics and clarifying the foundations of its validity.

7. INTERPRETATIONS OF PEANO'S PRIMITIVES

As a consequence of this result, the whole system of mathematics might be said to be true by virtue of mere definitions (namely, of the non-primitive mathematical terms) provided that the five Peano postulates are true. However, strictly speaking, we cannot, at this juncture, refer to the Peano postulates as propositions which are either true or false, for they contain three primitive terms which have not been assigned any specific meaning. All we can assert so far is that any specific interpretation of the primitives which satisfies the five postulates—i.e., turns them into true statements—will also satisfy all the theorems deduced from them. But for Peano's system, there are several—indeed, infinitely many—interpretations which will do this. For example, let us understand by o the origin of a half-line, by the successor of a point on that half-line the point 1 cm. behind it, counting from the origin, and by a number any point which is either the origin or can be reached from it by a finite succession of steps each of which leads from one point to its successor. It can then readily be seen that all the Peano postulates as well as the ensuing theorems turn into true propositions, although the interpretation given to the primitives is certainly not the customary one, which was mentioned earlier. More generally, it can be shown that every progression of elements of any kind provides a true interpretation, or a "model," of the Peano system. This example illustrates our earlier observation that a postulate system cannot be regarded as a set of "implicit definitions" for the primitive terms: The Peano system permits of many different interpretations, whereas in everyday as well as in scientific language, we attach one specific meaning to the concepts of arithmetic. Thus, e.g., in scientific and in everyday discourse,

---

among its consequences all true propositions which can be formulated within the language of arithmetic.

This fact does not, however, affect the result outlined above, namely, that it is possible to deduce, from the Peano postulates and the additional definitions of non-primitive terms, all those propositions which constitute the classical theory of arithmetic, algebra, and analysis; and it is to these propositions that I refer above and subsequently as the propositions of mathematics.

the concept 2 is understood in such a way that from the statement "Mr. Brown as well as Mr. Cope, but no one else is in the office, and Mr. Brown is not the same person as Mr. Cope," the conclusion "Exactly two persons are in the office" may be validly inferred. But the stipulations laid down in Peano's system for the natural numbers, and for the number 2 in particular, do not enable us to draw this conclusion; they do not "implicitly determine" the customary meaning of the concept 2 or of the other arithmetical concepts. And the mathematician cannot acquiesce in this deficiency by arguing that he is not concerned with the customary meaning of the mathematical concepts; for in proving, say, that every positive real number has exactly two real square roots, he is himself using the concept 2 in its customary meaning, and his very theorem cannot be proved unless we presuppose more about the number 2 than is stipulated in the Peano system.

If therefore mathematics is to be a correct theory of the mathematical concepts in their intended meaning, it is not sufficient for its validation to have shown that the entire system is derivable from the Peano postulates plus suitable definitions; rather, we have to inquire further whether the Peano postulates are actually true when the primitives are understood in their customary meaning. This question, of course, can be answered only after the customary meaning of the terms "o," "natural number," and "successor" has been clearly defined. To this task we now turn.

8. DEFINITION OF THE CUSTOMARY MEANING OF THE CONCEPTS OF ARITHMETIC IN PURELY LOGICAL TERMS

At first blush, it might seem a hopeless undertaking to try to define these basic arithmetical concepts without presupposing other terms of arithmetic, which would involve us in a circular procedure. However, quite rigorous definitions of the desired kind can indeed be formulated, and it can be shown that for the concepts so defined, all Peano postulates turn into true statements. This important result is due to the research of the German logician G. Frege (1848–1925) and to the subsequent systematic and detailed work of the contemporary English logicians and philosophers B. Russell and A. N. Whitehead. Let us consider briefly the basic ideas underlying these definitions.[7]

A natural number—or, in Peano's term, a number—in its customary meaning can be considered as a characteristic of certain *classes* of objects. Thus, e.g., the class of the apostles has the number 12, the class of the

---

[7] For a more detailed discussion, cf. Russell, *loc. cit.*, chs. II, III, IV. A complete technical development of the idea can be found in the great standard work in mathematical logic, A. N. Whitehead and B. Russell, *Principia Mathematica*, Cambridge, England, 1910–1913. For a very precise recent development of the theory, see W. V. O. Quine, *Mathematical Logic*, New York, 1940. A specific discussion of the Peano system and its interpretations from the viewpoint of semantics is included in R. Carnap, *Foundations of Logic and Mathematics*, International Encyclopedia of Unified Science, Vol. I, no. 3, Chicago, 1939; especially sections 14, 17, 18.

Dionne quintuplets the number 5, any couple the number 2, and so on. Let us now express precisely the meaning of the assertion that a certain class C has the number 2, or briefly, that $n(C) = 2$. Brief reflection will show that the following definiens is adequate in the sense of the customary meaning of the concept 2: There is some object x and some object y such that (1) $x \epsilon C$ (i.e., x is an element of C) and $y \epsilon C$, (2) $x \neq y$, and (3) if z is any object such that $z \epsilon C$, then either $z = x$ or $z = y$. (Note that on the basis of this definition it becomes indeed possible to infer the statement "The number of persons in the office is 2" from "Mr. Brown as well as Mr. Cope, but no one else is in the office, and Mr. Brown is not identical with Mr. Cope"; C is here the class of persons in the office.) Analogously, the meaning of the statement that $n(C) = 1$ can be defined thus: There is some x such that $x \epsilon C$, and any object y such that $y \epsilon C$, is identical with x. Similarly, the customary meaning of the statement that $n(C) = 0$ is this: There is no object such that $x \epsilon C$.

The general pattern of these definitions clearly lends itself to the definition of any natural number. Let us note especially that in the definitions thus obtained, the definiens never contains any arithmetical term, but merely expressions taken from the field of formal logic, including the signs of identity and difference. So far, we have defined only the meaning of such phrases as "$n(C) = 2$," but we have given no definition for the numbers 0, 1, 2, . . . apart from this context. This desideratum can be met on the basis of the consideration that 2 is that property which is common to all couples, i.e., to all classes C such that $n(C) = 2$. This common property may be conceptually represented by the class of all those classes which share this property. Thus we arrive at the definition: 2 is the class of all couples, i.e., the class of all classes C for which $n(C) = 2$.—This definition is by no means circular because the concept of couple—in other words, the meaning of "$n(C) = 2$"—has been previously defined without any reference to the number 2. Analogously, 1 is the class of all unit classes, i.e., the class of all classes C for which $n(C) = 1$. Finally, 0 is the class of all null classes, i.e., the class of all classes without elements. And as there is only one such class, 0 is simply the class whose only element is the null class. Clearly, the customary meaning of any given natural number can be defined in this fashion.[8] In order to characterize the intended interpretation of Peano's primitives, we actually need, of all the definitions

[8] The assertion that the definitions given above state the "customary" meaning of the arithmetical terms involved is to be understood in the logical, not the psychological sense of the term "meaning." It would obviously be absurd to claim that the above definitions express "what everybody has in mind" when talking about numbers and the various operations that can be performed with them. What is achieved by those definitions is rather a "logical reconstruction" of the concepts of arithmetic in the sense that if the definitions are accepted, then those statements in science and everyday discourse which involve arithmetical terms can be interpreted coherently and systematically in such a manner that they are capable of objective validation. The statement about the two persons in the office provides a very elementary illustration of what is meant here.

here referred to, only that of the number o. It remains to define the terms "successor" and "integer."

The definition of "successor," whose precise formulation involves too many niceties to be stated here, is a careful expression of a simple idea which is illustrated by the following example: Consider the number 5, i.e., the class of all quintuplets. Let us select an arbitrary one of these quintuplets and add to it an object which is not yet one of its members. 5', the successor of 5, may then be defined as the number applying to the set thus obtained (which, of course, is a sextuplet). Finally, it is possible to formulate a definition of the customary meaning of the concept of natural number; this definition, which again cannot be given here, expresses, in a rigorous form, the idea that the class of the natural numbers consists of the number o, its successor, the successor of that successor, and so on.

If the definitions here characterized are carefully written out—this is one of the cases where the techniques of symbolic, or mathematical, logic prove indispensable—it is seen that the definiens of every one of them contains exclusively terms from the field of pure logic. In fact, it is possible to state the customary interpretation of Peano's primitives, and thus also the meaning of every concept definable by means of them—and that includes every concept of mathematics—in terms of the following seven expressions (in addition to variables such as "x" and "C"): *not, and, if—then; for every object x it is the case that* . . . ; *there is some object x such that* . . . ; x *is an* element *of class* C; *the class of all things x such that* . . . And it is even possible to reduce the number of logical concepts needed to a mere four: The first three of the concepts just mentioned are all definable in terms of "*neither—nor,*" and the fifth is definable by means of the fourth and "*neither—nor.*" Thus, all the concepts of mathematics prove definable in terms of four concepts of pure logic. (The definition of one of the more complex concepts of mathematics in terms of the four primitives just mentioned may well fill hundreds or even thousands of pages; but clearly this affects in no way the theoretical importance of the result just obtained; it does, however, show the great convenience and indeed practical indispensability for mathematics of having a large system of highly complex defined concepts available.)

9. THE TRUTH OF PEANO'S POSTULATES IN THEIR CUSTOMARY INTERPRETATION

The definitions characterized in the preceding section may be said to render precise and explicit the customary meaning of the concepts of arithmetic. Moreover—and this is crucial for the question of the validity of mathematics—it can be shown that the Peano postulates all turn into true propositions if the primitives are construed in accordance with the definitions just considered.

Thus, P1 (o is a number) is true because the class of all numbers—i.e., natural numbers—was defined as consisting of o and all its successors. The truth of P2 (the successor of any number is a number) follows from the same definition. This is true also of P5, the principle of mathematical induction. To prove this, however, we would have to resort to the precise definition of "integer" rather than the loose description given of that definition above. P4 (o is not the successor of any number) is seen to be true as follows: By virtue of the definition of "successor," a number which is a successor of some number can apply only to classes which contain at least one element; but the number o, by definition, applies to a class if and only if that class is empty. While the truth of P1, P2, P4, P5 can be inferred from the above definitions simply by means of the principles of logic, the proof of P3 (no two numbers have the same successor) presents a certain difficulty. As was mentioned in the preceding section, the definition of the successor of a number n is based on the process of adding, to a class of n elements, one element not yet contained in that class. Now if there should exist only a finite number of things altogether then this process could not be continued indefinitely, and P3, which (in conjunction with P1 and P2) implies that the integers form an infinite set, would be false. This difficulty can be met by the introduction of a special "axiom of infinity" [9] which asserts, in effect, the existence of infinitely many objects, and thus makes P3 demonstrable. The axiom of infinity does not belong to the generally recognized laws of logic; but it is capable of expression in purely logical terms and may be considered as an additional postulate of modern logical theory.

10. MATHEMATICS AS A BRANCH OF LOGIC

As was pointed out earlier, all the theorems of arithmetic, algebra, and analysis can be deduced from the Peano postulates and the definitions of those mathematical terms which are not primitives in Peano's system. This deduction requires only the principles of logic plus, in certain cases, the axiom of choice. By combining this result with what has just been said about the Peano system, the following conclusion is obtained, which is also known as *the thesis of logicism concerning the nature of mathematics*:

Mathematics is a branch of logic. It can be derived from logic in the following sense:

a. All the concepts of mathematics, i.e., of arithmetic, algebra, and analysis, can be defined in terms of four concepts of pure logic.

b. All the theorems of mathematics can be deduced from those definitions by means of the principles of logic (including the axioms of infinity and choice).[10]

[9] Cf. Bertrand Russell, *loc. cit.*, p. 24 and ch. XIII.

[10] The principles of logic developed in modern systems of formal logic embody certain restrictions as compared with those logical rules which had been rather generally accepted as sound until about the turn of the 20th century. At that time, the discovery of the famous paradoxes of logic, especially of Russell's paradox (cf. Russell, *loc. cit.*,

In this sense it can be said that the propositions of the system of mathematics as here delimited are true by virtue of the definitions of the mathematical concepts involved, or that they make explicit certain characteristics with which we have endowed our mathematical concepts by definition. The propositions of mathematics have, therefore, the same unquestionable certainty which is typical of such propositions as "All bachelors are unmarried," but they also share the complete lack of empirical content which is associated with that certainty: The propositions of mathematics are devoid of all factual content; they convey no information whatever on any empirical subject matter.

11. ON THE APPLICABILITY OF MATHEMATICS TO EMPIRICAL SUBJECT MATTER.

This result seems to be irreconcilable with the fact that after all mathematics has proved to be eminently applicable to empirical subject matter, and that indeed the greater part of present-day scientific knowledge has been reached only through continual reliance on and application of the propositions of mathematics. Let us try to clarify this apparent paradox by reference to some examples.

Suppose that we are examining a certain amount of some gas, whose volume v, at a certain fixed temperature, is found to be 9 cubic feet when the pressure p is 4 atmospheres. And let us assume further that the volume of the gas for the same temperature and $p = 6$ at., is predicted by means of Boyle's law. Using elementary arithmetic we reason thus: For corresponding values of v and p, $vp = c$, and $v = 9$ when $p = 4$; hence $c = 36$: Therefore, when $p = 6$, then $v = 6$. Suppose that this prediction is borne out by subsequent test. Does that show that the arithmetic used has a predictive power of its own, that its propositions have factual implications? Certainly not. All the predictive power here deployed, all the empirical content exhibited stems from the initial data and from Boyle's law, which asserts that $vp = c$ for *any* two corresponding values of v and p, hence also for $v = 9$, $p = 4$, and for $p = 6$ and the corresponding value of v.[11] The function of the mathematics here applied is not predictive at all; rather, it is analytic or explicative: it renders explicit certain assumptions or assertions which are included in the content of the premises of the argument (in our case, these consist of Boyle's law plus the additional data); mathematical reasoning reveals that those premises contain—hidden in them, as it were,—an assertion about the case as yet unobserved. In accepting our premises—so arithmetic reveals—we have—knowingly or

---

ch. XIII), revealed the fact that the logical principles implicit in customary mathematical reasoning involved contradictions and therefore had to be curtailed in one manner or another.

[11] Note that we may say "hence" by virtue of the rule of substitution, which is one of the rules of logical inference.

unknowingly—already accepted the implication that the p-value in question is 6. Mathematical as well as logical reasoning is a conceptual technique of making explicit what is implicitly contained in a set of premises. The conclusions to which this technique leads assert nothing that is *theoretically new* in the sense of not being contained in the content of the premises. But the results obtained may well be *psychologically new:* we may not have been aware, before using the techniques of logic and mathematics, what we committed ourselves to in accepting a certain set of assumptions or assertions.

A similar analysis is possible in all other cases of applied mathematics, including those involving, say, the calculus. Consider, for example, the hypothesis that a certain object, moving in a specified electric field, will undergo a constant acceleration of 5 feet/sec². For the purpose of testing this hypothesis, we might derive from it, by means of two successive integrations, the prediction that if the object is at rest at the beginning of the motion, then the distance covered by it at any time t is $\frac{5}{2}t^2$ feet. This conclusion may clearly be psychologically new to a person not acquainted with the subject, but it is not theoretically new; the content of the conclusion is already contained in that of the hypothesis about the constant acceleration. And indeed, here as well as in the case of the compression of a gas, a failure of the prediction to come true would be considered as indicative of the factual incorrectness of at least one of the premises involved (*f.ex.*, of Boyle's law in its application to the particular gas), but never as a sign that the logical and mathematical principles involved might be unsound.

Thus, in the establishment of empirical knowledge, mathematics (as well as logic) has, so to speak, the function of a theoretical juice extractor: the techniques of mathematical and logical theory can produce no more juice of factual information than is contained in the assumptions to which they are applied; but they may produce a great deal more juice of this kind than might have been anticipated upon a first intuitive inspection of those assumptions which form the raw material for the extractor.

At this point, it may be well to consider briefly the status of those mathematical disciplines which are not outgrowths of arithmetic and thus of logic; these include in particular topology, geometry, and the various branches of abstract algebra, such as the theory of groups, lattices, fields, etc. Each of these disciplines can be developed as a purely deductive system on the basis of a suitable set of postulates. If P be the conjunction of the postulates for a given theory, then the proof of a proposition T of that theory consists in deducing T from P by means of the principles of formal logic. What is established by the proof is therefore not the truth of T, but rather the fact that T is true provided that the postulates are. But since both P and T contain certain primitive terms of the theory, to which no specific meaning is assigned, it is not strictly possible to speak of the truth of either P or T; it is therefore more adequate to state the point as follows: If a proposition T is logically deduced from P, then every specific interpretation of the primitives which turns all the postulates of P into true statements, will also render T a true statement. Up to this point, the analysis is exactly analogous to that of arithmetic as based on Peano's set of postulates. In the case of arithmetic, however, it proved possible to go a step further, namely to define the customary meanings of the primitives in terms of purely logical concepts and to show that the postulates—and therefore also the theorems—of arithmetic are unconditionally true by virtue of these definitions. An analogous procedure is not applicable to those disciplines which are not outgrowths of arithmetic: The primitives of the various branches of abstract algebra have no specific "customary meaning"; and if geometry in its customary interpretation is thought of as a theory of the structure of physical space, then its primitives have to be construed as referring to certain types of physical entities, and the question of the truth of a geometrical theory in this interpretation turns into an *empirical* problem.[12] For the purpose of applying any one of these non-arithmetical disciplines to some specific field of mathematics or empirical science, it is therefore necessary first to assign to the primitives some specific meaning and then to ascertain whether in this interpretation the postulates turn into true statements. If this is the case, then we can be sure that all the theorems are true statements too, because they are logically derived from the postulates and thus simply explicate the content of the latter in the given interpretation. In their application to empirical subject matter, therefore, these mathematical theories no less than those which grow out of arithmetic and ultimately out of pure logic, have the function of an analytic tool, which brings to light the implications of a given set of assumptions but adds nothing to their content.

But while mathematics in no case contributes anything to the content of our knowledge of empirical matters, it is entirely indispensable as an instrument for the validation and even for the linguistic expression of such knowledge: The majority of the more far-reaching theories in empirical science—including those which lend themselves most eminently to prediction or to practical application—are stated with the help of mathematical concepts; the formulation of these theories makes use, in particular, of the number system, and of functional relationships among different metrical variables. Furthermore, the scientific test of these theories, the establishment of predictions by means of them, and finally their practical application, all require the deduction, from the general theory, of certain specific consequences; and such deduction would be entirely impossible without the techniques of mathematics which reveal what the given general theory implicitly asserts about a certain special case.

---

[12] For a more detailed discussion of this point, cf. the next article in this collection.

Thus, the analysis outlined on these pages exhibits the system of mathematics as a vast and ingenious conceptual structure without empirical content and yet an indispensable and powerful theoretical instrument for the scientific understanding and mastery of the world of our experience.

Geometry and Empirical Science *

CARL G. HEMPEL

1. INTRODUCTION

The most distinctive characteristic which differentiates mathematics from the various branches of empirical science, and which accounts for its fame as the queen of the sciences, is no doubt the peculiar certainty and necessity of its results. No proposition in even the most advanced parts of empirical science can ever attain this status; a hypothesis concerning "matters of empirical fact" can at best acquire what is loosely called a high probability or a high degree of confirmation on the basis of the relevant evidence available; but however well it may have been confirmed by careful tests, the possibility can never be precluded that it will have to be discarded later in the light of new and disconfirming evidence. Thus, all the theories and hypotheses of empirical science share this provisional character of being established and accepted "until further notice," whereas a mathematical theorem, once proved, is established once and for all; it holds with that particular certainty which no subsequent empirical discoveries, however unexpected and extraordinary, can ever affect to the slightest extent. It is the purpose of this paper to examine the nature of that proverbial "mathematical certainty" with special reference to geometry, in an attempt to shed some light on the question as to the validity of geometrical theories, and their significance for our knowledge of the structure of physical space.

The nature of mathematical truth can be understood through an analysis of the method by means of which it is established. On this point I can be very brief: it is the method of mathematical demonstration, which consists in the logical deduction of the proposition to be proved from other propositions, previously established. Clearly, this procedure would involve an infinite regress unless some propositions were accepted without proof; such propositions are indeed found in every mathematical discipline which is rigorously developed; they are the *axioms* or *postulates* (we shall use these terms interchangeably) of the theory. Geometry provides the historically first example of the axiomatic presentation of a mathematical discipline. The classical set of postulates, however, on which Euclid based

* Reprinted by kind permission of the author and the editors from the *American Mathematical Monthly*, 52, 1945.

his system, has proved insufficient for the deduction of the well-known theorems of so-called euclidean geometry; it has therefore been revised and supplemented in modern times, and at present various adequate systems of postulates for euclidean geometry are available; the one most closely related to Euclid's system is probably that of Hilbert.

2. THE INADEQUACY OF EUCLID'S POSTULATES

The inadequacy of Euclid's own set of postulates illustrates a point which is crucial for the axiomatic method in modern mathematics: Once the postulates for a theory have been laid down, every further proposition of the theory must be proved exclusively by logical deduction from the postulates; any appeal, explicit or implicit, to a feeling of self-evidence, or to the characteristics of geometrical figures, or to our experiences concerning the behavior of rigid bodies in physical space, or the like, is strictly prohibited; such devices may have a heuristic value in guiding our efforts to find a strict proof for a theorem, but the proof itself must contain absolutely no reference to such aids. This is particularly important in geometry, where our so-called intuition of geometrical relationships, supported by reference to figures or to previous physical experiences, may induce us tacitly to make use of assumptions which are neither formulated in our postulates nor provable by means of them. Consider, for example, the theorem that in a triangle the three medians bisecting the sides intersect in one point which divides each of them in the ratio of 1:2. To prove this theorem, one shows first that in any triangle ABC (see figure) the line segment MN which connects the centers of AB and AC is parallel to BC and therefore half as long as the latter side. Then the lines BN and CM are drawn, and an examination of the triangles MON and BOC leads to the proof of the theorem. In this procedure, it is usually taken for granted that BN and CM intersect in a point O which lies between B and N as well as between C and M. This assumption is based on geometrical

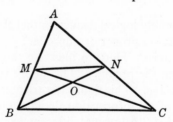

intuition, and indeed, it cannot be deduced from Euclid's postulates; to make it strictly demonstrable and independent of any reference to intuition, a special group of postulates has been added to those of Euclid; they are the postulates of order. One of these—to give an example—asserts that if A, B, C are points on a straight line l, and if B lies between A and C, then B also lies between C and A. Not even as "trivial" an assumption as this may be taken for granted; the system of postulates has to be made so complete that all the required propositions can be deduced from it by purely logical means.

Another illustration of the point under consideration is provided by the proposition that triangles which agree in two sides and the enclosed angle, are congruent. In Euclid's Elements, this proposition is presented as a theorem; the alleged proof, however, makes use of the ideas of motion and superimposition of figures and thus involves tacit assumptions which are based on our geometric intuition and on experiences with rigid bodies, but which are definitely not warranted by—i.e., deducible from—Euclid's postulates. In Hilbert's system, therefore, this proposition (more precisely: part of it) is explicitly included among the postulates.

3. MATHEMATICAL CERTAINTY

It is this purely deductive character of mathematical proof which forms the basis of mathematical certainty: What the rigorous proof of a theorem —say the proposition about the sum of the angles in a triangle—establishes is not the truth of the proposition in question but rather a conditional insight to the effect that that proposition is certainly true *provided that* the postulates are true; in other words, the proof of a mathematical proposition establishes the fact that the latter is logically implied by the postulates of the theory in question. Thus, each mathematical theorem can be cast into the form

$$(P_1 \cdot P_2 \cdot P_3 \cdot \; \ldots \; . P_n) \to T$$

where the expression on the left is the conjunction (joint assertion) of all the postulates, the symbol on the right represents the theorem in its customary formulation, and the arrow expresses the relation of logical implication or entailment. Precisely this character of mathematical theorems is the reason for their peculiar certainty and necessity, as I shall now attempt to show.

It is typical of any purely logical deduction that the conclusion to which it leads simply re-asserts (a proper or improper) part of what has already been stated in the premises. Thus, to illustrate this point by a very elementary example, from the premise, "This figure is a right triangle," we can deduce the conclusion, "This figure is a triangle"; but this conclusion clearly reiterates part of the information already contained in the premise. Again, from the premises, "All primes different from 2 are odd" and "n is a prime different from 2," we can infer logically that n is odd; but this consequence merely repeats part (indeed a relatively small part) of the information contained in the premises. The same situation prevails in all other cases of logical deduction; and we may, therefore, say that logical deduction —which is the one and only method of mathematical proof—is a technique of conceptual analysis: it discloses what assertions are concealed in a given set of premises, and it makes us realize to what we committed ourselves in accepting those premises; but none of the results obtained by this technique ever goes by one iota beyond the information already contained in the initial assumptions.

Since all mathematical proofs rest exclusively on logical deductions from certain postulates, it follows that a mathematical theorem, such as the Pythagorean theorem in geometry, asserts nothing that is *objectively* or *theoretically new* as compared with the postulates from which it is derived, although its content may well be *psychologically new* in the sense that we were not aware of its being implicitly contained in the postulates.

The nature of the peculiar certainty of mathematics is now clear: A mathematical theorem is certain *relatively* to the set of postulates from which it is derived; i.e., it is necessarily true *if* those postulates are true; and this is so because the theorem, if rigorously proved, simply re-asserts part of what has been stipulated in the postulates. A truth of this conditional type obviously implies no assertions about matters of empirical fact and can, therefore, never get into conflict with any empirical findings, even of the most unexpected kind; consequently, unlike the hypotheses and theories of empirical science, it can never suffer the fate of being disconfirmed by new evidence: A mathematical truth is irrefutably certain just because it is devoid of factual, or empirical content. Any theorem of geometry, therefore, when cast into the conditional form described earlier, is analytic in the technical sense of logic, and thus true *a priori;* i.e., its truth can be established by means of the formal machinery of logic alone, without any reference to empirical data.

4. POSTULATES AND TRUTH

Now it might be felt that our analysis of geometrical truth so far tells only half of the relevant story. For while a geometrical proof no doubt enables us to assert a proposition conditionally—namely on condition that the postulates are accepted—is it not correct to add that geometry also unconditionally asserts the truth of its postulates and thus, by virtue of the deductive relationship between postulates and theorems, enables us unconditionally to assert the truth of its theorems? Is it not an unconditional assertion of geometry that two points determine one and only one straight line that connects them, or that in any triangle, the sum of the angles equals two right angles? That this is definitely not the case, is evidenced by two important aspects of the axiomatic treatment of geometry which will now be briefly considered.

The first of these features is the well-known fact that in the more recent development of mathematics, several systems of geometry have been constructed which are incompatible with euclidean geometry, and in which, for example, the two propositions just mentioned do not necessarily hold. Let us briefly recollect some of the basic facts concerning these *non-*

euclidean geometries. The postulates on which euclidean geometry rests include the famous postulate of the parallels, which, in the case of plane geometry, asserts in effect that through every point P not on a given line l there exists exactly one parallel to l, i.e., one straight line which does not meet l. As this postulate is considerably less simple than the others, and as it was also felt to be intuitively less plausible than the latter, many efforts were made in the history of geometry to prove that this proposition need not be accepted as an axiom, but that it can be deduced as a theorem from the remaining body of postulates. All attempts in this direction failed, however; and finally it was conclusively demonstrated that a proof of the parallel principle on the basis of the other postulates of euclidean geometry (even in its modern, completed form) is impossible. This was shown by proving that a perfectly self-consistent geometrical theory is obtained if the postulate of the parallels is replaced by the assumption that through any point P not on a given straight line l there exist at least two parallels to l. This postulate obviously contradicts the euclidean postulate of the parallels, and if the latter were actually a consequence of the other postulates of euclidean geometry, then the new set of postulates would clearly involve a contradiction, which can be shown not to be the case. This first non-euclidean type of geometry, which is called hyperbolic geometry, was discovered in the early 20's of the last century almost simultaneously, but independently by the Russian N. I. Lobatschefskij, and by the Hungarian J. Bolyai. Later, Riemann developed an alternative geometry, known as elliptical geometry, in which the axiom of the parallels is replaced by the postulate that no line has any parallels. (The acceptance of this postulate, however, in contradistinction to that of hyperbolic geometry, requires the modification of some further axioms of euclidean geometry, if a consistent new theory is to result.) As is to be expected, many of the theorems of these non-euclidean geometries are at variance with those of euclidean theory; thus, e.g., in the hyperbolic geometry of two dimensions, there exist, for each straight line l, through any point P not on l, infinitely many straight lines which do not meet l; also, the sum of the angles in any triangle is less than two right angles. In elliptic geometry, this angle sum is always greater than two right angles; no two straight lines are parallel; and while two different points usually determine exactly one straight line connecting them (as they always do in euclidean geometry), there are certain pairs of points which are connected by infinitely many different straight lines. An illustration of this latter type of geometry is provided by the geometrical structure of that curved two-dimensional space which is represented by the surface of a sphere, when the concept of straight line is interpreted by that of great circle on the sphere. In this space, there are no parallel lines since any two great circles intersect; the endpoints of any diameter of the sphere are points connected by infinitely many different "straight lines," and the sum of the angles in a triangle is always in excess of two right angles. Also, in this space, the ratio between the circumference and the diameter of a circle (not necessarily a great circle) is always less than 2π.

Elliptic and hyperbolic geometry are not the only types of non-euclidean geometry; various other types have been developed; we shall later have occasion to refer to a much more general form of non-euclidean geometry which was likewise devised by Riemann.

The fact that these different types of geometry have been developed in modern mathematics shows clearly that mathematics cannot be said to assert the truth of any particular set of geometrical postulates; all that pure mathematics is interested in, and all that it can establish, is the deductive consequences of given sets of postulates and thus the necessary truth of the ensuing theorems relatively to the postulates under consideration.

A second observation which likewise shows that mathematics does not assert the truth of any particular set of postulates refers to *the status of the concepts in geometry*. There exists, in every axiomatized theory, a close parallelism between the treatment of the propositions and that of the concepts of the system. As we have seen, the propositions fall into two classes: the postulates, for which no proof is given, and the theorems, each of which has to be derived from the postulates. Analogously, the concepts fall into two classes: the primitive or basic concepts, for which no definition is given, and the others, each of which has to be precisely defined in terms of the primitives. (The admission of some undefined concepts is clearly necessary if an infinite regress in definition is to be avoided.) The analogy goes farther: Just as there exists an infinity of theoretically suitable axiom systems for one and the same theory—say, euclidean geometry—so there also exists an infinity of theoretically possible choices for the primitive terms of that theory; very often—but not always—different axiomatizations of the same theory involve not only different postulates, but also different sets of primitives. Hilbert's axiomatization of plane geometry contains six primitives: point, straight line, incidence (of a point on a line), betweenness (as a relation of three points on a straight line), congruence for line segments, and congruence for angles. (Solid geometry, in Hilbert's axiomatization, requires two further primitives, that of plane and that of incidence of a point on a plane.) All other concepts of geometry, such as those of angle, triangle, circle, etc., are defined in terms of these basic concepts.

But if the primitives are not defined within geometrical theory, what meaning are we to assign to them? The answer is that it is entirely unnecessary to connect any particular meaning with them. True, the words "point," "straight line," etc., carry definite connotations with them which relate to the familiar geometrical figures, but the validity of the propositions is completely independent of these connotations. Indeed, suppose that in axiomatized euclidean geometry, we replace the over-suggestive terms "point," "straight line," "incidence," "betweenness," etc., by the neutral terms "object of kind 1," "object of kind 2," "relation No. 1," "relation No. 2," etc., and suppose that we present this modified wording of geometry to a competent mathematician or logician who, however, knows nothing of the customary connotations of the primitive terms. For this logician, all proofs would clearly remain valid, for as we saw before, a rigorous proof in geometry rests on deduction from the axioms alone without any reference to the customary interpretation of the various geometrical concepts used. We see therefore that indeed no specific meaning has to be attached to the primitive terms of an axiomatized theory; and in a precise logical presentation of axiomatized geometry the primitive concepts are accordingly treated as so-called logical variables.

As a consequence, geometry cannot be said to assert the truth of its postulates, since the latter are formulated in terms of concepts without any specific meaning; indeed, for this very reason, the postulates themselves do not make any specific assertion which could possibly be called true or false! In the terminology of modern logic, the postulates are not sentences, but sentential functions with the primitive concepts as variable arguments. This point also shows that the postulates of geometry cannot be considered as "self-evident truths," because where no assertion is made, no self-evidence can be claimed.

5. PURE AND PHYSICAL GEOMETRY

Geometry thus construed is a purely formal discipline; we shall refer to it also as *pure geometry*. A pure geometry, then,—no matter whether it is of the euclidean or of a non-euclidean variety—deals with no specific subject-matter; in particular, it asserts nothing about physical space. All its theorems are analytic and thus true with certainty precisely because they are devoid of factual content. Thus, to characterize the import of pure geometry, we might use the standard form of a movie-disclaimer: No portrayal of the characteristics of geometrical figures or of the spatial properties or relationships of actual physical bodies is intended, and any similarities between the primitive concepts and their customary geometrical connotations are purely coincidental.

But just as in the case of some motion pictures, so in the case at least of euclidean geometry, the disclaimer does not sound quite convincing: Historically speaking, at least, euclidean geometry has its origin in the generalization and systematization of certain empirical discoveries which were made in connection with the measurement of areas and volumes, the practice of surveying, and the development of astronomy. Thus understood, geometry has factual import; it is an empirical science which might be called, in very general terms, the theory of the structure of physical space, or briefly, *physical geometry*. What is the relation between pure and physical geometry?

When the physicist uses the concepts of point, straight line, incidence, etc., in statements about physical objects, he obviously connects with each of them a more or less definite physical meaning. Thus, the term "point" serves to designate physical points, i.e., objects of the kind illustrated by pin-points, cross hairs, etc. Similarly, the term "straight line" refers to straight lines in the sense of physics, such as illustrated by taut strings or by the path of light rays in a homogeneous medium. Analogously, each of the other geometrical concepts has a concrete physical meaning in the statements of physical geometry. In view of this situation, we can say that physical geometry is obtained by what is called, in contemporary logic, a semantical interpretation of pure geometry. Generally speaking, a semantical interpretation of a pure mathematical theory, whose primitives are not assigned any specific meaning, consists in giving each primitive (and thus, indirectly, each defined term) a specific meaning or designatum. In the case of physical geometry, this meaning is physical in the sense just illustrated; it is possible, however, to assign a purely arithmetical meaning to each concept of geometry; the possibility of such an arithmetical interpretation of geometry is of great importance in the study of the consistency and other logical characteristics of geometry, but it falls outside the scope of the present discussion.

By virtue of the physical interpretation of the originally uninterpreted primitives of a geometrical theory, physical meaning is indirectly assigned also to every defined concept of the theory; and if every geometrical term is now taken in its physical interpretation, then every postulate and every theorem of the theory under consideration turns into a statement of physics, with respect to which the question as to truth or falsity may meaningfully be raised—a circumstance which clearly contradistinguishes the propositions of physical geometry from those of the corresponding uninterpreted pure theory. Consider, for example, the following postulate of pure euclidean geometry: For any two objects x, y of kind 1, there exists exactly one object l of kind 2 such that both x and y stand in relation No. 1 to l. As long as the three primitives occurring in this postulate are uninterpreted, it is obviously meaningless to ask whether the postulate is true. But by virtue of the above physical interpretation, the postulate turns into the following statement: For any two physical points x, y there exists exactly one physical straight line l such that both x and y lie on l. But this is a physical hypothesis, and we may now meaningfully ask whether it is true or false. Similarly, the theorem about the sum of the angles in a triangle turns into the assertion that the sum of the angles (in the physical sense) of a figure bounded by the paths of three light rays equals two right angles.

Thus, the physical interpretation transforms a given pure geometrical theory—euclidean or non-euclidean—into a system of physical hypotheses which, if true, might be said to constitute a theory of the structure of physical space. But the question whether a given geometrical theory in physical interpretation is factually correct represents a problem not of pure mathematics but of empirical science; it has to be settled on the basis of suitable experiments or systematic observations. The only assertion the mathematician can make in this context is this: If all the postulates of a given geometry, in their physical interpretation, are true, then all the theorems of that geometry, in their physical interpretation, are necessarily true, too, since they are logically deducible from the postulates. It might seem, therefore, that in order to decide whether physical space is euclidean or non-euclidean in structure, all that we have to do is to test the respective postulates in their physical interpretation. However, this is not directly feasible; here, as in the case of any other physical theory, the basic hypotheses are largely incapable of a direct experimental test; in geometry, this is particularly obvious for such postulates as the parallel axiom or Cantor's axiom of continuity in Hilbert's system of euclidean geometry, which makes an assertion about certain infinite sets of points on a straight line. Thus, the empirical test of a physical geometry no less than that of any other scientific theory has to proceed indirectly; namely, by deducing from the basic hypotheses of the theory certain consequences, or predictions, which are amenable to an experimental test. If a test bears out a prediction, then it constitutes confirming evidence (though, of course, no conclusive proof) for the theory; otherwise, it disconfirms the theory. If an adequate amount of confirming evidence for a theory has been established, and if no disconfirming evidence has been found, then the theory may be accepted by the scientist "until further notice."

It is in the context of this indirect procedure that pure mathematics and logic acquire their inestimable importance for empirical science: While formal logic and pure mathematics do not in themselves establish any assertions about matters of empirical fact, they provide an efficient and entirely indispensable machinery for deducing, from abstract theoretical assumptions, such as the laws of Newtonian mechanics or the postulates of euclidean geometry in physical interpretation, consequences concrete and specific enough to be accessible to direct experimental test. Thus, e.g., pure euclidean geometry shows that from its postulates there may be deduced the theorem about the sum of the angles in a triangle, and that this deduction is possible no matter how the basic concepts of geometry are interpreted; hence also in the case of the physical interpretation of euclidean geometry. This theorem, in its physical interpretation, is accessible to experimental test; and since the postulates of elliptic and of hyperbolic geometry imply values different from two right angles for the angle sum of a triangle, this particular proposition seems to afford a good opportunity for a crucial experiment. And no less a mathematician than Gauss did indeed perform this test; by means of optical methods—and thus using the interpretation of physical straight lines as paths of light rays—he ascertained the angle sum of a large triangle determined by three mountain tops. Within the limits of experimental error, he found it equal to two right angles.

6. ON POINCARÉ'S CONVENTIONALISM CONCERNING GEOMETRY

But suppose that Gauss had found a noticeable deviation from this value; would that have meant a refutation of euclidean geometry in its physical interpretation, or, in other words, of the hypothesis that physical space is euclidean in structure? Not necessarily; for the deviation might have been accounted for by a hypothesis to the effects that the paths of the light rays involved in the sighting process were bent by some disturbing force and thus were not actually straight lines. The same kind of reference to deforming forces could also be used if, say, the euclidean theorems of congruence for plane figures were tested in their physical interpretation by means of experiments involving rigid bodies, and if any violations of the theorems were found. This point is by no means trivial; Henri Poincaré, the great French mathematician and theoretical physicist, based on considerations of this type his famous *conventionalism concerning geometry*. It was his opinion that no empirical test, whatever its outcome, can conclusively invalidate the euclidean conception of physical space; in other words, the validity of euclidean geometry in physical science can always be preserved—if necessary, by suitable changes in the theories of physics, such as the introduction of new hypotheses concerning deforming or deflecting forces. Thus, the question as to whether physical space has a euclidean or a non-euclidean structure would become a matter of convention, and the decision to preserve euclidean geometry at all costs would recommend itself, according to Poincaré, by the greater simplicity of euclidean as compared with non-euclidean geometrical theory.

It appears, however, that Poincaré's account is an oversimplification. It rightly calls attention to the fact that the test of a physical geometry G always presupposes a certain body P of non-geometrical physical hypotheses (including the physical theory of the instruments of measurement and observation used in the test), and that the so-called test of G actually bears on the combined theoretical system $G \cdot P$ rather than on G alone. Now, if predictions derived from $G \cdot P$ are contradicted by experimental findings, then a change in the theoretical structure becomes necessary. In classical physics, G always was euclidean geometry in its physical interpretation, GE; and when experimental evidence required a modification of the theory, it was P rather than GE which was changed. But Poincaré's assertion that this procedure would always be distinguished by its greater simplicity is not entirely correct; for what has to be taken into consideration is the simplicity of the total system $G \cdot P$, and not just that of its geometrical part. And here it is clearly conceivable that a simpler total theory in accordance with all the relevant empirical evidence is obtainable by going over to a non-euclidean form of geometry rather than by preserving the euclidean structure of physical space and making adjustments only in part P.

And indeed, just this situation has arisen in physics in connection with the development of the general theory of relativity: If the primitive terms of geometry are given physical interpretations along the lines indicated before, then certain findings in astronomy represent good evidence in favor of a total physical theory with a non-euclidean geometry as part G. According to this theory, the physical universe at large is a three-dimensional curved space of a very complex geometrical structure; it is finite in volume and yet unbounded in all directions. However, in comparatively small areas, such as those involved in Gauss' experiment, euclidean geometry can serve as a good approximative account of the geometrical structure of space. The kind of structure ascribed to physical space in this theory may be illustrated by an analogue in two dimensions; namely, the surface of a sphere. The geometrical structure of the latter, as was pointed out before, can be described by means of elliptic geometry, if the primitive term "straight line" is interpreted as meaning "great circle," and if the other primitives are given analogous interpretations. In this sense, the surface of a sphere is a two-dimensional curved space of non-euclidean structure, whereas the plane is a two-dimensional space of euclidean structure. While the plane is unbounded in all directions, and infinite in size, the spherical surface is finite in size and yet unbounded in all directions: a two-dimensional physicist, travelling along "straight lines" of that space would never encounter any boundaries of his space; instead, he would finally return to his point of departure, provided that his life span and his technical facilities were sufficient for such a trip in consideration of the size of his "universe." It is interesting to note that the physicists of that world, even if they lacked any intuition of a three-dimensional space, could empirically ascertain the fact that their two-dimensional space was curved. This might be done by means of the method of travelling along straight lines; another, simpler test would consist in determining the angle sum in a triangle; again another in determining, by means of measuring tapes, the ratio of the circumference of a circle (not necessarily a great circle) to its diameter; this ratio would turn out to be less than π.

The geometrical structure which relativity physics ascribes to physical space is a three-dimensional analogue to that of the surface of a sphere, or, to be more exact, to that of the closed and finite surface of a potato, whose curvature varies from point to point. In our physical universe, the curvature of space at a given point is determined by the distribution of masses in its neighborhood; near large masses such as the sun, space is strongly curved, while in regions of low mass-density, the structure of the universe is approximately euclidean. The hypothesis stating the connection between the mass distribution and the curvature of space at a point has been approximately confirmed by astronomical observations concerning the paths of light rays in the gravitational field of the sun.

The geometrical theory which is used to describe the structure of the physical universe is of a type that may be characterized as a generalization of elliptic geometry. It was originally constructed by Riemann as a purely mathematical theory, without any concrete possibility of practical application at hand. When Einstein, in developing his general theory of relativity, looked for an appropriate mathematical theory to deal with the structure of physical space, he found in Riemann's abstract system the conceptual tool he needed. This fact throws an interesting sidelight on the importance for scientific progress of that type of investigation which the "practical-minded" man in the street tends to dismiss as useless, abstract mathematical speculation.

Of course, a geometrical theory in physical interpretation can never be validated with mathematical certainty, no matter how extensive the experimental tests to which it is subjected; like any other theory of empirical science, it can acquire only a more or less high degree of confirmation. Indeed, the considerations presented in this article show that the demand for mathematical certainty in empirical matters is misguided and unreasonable; for, as we saw, mathematical certainty of knowledge can be attained only at the price of analyticity and thus of complete lack of factual content. Let me summarize this insight in Einstein's words:

"As far as the laws of mathematics refer to reality, they are not certain; and as far as they are certain, they do not refer to reality."

Truth by Convention [*]

W. V. QUINE

The less a science has advanced, the more its terminology tends to rest on an uncritical assumption of mutual understanding. With increase of rigor this basis is replaced piecemeal by the introduction of definitions. The interrelationships recruited for these definitions gain the status of analytic principles; what was once regarded as a theory about the world becomes reconstrued as a convention of language. Thus it is that some flow from the theoretical to the conventional is an adjunct of progress in the logical foundations of any science. The concept of simultaneity at a distance affords a stock example of such development: in supplanting the uncritical use of this phrase by a definition, Einstein so chose the definitive relationship as to verify conventionally the previously paradoxical principle of the absoluteness of the speed of light. But whereas the physical sciences are generally recognized as capable only of incomplete evolution in this direction, and as destined to retain always a nonconventional kernel of doctrine, developments of the past few decades have led to a widespread conviction that logic and mathematics are purely analytic or conventional. It is less the purpose of the present inquiry to question the validity of this contrast than to question its sense.

I

A definition, strictly, is a convention of notational abbreviation.[1] A *simple* definition introduces some specific expression, e.g., 'kilometer', or '*e*', called the *definiendum*, as arbitrary shorthand for some complex expression, e.g., 'a thousand meters' or '$\lim_{n \to \infty} (1 + \frac{1}{n})^n$', called the *definiens*. A *contextual* definition sets up indefinitely many mutually analogous pairs of definienda and definientia according to some general scheme; an example is the definition whereby expressions of the form '$\frac{\sin\text{---}}{\cos\text{---}}$' are abbreviated as 'tan---'. From a formal standpoint the signs thus introduced are wholly

[*] Reprinted by kind permission of the author as well as the editor and publishers of *Philosophical Essays for A. N. Whitehead*, copyright 1936 by Otis H. Lee; Longmans, Green and Co., New York.
[1] Cf. Russell, *Principles of Mathematics* (Cambridge, 1903), p. 429.

arbitrary; all that is required of a definition is that it be theoretically immaterial, i.e., that the shorthand which it introduces admit in every case of unambiguous elimination in favor of the antecedent longhand.[2]

Functionally a definition is not a premiss to theory, but a license for rewriting theory by putting definiens for definiendum or vice versa. By allowing such replacements a definition transmits truth: it allows true statements to be translated into new statements which are true by the same token. Given the truth of the statement 'The altitude of Kibo exceeds six thousand meters', the definition of 'kilometer' makes for the truth of the statement 'The altitude of Kibo exceeds six kilometers'; given the truth of the statement '$\frac{\sin \pi}{\cos \pi} = \frac{\sin \pi}{\cos \pi}$,' of which logic assures us in its earliest pages, the contextual definition cited above makes for the truth of the statement 'tan $\pi = \frac{\sin \pi}{\cos \pi}$.' In each case the statement inferred through the definition is true only because it is shorthand for another statement which was true independently of the definition. Considered in isolation from all doctrine, including logic, a definition is incapable of grounding the most trivial statement; even 'tan $\pi = \frac{\sin \pi}{\cos \pi}$' is a definitional transformation of an antecedent self-identity, rather than a spontaneous consequence of the definition.

What is loosely called a logical consequence of definitions is therefore more exactly describable as a logical truth definitionally abbreviated: a statement which becomes a truth of logic when definienda are replaced by definientia. In this sense 'tan $\pi = \frac{\sin \pi}{\cos \pi}$' is a logical consequence of the contextual definition of the tangent. 'The altitude of Kibo exceeds six kilometers' is not *ipso facto* a logical consequence of the given definition of 'kilometer'; on the other hand it would be a logical consequence of a quite suitable but unlikely definition introducing 'Kibo' as an abbreviation of the phrase 'the totality of such African terrain as exceeds six kilometers in altitude', for under this definition the statement in question is an abbreviation of a truth of logic, viz., 'The altitude of the totality of such African terrain as exceeds six kilometers in altitude exceeds six kilometers.'

Whatever may be agreed upon as the exact scope of logic, we may expect definitional abbreviations of logical truths to be reckoned as logical rather than extralogical truths. This being the case, the preceding conclusion shows logical consequences of definitions to be themselves truths of logic.

---

[2] From the present point of view a contextual definition may be recursive, but can then count among its definienda only those expressions in which the argument of recursion has a constant value, since otherwise the requirement of eliminability is violated. Such considerations are of little consequence, however, since any recursive definition can be turned into a direct one by purely logical methods. Cf. Carnap, *Logische Syntax der Sprache*, Vienna, 1934, pp. 23. 79.

To claim that mathematical truths are conventional in the sense of following logically from definitions is therefore to claim that mathematics is part of logic. The latter claim does not represent an arbitrary extension of the term 'logic' to include mathematics; agreement as to what belongs to logic and what belongs to mathematics is supposed at the outset, and it is then claimed that definitions of mathematical expressions can so be framed on the basis of logical ones that all mathematical truths become abbreviations of logical ones.

Although signs introduced by definition are formally arbitrary, more than such arbitrary notational convention is involved in questions of definability; otherwise any expression might be said to be definable on the basis of any expressions whatever. When we speak of definability, or of finding a definition for a given sign, we have in mind some traditional usage of the sign antecedent to the definition in question. To be satisfactory in this sense a definition of the sign not only must fulfill the formal requirement of unambiguous eliminability, but must also conform to the traditional usage in question. For such conformity it is necessary and sufficient that every context of the sign which was true and every context which was false under traditional usage be construed by the definition as an abbreviation of some other statement which is correspondingly true or false under the established meanings of its signs. Thus when definitions of mathematical expressions on the basis of logical ones are said to have been framed, what is meant is that definitions have been set up whereby every statement which so involves those mathematical expressions as to be recognized traditionally as true, or as false, is construed as an abbreviation of another correspondingly true or false statement which lacks those mathematical expressions and exhibits only logical expressions in their stead.[3]

An expression will be said to occur *vacuously* in a given statement if its replacement therein by any and every other grammatically admissible expression leaves the truth or falsehood of the statement unchanged. Thus for any statement containing some expressions vacuously there is a class of statements, describable as *vacuous variants* of the given statement, which are like it in point of truth or falsehood, like it also in point of a certain skeleton of symbolic make-up, but diverse in exhibiting all grammatically possible variations upon the vacuous constituents of the given statement. An expression will be said to occur *essentially* in a statement if it occurs in all the vacuous variants of the statement, i.e., if it forms part of the aforementioned skeleton. (Note that though an expression occur non-vacuously in a statement it may fail of essential occurrence because some of its parts occur vacuously in the statement.)

---

[3] Note that an expression is said to be defined, in terms, e.g., of logic, not only when it is a single sign whose elimination from a context in favor of logical expressions is accomplished by a single application of one definition, but also when it is a complex expression whose elimination calls for successive application of many definitions.

Now let S be a truth, let the expressions E_i occur vacuously in S, and let the statements S_i be the vacuous variants of S. Thus the S_i will likewise be true. On the sole basis of the expressions belonging to a certain class a, let us frame a definition for one of the expressions F occurring in S outside the E_i. S and the S_i thereby become abbreviations of certain statements S' and S'_i which exhibit only members of a instead of those occurrences of F, but which remain so related that the S'_i are all the results of replacing the E_i in S' by any other grammatically admissible expressions. Now since our definiton of F is supposed to conform to usage, S' and the S'_i will, like S and the S_i be uniformly true; hence the S'_i will be vacuous variants of S', and the occurrences of the E_i in S' will be vacuous. The definition thus makes S an abbreviation of a truth S' which, like S, involves the E_i vacuously, but which differs from S in exhibiting only members of a instead of the occurrences of F outside the E_i. Now it is obvious that an expression cannot occur essentially in a statement if it occurs only within expressions which occur vacuously in the statement; consequently F, occurring in S' as it does only within the E_i if at all, does not occur essentially in S'; members of a occur essentially in its stead. Thus if we take F as any non-member of a occurring essentially in S, and repeat the above reasoning for each such expression, we see that, through definitions of all such expressions in terms of members of a, S becomes an abbreviation of a truth S'' involving only members of a essentially.

Thus if in particular we take a as the class of all logical expressions, the above tells us that if logical definitions be framed for all non-logical expressions occurring essentially in the true statement S, S becomes an abbreviation of a truth S'' involving only logical expressions essentially. But if S'' involves only logical expressions essentially, and hence remains true when everything except that skeleton of logical expressions is changed in all grammatically possible ways, then S'' depends for its truth upon those logical constituents alone, and is thus a truth of logic. It is therefore established that if all non-logical expressions occurring essentially in a true statement S be given definitions on the basis solely of logic, then S becomes an abbreviation of a truth S'' of logic. In particular, then, if all mathematical expressions be defined in terms of logic, all truths involving only mathematical and logical expressions essentially become definitional abbreviations of truths of logic.

Now a mathematical truth, e.g., 'Smith's age plus Brown's equals Brown's age plus Smith's,' may contain non-logical, non-mathematical expressions. Still any such mathematical truth, or another whereof it is a definitional abbreviation, will consist of a skeleton of mathematical or logical expressions filled in with non-logical, non-mathematical expressions all of which occur vacuously. Thus every mathematical truth either is a truth in which only mathematical and logical expressions occur essentially, or is a definitional abbreviation of such a truth. Hence, granted definitions of all mathematical expressions in terms of logic, the preceding conclusion shows that all mathematical truths become definitional abbreviations of truths of logic —therefore truths of logic in turn. For the thesis that mathematics is logic it is thus sufficient that all mathematical notation be defined on the basis of logical notation.

If on the other hand some mathematical expressions resist definition on the basis of logical ones, then every mathematical truth containing such recalcitrant expressions must contain them only inessentially, or be a definitional abbreviation of a truth containing such expressions only inessentially, if all mathematics is to be logic: for though a logical truth, e.g., the above one about Africa, may involve non-logical expressions, it or some other logical truth whereof it is an abbreviation must involve only logical expressions essentially. It is of this alternative that those [4] avail themselves who regard mathematical truths, insofar as they depend upon non-logical notions, as elliptical for hypothetical statements containing as tacit hypotheses all the postulates of the branch of mathematics in question. Thus, suppose the geometrical terms 'sphere' and 'includes' to be undefined on the basis of logical expressions, and suppose all further geometrical expressions defined on the basis of logical expressions together with 'sphere' and 'includes', as with Huntington.[5] Let Huntington's postulates for (Euclidean) geometry, and all the theorems, be expanded by thoroughgoing replacement of definienda by definientia, so that they come to contain only logical expressions and 'sphere' and 'includes', and let the conjunction of the thus expanded postulates be represented as 'Hunt (sphere, includes).' Then, where 'Φ (sphere, includes)' is any of the theorems, similarly expanded into primitive terms, the point of view under consideration is that 'Φ (sphere, includes),' insofar as it is conceived as a mathematical truth, is to be construed as an ellipsis for 'If Hunt (sphere, includes) then Φ (sphere, includes).' Since 'Φ (sphere, includes)' is a logical consequence of Huntington's postulates, the above hypothetical statement is a truth of logic; it involves the expressions 'sphere' and 'includes' inessentially, in fact vacuously, since the logical deducibility of the theorems from the postulates is independent of the meanings of 'sphere' and 'includes' and survives the replacement of those expressions by any other grammatically admissible expressions whatever. Since, granted the fitness of Huntington's postulates, all and only those geometrical statements are truths of geometry which are logical consequences in this fashion of 'Hunt (sphere, includes),' all geometry becomes logic when interpreted in the above manner as a conventional ellipsis for a body of hypothetical statements.

But if, as a truth of mathematics, 'Φ (sphere, includes)' is short for 'If

---

[4] E.g. Russell, *op. cit.*, pp. 429–430; Behmann, "Sind die mathematischen Urteile analytisch oder synthetisch?" *Erkenntnis*, 4 (1934), pp. 8–10.

[5] "A Set of Postulates for Abstract Geometry", *Mathematische Annalen*, 73 (1913), pp. 522–559.

Hunt (sphere, includes) then Φ (sphere, includes),' still there remains, as part of this expanded statement, the original statement 'Φ (sphere, includes)'; this remains as a presumably true statement within some body of doctrine, say for the moment "non-mathematical geometry", even if the title of mathematical truth be restricted to the entire hypothetical statement in question. The body of all such hypothetical statements, describable as the "theory of deduction of non-mathematical geometry," is of course a part of logic; but the same is true of any "theory of deduction of sociology," "theory of deduction of Greek mythology," etc., which we might construct in parallel fashion with the aid of any set of postulates suited to sociology or to Greek mythology. The point of view toward geometry which is under consideration thus reduces merely to an exclusion of geometry from mathematics, a relegation of geometry to the status of sociology or Greek mythology; the labelling of the "theory of deduction of non-mathematical geometry" as "mathematical geometry" is a verbal *tour de force* which is equally applicable in the case of sociology or Greek mythology. To incorporate mathematics into logic by regarding all recalcitrant mathematical truths as elliptical hypothetical statements is thus in effect merely to restrict the term 'mathematics' to exclude those recalcitrant branches. But we are not interested in renaming. Those disciplines, geometry and the rest, which have traditionally been grouped under mathematics are the objects of the present discussion, and it is with the doctrine that mathematics in this sense is logic that we are here concerned.[6]

Discarding this alternative and returning, then, we see that if some mathematical expressions resist definition on the basis of logical ones, mathematics will reduce to logic only if, under a literal reading and without the gratuitous annexation of hypotheses, every mathematical truth contains (or is an abbreviation of one which contains) such recalcitrant expressions only inessentially if at all. But a mathematical expression sufficiently troublesome to have resisted trivial contextual definition in terms of logic can hardly be expected to occur thus idly in all its mathematical contexts. It would thus appear that for the tenability of the thesis that mathematics is logic it is not only sufficient but also necessary that all mathematical expressions be capable of definition on the basis solely of logical ones.

Though in framing logical definitions of mathematical expressions the ultimate objective be to make all mathematical truths logical truths, attention is not to be confined to mathematical and logical truths in testing the conformity of the definitions to usage. Mathematical expressions belong to the general language, and they are to be so defined that all statements containing them, whether mathematical truths, historical truths, or falsehoods under traditional usage, come to be construed as abbreviations of other statements which are correspondingly true or false. The definition intro-

---

[6] Obviously the foregoing discussion has no bearing upon postulate method as such, nor upon Huntington's work.

ducing 'plus' must be such that the mathematical truth 'Smith's age plus Brown's equals Brown's age plus Smith's' becomes an abbreviation of a logical truth, as observed earlier; but it must also be such that 'Smith's age plus Brown's age equals Jones' age' becomes an abbreviation of a statement which is empirically true or false in conformity with the county records and the traditional usage of 'plus'. A definition which fails in this latter respect is no less Pickwickian than one which fails in the former; in either case nothing is achieved beyond the transient pleasure of a verbal recreation.

But for these considerations, contextual definitions of any mathematical expressions whatever could be framed immediately in purely logical terms, on the basis of any set of postulates adequate to the branch of mathematics in question. Thus, consider again Huntington's systematization of geometry. It was remarked that, granted the fitness of Huntington's postulates, a statement will be a truth of geometry if and only if it is logically deducible from 'Hunt (sphere, includes)' without regard to the meanings of 'sphere' and 'includes'. Thus 'Φ (sphere, includes)' will be a truth of geometry if and only if the following is a truth of logic: 'If a is any class and R any relation such that Hunt (a, R), then Φ (a, R).' For 'sphere' and 'includes' we might then adopt the following contextual definition: Where '‒‒‒' is any statement containing 'a' or 'R' or both, let the statement 'If a is any class and R any relation such that Hunt (a, R), then ‒‒‒' be abbreviated as that expression which is got from '‒‒‒' by putting 'sphere' for 'a' and 'includes' for 'R' throughout. (In the case of a compound statement involving 'sphere' and 'includes', this definition does not specify whether it is the entire statement or each of its constituent statements that is to be accounted as shorthand in the described fashion; but this ambiguity can be eliminated by stipulating that the convention apply only to whole contexts.) 'Sphere' and 'includes' thus receive contextual definition in terms exclusively of logic, for any statement containing one or both of those expressions is construed by the definition as an abbreviation of a statement containing only logical expressions (plus whatever expressions the original statement may have contained other than 'sphere' and 'includes'). The definition satisfies past usage of 'sphere' and 'includes' to the extent of verifying all truths and falsifying all falsehoods of geometry; all those statements of geometry which are true, and only those, become abbreviations of truths of logic.

The same procedure could be followed in any other branch of mathematics, with the help of a satisfactory set of postulates for the branch. Thus nothing further would appear to be wanting for the thesis that mathematics is logic. And the royal road runs beyond that thesis, for the described method of logicizing a mathematical discipline can be applied likewise to any non-mathematical theory. But the whole procedure rests on failure to conform the definitions to usage; what is logicized is not the intended subject-matter. It is readily seen, e.g., that the suggested contextual definition of 'sphere' and 'includes', though transforming purely geometrical truths and falsehoods respectively into logical truths and falsehoods, transforms certain empirical truths into falsehoods and vice versa. Consider, e.g., the true statement 'A baseball is roughly a sphere,' more rigorously 'The whole of a baseball, except for a certain very thin, irregular peripheral layer, constitutes a sphere.' According to the contextual definition, this statement is an abbreviation for the following: 'If a is any class and R any relation such that Hunt (a, R), then the whole of a baseball, except for a thin peripheral layer, constitutes an [a member of] a.' This tells us that the whole of a baseball, except for a thin peripheral layer, belongs to every class a for which a relation R can be found such that Huntington's postulates are true of a and R. Now it happens that 'Hunt $(a, \text{includes})$' is true not only when a is taken as the class of all spheres, but also when a is restricted to the class of spheres a foot or more in diameter; [7] yet the whole of a baseball, except for a thin peripheral layer, can hardly be said to constitute a sphere a foot or more in diameter. The statement is therefore false, whereas the preceding statement, supposedly an abbreviation of this one, was true under ordinary usage of words. The thus logicized rendering of any other discipline can be shown in analogous fashion to yield the sort of discrepancy observed just now for geometry, provided only that the postulates of the discipline admit, like those of geometry, of alternative applications; and such multiple applicability is to be expected of any postulate set.[8]

Definition of mathematical notions on the basis of logical ones is thus a more arduous undertaking than would appear from a consideration solely of the truths and falsehoods of pure mathematics. Viewed *in vacuo*, mathematics is trivially reducible to logic through erection of postulate systems into contextual definitions; but "cette science n'a pas uniquement pour objet de contempler éternellement son propre nombril." [9] When mathematics is recognized as capable of use, and as forming an integral part of general language, the definition of mathematical notions in terms of logic becomes a task whose completion, if theoretically possible at all, calls for mathematical genius of a high order. It was primarily to this task that Whitehead and Russell addressed themselves in their *Principia Mathematica*. They adopt a meager logical language as primitive, and on its basis alone they undertake to endow mathematical expressions with definitions which conform to usage in the full sense described above: definitions which not only reduce mathematical truths and falsehoods to logical ones, but reduce *all* statements, containing the mathematical expressions in question, to

[7] Cf. Huntington, *op. cit.*, p. 540.

[8] Note that a postulate set is superfluous if it *demonstrably* admits of one and only one application: for it then embodies an adequate defining property for each of its constituent primitive terms. Cf. Tarski, "Einige methodologische Untersuchungen über die Definierbarkeit der Begriffe," *Erkenntnis*, 5 (1934), p. 85 (*Satz* 2).

[9] Poincaré, *Science et Méthode*, Paris, 1908, p. 199.

equivalent statements involving logical expressions instead of the mathematical ones. Within *Principia* the program has been advanced to such a point as to suggest that no fundamental difficulties stand in the way of completing the process. The foundations of arithmetic are developed in *Principia,* and therewith those branches of mathematics are accommodated which, like analysis and theory of number, spring from arithmetic. Abstract algebra proceeds readily from the relation theory of *Principia.* Only geometry remains untouched, and this field can be brought into line simply by identifying *n*-dimensional figures with those *n*-adic arithmetical relations ("equations in *n* variables") with which they are correlated through analytic geometry.[10] Some question Whitehead and Russell's reduction of mathematics to logic,[11] on grounds for whose exposition and criticism there is not space; the thesis that all mathematics reduces to logic is, however, substantiated by *Principia* to a degree satisfactory to most of us. There is no need here to adopt a final stand in the matter.

If for the moment we grant that all mathematics is thus definitionally constructible from logic, then mathematics becomes true by convention in a relative sense: mathematical truths become conventional transcriptions of logical truths. Perhaps this is all that many of us mean to assert when we assert that mathematics is true by convention; at least, an *analytic* statement is commonly explained merely as one which proceeds from logic and definitions, or as one which, on replacement of definienda by definientia, becomes a truth of logic.[12] But in strictness we cannot regard mathematics as true purely by convention unless all those logical principles to which mathematics is supposed to reduce are likewise true by convention. And the doctrine that mathematics is *analytic* accomplishes a less fundamental simplification for philosophy than would at first appear, if it asserts only that mathematics is a conventional transcription of logic and not that logic is convention in turn: for if in the end we are to countenance any *a priori* principles at all which are independent of convention, we should not scruple to admit a few more, nor attribute crucial importance to conventions which serve only to diminish the number of such principles by reducing some to others.

But if we are to construe logic also as true by convention, we must rest logic ultimately upon some manner of convention other than definition: for it was noted earlier that definitions are available only for transforming truths, not for founding them. The same applies to any truths of

[10] Cf. Study, *Die realistische Weltansicht und die Lehre vom Raume,* Brunswick, 1914, pp. 86–92.

[11] Cf. e.g., Dubislav, "Ueber das Verhältnis der Logik zur Mathematik", *Annalen der Philosophie,* 5 (1925), pp. 193–208; Hilbert, *Die Grundlagen der Mathematik,* Leipzig, 1928, pp. 12, 21.

[12] Cf. Frege, *Grundlagen der Arithmetik,* Breslau, 1884, p. 4; Behmann, *op. cit.,* p. 5. Carnap, *op. cit.,* uses the term in essentially the same sense but subject to more subtle and rigorous treatment.

mathematics which, contrary to the supposition of a moment ago, may resist definitional reduction to logic; if such truths are to proceed from convention, without merely being reduced to antecedent truths, they must proceed from conventions other than definitions. Such a second sort of convention, generating truths rather than merely transforming them, has long been recognized in the use of postulates.[18] Application of this method to logic will occupy the next section; customary ways of rendering postulates and rules of inference will be departed from, however, in favor of giving the whole scheme the explicit form of linguistic convention.

II

Let us suppose an approximate maximum of definition to have been accomplished for logic, so that we are left with about as meager as possible an array of primitive notational devices. There are indefinitely many ways of framing the definitions, all conforming to the same usage of the expressions in question; apart from the objective of defining much in terms of little, choice among these ways is guided by convenience or chance. Different choices involve different sets of primitives. Let us suppose our procedure to be such as to reckon among the primitive devices the *not*-idiom, the *if*-idiom ('If . . . then . . .'), the *every*-idiom ('No matter what x may be, $---x---$'), and one or two more as required. On the basis of this much, then, all further logical notation is to be supposed defined; all statements involving any further logical notation become construed as abbreviations of statements whose logical constituents are limited to those primitives.

'Or', as a connective joining statements to form new statements, is amenable to the following contextual definition in terms of the *not*-idiom and the *if*-idiom: A pair of statements with 'or' between is an abbreviation of the statement made up successively of these ingredients: first, 'If'; second, the first statement of the pair, with 'not' inserted to govern the main verb (or, with 'it is false that' prefixed); third, 'then'; fourth, the second statement of the pair. The convention becomes clearer if we use the prefix '$\sim$' as an artificial notation for denial, thus writing '$\sim$ ice is hot' instead of 'Ice is not hot' or 'It is false that ice is hot.' Where '$---$' and '$\underline{\quad}$' are any statements, our definition then introduces '$---$ or $\underline{\quad}$' as an abbreviation of 'If $\sim$ $---$ then $\underline{\quad}$.' Again 'and', as a connective joining statements, can be defined contextually by construing '$---$ and $\underline{\quad}$' as an abbreviation for '$\sim$ if $---$ then $\sim$ $\underline{\quad}$.' Every such idiom is what is known as a *truth-function*, and is characterized by the fact that the truth or falsehood of the complex statement which it generates is uniquely determined by the truth or falsehood of the several statements which it combines. All truth-functions

---

[18] The function of postulates as conventions seems to have been first recognized by Gergonne, "Essai sur la théorie des définitions", *Annales des mathématiques pures et appliquées* (1819). His designation of them as "implicit definitions", which has had some following in the literature, is avoided here.

are known to be constructible in terms of the *not-* and *if-*idioms as in the above examples.[14] On the basis of the truth-functions, then, together with our further primitives—the *every*-idiom *et al.*—all further logical devices are supposed defined.

A word may, through historical or other accidents, evoke a train of ideas bearing no relevance to the truth or falsehood of its context; in point of *meaning*, however, as distinct from connotation, a word may be said to be determined to whatever extent the truth or falsehood of its contexts is determined. Such determination of truth or falsehood may be outright, and to that extent the meaning of the word is absolutely determined; or it may be relative to the truth or falsehood of statements containing other words, and to that extent the meaning of the word is determined relatively to those other words. A definition endows a word with complete determinacy of meaning relative to other words. But the alternative is open to us, on introducing a new word, of determining its meaning *absolutely* to whatever extent we like by specifying contexts which are to be true and contexts which are to be false. In fact, we need specify only the former: for falsehood may be regarded as a derivative property depending on the word '∼', in such wise that falsehood of '−−−' means simply truth of '∼−−−.' Since all contexts of our new word are meaningless to begin with, neither true nor false, we are free to run through the list of such contexts and pick out as true such ones as we like; those selected become true by fiat, by linguistic convention. For those who would question them we have always the same answer, 'You use the word differently.' The reader may protest that our arbitrary selection of contexts as true is subject to restrictions imposed by the requirement of *consistency*—e.g., that we must not select both '−−−' and '∼−−−'; but this consideration, which will receive a clearer status a few pages hence, will be passed over for the moment.

Now suppose in particular that we abstract from existing usage of the locutions 'if-then', 'not' (or '∼'), and the rest of our logical primitives, so that for the time being these become meaningless marks, and the erstwhile statements containing them lose their status as statements and become likewise meaningless, neither true nor false; and suppose we run through all those erstwhile statements, or as many of them as we like, segregating various of them arbitrarily as true. To whatever extent we carry this process, we to that extent determine meaning for the initially meaningless marks 'if', 'then', '∼', and the rest. Such contexts as we render true are true by convention.

We saw earlier that if all expressions occurring essentially in a true state-

---

[14] Sheffer ("A Set of Five Independent Postulates for Boolean Algebras", *Trans. Amer. Math. Soc.*, 14 (1913), pp. 481–488) has shown ways of constructing these two, in turn, in terms of one; strictly, therefore, such a one should supplant the two in our ostensibly minimal set of logical primitives. Exposition will be facilitated, however, by retaining the redundancy.

ment S and not belonging to a class a are given definitions in terms solely of members of a, than S becomes a definitional abbreviation of a truth S'' involving only members of a essentially. Now let a comprise just our logical primitives, and let S be a statement which, under ordinary usage, is true and involves only logical expressions essentially. Since all logical expressions other than the primitives are defined in terms of the primitives, it then follows that S is an abbreviation of a truth S'' involving only the primitives essentially. But if one statement S is a definitional abbreviation of another S'', the truth of S proceeds wholly from linguistic convention if the truth of S'' does so. Hence if, in the above process of arbitrarily segregating statements as true by way of endowing our logical primitives with meaning, *we assign truth to those statements which, according to ordinary usage, are true and involve only our primitives essentially*, then not only will the latter statements be true by convention, but so will all statements which are true under ordinary usage and involve only logical expressions essentially. Since, as remarked earlier, every logical truth involves (or is an abbreviation of another which involves) only logical expressions essentially, the described scheme of assigning truth makes all logic true by convention.

Not only does such assignment of truth suffice to make all those statements true by convention which are true under ordinary usage and involve only logical expressions essentially, but it serves also to make all those statements false by convention which are false under ordinary usage and involve only logical expressions essentially. This follows from our explanation of the falsehood of '---' as the truth of '$\sim$---', since '---' will be false under ordinary usage if and only if '$\sim$---' is true under ordinary usage. The described assignment of truth thus goes far toward fixing all logical expressions in point of meaning, and fixing them in conformity with usage. Still many statements containing logical expressions remain unaffected by the described assignments: all those statements which, from the standpoint of ordinary usage, involve some non-logical expressions essentially. There is hence room for supplementary conventions of one sort or another, over and above the described truth-assignments, by way of completely fixing the meanings of our primitives—and fixing them, it is to be hoped, in conformity with ordinary usage. Such supplementation need not concern us now; the described truth-assignments provide partial determinations which, as far as they go, conform to usage, and which go far enough to make all logic true by convention.

But we must not be deceived by schematism. It would appear that we sit down to a list of expressions and check off as arbitrarily true all those which, under ordinary usage, are true statements involving only our logical primitives essentially; but this picture wanes when we reflect that the number of such statements is infinite. If the convention whereby those statements are singled out as true is to be formulated in finite terms, we must avail ourselves of conditions finite in length which determine infinite classes of expressions.[15]

Such conditions are ready at hand. One, determining an infinite class of expressions all of which, under ordinary usage, are true statements involving only our primitive *if*-idiom essentially, is the condition of being obtainable from

(1) 'If if p then q then if if q then r then if p then r'

by putting a statement for 'p', a statement for 'q', and a statement for 'r'. In more customary language the form (1) would be expanded, for clarity, in some such fashion as this: 'If it is the case that if p then q, then, if it is the case further that if q then r, then, if p, r.' The form (1) is thus seen to be the principle of the syllogism. Obviously it is true under ordinary usage for all substitutions of statements for 'p', 'q', and 'r'; hence such results of substitution are, under ordinary usage, true statements involving only the *if*-idiom essentially. One infinite part of our program of assigning truth to all expressions which, under ordinary usage, are true statements involving only our logical primitives essentially, is thus accomplished by the following convention:

(I) Let all results of putting a statement for 'p', a statement for 'q', and a statement for 'r' in (1) be true.

Another infinite part of the program is disposed of by adding this convention:

(II) Let any expression be true which yields a truth when put for 'q' in the result of putting a truth for 'p' in 'If p then q.'

Given truths '---' and 'If --- then ----,' (II) yields the truth of '----'. That (II) conforms to usage, i.e., that from statements which are true under ordinary usage (II) leads only to statements which are likewise true under ordinary usage, is seen from the fact that under ordinary usage a statement '----' is always true if statements '---' and 'If --- then ----' are true. Given all the truths yielded by (I), (II) yields another infinity of truths which, like the former, are under ordinary usage truths involving only the *if*-idiom essentially. How this comes about is seen roughly as follows. The truths yielded by (I), being of the form of (1), are complex statements of the form 'If --- then ----.' The statement '---' here may in particular be of the form (1) in turn, and hence likewise be true according to (I). Then, by (II), '----' becomes true. In general '----' will not be of the form (1), hence would not have been obtainable by (I) alone. Still '----' will in every such case be a statement which, under

---

[15] Such a condition is all that constitutes a *formal system*. Usually we assign such meanings to the signs as to construe the expressions of the class as statements, specifically true statements, theorems; but this is neither intrinsic to the system nor necessary in all cases for a useful application of the system.

ordinary usage, is true and involves only the *if*-idiom essentially; this follows from the observed conformity of (I) and (II) to usage, together with the fact that the above derivation of '——' demands nothing of '——' beyond proper structure in terms of 'if-then'. Now our stock of truths embraces not only those yielded by (I) alone, i.e., those having the form (1), but also all those thence derivable by (II) in the manner in which '——' has just now been supposed derived.[16] From this increased stock we can derive yet further ones by (II), and these likewise will, under ordinary usage, be true and involve only the *if*-idiom essentially. The generation proceeds in this fashion *ad infinitum*.

When provided only with (I) as an auxiliary source of truth, (II) thus yields only truths which under ordinary usage are truths involving only the *if*-idiom essentially. When provided with further auxiliary sources of truths, however, e.g., the convention (III) which is to follow, (II) yields truths involving further locutions essentially. Indeed, the effect of (II) is not even confined to statements which, under ordinary usage, involve only logical locutions essentially; (II) also legislates regarding other statements, to the extent of specifying that no two statements '———' and 'If ——— then ——' can both be true unless '——' is true. But this overflow need not disturb us, since it also conforms to ordinary usage. In fact, it was remarked earlier that room remained for supplementary conventions, over and above the described truth-assignments, by way of further determining the meanings of our primitives. This overflow accomplishes just that for the *if*-idiom; it provides, with regard even to a statement 'If ——— then ——' which from the standpoint of ordinary usage involves non-logical expressions essentially, that the statement is not to be true if '———' is true and '——' not.

But present concern is with statements which, under ordinary usage, involve only our logical primitives essentially; by (I) and (II) we have provided for the truth of an infinite number of such statements, but by no means all. The following convention provides for the truth of another infinite set of such statements; these, in contrast to the preceding, involve not only the *if*-idiom but also the *not*-idiom essentially (under ordinary usage).

(III) Let all results of putting a statement for 'p' and a statement for 'q', in 'If p then if $\sim p$ then q' or 'If if $\sim p$ then p then p,' be true.[17]

Statements generated thus by substitution in 'If p then if $\sim p$ then q' are statements of hypothetical form in which two mutually contradictory

---

[16] The latter in fact comprise all and only those statements which have the form 'If if if q then r then if p then r then s then if if p then q then s'.

[17] (1) and the two formulae in (III) are Łukasiewicz's three postulates for the propositional calculus.

statements occur as premisses; obviously such statements are trivially true, under ordinary usage, no matter what may figure as conclusion. Statements generated by substitution in 'If [it is the case that] if $\sim p$ then p, then p' are likewise true under ordinary usage, for one reasons as follows: Grant the hypothesis, viz., that if $\sim p$ then p; then we must admit the conclusion, viz., that p, since even denying it we admit it. Thus all the results of substitution referred to in (III) are true under ordinary usage no matter what the substituted statements may be; hence such results of substitution are, under ordinary usage, true statements involving nothing essentially beyond the *if*-idiom and the *not*-idiom ('$\sim$').

From the infinity of truths adopted in (III), together with those already at hand from (I) and (II), infinitely more truths are generated by (II). It happens, curiously enough, that (III) adds even to our stock of statements which involve only the *if*-idiom essentially (under ordinary usage); there are truths of that description which, though lacking the *not*-idiom, are reached by (I)-(III) and not by (I) and (II). This is true, e.g., of any instance of the principle of identity, say

(2) 'If time is money then time is money.'

It will be instructive to derive (2) from (I)-(III), as an illustration of the general manner in which truths are generated by those conventions. (III), to begin with, directs that we adopt these statements as true:

(3) 'If time is money then if time is not money then time is money.'

(4) 'If if time is not money then time is money then time is money.'

(I) directs that we adopt this as true:

(5) 'If if time is money then if time is not money then time is money then if if if time is not money then time is money then time is money then if time is money then time is money.'

(II) tells us that, in view of the truth of (5) and (3), this is true:

(6) 'If if if time is not money then time is money then time is money then if time is money then time is money.'

Finally (II) tells us that, in view of the truth of (6) and (4), (2) is true.

If a statement S is generated by (I)-(III), obviously only the structure of S in terms of 'if-then' and '$\sim$' was relevant to the generation; hence all those variants S_i of S which are obtainable by any grammatically admissible substitutions upon constituents of S not containing 'if', 'then', or '$\sim$', are likewise generated by (I)-(III). Now it has been observed that (I)-(III) conform to usage, i.e., generate only statements which are true under ordinary usage; hence S and all the S_i are uniformly true under ordinary usage, the S_i are therefore vacuous variants of S, and hence only 'if', 'then', and '∼' occur essentially in S. Thus (I)-(III) generate only statements which under ordinary usage are truths involving only the *if*-idiom and the *not*-idiom essentially.

It can be shown also that (I)-(III) generate *all* such statements.[18] Consequently (I)-(III), aided by our definitions of logical locutions in terms of our primitives, are adequate to the generation of all statements which under ordinary usage are truths which involve any of the so-called truth-functions but nothing else essentially: for it has been remarked that all the truth-functions are definable on the basis of the *if*-idiom and the *not*-idiom. All such truths thus become true by convention. They comprise all those statements which are instances of any of the principles of the so-called propositional calculus.

To (I)-(III) we may now add a further convention or two to cover another of our logical primitives—say the *every*-idiom. A little more in this direction, by way of providing for our remaining primitives, and the program is completed; all statements which under ordinary usage are truths involving only our logical primitives essentially become true by convention. Therewith, as observed earlier, all logic becomes true by convention. The conventions with which (I)-(III) are thus to be supplemented will be more complex than (I)-(III), and considerable space would be needed to present them. But there is no need to do so, for (I)-(III) provide adequate illustration of the method; the complete set of conventions would be an adaptation of one of various existing systematizations of general logistic, in the same way in which (I)-(III) are an adaptation of a systematization of the propositional calculus.

Let us now consider the protest which the reader raised earlier, viz., that our freedom in assigning truth by convention is subject to restrictions imposed by the requirement of consistency.[19] Under the fiction, implicit in an earlier stage of our discussion, that we check off our truths one by one in an exhaustive list of expressions, consistency in the assignment of truth is nothing more than a special case of conformity to usage.

[18] The proof rests essentially upon Łukasiewicz's proof (in his *Elementy logiki matematycznej*, Warsaw, 1929) that his three postulates for the propositional calculus, viz., (1) and the formulae in (III), are *complete*. Adaptation of his result to present purposes depends upon the fact, readily established, that any formula generable by his two rules of inference (the so-called rule of substitution and a rule answering to (II)) can be generated by applying the rules in such order that all applications of the rule of substitution precede all applications of the other rule. This fact is relevant because of the manner in which the rule of substitution has been absorbed, here, into (I) and (III). The adaptation involves also two further steps, which however present no difficulty: we must make connection between Łukasiewicz's *formulae*, containing variables '*p*', '*q*', etc., and the concrete *statements* which constitute the present subject-matter; also between *completeness*, in the sense (Post's) in which Łukasiewicz uses the term, and the generability of all statements which under ordinary usage are truths involving only the *if*-idiom or the *not*-idiom essentially.

[19] So, e.g., Poincaré, *op. cit.*, pp. 162–163, 195–198; Schlick, *Allgemeine Erkenntnislehre*, Berlin, 1925, pp. 36, 327.

If we make a mark in the margin opposite an expression '---', and another opposite '∼---', we sin only against the established usage of '∼' as a denial sign. Under the latter usage '---' and '∼---' are not both true; in taking them both by convention as true we merely endow the sign '∼', roughly speaking, with a meaning other than denial. Indeed, we might so conduct our assignments of truth as to allow no sign of our language to behave analogously to the denial locution of ordinary usage; perhaps the resulting language would be inconvenient, but conventions are often inconvenient. It is only the objective of ending up with our mother tongue that dissuades us from marking both '---' and '∼---', and this objective would dissuade us also from marking 'It is always cold on Thursday.'

The requirement of consistency still retains the above status when we assign truth wholesale through general conventions such as (I)-(III). Each such convention assigns truth to an infinite sheaf of the entries in our fictive list, and in this function the conventions cannot conflict; by overlapping in their effects they reinforce one another, by not overlapping they remain indifferent to one another. If some of the conventions specified entries to which truth was *not* to be assigned, genuine conflict might be apprehended; such negative conventions, however, have not been suggested. (II) was, indeed, described earlier as specifying that 'If --- then ——' is not to be true if '---' is true and '——' not; but within the framework of the conventions of truth-assignment this apparent proscription is ineffectual without antecedent proscription of '——'. Thus any inconsistency among the general conventions will be of the sort previously considered, viz., the arbitrary adoption of both '---' and '∼---' as true; and the adoption of these was seen merely to impose some meaning other than denial upon the sign '∼'. As theoretical restrictions upon our freedom in the conventional assignment of truth, requirements of consistency thus disappear. Preconceived usage may lead us to stack the cards, but does not enter the rules of the game.

III

Circumscription of our logical primitives in point of meaning, through conventional assignment of truth to various of their contexts, has been seen to render all logic true by convention. Then if we grant the thesis that mathematics is logic, i.e., that all mathematical truths are definitional abbreviations of logical truths, it follows that mathematics is true by convention.

If on the other hand, contrary to the thesis that mathematics is logic, some mathematical expressions resist definition in terms of logical ones, we can extend the foregoing method into the domain of these recalcitrant expressions: we can circumscribe the latter through conventional assignment of truth to various of their contexts, and thus render mathematics conventionally true in the same fashion in which logic has been rendered so. Thus, suppose some mathematical expressions to resist logical definition, and suppose them to be reduced to as meager as possible a set of mathematical primitives. In terms of these and our logical primitives, then, all further mathematical devices are supposed defined; all statements containing the latter become abbreviations of statements containing by way of mathematical notation only the primitives. Here, as remarked earlier in the case of logic, there are alternative courses of definition and therewith alternative sets of primitives; but suppose our procedure to be such as to count 'sphere' and 'includes' among the mathematical primitives. So far we have a set of conventions, (I)-(III) and a few more, let us call them (IV)-(VII), which together circumscribe our logical primitives and yield all logic. By way of circumscribing the further primitives 'sphere' and 'includes', let us now add this convention to the set:

(VIII) Let 'Hunt (sphere, includes)' be true.

Now we saw earlier that where 'Φ (sphere, includes)' is any truth of geometry, supposed expanded into primitive terms, the statement

(7) 'If Hunt (sphere, includes) then Φ (sphere, includes)'

is a truth of logic. Hence (7) is one of the expressions to which truth is assigned by the conventions (I)-(VII). Now (II) instructs us, in view of convention (VIII) and the truth of (7), to adopt 'Φ (sphere, includes)' as true. In this way each truth of geometry is seen to be present among the statements to which truth is assigned by the conventions (I)-(VII).

We have considered four ways of construing geometry. One way consisted of straightforward definition of geometrical expressions in terms of logical ones, within the direction of development represented by *Principia Mathematica;* this way, presumably, would depend upon identification of geometry with algebra through the correlations of analytic geometry, and definition of algebraic expressions on the basis of logical ones as in *Principia Mathematica.* By way of concession to those who have fault to find with certain technical points in *Principia,* this possibility was allowed to retain a tentative status. The other three ways all made use of Huntington's postulates, but are sharply to be distinguished from one another. The first was to include geometry in logic by construing geometrical truths as elliptical for hypothetical statements bearing 'Hunt (sphere, includes)' as hypothesis; this was seen to be a mere evasion, tantamount, under its verbal disguise, to the concession that geometry is not logic after all. The next procedure was to define 'sphere' and 'includes' contextually in terms of logical expressions by construing 'Φ (sphere, includes)' in every case as an abbreviation of 'If a is any class and R any relation such that Hunt (a, R), then Φ (a, R).' This definition was condemned on the grounds that it fails to yield the intended usage of the defined terms. The last procedure finally, just now presented, renders geometry true by convention without making it part of logic. Here 'Hunt (sphere, includes)' is made true by fiat, by way of conventionally delimiting the meanings of 'sphere' and 'includes'. The truths of geometry then emerge not as truths of logic, but in parallel fashion to the truths of logic.

This last method of accommodating geometry is available also for any other branch of mathematics which may resist definitional reduction to logic. In each case we merely set up a conjunction of postulates for that branch as true by fiat, as a conventional circumscription of the meanings of the constituent primitives, and all the theorems of the branch thereby become true by convention: the convention thus newly adopted together with the conventions (I)-(VII). In this way all mathematics becomes conventionally true, not by becoming a definitional transcription of logic, but by proceeding from linguistic convention in the same way as does logic.

But the method can even be carried beyond mathematics, into the so-called empirical sciences. Having framed a maximum of definitions in the latter realm, we can circumscribe as many of our "empirical" primitives as we like by adding further conventions to the set adopted for logic and mathematics; a corresponding portion of "empirical" science then becomes conventionally true in precisely the manner observed above for geometry.

The impossibility of defining any of the "empirical" expressions in terms exclusively of logical and mathematical ones may be recognized at the outset: for if any proved to be so definable, there can be no question but that it would thenceforward be recognized as belonging to pure mathematics. On the other hand vast numbers of "empirical" expressions are of course definable on the basis of logical and mathematical ones together with other "empirical" ones. Thus 'momentum' is defined as 'mass times velocity'; 'event' may be defined as 'referent of the *later*-relation', i.e., 'whatever is later than something'; 'instant' may be defined as 'class of events no one of which is later than any other event of the class'; 'time' may be defined as 'the class of all instants'; and so on. In these examples 'momentum' is defined on the basis of mathematical expressions together with the further expressions 'mass' and 'velocity'; 'event', 'instant', and 'time' are all defined on the basis ultimately of logical expressions together with the one further expression 'later than'.

Now suppose definition to have been performed to the utmost among such non-logical, non-mathematical expressions, so that the latter are reduced to as few "empirical" primitives as possible.[20] *All* statements then

---

[20] In *Der Logische Aufbau der Welt*, Berlin, 1928, Carnap has pursued this program with such amazing success as to provide grounds for expecting all the expressions to be definable ultimately in terms of logic and mathematics plus just one "empirical" primitive, representing a certain dyadic relation described as *recollection of resemblance*. But for the present cursory considerations no such spectacular reducibility need be presupposed.

become abbreviations of statements containing nothing beyond the logical and mathematical primitives and these "empirical" ones. Here, as before, there are alternatives of definition and therewith alternative sets of primitives; but suppose our primitives to be such as to include 'later than', and consider the totality of those statements which under ordinary usage are truths involving only 'later than' and mathematical or logical expressions essentially. Examples of such statements are 'Nothing is later than itself'; 'If Pompey died later than Brutus and Brutus died later than Caesar then Pompey died later than Caesar.' All such statements will be either very general principles, like the first example, or else instances of such principles, like the second example. Now it is a simple matter to frame a small set of general statements from which all and only the statements under consideration can be derived by means of logic and mathematics. The conjunction of these few general statements can then be adopted as true by fiat, as 'Hunt (sphere, includes)' was adopted in (VIII); their adoption is a conventional circumscription of the meaning of the primitive 'later than'. Adoption of this convention renders all those statements conventionally true which under ordinary usage are truths essentially involving any logical or mathematical expressions, or 'later than', or any of the expressions which, like 'event', 'instant', and 'time', are defined on the basis of the foregoing, and inessentially involving anything else.

Now we can pick another of our "empirical" primitives, perhaps 'body' or 'mass' or 'energy', and repeat the process. We can continue in this fashion to any desired point, circumscribing one primitive after another by convention, and rendering conventionally true all statements which under ordinary usage are truths essentially involving only the locutions treated up to that point. If in disposing successively of our "empirical" primitives in the above fashion we take them up in an order roughly describable as leading from the general to the special, then as we progress we may expect to have to deal more and more with statements which are true under ordinary usage only with reservations, only with a probability recognized as short of certainty. But such reservations need not deter us from rendering a statement true by convention; so long as under ordinary usage the presumption is rather for than against the statement, our convention conforms to usage in verifying it. In thus elevating the statement from putative to conventional truth, we still retain the right to falsify the statement tomorrow if those events should be observed which would have occasioned its repudiation while it was still putative: for conventions are commonly revised when new observations show the revision to be convenient.

If in describing logic and mathematics as true by convention what is meant is that the primitives *can* be conventionally circumscribed in such fashion as to generate all and only the so-called truths of logic and mathematics, the characterization is empty; our last considerations show that the same might be said of any other body of doctrine as well. If on the other hand it is meant merely that the speaker adopts such conventions for those fields but not for others, the characterization is uninteresting; while if it is meant that it is a general practice to adopt such conventions explicitly for those fields but not for others, the first part of the characterization is false.

Still, there is the apparent contrast between logico-mathematical truths and others that the former are *a priori*, the latter *a posteriori*; the former have "the character of an inward necessity", in Kant's phrase, the latter do not. Viewed behavioristically and without reference to a metaphysical system, this contrast retains reality as a contrast between more and less firmly accepted statements; and it obtains antecedently to any *post facto* fashioning of conventions. There are statements which we choose to surrender last, if at all, in the course of revamping our sciences in the face of new discoveries; and among these there are some which we will not surrender at all, so basic are they to our whole conceptual scheme. Among the latter are to be counted the so-called truths of logic and mathematics, regardless of what further we may have to say of their status in the course of a subsequent sophisticated philosophy. Now since these statements are destined to be maintained independently of our observations of the world, we may as well make use here of our technique of conventional truth-assignment and thereby forestall awkward metaphysical questions as to our *a priori* insight into necessary truths. On the other hand this purpose would not motivate extension of the truth-assignment process into the realm of erstwhile contingent statements. On such grounds, then, logic and mathematics may be held to be conventional while other fields are not; it may be held that it is philosophically important to circumscribe the logical and mathematical primitives by conventions of truth-assignment which yield all logical and mathematical truths, but that it is idle elaboration to carry the process further. Such a characterization of logic and mathematics is perhaps neither empty nor uninteresting nor false.

In the adoption of the very conventions (I)-(III) etc. whereby logic itself is set up, however, a difficulty remains to be faced. Each of these conventions is general, announcing the truth of every one of an infinity of statements conforming to a certain description; derivation of the truth of any specific statement from the general convention thus requires a logical inference, and this involves us in an infinite regress. E.g., in deriving (6) from (3) and (5) on the authority of (II) we *infer*, from the general announcement (II) and the specific premiss that (3) and (5) are true statements, the conclusion that

(7) (6) is to be true.

An examination of this inference will reveal the regress. For present purposes it will be simpler to rewrite (II) thus:

(II′) No matter what x may be, no matter what y may be, no matter what z may be, if x and z are true [statements] and z is the result of putting x for 'p' and y for 'q' in 'If p then q' then y is to be true.

We are to take (II′) as a premiss, then, and in addition the premiss that (3) and (5) are true. We may also grant it as known that (5) is the result of putting (3) for 'p' and (6) for 'q' in 'If p then q.' Our second premiss may thus be rendered compositely as follows:

(8) (3) and (5) are true and (5) is the result of putting (3) for 'p' and (6) for 'q' in 'If p then q.'

From these two premisses we propose to infer (7). This inference is obviously sound logic; as logic, however, it involves use of (II′) and others of the conventions from which logic is supposed to spring. Let us try to perform the inference on the basis of those conventions. Suppose that our convention (IV), passed over earlier, is such as to enable us to infer specific instances from statements which, like (II′), involve the *every*-idiom; i.e., suppose that (IV) entitles us in general to drop the prefix 'No matter what x [or y, etc.] may be' and simultaneously to introduce a concrete designation instead of 'x' [or 'y', etc.] in the sequel. By invoking (IV) three times, then, we can infer the following from (II′):

(9) If (3) and (5) are true and (5) is the result of putting (3) for 'p' and (6) for 'q' in 'If p then q' then (6) is to be true.

It remains to infer (7) from (8) and (9). But this is an inference of the kind for which (II′) is needed; from the fact that

(10) (8) and (9) are true and (9) is the result of putting (8) for 'p' and (7) for 'q' in 'If p then q'

we are to infer (7) with help of (II′). But the task of getting (7) from (10) and (II′) is exactly analogous to our original task of getting (6) from (8) and (II′); the regress is thus under way.[21] (Incidentally the derivation of (9) from (II′) by (IV), granted just now for the sake of argument, would encounter a similar obstacle; so also the various unanalyzed steps in the derivation of (8).)

In a word, the difficulty is that if logic is to proceed *mediately* from conventions, logic is needed for inferring logic from the conventions. Alternatively, the difficulty which appears thus as a self-presupposition of doctrine can be framed as turning upon a self-presupposition of primitives. It is supposed that the *if*-idiom, the *not*-idiom, the *every*-idiom, and so on, mean nothing to us initially, and that we adopt the conventions

---

[21] Cf. Lewis Carroll, "What the Tortoise Said to Achilles", *Mind*, 4, N. S. (1895), pp. 278–280.

(I)-(VII) by way of circumscribing their meaning; and the difficulty is that communication of (I)-(VII) themselves depends upon free use of those very idioms which we are attempting to circumscribe, and can succeed only if we are already conversant with the idioms. This becomes clear as soon as (I)-(VII) are rephrased in rudimentary language, after the manner of (II').[22] It is important to note that this difficulty besets only the method of wholesale truth-assignment, not that of definition. It is true, e.g., that the contextual definition of 'or' presented at the beginning of the second section was communicated with the help of logical and other expressions which cannot be expected to have been endowed with meaning at the stage where logical expressions are first being introduced. But a definition has the peculiarity of being theoretically dispensable; it introduces a scheme of abbreviation, and we are free, if we like, to forego the brevity which it affords until enough primitives have been endowed with meaning, through the method of truth-assignment or otherwise, to accommodate full exposition of the definition. On the other hand the conventions of truth-assignment cannot be thus withheld until preparations are complete, because they are needed in the preparations.

If the truth-assignments were made one by one, rather than an infinite number at a time, the above difficulty would disappear; truths of logic such as (2) would simply be asserted severally by fiat, and the problem of inferring them from more general conventions would not arise. This course was seen to be closed to us, however, by the infinitude of the truths of logic.

It may still be held that the conventions (I)-(VIII) etc. are *observed* from the start, and that logic and mathematics thereby become conventional. It may be held that we can adopt conventions through behavior, without first announcing them in words; and that we can return and formulate our conventions verbally afterward, if we choose, when a full language is at our disposal. It may be held that the verbal formulation of conventions is no more a prerequisite of the adoption of the conventions than the writing of a grammar is a prerequisite of speech; that explicit exposition of conventions is merely one of many important uses of a completed language. So conceived, the conventions no longer involve us in vicious regress. Inference from general conventions is no longer demanded initially, but remains to the subsequent sophisticated stage where we frame

---

[22] Incidentally the conventions presuppose also some further locutions, e.g., 'true' ('a true statement'), 'the result of putting . . . for . . . in . . .', and various nouns formed by displaying expressions in quotation marks. The linguistic presuppositions can of course be reduced to a minimum by careful rephrasing; (II'), e.g., can be improved to the following extent:

> (II") No matter what x may be, no matter what y may be, no matter what z may be, if x is true then if z is true then if z is the result of putting x for 'p' in the result of putting y for 'q' in 'If p then q' then y is true.

This involves just the *every*-idiom, the *if*-idiom, 'is', and the further locutions mentioned above.

general statements of the conventions and show how various specific conventional truths, used all along, fit into the general conventions as thus formulated.

It must be conceded that this account accords well with what we actually do. We discourse without first phrasing the conventions; afterwards, in writings such as this, we formulate them to fit our behavior. On the other hand it is not clear wherein an adoption of the conventions, antecedently to their formulation, consists; such behavior is difficult to distinguish from that in which conventions are disregarded. When we first agree to understand 'Cambridge' as referring to Cambridge in England failing a suffix to the contrary, and then discourse accordingly, the rôle of linguistic convention is intelligible; but when a convention is incapable of being communicated until after its adoption, its rôle is not so clear. In dropping the attributes of deliberateness and explicitness from the notion of linguistic convention we risk depriving the latter of any explanatory force and reducing it to an idle label. We may wonder what one adds to the bare statement that the truths of logic and mathematics are *a priori*, or to the still barer behavioristic statement that they are firmly accepted, when he characterizes them as true by convention in such a sense.

The more restricted thesis discussed in the first section, viz. that mathematics is a conventional transcription of logic, is far from trivial; its demonstration is a highly technical undertaking and an important one, irrespectively of what its relevance may be to fundamental principles of philosophy. It is valuable to show the reducibility of any principle to another through definition of erstwhile primitives, for every such achievement reduces the number of our presuppositions and simplifies and integrates the structure of our theories. But as to the larger thesis that mathematics and logic proceed wholly from linguistic conventions, only further clarification can assure us that this asserts anything at all.

IV

IS THERE SYNTHETIC *A PRIORI* KNOWLEDGE?

Is There a Factual *a Priori?* *

MORITZ SCHLICK

The future historian of the philosophy of the nineteenth and twentieth centuries will find himself forced to the conclusion that in the systems which followed Kant, very little remained of the spirit of the Critical Philosophy even among those who either appealed directly to Kant, or believed themselves to be giving a further development to his ideas. That this is true of the *metaphysical* systems which followed Kant up to the time of Schopenhauer and after, is reasonably clear. It is equally true, however, of those admirers of kantian methods who believed themselves able to transfer his theory of knowledge, oriented as it was to Newtonian physics, to the sciences of mind and culture; and, finally, it is true of those critics of Kant who use his terminology, but who would like to give it a new meaning.

The signal merit which must be allowed Kant, of having most clearly delimited and applied his concept of the *a priori*, has come to be neglected and misunderstood today, particularly by the phenomenologists, in that they employ the term "*a priori*" in a completely unkantian way, and invent new definitions for it. Thus Scheler writes,[1] in explicit agreement with the position of Husserl, "We characterize as '*a priori*' all those ideal meaning-wholes and propositions which, irrespective of any mode in which they are considered by the subject which thinks them and of the nature of that subject, as well as irrespective of any mode in which an object is posited to which they might be applicable, are bodily given through the content of an immediate intuition." Such a usage of the term "*a priori*" would naturally be quite inadmissible if that which is set down by the definition had nothing in common with the meaning established by Kant—and it is certainly the opinion of the phenomenologists themselves that such a common element exists. Indeed, it clearly consists in the fact that they as well as Kant intend this term to refer to the source of propositions of absolutely universal validity. To be sure, Scheler and others of like mind speak of a phenomenological "experience" as the source of such propositions, but this signifies nothing more than confusion confounded,

* First published in "*Wissenschaftlicher Jahresbericht der Philosophischen Gesellschaft an der Universitaet zu Wien fuer das Vereinsjahr 1930/31*". Translated by W. S. and reprinted by kind permission of Mrs. Schlick.
[1] *Der Formalismus in der Ethik und die Materiale Wertethik*, 2nd ed., p. 43.

since they also give a new meaning to the term "experience". To what extent this so differently defined "*a priori*" shares further significant characteristics with that of Kant, is a matter on which there is room for difference of opinion. The phenomenologists, in any case, believe themselves justified in blaming Kant for making the *a priori* co-extensive with the formal. Scheler puts it as follows: [2] "The identification of the '*a priori*' with the 'formal' is a fundamental mistake of the Kantian doctrine." It is clearly implied by this assertion that propositions whose universal validity is absolute need not be of a purely formal character. As a matter of fact the decisive difference between the "*Wesensschau*" (intuition of essences) of Husserl and the pure intuition of Kant is that the former leads to propositions of absolute validity which nevertheless have something to say concerning the stuff or material of experience.

Husserl himself writes: [3] "Finally all the basic confusions of the Kantian critique of reason hang together . . . in that he lacked the phenomenologically correct concept of the *a priori*." We get an inkling as to how clear, in Husserl's opinion, the philosophy of Kant might have turned out to be after phenomenological correction, when we go on to read: "It was disastrous that Kant held the domain of the purely logical in the narrowest sense to be adequately taken care of by the remark that it falls under the principle of contradiction. Not only did he never see how little the laws of logic have the character of analytic propositions in the sense which he laid down as a matter of definition; he didn't even see how little is gained in the way of a clarification of the function of analytic thought, by a reference to a self-evident principle of analytic propositions."

The truth of the matter is that analytic judgments, that is, tautological propositions, actually need no clarification, the theoretical task with respect to them consisting at most in coming to see that this is indeed the case (which, of course, is not a matter of a psychological investigation of thought). Kant's insight was quite correct, and his opinion that logic as a whole is to be understood in terms of the principle of contradiction can accordingly be interpreted as a recognition of its purely tautological character. This conclusion is not weakened by the fact that the verbal form in which Kant clothed his definition of analytic propositions no longer satisfies us. Moreover, Husserl's conception of the principle of contradiction, which he characterizes as a "self-evident principle," is far more psychologistic than that of Kant.

An analytic proposition is one which is true by virtue of its form alone. Whoever has grasped the meaning of a tautology, has in doing so seen it to be true. It is because of this that it is *a priori*. In the case of a synthetic proposition, on the other hand, one must first understand its mean-

[2] *Ibid.*, p. 49.
[3] *Logische Untersuchungen*, II, 2, p. 203.

ing, and afterwards determine whether it is true or false. It is because of this that it is *a posteriori*.

Let us next ask by what way Kant arrived at an inseparable connection between the *a priori* and the formal. His point of departure was, of course, an amazement over the presence of synthetic and yet universally valid judgments in the exact sciences; and the entire labor of the *Critique of Pure Reason* was dedicated to the task of solving the problem of how this was possible. He concluded that it was entirely impossible, if these judgments claimed to assert anything concerning the stuff of experience, and the only solution for his problem that came to him after unspeakable toil was this, that the *a priori* validity of these judgments can only be understood on the condition that they express nothing but the *form* of experience which consciousness gives to all knowledge.

The identification of the *a priori* with the formal was for Kant neither presupposition nor prejudice, but rather a conclusion to which he was led by sheer force of argument, and, so to speak, against his rationalistic instinct. If in this process he made an error, then the problem of synthetic *a priori* judgments remains unsolved. Whoever stands by the existence of such judgments and yet rejects Kant's solution, must take the finding of another solution to be his most important task. Now the phenomenologists not only believe in these judgments so astounding in their implications for knowledge, they even fix their boundaries astonishingly wider than Kant. Thus, they would certainly seem to be under an obligation to explain their possibility. This they have in no way attempted to do. They are clearly undisturbed by the problems to which the *Critique of Pure Reason* owes its origin. They have either forgotten the issue, or seem to make a detour whenever they get in its neighborhood. Thus Scheler writes [4] in connection with a critique of Kant's proposal to equate the "material" (that is, the non-formal) with "sensuous" content: "It is, it seems to me, the πρῶτον ψεῦδος of this identification that instead of asking the simple question, 'What *is* given?', one asks, 'What *can* be given?'" In Phenomenology we do not meet with the question as to the "can", the question of "possibility" in the kantian sense. Is this not, however, a genuine problem? May one not go on to ask how the "*Wesensschau*" goes about the business of delivering synthetic, universally valid knowledge to us, or must we accept this as a simple matter of fact? Even in Husserl himself we find on this point only obscure passages concerning "self-evidence" which are of highly dubious propriety, coming as they do, from the great warrior against psychologism.

The defenders of the factual *a priori*, the ranks of which include others beside the phenomenologists, have, I repeat, far more reason than Kant to ask the question: "How are synthetic *a priori* judgments possible?" In the

[4] *Op. cit.*, p. 50.

first place, because according to them the domain of such judgments is much more inclusive, and in the second place, because they explicitly reject the answer given by Kant. We have every cause to raise in the presence of this philosophy the still more penetrating question, which forced our empiricism to take a stand in opposition to the kantian system, and which it had to answer in the negative, "Are the judgments actually synthetic and *a priori* which you take to be so?" And if the answer should be in the affirmative with respect to the judgments arising from "*Wesensschau*" (intuition of essences), we ought not to rest until we had clarified their puzzling existence, their possibility. Indeed, as long as we had not succeeded in doing this, we should be in a state of constantly recurring doubt lest we had been deceived in the very assertion of their existence, and should reckon with the possibility that further insight would lead us to a more adequate account, just as an improved insight into the nature of mathematics and the natural sciences has shown the kantian thesis that they contain synthetic *a priori* judgments, to be untenable. For we are today of the opinion that the propositions of pure mathematics are not synthetic, while those of the science of nature (to which geometry belongs, in so far as it is conceived to be the science of Space) are not *a priori*. Our empiricism makes the assertion that there are no other *a priori* judgments than the analytic, or rather, as we prefer to say today, that only tautological propositions are *a priori*. It willingly admits, however, that the propositions which the phenomenologist traces to "*Wesensschau*" and characterizes as constituting a factual *a priori* are worthy of the most exacting test, and appear to be a more serious threat to its position than those with which the *Critique of Pure Reason* is concerned. It is ready to revise its standpoint, if the result of the test should not be in its favor.

(A philosopher who believes in a factual *a priori*, and would like to clarify its possibility, would have, as far as I can see, no other way out than to carry over the kantian theory from the form to the content of experience. He would have to assume that not only the form of our cognitions, but also their matter springs from the knowing consciousness —for only thus could *a priori* propositions relating to them be made intelligible. This would amount to a subjective Idealism of the Fichtean variety; one would find oneself entangled in a weird metaphysics.)

*   *   *

What, then, are the propositions which the phenomenologist brings forward to substantiate his contention, and which he believes, as Husserl put it, to found a science which "achieves an abundance of knowledge of the most rigorous type decisive in its import for all philosophy to come"? It is common knowledge that they are such judgments as these, that every tone has an intensity and a pitch, that one and the same surface cannot be simultaneously red and green, that (according to Scheler) "spiritual values have a higher place in the scale of values than vital values, and the values of the Holy a higher place than the spiritual",[5] and so on. In the analysis which follows, we shall limit ourselves to propositions of the type represented by the first two examples, since the ethical proposition, because of its lack of clarity, offers no foothold for an exact analysis. We ask first whether these propositions are genuinely *a priori*, or are *a posteriori* in the same way as the proposition: "This organ pipe emits the note A" or "This cloth is red".

All those who share a still widespread childish conception of the nature of empiricism will believe that it must be predisposed from the very first to regard the sentences in question as giving expression to facts of experience, and that it will attempt to defend this assertion of their *a posteriori* character in all possible ways. But such a naïve conception, which would accord perhaps with the standpoint of John Stuart Mill, is wide of the mark as far as our empiricism is concerned, which owes its entire force to purely logical insights. When it is confronted by an assertion such as "A surface cannot be simultaneously red and green," it does nothing more than simply and without prejudice make clear the meaning of the assertion. For this is in general the true task of philosophical activity; its problems are solved not by means of proofs which yield fresh knowledge, but rather by the mere process of reflecting on what is actually meant by the sentences which have come to be so puzzling; on what one is trying to say by means of them. And in order to see this, one only needs to realize how these sentences are properly used.

A synthetic sentence, that is to say, one that actually gives expression to a cognition, is always used in science and life to communicate a state of affairs, and, indeed, that state of affairs the cognition of which is formulated by the sentence. On the other hand, an analytic sentence, or, to put it more clearly, a tautology, has a quite different function; it represents only a purely formal transformation of equivalent expressions, and serves, therefore, only as a technical device within a proof, a deduction, a calculus. A tautology is naturally an *a priori* truth, but gives expression to no state of affairs, and the validity of a tautology rests in no way upon experience. For in order to know whether or not two expressions are equivalent, I need only know their established meaning, and not any state of affairs in the world.

The empiricism which I represent believes itself to be clear on the point that, as a matter of principle, all propositions are either synthetic *a posteriori* or tautologous; synthetic *a priori* propositions seem to it to be a logical impossibility. Must it abandon this position which it has been able to defend with ease against the kantian philosophy, in the face of the propositions which Husserl and his school have apparently made the foundation of a new philosophy?

[5] *Ibid.*, p. 109.

Is it perhaps a synthetic *a priori* proposition that every tone has a determinate pitch, that a green spot is not also red?

In accordance with our program, we ask how these sentences are actually used, in what circumstances they make their appearance. Here we note the remarkable fact that they are to be met with neither in science, nor in life, with the exception of a purely rhetorical usage (thus an orator might say, "After all, what is black is not white"). Only in the phenomenological philosophy do they play a rôle. This is already a startling fact. It is beyond doubt that exactly those phenomenological judgments which are recognized on all sides as true, are never encountered in the language of everyday life. The reason for this is obvious; they are recognized to be completely trivial. Should anybody tell me that a certain lady wore a green dress, it would surely strike him as odd were I then to ask, "Can I take it that the dress wasn't red?" He would insist, "I have already told you that it was green".

Nobody denies that it is only through experience that we can come to know that a (uniformly colored) dress worn by a given person at a given time was green or red or of some other color. But it is equally impossible to deny that once we know it to be green we need no further experience in order to know that it isn't red. The two cases stand on completely different levels. Every attempt to explain the difference between them as one of degree, by claiming, perhaps, that while in the first we have to do with a direct report of experience, the second, in the last analysis, can be traced back to experiences (on the ground that only through such could we know that red and green cannot be associated with the same spot), is fruitless. One must have a strong prejudice in favor of the so-called "empiristical" tendencies represented by Mill in order not to see that this approach is completely untenable. Even if all humanity always wore green clothes, and we had confirmed by examining millions of cases that red clothes were not to be found, we should have not the least difficulty in imagining people dressed in red, and it would never enter our heads to deny the possibility that in distant lands or times it might be the fashion to wear red. We know exactly how dark blue lions would look, even though all we have seen have been yellow.

Suppose that an explorer assured us that in Africa he had run across lions of normal yellow color, which, however, were also blue from tip to toe! What would the situation be then? We should, of course, immediately point out that this is impossible. And if he replied that our disbelief was due merely to the fact that by chance we had never happened to see a color that was yellow all over, but also entirely blue, this would not lead us to change our opinion. Nothing could convince us that this case resembles that of the green clothes and the red clothes. We must admit an unbridgeable difference, a difference of principle between the two cases. It simply amounts to this: We have only *a posteriori* knowledge concerning the qualities of the clothes worn by this or that person, or by people generally; whereas we know *a priori* that a green dress is not a red dress, nor a yellow hide, blue.

In other words, the propositions in question are beyond a doubt *a priori*. The contention of the phenomenologists that the validity of such judgments is of a completely different type from that of ordinary judgments of experience, is correct. We are not to be diverted from this insight by the fact that many wish to speak of a special kind of "experience", the phenomenological, which is to be identified with "*Wesensschau*".

What, however, is to be said about the second part of the contention, namely that these propositions give rise to genuine knowledge, that they have factual content, that they have a material, not merely formal character?

The fact that they have to do with colors, sounds, in short, with the content, the stuff of sense experience seems to point in this direction. Against it, however, seems to stand the triviality of the propositions in question, a triviality which we find elsewhere only in the case of tautological propositions, which say nothing, are true by virtue of their form alone, and give no information about the world.

A decision should not be difficult, for on the first alternative, the necessary validity of these truths would be a factual one, somehow grounded in the nature of things, whereas on the second alternative, the validity would be a purely logical one—and it seems hardly possible that the two should be confused. Have we not yet learned to draw a line between that special kind of validity which is the purely logical and all that imitates it?

The confusion of *causa* and *ratio*, which Spinoza erected into a principle, is today rarely encountered (for which reason we are the more astonished at the fundamental notion of Meyerson's *Identity and Reality*) and we are, in general, equally little inclined to follow Schopenhauer's example by slipping in between *ratio cognoscendi* and *ratio fiendi* (or *causa*) an additional *ratio essendi* which would be difficult to distinguish from the former. But as a matter of fact, necessity in the sense in which it characterizes, according to the phenomenologists, the results of "*Wesensschau*", is nothing other than the Schopenhauerian *ratio essendi*, the very "intuitive necessity" which, according to Kant (whose teachings on this point have been taken up again by the followers of Husserl; see, for example, O. Becker), characterizes geometrical knowledge. I, personally, hold it to be fully established that the sole necessity of which we can speak in connection with geometry, is the purely logical necessity which is the deductive relationship of the propositions to one another, a necessity which leaves entirely open the question as to whether or not these propositions apply to "real" intuitive space, and I shall waste no words in this connection. Is, however, "*a priori* intuition" to gain entrance into philosophy by a new door? Does it determine the matter of our experiences? Is it the expression of a remarkable *Gesetzmaessigkeit des "Soseins"* (lawful structure of essences), which forbids a green surface to be at the same time red, or forbids a tone to exist unless it has a determinate pitch?

If this were the case, then there would be a factual *a priori*, and the question as to its possibility would have to be posed in exactly the same sense as it was by Kant in the *Critique of Pure Reason*, though he was not able to solve it. But this time the problem would be far more formidable, particularly since the entire distance we have traveled since Kant has been in a different direction.

Fortunately, however, the matter is quite otherwise. ("Fortunately" in this connection does not imply "by chance"; rather we shall see that it couldn't be otherwise.) Our "materially" *a priori* propositions are in truth of a purely conceptual nature, their validity is a logical validity, they have a tautological, formal character.

This stands out clearly by way of contrast as soon as we confront their meaning with that of empirical-synthetic judgments. If I hear that the Queen wore a green dress, the assertion is an empirical one, since I know that she could equally well have worn a red one (even though green dresses alone are in fashion). But what does this mean? Nothing else than that the sentence "The Queen wore a red dress" is just as meaningful as the sentence "The Queen wore a green dress"; I know exactly what is meant by both sentences, even if by chance I have never seen green or red dresses. On the other hand, if I hear that the dress was both green and red, I am unable to give a meaning to this combination of words; I just do not know what it is supposed to mean. If someone speaks of a tone that lacked a determinate pitch, I know beyond question that it was no simple musical tone; and if someone speaks of a green dress, I know beyond question that it wasn't a red dress; in the same way I know that a man who is 1.60 meters tall, isn't at the same time 1.80 meters tall. Everyone will admit that it requires no special kind of experience or insight in order to know that the lengths corresponding to 1.60 and 1.80 meters are incompatible with one another, for this follows from the nature of the concepts. As long as I take them to be compatible, I simply have not understood what is meant by the words "1.60 meters long". And the case is not different by even the breadth of a hair with respect to colors, tones, or whatever else might be brought forward by way of example. Red and green are incompatible, not because I happen never to have observed such a joint appearance, but because the sentence "This spot is both red and green" is a meaningless combination of words. The logical rules which underlie our employment of color-words forbid such a usage, just as they would forbid us to say "Light red is redder than dark red."

In the last analysis no one doubts this, and what difficulty there is consists merely in coming to see that the matter is a purely logical one, and that with this insight the whole issue is disposed of, and gives rise to no further problem. The meaning of a word is solely determined by the rules which hold for its use. Whatever follows from these rules, follows from the mere meaning of the word, and is therefore purely analytic, tautological, formal. The error committed by the proponents of the factual *a priori* can be understood as arising from the fact that it was not clearly realized that such concepts as those of the colors have a formal structure just as do numbers or spatial concepts, and that this structure determines their meaning without remainder. The first who, to my knowledge, has given the correct solution of the problem is Ludwig Wittgenstein (see his *Tractatus Logico-Philosophicus* and essay in the *Proceedings of the Aristotelian Society*, 1929), to whom we owe fundamental logical clarifications which will decisively influence the future course of philosophy.

Should I assert that the height of a certain person is 160 cm., no one would take a statement to the effect that the individual in question isn't 180 cm. tall to give new insight or information. For everyone knows that the second piece of information is already included in the first by virtue of the meaning of the number symbols. He knows this as well as he knows that by the use of the above number nothing is said as to whether the person is a Frenchman or a Spaniard, whether polite or rude. Just as it belongs to the meaning of a statement giving someone's age that a person has only one age at a given time, and cannot be, for example, both 30 and 40 years old, so it belongs to the meaning of the word "tone" that one and only one determinate pitch characterizes a tone, and so it belongs to the logical grammar of color words that a word of this kind designates a specific property only on condition that I cannot designate this same property by means of a different color word. Should I permit this, the color words I use would have an entirely different meaning from that which we give them in everyday usage. In that case, the sentences which are the showpieces of the phenomenological philosophy would no longer be correct. Thus, they say nothing about existence, or about the nature of anything, but rather only exhibit the content of our concepts, that is, the mode and manner in which we employ the words of our language. Given the meanings of the words, they are *a priori*, but purely formal-tautological, as indeed are all other *a priori* propositions. As expressions which have nothing to say, they bring no knowledge, and cannot serve as the foundation of a special science. Such a science as the phenomenologists have promised us just does not exist.

A Pragmatic Conception of the *a Priori**

C. I. LEWIS [1]

The conception of the *a priori* points two problems which are perennial in philosophy; the part played in knowledge by the mind itself, and the possibility of "necessary truth" or of knowledge "independent of experience." But traditional conceptions of the *a priori* have proved untenable. That the mind approaches the flux of immediacy with some godlike foreknowledge of principles which are legislative for experience, that there is any natural light or any innate ideas, it is no longer possible to believe.

Nor shall we find the clue to the *a priori* in any compulsion of the mind to incontrovertible truth or any peculiar kind of demonstration which establishes first principles. All truth lays upon the rational mind the same compulsion to belief; as Mr. Bosanquet has pointed out, this character belongs to all propositions or judgments once their truth is established.

The difficulties of the conception are due, I believe, to two mistakes: whatever is *a priori* is necessary, but we have misconstrued the relation of necessary truth to mind. And the *a priori* is independent of experience, but in so taking it, we have misunderstood its relation to empirical fact. What is *a priori* is necessary truth not because it compels the mind's acceptance, but precisely because it does not. It is given experience, brute fact, the *a posteriori* element in knowledge which the mind must accept willy-nilly. The *a priori* represents an attitude in some sense freely taken, a stipulation of the mind itself, and a stipulation which might be made in some other way if it suited our bent or need. Such truth is necessary as opposed to contingent, not as opposed to voluntary. And the *a priori* is independent of experience not because it prescribes a form which the data of sense must fit, or anticipates some preëstablished harmony of experience with the mind, but precisely because it prescribes nothing to experience. That is *a priori* which is true, *no matter what*. What it anticipates is not the given, but our attitude toward it: it concerns the uncompelled initiative of mind or, as Josiah Royce would say, our categorical ways of acting.

The traditional example of the *a priori par excellence* is the laws of

---

* Reprinted from *The Journal of Philosophy*, 20, 1923, by kind permission of the author and the editors.

[1] Read at the meeting of the American Philosophical Association, Dec. 27, 1922.

logic. These can not be derived from experience since they must first be taken for granted in order to prove them. They make explicit our general modes of classification. And they impose upon experience no real limitation. Sometimes we are asked to tremble before the spectre of the "alogical," in order that we may thereafter rejoice that we are saved from this by the dependence of reality upon mind. But the "alogical" is pure bogey, a word without a meaning. What kind of experience could defy the principle that everything must either be or not be, that nothing can both be and not be, or that if x is y and y is z, then x is z? If anything imaginable or unimaginable could violate such laws, then the ever-present fact of change would do it every day. The laws of logic are purely formal; they forbid nothing but what concerns the use of terms and the corresponding modes of classification and analysis. The law of contradiction tells us that nothing can be both white and not-white, but it does not and can not tell us whether black is not-white, or soft or square is not-white. To discover *what contradicts what* we must always consult the character of experience. Similarly the law of the excluded middle formulates our decision that whatever is not designated by a certain term shall be designated by its negative. It declares our purpose to make, for every term, a complete dichotomy of experience, instead—as we might choose—of classifying on the basis of a tripartite division into opposites (as black and white) and the middle ground between the two. Our rejection of such tripartite division represents only our penchant for simplicity.

Further laws of logic are of similar significance. They are principles of procedure, the parliamentary rules of intelligent thought and speech. Such laws are independent of experience because they impose no limitations whatever upon it. They are legislative because they are addressed to ourselves—because definition, classification, and inference represent no operations of the objective world, but only our own categorical attitudes of mind.

And further, the ultimate criteria of the laws of logic are pragmatic. Those who suppose that there is, for example, *a* logic which everyone would agree to if he understood it and understood himself, are more optimistic than those versed in the history of logical discussion have a right to be. The fact is that there are several logics, markedly different, each self-consistent in its own terms and such that whoever, using it, avoids false premises, will never reach a false conclusion. Mr. Russell, for example, bases *his* logic on an implication relation such that if twenty sentences be cut from a newspaper and put in a hat, and then two of these be drawn at random, one of them will certainly imply the other, and it is an even bet that the implication will be mutual. Yet upon a foundation so remote from ordinary modes of inference the whole structure of *Principia Mathematica* is built. This logic—and there are others even more strange—is utterly consistent and the results of it entirely valid. Over and above all questions of consistency, there are issues of logic which can not be determined—nay, can not even be argued—except on pragmatic grounds of conformity to human bent and intellectual convenience. That we have been blind to this fact, itself reflects traditional errors in the conception of the *a priori*.

We may note in passing one less important illustration of the *a priori*—the proposition "true by definition." Definitions and their immediate consequences, analytic propositions generally, are necessarily true, true under all possible circumstances. Definition is legislative because it is in some sense arbitrary. Not only is the meaning assigned to words more or less a matter of choice—that consideration is relatively trivial—but the manner in which the precise classifications which definition embodies shall be effected, is something not dictated by experience. If experience were other than it is, the definition and its corresponding classification might be inconvenient, fantastic, or useless, but it could not be false. Mind makes classifications and determines meanings; in so doing it creates the *a priori* truth of analytic judgments. But that the manner of this creation responds to pragmatic considerations, is so obvious that it hardly needs pointing out.

If the illustrations so far given seem trivial or verbal, that impression may be corrected by turning to the place which the *a priori* has in mathematics and in natural science. Arithmetic, for example, depends *en toto* upon the operation of counting or correlating, a procedure which can be carried out at will in any world containing identifiable things—even identifiable ideas—regardless of the further characters of experience. Mill challenged this *a priori* character of arithmetic. He asked us to suppose a demon sufficiently powerful and maleficent so that every time two things were brought together with two other things, this demon should always introduce a fifth. The implication which he supposed to follow is that under such circumstances $2 + 2 = 5$ would be a universal law of arithmetic. But Mill was quite mistaken. In such a world we should be obliged to become a little clearer than is usual about the distinction between arithmetic and physics, that is all. If two black marbles were put in the same urn with two white ones, the demon could take his choice of colors, but it would be evident that there were more black marbles or more white ones than were put in. The same would be true of all objects in any wise identifiable. We should simply find ourselves in the presence of an extraordinary physical law, which we should recognize as universal in our world, that whenever two things were brought into proximity with two others, an additional and similar thing was always created by the process. Mill's world would be physically most extraordinary. The world's work would be enormously facilitated if hats or locomotives or tons of coal could be thus multipled by anyone possessed originally of two pairs. But the laws of mathematics would remain unaltered. It is because this is true that arithmetic is *a priori*. Its laws prevent *nothing;* they are compatible with anything which happens or could conceivably happen in nature. They would be true in any possible world. Mathematical addition is not a physical transformation. Physical changes which result in an increase or decrease of the countable things involved are matters of everyday occurrence. Such physical processes present us with phenomena in which the purely mathematical has to be separated out by abstraction. Those laws and those laws only have necessary truth which we are prepared to maintain, no matter what. It is because we shall always separate out that part of the phenomenon not in conformity with arithmetic and designate it by some other category—physical change, chemical reaction, optical illusion—that arithmetic is *a priori*.

The *a priori* element in science and in natural law is greater than might be supposed. In the first place, all science is based upon definitive concepts. The formulation of these concepts is, indeed, a matter determined by the commerce between our intellectual or our pragmatic interests and the nature of experience. Definition is classification. The scientific search is for such classification as will make it possible to correlate appearance and behavior, to discover law, to penetrate to the "essential nature" of things in order that behavior may become predictable. In other words, if definition is unsuccessful, as early scientific definitions mostly have been, it is because the classification thus set up corresponds with no natural cleavage and does not correlate with any important uniformity of behavior. A name itself must represent *some* uniformity in experience or it names nothing. What does not repeat itself or recur in intelligible fashion is not a thing. Where the definitive uniformity is a clue to other uniformities, we have successful scientific definition. Other definitions can not be said to be false; they are merely useless. In scientific classification the search is, thus, for *things worth naming*. But the naming, classifying, defining activity is essentially prior to investigation. We can not interrogate experience in general. Until our meaning is definite and our classification correspondingly exact, experience can not conceivably answer our questions.

In the second place, the fundamental laws of any science—or those treated as fundamental—are *a priori* because they formulate just such definitive concepts or categorical tests by which alone investigation becomes possible. If the lightning strikes the railroad track at two places, *A* and *B*, how shall we tell whether these events are simultaneous? "We . . . require a definition of simultaneity such that this definition supplies us with the method by means of which . . . we can decide whether or not both the lightning strokes occurred simultaneously. As long as this requirement is not satisfied, I allow myself to be deceived as a physicist (and of course the same applies if I am not a physicist), when I imagine that I am able to attach a meaning to the statement of simultaneity. . . .

"After thinking the matter over for some time you then offer the following suggestion with which to test simultaneity. By measuring along the rails, the connecting line AB should be measured up and an observer placed at the mid-point M of the distance AB. This observer should be supplied with an arrangement (e.g., two mirrors inclined at 90°) which allows him visually to observe both places A and B at the same time. If the observer perceives the two flashes at the same time, then they are simultaneous.

"I am very pleased with this suggestion, but for all that I can not re-gard the matter as quite settled, because I feel constrained to raise the following objection: 'Your definition would certainly be right, if I only knew that the light by means of which the observer at M perceives the lightning flashes travels along the length A—M with the same velocity as along the length B—M. But an examination of this supposition would only be possible if we already had at our disposal the means of measuring time. It would thus appear as though we were moving here in a logical circle.'

"After further consideration you cast a somewhat disdainful glance at me—and rightly so—and you declare: 'I maintain my previous definition nevertheless, because in reality it assumes absolutely nothing about light. There is only *one* demand to be made of the definition of simultaneity, namely, that in every real case it must supply us with an empirical deci-sion as to whether or not the conception which has to be defined is ful-filled. That light requires the same time to traverse the path A—M as for the path B—M is in reality *neither a supposition nor a hypothesis* about the physical nature of light, but a *stipulation* which I can make of my own free-will in order to arrive at a definition of simultaneity.' . . . We are thus led also to a definition of 'time' in physics." [2]

As this example from the theory of relativity well illustrates, we can not even ask the questions which discovered law would answer until we have first by *a priori* stipulation formulated definitive criteria. Such con-cepts are not verbal definitions, nor classifications merely; they are them-selves laws which prescribe a certain uniformity of behavior to whatever is thus named. Such definitive laws are *a priori;* only so can we enter upon the investigation by which further laws are sought. Yet it should also be pointed out that such *a priori* laws are subject to abandonment if the struc-ture which is built upon them does not succeed in simplifying our inter-pretation of phenomena. If, in the illustration given, the relation "simul-taneous with," as defined, should not prove transitive—if event A should prove simultaneous with B, and B with C, but not A with C—this defini-tion would certainly be rejected.

And thirdly, there is that *a priori* element in science—as in other hu-man affairs—which constitutes the criteria of the real as opposed to the unreal in experience. An object itself is a uniformity. Failure to behave in

[2] Einstein, *Relativity*, pp. 26-28: italics are the author's.

certain categorical ways marks it as unreal. Uniformities of the type called "natural law" are the clues to reality and unreality. A mouse which disappears where no hole is, is no real mouse; a landscape which recedes as we approach is but illusion. As the queen remarked in the episode of the wishing-carpet, "If this were real, then it would be a miracle. But miracles do not happen. Therefore I shall wake presently." That the uniformities of natural law are the only reliable criteria of the real, is inescapable. But such a criterion is *ipso facto a priori*. No conceivable experience could dictate the alteration of a law so long as failure to obey that law marked the content of experience as unreal.

This is one of the puzzles of empiricism. We deal with experience: what any reality may be which underlies experience, we have to learn. What we desire to discover is natural law, the formulation of those uniformities which obtain amongst the real. But experience as it comes to us contains not only the real but all the content of illusion, dream, hallucination, and mistake. The *given* contains both real and unreal, confusingly intermingled. If we ask for uniformities of this unsorted experience, we shall not find them. Laws which characterize all experience, of real and unreal both, are non-existent and would in any case be worthless. What we seek are the uniformities of the *real;* but *until we have such laws, we can not sift experience and segregate the real.*

The obvious solution is that the enrichment of experience, the separation of the real from the illusory or meaningless, and the formulation of natural law, all grow up together. If the criteria of the real are *a priori*, that is not to say that no conceivable character of experience would lead to alteration of them. For example, spirits can not be photographed. But if photographs of spiritistic phenomena, taken under properly guarded conditions, should become sufficiently frequent, this *a priori* dictum would be called in question. What we should do would be to redefine our terms. Whether "spook" was spirit or matter, whether the definition of "spirit" or of "matter" should be changed; all this would constitute one interrelated problem. We should reopen together the question of definition or classification, of criteria for this sort of real, and of natural law. And the solution of one of these would mean the solution of all. Nothing could *force* a redefinition of spirit or of matter. A sufficiently fundamental relation to human bent, to human interests, would guarantee continuance unaltered even in the face of unintelligible and baffling experiences. In such problems, the mind finds itself uncompelled save by its own purposes and needs. I *may* categorize experience as I will; but *what* categorical distinctions will best serve my interests and objectify my own intelligence? What the mixed and troubled experience shall be—that is beyond me. But what I shall do with it—that is my own question, when the character of experience is sufficiently before me. I am coerced only by my own need to understand.

It would indeed be inappropriate to characterize as *a priori* a law which we are wholly prepared to alter in the light of further experience, even though in an isolated case we should discard as illusory any experience which failed to conform. But the crux of the situation lies in this; beyond such principles as those of logic, which we seem fully prepared to maintain no matter what, there must be further and more particular criteria of the real prior to any investigation of nature whatever. We can not even interrogate experience without a network of categories and definitive concepts. And we must further be prepared to say what experimental findings will answer what questions, and how. Without tests which represent anterior principle, there is no question which experience could answer at all. Thus the most fundamental laws in any category—or those which we regard as most fundamental—are *a priori*, even though continued failure to render experience intelligible in such terms might result eventually in the abandonment of that category altogether. Matters so comparatively small as the behavior of Mercury and of starlight passing the sun's limb may, if there be persistent failure to bring them within the field of previously accepted modes of explanation, result in the abandonment of the independent categories of space and time. But without the definitions, fundamental principles, and tests, of the type which constitute such categories, no experience whatever could prove or disprove anything. And to that mind which should find independent space and time absolutely necessary conceptions, no possible experiment could prove the principles of relativity. "There must be some error in the experimental findings, or some law not yet discovered," represents an attitude which can never be rendered impossible. And the only sense in which it could be proved unreasonable would be the pragmatic one of comparison with another method of categorical analysis which more successfully reduced all such experience to order and law.

At the bottom of all science and all knowledge are categories and definitive concepts which represent fundamental habits of thought and deeply-lying attitudes which the human mind has taken in the light of its total experience. But a new and wider experience may bring about some alteration of these attitudes, even though by themselves they dictate nothing as to the content of experience, and no experience can conceivably prove them invalid.

Perhaps some will object to this conception on the ground that only such principles should be designated *a priori* as the human mind *must* maintain, no matter what; that if, for example, it is shown possible to arrive at a consistent doctrine of physics in terms of relativity, even by the most arduous reconstruction of our fundamental notions, then the present conceptions are by that fact shown not to be *a priori*. Such objection is especially likely from those who would conceive the *a priori* in terms of an absolute mind or an absolutely universal human nature. We should readily agree that a decision by popular approval or a congress of scientists or anything short of such a test as would bring to bear the full weight of human capacity and interest, would be ill-considered as having to do with the *a priori*. But we wish to emphasize two facts: first, that in the field of those conceptions and principles which have altered in human history, there are those which could neither be proved nor disproved by any experience, but represent the uncompelled initiative of human thought—that without this uncompelled initiative no growth of science, nor any science at all, would be conceivable. And second, that the difference between such conceptions as are, for example, concerned in the decision of relativity versus absolute space and time, and those more permanent attitudes such as are vested in the laws of logic, there is only a difference of degree. The dividing line between the *a priori* and the *a posteriori* is that between principles and definitive concepts which *can* be maintained in the face of all experience and those genuinely empirical generalizations which *might* be proven flatly false. The thought which both rationalism and empiricism have missed is that there are principles, representing the initiative of mind, which impose upon experience no limitations whatever, but that such conceptions are still subject to alteration on pragmatic grounds when the expanding boundaries of experience reveal their infelicity as intellectual instruments.

Neither human experience nor the human mind has a character which is universal, fixed, and absolute. "The human mind" does not exist at all save in the sense that all humans are very much alike in fundamental respects, and that the language habit and the enormously important exchange of ideas has greatly increased our likeness in those respects which are here in question. Our categories and definitions are peculiarly social products, reached in the light of experiences which have much in common, and beaten out, like other pathways, by the coincidence of human purposes and the exigencies of human coöperation. Concerning the *a priori* there need be neither universal agreement nor complete historical continuity. Conceptions, such as those of logic, which are least likely to be affected by the opening of new ranges of experience, represent the most stable of our categories; but none of them is beyond the possibility of alteration.

Mind contributes to experience the element of order, of classification, categories, and definition. Without such, experience would be unintelligible. Our knowledge of the validity of these is simply consciousness of our own fundamental ways of acting and our own intellectual intent. Without this element, knowledge is impossible, and it is here that whatever truths are necessary and independent of experience must be found. But the commerce between our categorical ways of acting, our pragmatic interests, and the particular character of experience, is closer than we have realized. No explanation of any one of these can be complete without consideration of the other two.

Pragmatism has sometimes been charged with oscillating between two contrary notions; the one, that experience is "through and through malleable to our purpose," the other, that facts are "hard" and uncreated by the mind. We here offer a mediating conception: through all our knowledge runs the element of the *a priori*, which is indeed malleable to our purpose and responsive to our need. But throughout, there is also that other element of experience which is "hard," "independent," and unalterable to our will.

V

INDUCTION AND PROBABILITY

The Logical Character of the Principle of Induction *

HERBERT FEIGL

The purpose of this paper is to make clear (1) that the widely recognized formulations of the principle of induction do not express the most fundamental rule of induction; (2) that the current view concerning the probability of induction must be revised in terms of a frequency theory of probability; (3) that on this basis the problem of induction in its traditional form is a pseudo-problem; and (4) that the principle of induction must be interpreted as a *pragmatic* or *operational* maxim.

I

Let us begin with a brief summary of those views concerning the problem of induction which seem to have received the most general approval among contemporary logicians and philosophers.

1. Induction is essentially different from deductive inference. It can never attain certainty. All attempts to transform inductive into deductive inference fail because they necessitate the introduction of *inductive* premises. Hume has shown that induction can be proved certain neither on logical grounds nor on the basis of its own success.

2. Induction is the indispensable foundation of all factual science, although it is admitted that the more advanced factual sciences do not actually proceed by inductive generalization. Their method consists rather in the construction of hypothetico-deductive systems. The strength of such systems lies in the high degree of internal connectedness by which the various parts of a system reinforce one another. But logically, if not genetically, a theory is inductive. This is clear from the fact that any verification establishes the truth only of singular or particular propositions but not of general hypotheses.

3. The principle of induction expresses the increase of the *probability* of inductions in dependence upon the accumulation of factual evidence. Such evidence consists in the elimination of irrelevant circumstances, as

* Reprinted, with slight alterations, by kind permission of the publishers, The Williams and Wilkins Co., Baltimore, from *Philosophy of Science*, Vol. I, 1934. This paper, written in 1931, was read at a meeting of the Western Division of the American Philosophical Association at Ann Arbor, Michigan, March, 1932.

well as in the positive confirmation of a specific connection, uniformity, or regularity.

4. This principle of induction is not a consequence of the purely logical axioms of the calculus of probabilities. It can be demonstrated only on the basis of *assumptions concerning the general constitution of nature.* Thus, Jevons took nature to be something like an urn to which we can apply Bayes' Theorem. Peirce, similarly, assumed that our observations represent "fair samples" of a thoroughly statistical world. Zilsel, Broad, Keynes and Nicod introduce more refined formulations of the "Principle of the Uniformity of Nature" such as the "Principle of Limited Depth and Variety," or at least the antecedent probability of such assumptions.[1]

5. The quantitative value of probabilities and their convergence toward certainty can be derived only from the presupposition of rather arbitrary and artificial conditions whose fulfilment is by no means warranted in any case of scientifically significant induction. The idea of determining the numerical value of the probability of scientific theories seems preposterous.

6. Since these general hypotheses underlying induction are interpreted as significant assumptions concerning the structure of reality, they must be logically synthetic and, therefore, themselves *inductive.* This is the fundamental difficulty. *What can be meant by the probability of these presuppositions of the probability of all particular inductions?* It is held that even these presuppositions can be rendered increasingly probable by the verification of their consequences. Keynes and Nicod believe that they have proved this argument to be free from circularity. To many thinkers the whole issue appears highly problematic.

II

The unsatisfactory state of the problem of induction seems to me to be due to the preoccupation with the problem of the *validity* of induction. The more fundamental question concerning the *meaning* of the principle of induction is rather neglected and it is this which needs a careful, logical analysis.

The chief difficulty, undoubtedly, lies in the interpretation of the concept of probability. To Hume, the probability of induction was a subjective or psychological matter. It was a degree of belief or an intensity of expectation, based on habit. In contrast with this reduction of probability to something irrational and in opposition to the classical *subjective* interpretation of mathematical probability, two types of *objective* interpretations have been advanced:

1. *Probability as a Logical Relation*—the theory of Leibniz, Bolzano and

---

[1] E. Zilsel: *Das Anwendungsproblem,* Leipzig, 1916. C. D. Broad: "The Principles of Problematic Induction", *Proc. Aristot. Soc.,* 1927-8. J. M. Keynes: *A Treatise on Probability,* 1921. Nicod: *Foundations of Geometry and Induction,* 1930.

W. E. Johnson, most fully expounded in Keynes' *Treatise*, and accepted by C. D. Broad, Nicod and others.

2. *Probability as the Limit of a Statistical Frequency*—the theory of Venn and Peirce, rejected by Keynes, but recently restated, defended and mathematically systematized by the Berlin mathematician, R. v. Mises.

According to the logical interpretation, which still seems generally favored, probability is the relation of partial or inconclusive implication between one proposition and another. But this account is for Keynes merely a characterization, not a definition, of the fundamentally unanalyzable and indefinable probability relation. Here, I believe, Keynes is fundamentally in error. I do not mean to deny that the probability relation can be chosen as a primitive notion in an axiomatization of the probability calculus. That can of course be done, and has in fact been done by Keynes, and more recently by Reichenbach.[2] But probability is also applied to empirical facts and in this case we need rules in order to determine the value of the applied probability. These rules, if they can be stated at all, are then the *definition of the empirical or applied probability concept*. I have not time here to prove in detail that in any significant application of the probability concept its essential meaning is statistical. However, I shall discuss a few of the relevant points.

If the principle of indifference operates not on the basis of equal ignorance, as did its predecessor, the "principle of insufficient reason," but on positive grounds, it must inevitably make use of statistical assumptions. Often these assumptions are tacit and in many cases their statistical character is not recognized, but they are the true source of every fruitful probability argument. The "indifference" or "irrelevancy," which is the crucial concept in the principle, means generally *causal irrelevance*. Causal irrelevance, however, is identical with random distribution, and random distribution is a fact which can be established only by statistical investigation. The essential and final test for the correctness of any estimate of probabilities is always the comparison with the statistical frequencies. Confronted with an "a priori" probability, one can take only one reasonable attitude, and that is to ask the direct question: What bearing does it have on observable facts? It is understandable that Peirce, who introduced this pragmatic question as a general criterion of meaning, was at the same time perhaps the most convincing advocate of the frequency theory.

III

If probability is to be a significant guide for our expectations and predictions, inductive probability must be interpreted in terms of the frequency theory. Once it is granted that induction is not an infallible procedure, all our care must be directed toward attaining success at least

---

[2] H. Reichenbach: "Axiomatik der Wahrscheinlichkeitsrechnung", *Math. Zeitschrift*, 34, 1932.

with a maximal frequency. Mill's famous question—Why are the experimental methods (as stated in his own canons) much more efficient than induction by pure enumeration?—means precisely: Why are the experimental methods successful more frequently than simple induction in the discovery of a law? The fact that they are more successful has stimulated the desire for a more profound explanation in terms of assumptions about the structure of the world. The assumption that there are at the bottom of nature strictly deterministic laws, on the one hand, and complete independencies on the other, seemed to account for the superior reliability of experimental methods. For if we follow the simpler method of pure enumeration, we can always be deceived by strong statistical correlations which we may mistake for laws. Only the experimental methods are capable of splitting up such correlations into their strictly causal and strictly random components.

This hypothesis of the "All or None" character of nature has been one of the most fundamental and fruitful guiding principles in almost every field of science. But the recent development of Quantum Physics has proved that it is not an *a priori* or necessary truth. According to Quantum Physics some of the elementary laws of nature are statistical correlations which will probably never be reduced to a deterministic scheme. The change in attitude is fundamental, and even if determinism should be re-established as a result of surprising new discoveries, the lesson taught by modern physics would remain of great importance to the theory of induction. Any assumption or "Inductive Hypothesis" (in the sense of Broad and Keynes) about the general constitution of nature is subject to possible correction in the light of new experimental facts, and can therefore be regarded only as a tentative frame-work for more special research. Any such assumption is simply one of an infinity of possibilities, and unless it is accompanied by still more general and precarious suppositions, it can not be assigned a finite probability. On this point the theories of Keynes, Broad and Nicod are seriously in error. Even on the basis of the logical interpretation of probability, the assumption of the finite antecedent probability of an "Inductive Hypothesis" is untenable. These able thinkers are mistaken when they assert that a singular fact can confer a finite probability upon a general assumption. This is possible only by the exclusion of alternative assumptions. Therefore, the whole issue is prejudged. It can never be demonstrated that the principle of induction has the faintest probability except by a *petitio principii*.

But even if we accept the "Principle of Limited Variety" as a necessary condition of induction, it is easy to see that it is by no means sufficient. Unless we are allowed to infer from the probabilities of the chance coincidences of causally independent characters (or events) something concerning their corresponding frequencies, the principle of induction can have no significance. It is precisely the assumption of the stability of statistical frequencies which is necessary here. But of this assumption we can never be sure. The occurrence of a long chain of extremely improbable coincidences can always mislead our inductions. And there is no way to make sure that we are not living in just such an unfavorable world epoch. If we actually believed that we were so situated we would terminate all investigations and wait until the world passed into a more propitious stage. But the peculiar fact is that we are optimists, and refuse to abandon the belief that we can obtain "fair samples" of the world.

The probability of induction is therefore established on the basis of generalizations for which there is no probability at all. These generalizations extrapolate statistical frequencies, but only more special hypotheses can acquire probability with reference to such frequencies. The probability of a natural law is determined, roughly speaking, by the success-frequency of the inductive method by which it was discovered. The principle of induction, formulated in terms of the frequency theory, states simply that those regularities which have held so far without exception will be found to hold most frequently in the future.[3] According to this analysis, the probability of induction is always secondary and hypothetical, and can never be a genuine attribute of pure generalization.

But if, as we have seen, this most general presupposition of all induction cannot be shown to be appreciably probable, is there any other justification for accepting it? The usual reply—and here the influence of Kant is noticeable—is that such assumptions are necessary conditions for the possibility of knowledge in general. It is true, of course, that knowledge of nature would be impossible if there were not a certain amount of order and simplicity. But what are we to infer from this? That in our scientific investigations we must always begin with the postulate or demand of order and simplicity? But obviously from the fact that we demand something, it does not follow that we get it.

Our critique must seem very destructive, and it is destructive as regards illusory solutions of the problem. After the failure of all these attempts to achieve anything like an objective vindication of induction are we finally driven back to Hume's scepticism?

There are thinkers, however, who deny that Hume's analysis of causality and induction has any sceptical consequences. R. E. Hobart [4] has most convincingly shown that Hume's arguments appear sceptical only to those who desire to prove what cannot possibly be proved. Moreover, he has shown that almost everything that we call reasonable, rational or justifiable in our active life is absolutely dependent upon belief as the ultimate basis of all our significant knowledge. This ultimate belief, according to Ho-

---

[3] It should be noted that the frequency theory is still in process of completion and reconciliation with the logical theory. There are difficulties, but they do not appear insurmountable.

[4] "Hume Without Scepticism", *Mind*, 1930.

bart, is present as an immediate fact in every cognitive situation. Although I fully agree with him, yet I feel that for the purposes of a logical analysis of knowledge his formulations are not adequate. For, as he admits, to speak of belief is to speak in terms of psychology. Yet psychology itself is possible only through the belief in induction. Every explanation of belief in the context of psychological or biological theories presupposes induction, because it is by induction that we establish explanations. It is quite legitimate to study the phenomenon of belief from the scientific point of view, but in a systematic logical account of the structure of knowledge the principle of induction is prior to the recognition of its embodiments in psychological or biological processes.

IV

What then is the nature of this principle? Its peculiarly elusive character is startling. If it is a meaningful assumption about the world, then it is no longer the most general principle of induction, it is itself inductive. And if it is stated in such terms that it can never be verified or proven false, then it does not say anything at all. How can we escape this dilemma?

A glance at the logic of deduction will provide us with an instructive analogy. In any axiomatic, deductive system the starting point of our deductions is a set of primitive propositions or postulates whose truth is either "evident" or assumed. From these we derive other propositions. But in order to do this we must have methods or rules of deduction. Important examples are the Rule of Substitution and the Rule of Inference. The one allows us to substitute logically equivalent terms for each other, the other allows us to drop true premises and assert the conclusion. These rules are not commands, but anyone who wants to perform deductions must employ them. (Professor Sheffer of Harvard calls these rules "prescripts," in contradistinction to the postulates which are "descriptive" either of facts or of logical structures.)

Analogously, the principle of induction is not a bit of knowledge, it is neither analytic nor synthetic, neither *a priori* nor *a posteriori, it is not a proposition at all. It is, rather, the principle of a procedure, a regulative maxim, an operational rule.*

According to the viewpoint of logical analysis, all empirical knowledge is a construction erected upon immediate experience. What this immediately given really is can be disputed, but that there must be some such "groundfloor" of knowledge is necessary if any empirical proposition is to have a meaning. If it is the possibility of verification which establishes meaning, then verification itself must consist in the comparison of elementary or atomic propositions with the given. These elementary propositions are the raw material of knowledge. Moreover, as in the case of deductive systems, inductive science too has its prescriptive rules, and the principle of induction is undoubtedly the most significant among them. Its nature, just as the nature of the rules of deduction, can be determined only through the recognition of the function that it fulfills with regard to the goal of science.

Now the ultimate goal of science is not the achievement of a loosely connected miscellany of descriptions, but the establishment of a systematic structure of laws as a basis for explanation and prediction. The prescriptive rule, which is a direct consequence of this objective, is then the real principle of induction. It reads: "*Seek to achieve a maximum of order by logical operations upon elementary propositions. Generalize this order (whatever its form be: causal, statistical or other), with a minimum of arbitrariness, that is, according to the principle of simplicity.*" The condition of simplicity is essential, because it restricts the ambiguity of the procedure. But, since simplicity is measurable, if at all, only with great difficulty, there will usually be several ways of generalizing. This explains the case of competing scientific theories. Only when new experimental evidence is supplied, can it be determined that the one or the other theory is more complicated in that it employs more arbitrary hypotheses.

There can be no guaranty for the validity of generalizations, be they simple enumerative inductions or hypotheses of the more advanced scientific type. At any stage of scientific progress (as we know it) there will be outstanding premises, from which the more specific statements can be derived, with—indeed—(*deductive*) certainty; but those premises in themselves are *assumptions*, ever ready for revision, valid only "until further notice."

The principle underlying all induction can therefore have only *pragmatic* significance. Its meaning is not factual but "motivational" (directive); it simply tells us "to go ahead" with our generalizations from past experience and with the establishing of hypotheses-systems. There is no proof that these procedures, even if conducted as carefully as they may, will lead to the success aimed at, i.e., the truth of predictions. But the principle is nonetheless more than an arbitrary prescription and it is certainly not a categorical imperative. To use classical terms, its nature is best expressed as the *hypothetical imperative: If you intend to predict correctly use the method of simplest generalization on the basis of as broad an experiential (observational, experimental, statistical, etc.) background as you can secure*. This imperative, however, does not and cannot promise the desired success. Its only claim is: If you desire to proceed according to a *method*, i.e., if you are not interested in capriciously guessing, gambling or mystically intuiting the future (more generally the yet unknown, but knowable) then you have *no choice*. Any other "method" (like expecting systematic deviations from past regularities or not employing all available experience) would be "madness" because it would not in any typical sense be distinguished from an indefinite number (a continuum, virtually) of equally arbitrary "methods." (The old principle of sufficient reason con-

strued as an operational maxim.) The *justification* of the inductive procedure lies precisely in this uniqueness (extremum character) of the only
rational method capable (but not guaranteed) of success. This then is the
small step we can go beyond Hume's view of the matter. The step may
seem too small to those who still cherish hopes for a better vindication
of induction. But those who acknowledge the very simple fact that we
don't know what we really don't *know* will be satisfied with having at
least a rational way of taking a chance of knowing what we don't know.

I hope that these remarks will suffice to make clear why I thought it
so important to formulate the principle of induction in such a way that
its meaning would express the basic regulative maxim of factual knowledge. If, in the analysis that led me to my result, I have made use of induction, such as in taking it for granted that the essential features of human
knowledge will remain the same in the future as they have been in the
past, I would reject the charge of vicious circularity. I was not forced to
use some theory of induction as a *presupposition* of my account of induction. And this for the simple reason that my aim as well as my method
were analytic and not inductive. I did not try to establish the certainty
or probability of inductive generalization—this I had shown to be an illusory problem—but my goal was merely to analyze factual knowledge and
to disclose one of its most fundamental rules of procedure.

If foreknowledge is to be distinguished from arbitrary or capricious
guessing, if it is to be different from dream and inspiration, no other definition can be given of the procedure of science. However, the principle does
not carry in itself the guaranty of its own success. In this it is radically
different from the rules of deductive inference. Here the analogy breaks
down. Hume's scepticism is irrefutable if it simply emphasizes this difference. But with regard to operational rules doubt has no meaning. As long
as there is knowledge in the sense in which we have hitherto understood
knowledge, the principle of induction will be its inescapable guiding
maxim. This is in itself an analytic proposition, the sheerest tautology, because it merely makes explicit the definition of knowledge. The attempt
to know, to grasp an order, to adjust ourselves to the world in which we
are embedded, is just as genuine as, indeed, is identical with, the attempt
to live. Confronted with a totally different universe, we would nonetheless try again and again to generalize from the known to the unknown.
Only if extended and strenuous efforts led invariably to complete failure,
would we abandon the hope of finding order. And even that would be
an induction.

The Logical Foundations of the Concept of Probability *

HANS REICHENBACH

In an earlier paper [1] I presented my ideas of a solution of the problem of probability. They culminated in the project of a probability logic in which the alternative "true-false" of classical logic is replaced by a continuous scale of probability values; such an extension proved to be necessary in order to overcome the peculiar difficulties of the problem of convergence, which appear in the interpretation of probability as the limit of a frequency. In the meantime I have developed these ideas, published originally only in the form of a program, into a system of probability logic and have arrived at a solution of the problem which appears to me to be final. I should like to give in this paper a summary of my results. I regard it as a particular merit of the new theory that it makes possible a solution of the problem of induction, for which no satisfactory philosophical solution had been known ever since David Hume's outstanding formulation of the problem.

The new theory required a number of mathematical investigations, the results of which, at least in part, I published in other papers.[2] A presentation which includes both the mathematical and the philosophical problems of this complex, will be published in the form of a book in the near future.† In the present article I should like first to speak briefly about the results of the mathematical studies and then to proceed to an exposition, in the form of a survey, of the ensuing philosophical considerations.

* * *

It was of prime importance for the mathematical investigations of this problem to carry through an axiomatic construction of the calculus of

---

* Translated by Maria Reichenbach from the German original which appeared in *Erkenntnis*, 3, 1932/33 and reprinted with the kind permission of the author and the publisher, Felix Meiner, Leipzig. A few footnotes were added to this translation by the author; they are distinguished from the original footnotes by inclusion in brackets.
1 "Kausalität und Wahrscheinlichkeit", *Erkenntnis*, 1, 1930, p. 158.
2 "Axiomatik der Wahrscheinlichkeitsrechnung," *Math. Zeitschrift*, 34, 1932, p. 568.
"Wahrscheinlichkeitslogik," *Ber. d. Preuss. Akad. d. Wiss.*, phys.-math. Kl., 1932.
† [This remark refers to my book *Wahrscheinlichkeitslehre*, published 1935 in Leiden, Holland, at A. W. Sijthoff's. An English translation is in preparation. A short exposition in French language was published in *Les Fondements Logiques du Calcul des Probabilités* (Extrait des Annales de l'Institut Henri Poincaré, tome VII, fascicule V, pages 267–348).]

probability, which satisfies both mathematical and logical requirements. Such an inquiry was necessary because, first of all, the assumptions contained in the mathematical calculus of probability had to be formulated. Only when we know these assumptions can we find out which assumptions are made in the application of the calculus of probability to physical reality and which assumptions thus constitute the subject to which the philosophical investigation has to refer. It has turned out that all these assumptions can be reduced to one. In order to explain this result I shall briefly outline the axiomatic construction of the theory of probability.

The construction of the calculus of probability starts with the characterization of the logical structure of the probability statement. The probability is treated as a relation, which is called probability implication. This relation holds between the elements of two classes, with the qualification that these elements must be arranged in the form of a sequence. The probability implication is written in the form [3]

$$(i)\,(x_i \epsilon A \underset{p}{\rightarrow} y_i \epsilon B) \tag{1}$$

Let us take the following example: if the event x_i is the throw of a die (class A), there exists a probability $p = \frac{1}{6}$ that the coördinated result y_i belongs to the class B of throws of face "six"; this holds for all elements x_i and y_i. Or another example: if x_i suffers from tuberculosis (class A), there exists a certain probability p that the son y_i of x_i will die of tuberculosis (class B); this holds again for all x_i and y_i. The one-to-one coördination of the x_i and y_i must be known, i.e., there must exist two sequences (x_i) and (y_i) whose elements are coördinated to each other by pairs.

Instead of the notation (1) we shall use the abbreviated form

$$(A \underset{p}{\rightarrow} B) \tag{2}$$

This expression means the same as (1). It is expedient in many cases to replace (2) by the notation

$$P(A,B) = p \tag{3}$$

whose meaning is identical with (2).

In addition to the sign for probability the logistic signs enter into the probability formulas. For instance, we can ask for the probability of a disjunction BvC (B or C) or for the probability of a conjunction

[3] By ϵ we denote according to Russell the membership of the element x_i in the class A. The parenthesis (i) denotes the all-operator and is to be read "for all i". In a more complete notation we would have to write $(x_i)\,(y_i)$, i.e., "for all x_i and y_i". The sign $\underset{p}{\rightarrow}$ denotes the probability implication and is to be read "implies with the probability p". [In adaptation to the English language the German symbol "W" is replaced by "P", standing for "probability". The letters "O", "P", "Q", of the German notation are replaced by "A", "B", "C". The same change was carried through in the exposition in French language, mentioned above, and will also be used in the English translation of my book *Wahrscheinlichkeitslehre*.]

$B \cdot C \cdot$ (B and C). The logistic signs inside probability formulas are treated according to the rules of logistics. For instance, the expression

$$P(A, B \cdot [C \vee D]) \qquad (4)$$

can be replaced by

$$P(A, B \cdot C \vee B \cdot D). \qquad (5)$$

In this manner the application of the logistic algebra is made possible within the P-symbols.

The whole expression $P(\quad)$, for instance the expression (5), possesses the character of a mathematical variable; it stands for a degree of probability. Consequently, the P-symbols can be connected like mathematical quantities, and probability equations can be constructed which determine relations between probabilities. For instance, for mutually exclusive events B and C the relation

$$P(A, B \vee C) = P(A, B) + P(A, C) \qquad (6)$$

holds. In this way a calculus is constructed which combines logistics with mathematical methods; within the P-symbols logistics holds, while the P-symbols as wholes are subject to the rules of the mathematical methods of equations. This combined calculus proves to be very expedient, not only for theoretical, but also for practical applications, and makes possible the strict formulation of all theorems of the calculus of probability.

The axioms of the calculus of probability appear as a series of formulas, which contain in addition to logistic signs the sign $\underset{p}{+}$, or, in another way of writing, the sign $P(\quad)$. These formulas contain rules for the usage of the new sign $\underset{p}{+}$, or $P(\quad)$, respectively. They are to be conceived as a series of implicit definitions of the concept of probability. Consequently, we can apply the considerations known from the method of implicit definitions, according to which such an axiom system can be conceived in two ways. In the first conception a system can be used formally, i.e., operations with the formulas can be performed although the new sign for probability is not given any interpretation. In the second conception the new sign is given a meaning, or interpretation. Any interpretation is admissible which is compatible with the properties of the sign as formulated in the axioms. The situation is analogous to that of the axiomatic construction of geometry: geometry can be conceived as purely formal; but it is also possible to give to the fundamental geometrical concepts, such as "point", "straight line", etc., an interpretation in terms of small particles, light rays, etc., and thus to proceed to an applied geometry. The coördination of an interpretation to a sign is called coördinating definition.

This double manipulation of the axiomatic system proves to be very valuable for the calculus of probability. We can derive all known theorems of the calculus of probability without referring to an interpretation of the concept of probability. On the other hand, we can transform the formal calculus of probability thus constructed into an interpreted calculus by interpreting the term "probability". For instance, we can interpret probability as a frequency; then our theory comprises all theorems of a calculus of probability based on the frequency interpretation.

The frequency interpretation is introduced by a definition according to which we understand by probability the limit of a frequency, a definition which has first been carried through by R. v. Mises.[4] Our theory, however, differs from v. Mises' theory in that we do not demand any further properties for the concept of probability. In particular, we renounce any rules for the order of probability sequences, as are given by v. Mises in the principle of randomness. Any sequence in which the frequency of events converges towards a limit is a probability sequence in our interpretation. It turns out that, if the frequency interpretation of probability is assumed, all the axioms of the calculus of probability can be proved to be tautologies. This fact proves that the frequency interpretation supplies an admissible model of our axiomatic system.

The calculus of probability so constructed must of course include conceptions concerning the order of probability sequences. It turns out that this task can be accomplished and that a number of different types of order can be defined for probability sequences. Among these types of order the type of extreme randomness is only a special case, which we call *normal sequence;* in addition there are types of a higher degree of order, which step by step lead to the extremely ordered sequence, as is given, for instance, in the alternating sequence $B \; \bar{B} \; B \; \bar{B} \; B \; \bar{B}$ . . . The characterization of the types of order can be carried through by means of rules laying down that certain probabilities referring to sub-sequences are equal to each other. For instance, the normal sequence has the property that in the sub-sequence selected by B as predecessor the frequency of B is equal to that in the main sequence; on the other hand, the alternating sequence mentioned above does not possess this property. This illustration indicates the general method by means of which the characterization of special cases of probability sequences can be carried through. Every such characterization consists in the statement that certain probabilities are equal to each other.

I shall not go into the multiple mathematical applications of this theory, but will refer only to one of its results which is essential for the following philosophical considerations. This result is found in the fact that we need only one assumption for the application of the calculus of probability to physical reality. If we possess a method by means of which we can de-

[4] "Grundlagen der Wahrscheinlichkeitsrechnung", *Mathematische Zeitschrift*, 5, 1919, p. 52.
Cf. the bibliography of literature on probability in *Erkenntnis*, 2, 1931, p. 189.

termine the limit of the frequency in a sequence of events, in case there is one, the applicability of the calculus of probability is assured. All that is added by the calculus is tautological transformations, since all the axioms of the calculus of probability are tautologically satisfied for sequences of a limit character. Furthermore we shall determine by the same method, whether a given probability problem possesses the properties of certain special cases. If we can determine the limit of the frequency of a sequence, we can also determine whether two different sequences have the same limit, that is, whether the conditions of the special case are satisfied.

This result has a great bearing upon the philosophical critique of the calculus of probability. Nobody could know *a priori* whether the calculus of probability does not contain further assumptions. For an illustration we might refer to the difficulties which resulted for logic as long as the introduction of the axiom of reducibility was regarded as necessary. We are free from such difficulties with respect to the calculus of probability and have to answer only the question how to find the limit of the frequency of a sequence. With this investigation, however, we touch upon a number of peculiar problems, which represent the very difficulty of a philosophical solution of the problem of probability.

* * *

The character of these difficulties has repeatedly been treated in the recent literature on probability. These difficulties derive from the fact that the probability sequences occurring in nature are never given by a rule, i.e., are not *intensionally* given, but are presented to us only by enumeration of their elements, i.e., are *extensionally* given. Consequently only an initial section of a finite length is known to us, and we cannot make a definite statement about the infinite rest of the sequence. In particular, it is undetermined towards which limit the frequency of the sequence will converge, because a given initial section can be continued in terms of a different frequency, so that the given beginning can always be made compatible with any value of the limit. The fact that the limit cannot be determined from the initial section makes the meaning of the limit statement questionable. If we assert that a sequence has a certain limit of the frequency, no matter what source we have for our statement, we lack the possibility of verifying this assertion as true or false. It is therefore doubtful whether we can ascribe a meaning to the statement. For a meaningful statement we demand that there exist a method in terms of which the statement, in principle, can be verified as true or false.[5]

We pointed out in the beginning that a way out of this difficulty seems to be possible only if we abandon the alternative *true-false* of classical logic and introduce in its place a continuous scale of probability values.

[5] Cf. Rudolf Carnap, "Die Überwindung der Metaphysik durch logische Analyse der Sprache", *Erkenntnis*, 2, 1931, p. 219.

As explained in the paper mentioned above, such a probability logic cor-responds to the actual behavior which the man in the street as well as the scientist displays in face of this situation with respect to probability statements. If a long enough section of the sequence with a frequency close to a predicted value p is observed, it will be taken as a confirmation of the prediction, whereas a value of the frequency deviating very much from p will be regarded as a disproof of the prediction. The peculiarity of this judgment consists in the fact that it includes intermediate steps, according as the observed frequency is more or less different from p. Therefore we are no longer concerned with an alternative of judgments but with a judgment in terms of higher or lower probabilities. At first it appears inexplicable on what grounds we base such a judgment about the probability, since there is no reason why we should believe in an un-changed continuation of the observed section of the sequence. I shall post-pone the discussion of this problem, which is nothing but the problem of the inductive inference, and develop first the structural form of such a probability logic. The construction of this logic opens up a specific kind of logistic problem, which had to be solved by the use of the mathematico-logical form of the calculus of probability. I shall present briefly the out-lines of this solution.

* * *

If the question of a generalization of two-valued logic into a multi-valued logic is to be considered, the grounds of the two-valued character of our logic must first be examined. When we analyze the statements of every-day life or of science from this point of view, we find that the dichotomy can by no means be called necessary. From the example "the weather is summery" it is easily seen that this statement could very well be called "more or less true." If the weather is warm and the sky cloudless, the state-ment would be better justified than if clouds appear or a light shower falls, and in the event of extensive cloudiness or heavy downpours the state-ment will scarcely be regarded as adequate. It would be natural to ascribe to the statement a continuously variable degree w of truth, so that the current meteorological situation would make the statement "true to the degree w". But this treatment of statements is unusual; what is used in-stead is a division of all meteorological situations into summery and non-summery ones by means of an artificial line of demarcation. In fact, the meteorologists have defined summery weather by reference to a certain minimum duration of sunlight, a certain minimum value of day-time tem-perature, and of a certain maximum quantity of rain. In this manner the continuous scale has been transformed into a dichotomy.

This method evidently represents an arbitrary rule, and we have in fact to regard the two-valuedness of our logic as a convention, which could very well be replaced by another rule. All such rules constitute equivalent descriptions in the sense that any such description of nature will be adequate and that it is possible to transform one kind of description into the other. The transition from a continuous scale of truth values to the two-valued one can always be reached by means of an arbitrary dichotomy. We can compare the convention represented by the two-valuedness of our logic with the decimal character of our system of numbers, in which number 10 plays a similar part as the number 2 in two-valued logic; the possibility of translating every multi-valued description into a two-valued one corresponds to the possibility of translating any system of numbers, for instance, the duodecimal system, into the decimal one.

If from this point of view the two-valuedness of our logic appears as a property that can easily be eliminated, these considerations show, on the other hand, that nothing is gained by such an introduction of a multi-valuedness, because we arrive at equivalent descriptions. And indeed, the logic of the probability statement is not identical with a multi-valuedness of the type just described in the example of the summery weather. This is clear from the fact that the characterization of the weather as "summery to a certain degree" has no degree of indeterminacy attached to it, of the kind typical for probability statements. The multi-valued characterization of individual statements with respect to the varying degree of their exactness can, therefore, not represent that generalization of logic which we need for probability logic.

The unique problem of probability logic consists rather in the peculiarity that a multi-valued logic has to be constructed which applies although for individual statements we keep to two-valuedness. We call a future event probable, even though we know that a statement about it will be verified as true or false after its occurrence. The problem is to construct a multi-valued logic within the frame of a two-valued logic. This can be done if the concept of probability is given an interpretation, which has always been employed for a solution of the concept of probability: the frequency interpretation. The frequency interpretation derives the degree of probability from an enumeration of the truth values of individual statements and thus reduces the concept of probability to the concept of truth. This is the reason why the degree of probability cannot be conceived as a predicate of individual statements, but has to be referred to more general logical constructions, which are built up from individual statements in a similar way as a sequence is constructed from individual elements.

In carrying through this idea we meet a certain difficulty. Truth is a *property* of statements, i.e., it refers to one statement. Probability, however, is to be conceived as a *relation*, as was formulated in (1) and (2); a sequence of events possesses a probability only with regard to another sequence. It seems therefore difficult to interpret the concept of probability as an analogue of the concept of truth.*

We can overcome this difficulty by means of the following device. All those x_i in the sequence of events (x_i), which do not belong to the class A, can be canceled; the remaining elements are renumbered, that is, receive a new subscript i, so that a reduced sequence (x_i) results, for which all x_i belong to A and which we shall call "compact". Likewise we omit all those elements y_i whose corresponding x_i are omitted and renumber the remaining elements y_i. The reduced sequence (x_i) can then be dispensed with; its function for the sequence (y_i) can be assigned to the subscript i, which expresses the enumeration. The frequency of B in the sequence (y_i) is now counted with respect to all elements y_i, no selection from this sequence being referred to. We then can conceive the probability as a property of the sequence (y_i) alone; we count the frequency of B in the sequence (y_i) and call this frequency the probability of B.

The sequence (y_i) so constructed can also be conceived in a different way. We explained above that the enumeration proceeds in terms of $y_i \epsilon B$ being valid or not. Because of the equivalence of classes and propositional functions we can also consider the propositional function ϕy_i, which is identical with $y_i \epsilon B$; the counting of the frequency is then equivalent to counting whether the individual values of the propositional function ϕ are true or false. The aggregate (ϕy_i), which consists of a sequence of individual statements of the form ϕy_i, may be called a *propositional sequence*.

The propositional sequence can be conceived as an extension of the concept of statement. The statement is derived from a propositional function by means of a coördination of a special value y_0 of the argument to the propositional function. In a similar way we can conceive the propositional sequence as being constructed by means of a coördination of the argument sequence (y_i) to the propositional function ϕ. Just as the aggregate constructed by the coördination of an individual argument to a propositional function possesses a truth value, the aggregate resulting from the coördination of an argument sequence to a propositional function possesses a probability value. Probability is thus a property of propositional sequences in the same sense as truth is a property of statements. In-

---

* [My paper of 1933 does not mention the fact that in order to make probability an analogue of truth a certain change in the interpretation of probability is necessary: probability then is not regarded as a property of events, or things, but as a property of linguistic expressions. In other words, the calculus of probability is then incorporated in the metalanguage. This transition is easily achieved for the frequency interpretation, since the numerical value of a probability will be the same whether we count events or the corresponding sentences about the occurrence of the events. Although the paper correctly employs the second interpretation, it would have been advisable to mention the duality of interpretation, which, incidentally, was clearly explained by Boole (G. Boole, *An Investigation of the Laws of Thought*, London, 1854, pp. 247-248.)

This remark is the only correction I have to add to my paper of 1933. A correct exposition of the duality was given in my paper: "Über die semantische und die Objekt-Auffassung von Wahrscheinlichkeitsausdrücken", *Erkenntnis* 8, 1939, pp. 50-68.]

cidentally, propositional sequences need not be infinite; our considerations can also be carried through for finite propositional sequences. This fact makes possible a transition from a propositional sequence to an individual statement: the statement appears as the special case of a propositional sequence in which the argument sequence coördinated to the propositional function consists of only one element.

The preceding considerations supply the fundamentals of probability logic. Probability logic is a logic of propositional sequences and appears as a generalization of the logic of statements, which may be likened to the transition from Euclidean geometry to Riemannian geometry. Riemannian geometry is based on the principle that the geometry of the large dimensions can have properties different from those of the geometry of the small dimensions. Similarly the aggregate *propositional sequence* is imbedded in a more general frame than is employed for individual statements, although statements are elements of propositional sequences. The logic of propositional sequences is so to speak a "logic of the large dimensions" and can therefore possess more general properties than the "logic of the small dimensions".

In order to carry through probability logic it is necessary to construct truth tables by analogy with classical logic. This is relatively easy, if the logistic conception of the calculus of probability is taken as a basis. It then is in fact possible to construct truth tables for the logical operations "and", "or", "implication", etc., which on the one hand satisfy the laws of the calculus of probability and on the other hand can be conceived as generalizations of the familiar logistic truth tables. This proof is given by the fact that the truth tables of probability logic, for the special case in which the propositional sequence consists of only one element, become identical with the logistic truth tables. For the formulation of these truth tables and the form of the transition to logistic truth tables we must refer to the paper *Probability Logic* mentioned above.

* * *

It is a peculiarity of the probability logic so constructed that it makes use of the frequency interpretation in the same sense as this interpretation is usually applied in the calculus of probability. Within the calculus of probability the character of being probable is not attached to the individual statement, but to the propositional sequence. The reduction of the probability value to an enumeration of truth values, which is thus accomplished, can be called the *extensional reduction* of probability logic. According to this interpretation we need not regard probability as a property existing independent of the truth value and belonging to the meaning of the statement, but can consider the probability of the propositional sequence as completely determined by the truth values of its individual elements.

With this extensional reduction, however, a fundamental difficulty inherent in the frequency interpretation is transmitted to probability logic. If probability is only a property of propositional sequences, what is the meaning of the degree of probability for the single case? There are numerous instances in everyday life as well as in science where we apparently deal with the probability of a single case; for instance, we may ask for the probability that the weather will be fine tomorrow, or that a certain planned action will be successful, or that a scientific experiment will furnish the result expected. How can probability logic help us in these cases, if probability concerns only a propositional sequence, i.e., a series of propositions similar to each other? This question has often been regarded a fundamental difficulty for any frequency interpretation; but it seems to me that this objection is not tenable. There is a way out which leads to a satisfactory solution of the problem of the single case without a renunciation of the frequency interpretation. We can illustrate this solution by recalling the behavior of a gambler: The gambler has to make a prediction before every game, although he knows that the calculated probability has a meaning only for larger numbers; and he makes his decision by betting, or as we shall say, by *positing* the more probable event. This positing does not mean that he is certain of the result. As a matter of fact, it does not mean any judgment about the single case under consideration; it means only that the decision for the more probable case represents a more favorable action than the opposite decision. The concept "more favorable" can be interpreted by a frequency statement: if the gambler follows the principle of positing always the more probable case, he can count on a greater number of successes in the long run than would obtain for the opposite behavior. The frequency interpretation justifies, indeed, a *posit* on the more probable case. It is true that it cannot give us a guarantee that we shall be successful in the particular instance considered; but instead it supplies us with a principle which in repeated application leads to a greater number of successes than would obtain if we acted against it.

The decisive logical tool in this consideration is the concept of *posit*. To posit a case does not mean to regard it as a necessary event or to regard the statement about it as true; nor, of course, does it mean the contrary. By positing an event we do not assert anything about the event considered, but perform an action about which we know only something more general: that it conforms to a principle which, when honored, leads to the greatest possible number of successes. If from this point of view we look at the numerous actions of daily life where we deal with the "probability of a single case", we notice that the concept of posit supplies a complete solution: we posit that the weather of tomorrow will have the most probable character, or that a planned action will have the most probable result, and although we do not know anything for the single case, we know that in this way we do the most favorable thing that we can do at all—we behave in such a way that we can count on the greatest number of successes.

The concept of posit represents the bridge between the probability of the propositional sequence and the compulsion to make a decision in a single case. It is important to realize that the principle of the greatest number of successes is even applicable if we are not concerned with a repetition of cases of the same kind. If we posit in one case fine weather, in another one the satisfactory result of a financial transaction, in a third one the winning of a certain horse in a race, such cases constitute a sequence to which the frequency interpretation is applicable. The calculus of probability includes a theory of sequences which are played from element to element with a variable probability.[6]

We shall call a posit that conforms to the principle of the greatest number of successes the *best posit*. The probability belonging to this posit we call its *weight;* the weight is therefore the probability of the propositional sequence whose element is the posit under consideration. The concept of weight replaces the untenable concept of the probability of a single statement; we cannot coördinate a probability to a single statement, but we can coördinate a weight to it, by which the probability of the corresponding propositional sequence assumes an indirect meaning for the single case.

The best posit has only a restricted use, since it presupposes that we know the corresponding weight, i.e., the probability of the corresponding propositional sequence. There are cases where the probabilities are unknown, and we have to find out what constitutes the most favorable behavior in such cases.

*   *   *

With this question we enter into the fundamental problem of the concept of probability. We said above that the application of the calculus of probability to physical reality contains only one unsolved problem: in order to apply the calculus of probability we must determine the limit of an extensionally given sequence, of which only a first finite section is known. All other operations of the calculus of probability, we found, are of a tautological nature; only this one method requires critical analysis.

It is evidently the concept of *posit* which we have to employ for an explanation of this method. If in the finite section given we have observed a certain frequency * f^n, we *posit* that the sequence, on further continuation, will converge towards a limit f^n (more precisely: within the interval $f^n \pm \delta$). We *posit* this; we do not say that it is true, we only posit it in the same sense as the gambler lays a wager on the horse which he believes to be the fastest. We perform an action which appears to us the most favorable one, without knowing anything about the success of this individual action.

[6] Problems of this kind are treated by means of a *sequence lattice;* cf. the axiomatic construction of the calculus of probability mentioned above.

* For notational reasons the number of the element at which the frequency f is considered is indicated by the superscript n.

In this instance, however, we are concerned with a kind of posit different from the one employed in the case of the best posit. The best posit can be chosen, if its corresponding weight, i.e., the probability of the corresponding propositional sequence, is known. It is true that we can also speak of a corresponding weight for the case of a posit concerning a limit; this weight is given by the probability of the occurrence of a certain probability, i.e., by a probability of the second level. It is very well possible to extend the theory of probability to such probabilities of a higher level. The frequency interpretation is likewise applicable; the individual sequence is then to be conceived as an element in a series of sequences in which the frequency of a sequence possessing a limit of a certain value is counted. But this determination can only be carried through, if a series of sequences exists; in general we deal only with an individual sequence and are then unable to determine the probability of the second level. Although the determination of a corresponding weight is possible in principle, we are in the peculiar situation that we have to make a posit without knowing the corresponding weight. We do not know, therefore, whether positing the value f^n of the limit is the best posit—yet we make this posit.

These considerations represent the peculiar problem of the inductive inference, since the ascertainment of a limit by the method discussed is identical with the inductive inference. It is true that this inference is usually only considered in the narrower form that an event occurs without exceptions in a great number of cases and we conclude that it will always occur; but this case must be regarded as the special case where the limit has the value 1; the logical problem is the same when the limit possesses any other value f^n. It is an important step to recognize that the inductive inference is not meant to supply a true statement, but a *posit*: we posit that the sequence will go on in the same way as observed. The difficulty lies in the fact that we must make this posit without knowing its weight.

And yet it is possible to give a justification even for this kind of posit. The following consideration will help us. Let us assume for the moment that there is a limit towards which the sequence converges, then there must be an n from which on our posit leads to the correct result; this follows from the definition of the limit, which requires that there be an n from which on the frequency remains within a given interval δ. If we were to adopt, on the contrary, the principle of always positing a limit outside $f^n \pm \delta$ when a frequency f^n has been observed, such a procedure would certainly lead us to a false result from a certain n on. This does not mean that there could not be other principles which like the first would lead to the correct limit. But we can make the following statement about these principles: even if they determine a posit outside $f^n \pm \delta$ for a smaller n, they must, from a certain n on, determine the posit within $f^n \pm \delta$. All other principles of positing must converge asymptotically with the first principle. This is the property which distinguishes the first principle from others: we know that it must eventually lead to the right result, whereas we know nothing about other principles—except that, if they are to be successful, they must eventually converge with the first.

We call such a posit an *approximative posit;* it represents an approximative method because it anticipates the aim and is used as though the aim had already been reached. Positing that the frequency will remain at the value last observed finds a justification, as we saw, by the fact that it will finally lead to the correct result, *if a limit of the frequency exists.* Let us assume temporarily this condition and postpone the question of how to dispense with it to a later discussion.

* * *

The method of the approximative posit requires a supplementation, which we must now explain. These considerations will show us at the same time the part played by probability logic in this connection.

We mentioned before that even the approximate posit is capable of receiving a weight, and that this weight can be found by considering the posit within the frame of a class of similar posits. Such an incorporation of individual posits in a comprehensive class actually occurs when scientific statements are made. Our judgment in the case of a series of individual observations is never based upon this observational series alone, but is also determined by a number of earlier experiences in other fields. If we throw a die, we shall not base the assumption of a probability $\frac{1}{6}$ on the present observational series alone; our judgment will also be influenced by experiences with earlier throws. If we want to be sure, we shall examine the center of gravity of the die by physical experiments and thereby include experiences of a mechanical type in our considerations. In this way a concatenation of all experiences obtains; this concatenation carries the advantage that we can construct probabilities of a higher level, which enable us to assign a weight to the posit pertaining to our series of experiments. This method applies likewise to very different examples. If the physicist measures a number of spectral lines and finds that the observational series can be extrapolated according to a certain rule, his confidence in this rule will be strengthened considerably, if the same rule is confirmed by other series of spectral lines. It is this method by means of which, for instance, a rule like Bohr's rule of the quanta is tested. The probability of the validity of Bohr's rule is thus made a probability of a higher level. This method can lead to the result that the original rules are to be subjected to a correction. If we find after 100 throws, for instance, that for a certain die the frequency is still very far from the required value $\frac{1}{6}$ for a certain face, and if we have made sure by mechanical tests that the die is not loaded, we shall keep to the posit $\frac{1}{6}$ for the limit of the frequency. The original posit is subject to a correction in terms of the corresponding weight, which says in this case that there exists a high probability of the second level that the frequency of the sequence will converge toward the limit $\frac{1}{6}$.

This method of correction finds an extensive application in science; we may even say that scientific method is nothing but a continuous correction of posits by incorporating them into more general considerations. If the scientist predicts the orbit of a new planet, this prediction is essentially based upon experiences concerning other planets, and the laws which he applies to the movements of the planets are in turn connected with experiences concerning very different objects by means of a concatenation with other mechanical phenomena. The system of scientific knowledge can be conceived as a method of correction, which relates every individual statement to the total system of experience. It is the significance of scientific method that for the prediction of a new phenomenon we are never dependent on the specific observations alone to which the prediction refers, but that we can also make use of the vast domain of experiences in very different fields.

This concatenation of experiences is not so rigid, on the other hand, as to deprive the single event of its independence. If we find that a certain individual sequence *retains* its frequency in repeated continuation, although the total system of experiences makes another limit more probable, we shall finally believe in the deviating value for this single case. The system presents us only with a *probability* for the single case, not with an absolute *certainty*. The peculiar tension between individual fact and system, which is characteristic of all scientific research and which is expressed in the old struggle between experiment and theory, receives its strict formulation within the frame of probability logic. It appears as an interrelation between the individual posit and its weight and obtains in this way its mathematical expression.

Let us analyze more precisely the determination of the probability of the second level. It is based again on a posit, which we may call a secondary posit, in contradistinction to the primary posits. That we deal only with a posit follows from the fact that, as always, we are given only a finite number of observed cases and are dependent on the method of the approximate posit. The method of correction can thus be described as follows: at first we make a number of primary posits; by regarding them as valid, we arrived at secondary posits. We can use the secondary posits, on the other hand, to correct the primary posits for an individual case. This is no contradiction, although the determination of the secondary posits presupposes the primary posits as valid. The reason is that certain changes in the primary posits furnish only very small changes for the secondary posits. For example: if an electric current flows through a wire, the wire will generally be heated; the posit that in a certain individual case the wire will be heated by the current is therefore corroborated by the secondary posit that in general the flowing of a current produces heat. If the wire is submerged in liquid helium, the primary posit will be false in this individual case (because of supraconductivity), but this does not mean that in general the secondary posit will be false. Often we even have to retain the secondary posits in order to prove that the primary posit is false in the individual case considered. For instance, the current flowing through the supraconductor may be measured in another sector of the circuit by a heat-ampèremeter so that the statement "in the supracon-ductor there flows a current which does not cause any heat there" is based upon an observation which assumes the heating as a criterion of the flow of the current. The importance of the method of correction and the adaptability of scientific method to new observational discoveries is founded on the relative independence of secondary posits.

The logical schema explained above can now be incorporated into the frame of probability logic. Scientific knowledge starts with primary posits; but we do not stop with them and go on to secondary posits, which fur-nish a weight of the primary posits and thereby coördinate to them a degree of probability. The primary posits acquire the character of state-ments which are not judged as true or false, but as more or less probable. On the basis of the probabilities so determined the primary posits can thus be transformed into best posits on the basis of a known weight. On this step, however, the secondary posits remain without any weight, that is, we do not know whether they are the best ones; they are approximate posits in the sense of our definition. But we can repeat the same method and proceed to tertiary posits, which admit of the determination of weights of secondary posits. The approximative character is thereby shifted to the tertiary posits, and so on. We thus obtain a concatenated system of posits, in which weights are known for the posits of lower levels; only the posits of the last level are made without the knowledge of a correspond-ing weight.

Scientific knowledge represents, therefore, a system of concatenated posits which has an inner order in terms of the principle of the best posit, but which as a whole is so to speak suspended in midair, since there is no weight known for the posits of the last level. In spite of this apparent in-determinacy we can point out the advantage of such a concatenated system. For the justification of the approximative posits we made use of the idea that if there is a limit of the frequency, the approximative posit will finally lead to success. The difficulty arising for this approximative method originates from the fact that we do not know at which place n of the sequence the convergence is reached, so that under certain conditions we continue to make bad posits for a long time, that is, as long as we are very far away from the place of convergence. It is the significance of the method of correction to make possible a faster convergence. It can be shown that the system as a whole converges better than an individual primary posit. The reason is that the posits of a higher level are relatively independent of the posits of a lower level. Consequently we can count on a faster convergence for a primary posit which has been corrected by the total system.

Let us illustrate this correction by an example. If an observer finds that a low position of the barometer is frequently connected with rain, he will posit rain when he observes a low position of the barometer. This primary posit is not very good, and the observer will be disappointed relatively often. Now the system of scientific experiences shows that we arrive at better predictions, if in addition to the position of the barometer we take into account the humidity of the air; in other words, we find that in those cases in which rain was posited for a low position of the barometer the prediction was confirmed mainly within the narrower class of cases in which the low position of the barometer was associated with a high position of the hygrometer. In this way the primary posit is corrected by a system of more comprehensive experiences. If the scientist belittles the advocate of a primitive empiricism, whose knowledge consists merely in "empirical rules", he is justified in so far as he asks that the total system of experience, at the disposition of the scientist, should be used for a correction of the primary empirical rules. It would be a mistake, however, to believe that the scientist applies a method different in principle from that of the pure empiricist. Even the theorems established by scientific method represent posits; but the superiority of these posits derives from the fact that they are posits of a higher level and therefore lead to a faster convergence.

We must therefore conceive the system of scientific statements, not as a system of true statements in the sense of two-valued logic, but as a system of posits ordered within the frame of probability logic. The inductive inference is the only assumption of a non-analytic nature contained in this system, and we found that this inference is to be interpreted by the concept of the approximate posit. It represents a method of approximation which we are justified to use if the occurring sequences possess a limit character. It is the only approximative system of which, on this condition, we know something positive: we know that this method will lead to our aim if the condition is satisfied. A further result is added by the analysis of the method of concatenation: we know the concatenated system converges better than the individual posit.

This is indeed a far-reaching justification of the inductive inference; but we still have to free ourselves from the last condition which we have used.

*　　*　　*

This condition consists in the assumption that we know a limit of the frequency to exist for the sequences considered. Only on this condition does the method of the approximative posit lead to the correct value. If no limit exists, we shall never have success when we posit the persistence of the frequency; and the method of correction is useless, too, because it cannot lead to success either.

It would be all too audacious to contend that for some reason or other all sequences occurring in nature must have a limit of the frequency. The philosophy of the *a priori* would certainly be ready for such a pseudo-proof. We must realize, however, that an assumption of this kind, i.e., an assumption about the content of all possible experience, is undemonstrable and that we have no reason to believe it. In spite of this difficulty it can be shown that we may continue the path of our considerations.

What would be the case if the sequences occurring in nature would not possess a limit of the frequency? All systematic predictions would be impossible. A prediction might come true by chance once in a while, but we would have to renounce the possibility of consistently confirming the prediction as well as the possibility of constructing a system of better convergence. The attempt of science to arrive at a system of reliable predictions would be futile.

What conclusion can be drawn? It follows that the approximative posit, i.e., the inductive inference, has *no* justification if we know that the sequences occurring in nature have no limit of the frequency. But this is by no means our situation. It would be false to say: "*we know* that there *exists* a limit of the frequency" but it would likewise be false to say: "*we know* that a limit of the frequency does *not exist*". We are confronted by an indeterminacy: *we do not know* whether there exists a limit of the frequency.

In this situation the approximative posit carries a decisive advantage over all other posits. We know: if the sequences occurring in nature possess a limit of the frequency we shall eventually arrive at reliable predictions by applying the method of the approximative posit; and if there is no limit we shall never attain this goal. If anything can be achieved at all, we shall reach our aim by applying the method of the approximative posit; otherwise we shall not attain anything.

With these considerations the method of the approximative posit, that is, the inductive inference, finds its justification. The inductive inference is the only method of which we know that it leads to the aim if the aim can be reached; this is the reason why we must use it, if we want to reach the aim. The problem of the inductive inference finds its solution by means of the argument that it is not necessary for the application of this inference to know a *positive* condition to hold, but that the application is already justified if a *negative* condition is *not* known to hold.

We are often confronted by similar situations in daily life. We want to reach a certain aim and we know of a necessary step, which we shall have to take in order to attain this aim, but we do not know whether this step is sufficient. He who wants to reach the aim will have to take the step, even if it is uncertain whether he will reach his aim in this way. The businessman who keeps his store well stocked so that he can sell something when a customer comes in, the unemployed who makes an application with reference to an advertisement in the paper, although he does not know whether he will receive an answer, the ship-wrecked man who climbs a cliff, although he does not know whether a rescue-ship will spot him—all these persons find themselves in an analogous situation; they satisfy the *necessary* conditions of reaching an aim without knowing whether the *sufficient* conditions are satisfied. We can apply this analogy because we know that the inductive inference must not be construed as an instrument of finding a true statement, but of finding a posit, and that we derive the conclusion not from the viewpoint of truth, but from the viewpoint of the most favorable step which we can take. The most favorable step toward the aim of prediction is that step of which we know that on repetition it must eventually lead to the aim if this aim is attainable at all—and this is the step made in the inductive inference.

With this result we also overcome an objection which was seen in the fact that the *n* of the place of convergence will for ever remain unknown. The argument has been advanced that the limit-character of the sequences is useless for us, because the convergence may start after such a large number of elements that it will remain unattainable during the restricted life time of human beings. It is true that in the case of such badly converging sequences predictions would be impossible; this case would in all practical respects have the same consequence as the case in which the sequences do not converge at all. Since we could show, however, that we can even include this more general case into our considerations and still arrive at a justification of the approximative posit, the case of the badly converging sequences is also taken care of. Similar to the situation previously discussed, we must say, not that we *know* of the bad convergence, but that we *do not know* whether a good convergence will take place.

If we now analyze critically the considerations leading to a justification of the inductive inference, we should like to point out the significance of this justification as follows. It has been shown for a long time that a logical justification in the sense of a guarantee of success cannot be given for the inductive inference. It would be incorrect, however, to infer that the inductive inference represents a perfectly arbitrary action, that it is so to speak the private affair of everybody whether or not he wants to act according to the principle of the inductive inference. If this were the case, if we had no reason to prefer the posit determined by the inductive inference to other posits, we would be completely lost in all situations of everyday life. But all our behavior, our persistent adherence to the inductive inference, proves that we believe by no means in an equivalence of all kinds of posits, but that we prefer a certain kind of posit, i.e., the one in accordance with the inductive inference. It is the significance of our theory that it succeeds in establishing the preëminence of this posit. The method of correction which we described can be conceived as the establishment of an order for all posits; although we can in no way claim certainty of success for the method described, we can at least maintain that we have arranged the possible posits in the best order attainable, if success can be reached at all. This is the reason why we may regard our theory of the inductive inference as a solution of the problem; in spite of the uncertainty of future happenings we can prove a logical superiority for all those actions which are performed according to the principle of induction.

Our investigation has come to an end. We could show that the non-analytic assumptions for the application of the calculus of probability to physical reality, and thus in all empirical sciences, are reducible to one, to the inductive inference. And we are in a position to give an explanation for this inference, which since Hume has been recognized by all empiricists to be the central problem of epistemology. This explanation is achieved by the incorporation of the inductive inference in the frame of probability logic and the proof that it represents a method of approximation which has the character of a necessary condition for the making of predictions. He who wants greater certainty, who does not want to make any predictions before he can believe with certainty in their coming true, cannot be helped. We others are satisfied if we know a method by means of which we can at least *posit* the future—if we know we are doing our best to attain success, since a guarantee for success is not given to us.

On the Justification of Induction *

HANS REICHENBACH

Miss Creed's paper [1] gives me the welcome opportunity to explain more fully what I understand by a justification of induction. We both agree that the question of justification can be raised only if a decision on a certain aim has been made; i.e., justification concerns the question of the appropriateness of a certain means in respect to a chosen aim, not the question of the choice of the aim itself. The question of appropriateness, however, includes the question of the attainability of the aim; thus we have to distinguish different kinds of justification according to differences in what we know about the attainability of the aim. I say "differences in *what we know*," for a man's actions can be guided only by his knowledge of the world, and not by unknown features of the world; if we have to decide whether his actions are reasonable we have to ask whether they are reasonable in relation to what he knows.

Now as to our knowledge of the attainability of the aim I would distinguish the following cases:

1. We know something about the objective possibility of reaching the aim A by applying the means M. We can introduce here the subdivisions:

   a we know that by applying the means M we shall certainly reach the aim A;

   β we know the probability p that A will occur if M is applied;

   γ we know at least that $p > 0$;

   δ we know that although p may be $= 0$ the aim is possible.

The difference between γ and δ is here not very great; we have to distinguish these cases only because the probability $p = 0$ is not equivalent to impossibility (i.e., the limit of the frequency may be 0 although the event sometimes happens). For the same reason case a is slightly different from the case $p = 1$. But these differences are not very important for our problem.

2. We do not know whether or not application of the means M will lead to the aim A.

---

* Reprinted by kind permission of the author and the editors from *The Journal of Philosophy*, 37, 1940.

[1] Isabel P. Creed, "The Justification of the Habit of Induction", *The Journal of Philosophy*, 37, 1940.

3. We know that by applying the means M we shall never reach the aim A.

Now we certainly agree that in case 3 a justification of the procedure M can not be given. But it seems to me that in all the other cases it can be given. Although we know only in case 1a that the means will lead to success we should call the procedure justified also in the cases 1β, γ, δ, and 2, if the means M can be shown to be the best means we know in respect to A. Miss Creed would agree with me as far as 1a, β, γ are concerned; her condition b is equivalent to my case 1γ. The difference then would be that a justification is not considered possible in the cases 1δ and 2.

Instead Miss Creed considers another case which is called b' and defined by the clause "that it be assumed or believed that success is practically possible, though there be no evidence to support the assumption or belief." I confess that this seems to me a rather strange case. Belief can be the *motive* of an action, but belief as such can never *justify* an action; only a *justified* belief can do that. But if according to the definition of case b', the belief is unjustified—how can it lead to a justification of induction?

This is a point in which, it seems to me, Miss Creed's paper reveals the tracks of David Hume, and unfortunately of that part of his theory of induction which has brought so much confusion into the empiricist camp. It seems to me that after his brilliant criticism of induction, the merits of which cannot be overestimated, Hume ran the problem into a side track by his defense of inductive belief as a habit. Even today the consideration of this habit, and belief, is in the foreground of the philosophic discussion of the inductive problem, and eclipses the logical problem behind this psychological fact. Miss Creed speaks in the title of her paper of the justification of the *habit* of induction. I do not think she would ever have written a paper on the habit of the syllogism. Although syllogistic inference is a habit also, as well as inductive inference, nobody would mention this fact within a logical analysis. Unfortunately, ever since David Hume's turning of the problem of the inference into the problem of a habit logicians have shared his escape from logic into psychology. But unwarranted belief, even if it is a habit, can never confer any title of justification to the scientific procedure of induction.

So what we have in case b' is, logically speaking, nothing but the clause added, that there is no evidence against the possibility of success. But this is exactly my case 2, the very case which corresponds to the logical situation of the problem of induction. The fact that even in this case a justification can be given, though overlooked in the traditional exposition of the problem, seems to me to open the way to a solution of the inductive problem.

The situation is obscured by some ambiguity in the word "possible." We have to consider first *objective possibility*; by this term we mean cases in which an event sometimes happens. For instance, we say it is possible that it will rain tomorrow, and mean by this that there are summer days on which it rains. Besides this, there is what we might call *epistemic possibility*, i.e., the case that we know the objective possibility. Whereas the terms "objective possibility" and "objective impossibility" form a complete disjunction, the epistemic terms lead to a trichotomy: either we know the possibility of an event, or we know the impossibility, or we do not know anything about the possibility or impossibility. Thus "not impossible" in the epistemic sense is not equivalent to "possible"; it would include the case of indeterminacy. Sometimes, however, we understand by epistemic "possibility" the same as the epistemic "not impossible," that is, we include the case of indeterminacy into the term "possible." I think that if somebody insists that a justification should include a demonstration of the possibility of success he means "possibility" in this sense. If this is meant I would, of course, agree with such a postulate. It is clear that in this sense success of the inductive procedure is possible.

I turn now to a consideration of condition *c*. Miss Creed is certainly right in saying that if we speak of the justification of a means, or procedure, this justification is conditional in so far as it refers to a certain aim. If somebody does not want the aim in question an application of the means by him would not be justified. But it would mean misunderstanding my theory of induction if it is said that for a justification I should have to prove condition *c*, or *c'*, both of which certainly are synthetic propositions of a psychological content. It is not my task to prove these propositions; they stand in the implicans of my theorem, and all I want to maintain, and need to maintain for a justification, is an implication of the form: if a man fulfills condition *c*, or *c'*, i.e., if he wants to predict, he should make inductions.

But apart from this easily corrigible misunderstanding I readily consent to Miss Creed's very pertinent distinction between *c* and *c'*, between the case of wanting the aim in general, and wanting it in face of the more or less problematic chance of success. It is quite right that my implication presupposes *c'*, and that *c* is not sufficient. I am glad Miss Creed pointed this out so clearly; my writings are perhaps not clear enough on this point although I never wished to maintain anything else.

It seems, however, Miss Creed considers condition *c'* unsatisfactory. She would prefer to have a method which permits us to deduce *c'* from *c*. This refers to the methods using the concept of "mathematical expectation" which determine whether or not a bet is acceptable. If *a* is the amount of pleasure attached to the aim *A*, *m* the amount of displeasure combined with the application of the means *M*, *p* the probability that *A* will occur if *M* is applied, then the mathematical theory furnishes the result that the bet is acceptable if the "valuational balance"

$$p \cdot a - m$$

is greater than o. This condition is easily deducible if a means the amount of money to be gained in a game, m the amount of money to be paid in advance, i.e., the individual stake. We sometimes extend this condition to cases in which a and m mean emotional values, assuming that there is a possibility of measuring them. Only such a calculation of the valuational balance, so far as I see, would be considered by Miss Creed as a perfect justification of induction; if she denies to my theory of induction the predicate of justification it seems to be because I do not give an analysis of this kind. That is, I am invited to prove that the pleasure of successful prediction multiplied by the chance of success exceeds the displeasure of the troublesome procedure of induction.

Now I will not deny that in some cases of volitional decisions we engage in considerations which at least qualitatively may be represented by the mathematical calculation described. However, such an analysis of the volitional decision to act is not always possible; and even if it is possible it mostly is not relevant. It is not possible if p is not known; thus already in case 1γ it is not possible unless we are ready to consider a as an infinite value which seems to me rather absurd. And if it is possible it is not relevant because it does not free the volitional decision from a subjective element. That is, instead of having in the implicans the subjective decision to act, we have there now the subjective constants a and m; and if a man rejects our suggestion to act he may always defend himself by saying that his emotional constants do not furnish a positive valuational balance.

Moreover, it is very dubitable whether we are entitled to assume the existence of such emotional constants as a and m. Emotional values vary widely with the situation. The means M may appear very unpleasant to us if considered in isolation but if we know it is the means to reach the coveted aim A our dislike for M may turn into a liking for it. Any intellectual calculation of the valuational balance does violence to the actual psychological processes by which the volitional decision is made. What actually happens in most cases is that when confronted by the situation, we perform a decision *en bloc*, i.e., we perform an act not analyzable into the components p, a, m. Thus Miss Creed's condition c' is a much better representation of the actual situation than would be a deduction of c' from c.

I may add here the remark that even if such a calculation of the valuational balance could be given, a positive value for this balance would not involve an obligation to act. Our man might object that he accepts a bet only if the valuational balance is greater than a certain valuational threshold t. This is, for instance, the practice of insurance companies which calculate the premiums so that statistical laws guarantee to them a profit. Or our man might object that he accepts a bet only if the probability p is greater than a certain safety quantity s; if p is smaller than s he considers the event as practically impossible. The case then would be better represented by case 3 in which the action is not justifiable. I think this is a principle which we all more or less apply because "impossible" never means for us more than "practically impossible." If, for instance—to make use of Miss Creed's interesting example—we refuse to recognize an obligation to comply with the rites of a certain church in spite of there being a slight chance of truth in the promise that such a behavior would lead us to eternal happiness, this negative decision I think is best explained by the introduction of the principle that a probability of so small a degree is considered as a practical impossibility. (It follows, by the way, that cases 1γ, δ, and 2 will permit a better justification than case 1β, if in the last case p is known to be small; knowing nothing about p is a less unfavorable situation than knowing that p is small.) With these considerations two further subjective constants t and s are introduced, which make the relation between wanting the aim in general, and deciding under given conditions for an action in its favor, more flexible and questionable.

On the other hand there are cases in which the calculation of the valuational balance is unnecessary because its positive value can immediately be asserted. This is the case if m is not a displeasure but a pleasure; the sign of the m-term in the valuational balance then would be positive. There are many examples of this kind. Imagine the father saying to his son: If you want to have a car of your own take the old car in the garage and repair it. The boy may be glad to have, not only a car, but also the opportunity to repair a car. This case, I suppose, corresponds best to our actual behavior in face of the problem of induction. I think most of us would not envy the lazy man who waits until the fried pigeons fly into his mouth; we like to work, to try success, to gamble—at least as long as we like to live. I do not say this with the intention of giving an exhaustive psychological analysis of the decision to attempt to predict. I should have no objection if one should speak here of the great contribution which habit adds to our decision to act, for this is a point where we have left the logical field and are concerned with the psychological motives of our actions. Habit, though never a permissible argument for the choice of the *means* of prediction, may well be accepted as the motive which determines the *aim*. Miss Creed speaks so charmingly of the "gentle force of the habit of induction" which leads us, instead of "an intellectual calculation of values"; let us consider this idea together with the joy of gambling as the psychological motives of our decision to act. But let us carefully distinguish between the psychological question of the motives of our decision, and the logical question of the best means we can choose in order to reach the aim of our decision.

This logical question remains unchanged whatever may be the result of the psychological analysis as to the motives of our pursuit of the aim. Even if the application of the means M is combined, not with displeasure, but with pleasure, the question whether it is an appropriate means for the aim A has to be decided independently of this psychological fact. M involves pleasure for us only because it is the way towards A.

I shall summarize. The problem of the justification of induction includes both the question of the decision to attempt predictions and the question of the choice of the best means of making them. The decision on the attempt is justified if the aim is not proved to be unattainable. To demand more, to show that the aim will be reached with a probability p and that the valuational balance is positive would be equivalent to an analysis of the volitional decision which seems inappropriate from a psychological viewpoint and which would not eliminate the subjective element reappearing in the emotional constants a, m, t, s. I therefore can not consider such an analysis as necessary for a justification; a decision *en bloc* is permissible in the implicans of our proof. The word "justification" is chosen with the very intention of indicating the subjective element; otherwise we should speak of a demonstration of an *obligation* to pursue the aim. Only when we turn to the second point are we confronted by a problem free from subjective elements, as the question of the choice of the best means is purely logical. Justification of the choice of the means is therefore equivalent to the logical demonstration that the means is the best we have. If this proof is given the problem of justification is solved, since it is obvious that the first condition, the lack of a disproof of the possibility of success, is fulfilled.

The Two Concepts of Probability *

RUDOLF CARNAP

I. THE PROBLEM OF PROBABILITY

The problem of probability may be regarded as the task of finding an adequate definition of the concept of probability that can provide a basis for a theory of probability. This task is not one of defining a new concept but rather of redefining an old one. Thus we have here an instance of that kind of problem—often important in the development of science and mathematics—where a concept already in use is to be made more exact or, rather, is to be replaced by a more exact new concept. Let us call these problems (in an adaptation of the terminology of Kant and Husserl) problems of *explication;* in each case of an explication, we call the old concept, used in a more or less vague way either in every-day language or in an earlier stage of scientific language, the *explicandum;* the new, more exact concept which is proposed to take the place of the old one the *explicatum.* Thus, for instance, the definition of the cardinal number three by Frege and Russell as the class of all triples was meant as an explication; the explicandum was the ordinary meaning of the word 'three' as it appears in every-day life and in science; the concept of the class of all triples (defined not by means of the word 'triple' but with the help of existential quantifiers and the sign of identity) was proposed as an explicatum for the explicandum mentioned.

Using these terms, we may say that the problem of probability is the problem of finding an adequate explication of the word 'probability' in its ordinary meaning, or in one of its meanings if there are several.

II. THE LOGICAL CONCEPTS OF CONFIRMATION

In the preparation for our subsequent discussion of the problem of probability, let us examine some concepts which are connected with the scientific procedure of confirming or disconfirming hypotheses on the basis of results found by observation.

The procedure of confirmation is a complex one consisting of components of different kinds. In the present discussion, we shall be concerned only with what may be called the logical side of confirmation,

* Reprinted by kind permission of the author and the editors from *Philosophy and Phenomenological Research*, 5, 1945.

namely, with certain logical relations between sentences (or propositions expressed by these sentences). Within the procedure of confirmation, these relations are of interest to the scientist, for instance, in the following situation: He intends to examine a certain hypothesis *h;* he makes many observations of particular events which he regards as relevant for judging the hypothesis *h;* he formulates this evidence, the results of all observations made, or as many of them as are relevant, in a report *e,* which is a long sentence. Then he tries to decide whether and to what degree the hypothesis *h* is confirmed by the observational evidence *e.* It is with this decision alone that we shall be concerned. Once the hypothesis is formulated by *h* and the observational results by *e,* then this question as to whether and how much *h* is confirmed by *e* can be answered merely by a logical analysis of *h* and *e* and their relations. Therefore the question is a logical one. It is not a question of fact in the sense that knowledge of empirical fact is required to find the answer. Although the sentences *h* and *e* under consideration do themselves certainly refer to facts, nevertheless once *h* and *e* are given, the question of confirmation requires only that we are able to understand them, i.e., grasp their meanings, and to discover certain relations which are based upon their meanings. If by semantics [1] we understand the theory of the meanings of expressions, and especially of sentences, in a language then the relations to be studied between *h* and *e* may be regarded as semantical.

The question of confirmation in which we are here interested has just been characterized as a logical question. In order to avoid misunderstanding, a qualification should be made. The question at issue does not belong to deductive but to inductive logic. Both branches of logic have this in common: solutions of their problems do not require factual knowledge but only analysis of meaning. Therefore, both parts of logic (if formulated with respect to sentences rather than to propositions) belong to semantics. This similarity makes it possible to explain the logical character of the relations of confirmation by an analogy with a more familiar relation in deductive logic, viz., the relation of logical consequence or its converse, the relation of L-implication (i.e., logical implication or entailment in distinction to material implication). Let *i* be the sentence 'all men are mortal, and Socrates is a man,' and *j* the sentence 'Socrates is mortal.' Both *i* and *j* have factual content. But in order to decide whether *i* L-implies *j*, we need no factual knowledge, we need not know whether *i* is true or false, whether *j* is true or false, whether anybody believes in *i*, and if so, on what basis. All that is required is a logical analysis of the meanings of the two sentences. Analogously, to decide to what degree *h* is confirmed by *e*—a question in logic, but here in inductive, not in deductive, logic

[1] Compare Alfred Tarski, "The Semantic Conception of Truth and the Foundations of Semantics", *Philosophy and Phenomenological Research*, 4, 1944, pp. 341-376 [pp. 52-83 in the present collection]; and R. Carnap, *Introduction to Semantics*, 1942.

—we need not know whether *e* is true or false, whether *h* is true or false, whether anybody believes in *e*, and, if so, whether on the basis of observation or of imagination or of anything else. All we need is a logical analysis of the meanings of the two sentences. For this reason we call our problem the logical or semantical problem of confirmation, in distinction to what might be called the methodological problems of confirmation, e.g., how best to construct and arrange an apparatus for certain experiments in order to test a given hypothesis, how to carry out the experiments, how to observe the results, etc.

We may distinguish three logical concepts of confirmation, concepts which have to do with the logical side only of the problem of confirmation. They are all logical and hence semantical concepts. They apply to two sentences, which we call hypothesis and evidence and which in our example were designated by "*h*" and "*e*" respectively. Although the basis is usually an observational report, as in the application sketched above, and the hypothesis a law or a prediction, we shall not restrict our concepts of confirmation to any particular content or form of the two sentences. We distinguish the positive, the comparative, and the metrical concepts of confirmation in the following way.

(i) *The positive concept of confirmation* is that relation between two sentences *h* and *e* which is usually expressed by sentences of the following forms:

"*h* is confirmed by *e*."
"*h* is supported by *e*."
"*e* gives some (positive) evidence for *h*."
"*e* is evidence substantiating (or corroborating) the assumption of *h*."

Here *e* is ordinarily, as in the previous example, an observational report, but may also refer to particular states of affairs not yet known but merely assumed, and may even include assumed laws; *h* is usually a statement about an unknown state of affairs, e.g., a prediction, or it may be a law or any other hypothesis. It is clear that this concept of confirmation is a relation between two sentences, not a property of one of them. Customary formulations which mention only the hypothesis are obviously elliptical; the basis is tacitly understood. For instance, when a physicist says: "This hypothesis is well confirmed," he means ". . . on the evidence of the observational results known today to physicists."

(ii) *The comparative* (or topological) *concept of confirmation* is usually expressed in sentences of the following forms (*a*), (*b*), (*c*), or similar ones.
(*a*) "*h* is more strongly confirmed (or supported, substantiated, corroborated etc.) by *e* than *h'* by *e'*."
Here we have a tetradic relation between four sentences. In general,

the two hypotheses h and h' are different from one another, and likewise the two evidences e and e'. Some scientists will perhaps doubt whether a comparison of this most general form is possible, and may, perhaps, restrict the application of the comparative concept only to those situations where two evidences are compared with respect to the same hypothesis [example (b)], or where two hypotheses are examined with respect to one evidence [example (c)]. In either case the comparative concept is a triadic relation between three sentences.

(b) "The general theory of relativity is more highly confirmed by the results of laboratory experiments and astronomical observations known today than by those known in 1905."

(c) "The optical phenomena available to physicists in the 19th century were more adequately explained by the wave theory of light than by the corpuscular theory; in other words, they gave stronger support to the former theory than to the latter."

(iii) *The metrical* (or quantitative) *concept of confirmation*, the concept of *degree of confirmation*. Opinion seems divided as to whether or not a concept of this kind ever occurs in the customary talk of scientists, that is to say, whether they ever assign a numerical value to the degree to which a hypothesis is supported by given observational material or whether they use only positive and comparative concepts of confirmation. For the present discussion, we leave this question open; even if the latter were the case, an attempt to find a metrical explicatum for the comparative explicandum would be worth while. (This would be analogous to many other cases of scientific explication, to the introduction, for example, of the metrical explicatum "temperature" for the comparative explicandum 'warmer', or of the metrical explicatum 'I.Q.' for the comparative explicandum 'higher intelligence'.)

III. THE TWO CONCEPTS OF PROBABILITY

The history of the theory of probability is the history of attempts to find an explication for the pre-scientific concept of probability. The number of solutions which have been proposed for this problem in the course of its historical development is rather large. The differences, though sometimes slight, are in many cases considerable. To bring some order into the bewildering multiplicity, several attempts have been made to arrange the many solutions into a few groups. The following is a simple and plausible classification of the various conceptions of probability into three groups: [2] (i) the classical conception, originated by Jacob Bernoulli and Laplace, and represented by their followers in various forms; here, probability is defined as the ratio of the number of favorable cases to

[2] See Ernest Nagel, "Principles of the Theory of Probability" (*International Encyclopedia of Unified Science*, Vol. I, 1939, No. 6).

the number of all possible cases; (ii) the conception of probability as a certain objective logical relation between propositions (or sentences); the chief representatives of this conception are Keynes [3] and Jeffreys; [4] (iii) the conception of probability as relative frequency, developed most completely by von Mises [5] and Reichenbach. [6]

In this paper, a discussion of these various conceptions is not intended. While the main point of interest both for the authors and for the readers of the various theories of probability is normally the solutions proposed in those theories, we shall inspect the theories from a different point of view. We shall not ask what solutions the authors offer but rather which problems the solutions are intended to solve; in other words, we shall not ask what explicata are proposed but rather which concepts are taken as explicanda.

This question may appear superfluous, and the fact obvious that the explicandum for every theory of probability is the pre-scientific concept of probability, i.e., the meaning in which the word 'probability' is used in the pre-scientific language. Is the assumption correct, however, that there is only one meaning connected with the word 'probability' in its customary use, or at the least that only one meaning has been chosen by the authors as their explicandum? When we look at the formulations which the authors themselves offer in order to make clear which meanings of 'probability' they intend to take as their explicanda, we find phrases as different as "degree of belief," "degree of reasonable expectation," "degree of possibility," "degree of proximity to certainty," "degree of partial truth," "relative frequency," and many others. This multiplicity of phrases shows that any assumption of a unique explicandum common to all authors is untenable. And we might even be tempted to go to the opposite extreme and to conclude that the authors are dealing not with one but with a dozen or more different concepts. However, I believe that this multiplicity is misleading. It seems to me that the number of explicanda in all the various theories of probability is neither just one nor about a dozen, but in all essential respects—leaving aside slight variations—very few, and chiefly two. In the following discussion we shall use subscripts in order to distinguish these two meanings of the term 'probability' from which most of the various theories of probability start; we are, of course, distinguishing between two explicanda and not between the various explicata offered by these theories, whose number is much greater. The two concepts are: (i) $probability_1$ = degree of confirmation; (ii) $probability_2$ = relative frequency in the long run. Strictly speaking, there are two groups of concepts, since both for (i) and for (ii) there is a positive,

[3] John Maynard Keynes, *A Treatise on Probability*, 1921.
[4] Harold Jeffreys, *Theory of Probability*, 1939.
[5] Richard von Mises, *Probability, Statistics, and Truth* (orig. 1928), 1939.
[6] Hans Reichenbach, *Wahrscheinlichkeitslehre*, 1935.

a comparative, and a metrical concept; however, for our discussion, we may leave aside these distinctions.

Let me emphasize again that the distinction made here refers to two explicanda, not to two explicata. That there is more than one explicatum is obvious; and indeed, their number is much larger than two. But most investigators in the field of probability apparently believe that all the various theories of probability are intended to solve the same problem and hence that any two theories which differ fundamentally from one another are incompatible. Consequently we find that most representatives of the frequency conception of probability reject all other theories; and, vice versa, that the frequency conception is rejected by most of the authors of other theories. These mutual rejections are often formulated in rather strong terms. This whole controversy seems to me futile and unnecessary. The two sides start from different explicanda, and both are right in maintaining the scientific importance of the concepts chosen by them as explicanda—a fact which does not, however, imply that on either side all authors have been equally successful in constructing a satisfactory explicatum. On the other hand, both sides are wrong in most of their polemic assertions against the other side.

A few examples may show how much of the futile controversy between representatives of different conceptions of probability is due to the blindness on both sides with respect to the existence and importance of the probability concept on the other side. We take as examples a prominent contemporary representative of each conception: von Mises, who constructed the first complete theory based on the frequency conception, and Jeffreys, who constructed the most advanced theory based on probability$_1$. Von Mises [7] seems to believe that probability$_2$ is the only basis of the Calculus of Probability. To speak of the probability of the death of a certain individual seems to him meaningless. Any use of the term "probability" in everyday life other than in the statistical sense of probability$_2$ has in his view nothing to do with the Calculus of Probability and cannot take numerical values. That he regards Keynes' conception of probability as thoroughly subjectivistic [8] indicates clearly his misunderstanding.

On the other hand, we find Jeffreys similarly blind in the other direction. Having laid down certain requirements which every theory of probability (and that means for him probability$_1$) should fulfill, he then rejects all frequency theories, that is, theories of probability$_2$, because they do not fulfill his requirements. Thus he says: [9] "No 'objective' definition of probability in terms of actual or possible observations . . . is admissible," because the results of observations are initially unknown and, consequently, we could not know the fundamental principles of the theory and would

[7] *Op. cit.*, First Lecture.
[8] *Op. cit.*, Third Lecture.
[9] *Op. cit.*, p. 11.

have no starting point. He even goes so far as to say that "in practice, no statistician ever uses a frequency definition, but that all use the notion of degree of reasonable belief, usually without ever noticing that they are using it." [10] While von Mises' concern with explicating the empirical concept of probability$_2$ by the limit of relative frequency in an infinite sequence has led him to apply the term "probability" only in cases where such a limit exists, Jeffreys misunderstands his procedure completely and accuses the empiricist von Mises of apriorism: "The existence of the limit is taken as a postulate by von Mises. . . . The postulate is an *a priori* statement about possible experiments and is in itself objectionable." [11] Thus we find this situation: von Mises and Jeffreys both assert that there is only one concept of probability that is of scientific importance and that can be taken as the basis of the Calculus of Probability. The first maintains that this concept is probability$_2$ and certainly not anything like probability$_1$; the second puts it just the other way round; and neither has anything but ironical remarks for the concept proposed by the other.

When we criticize the theory of probability proposed by an author, we must clearly distinguish between a rejection of his explicatum and a rejection of his explicandum. The second by no means follows from the first. Donald Williams, in his paper in this symposium, [12] raises serious objections against the frequency theory of probability, especially in von Mises' form. The chief objection is that von Mises' explicatum for probability, viz., the limit of the relative frequency in an infinite sequence of events with a random distribution, is not accessible to empirical confirmation—unless it be supplemented by a theory of inductive probability, a procedure explicitly rejected by von Mises. I think Williams is right in this objection. This, however, means merely that the concept proposed by von Mises is not yet an adequate explicatum. On the other hand, I believe the frequentists are right in the assertion that their explicandum, viz., the statistical concept of probability$_2$, plays an important rôle in all branches of empirical science and especially in modern physics, and that therefore the task of explicating this concept is of great importance for science.

It would likewise be unjustified to reject the concept of probability$_1$ as an explicandum merely because the attempts so far made at an explication are not yet quite satisfactory. It must be admitted that the classical Laplacean definition is untenable. It defines probability as the ratio of the number of favorable cases to the total number of equipossible cases, where equipossibility is determined by the principle of insufficient reason (or indifference). This definition is in certain cases inapplicable, in other cases it yields inadequate values, and in some cases it leads even to contra-

[10] *Op. cit.*, p. 300.

[11] *Op. cit.*, p. 304.

[12] "On the Derivation of Probabilities from Frequencies", *Philosophy and Phenomenological Research*, 5, 1945.

dictions, because for any given proposition there are, in general, several ways of analyzing it as a disjunction of other, logically exclusive, propositions.[13] Modern authors, especially Keynes, Jeffreys, and Hosiasson,[14] proceed more cautiously, but at the price of restricting themselves to axiom systems which are rather weak and hence far from constituting an explicit definition. I have made an attempt to formulate an explicit definition of the concept of degree of confirmation (with numerical values) as an explicatum for probability$_1$, and to construct a system of metrical inductive logic based on that definition.[15] No matter whether this first attempt at an explication with the help of the methods of modern logic and in particular those of semantics will turn out to be satisfactory or not, I think there is no reason for doubting that an adequate explication will be developed in time through further attempts.

The distinction between the two concepts which serve as explicanda is often overlooked on both sides. This is primarily due to the unfortunate fact that both concepts are designated by the same familiar, but ambiguous word 'probability'. Although many languages contain two words (e.g., English 'probable' and 'likely', Latin *'probabilis'* and *'verisimilis'*, French *'probable'* and *'vraisemblable'*), these words seem in most cases to be used in about the same way or at any rate not to correspond to the two concepts we have distinguished. Some authors (e.g., C. S. Peirce and R. A. Fisher) have suggested utilizing the plurality of available words for the distinction of certain concepts (different from our distinction); however, the proposals were made in an artificial way, without relation to the customary meanings of the words. The same would hold if we were to use the two words for our two concepts; therefore we prefer to use subscripts as indicated above.

Probability$_1$, in other words, the logical concept of confirmation in its different forms (positive, comparative, and metrical), has been explained in the preceding section. A brief explanation may here be given of probability$_2$, merely to make clear its distinction from probability$_1$. A typical example of the use of this concept is the following statement: "The probability$_2$ of casting an ace with this die is $1/6$." Statements of this form refer to two properties (or classes) of events: (i) the reference property M_1, here the property of being a throw with this die; (ii) the specific prop-

---

[13] Williams' indications (*op. cit.*, pp. 450 and 469) to the effect that he intends to maintain Laplace's definition even in a simplified form and without the principle of indifference are rather puzzling. We have to wait for the full formulation of his solution, which his present paper does not yet give (*op. cit.*, p. 481), in order to see how it overcomes the well-known difficulties of Laplace's definition.

[14] Janina Hosiasson-Lindenbaum, "On Confirmation", *Journal of Symbolic Logic*, Vol. V, 1940, pp. 133–148.

[15] A book exhibiting this system is in preparation. The present paper is a modified version of a chapter of the book. The definition is explained and some of the theorems of my system of inductive logic are summarized in the paper "On Inductive Logic", which will appear in *Philosophy of Science*, Vol. XII, 1945.

erty M_2, here the property of being a throw with any die resulting in an ace. The statement says that the probability$_2$ of M_2 with respect to M_1 is 1/6. The statement is tested by statistical investigations. A sufficiently long series of, say, n throws of the die in question is made, and the number m of these throws which yield an ace is counted. If the relative frequency m/n of aces in this series is sufficiently close to 1/6, the statement is regarded as confirmed. Thus, the other way round, the statement is understood as predicting that the relative frequency of aces thrown with this die in a sufficiently long series will be about 1/6. This formulation is admittedly inexact; but it intends no more than to indicate the meaning of 'probability$_2$' as an explicandum. To make this concept exact is the task of the explication; our discussion concerns only the two explicanda.

IV. THE LOGICAL NATURE OF THE TWO PROBABILITY CONCEPTS

On the basis of the preceding explanations, let us now characterize the two probability concepts, not with respect to what they mean but merely with respect to their logical nature, more specifically, with respect to the kind of entities to which they are applied and the logical nature of the simplest sentences in which they are used. (Since the pre-scientific use of both concepts is often too vague and incomplete, e.g., because of the omission of the second argument [viz., the evidence or the reference class], we take here into consideration the more careful use by authors on probability. However, we shall be more concerned with their general discussions than with the details of their constructed systems.) For the sake of simplicity, let us consider the two concepts in their metrical forms only. They may be taken also in their comparative and in their positive forms (as explained for probability$_1$, i.e., confirmation, in section II), and these other forms would show analogous differences. Probability$_1$ and probability$_2$, taken as metrical concepts, have the following characteristics in common: each of them is a function of two arguments; their values are real numbers belonging to the interval 0 to 1 (according to the customary convention, which we follow here). Their characteristic differences are as follows:

1. *Probability$_1$* (degree of confirmation).

(*a*) The *two arguments* are variously described as events (in the literal sense, see below), states of affairs, circumstances, and the like. Therefore each argument is expressible by a declarative sentence and hence is, in our terminology, a proposition. Another alternative consists in taking as arguments the sentences expressing the propositions, describing the events, etc. If we choose this alternative, probability$_1$ is a semantical concept (as in section II). (Fundamentally it makes no great difference whether propositions or sentences are taken as arguments; but the second method has certain technical advantages, and therefore we use it for our discussion.)

(*b*) A simple *statement* of probability$_1$, i.e., one attributing to two given arguments a particular number as value of probability$_1$, is either L-true (logically true, analytic) or L-false (logically false, logically self-contradictory), hence in any case L-determinate, not factual (synthetic). Therefore, a statement of this kind is to be established by logical analysis alone, as has been explained earlier (section II). It is independent of the contingency of facts because it does not say anything about facts (although the two arguments do in general refer to facts).

2. *Probability$_2$* (relative frequency).

(*a*) The *two arguments* are properties, kinds, classes, usually of events or things. [As an alternative, the predicate expressions designating the properties might be taken as arguments; then the concept would become a semantical one. In the present case, however, in distinction to (1), there does not seem to be any advantage in this method. On the contrary, it appears to be more convenient to have the probability$_2$ statements in the object language instead of the metalanguage; and it seems that all authors who deal with probability$_2$ choose this form.]

(*b*) A simple *statement* of probability$_2$ is factual and empirical, it says something about the facts of nature, and hence must be based upon empirical procedure, the observation of relevant facts. From these simple statements the theorems of a mathematical theory of probability$_2$ must be clearly distinguished. The latter do not state a particular value of probability$_2$ but say something about connections between probability$_2$ values in a general way, usually in a conditional form (for example: "if the values of such and such probabilities$_2$ are q_1 and q_2, then the value of a probability$_2$ related to the original ones in a certain way is such and such a function, say, product or sum, of q_1 and q_2"). These theorems are not factual but L-true (analytic). Thus a theory of probability$_2$, e.g., the system constructed by von Mises or that by Reichenbach, is not of an empirical but of a logico-mathematical nature; it is a branch of mathematics, like arithmetic, fundamentally different from any branch of empirical science, e.g., physics.

It is very important to distinguish clearly between *kinds of events* (war, birth, death, throw of a die, throw of this die, throw of this die yielding an ace, etc.) and *events* (Caesar's death, the throw of this die made yesterday at 10 A.M., the series of all throws of this die past and future). This distinction is doubly important for discussions on probability, because one of the characteristic differences between the two concepts is this: the first concept refers sometimes to two events, the second to two kinds of events [see 1(*a*) and 2(*a*)]. Many authors of probability use the word 'event' (or the corresponding words 'Ereignis' and 'évènement') when they mean to speak, not about events, but about kinds of events. This usage is of long standing in the literature on probability, but it is very unfortunate. It has only served to reinforce the customary neglect of the fundamental difference between the two probability concepts which arose originally out of the ambiguous use of the word 'probability', and thereby to increase the general confusion in discussions on probability. The authors who use the term 'event' when they mean kinds of events get into trouble, of course, whenever they want to speak about specific events. The traditional solution is to say 'the happenings (or occurrences) of a certain event' instead of 'the events of a certain kind'; sometimes the events are referred to by the term 'single events'. But this phrase is rather misleading; the important difference between events and kinds of events is not the same as the inessential difference between single events (the first throw I made today with this die) and multiple or compound events (the series of all throws made with this die). Keynes, if I interpret him correctly, has noticed the ambiguity of the term 'event'. He says [16] that the customary use of phrases like 'the happening of events' is "vague and unambiguous," which I suppose to be a misprint for "vague and ambiguous"; but he does not specify the ambiguity. He proposes to dispense altogether with the term 'event' and to use instead the term 'proposition'. Subsequent authors dealing with probability$_1$, like Jeffreys, for example, have followed him in this use.

Many authors have made a distinction between two (or sometimes more) kinds of probability, or between two meanings of the word 'probability'. Some of these distinctions are quite different from the distinction made here between probability$_1$ and probability$_2$. For instance, a distinction is sometimes made between mathematical probability and philosophical probability; their characteristic difference appears to be that the first has numerical values, the second not. However, this difference seems hardly essential; we find a concept with numerical values and one without, in other words, both a metrical and a comparative concept on either side of our distinction between the two fundamentally different meanings of 'probability'. Another distinction has been made between subjective and objective probability. However, I believe that practically all authors really have an objective concept of probability in mind, and that the appearance of subjectivist conceptions is in most cases caused only by occasional unfortunate formulations; this will soon be discussed.

Other distinctions which have been made are more or less similar to our distinction between probability$_1$ and probability$_2$. For instance, Ramsey [17] says: ". . . the general difference of opinion between statisticians who for the most part adopt the frequency theory of probability and logicians who mostly reject it renders it likely that the two schools are really discussing different things, and that the word 'probability' is used by logicians in one sense and by statisticians in another."

[16] *Op. cit.*, p. 5.
[17] F. P. Ramsey, *The Foundations of Mathematics*, 1931; see p. 157.

It seems that many authors have taken either probability$_1$ or probability$_2$ as their explicandum. I believe moreover that practically all authors on probability have intended one of these two concepts as their explicandum, despite the fact that their various explanations appear to refer to a number of quite different concepts.

For one group of authors, the question of their explicandum is easily answered. In the case of all those who support a frequency theory of probability, i.e., who define their explicata in terms of relative frequency (as a limit or in some other way), there can be no doubt that their explicandum is probability$_2$. Their formulations are, in general, presented in clear and unambiguous terms. Often they state explicitly that their explicandum is relative frequency. And even in the cases where this is not done, the discussion of their explicata leaves no doubt as to what is meant as explicandum.

This, however, covers only one of the various conceptions, i.e., explicata proposed, and only one of the many different explanations of explicanda which have been given and of which some examples were mentioned earlier. It seems clear that the other explanations do not refer to the statistical, empirical concept of relative frequency; and I believe that practically all of them, in spite of their apparent dissimilarity, are intended to refer to probability$_1$. Unfortunately, many of the phrases used are more misleading than helpful in our efforts to find out what their authors actually meant as explicandum. There is, in particular, one point on which many authors in discussions on probability$_1$, or on logical problems in general, commit a certain typical confusion or adopt incautiously other authors' formulations which are infected by this confusion. I am referring to what is sometimes called psychologism in logic.

Many authors in their general remarks about the nature of (deductive) logic say that it has to do with ways and forms of thinking or, in more cautious formulations, with forms of correct or rational thinking. In spite of these subjectivistic formulations, we find that in practice these authors use an objectivistic method in solving any particular logical problem. For instance, in order to find out whether a certain conclusion follows from given premises, they do not in fact make psychological experiments about the thinking habits of people but rather analyze the given sentences and show their conceptual relations. In inductive logic or, in other words, the theory of probability$_1$, we often find a similar psychologism. Some authors, from Laplace and other representatives of the classical theory of probability down to contemporary authors like Keynes and Jeffreys, use subjectivistic formulations when trying to explain what they take as their explicandum; they say that it is probability in the sense of degree of belief or, if they are somewhat more cautious, degree of reasonable or justified belief. However, an analysis of the work of these authors comes to quite different results if we pay more attention to the methods the authors actually use in solving problems of probability than to the general remarks in which they try to characterize their own aims and methods. Such an analysis, which cannot be carried out within this paper, shows that most and perhaps all of these authors use objectivistic rather than subjectivistic methods. They do not try to measure degrees of belief by actual, psychological experiments, but rather carry out a logical analysis of the concepts and propositions involved. It appears, therefore, that the psychologism in inductive logic is, just like that in deductive logic, merely a superficial feature of certain marginal formulations, while the core of the theories remains thoroughly objectivistic. And, further, it seems to me that for most of those authors who do not maintain a frequency theory, from the classical period to our time, the objective concept which they take as their explicandum is probability$_1$, i.e., degree of confirmation.

V. EMPIRICISM AND THE LOGICAL CONCEPT OF PROBABILITY

Many empiricist authors have rejected the logical concept of probability$_1$ as distinguished from probability$_2$ because they believe that its use violates the principle of empiricism and that, therefore, probability$_2$ is the only concept admissible for empiricism and hence for science. We shall now examine some of the reasons given for this view.

The concept of probability$_1$ is applied also in cases in which the hypothesis h is a prediction concerning a particular "single event," e.g., the prediction that it will rain tomorrow or that the next throw of this die will yield an ace. Some philosophers believe that an application of this kind violates the principle of verifiability (or confirmability). They might say, for example: "How can the statement 'the probability of rain tomorrow on the evidence of the given meteorological observations is one-fifth' be verified? We shall observe either rain or not-rain tomorrow, but we shall not observe anything that can verify the value one-fifth." This objection, however, is based on a misconception concerning the nature of the probability$_1$ statement. This statement does not ascribe the probability$_1$ value $1/5$ to tomorrow's rain but rather to a certain logical relation between the prediction of rain and the meteorological report. Since the relation is logical, the statement is, if true, L-true; therefore it is not in need of verification by observation of tomorrow's weather or of any other facts.

It must be admitted that earlier authors on probability have sometimes made inferences which are inadmissible from the point of view of empiricism. They calculated the value of a logical probability and then inferred from it a frequency, hence making an inadvertent transition from probability$_1$ to probability$_2$. Their reasoning might be somewhat like this: "On the basis of the symmetry of this die the probability of an ace is $1/6$; therefore, one-sixth of the throws of this die will result in an ace." Later authors have correctly criticized inferences of this kind. It is clear that from a probability$_1$ statement a statement on frequency can never be inferred, because the former is purely logical while the latter is factual. Thus the source of the mistake was the confusion of probability$_1$ with probability$_2$. The use of probability$_1$ statements cannot in itself violate the principle of empiricism so long as we remain aware of the fact that those statements are purely logical and hence do not allow the derivation of factual conclusions.

The situation with respect to both objections just discussed may be clarified by a comparison with deductive logic. Let h be the sentence 'there will be rain tomorrow' and j the sentence 'there will be rain and wind tomorrow'. Suppose somebody makes the statement in deductive logic: "h follows logically from j." Certainly nobody will accuse him of apriorism either for making the statement or for claiming that for its verification no factual knowledge is required. The statement "the probability$_1$ of h on the evidence e is $1/5$" has the same general character as the former statement; therefore it cannot violate empiricism any more than the first. Both statements express a purely logical relation between two sentences. The difference between the two statements is merely this: while the first states a complete logical implication, the second states only, so to speak, a partial logical implication; hence, while the first belongs to deductive logic, the second belongs to inductive logic. Generally speaking, the assertion of purely logical sentences, whether in deductive or in inductive logic, can never violate empiricism; if they are false, they violate the rules of logic. The principle of empiricism can be violated only by the assertion of a factual (synthetic) sentence without a sufficient empirical foundation, or by the thesis of apriorism when it contends that for knowledge with respect to certain factual sentences no empirical foundation is required.

According to Reichenbach's view,[18] the concept of logical probability or weight, in order to be in accord with empiricism, must be identified with the statistical concept of probability. If we formulate his view with the help of our terms with subscripts, it says that probability$_1$ is identical with probability$_2$, or, rather, with a special kind of application of it. He argues for this "identity conception" against any "disparity conception," like the one presented in this paper, which regards the two uses of 'probability' as essentially different. Reichenbach tries to prove the identity conception by showing how the concept which we call probability$_1$, even when applied to a "single event," leads back to a relative frequency. I agree that in certain cases there is a close relationship between probability$_1$ and relative frequency. The decisive question is, however, the nature of this relationship. Let us consider a simple example. Let the evidence e say that among 30 observed things with the property M_1 20 have been

[18] Hans Reichenbach, *Experience and Prediction*, 1938, see §§ 32–34.

found to have the property M_2, and hence that the relative frequency of M_2 with respect to M_1 in the observed sample is $2/3$; let e say, in addition, that a certain individual b not belonging to the sample is M_1. Let h be the prediction that b is M_2. If the degree of confirmation c is defined in a suitable way as an explicatum for probability$_1$, $c(h,e)$ will be equal or close to $2/3$; let us assume for the sake of simplicity that $c = 2/3$.[19] However, the fact that, in this case, the value of c or probability$_1$ is equal to a certain relative frequency by no means implies that probability$_1$ is here the same as probability$_2$; these two concepts remain fundamentally different even in this case. This becomes clear by the following considerations (i) to (iv).

(i) The c-statement '$c(h,e) = 2/3$' does not itself state a relative frequency although the value of c which it states is calculated on the basis of a known relative frequency and, under our assumptions, is in this case exactly equal to it. A temperature is sometimes determined by the volume of a certain body of mercury and is, under certain conditions, equal to it; this, however, does not mean that temperature and volume are the same concept. The c-statement, being a purely logical statement, cannot possibly state a relative frequency for two empirical properties like M_1 and M_2. Such a relative frequency can be stated only by a factual sentence; in the example, it is stated by a part of the factual sentence e. The c-statement does not imply either e or the part of e just mentioned; it rather speaks about e, stating a logical relation between e and h. It seems to me that Reichenbach does not realize this fact sufficiently clearly. He feels, correctly, that the c-value $2/3$ stated in the c-statement is in some way based upon our empirical knowledge of the observed relative frequency. This leads him to the conception, which I regard as incorrect, that the c-statement must be interpreted as stating the relative frequency and hence as being itself a factual, empirical statement. In my conception, the factual content concerning the observed relative frequency must be ascribed, not to the c-statement, but to the evidence e referred to in the c-statement.

(ii) The relative frequency $2/3$, which is stated in e and on which the value of c is based, is not at all a probability$_2$. The probability$_2$ of M_2 with respect to M_1 is the relative frequency of M_2 with respect to M_1 in the whole sequence of relevant events. The relative frequency stated by e, on the other hand, is the relative frequency observed within the given sample. It is true that our estimate of the value of probability$_2$ will be based on the observed relative frequency in the sample. However, observations of several samples may yield different values for the observed relative frequency. Therefore we cannot identify observed relative fre-

---

[19] According to Reichenbach's inductive logic, in the case described $c = 2/3$. According to my inductive logic, c is close to but not exactly equal to $2/3$. My reason for regarding a value of the latter kind as more adequate has been briefly indicated in the paper mentioned above "On Inductive Logic", § 10. For our present discussion, we may leave aside this question.

quency with probability$_2$, since the latter has only one value, which is unknown. (I am using here the customary realistic language as it is used in everyday life and in science; this use does not imply acceptance of realism as a metaphysical thesis but only of what Feigl calls "empirical realism." [20])

(iii) As mentioned, an estimate of the probability$_2$, the relative frequency in the whole sequence, is based upon the observed relative frequency in the sample. I think that, in a sense, the statement '$c(h,e) = 2/3$' itself may be interpreted as stating such an estimate; it says the same as: "The best estimate on the evidence e of the probability$_2$ of M_2 with respect to M_1 is $2/3$." If somebody should like to call this a frequency interpretation of probability$_1$, I should raise no objection. It need, however, be noticed clearly that this interpretation identifies probability$_1$ not with probability$_2$ but with the best estimate of probability$_2$ on the evidence e; and this is something quite different. The best estimate may have different values for different evidences; probability$_2$ has only one value. A statement of the best estimate on a given evidence is purely logical; a statement of probability$_2$ is empirical. The reformulation of the statement on probability$_1$ or c in terms of the best estimate of probability$_2$ may be helpful in showing the close connection between the two probability concepts. This formulation must, however, not be regarded as eliminating probability$_1$. The latter concept is still implicitly contained in the phrase "the best estimate," which means nothing else but "the most probable estimate," that is, "the estimate with the highest probability$_1$." Generally speaking, any estimation of the value of a physical magnitude (length, temperature, probability$_2$, etc.) on the evidence of certain observations or measurements is an inductive procedure and hence necessarily involves probability$_1$, either in its metrical or in its comparative form.

(iv) The fundamental difference between probability$_1$ and probability$_2$ may be further elucidated by analyzing the sense of the customary references to *unknown probabilities*. As we have seen under (ii), the value of a certain probability$_2$ may be unknown to us at a certain time in the sense that we do not possess sufficient factual information for its calculation. On the other hand, the value of a probability$_1$ for two given sentences cannot be unknown in the same sense. (It may, of course, be unknown in the sense that a certain logico-mathematical procedure has not yet been accomplished, that is, in the same sense in which we say that the solution of a certain arithmetical problem is at present unknown to us.) In this respect also, a confusion of the two concepts of probability has sometimes been made in formulations of the classical theory. This theory deals, on the whole, with probability$_1$; and the principle of indifference, one of

[20] Herbert Feigl, "Logical Empiricism", in *Twentieth Century Philosophy*, ed. D. Runes, 1943, pp. 373-416 [pp. 3-26 in the present collection]; see pp. 390 ff. [pp. 15 ff. above].

the cornerstones of the theory, is indeed valid to a certain limited extent for this concept. However, this principle is absurd for probability$_2$, as has often been pointed out. Yet the classical authors sometimes refer to unknown probabilities or to the probability (or chance) of certain probability values, e.g., in formulations of Bayes' theorem. This would not be admissible for probability$_1$, and I believe that here the authors inadvertently go over to probability$_2$. Since a probability$_2$ value is a physical property like a temperature, we may very well inquire into the probability$_1$, on a given evidence, of a certain probability$_2$ (as in the earlier example, at the end of (iii)). However, a question about the probability$_1$ of a probability$_1$ statement has no more point than a question about the probability$_1$ of the statement that $2 + 2 = 4$ or that $2 + 2 = 5$, because a probability$_1$ statement is, like an arithmetical statement, either L-true or L-false; therefore its probability$_1$, with respect to any evidence, is either 1 or zero.

VI. PROBABILITY AND TRUTH

It is important to distinguish clearly between a concept characterizing a thing independently of the state of our knowledge (e.g., the concept 'hard') and the related concept characterizing our state of knowledge with respect to the thing (e.g., the concept 'known to be hard'). It is true that a person will, as a rule, attribute the predicate 'hard' to a thing b only if he knows it to be hard, hence only if he is prepared to attribute to it also the predicate 'known to be hard'. Nevertheless, the sentences 'b is hard' and 'b is known to be hard' are obviously far from meaning the same. One point of difference becomes evident when we look at the sentences in their complete form; the second sentence, in distinction to the first (if we regard hardness as a permanent property), must be supplemented by references to a person and a time point: 'b is known to X at the time t to be hard'. The distinction between the two sentences becomes more conspicuous if they occur within certain larger contexts. For example, the difference between the sentences 'b is not hard' and 'b is not known to X at the time t to be hard' is clear from the fact that we can easily imagine a situation where we would be prepared to assert the second but not the first.

The distinction just explained may appear as obvious beyond any need of emphasis. However, a distinction of the same general form, where 'true' is substituted for 'hard', is nevertheless often neglected by philosophers. A person will, in general, attribute the predicate 'true' to a given sentence (or proposition) only if he knows it to be true, hence only if he is prepared to attribute to it also the predicate 'known to be true' or 'established as true' or 'verified'. Nevertheless 'true' and 'verified (by the person X at the time t)' mean quite different things; and so do 'false' and 'falsified' (in the sense of 'known to be false', 'established as false'). A given sentence is often neither verified nor falsified; nevertheless it is either true or false, whether anybody knows it or not. (Some empiricists shy away from the latter formulation because they believe it to involve an anti-empiricist absolutism. This, however, is not the case. Empiricism admits as meaningful any statement about unknown fact and hence also about unknown truth, provided only the fact or the truth is know*able*, or confirmable.) In this way an inadvertent confusion of 'true' and 'verified' may lead to doubts about the validity of the principle of excluded middle. The question of whether and to what extent a confusion of this kind has actually contributed to the origin of some contemporary philosophical doctrines rejecting that principle is hard to decide and will not be investigated here.

A statement like 'this thing is made of iron' can never be verified in the strictest sense, i.e., definitively established as true so that no possibility remains of refuting it by future experience. The statement can only be more or less confirmed. If it is highly confirmed, that is to say, if strong evidence for it is found, then it is often said to be verified; but this is a weakened, non-absolutistic sense of the term. I think it is fair to say that most philosophers, and at least all empiricists, agree today that the concept 'verified' in its strict sense is not applicable to statements about physical things. Some philosophers, however, go further; they say that, because we can never reach absolutely certain knowledge about things, we ought to abandon the concept of truth. It seems to me that this view is due again to an unconscious confusion of 'true' and 'verified'.[21] Some of these philosophers say that, in order to avoid absolutism, we should not ask whether a given statement is true but only whether it has been confirmed, corroborated, or accepted by a certain person at a certain time.[22] Others think that 'true' should be abandoned in favor of 'highly confirmed' or 'highly probable.' Reichenbach[23] has been led by considerations of this kind to the view that the values of probability (the logical concept of probability$_1$) ought to take the place of the two truth-values, truth and falsity, of ordinary logic, or, in other words, that probability logic is a multivalued logic superseding the customary two-valued logic. I agree with Reichenbach that here a concept referring to an absolute and unobtainable maximum should be replaced by a concept referring to a high degree in a continuous scale. However, what is superseded by 'highly probable' or 'confirmed to a high degree' is the concept 'confirmed to the maximum degree' or 'verified', and not the concept 'true'.

[21] I have given earlier warnings against this confusion in "Wahrheit und Bewährung", *Actes du Congrès International de Philosophic Scientifique*, Paris, 1936, Vol. IV, pp. 1–6 [included, in an English translation with modifications and additions, in the present collection, under the title "Truth and Confirmation"]; and in *Introduction to Semantics*, p. 28.

[22] See, e.g., Otto Neurath, "Universal Jargon and Terminology", *Proceedings Aristotelian Society*, 1940–1941, pp. 127–148, see esp. pp. 138 f.

[23] *Experience and Prediction.* §§ 22, 35.

Values of probability$_1$ are fundamentally different from truth-values. Therefore inductive logic, although it introduces the continuous scale of probability$_1$ values, remains like deductive logic two-valued. While it is true that to the multiplicity of probability$_1$ values in inductive logic only a dichotomy corresponds in deductive logic, nevertheless, this dichotomy is not between truth and falsity of a sentence but between L-implication and non-L-implication for two sentences. If, to take our previous example, $c(h,e) = 2/3$, then h is still either true or false and does not have an intermediate truth-value of $2/3$.

* * *

It has been the chief purpose of this paper to explain and discuss the two concepts of probability in their rôle as explicanda for theories of probability. I think that in the present situation clarification of the explicanda is the most urgent task. When every author has not only a clear understanding of his own explicandum but also some insight into the existence, the importance, and the meaning of the explicandum on the other side, then it will be possible for each side to concentrate entirely on the positive task of constructing an explication and a theory of the chosen explicatum without wasting energy in futile polemics against the explicandum of the other side.

VI

DATA, REALITY, AND THE MIND-BODY PROBLEM

Hume's Philosophy *

G. E. MOORE

In both of his two books on the Human Understanding, Hume had, I think, one main general object. He tells us that it was his object to discover "the extent and force of human understanding," to give us "an exact analysis of its powers and capacity." And we may, I think, express what he meant by this in the following way. He plainly held (as we all do) that some men sometimes entertain opinions which they cannot know to be true. And he wished to point out what characteristics are possessed by those of our opinions which we *can* know to be true, with a view of persuading us that any opinion which does *not* possess any of these characteristics is of a kind which we *cannot* know to be so. He thus tries to lay down certain rules to the effect that the *only* propositions which we can, any of us, know to be true are of certain definite kinds. It is in this sense, I think, that he tries to define the limits of human understanding.

With this object he, first of all, divides all the propositions, which we can even so much as conceive, into two classes. They are all, he says, either propositions about "relations of ideas" or else about "matters of fact." By propositions about "relations of ideas" he means such propositions as that twice two are four, or that black differs from white; and it is, I think, easy enough to see, though by no means easy to define, what kind of propositions it is that he means to include in this division. They are, he says, the only kind of propositions with regard to which we can have "intuitive" or "demonstrative" certainty. But the vast majority of the propositions in which we believe and which interest us most, belong to the other division: they are propositions about "matters of fact." And these again he divides into two classes. So far as his words go, this latter division is between "matters of fact, beyond the present testimony of our senses, or the records of our memory," on the one hand, and matters of fact for which we *have* the evidence of our memory or senses, on the other. But it is, I think, quite plain that these words do not represent quite accurately the division which he really means to make. He plainly intends to reckon along with facts for which we have the evidence of our *senses*

* Reprinted by kind permission of the author and the publishers of his *Philosophical Studies*, Kegan Paul, Trench, Trubner & Co. Ltd., London, 1922.

all facts for which we have the evidence of *direct observation*—such facts, for instance, as those which I observe when I observe that I am angry or afraid, and which cannot be strictly said to be apprehended by my *senses*. The division, then, which he really intends to make is (to put it quite strictly) into the two classes—(1) propositions which assert some matter of fact which I am (in the strictest sense) *observing* at the moment, or which I have so observed in the past and now remember; and (2) propositions which assert any matter of fact which I am not now observing and never have observed, or, if I have, have quite forgotten.

We have, then, the three classes—(1) propositions which assert "relations of ideas"; (2) propositions which assert "matters of fact" for which we have the evidence of direct observation or personal memory; (3) propositions which assert "matters of fact" for which we have *not* this evidence. And as regards propositions of the first two classes, Hume does not seem to doubt our capacity for knowledge. He does not doubt that we can know *some* (though, of course, not *all*) propositions about "relations of ideas" to be true; he never doubts, for instance, that we can know that twice two are four. And he generally assumes also that each of us can know the truth of *all* propositions which merely assert some matter of fact which we ourselves are, in the strictest sense, directly observing, or which we have so observed and now remember. He does, indeed, in one place, suggest a doubt whether our memory is *ever* to be implicitly trusted, but he generally assumes that it *always* can. It is with regard to propositions of the third class that he is chiefly anxious to determine which of them (if any) we can know to be true and which not. In what cases can any man know any matter of fact which he himself has not directly observed? It is Hume's views on this question which form, I think, the main interest of his philosophy.

He proposes, first of all, by way of answer to it, a rule which may, I think, be expressed as follows: No man, he says, can ever know any matter of fact, which he has not himself observed, unless he can know that it is connected by "the relation of cause and effect," with some fact which he *has* observed. And no man can ever know that any two facts are connected by this relation, except by the help of his own past *experience*. In other words, if I am to know any fact, A, which I have not myself observed, my past experience must give me some foundation for the belief that A is causally connected with some fact, B, which I have observed. And the only kind of past experience which can give me any foundation for such a belief is, Hume seems to say, as follows: I must, he says, have found *facts like* A "constantly conjoined" in the past with *facts like* B. This is what he *says;* but we must not, I think, press his words too strictly. I may, for instance, know that A is *probably* a fact, even where the conjunction of facts like it with facts like B has not been quite constant. Or instead of observing facts like A conjoined with facts like B, I may have

observed a whole series of conjunctions—for instance, between A and C,
C and D, D and E, and E and B; and such a series, however long, will do
quite as well to establish a causal connection between A and B, as if I
had directly observed conjunctions between A and B themselves. Such
modifications as this, Hume would, I think, certainly allow. But, allowing for them, his principle is, I think, quite clear. I can, he holds, never
know any fact whatever, which I have not myself observed, unless I have
observed similar facts in the past and have observed that they were "conjoined" (directly or indirectly) with facts similar to some fact which I
do now observe or remember. In this sense, he holds, *all* our knowledge
of facts, beyond the reach of our own observation, is founded on *experience*.

This is Hume's primary principle. But what consequences does he think
will follow from it, as to the kind of facts, beyond our own observation,
which we can know? We may, I think, distinguish three entirely different
views as to its consequences, which he suggests in different parts of his
work.

In the first place, where he is specially engaged in explaining this primary
principle, he certainly seems to suppose that all propositions of the kind,
which we assume most universally in everyday life, may be founded on
experience in the sense required. He supposes that we have this foundation
in experience for such beliefs as that "a stone will fall, or fire burn"; that
Julius Cæsar was murdered; that the sun will rise to-morrow; that all men
are mortal. He speaks as if experience did not merely render such beliefs
probable, but actually *proved* them to be true. The "arguments from experience" in their favour are, he says, such as "leave no room for doubt
or opposition." The only kinds of belief, which he definitely mentions as
not founded on experience, are "popular superstitions" on the one hand,
and certain religious and philosophical beliefs, on the other. He seems
to suppose that a few (a very few) religious beliefs may, perhaps, be
founded on experience. But as regards most of the specific doctrines of
Christianity, for example, he seems to be clear that they are not so founded.
The belief in miracles is not founded on experience; nor is the philosophical belief that every event is caused by the direct volition of the
Deity. In short, it would seem, that in this doctrine that our knowledge of
unobserved facts is confined to such as are "founded on experience," he
means to draw the line very much where it is drawn by the familiar doctrine which is called "Agnosticism." We can know such facts as are asserted in books on "history, geography or astronomy," or on "politics,
physics and chemistry," because such assertions may be "founded on experience"; but we cannot know the greater part of the facts asserted in
books "of divinity or school metaphysics," because such assertions have
no foundation in experience.

This, I think, was clearly one of Hume's views. He meant to fix the limits of our knowledge at a point which would *exclude* most religious propositions and a great many philosophical ones, as incapable of being known; but which would *include* all the other kinds of propositions, which are most universally accepted by common-sense, as capable of being known. And he thought that, so far as matters of fact beyond the reach of our personal observation are concerned, this point coincided with that at which the possibility of "foundation on experience" ceases.

But, if we turn to another part of his work, we find a very different view suggested. In a quite distinct section of both his books, he investigates the beliefs which we entertain concerning the existence of "external objects." And he distinguishes two different kinds of belief which may be held on this subject. "Almost all mankind, and philosophers themselves, for the greatest part of their lives," believe, he says, that "the very things they feel and see" *are* external objects, in the sense that they continue to exist, even when we cease to feel or see them. Philosophers, on the other hand, have been led to reject this opinion and to suppose (when they reflect) that what we actually perceive by the senses never exists except when we perceive it, but that there are other external objects, which do exist independently of us, and which *cause* us to perceive what we do perceive. Hume investigates both of these opinions, at great length in the *Treatise*, and much more briefly in the *Enquiry*, and comes to the conclusion, in both books, that neither of them can be "founded on experience," in the sense he has defined. As regards the first of them, the vulgar opinion, he does seem to admit in the *Treatise* that it is, in a sense, founded on experience; but not, he insists, in the sense defined. And he seems also to think that, apart from this fact, there are conclusive reasons for holding that the opinion cannot be true. And as regards the philosophical opinion, he says that any belief in external objects, which we never perceive but which cause our perceptions, cannot possibly be founded on experience, for the simple reason that if it were, we should need to have directly observed some of these objects and their "conjunction" with what we do perceive, which *ex hypothesi*, we cannot have done, since we never do directly observe any external object.

Hume, therefore, concludes, in this part of his work, that we cannot know of the existence of any "external object" whatever. And though in all that he says upon this subject, he is plainly thinking only of *material* objects, the principles by which he tries to prove that we cannot know these must, I think, prove equally well that we cannot know any "external object" whatever—not even the existence of any other human mind. His argument is: We cannot directly observe any object whatever, except such as exist only when we observe them; we cannot, therefore, observe any "constant conjunctions" except between objects of this kind: and hence we can have no foundation in experience for any proposition which asserts the existence of any other kind of object, and cannot, therefore, know any such proposition to be true. And this argument must plainly apply to all the feelings, thoughts and perceptions of other men just as much as to material objects. I can never know that any perception of mine, or anything which I do observe, must have been caused by any other man, because I can never directly observe a "constant conjunction" between any other man's thoughts or feelings or intentions and anything which I directly observe: I cannot, therefore, know that any other man ever had any thoughts or feelings—or, in short, that any man beside myself ever existed. The view, therefore, which Hume suggests in this part of his work, flatly contradicts the view which he at first seemed to hold. He now says we *cannot* know that a stone will fall, that fire will burn, or the sun will rise to-morrow. All that I can possibly know, according to his present principles, is that *I shall see* a stone fall, shall feel the fire burn, shall see the sun rise to-morrow. I cannot even know that any other men will see these things; for I cannot know that any other men exist. For the same reason, I cannot know that Julius Cæsar was murdered, or that all men are mortal. For these are propositions asserting "external" facts—facts which don't exist only at the moment when I observe them; and, according to his present doctrine, I cannot possibly know any such proposition to be true. No man, in short, can know any proposition about "matters of fact" to be true, except such as merely assert something about *his own* states of mind, past, present or future—about these or about what *he himself* has directly observed, is observing, or will observe.

Here, therefore, we have a very different view suggested, as to the limits of human knowledge. And even this is not all. There is yet a third view, inconsistent with both of these, which Hume suggests in some parts of his work.

So far as we have yet seen, he has not in any way contradicted his original supposition that we can know *some* matters of fact, which we have never ourselves observed. In the second theory, which I have just stated, he does not call in question the view that I can know all such matters of fact as I know to be causally connected with facts which I have observed, nor the view that I can know some facts to be thus causally connected. All that he has done is to question whether I can know any *external* fact to be causally connected with anything which I observe; he would still allow that I may be able to know that future states of my own, or past states, which I have forgotten, are causally connected with those which I now observe or remember; and that I may know therefore, in some cases, what I shall experience in the future, or have experienced in the past but have now forgotten. But in some parts of his work he does seem to question whether any man can know even as much as this: he seems to question whether we can ever know any fact whatever to be causally connected with any other fact. For, after laying it down, as we saw above, that we cannot know any fact, A, to be causally connected with another, B, unless we have experienced in the past a constant conjunction between facts like A and facts like B, he goes on to ask what foundation we have for the conclusion that A and B *are* causally connected, even when we *have* in the past experienced a constant conjunction between them. He points out that from the fact that A has been constantly conjoined with B in the past, it does not follow that it ever will be so again. It does not follow, therefore, that the two really are causally connected in the sense that, when the one occurs, the other *always* will occur also. And he concludes, for this and other reasons, that *no argument* can assure us that, because they have been constantly conjoined in the past, therefore they really are causally connected. What, then, he asks, is the foundation for such an inference? *Custom,* he concludes, is the only foundation. It is nothing but custom which induces us to believe that, because two facts have been constantly conjoined on many occasions, therefore they will be so on *all* occasions. We have, therefore, no better foundation than custom for any conclusion whatever as to facts which we have not observed. And can we be said really to *know* any fact, for which we have no better foundation than this? Hume himself, it must be observed, never says that we can't. But he has been constantly interpreted as if the conclusion that we can't really know any one fact to be causally connected with any other, did follow from this doctrine of his. And there is, I think, certainly much excuse for this interpretation in the tone in which he speaks. He does seem to suggest that a belief which is *merely* founded on custom, can scarcely be one which we *know* to be true. And, indeed, he owns himself that, when he considers that this is our only foundation for any such belief, he is sometimes tempted to doubt whether we do know any fact whatever, except those which we directly observe. He does, therefore, at least suggest the view that every man's knowledge is entirely confined to those facts, which he is directly observing at the moment, or which he has observed in the past, and now remembers.

We see, then, that Hume suggests, at least, three entirely different views as to the consequences of his original doctrine. His original doctrine was that, as regards matters of fact beyond the reach of our own actual observation, the knowledge of each of us is strictly limited to those for which we have a basis in our own experience. And his first view as to the consequences of this doctrine was that it does show us to be incapable of knowing a good many religious and philosophical propositions, which many men have claimed that they knew; but that it by no means denies our capacity of knowing the vast majority of facts beyond our own observation, which we all commonly suppose that we know. His second view, on the other hand, is that it cuts off at once all possibility of our knowing the vast majority of these facts; since he implies that we cannot have any basis in experience for asserting any *external* fact whatever—any fact, that is, except facts relating to our own actual past and future observations.

And his third view is more sceptical still, since it suggests that we cannot really know any fact whatever, beyond the reach of our present observation or memory, even where we *have* a basis in experience for such a fact: it suggests that experience cannot ever let us *know* that any two things are causally connected, and therefore that it cannot give us *knowledge* of any fact based on this relation.

What are we to think of these three views, and of the original doctrine from which Hume seems to infer them?

As regards the last two views, it may perhaps be thought that they are too absurd to deserve any serious consideration. It is, in fact, absurd to suggest that I do not know any external facts whatever; that I do not know, for instance, even that there are any men beside myself. And Hume himself, it might seem, does not seriously expect or wish us to accept these views. He points out, with regard to all such excessively sceptical opinions that we cannot continue to believe them for long together—that, at least, we cannot, for long together, avoid believing things flatly inconsistent with them. The philosopher may believe, when he is philosophising, that no man knows of the existence of any other man or of any material object; but at other times he will inevitably believe, as we all do, that he does know of the existence of this man and of that, and even of this and that material object. There can, therefore, be no question of making all our beliefs consistent with such views as this, of never believing anything that is inconsistent with them. And it may, therefore, seem useless to discuss them. But in fact, it by no means follows that, because we are not able to adhere consistently to a given view, therefore that view is false; nor does it follow that we may not sincerely believe it, whenever we are philosophising, even though the moment we cease to philosophise, or even before, we may be forced to contradict it. And philosophers do, in fact, sincerely believe such things as this—things which flatly contradict the vast majority of the things which they believe at other times. Even Hume, I think, does sincerely wish to persuade us that we cannot know of the existence of external material objects—that this is a philosophic truth, which we ought, if we can, so long as we are philosophising, to believe. Many people, I think, are certainly tempted, in their philosophic moments, to believe such things; and, since this is so, it is, I think, worth while to consider seriously what arguments can be brought against such views. It is worth while to consider whether they are views which we ought to hold as philosophical opinions, even if it be quite certain that we shall never be able to make the views which we entertain at other times consistent with them. And it is the more worth while, because the question how we can prove or disprove such extreme views as these, has a bearing on the question how we can, in any case whatever, prove or disprove that we do really *know*, what we suppose ourselves to know.

What arguments, then, are there for or against the extreme view that

no man can know any external fact whatever; and the still more extreme
view that no man can know any matter of fact whatever, except those
which he is directly observing at the moment, or has observed in the past
and now remembers?

It may be pointed out, in the first place, that, if these views are true,
then at least no man can possibly know them to be so. What these views
assert is that I cannot know any external fact whatever. It follows, therefore, that I cannot know that there are any other men, beside myself, and
that they are like me in this respect. Any philosopher who asserts positively
that other men, equally with himself, are incapable of knowing any external facts, is, in that very assertion, contradicting himself, since he implies that he *does* know a great many facts about the knowledge of other
men. No one, therefore, can be entitled to assert positively that human
knowledge is limited in this way, since, in asserting it positively, he is
implying that his own knowledge is not so limited. It cannot be proper,
even in our philosophic moments, to take up such an attitude as this.

No one, therefore, can know positively that men, in general, are incapable of knowing external facts. But still, although we cannot *know* it,
it remains possible that the view should be a true one. Nay, more, it remains possible that a man should know that *he himself* is incapable of
knowing any external facts, and that, *if* there are any other men whose
faculties are only similar to his own, they also must be incapable of knowing any. The argument just used obviously does not apply against such
a position as this. It only applies against the position that men in general
positively are incapable of knowing external facts: it does not apply against
the position that the philosopher himself is incapable of knowing any,
or against the position that there are *possibly* other men in the same case,
and that, if their faculties are similar to the philosopher's, they certainly
would be in it. I do not contradict myself by maintaining positively that *I*
know no external facts, though I do contradict myself if I maintain
that I am only one among other men, and that no man knows any external facts. So far, then, as Hume merely maintains that *he* is incapable
of knowing any external facts, and that there *may* be other men like him
in this respect, the argument just used is not valid against his position.
Can any conclusive arguments be found against it?

It seems to me that such a position must, in a certain sense, be quite
incapable of disproof. So much must be granted to any sceptic who feels
inclined to hold it. Any valid argument which can be brought against it
must be of the nature of a *petitio principii*: it must beg the question at
issue. How is the sceptic to prove to himself that he does know any external facts? He can only do it by bringing forward some instance of an
external fact, which he does know; and, in assuming that he does know
this one, he is, of course, begging the question. It is therefore quite impossible for any one to *prove*, in one strict sense of the term, that he does

know any external facts. I can only prove that I do, by assuming that in some particular instance, I actually do know one. That is to say, the so-called proof must assume the very thing which it pretends to prove. The only proof that we do know external facts lies in the simple fact that we do know them. And the sceptic can, with perfect internal consistency, deny that he does know any. But it can, I think, be shown that he has no reason for denying it. And in particular it may, I think, be easily seen that the arguments which Hume uses in favour of this position have no conclusive force.

To begin with, his arguments, in both cases, depend upon the two original assumptions, (1) that we cannot know any fact, which we have not observed, unless we know it to be causally connected with some fact which we have observed, and (2) that we have no reason for assuming any causal connection, except where we have experienced some instances of conjunction between the two facts connected. And both of these assumptions may, of course, be denied. It is just as easy to deny them, as to deny that I do know any external facts. And, if these two assumptions did really lead to the conclusion that I cannot know any, it would, I think, be proper to deny them: we might fairly regard the fact that they led to this absurd conclusion as disproving them. But, in fact, I think it may be easily seen that they do not lead to it.

Let us consider, first of all, Hume's most sceptical argument (the argument which he merely suggests). This argument suggests that, since our only reason for supposing two facts to be causally connected is that we have found them constantly conjoined in the past, and since it does not follow from the fact that they have been conjoined ever so many times, that they *always* will be so, therefore we cannot *know* that they always will be so, and hence cannot know that they are causally connected. But obviously the conclusion does not follow. We must, I think, grant the premiss that, from the fact that two things have been conjoined, no matter how often, it does not strictly *follow* that they *always* are conjoined. But it by no means follows from this that we may not *know* that, as a matter of fact, when two things are conjoined sufficiently often, they are also *always* conjoined. We may quite well *know* many things which do not logically follow from anything else which we know. And so, in this case, we may *know* that two things are causally connected, although this does not logically follow from our past experience, nor yet from anything else that we know. And, as for the contention that our belief in causal connections is merely based on *custom*, we may, indeed, admit that custom would not be a sufficient *reason* for concluding the belief to be true. But the mere fact (if it be a fact) that the belief is only caused by custom, is also no sufficient reason for concluding that we can *not* know it to be true. Custom *may* produce beliefs, which we do know to be true, even though it be admitted that it does not *necessarily* produce them.

And as for Hume's argument to prove that we can never know any *external* object to be causally connected with anything which we actually observe, it is, I think, obviously fallacious. In order to prove this, he has, as he recognises, to disprove both of two theories. He has, first of all, to disprove what he calls the vulgar theory—the theory that we can know the very things which we see or feel to be external objects; that is to say, can know that these very things exist at times when we do not observe them. And even here, I think, his arguments are obviously inconclusive. But we need not stay to consider them, because, in order to prove that we cannot know any external objects, he has also to disprove what he calls the philosophic theory—the theory that we can know things which we do observe, to be caused by external objects which we never observe. If, therefore, his attempt to disprove this theory fails, his proof that we cannot know any external objects also fails; and I think it is easy to see that his disproof does fail. It amounts merely to this: That we cannot, *ex hypothesi*, ever observe these supposed external objects, and therefore cannot observe them to be constantly conjoined with any objects which we do observe. But what follows from this? His own theory about the knowledge of causal connection is not that in order to know A to be the cause of B, we must have observed A *itself* to be conjoined with B; but only that we must have observed objects *like* A to be constantly conjoined with objects *like* B. And what is to prevent an external object from being *like* some object which we have formerly observed? Suppose I have frequently observed a fact *like* A to be conjoined with a fact *like* B: and suppose I now observe B, on an occasion when I do not observe anything like A. There is no reason, on Hume's principles, why I should not conclude that A does exist on this occasion, even though I do not observe it; and that it is, therefore, an external object. It will, of course, differ from any object which I have ever observed, in respect of the simple fact that it is *not* observed by me, whereas they were. There is, therefore, this one respect in which it must be *unlike* anything which I have ever observed. But Hume has never said anything to show that unlikeness in this single respect is sufficient to invalidate the inference. It may quite well be like objects which I have observed in all other respects; and this degree of likeness may, according to his principles, be quite sufficient to justify us in concluding its existence. In short, when Hume argues that we cannot possibly learn by experience of the existence of any external objects, he is, I think, plainly committing the fallacy of supposing that, because we cannot, *ex hypothesi*, have ever observed any object which actually is "external," therefore we can never have observed any object *like* an external one. But plainly we may have observed objects like them in all respects except the single one that these have been observed whereas the others have not. And even a less degree of likeness than this would, according to his principles, be quite sufficient to justify an inference of causal connection.

Hume does not, therefore, bring forward any arguments at all sufficient to prove either that he cannot know any one object to be causally connected with any other or that he cannot know any external fact. And, indeed, I think it is plain that no conclusive argument could possibly be advanced in favour of these positions. It would always be at least as easy to deny the argument as to deny that we do know external facts. We may, therefore, each one of us, safely conclude that we do know external facts; and, if we do, then there is no reason why we should not also know that other men do the same. There is no reason why we should not, in this respect, make our philosophical opinions agree with what we necessarily believe at other times. There is no reason why I should not confidently assert that I do really *know* some external facts, although I cannot prove the assertion except by simply assuming that I do. I am, in fact, as certain of this as of anything; and as reasonably certain of it. But just as I am certain that I do know *some* external facts, so I am also certain that there are others which I do not know. And the question remains: Does the line between the two fall, where Hume says it falls? Is it true that the only external facts I know are facts for which I have a basis in my own experience? And that I cannot know any facts whatever, beyond the reach of my own observation and memory, except those for which I have such a basis?

This, it seems to me, is the most serious question which Hume raises. And it should be observed that his own attitude towards it is very different from his attitude towards the sceptical views which we have just been considering. These sceptical views he did not expect or wish us to accept, except in philosophic moments. He declares that we cannot, in ordinary life, avoid believing things which are inconsistent with them; and, in so declaring, he, of course, implies incidentally that they are false: since he implies that he himself has a great deal of knowledge as to what we can and cannot believe in ordinary life. But, as regards the view that our knowledge of matters of fact beyond our own observation is entirely confined to such as are founded on experience, he never suggests that it is impossible that all our beliefs should be consistent with this view, and he does seem to think it eminently desirable that they should be. He declares that any assertion with regard to such matters, which is not founded on experience, can be nothing but "sophistry and illusion"; and that all books which are composed of such assertions should be "committed to the flames." He seems, therefore, to think that here we really have a test by which we may determine what we should or should not believe, on all occasions: any view on such matters, for which we have no foundation in experience, is a view which we cannot know to be even probably true, and which we should *never* accept, if we can help it. Is there any justification for this strong view?

It is, of course, abstractly possible that we do really know, *without* the help of experience, some matters of fact, which we never have observed. Just as we know matters of fact, which we *have* observed, without the need of any further evidence, and just as we know, for instance, that $2 + 2 = 4$, without the need of any proof, it is possible that we may know, directly and immediately, without the need of any basis in experience, some facts which we never have observed. This is certainly possible, in the same sense in which it is possible that I do not really know any external facts: no conclusive disproof can be brought against either position. We must make assumptions as to what facts we do know and do not know, before we can proceed to discuss whether or not all of the former are based on experience; and none of these assumptions can, in the last resort, be conclusively proved. We may offer one of them in proof of another; but it will always be possible to dispute the one which we offer in proof. But there are, in fact, certain kinds of things which we universally assume that we do know or do not know, just as we assume that we do know some external facts; and if among all the things which we know as certainly as this, there should turn out to be none for which we have no basis in experience, Hume's view would, I think, be as fully proved as it is capable of being. The question is: Can it be proved in this sense? Among all the facts beyond our own observation, which we know most certainly, are there any which are certainly not based upon experience? For my part, I confess, I cannot feel certain what is the right answer to this question: I cannot tell whether Hume was right or wrong. But if he was wrong— if there are any matters of fact, beyond our own observation, which we know for certain, and which yet we know directly and immediately, without any basis in experience, we are, I think, faced with an eminently interesting problem. For it is, I think, as certain as anything can be that there are *some* kinds of facts with regard to which Hume was right—that there are *some* kinds of facts which we cannot know without the evidence of experience. I could not know, for instance, without some such evidence, such a fact as that Julius Cæsar was murdered. For such a fact I must, in the first instance, have the evidence of other persons; and if I am to know that their evidence is trustworthy, I must have some ground in experience for supposing it to be so. There are, therefore, some kinds of facts which we cannot know without the evidence of experience and observation. And if it is to be maintained that there are others, which we can know without any such evidence, it ought to be pointed out exactly what kind of facts these are, and in what respects they differ from those which we cannot know without the help of experience. Hume gives us a very clear division of the kinds of propositions which we can know to be true. There are, first of all, some propositions which assert "relations of ideas";

there are, secondly, propositions which assert "matters of fact" which we ourselves are actually observing, or have observed and now remember; and there are, thirdly, propositions which assert "matters of fact" which we have never actually observed, but for believing in which we have some foundation in our past observations. And it is, I think, certain that some propositions, which we know as certainly as we know anything, do belong to each of these three classes. I know, for instance, that twice two are four; I know by direct observation that I am now seeing these words, that I am writing, and by memory that this afternoon I saw St. Paul's; and I know also that Julius Cæsar was murdered, and I have some foundation in experience for this belief, though I did not myself witness the murder. Do any of those propositions, which we know as certainly as we know these and their like, *not* belong to either of these three classes? Must we add a fourth class consisting of propositions which resemble the two last, in respect of the fact that they do assert "matters of fact," but which differ from them, in that we know them neither by direct observation nor by memory, nor yet as a result of previous observations? There may, perhaps, be such a fourth class; but, if there is, it is, I think, eminently desirable that it should be pointed out exactly what propositions they are which we do know in this way; and this, so far as I know, has never yet been done, at all clearly, by any philosopher.

The Refutation of Realism *

W. T. STACE

More than thirty years have now elapsed since Prof. Moore published in *Mind* his famous article, "The Refutation of Idealism". Therewith the curtain rose upon the episode of contemporary British realism. After three decades perhaps the time is now ripe for the inauguration of another episode. And it is but fitting that "The Refutation of Realism" should appear on the same stage as its famous predecessor.

I shall not gird at realism because its exponents disagree among themselves as to what precisely their philosophy teaches. But disagreements certainly exist, and they make it difficult for a would-be refuter to know precisely what is the proposition which he ought to refute. It is far from certain that all idealists would agree that the idealism which Prof. Moore purported to refute represented adequately, or even inadequately, their views. And it may be that a similar criticism will be urged by realists against what I shall here have to say. But I must take my courage in my hands. Realists, it seems to me, agree in asserting that "some entities sometimes exist without being experienced by any finite mind". This, at any rate, is the proposition which I shall undertake to refute.

I insert the word "finite" in this formula because if I wrote "some entities exist without being experienced by any mind", it might be objected that the proposition so framed would imply that some entities exist of which God is ignorant, if there is such a being as God, and that it is not certain that all realists would wish to assert this. I think that we can very well leave God out of the discussion. In front of me is a piece of paper. I assume that the realist believes that this paper will continue to exist when it is put away in my desk for the night, and when no finite mind is experiencing it. He *may* also believe that it will continue to exist even if God is not experiencing it. But he must *at least* assert that it will exist when no finite mind is experiencing it. That, I think, is essential to his position. And therefore to refute that proposition will be to refute realism. In what follows, therefore, when I speak of minds I must be understood as referring to finite minds.

Possibly I shall be told that although realists probably do as a matter of fact believe that some entities exist unexperienced, yet this is not the

* Reprinted by kind permission of the author and the editors from *Mind*, 53, 1934.

essence of realism. Its essence, it may be said, is the belief that the relation between knowledge and its object is such that the knowledge makes no difference to the object, so that the object *might* exist without being known, whether as a matter of fact it does so exist or not.

But it would seem that there could be no point in asserting that entities *might* exist unexperienced, unless as a matter of fact they at least sometimes do so exist. To prove that the universe *might* have the property X, if as a matter of fact the universe has no such property, would seem to be a useless proceeding which no philosophy surely would take as its central contribution to truth. And I think that the only reason why realists are anxious to show that objects are such, and that the relation between knowledge and object is such, that objects might exist unexperienced, is that they think that this will lead on to the belief that objects actually do exist unexperienced. They have been anxious to prove that the existence of objects is not dependent on being experienced by minds because they wished to draw the conclusion that objects exist unexperienced. Hence I think that I am correct in saying that the essential proposition of realism, which has to be refuted, is that "some entities sometimes exist without being experienced by any finite mind".

Now, lest I should be misunderstood, I will state clearly at the outset that I cannot prove that no entities exist without being experienced by minds. For all I know completely unexperienced entities may exist, but what I shall assert is that we have not the slightest reason for believing that they do exist. And from this it will follow that the realistic position that they do exist is perfectly groundless and gratuitous, and one which ought not to be believed. It will be in exactly the same position as the proposition "there is a unicorn on the planet Mars". I cannot prove that there is no unicorn on Mars. But since there is not the slightest reason to suppose that there is one, it is a proposition which ought not to be believed.

And still further to clarify the issue, I will say that I shall not be discussing in this paper whether sense-objects are "mental". My personal opinion is that this question is a pointless one, but that if I am forced to answer it with a "yes" or "no", I should do so by saying that they are not mental; just as, if I were forced to answer the pointless question whether the mind is an elephant, I should have to answer that it is not an elephant. I will, in fact, assume for the purposes of this paper that sense-objects, whether they be colour patches or other sense-data, or objects, are not mental. My position will then be as follows: There is absolutely no reason for asserting that these non-mental, or physical, entities ever exist except when they are being experienced, and the proposition that they do so exist is utterly groundless and gratuitous, and one which ought not to be believed.

The refutation of realism will therefore be sufficiently accomplished if it can be shown that we do *not* know that any single entity exists unexperienced. And that is what I shall in this paper endeavour to show. I shall inquire how we could possibly know that unexperienced entities exist, even if, as a matter of fact, they do exist. And I shall show that there is no possible way in which we could know this, and that therefore we do *not* know it, and have no reason to believe it.

For the sake of clearness, let us take once again the concrete example of the piece of paper. I am at this moment experiencing it, and at this moment it exists, but how can I know that it existed last night in my desk when, so far as I know, no mind was experiencing it? How can I know that it will continue to exist to-night when there is no one in the room? The knowledge of these alleged facts is what the realists assert that they possess. And the question is, Whence could such knowledge have been obtained, and how can it be justified? What I assert is that it is absolutely impossible to have any such knowledge.

There are only two ways in which it could be asserted that the existence of any sense-object can be established. One is by sense-perception, the other by inference from sense-perception. I know of the existence of this paper *now* because I see it. I am supposed to know of the existence of the other side of the moon, which no one has ever seen, by inference from various actual astronomical observations, that is, by inference from things actually experienced. There are no other ways of proving the existence of a sense-object. Is either of them possible in the present case?

1. *Sense-perception.* I obviously cannot know by perception the existence of the paper when no one is experiencing it. For that would be self-contradictory. It would amount to asserting that I can experience the unexperienced.

2. *Inference.* Nor is it possible to prove by inference the existence of the paper when no mind is experiencing it. For how can I possibly pass by inference from the particular fact of the existence of the paper now, when I am experiencing it, to the quite different particular fact of the existence of the paper yesterday or to-morrow, when neither I nor any other mind is experiencing it? Strictly speaking, the onus of proving that such an inference is impossible is not on me. The onus of proving that it is possible is upon anyone who asserts it, and I am entitled to sit back and wait until someone comes forward with such an alleged proof. Many realists who know their business admit that no valid inference from an experienced to an unexperienced existence is possible. Thus Mr. Russell says, "Belief in the existence of things outside my own biography must, from the standpoint of theoretical logic, be regarded as a prejudice, not as a well-grounded theory." [1]

I might therefore adopt the strategy of masterly inaction. But I prefer

[1] *Analysis of Mind*, p. 133.

to carry the war into the enemy's camp. I propose to *prove* that no proof of the existence of unexperienced objects is possible.

It is clear in the first place that any supposed reasoning could not be inductive. Inductive reasoning proceeds always upon the basis that what has been found in certain observed cases to be true will also be true in unobserved cases. But there is no single case in which it has been observed to be true that an experienced object continues to exist when it is not being experienced; for, by hypothesis, its existence when it is not being experienced cannot be observed. Induction is generalisation from observed facts, but there is not a single case of an unexperienced existence having been observed on which could be based the generalisation that entities continue to exist when no one is experiencing them. And there is likewise not a single known instance of the existence of an unexperienced entity which could lead me to have even the slightest reason for supposing that this paper ever did exist, or will exist, when no one is experiencing it.

Since inductive reasoning is ruled out, the required inference, if there is to be an inference, must be of a formal nature. But deductive inference of all kinds depends upon the principle of consistency. If $P \supset Q$, then we can only prove Q, *if* P is admitted. From $P \supset Q$, therefore, all that can be deduced is that P and not-Q are inconsistent, and that we cannot hold both P and not-Q together, though we may hold either of them separately.

Hence, if it is alleged that a deductive inference can be drawn from the existence of the paper now, when I am experiencing it, to its existence when no one is experiencing it, this can only mean that to assert together the two propositions, (1) that it exists now, and (2) that it does not exist when no one is experiencing it, is an internally inconsistent position. But there is absolutely no inconsistency between these two propositions. If I believe that nothing whatever exists or ever did or will exist, except my own personal sense-data, this may be a view of the universe which no one would ever hold, but there is absolutely nothing internally inconsistent in it. Therefore, no deductive inference can prove the existence of an unexperienced entity. Therefore, by no reasoning at all, inductive or deductive, can the existence of such an entity be proved.

Nevertheless, arguments have been put forward from time to time by realists which are apparently intended to prove this conclusion. I will deal shortly with those with which I am acquainted. I am not bound to do this, since I have already proved that no proof of the realists' conclusion is possible. And for the same reason, if there are any arguments of this kind with which I am not acquainted, I am under no obligation to disprove them. But it will be better to meet at least the most well-known arguments.

a. It was Mr. Perry, I believe, who invented the phrase "egocentric predicament". The egocentric predicament was supposed to indicate where

lay a fallacy committed by idealists. It consisted in arguing from the fact
that it is impossible to discover anything which is not known to the
conclusion that all things are known. That any competent idealist ever
did use such an argument may well be doubted, but I will waive that point.
Mr. Perry's comment was that the egocentric predicament, as employed
by idealists, appeared to imply that from our ignorance of unexperienced
entities we could conclude to their nonexistence, and that to do so is a
fallacy.

No doubt such a procedure would be a fallacy. But though Mr. Perry's
argument may refute a supposed idealistic argument, *it does not prove anything whatever in favour of realism.* It would be a fallacy to argue that,
because we have never observed a unicorn on Mars, therefore there is no
unicorn there; but by pointing out this fallacy, one does not prove the
existence of a unicorn there. And by pointing out that our ignorance of
the existence of unexperienced entities does not prove their nonexistence,
one does nothing whatever towards proving that unexperienced entities
do exist. As regards the unicorn on Mars, the correct position, as far as
logic is concerned, is obviously that if anyone asserts that there is a unicorn there, the onus is on him to prove it; and that until he does prove it,
we ought not to believe it to be true. As regards the unexperienced entities,
the correct position, as far as logic is concerned, is that if realists assert
their existence, the onus is on them to prove it; and that until they do
prove it, we ought not to believe that they exist. Mr. Perry's argument,
therefore, proves nothing whatever in favour of realism.

Possibly all this is admitted and understood by realists. But there seems,
nevertheless, to have been a tendency to think that the overthrow of the
supposed idealistic argument was a very important matter in forwarding
the interests of realism. To point out, therefore, that it actually accomplishes nothing seems desirable.

b. Mr. Lovejoy, in his recent book, *The Revolt Against Dualism,* argues
that we can infer, or at least render probable, the existence of things during interperceptual intervals by means of the law of causation. He writes,
"The same uniform causal sequences of natural events which may be observed within experience appear to go on in the same manner when not
experienced. You build a fire in your grate of a certain quantity of coal,
of a certain chemical composition. Whenever you remain in the room
there occurs a typical succession of sensible phenomena according to an
approximately regular schedule of clock-time; in, say, half an hour the
coal is half consumed; at the end of the hour the grate contains only ashes.
If you build a fire of the same quantity of the same material under the
same conditions, leave the room, and return after any given time has
elapsed, you get approximately the same sense-experiences as you would
have had at the corresponding moment if you had remained in the room.
You infer, therefore, that the fire has been burning as usual during your

absence, and that being perceived is not a condition necessary for the occurrence of the process." [2]

This argument is simply a *petitio principii*. It assumes that we must believe that the law of causality continues to operate in the universe when
no one is observing it. But the law of causality is, it is clear, one aspect of
the universe, the unobserved existence of which is the very thing to be
proved.

Why must we believe that causation continues to operate during interperceptual intervals? Obviously, the case as regards unexperienced
processes and laws is in exactly the same position as the case regarding
unexperienced *things*. Just as we cannot perceive unexperienced things,
so we cannot perceive unexperienced processes and laws. Just as we cannot
infer from anything which we experience the existence of unexperienced things, so we cannot infer from anything we experience the existence of unexperienced processes and laws. There is absolutely no evidence (sense-experience) to show that the fire went on burning during
your absence, nor is any inference to that alleged fact possible. Any supposed inference will obviously be based upon our belief that the law of
causation operates continuously through time whether observed or unobserved. But this is one of the very things which has to be proved. Nor
is there the slightest logical inconsistency in believing that, when you first
observe the phenomena, unburnt coal existed, that there followed an interval in which nothing existed, not even a law, and that at the end of the
interval ashes began to exist.

No doubt this sounds very absurd and contrary to what we usually
believe, but that is nothing to the point. We usually believe that things go
on existing when no one is aware of them. But if we are enquiring how
this can be *proved*, we must, of course, begin from the position that we
do not know it, and therefore that it might not be true.

c. The distinction between sense-data and our awareness of them, which
was first emphasized, so far as I know, by Prof. Moore, has been made the
basis of an argument in favour of realism. Green, it is said, is not the same
thing as awareness of green. For if we compare a green sense-datum with
a blue sense-datum, we find a common element, namely awareness. The
awareness must be different from the green because awareness also exists
in the case of awareness of blue, and *that* awareness, at any rate, is not
green. Therefore, since green is not the same thing as awareness of green,
green might exist without awareness. Connected with this argument, too,
is the assertion of a special kind of relationship between the awareness
and the green.

Possibly this argument proves that green is not "mental". I do not
know whether it proves this or not, but the point is unimportant, since I
have already admitted that sense-data are not "mental". But whatever the

[2] *The Revolt against Dualism*, p. 268.

argument proves, it certainly does *not* prove that unexperienced entities exist. For suppose that it proves that green has the predicate x (which may be "non-mental" or "independent of mind", or anything else you please), it still can only prove that green has the predicate x during the period when green is related to the awareness in the alleged manner, that is, when some mind is aware of the green. It cannot possibly prove anything about green when no mind is aware of it. Therefore, it cannot prove that green exists when no mind is aware of it.

For the sake of clearness, I will put the same point in another way. Suppose we admit that green and awareness of green are two quite different things, and suppose we admit that the relation between them is r—which may stand for the special relation asserted in the argument. Now it is not in any way inconsistent with these admissions to hold that green begins to exist only when awareness of green begins to exist, and that when awareness of green ceases to exist, green ceases to exist. It may be the case that these two quite different things always co-exist, always accompany each other, and are co-terminous in the sense that they always begin and end simultaneously, and that while they co-exist, they have the relation r. And this will be so *whatever* the relation r may be. And not only is this supposition that they always co-exist not at all absurd or arbitrary. It is on the contrary precisely the conclusion to which such evidence as we possess points. For we never have evidence that green exists except when some mind is aware of green. And it will not be asserted that awareness of green exists when green does not exist.

The argument from the distinction between green and the awareness of it, therefore, does nothing whatever towards proving the realist conclusion that some entities exist unexperienced.

d. It has also been argued that if we identify a green or a square sense-datum with our awareness of it, then, since awareness is admittedly a state of mind, we shall have to admit that there exist green and square states of mind.

This argument is merely intended to support the previous argument that a sense-datum is different from our awareness of it. And as it has already been shown that this proposition, even if admitted, proves nothing in favour of realism, it is not necessary to say anything further about the present argument.

I will, however, add the following. It is not by any means certain, as is here assumed, that awareness is a state of mind, or indeed that such a thing as a *state* of mind exists. For the mind is not static. It is active. And what exists in it are *acts* of mind. Now the *attention* involved in being aware of a sense-datum is certainly an act of mind. But it is certainly arguable that *bare* awareness of a sense-datum (if there is such a thing as *bare* awareness) would be identical with the sense-datum and would not be an act of mind. For such bare awareness would be purely passive. In that case, the conclusion that there must exist green or square states of mind would not follow.

Moreover, even if we admit that there exist green and square states of mind, what then? I can see no reason why we should not admit it, except that (1) it is an unusual and unexplored view, and (2) it seems to smack of materialism, although I do not believe that it does really involve materialism. This shows that the whole argument is not really a logical argument at all. It is merely an attempt to throw dust in our eyes by appealing to the popular prejudices against (1) unfamiliar views, and (2) materialism.

It is not possible in the brief space at my disposal to make plausible the suggestions contained in the last two paragraphs. A full discussion of them would be necessary and this I have endeavoured to give elsewhere. In the present place, therefore, I must rely upon the strict logical position, which is, that this argument, since it is merely intended to support argument (c) above, and since argument (c) has already been refuted, proves nothing in favour of realism.

By the preceding discussion, I claim to have proved (1) that the existence of an unexperienced entity cannot be known by perception, (2) that it cannot be known by reasoning, and (3) that the arguments commonly relied upon by realists to prove it are all fallacies.

I think it is not worth while to discuss the possible suggestion that the arguments in favour of realism, although not proving their conclusion rigorously, render that conclusion probable. For what has been shown is that no valid reasoning of *any* kind can possibly exist in favour of this conclusion. Any conceivable reasoning intended to prove that unexperienced entities exist must, it has been shown, be *totally* fallacious. It cannot, therefore, lead even to a probable conclusion. The position, therefore, is that we have not even the faintest reason for believing in the existence of unexperienced entities.

That this is the correct logical position seems to be dimly perceived by many realists themselves, for it is common among them to assert that our belief in unexperienced existences is a "primitive belief", or is founded upon "instinctive belief", or upon "animal faith". This suggestion is obviously based upon the realisation that we cannot obtain a knowledge of unexperienced existences either from perception or from reasoning. Since this is so, realists are compelled to appeal to instinctive beliefs.

Such a weak position seems hardly to require discussion. A "primitive belief" is merely a belief which we have held for a long time, and may well be false. An "instinctive belief" is in much the same case. An "instinct", so far as I know, is some kind of urge to *action*, not an urge to believe a proposition. And it is therefore questionable whether there are such things as instinctive beliefs in any strict sense, although, of course, no one will deny that we have beliefs the grounds of which are only dimly, or not at all, perceived. Certainly the psychology of such alleged instinctive beliefs has not been adequately investigated. And certainly we have no good ground for supposing that an instinctive belief (if any such exists) might not be false.

And if we have such an instinctive or primitive belief in unexperienced existences, the question must obviously be asked How, When, and Why such a belief arose in the course of our mental evolution. Will it be alleged that the amoeba has this belief? And if not, why and when did it come into existence? Or did it at some arbitrarily determined stage in our evolution descend suddenly upon us out of the blue sky, like the immortal soul itself?

Is it not obvious that to base our belief in unexperienced existences on such grounds is a mere gesture of despair, an admission of the bankruptcy of realism in its attempt to find a rational ground for our beliefs?

Strictly speaking, I have here come to the end of my argument. I have refuted realism by showing that we have absolutely no good reason for believing in its fundamental proposition that entities exist unexperienced. Nothing I have said, of course, goes any distance towards proving that entities do *not* exist unexperienced. That, in my opinion, cannot be proved. The logically correct position is as follows. We have no reason whatever to believe that unexperienced entities exist. We cannot prove that they do not exist. The onus of proof is on those who assert that they do. Therefore, as such proof is impossible, the belief ought not to be entertained, any more than the belief that there is a unicorn on Mars ought to be entertained.

It is no part of the purpose of this essay to do more than arrive at this negative result. But lest it should be thought that this thinking necessarily leads to nothing but a negative result, or to a pure scepticism, I will indicate in no more than a dozen sentences that there is the possibility of a positive and constructive philosophy arising from it. That positive philosophy I have attempted to work out in detail in another place. Here, I will say no more than the following. Since our belief in unexperienced existences is not to be explained as either (1) a perception, or (2) an inference, or (3) an "instinctive belief", how is it to be explained? I believe that it can only be explained as a mental construction or fiction, a pure assumption which has been adopted, not because there is the slightest evidence for it, but solely because it simplifies our view of the universe. How it simplifies our view of the universe, and by what detailed steps it has arisen, I cannot discuss in this place. But the resulting conception is that, in the last analysis, nothing exists except minds and their sense-data (which are not "mental"), and that human minds have, out of these sense-data, slowly and laboriously constructed the rest of the solid universe of our knowledge. Unexperienced entities can only be said to exist in the sense that minds have chosen by means of a fiction to project them into the void of inter-perceptual intervals, and thus to construct or create their existence in imagination.

The Logical Analysis of Psychology *

CARL G. HEMPEL

I

One of the most important and most discussed problems of contemporary philosophy is that of determining how psychology should be characterized in the theory of science. This problem, overflowing the limits of epistemological analysis and leading to heated controversy in metaphysics itself, is brought to a focus by the familiar disjunction, "Is psychology a natural science, or is it one of the sciences of mind and culture (*Geisteswissenschaften*)?"

The present article attempts to sketch the general lines of a new analysis of psychology, one which makes use of rigorous logical tools, and which has made possible decisive advances towards the solution of the above problem.[1] This analysis was successfully undertaken by the "Vienna Circle" (*Wiener Kreis*), the members of which (M. Schlick, R. Carnap, Ph. Frank, O. Neurath, F. Waismann, H. Feigl, etc.) have, during the past ten years, developed an extremely fruitful method for the epistemological examination and critique of the various sciences, based in part on the work of L. Wittgenstein.[2] We shall limit ourselves essentially to the examination of psychology as carried out by Carnap and Neurath.

The method characteristic of the studies of the Vienna Circle can be briefly defined as a *logical analysis of the language of science*. This method became possible only with the development of an extremely subtle logical apparatus which makes use, in particular, of all the formal procedures

* Translated from the French by W. S. and reprinted from *Revue de Synthèse*, 1935, by kind permission of the author and the editors.

[1] I now (1947) consider the type of physicalism outlined in this paper as too restrictive; the thesis that all statements of empirical science are *translatable*, without loss of theoretical content, into the language of physics, should be replaced by the weaker assertion that all statements of empirical science are *reducible* to sentences in the language of physics, in the sense that for every empirical hypothesis, including, of course, those of psychology, it is possible to formulate certain test conditions in terms of physical concepts which refer to more or less directly observable physical attributes. But those test conditions are not asserted to exhaust the theoretical content of the given hypothesis in all cases.

For a more detailed development of this thesis, cf. R. Carnap, "Logical Foundations of the Unity of Science", in *International Encyclopedia of Unified Science*, The University of Chicago Press, Volume I, Number 1 (included in this volume).

[2] *Tractatus Logico-Philosophicus*, London, 1922.

of modern logistics.[3] However, in the following account, which does not pretend to give more than a broad orientation, we shall limit ourselves to the aim of bringing out the general principles of this new method, without making use of strictly formal procedures.

II

Perhaps the best way to bring out the meaning and scope of the position of the Vienna Circle as it relates to psychology, is to say that it is the exact antithesis of the current epistemological conviction that there is a fundamental difference between experimental psychology, as a natural science, and introspective psychology—in general, between the natural sciences as a whole, and the sciences of mind and culture.[4] The common content of the widely different formulae which are generally used to express this contention, which we reject, can be set down as follows: Apart from certain aspects clearly related to physiology, psychology is radically different, both as to subject-matter and as to method, from physics in the broad sense of the term. In particular, it is impossible to deal adequately with the subject-matter of psychology by means of physical methods. The subject-matter of physics includes such concepts as mass, wave length, temperature, field intensity, etc. In developing these, physics employs its distinctive method which makes a combined use of description and causal explanation. Psychology, on the other hand, has for its subject-matter notions which are, in a broad sense, mental. They are *toto genere* different from the concepts of physics, and the appropriate method for dealing with them scientifically is that of sympathetic insight, called "introspection", a method which is peculiar to psychology.

One of the essential differences between the two kinds of subject-matter, it is believed, consists in the fact that the objects investigated by psychology—in contradistinction to physics—possess an intrinsic meaningfulness. Indeed, several proponents of this idea state that the distinctive method of psychology consists in "understanding the sense of significant structures" (*sinnvolle Gebilde verstehend zu erfassen*). Take, for example, the case of a man who speaks. Within the framework of physics, this process is considered to be completely explained once one has traced the

---

[3] A recent presentation of logistics, based on the fundamental work of Whitehead and Russell, *Principia Mathematica*, is to be found in R. Carnap, *Abriss der Logistik*, 1929 (volume II of the series, *Schriften zur Wissenschaftlichen Weltauffassung*). It includes an extensive bibliography, as well as references to other logistic systems.

[4] The following are some of the principal publications of the Vienna Circle on the nature of psychology as a science: R. Carnap, *Scheinprobleme in der Philosophie. Das Fremdpsychische und der Realismusstreit*, Meiner, Leipsig, 1928; id., *Der Logische Aufbau der Welt*, Meiner, Leipsig, 1928, id., "Die Physikalische Sprache als Universalsprache der Wissenschaft", *Erkenntnis*, 2, 432; id., "Psychologie in physikalischer Sprache", *Erkenntnis*, 3, 107; id., "Ueber Protokollsaetze", *Erkenntnis*, 3, 215; O. Neurath, "Protokollsaetze", *Erkenntnis*, 3, 204; id., *Einheitswissenschaft und Psychologie*, 1933 (volume I of the series *Einheitswissenschaft*). See also the publications mentioned in the notes below.

movements which make up the utterance to their causes, that is to say, to certain physiological processes in the organism, and, in particular, to the central nervous system. But, it is said, this does not even broach the psychological problem. The latter begins with an understanding of what was said, and proceeds to integrate it into a wider context of meaning.

It is usually this latter idea which serves as a principle for the fundamental dichotomy that is introduced into the classification of the sciences. There is taken to be an *absolutely impassable gulf* between the *natural sciences* which have a subject-matter devoid of sense and the *sciences of mind and culture*, which have an intrinsically meaningful subject-matter, the appropriate methodological instrument for the scientific study of which is "insight into meaning".

III

The position in the theory of science which we have just sketched, has been attacked from several different points of view.[5] As far as psychology is concerned, one of the principal counter theses is that formulated by Behaviorism, a theory born in America shortly before the war. (In Russia, Pavlov has developed similar ideas.) Its principal methodological postulate is that a scientific psychology should limit itself to the study of the bodily behavior with which man and the animals respond to changes in their physical environment, every descriptive or explanatory step which makes use of such terms from introspective or "understanding" psychology as 'feeling', 'lived experience', 'idea', 'will', 'intention', 'goal', 'disposition', 'repression', being proscribed as non-scientific.[6] We find in Behaviorism, consequently, an attempt to construct a scientific psychology which would show by its success that even in psychology we have to do with purely physical processes, and that therefore there can be no impassable barrier between psychology and physics. However, this manner of undertaking the critique of a scientific thesis is not completely satisfactory. It seems, indeed, that the soundness of the behavioristic thesis expounded above depends on the possibility of fulfilling the program of behavioristic psychology. But one cannot expect the question as to the scientific status of psychology to be settled by empirical research in psychology itself. To achieve this is rather an undertaking in epistemology. We turn, therefore, to the considerations advanced by members of the Vienna Circle concerning this problem.

[5] P. Oppenheim, for example, in his book *Die Natuerliche Ordnung der Wissenschaften*, Fischer, Jena, 1926, opposes the view that there are fundamental differences between any of the different areas of science. On the analysis of "understanding", cf. M. Schlick, "Erleben, Erkennen, Metaphysik", *Kantstudien*, 31, 146.

[6] For further details see the statement of one of the founders of Behaviorism: J. B. Watson, *Behaviorism*, also A. A. Roback, *Behaviorism and Psychology*, Cambridge, 1923; and A. P. Weiss, *A Theoretical Basis of Human Behavior*, 2nd ed. rev., Columbus, Ohio, Adams, 1929; see also the work by Koehler cited in footnote 10 below.

IV

Before attacking the question as to whether the subject-matters of physics and psychology are essentially the same or different in nature, it is necessary first to clarify the very concept of the subject-matter of a science. The theoretical content of a science is to be found in propositions. It is necessary, therefore, to determine whether there is a fundamental difference between the propositions of psychology and those of physics. Let us therefore ask what it is which determines the content—one can equally well say the "meaning"—of a proposition. When, for example, do we know the meaning of the following statement: "Today at one o'clock, the temperature of such and such a place in the physics laboratory was 23.4° centigrade"? Clearly when, and only when, we know under what conditions we would characterize the statement as true, and under what circumstances we would characterize it as false. (Needless to say, it is not necessary to know whether or not the statement is true.) Thus, we understand the meaning of the above statement since we know that it is true when a tube of a certain kind, filled with mercury (in short, a thermometer with a centigrade scale) placed at the indicated time at the location in question, exhibits a coincidence between the level of the mercury and the mark of the scale numbered 23.4. It is also true if in the same circumstances one can observe certain coincidences on another instrument called an "alcohol thermometer"; and, again, if a galvanometer connected with a thermopile shows a certain deviation when the thermopile is placed there at the indicated time. Finally, there is a long series of other possibilities which make the statement true, each of which is defined by a "physical test sentence", as we should like to call it. The statement itself clearly affirms nothing other than this: all these physical test sentences obtain. (However, one verifies only some of these physical test sentences, and then "concludes by induction" that the others obtain as well.) The statement, therefore, is nothing but an abbreviated formulation of all these test sentences.

Before continuing the discussion, let us sum up this result as follows:

1. A proposition that specifies the temperature at a selected point in space-time can be "retranslated" without change of meaning into another proposition—doubtlessly longer—in which the word "temperature" no longer appears. This term functions solely as an abbreviation, making possible the concise and complete description of a state of affairs, the expression of which would otherwise be very complicated.

2. The example equally shows that *two propositions which differ in formulation* can nevertheless have the *same meaning*. A trivial example of a statement having the same meaning as the above would be: "Today at one o'clock, at such and such a location in the laboratory, the temperature was 19.44° Réaumur."

As a matter of fact, the preceding considerations show—and let us set it down as another result—that *the meaning of a proposition is established by the conditions of its verification.* In particular, two differently formulated propositions have the same meaning or the same effective content when, and only when, they are both true or both false in the same conditions. Furthermore, a proposition for which one can indicate absolutely no conditions which would verify it, which is in principle incapable of confrontation with test conditions, is wholly devoid of content and without meaning. In such a case we have to do with a "pseudo-proposition", that is to say, a sequence of words correctly constructed from the point of view of grammar, but without content, rather than with a proposition properly speaking.[7]

In view of these considerations, our problem reduces to one concerning the difference between the circumstances which verify psychological propositions and those which verify the propositions of physics. Let us therefore examine a proposition which involves a psychological concept, for example: "Paul has a toothache". What is the specific content of this proposition, that is to say, what are the circumstances in which it would be verified? It will be sufficient to indicate some test sentences which describe these circumstances.

  a. Paul weeps and makes gestures of such and such kinds.
  b. At the question, "What is the matter?", Paul utters the words "I have a toothache".
  c. Closer examination reveals a decayed tooth with exposed pulp.
  d. Paul's blood pressure, digestive processes, the speed of his reactions, show such and such changes.
  e. Such and such processes occur in Paul's central nervous system.

This list could be expanded considerably, but it is already sufficient to bring out the fundamental and essential point, namely, that all the circumstances which verify this psychological proposition are expressed by physical test sentences. [This is true even of test sentence *b*, which merely expresses the fact that in specified physical conditions (the propagation of vibrations produced in the air by the enunciation of the words, "What is the matter?") there occurs in the body of the subject a certain physical process (speech behavior of such and such a kind).]

The proposition in question, which is about someone's "pain", is therefore, equally with that concerning the temperature, simply an abbreviated expression of the fact that all its test sentences are verified. (Here, also, one verifies only some of the test sentences and then infers by way of induction that the others obtain as well.) It can be re-translated with-

---

[7] Space is lacking for a further discussion of the logical form of a test sentence (recently called "protocol-propositions" by Neurath and Carnap). On this question see Wittgenstein, *Tractatus Logico-Philosophicus*, as well as the articles by Neurath and Carnap which have appeared in *Erkenntnis* (above, footnote 4).

out loss of content into a proposition which no longer involves the term "pain", but only physical concepts. Our analysis has consequently established that a certain proposition belonging to psychology has the same content as a proposition belonging to physics; a result which is in direct contradiction with the thesis that there is an impassable gulf between the statements of psychology and those of physics.

The above reasoning can be applied to *any psychological proposition,* even to those which concern, as is said, "deeper psychological strata" than that of our example. Thus, the assertion that Mr. Jones suffers from intense inferiority feelings of such and such kinds can only be confirmed or falsified by observing Mr. Jones' behavior in various circumstances. To this behavior belong all the bodily processes of Mr. Jones, and, in particular, his gestures, the flushing and paling of his skin, his utterances, his blood pressure, the events that occur in his central nervous system, etc. In practice, when one wishes to test propositions concerning what are called the deeper layers of the psyche, one limits oneself to the observation of external bodily behavior, and, particularly, to speech movements aroused by certain physical stimuli (the asking of questions). But it is well known that experimental psychology has also developed techniques for making use of the subtler bodily states referred to above in order to confirm the psychological discoveries made by cruder methods. The statement concerning the inferiority feelings of Mr. Jones—whether true or false—means only this: such and such happenings take place in Mr. Jones' body in such and such circumstances.

We shall call a proposition which can be translated without change of meaning into the language of physics, a "physicalistic proposition," whereas we shall reserve the expression "proposition of physics" to those which are already formulated in the terminology of physical science. (Since every statement is in respect of content equivalent, or, better, equipollent to itself, every proposition of physics is also a physicalistic proposition.) The result of the preceding considerations can now be summed up as follows: *All psychological statements which are meaningful, that is to say, which are in principle verifiable, are translatable into propositions which do not involve psychological concepts, but only the concepts of physics. The propositions of psychology are consequently physicalistic propositions. Psychology is an integral part of physics.* If a distinction is drawn between psychology and the other areas of physics, it is only from the point of view of the practical aspects of research and the direction of interest, rather than a matter of principle. This logical analysis, of which the result shows a certain affinity with the fundamental ideas of behaviorism, constitutes the physicalistic conception of psychology.

V

It is customary to raise against the above conception the following fundamental objection: The physical test sentences of which you speak are absolutely incapable of formulating the intrinsic nature of a mental process; they merely describe the physical *symptoms* from which one infers, by purely psychological methods—notably that of understanding —the presence of a certain mental process. But it is not difficult to see that the use of the method of understanding or of other psychological procedures is bound up with the existence of certain observable physical data concerning the subject undergoing examination. There is no psychological understanding that is not tied up physically in one way or another with the person to be understood. Let us add that, for example, in the case of the proposition about the inferiority complex, even the "introspective" psychologist, the psychologist who "understands," can only confirm his conjecture if the body of Mr. Jones, when placed in certain circumstances (most frequently, subjected to questioning), reacts in a specified manner (usually, by giving certain answers). Consequently, even if the proposition in question had to be arrived at, *discovered*, by "sympathetic understanding," the only *information* it gives us is nothing more nor less than the following: under certain circumstances, certain specific events take place in the body of Mr. Jones. It is this which constitutes the meaning of the psychological statement.

The further objection will perhaps be raised that men can feign. Thus, though a criminal at the bar may show physical symptoms of mental disorder, one would nevertheless be justified in wondering whether his mental confusion was "real" or only simulated. One must note that in the case of the simulator, only some of the conditions are fulfilled which verify the statement "This man is mentally unbalanced," those, namely, which are most accessible to direct observation. A more penetrating examination —which should in principle take into account events occurring in the central nervous system—would give a decisive answer; and this answer would in turn clearly rest on a physicalistic basis. If, at this point, one wished to push the objection to the point of admitting that a man could show *all the "symptoms"* of a mental disease without being "really" ill, we reply that it would be absurd to characterize such a man as "really normal"; for it is obvious that by the very nature of the hypothesis we should possess no criterion in terms of which to distinguish this man from another who, while exhibiting the same bodily behavior down to the last detail, would "in addition" be "really ill." (To put the point more precisely, one can say that this hypothesis contains a *logical contradiction*, since it amounts to saying, "It is possible that a statement should be false even when the necessary and sufficient conditions of its truth are fulfilled.")

Once again we see clearly that the meaning of a psychological proposition consists merely in the function of abbreviating the description of certain modes of physical response characteristic of the bodies of man and the animals. An analogy suggested by O. Neurath may be of further assistance in clarifying the logical function of psychological statements.[8] The complicated statements that would describe the movements of the hands of a watch in relation to one another, and relatively to the stars, are ordinarily summed up in an assertion of the following form: "This watch runs well (runs badly, etc.)." The term "runs" is introduced here as an auxiliary defined expression which makes it possible to formulate briefly a relatively complicated system of statements. It would thus be absurd to say, for example, that the movement of the hands is only a "physical symptom" which reveals the presence of a running which is intrinsically incapable of being grasped by physical means, or to ask, if the watch should stop, what has become of the running of the watch.

It is in exactly the same way that abbreviating symbols are introduced into the language of physics, the concept of temperature discussed above being an example. The system of physical test sentences *exhausts* the meaning of the statement concerning the temperature at a place, and one should not say that these sentences merely have to do with "symptoms" of the existence of a certain temperature.

Our argument has shown that it is necessary to attribute to the characteristic concepts of psychology the same logical function performed by the concepts of "running" and of "temperature." They do nothing more than make possible the succinct formulation of propositions concerning the states or processes of animal or human bodies.

The introduction of new psychological concepts can contribute greatly to the progress of scientific knowledge. But it is accompanied by a danger, that, namely, of making an excessive and, consequently, harmful use of new concepts, which may result in questions and answers devoid of sense. This is frequently the case in metaphysics, notably with respect to the notions which we formulated in section II. Terms which are abbreviating symbols are taken to designate a special class of "psychological objects," and thus one is led to ask questions about the "essence" of these objects, and how they differ from "physical objects." The time-worn problem concerning the relation between mental and physical events is also based on this confusion concerning the logical function of psychological concepts. Our argument, therefore, enables us to see that *the psycho-physical problem is a pseudo-problem*, the formulation of which is based on an inadmissible use of scientific concepts; it is of the same logical nature as the question, suggested by the example above, concerning the relation of the running of the watch to the movement of the hands.[9]

---

[8] "Soziologie im Physicalismus", *Erkenntnis*, 2, 393, particularly p. 411.

[9] Carnap, *Der Logische Aufbau der Welt*, pp. 231–236; Id., *Scheinprobleme in der Philosophie*. See also note 4 above.

VI

In order to bring out the exact status of the fundamental idea of the physicalistic interpretation of psychology (or logical behaviorism), we shall contrast it with certain theses of psychological behaviorism and of classical materialism, which appear to be closely related.[10]

1. Logical behaviorism claims neither that minds, feelings, inferiority complexes, voluntary actions, etc., do not exist, nor that their existence is in the least doubtful. It insists that the very question as to whether these psychological constructs really exist is already a pseudo-problem, since these notions in their "legitimate use" appear only as abbreviations of physicalistic statements. Above all, one should not interpret the position sketched in this paper as amounting to the view that we can only know the "physical side" of psychological processes, and that the question as to whether there are mental phenomena behind the physical processes falls beyond the scope of science and must be left either to faith or to the conviction of each individual. On the contrary, the logical analyses originating in the Vienna Circle, of which one of the consequences is the physicalistic analysis of psychology, teach us that every meaningful question is, in principle, capable of a scientific answer. Furthermore, these analyses show that that which is, in the case of the mind-body problem, considered as an object of belief, is absolutely incapable of being expressed by a factual proposition. In other words, there can be no question here of an "article of faith." Nothing can be an object of faith which cannot, in principle, be known.

2. The thesis developed here, though related in certain ways to the fundamental idea of behaviorism, does not demand, as does the latter, that psychological research restrict itself methodologically to the study of the responses made by organisms to certain stimuli. It by no means offers a theory belonging to the domain of psychology, but rather a logical theory about the propositions of scientific psychology. Its position is that the latter are without exception physicalistic statements, by whatever means they may have been obtained. Consequently, it seeks to show that if in psychology only physicalistic statements are made, this is not a limitation because it is logically *impossible* to do otherwise.

3. In order for logical behaviorism to be acceptable, it is not necessary that we be able to describe the physical state of a human body which is referred to by a certain psychological statement—for example, one dealing with someone's feeling of pain—down to the most minute details of the phenomena of the central nervous system. No more does it presuppose a knowledge of all the physical laws governing human or animal bodily

---

[10] A careful discussion of the ideas of so-called "internal" behaviorism is to be found in *Psychologische Probleme* by W. Koehler, published by Springer, Berlin, 1933. See particularly the first two chapters [translated under the title *Gestalt Psychology*].

processes; nor *a fortiori* is the existence of rigorously deterministic laws relating to these processes a necessary condition of the truth of the behavioristic thesis. At no point does the above argument rest on such a concrete presupposition.

VII

In concluding, I should like to indicate briefly the clarification brought to the problem of the division of the sciences into totally different areas, by the method of the logical analysis of scientific statements, applied above to the special case of the place of psychology among the sciences. The considerations we have advanced can be extended to the domain of sociology, taken in the broad sense as the science of historical, cultural and economic processes. In this way one arrives at the result that every sociological assertion which is meaningful, that is to say, in principle verifiable, "has as its subject-matter nothing else than the states, processes and behavior of groups or of individuals (human or animal), and their responses to one another and to their environment," [11] and consequently that every sociological statement is a physicalistic statement. This view is characterized by Neurath as the thesis of "social behaviorism," which he adds to that of "individual behaviorism" which we have expounded above. Furthermore, we can show that every proposition of what are called the "sciences of mind and culture" is a sociological proposition in the above sense, provided it has genuine content. Thus we arrived at the "thesis of the unity of science":

The division of science into different areas rests exclusively on differences in research procedures and direction of interest; *one must not regard it as a matter of principle. On the contrary, all the branches of science are in principle of one and the same nature; they are branches of the unitary science, physics.*

VIII

The method of logical analysis which we have attempted to explicate in clarifying, by way of example, the propositions of psychology, leads, as we have been able to show only too briefly for the sciences of mind and culture, to a "physicalism" based on logic (Neurath): *Every proposition of the above-mentioned disciplines, and, in general, of experimental science as a whole, which is not merely a meaningless sequence of words, is translatable, without change of content, into a proposition in which appear only physicalistic terms, and consequently is a physicalistic proposition.*

This thesis frequently encounters a strong opposition arising from the

---

[11] R. Carnap, *Die Physikalische Sprache als Universalsprache*, p. 451. See also: O. Neurath, *Empirische Soziologie*, 1931, the fourth monograph in the series *Schriften zur wissenschaftlichen Weltauffassung*.

idea that such analyses violently and considerably reduce the richness of the life of mind or spirit, as though the aim of the discussion were purely and simply to eliminate vast and important areas of experience. Such a conception comes from a false interpretation of physicalism, the main elements of which we have already examined in section VII above. As a matter of fact, nothing can be more remote from a philosophy which has the methodological attitude we have characterized than the making of decisions, on its own authority, concerning the truth or falsity of particular scientific statements, or the desire to eliminate any matters of fact whatsoever. *The subject-matter of this philosophy is limited to the form of scientific statements, and the deductive relationships obtaining between them.* It is led by its analyses to the thesis of physicalism, and establishes on purely logical grounds that a certain class of venerable philosophical "problems" consists of pseudo-problems. It is certainly to the advantage of the progress of scientific knowledge that these imitation jewels in the coffer of scientific problems be known for what they are, and that the intellectual powers which have till now been devoted to a class of senseless questions which are by their very nature insoluble, become available for the formulation and study of new and fruitful problems. That the method of logical analysis stimulates research along these lines is shown by the numerous publications of the Vienna Circle and those who sympathize with its general point of view (H. Reichenbach, W. Dubislav, and others).

In the attitude of those who are so bitterly opposed to physicalism, an essential rôle is played by certain psychological factors relating to individuals and groups. Thus the contrast between the concepts (*Gebilde*) developed by the psychologist, and those developed by the physicist, or, again, the question as to the nature of the specific subject-matter of psychology and the cultural sciences (which present the appearance of a search for the essence and unique laws of "objective mind") is usually accompanied by a strong emotional coloring which has come into being during the long historical development of the "philosophical conception of the world," which was considerably less scientific than normative and intuitive. These emotional factors are still deeply rooted in the picture by which our epoch represents the world to itself. They are protected by certain affective dispositions which surround them like a rampart, and for all these reasons appear to us to have a verifiable content which a more penetrating analysis shows to be impossible.

A psychological and sociological study of the causes of the appearance of these "concomitant factors" of the metaphysical type would take us beyond the limits of this study; [12] but without tracing it back to its origins,

---

[12] O. Neurath has made interesting contributions along these lines in *Empirische Soziologie* and in *Soziologie im Physikalismus* (see above note 8), as has R. Carnap in his article "Ueberwindung der Metaphysik durch logische Analyse der Sprache," *Er-*

it is possible to say that if the logical analyses sketched above are correct, the fact that they necessitate at least a partial break with traditional philosophical ideas which are deeply dyed with emotion can certainly not justify an opposition to physicalism—at least if one admits that philosophy is to be something more than the expression of an individual vision of the world, that it aims at being a science.

kenntnis, 2, 219, which has been translated into French by General E. Vouillemin: *La science et la metaphysique devant l'analyse logique du language.* Introduction by Marcel Boll. *Actualités scientifiques et industriels,* Hermann, Paris, 1934, p. 45.

Some Logical Considerations Concerning the Mental *

C. I. LEWIS

It is a conception as old as Socrates and as modern as our current logical analyses that the central task in philosophic discussion of any topic is to arrive at and elucidate a definition. That, I take it, is what is properly meant by a philosophic "theory"; a theory of X is a more or less elaborate definitive statement having "X" as subject, together with such exposition as will remove difficulties of understanding and serve to show that this definition covers the phenomena to be taken into account.

I fear that what this occasion calls for is such a theory of mind. But if so, then I am unprepared for it. I am unable to present any statement of the form "Mind is . . ." (where "is" would express the relation of equivalence of meaning) which would satisfy me or which I should expect would satisfy you. I can only put forward certain statements intended to formulate attributes which are essential to mind; to point to phenomena of which we can say, "Whatever else is or is not comprehended under 'mind,' at least it is intended to include *these*." In particular, I shall wish to emphasize that whatever is called "content of consciousness" is so included, and to consider certain consequences of that simple fact.

In so doing, however, I am aware of one danger. Confronted with problems of analysis which there is trouble to resolve, one may sometimes circumvent them by changing the subject. We find ourselves unprepared to formulate any sufficient criterion of X which precisely accords with what is comprehended under "X" and what excluded. But we are—it may be—prepared to elaborate systematically and ingeniously some *other* definitive statement using the same term in a somewhat different signification; some definition of the *word* "X" devised with a view to skirting what is dark to our insight and ruling out whatever we find unmanageable in current usage of the term. Theories are sometimes achieved in this way. But this fallacy of changing the subject, I would above all else avoid. I can not express precisely and clearly what you and I mean by "mind"; but if anything I have to say should be found incompatible with that common meaning, then I should not wish to persist in maintaining it.

* Reprinted by kind permission of the author and the editors from *The Journal of Philosophy*, 38, 1941.

It is one such essential feature of what the word "mind" means that minds are private; that one's own mind is something with which one is directly acquainted—nothing more so—but that the mind of another is something which one is unable directly to inspect.

If that is, in fact, a required feature of what we should call "a mind," then indeed it must be admitted to be a question whether minds—anything having this character—exist. It must also be admitted that the statement itself, asserting the existence of mind in this sense, might contain some irremovable unclarity or some implicit inconsistency, rendering it a non-significant affirmation. However, any such possible doubts can, I think, be removed.

But first, let us observe that if the above statement is correct, when measured against the intended signification of "mind," that of itself is sufficient to preclude certain prevalent theories. Whatever else such theories may be true of or false of, as statements about what is meant by "mind" they are literally not pertinent. Behavioristic interpretations of mind are thus not pertinent, nor is any identification of mind with brain states or brain functionings.

The point has been raised often enough and will not need to be elaborated here. All men are directly acquainted with their own minds, but no one is directly acquainted with the present state of his brain. We know nothing about our brain states except by complicated and more or less uncertain inferences. And if technical difficulties of observing our own brains should be overcome, still the man who should be suffering pain and at the same time observing his own brain, would be aware of two things, not one; and only by an inductive inference would he be led to suppose that the one of them had anything to do with the other.

Sometimes when such arguments as this are put forward, however, it is not realized that they depend fundamentally upon what kind of thing is *meant* by "mind." That is the case: otherwise this type of objection to a behavioristic or brain state interpretation of mind could be easily met. It could be observed, for example, that one may see a thing held in the hand and at the same time feel it with the fingers. And one who thus saw and felt the same object might not know that what he visually observed was the same thing that he tactually observed. An infant or a man who suddenly receives the sense of sight, must learn to make such identification of the visually with the tactually perceived; it requires to be inductively inferred. Nevertheless, identification in this case is valid. And it might be argued that identification of the mental with the behavioral or with brain states is similarly valid, in spite of the objection. However, in such a case as this, in which an identification which is valid requires to be established by inductive inference, there are also two things—or more than two—whose *non*-identity is witnessed by the necessity of such learning. In our example, there is the tactually felt as such—the tactual datum—and there is the visually apprehended as such—the visual datum. There is also the object held in the hand; which is a different kind of entity from the other two. Thus in one signification of the phrases "what is seen" and "what is felt," they may denote the same thing, though this identity requires to be inferred from some course of experience. In another signification, what is seen is *not* identical with what is felt; and this non-identity is proved merely by the possibility of observing both without being able to identify them.

If, then, this kind of objection to behavioristic and brain-state interpretations of mind is sound, it is so because of the meaning of terms referring to the mental; because these are so intended that if *A* is a present phenomenon of my mind, then anything I can not directly inspect is not identical with *A*, and anything I could observe without being able to identify it with *A*, would be in fact not identical with *A*.

This characteristic of the intended meaning of terms applied to the mental is not peculiar to them; nor is the kind of controversy which can arise on account of the type of ambiguity here illustrated. The question whether the sound of music is or is not correctly identified with certain harmonic motions, is a closely similar issue, which depends on the meaning of the language which is used, and upon appeal to criteria which are different according as it is one or another of two possible meanings which is intended.

Apparently there are two classifications of namable things; one of them such that "*A*" and "*B*" can denote the same entity only if a person who directly observes what "*A*" names and what "*B*" names will also be able to observe that they name the same thing; and the other classification such that what "*A*" names can be identical with what "*B*" names even though one may observe what "*A*" names and what "*B*" names without being able to make the identification. If I knew how to draw a sharp and clear line between these two classifications of namable things, I suspect that this distinction might be important for our present topic. But I do not know how to draw it in a manner at once comprehensive and faithful to our actual intentions in the use of language.

There is, however, one consideration which seems pertinent and clear. Some terms—or some terms in some uses—name what presents itself, or could present itself, as such; name appearances or data. The intent of this use of terms we may, for convenience, label "phenomenal meaning"; and the language thus used may be called "phenomenal language." Other terms —or the same terms in a different and more frequent usage—name things which may appear but are in any case distinct from their appearances, that is, name something to which a given appearance may be attributable but something to which also more is attributable than could present itself to any single observer on one occasion. Physical objects are all of them included in this latter classification. And it is entities of this classification for which it may be true that *A* and *B* are identical, though one who observes what "*A*" names and observes also what "*B*" names may still be unable to make the identification. Phenomena of consciousness—it suggests itself—all of them belong in the former classification. They have universally the character here labelled "datum"; and language used to name or apply to any conscious content as such, has phenomenal meaning. It denotes an appearance or appearances. Such data, when given, are entities whose identity and character it is impossible to mistake—though admittedly any language used to name them may be inappropriate or inadequate and fail to express just what is intended. An appearance or datum is just what it seems to be, and is nothing more than or other than what it appears to be.

If this is correct, then it may serve to explain the pertinence of the argument that mental facts can not be identified with brain facts or facts of physical behavior because we directly inspect and are fully acquainted with the mental factuality but may be ignorant of the brain state or the behavior; or if we should be also aware of these latter, may still be ignorant of any connection between them and what is mental. Admitting this phenomenal meaning of language used to denote the mental, such argument is entirely sound, and proves its point.

These considerations may also serve to locate more precisely one issue between those who interpret the mental in terms of behavior or of brain states and those who would repudiate such interpretation. We who criticize these conceptions are talking about phenomenal entities as such when we use terms referring to the mental; they, by contrast, are in search of something belonging to the other classification; some entity to which these mental phenomena may be attributed, but a thing which by its nature transcends any possible phenomenal appearance which could be given at any one time. This thing is, on their account, a state of the physical brain or of the behaving organism.

If this does in fact correctly locate the issue—or *an* issue—then I think there is something further to be said about it which is obvious. It may well be that there are two kinds of namable entities to be talked about when the mental is under discussion; the directly given phenomena of consciousness, and a something—a substance, if you please—to which these are attributable. That there is such a thing or substance of which mental phenomena are attributes, and that this thing is the brain or the behaving organism, is one view, to be considered alongside others, including the dualistic conception of a non-physical substance as that to which mental states are attributable. But at least there are two things to be talked about: the substance of which the mental phenomena are attributes, and the directly given phenomena themselves which are to be attributed. There is a truth about these latter, and a kind of truth peculiarly patent, concerning which we can be mistaken only by some inadvertence. It is, moreover, this truth of the phenomenal which sets the problem in any search for that substance to which contents of consciousness are attributable. It is these phenomena which are to be accounted for, and the phenomenal facts about them which must be looked to in order to determine the correctness or incorrectness, or the plausibility, of any solution which may be offered for this problem which I have ventured to call the problem of substance.

In their preoccupation with this substance-problem, the proponents of behavioristic and brain-state theories of mind sometimes speak as if there *were* no such entities as the directly inspected contents of consciousness; or appear to deny that there is any truth which can be told about them except in terms of those things—on their view, physical things—of which the mental are manifestations. By implication, they seem to accuse us, who would try first of all to state facts about these directly presented phenomena themselves, of talking nonsense or speaking of what does not exist. Such implication, intended or not, is certainly without justification. Whoever would deny that there are directly inspectable facts of the content of consciousness, would deny that which alone makes a theory of mind desirable and significant, and that which supplies the only final test of such a theory.

There is a second point which is pertinent to these issues, and can also be approached from grounds of analysis or logic. A definition, or a philosophic theory, should explicate the subject of it by specifying that criterion by which the thing in question could be selected from amongst all possible things which could be presented to us or imagined. It is not sufficient in a definition—and it should not be thought satisfactory in a theory—to characterize A by reference to XYZ, where XYZ are characters which, under conceivable circumstances, might be determined as present but leave us still in doubt whether what is presented is A. If we know what we mean by "A" and if what we mean by "A" is expressed by "XYZ," then it could not conceivably happen that XYZ should be determined as present but there could be rational doubt whether what is presented is A.

Behavioristic and brain-state interpretations of mind do not satisfy this prime requisite of definition and adequate theory. They do not satisfy it for the same reasons that the relation between mental phenomena and behavior or brain states is something which can only be inferred inductively.

Let it be granted that there is some more or less complex character of behavior such that whenever behavior of just this character occurs there is consciousness, and whenever there is not behavior of this sort there is no consciousness. Let it be further granted that for every qualitative specificity of consciousness there is some equally specific and correlated character of behavior. Still the definitive explication of the mental in terms of the behavioral can not meet our requirement. First, because it would be possible, for example, to be in doubt whether the angle-worm on the fish-hook suffers pain; and we should be unable to dispel this doubt by observing its behavior. The criterion of consciousness in terms of behavior breaks down in such borderline cases, simply because nobody can specify this criterion except in some arbitrary fashion whose truth to what we mean by "consciousness" he merely guesses at. Second, the various modes of one's own consciousness—suffering pain, hearing music, seeing green—are directly distinguishable by inspection. But no one could recognize these specificities of his own mentality in terms of behavior, because neither he nor anyone else can state precisely what character of behavior is unexceptionably present when there is pain or heard music or the seeing of green, and unexceptionably absent when there is not this specific mode of consciousness.

It is sufficiently evident that identification of the mental with the behavioral, or with brain states, represents a locution comparable to the physicist's statement that a specific pitch *is* a particular frequency of harmonic motion, and that sound *is* harmonic motion within a certain range of frequencies. Such locution represents first an empirically discovered correlation of two independently recognizable phenomena, a pitch and a rate of vibration. If "middle C" did not *first* mean something identifiable without reference to vibration, and if "vibration of 256 per second" did not *first* mean something identifiable without reference to sound, this correlation of the two could never have been empirically established and statement of it would be unintelligible verbiage. Eventually we may come to have a degree of inductive assurance of this correlation which exceeds our confidence in identifications of pitch by other means than physical determination of this frequency. That being the case, our most trusted criterion of pitch, and of the objectivity of sound, comes to be this criterion in terms of harmonic motion. To that extent and in that sense, it becomes understandable and even justifiable if the phenomena of sound are *defined* in terms of harmonic motion.

Such definition, which represents a type quite common in science, is of a peculiar sort which may be called "definition by description" (definition by reference to some non-essential character but one uniformly found present in all actual cases of the thing in question and found absent in all other cases which are actual). A traditional example would be "Man is the animal that laughs." It is a distinguishing feature of such definition by description that the relation of definiens to definiendum which it states is one requiring to be established by induction and incapable of being established by logical analysis alone. Correlatively, the criterion of the definiendum which such a definition specifies is one (supposedly) sufficient for selecting what the definiendum denotes in all actual circumstances, but *not* sufficient to select what is defined under all thinkable circumstances or from amongst all imaginable things.

The behavioristic or the brain-state theory of mind involves such definition of the mental by description. The principal difference of it from the example just discussed is that, whereas the correlation between sound and harmonic motion is well substantiated in all details, the correlation of mental phenomena with equally specific brain states or modes of behavior is less well substantiated as a general thesis, and is quite undetermined in many of those specific details which the general truth of it requires. That being so, the definition of the utterly familiar specificities of the mental in terms of supposedly correlated brain functions or behavior, is definition of the known in terms of the unknown.

There is also the consideration that whereas in natural science, which concerns itself exclusively with the existent, such definition by description has its pragmatic justification, such justification is lacking in philosophy, whose concern is not that of establishing synthetic *a posteriori* truths. From this point of view, the behavioristic or the brain-state theory of mind substitutes an hypothesis which only the future development of natural science can corroborate or disprove for our more appropriate business of the analysis of meanings.

It has been regarded as a strong point in favor of interpreting the mental in terms of behavior or of brain functions, and a strong point against any theory of the sort indicated by what has here been said, that minds other than our own, as anything distinguishable from certain physical phenomena, are unverifiable entities. And affirmations of what is unverifiable have sometimes been said to be meaningless. You will not expect me to attempt, in the space that remains, any adequate discussion of the questions here involved. But one or two considerations which are pertinent may be briefly indicated.

All of us who earlier were inclined to say that unverifiable statements are meaningless—and I include myself—have since learned to be more careful. This dictum is unclear; and in the most readily suggested interpretations of it, is too sweeping to be plausible. Also, the main point here does not have to do with verification at all. With empiricists in general and pragmatists in particular, such references to verifiability as essential to meaning is only a roundabout way of pointing out that unless you are somehow prepared to recognize the factuality you assert, in case that factuality should be, or could be, presented to you, your verbal expression is not a matter-of-fact statement because it affirms nothing intelligible. Any conditions of verification over and above this one requirement that a matter-of-fact assertion must have empirical sense—whether these further conditions be "practical" or "theoretical"—are irrelevant to the question of meaningfulness. And clearly the belief in other consciousness than one's own satisfies this one requirement of the meaningful; that there must be some criterion for recognition, some sense content indicative of what is meant. We can envisage the conscious experience of another, by empathy, in terms of our own. And we do. Any denial of that would be too egregious for consideration.

We significantly believe in other minds than our own, but we can not *know* that such exist. This belief is a postulate. At least I should have said this earlier; and did say it. But I now think this statement was a concession to an over-rigorous conception of what deserves the name of "knowledge." For empirical knowledge, in distinction from merely meaningful belief, verification is required. But there is what we call "indirect verification" as well as "direct"; and there is "complete" or "decisive verification" and also "incomplete verification" or "confirmation" as more or less probable. There are reasons to think that these two distinctions—direct or indirect and complete or incomplete—reduce to one: that in any distinctive sense of "directly verifiable," that and that only is directly verifiable which is also completely and decisively verifiable. (The plausibility of this may be suggested by the thought that whatever is incompletely verified does not present itself in its full nature but is observed only in certain manifestations.) Most of what we call "knowledge" is not only incompletely verified at any time but—when the matter is considered carefully —must remain so forever. (It may be completely verifiable, or completely confirmable, in the sense that there is nothing which the truth of it requires which could not, given the conditions of verification, be found true or found false; but it is not completely verifiable in the sense that verification of it can be completed:—somewhat as there is no whole number which can not be counted, but counting of the whole numbers can not be completed.)

In view of these facts (if these suggestions indicate fact), it may be that there is no fundamental difference, by reference to its verifiability, between the belief in other minds and the belief, for example, in ultraviolet rays or in electrons. It might even be that the belief in other minds, though always incompletely verified and incapable of becoming otherwise, is supported by inductive evidence so extensive as to be better confirmed than some of the accepted theses of physical science.

On the Relation Between Psychological and Physical Concepts *

MORITZ SCHLICK

I

Recent philosophy has not been lacking in attempts to free the Cartesian problem of the relation between mind and body from its metaphysical obscurities, by refusing to pose it in terms of mental and physical substances; beginning, instead, with the harmless question as to how, in general, we have come by our physical and psychological concepts. That this is actually the correct way to approach the solution of the problem, I have no doubt. Indeed, I am convinced that the problem will already be solved the moment we become completely clear as to the rules in accordance with which we employ the words "mental" and "physical." For we shall then grasp the proper meaning of all physical and psychological propositions, and in doing so will know in what relation the propositions of physics stand to those of psychology.

When Descartes sought to define his "corporeal substance" by specifying the attribute *"extensio"* as its characteristic mark, he took the first step in a direction which must be followed to the end before one can hope to form a clear idea of the properties which belong to all "physical" concepts, and to these alone. *"Extensio"* refers, of course, to *spatial* extension; and it is indeed possible confidently to assert that an analysis of the concept of spatial extension yields without further ado a definition of the concept "physical."

The problem, however, is by no means so simple that it suffices to say "whatever is spatially extended is physical," for there are words which make sense when combined with the predicate "spatially extended," and which nevertheless refer to "mental" states; such words, for example, as "visual image," "tactual sensation," "pain," etc. Consequently, the difference we are seeking can be found along the above lines only if the word "extended" has different meanings in its psychological and physical usages.

Is this the case? Do I have the same thing in mind, or something different, when I say of a pain that it spreads over a certain area, as compared to when I ascribe a certain spatial extensity to a physical object, for ex-

* Translated by W. S. and reprinted with the kind permission of Mrs. Schlick and the editors of *Revue de Synthèse*. The original was published in 1935.

ample my hand? Is the visual image of the moon "extended" in the same sense as the moon itself? Do my visual impressions on looking at a book have extension in the same sense as the tactual impressions I obtain by holding it in my hand?

The answering of these questions is the first step in the process of clarifying our concepts, nay the second,—for the first and more difficult step is to ask these questions at all. This step was not taken by Descartes nor by those who follow him,—the possibility not even occurring to them that the word "*extensio*" is used in more than one sense. It would therefore not be correct to describe their use of this word by saying that they took it to have the *same* meaning in significantly different cases. They didn't even see that there were different cases. Berkeley alone was a famous exception. He posed the third of our three questions. The first two couldn't be raised in his system, since a by no means inconsiderable part of his philosophy consisted exactly in a proof that these questions do not exist. For him there is no other kind of extension than that which can be attributed to the representations of sight and touch; indeed, in Berkeley's philosophy it is already a mistake to speak of these as "representations," since there is nothing which is copied by them and is their original. Kant, who philosophized so much later than Berkeley, believed he had nothing to learn from him, and didn't succeed in raising our questions. He invariably speaks, as did Descartes before him, of extension, of Space, and omits any investigation as to whether it may not be necessary to distinguish between several space-concepts; first, between the physical and the psychological, and under the latter, between visual-space, tactual-space, etc. This neglect had unfortunate consequences for Kant's philosophy of geometry, and, through this, for his system as a whole. Physical space, the space of nature, is for him also psychological space, since nature is for him "mere appearance," that is, mere "idea," and this is a psychological term.

It is possible to regard Kant's distinction between "outer" and "inner" sense as an attempt to draw a boundary between the physical and the mental. His doctrine that Space, the form of intuition for outer sense, is lacking in the case of inner sense is indeed reminiscent of Descartes, as well as a forerunner of recent attempts to characterize the mental as simply the non-spatial. It is said that even where the mental has to do with the spatial (in ideas and perception), it is itself non-spatial. The idea of a red triangle is itself neither red nor triangular, nor is the perception of an extended object itself extended.

This assertion owes its appearance of plausibility to the fact that the words "perception" and "idea" are ambiguous. By them one can refer either to the content, that which is given (*une donnée actuelle*), or to the event, the act of perception, which is characterized as a "mental process" and concerning which there is indeed no question of "extension." (We leave unraised the question as to the justifiability of this distinction between content and act, and limit ourselves to pointing out that surely it first occurred to us to speak of an act of perception—and, later, of imaging —only after we had gained the knowledge that the occurrence of "contents" is somehow dependent on processes in the sense organs, and, furthermore that these processes are physical.) One can certainly not say of the contents of perception—at least in the cases of sight and touch —that they are "non-spatial"; rather they are beyond doubt extended. Indeed it is from them that we first derive this concept.

Nevertheless, we do not mean the same by "extension" in psychological and physical contexts. In order to make the difference clear it is best to examine exactly those cases where it is most difficult to distinguish psychological from physical space. We asked above if, for example, a pain is extended in the same sense as is a physical object, say, my hand. But what about the case where the pains are in my hand itself, where my whole hand aches? Do we not have here a mental datum the spatial extension of which is identical with that of the physical object which is "my hand"?

The answer is, "absolutely not!" Pain has its own space just as visual sensations have theirs and as do sensations of touch. The fact that several sensations of pain can occur *simultaneously* is sufficient to require us to speak of a "pain-space." Every arrangement of simultaneous items is a side-by-side (as opposed to a sequence) and it is customary to call such facts "spatial." It is experience which first brings about the coördination of the several spaces of visual and tactual sensations, feelings of pain, etc.

This can be made to stand out most clearly by conceiving of a man who lives in complete darkness and complete absence of motion. He would be acquainted with neither visual nor tactual sensations, but he could very well have "pain throughout his hand" (even though he would not use these words). Should he be freed from his cell, he would slowly form the customary spatial notions and on the basis of the observation of certain coexistences and sequences of events would gradually learn to interpret these pains as pains of the "hand," that is to say, of the five-fingered visual and tactual object which is connected with his body by another bodily structure, the "arm." For he would observe that his pains depend in a definite way on what befalls a physical object which he calls "my hand," which is visible in the visual field and touchable in the tactual field. Thus, a wounding or movement of this object would increase the pain, while other processes (medical treatment) would diminish them. In this way, the pain-space would be coördinated with the sight-space. Since experience alone teaches us that the several kinds of extension always appear together, the conclusion is to be drawn that there are several "spaces" rather than only one. If the world were otherwise than it actually is, if, for example, the person concerned always felt a pain when a certain object, for example the candlestick on the table, was violently disturbed, and, should the

candlestick move, perceived a sensation akin to the kinaesthetic sensation
which normally accompanies the movement of his hand, such experience
could lead him to coördinate the space of the "handache" with that of the
candlestick (and if, for example, the candlestick had five branches, its
extension would correspond to that of the five fingers). He could thus
meaningfully say, "I have a pain in the candlestick." (Similar and as yet
unpublished considerations have been advanced by Ludwig Wittgenstein
in another connection.) Thus, it is possible to conceive of experiences
which would result in the localization of the *same* handaches in quite
different physical spaces. It follows that mental pain-space and physical
space are entirely different things.

The difference is obvious in extreme cases. Let us compare, referring
back to our second example, the extension of the moon with that of the
visual image of the moon. The diameter of the moon, a physical magnitude,
can be given in miles; the diameter of the visual image, on the other hand,
is not even a "size." (Needless to say, the visual image must not be confused with the retinal image, which has physical magnitude, and, consequently, a diameter which can be specified in units of measure.) The
extensity of the visual image is frequently assigned an angular measure.
The latter is, indeed, a physical magnitude, but it does not make one of
the visual image itself. Rather, such a method of assigning a measure can be
justified only by means of a definitional coördination, which, however, is
not practical for many purposes. Thus, if one compares the visual image
of the moon at the zenith, with that of the moon at the horizon, the angle
is the same in both cases; nevertheless, as is well known, we call the extent of the mental visual image of the moon greater in the second case
than in the first. Whatever is meant by the "extension" or "size" of a
mental image, it is in any case something quite different from the extension or size of a physical object.

II

In what, then, does the difference consist which is to lead us to a definition of the "physical"?

Here we shall apply the method which seems to me the sole method
of true philosophy: We shall turn our attention to the way in which propositions about physical objects are *verified*. That which is common to all
the methods by which such propositions are verified, must then be that
which is characteristic of the physical. All propositions are tested with
respect to their truth or falsity by the performance of certain operations,
and to give an account of the meaning of the propositions consists in
specifying these operations. Of what sort, then, are these operations in the
case of propositions in which physical terms appear? In other words, in
what does the process of determining physical properties consist?

Physical properties are *measurable* properties. They are defined by the methods of measurement. (Bridgman's book, *The Logic of Modern Physics*, carries this thought through for physics as a whole.) It will suffice if we limit our discussion of these methods to the *scientific* methods of physics. There are, of course, pre-scientific ways of noting the presence of physical properties which continue to play a dominating rôle in everyday life, but there is no difference in principle between the procedures of everyday life and those of research. Since, however, the methods of science stand out more clearly, we shall limit ourselves to these. In everyday life, also, physical concepts arise only where measurements of one kind or another have taken place (even if by the thoroughly crude methods of pacing, touch, visual estimation, etc.), that is, *quantitative* determinations have been achieved. Every measurement springs from a counting, and can in the last analysis always be traced to a numbering of "coincidences," where by a coincidence is to be understood the spatial coming together of two previously separated singularities of the visual or tactual fields (marks, pointers, etc.). This characteristic of measurement whereby spatial extension is, as it were, mastered by division into discrete parts has often been pointed out. It is this way of determining the spatial which is the *physical*.

Why exactly do we make use of this procedure?

The only correct answer is, because of its objectivity, that is, because of its inter-sensual and inter-subjective validity. What this means can be easily clarified by an example. If I move the tips of my index fingers toward one another, there occurs in the visual field an event which is called "meeting of the finger tips," and another event in the tactual field which I call "contact of the finger tips." These two events, each of which is a discrete and distinguishable element in its field, always occur simultaneously. This is a fundamental empirical relation between them. Every time that a coincidence occurs in the field of touch, one also occurs in the visual field (at least under favorable circumstances of an exactly specifiable sort, for example, illumination, position of the eyes, etc.). This relationship is independent of the particular sense in question; it is inter-sensual. We also learn from experience that it is inter-subjective. That is to say, all other people who are present affirm (again under given, readily specifiable circumstances) that the same number of homologous coincidences occur in their visual and tactual fields. Thus, not only the different several senses, but also the different subjects agree in their testimony concerning the occurrence of coincidences. The order of these coincidences is nothing other than physical space-order (properly, space-time-order); it is an *objective* order (for by this word we bring together the two ideas of inter-sensual and inter-subjective).

In general, objectivity obtains only for these physical propositions which are tested by means of coincidences, and not for propositions which are concerned with qualities of color or sound, feelings such as sadness or joy, with memories and the like, in short, "psychological" propositions.

The meaning of all physical propositions thus consists in the fact that they formulate either coincidences or laws relating to coincidences; and these are spatio-temporal determinations. One may be tempted to say that this makes sense only if the coinciding items are specified, and that the propositions are incomplete without this addition. But closer examination shows that such specifications (which indeed must be made) refer us back to propositions concerning other coincidences. (Here we find the justification for the theses, elaborated particularly by A. S. Eddington, that physics as a whole is to be understood as geometry. "Geometry" in this connection clearly refers to an empirical science, rather than a purely formal mathematical discipline.) Even explication by means of ostensive gestures, which alone, in the last analysis, relates our concepts to the world, and makes them signs of objects in nature, is readily seen to consist in the bringing about of coincidences (for example, of a pointing finger with the object singled out). The fact that the spatial description of atomic processes does not occur in modern quantum theory does not alter the fact that all physical laws are verified by the occurrence of coincidences; for this holds also of the laws in which magnitudes relating to atoms appear. These magnitudes also have meaning only by their relation to physical space determinations.

According to what we have said above, the essential feature of physical concepts is that they are arrived at by selecting out of the infinite variety of events a special class, namely these "coincidences," and describing their inter-relationships with the help of numbers. Physical magnitudes are identical with the number-combinations which are thus arrived at. The question which we are seeking to answer (in principle) can therefore be put as follows: What is the relation of these coincidences to all other events, for example to the occurrence of a pain, to the change of a color, to a feeling of pleasure, to the emergence of a memory, and so forth?

III

It is usually claimed that the physicist simply and deliberately avoids reference to whatever is not a matter of space-time determinations. He ignores, it is said, the "qualitative" and limits himself to describing the quantitative relationships to be found in the world. This usually develops into the charge that physics is "one-sided"; that it plays a narrowly circumscribed rôle in our knowledge of reality; that it gives us only a fragment which must be supplemented, an empty space-time hull which must be filled with content. This content, it is urged, is the psychological. Psychology would therefore confront physics as an autonomous discipline. Indeed, we often hear the opinion that not even physics and psychology together exhaust the modes of describing the world, and that there remains a place where metaphysics is privileged to lay down the law.

To the assertion of the one-sidedness and limitations of the methods of physics, there stands in sharp opposition the claim that an absolutely complete description of the world is possible by the use of physical methods; that every event in the world can be described in the language of physics, and therefore specifically, that every psychological proposition can be translated into an expression in which physical concepts alone occur. This claim—which is referred to (in somewhat inelegant terminology) as the thesis of "physicalism"—is correct, if the physical language is not only objective, which we have already seen, but is in addition the *only* objective language; or, more accurately, if translatability into the physical language is a necessary condition of objectivity. This seems indeed to be the case. All experience up to now points to the conclusion that only physical concepts and concepts which are reducible to physical concepts fulfill the requirement of objectivity, which is, of course, essential to a language, for without it the language could not serve as a means by which different subjects could arrive at an understanding.

I therefore hold the thesis of physicalism to be correct (compare my *Allgemeine Erkenntnislehre*, 2nd ed., p. 271), but—and this can hardly be overemphasized—it is correct only on the basis of specific *experiences*. The thesis is therefore a factual one, an empirical proposition, as is, say, the proposition that England is an island, or the assertion that conservation of energy obtains in nature. The thesis is therefore not a philosophical discovery. The philosopher as such is not interested in facts of experience as such, for each fact is only one of indefinitely many possible facts. Rather he is interested in the *possibility* of facts. Since, in my opinion, his task is that of determining the meaning of propositions, and since a proposition has meaning only when it formulates a *possible* state of affairs (whether or not the state of affairs actually exists is irrelevant), it is one and the same thing to say that the philosopher is concerned with the meaning of propositions, and to say that he deals with the possibility of facts.

That the world is exactly as it is, that matters stand exactly as experience shows they do, is—in a readily intelligible sense—a contingent fact; and it is in exactly the same sense a contingent fact that the physical language is an inter-subjective universal language. (Even one of the most ardent exponents of "physicalism," Carnap, explains it as a stroke of good luck. Cf. *Erkenntnis* 2, p. 445.) As far as we are concerned, it follows directly from this that the word "physicalism" in no way designates a "philosophical movement." This is an admonition to us to evaluate and make use of the facts which the term brings to mind no differently than any other empirical matter of fact; to treat them, namely, as a paradigm, as one possibility among others. It is exactly by picturing other possible states of affairs from which the one that is actually realized stands out as against a background, that we shall first come to understand the latter correctly, and to grasp the rôle actually played by physical concepts, as well as their relation to psychological concepts.

IV

What, then, are the data of experience on which the objectivity and universality of the physical language rests? They consist in the fact that between the "coincidences" and all other events, there can be found systematic relationships such that to every difference in any of the other events, there corresponds a determinate difference in the coincidences so that, in principle, the world contains no variation nor constancy which does not go hand in hand with a variation or constancy in the domain of coincidences. If this is the case, then clearly the entire world of experience is uniquely determined by these coincidences; when these are known, so is it. It is from this that stems the universal character of the physical language. Two examples may suffice to illustrate. For the first we choose the relationship that exists between the psychological and the physical concepts of color. Physically, a color is defined by a frequency, a number of vibrations per second. This number, as is well known, is arrived at by the familiar procedure of counting the interference fringes of the light or measuring a spectrum, and from the resulting figures along with other measurements read off the apparatus, calculating the "frequency." That is to say, one observes the coincidence of a spectral line or of an interference fringe with certain marks on the measuring apparatus. Now experience shows that these coincidences always occur at the same places, and in accordance with the same general laws, whenever the light has visually the same color. For monochromatic light of an absolutely specific shade of red, I always get exactly the same frequency. Consequently, if I know that a source of light is emitting rays of this frequency, then I know what color I will see when it meets my eye. Thus, to designate the color, it is sufficient to give the frequency. Indeed, this physical designation is actually far more accurate than the corresponding color word (for example, "Bordeaux-red") used by the psychologist.

But is the correspondence of the frequency with the color as seen truly unambiguous? Do I always see the same color when I look at a source emitting the same frequency? Obviously not, for if my eye is tired, or has previously been affected by light of another color, or if my nervous system is under the influence of santonin, then I have different color impressions although objectively the radiation is the same. Doesn't experience refute the "thesis of physicalism"? No, for experience teaches that in all these cases in which, in spite of the identity of the frequency, I see a different color, *other* physical changes are detectable, namely those which concern the state of my organism, in particular my nervous system. The investigation of my nervous system, which is naturally a physical investigation, making use of the method of coincidences, shows (as far as our experience goes) that every difference in color quality goes hand in hand with a difference in the optical segment of the nervous system.

But without concerning ourselves as to whether a physiological investigation of the nervous system will be carried to completion, or is even a technical possibility, we find other physically describable processes which can be used in place of neural events to achieve an unambiguous correspondence between sense-quality and coincidence system, namely the physical behavior of the individual—in particular the reactions (speech, writing, etc.) by which he reports on his sensations when he is asked about their qualities. It will be supposed that the reason these reactions are as satisfactory for the purpose as the above-mentioned neural processes is because they in their turn can be unambiguously correlated with these processes (by virtue of the causal connection between them). But this is irrelevant to our purpose. What concerns us is solely the fact that it is possible unambiguously to coördinate quality of sensation with coincidence systems.

Every change of color quality thus corresponds to a change in the system of coincidences; but this is a matter not of those coincidences alone which are involved in the measuring of the frequency of the light, but also of other coincidences, observable on the body of the perceiver, the belonging of which to the sum-total of coincidences is a matter of empirical fact. With the taking into account of all relevant coincidences, the coördination of physical concepts with the qualities becomes completely unambiguous, as "physicalism" asserts.

One cannot reproach the physicist with the intentional overlooking of all qualities, for it is just not true that he overlooks them. On the contrary, every difference is for him an occasion and a hint to search for a difference of coincidences. If, for example, I were to say that I see blue under circumstances in which one is expected to have a sensation of yellow (say, at the place of the sodium line of the spectrum), the physicist would not rest until he had "explained" this unexpected fact, that is, until he had discovered physical peculiarities in my body, in other words, abnormal measurements shown by certain coincidences, which appear in this case and in no other. The world of qualities is thus of highest importance for him. He in no way forgets it, but on the contrary only regards his quantitative system as a satisfactory description of nature if the manifold of the world of qualities is represented in it by a corresponding multiplicity of numbers.

For our second example, let us take the question as to how the mental datum which is a feeling of grief is expressed and communicated. A feeling of this kind is neither localized, nor do we ascribe it a spatial extent, and its structure is essentially different from that of a sense quality. To be sure, grief is for the most part evoked by external events, that is to say, by events which occur outside the body of the griever, and which can be described in physical terms (for example, someone's death, or the news of a death). But the difference between this case and the preceding consists in the fact that no one believes that there exists a one-to-one correspondence between the quality of the feeling of grief and these external events. Rather, the dependence of the feeling on the state of the subject is so obvious that everybody looks to the body of the griever himself for the coincidences which are here principally in question. Once again we do not need to consider the events in the nervous system—which are for the most part unknown—for it is sufficient to pay attention to his expression, his utterances, his whole deportment. In these processes—which are describable in terms of coincidences—we have the facts by which feelings are expressible in the physical language.

Let it not be thought that the physicist must leave something out of his description, that there is something which he cannot formulate, which it remains, say, for the poet to express. For even the poet can only perceive someone's grief in terms of bodily behavior, and only in terms of bodily behavior can he make it intuitive for the listener. Indeed, the better a psychologist he is, the more he is a master of poetic language, the less he will make use of psychological terms to describe the grief. Instead he will attempt to achieve his purpose in an apparently indirect way by describing how the griever walks, his expression, how he holds his head, the weary movements of his hand, or by repeating his broken words,—occurrences, in short, which can also be described by the physicist, although he would make use of other symbols.

V

How exactly do we build our "psychological" concepts? Whereas the physical language gives formulation to events in their extensive spatial-temporal relationships, the psychologist brings them together from quite a different point of view, namely, in accordance with their "intensive similarity." Thus, each of a large number of different but resembling properties which occur in experience, is called by the common name "green", another manifold is called "yellow", and so on. Both of these manifolds exhibit such a resemblance to one another as well as to certain other qualities, that they are grouped under the common term "color". In addition, there are other elements which differ from these, but resemble each other and therefore receive a common name, as for example, "sound", "pleasure-feeling", "anger", "odor", "pain", "uneasiness", etc. Furthermore, there are families of events which are called "change of color," "intensification of sound," "decrease in brightness," "dying away of a feeling," "visual motion," "tactual motion," and so on. With these there naturally belong the classes of events, "visual coincidence" and "tactual coincidence."

We must therefore include the latter in the list of "psychological" concepts. If this strikes one as paradoxical or seems to contradict our earlier statements, then he is far removed from an understanding of the relation between physical and psychological concepts. It would be clearly a mistake to say: "The coincidences are of a much more complicated nature." If, for example, I dream that I am playing billiards, I see the balls come together in such a way that at certain points on their surfaces there occur coincidences which cannot, however (in this case), be used to construct a physical or objective space. For they are only dream-events. One cannot fit them into the same structure with the corresponding events of an actual game. They obey different laws. The "physical space" that one might construct with their aid, would be an unreal physical space, whereas the visual coincidences of a dream as mental events have naturally the same reality as the fact of waking life. But they do not have the inter-subjectivity which distinguishes the coincidences observed in real life. Indeed, the difference from an actual billiard game consists exactly in the fact that the coincidences of the dream are not suited to the construction of an inter-subjective space, whereas the coincidences of normal life fit in a direct and easy way into the system of physical space and natural law. Thus, it is not the coincidences as such, which constitute the "physical world", rather it is their incorporation into a certain system (the system of objective space) which makes possible the formation of physical concepts. The adjectives "physical" and "mental" formulate only two different representational modes by which the data of experience are ordered; they are different ways of describing reality. That in which one counts ordered coincidences in inter-subjective space, is the physical; whereas that which operates by the grouping of intensive properties is a psychological description.

The so-called "psycho-physical problem" arises from the mixed employment of both modes of representation in one and the same sentence. Words are put side by side which, when correctly used, really belong to different languages. This gives rise to no difficulties in everyday life, because there language isn't pushed to the critical point. This occurs first in philosophical reflection on the propositions of science. Here the physicist must needs assure us that, for example, the sentence, "The leaf is green" merely means that a certain spatial object reflects rays of a certain frequency only: while the psychologist must needs insist that the sentence says something about the quality of a perceptual content. The different "mind-body theories" are only outgrowths of subsequent puzzled attempts to make these interpretations accord with one another. Such theories speak for the most part of a duality of percept and object, inner-world, outer-world, etc., where it is actually only a matter of two linguistic groupings of the events of the world. The circumstance that the physical language as a matter of experience seems to suffice for a complete description of the world, has, as history teaches, not made easy the understanding of the true situation, but has favored the growth of a materialistic meta-physics, which is as much a hindrance to the clarification of the problem as any other metaphysics.

VI

In our world, the physical language has the character of objectivity and universality, which the psychological language seems to lack. It is possible to conceive that matters were turned around—that the formation of psychological concepts was inter-sensual and inter-subjective, while no universal agreement could be achieved in the case of assertions concern-ing coincidences. Such a world would bear no resemblance to the actual world, but one could nevertheless picture it to oneself—as consisting, for example, of a finite number of discrete qualities (classifiable in various resemblance-classes) the simultaneous or successive occurrence of which was shown by experience to be governed by certain laws, but which were never clearly distinguished from one another by clear-cut boundaries. Naturally, in this world, the means of communication, the linguistic sym-bols, would be constructed of entirely different material than our words, and the individuals who speak with one another would not possess spatial bodies of the sort to which we are accustomed,—but all this is not im-possible.

The reason for the fact that exactly the physical language, the language of spatial coincidences, is for us an inter-subjective means of communica-tion, lies naturally in the fact that it is by spatial relationships that indi-viduals are both distinguished from and yet bound up with one another. Putting it somewhat differently: The external world is a spatial world. Indeed, the word "external" serves to designate a spatial relation; and it is easy to see that the opposition between "I" and "external world" is as a matter of fact only the difference between "one's own" body and other physical objects. But the clarification of such complicated concepts as "I" or even "consciousness" lies beyond the scope of this paper. We con-tent ourselves here with the examination of the employment of certain simple psychological and physical terms. It is a preliminary task which prevents the emergence of those difficulties which hide behind the words "psycho-physical problem."

VII

We have emphasized that the circumstances on which rests the uni-versality of the physical language, that is to say, the "thesis of physical-ism," are of an empirical rather than a logical character. They are, how-ever, of such a pervasive sort, and we are so thoroughly accustomed to them, that it is by no means easy to form an idea as to how the world would look if only these decisive relationships did not obtain, though everything else remained the same. It would be a world enormously different from the actual world.

In it there would be no uniform one-to-one correspondence between coincidences and qualities. Perhaps we can imagine this most easily if we consider *feelings*. I can, for example, imagine that my feeling of grief corresponded in no way to any bodily condition. If, for example, I laughed, skipped around, sang and told witty stories, no one would be able to conclude from this that I was gay, rather this behavior would be as compatible with a sorrowful as with a cheerful mood. Above all, and this is a significant point, it would have to be impossible for me to communicate my state of feeling under interrogation. I must not be able, even if I desired, to give information concerning my feelings. (It is extremely difficult to express oneself accurately on such considerations; in our case, the correct formulation would be: in the changed world it would be a law of nature relating to my will, that there was no such thing as a wish to give expression to a feeling.) For if I could say something concerning my feelings, then there would be spatially describable processes, namely, speech movements and speech sounds—by reference to which the feeling qualities could be unambiguously described, and that would contradict our hypothesis. There must be no uniform relation between any kind of external events and the occurrence of my feelings, for otherwise someone could describe my feeling-state as "that which one has on the death of a friend or relative." Only if my feelings occurred entirely without connection with my sense-perceptions, would it be impossible to designate that which in the actual world we call "grief" by a word belonging to inter-subjective language which anyone can understand. It would be impossible to give a definition for such a word.

In the described case there would be a world of feeling which could not be talked about in the physical language. To be sure, all that I could communicate would be expressible in this language. It would be the sole inter-subjective language (in contrast with the possibility suggested in the preceding section), but it would no longer be universal, for in addition to it there would be a private language in which I could reflect about the world of feeling.

Similar considerations arise in connection with the "sense qualities." It is, for example, possible that although all visual coincidences continue as before, they should be accompanied by entirely different perceptual contents from those to which we are accustomed, and, indeed, in a fully irregular way. For example, in the case of the observation of optical spectra, the lines might preserve their exact position, but appear in varying colors, so that the location of the D-line of sodium appeared first as yellow, then as red, then green, etc., without my being able to discover any rule by which the appearance of a specific color was bound up with determinate external conditions capable of being specified by means of coincidences. In this case, while I could always order the colors in classes and assign them symbols, these symbols would not belong to an objective language; they would have only a private use.

With the aid of these symbols I could formulate such regularities as might very well be present and discoverable in the domain of the qualities. Here are a few examples of such possibilities:

1. At every moment, the entire visual field has only one color—with different intensity at different places—but undergoes a temporal variation such that the various colors appear in their spectral order: red, yellow, green, blue, etc.

2. We see the world as red when we are in a cheerful mood; as blue, on the other hand, when we are in an unpleasant mood. These feelings—in accordance with our assumption—must be in no way bound up with bodily events.

3. I have the ability to bring about "arbitrary" changes of quality; I can act in this domain. This, however, can only be allowed on the assumption that the motive for such activity always lies in the qualities themselves, and never in the coincidences. These would not, if I may so express myself, influence my will in so far as it was concerned with qualities; nor, on the other hand, could my will be influenced (if we are to be consistent with our assumptions) by the qualities in so far as it was concerned with coincidences (actions in the external world).

4. If I feel warm, the color qualities change in one direction of the spectrum, if I feel cold, in the other—here as well, needless to say, warmth and coldness must be independent of coincidences.—etc., etc.

In circumstances such as those described, and in a thousand others more or less phantastic, there would be no possibility of assigning words for the color-qualities in an inter-subjective language. We would as a matter of course think of language *qua* means of communication as something which belongs only to the domain of coincidences. We wouldn't even conceive of an alternative possibility, for it wouldn't even occur to us that there could be a connection between coincidences and changes of quality,—just as now many a physicalist may think that there couldn't fail to be such a connection.

The notion of worlds which differ from actuality in the ways we have indicated perhaps makes by no means inconsiderable demands on our imagination; the laws of such a world—and with them the conditions of our own existence—would strike us as extremely strange and would have an entirely different form. But is imagination a privilege of the poet alone? May we not assume it in the philosopher?

VIII

What could be said about such a non-physicalistic world as we have pictured in several examples? First of all perhaps this, that we should hardly speak of it as *one* world but rather as two different domains, one physical, public, and common, and one private, psychological and suited only to monologue. The latter would be to such an extent mine alone, that I couldn't even arrive at the thought of communicating facts concerning it to others. The two worlds would run on side by side. Yet they would not be lacking in all connection. There would be certain relations between the spatial characteristics of the two, for the coincidences would in any case mark the boundaries of the qualities.

By means of a comparison of the constructed example with the actual world we first learn to understand and evaluate the structure of the latter. It is, as far as experience tells us, so constructed that it is fully describable by means of the spatio-temporal conceptual apparatus of Physics; this implies the existence in the world of a certain determinate mode of interconnection. The instant we think away this property of the world, reality falls apart into several domains; it ceases to be a *universe*.

We have therefore to do with an empirical fact of far-reaching significance. But only with an empirical fact. We can be saved from attaching too much weight to this fact by noting that we can conceive of different degrees of the separation of the domain of qualities from that of the coincidences, so that a gradual transition from the actual world to our so completely different imaginary world is conceivable. For example, qualities in general might be strictly bound up with coincidences, with the exception, for example, of a limited domain of colors, let us say, shades of green, for which all our earlier assumptions would be true. In this case, the private domain excluded from physics would be of extremely limited scope. We can, however, think of it as broadened to any desired degree, first to include all visual, then all acoustic qualities, etc., so that the validity of the physicalistic assertion would be ever more restricted.

Moreover, we can think of the worlds of sight, sound, smell, etc., as related to one another in certain uniform ways or not, as we choose. In the latter case we are led to conceive of as many mutually independent domains as there are kinds of quality. Needless to say there is here no question of metaphysical pluralism any more than it would be a metaphysical dualism to contrast the world of qualities uniformly interrelated in accordance with empirical laws with the world of coincidences. Rather we would have to do with an empirical, contingent division of the world, just as it is an empirical contingent fact that we have exactly the number of sense-organs we do, neither more nor less.

If, as a matter of fact, the physical language is characterized by complete universality, the setting down of this circumstance is in no way the assertion of a metaphysical "monism." But one could hardly go wrong with the assumption that it is exactly this empirical fact which impressed the great system builders of the monistic tradition, particularly Spinoza and Leibnitz, even though it was impossible at their time to find the correct way of expressing it. Here, however, we are getting off the main track of our remarks. Our aim has been so to loosen up thought by the consideration of various logical possibilities, as to dispel the traditional associations which have so often hindered the understanding of the relation between physical and psychological propositions.

Logical Foundations of the Unity of Science *

RUDOLF CARNAP

I. WHAT IS LOGICAL ANALYSIS OF SCIENCE?

The task of analyzing science may be approached from various angles.
The analysis of the subject matter of the sciences is carried out by science
itself. Biology, for example, analyzes organisms and processes in organisms, and in a similar way every branch of science analyzes its subject
matter. Mostly, however, by 'analysis of science' or 'theory of science' is
meant an investigation which differs from the branch of science to which
it is applied. We may, for instance, think of an investigation of scientific
activity. We may study the historical development of this activity. Or we
may try to find out in which way scientific work depends upon the individual conditions of the men working in science, and upon the status of
the society surrounding them. Or we may describe procedures and ap-
pliances used in scientific work. These investigations of scientific activity
may be called history, psychology, sociology, and methodology of science.
The subject matter of such studies is science as a body of actions carried
out by certain persons under certain circumstances. Theory of science in
this sense will be dealt with at various other places in this *Encyclopedia;*
it is certainly an essential part of the foundation of science.

We come to a theory of science in another sense if we study not the
actions of scientists but their results, namely, science as a body of ordered
knowledge. Here, by 'results' we do not mean beliefs, images, etc., and
the behavior influenced by them. That would lead us again to psychology
of science. We mean by 'results' certain linguistic expressions, viz., the
statements asserted by scientists. The task of the theory of science in this
sense will be to analyze such statements, study their kinds and relations,
and analyze terms as components of those statements and theories as ordered systems of those statements. A statement is a kind of sequence of
spoken sounds, written marks, or the like, produced by human beings for
specific purposes. But it is possible to abstract in an analysis of the statements of science from the persons asserting the statements and from the
psychological and sociological conditions of such assertions. The analysis

* Reprinted by kind permission of the author and the publishers, the University
of Chicago Press, from *International Encyclopedia of Unified Science*, I, 1. 1938.

of the linguistic expressions of science under such an abstraction is *logic of science*.

Within the logic of science we may distinguish between two chief parts. The investigation may be restricted to the forms of the linguistic expressions involved, i.e., to the way in which they are constructed out of elementary parts (e.g., words) without referring to anything outside of language. Or the investigation goes beyond this boundary and studies linguistic expressions in their relation to objects outside of language. A study restricted in the first-mentioned way is called *formal;* the field of such formal studies is called formal logic or *logical syntax.* Such a formal or syntactical analysis of the language of science as a whole or in its various branches will lead to results of the following kinds. A certain term (e.g., a word) is defined within a certain theory on the basis of certain other terms, or it is definable in such a way. A certain term, although not definable by certain other terms, is reducible to them (in a sense to be explained later). A certain statement is a logical consequence of (or logically deducible from) certain other statements; and a deduction of it, given within a certain theory, is, or is not, logically correct. A certain statement is incompatible with certain other statements, i.e., its negation is a logical consequence of them. A certain statement is independent of certain other statements, i.e., neither a logical consequence of them nor incompatible with them. A certain theory is inconsistent, i.e., some of its statements are incompatible with the other ones. The last sections of this essay will deal with the question of the unity of science from the logical point of view, studying the logical relations between the terms of the chief branches of science and between the laws stated in these branches; thus it will give an example of a syntactical analysis of the language of science.

In the second part of the logic of science, a given language and the expressions in it are analyzed in another way. Here also, as in logical syntax, abstraction is made from the psychological and sociological side of the language. This investigation, however, is not restricted to formal analysis but takes into consideration one important relation between linguistic expressions and other objects—that of designation. An investigation of this kind is called *semantics.* Results of a semantical analysis of the language of science may, for instance, have the following forms. A certain term designates a certain particular object (e.g., the sun), or a certain property of things (e.g., iron), or a certain relation between things (e.g., fatherhood), or a certain physical function (e.g., temperature); two terms in different branches of science (e.g., 'homo sapiens' in biology and 'person' in economics, or, in another way, 'man' in both cases) designate (or: do not designate) the same. What is designated by a certain expression may be called its *designatum.* Two expressions designating the same are called *synonymous.* The term 'true,' as it is used in science and in everyday life, can also be defined within semantics. We see that the chief subject matter of a semantical analysis of the language of science are such properties and relations of expressions, and especially of statements, as are based on the relation of designation. (Where we say 'the designatum of an expression,' the customary phrase is 'the meaning of an expression.' It seems, however, preferable to avoid the word 'meaning' wherever possible because of its ambiguity, i.e., the multiplicity of its designata. Above all, it is important to distinguish between the semantical and the psychological use of the word 'meaning.')

It is a question of terminological convention whether to use the term 'logic' in the wider sense, including the semantical analysis of the designata of expressions, or in the narrower sense of logical syntax, restricted to formal analysis, abstracting from designation. And accordingly we may distinguish between logic of science in the narrower sense, as the syntax of the language of science, and logic of science in the wider sense, comprehending both syntax and semantics.

II. THE MAIN BRANCHES OF SCIENCE

We use the word 'science' here in its widest sense, including all theoretical knowledge, no matter whether in the field of natural sciences or in the field of the social sciences and the so-called humanities, and no matter whether it is knowledge found by the application of special scientific procedures, or knowledge based on common sense in everyday life. In the same way the term 'language of science' is meant here to refer to the language which contains all statements (i.e., theoretical sentences as distinguished from emotional expressions, commands, lyrics, etc.) used for scientific purposes or in everyday life. What usually is called science is merely a more systematic continuation of those activities which we carry out in everyday life in order to know something.

The first distinction which we have to make is that between *formal science* and *empirical science*. Formal science consists of the analytic statements established by logic and mathematics; empirical science consists of the synthetic statements established in the different fields of factual knowledge. The relation of formal to empirical science will be dealt with at another place; here we have to do with empirical science, its language, and the problem of its unity.

Let us take 'physics' as a common name for the nonbiological field of science, comprehending both systematic and historical investigations within this field, thus including chemistry, mineralogy, astronomy, geology (which is historical), meteorology, etc. How, then, are we to draw the boundary line between physics and biology? It is obvious that the distinction between these two branches has to be based on the distinction between two kinds of things which we find in nature: organisms and nonorganisms. Let us take this latter distinction as granted; it is the task of biologists to lay down a suitable definition for the term 'organism,' in other words, to tell us the features of a thing which we take as characteristic for its being an organism. How, then, are we to define 'biology' on the basis of 'organism'? We could perhaps think of trying to do it in this way: biology is the branch of science which investigates organisms and the processes occurring in organisms, and physics is the study of non-organisms. But these definitions would not draw the distinction as it is usually intended. A law stated in physics is intended to be valid universally, without any restriction. For example, the law stating the electrostatic force as a function of electric charges and their distance, or the law determining the pressure of a gas as a function of temperature, or the law determining the angle of refraction as a function of the coefficients of refraction of the two media involved, are intended to apply to the processes in organisms no less than to those in inorganic nature. The biologist has to know these laws of physics in studying the processes in organisms. He needs them for the explanation of these processes. But since they do not suffice, he adds some other laws, not known by the physicist, viz., the specifically biological laws. Biology presupposes physics, but not vice versa.

These reflections lead us to the following definitions. Let us call those terms which we need—in addition to logico-mathematical terms—for the description of processes in inorganic nature *physical terms*, no matter whether, in a given instance, they are applied to such processes or to processes in organisms. That sublanguage of the language of science, which contains—besides logico-mathematical terms—all and only physical terms, may be called *physical language*. The system of those statements which are formulated in the physical language and are acknowledged by a certain group at a certain time is called the physics of that group at that time. Such of these statements as have a specific universal form are called *physical laws*. The physical laws are needed for the explanation of processes in inorganic nature; but, as mentioned before, they apply to processes in organisms also.

The whole of the rest of science may be called *biology (in the wider sense)*. It seems desirable, at least for practical purposes, e.g., for the division of labor in research work, to subdivide this wide field. But it seems questionable whether any distinctions can be found here which, although not of a fundamental nature, are at least clear to about the same degree as the distinction between physics and biology. At present, it is scarcely possible to predict which subdivisions will be made in the future. The traditional distinction between bodily (or material) and mental (or psychical) processes had its origin in the old magical and later metaphysical mind-body dualism. The distinction as a practical device for the classification of branches of science still plays an important role, even for those scientists who reject that metaphysical dualism; and it will probably continue to do so for some time in the future. But when the aftereffect of such prescientific issues upon science becomes weaker and weaker, it may be that new boundary lines for subdivisions will turn out to be more satisfactory.

One possibility of dividing biology in the wider sense into two fields is such that the first corresponds roughly to what is usually called biology, and the second comprehends among other parts those which usually are called psychology and social science. The second field deals with the behavior of individual organisms and groups of organisms within their environment, with the dispositions to such behavior, with such features of processes in organisms as are relevant to the behavior, and with certain features of the environment which are characteristic of and relevant to the behavior, e.g., objects observed and work done by organisms.

The first of the two fields of biology in the wider sense may be called biology in the narrower sense, or, for the following discussions, simply *biology*. This use of the term 'biology' seems justified by the fact that, in terms of the customary classification, this part contains most of what is usually called biology, namely, general biology, botany, and the greater part of zoölogy. The terms which are used in this field in addition to logico-mathematical and physical terms may be called biological terms in the narrower sense, or simply *biological terms*. Since many statements of biology contain physical terms besides biological ones, the *biological language* cannot be restricted to biological terms; it contains the physical language as a sublanguage and, in addition, the biological terms. Statements and laws belonging to this language but not to physical language will be called *biological statements* and *biological laws*.

The distinction between the two fields of biology in the wider sense has been indicated only in a very vague way. At the present time it is not yet clear as to how the boundary line may best be drawn. Which processes in an organism are to be assigned to the second field? Perhaps the connection of a process with the processes in the nervous system might be taken as characteristic, or, to restrict it more, the connection with speaking activities, or, more generally, with activities involving signs. Another way of characterization might come from the other direction, from outside, namely, selecting the processes in an organism from the point of view of their relevance to achievements in the environment (see Brunswik and Ness). There is no name in common use for this second field. (The term 'mental sciences' suggests too narrow a field and is connected too closely with the metaphysical dualism mentioned before.) The term 'behavioristics' has been proposed. If it is used, it must be made clear that the word 'behavior' has here a greater extension than it had with the earlier behaviorists. Here it is intended to designate not only the overt behavior which can be observed from outside but also internal behavior (i.e., processes within the organism); further, dispositions to behavior which may not be manifest in a special case; and, finally, certain effects upon the environment. Within this second field we may distinguish roughly between two parts dealing with individual organisms and with groups of organisms. But it seems doubtful whether any sharp line can be drawn between these two parts. Compared with the customary classification of science, the first part would include chiefly psychology, but also some parts of physiology and the humanities. The second part would chiefly include social science and, further, the greater part of the humanities and history, but it has not only to deal with groups of human beings but also to deal with groups of other organisms. For the following discussion, the terms 'psychology' and 'social science' will be used as names of the two parts because of lack of better terms. It is clear that both the question of boundary lines and the question of suitable terms for the sections is still in need of much more discussion.

III. REDUCIBILITY

The question of the unity of science is meant here as a problem of the logic of science, not of ontology. We do not ask: "Is the world one?" "Are all events fundamentally of one kind?" "Are the so-called mental processes really physical processes or not?" "Are the so-called physical processes really spiritual or not?" It seems doubtful whether we can find any theoretical content in such philosophical questions as discussed by monism, dualism, and pluralism. In any case, when we ask whether there is a unity in science, we mean this as a question of logic, concerning the logical relationships between the terms and the laws of the various branches of science. Since it belongs to the logic of science, the question concerns scientists and logicians alike.

Let us first deal with the question of terms. (Instead of the word 'term' the word 'concept' could be taken, which is more frequently used by logicians. But the word 'term' is more clear, since it shows that we mean signs, e.g., words, expressions consisting of words, artificial symbols, etc., of course with the meaning they have in the language in question. We do not mean 'concept' in its psychological sense, i.e., images or thoughts somehow connected with a word; that would not belong to logic.) We know the meaning (designatum) of a term if we know under what conditions we are permitted to apply it in a concrete case and under what conditions not. Such a knowledge of the conditions of application can be of two different kinds. In some cases we may have a merely practical knowledge, i.e., we are able to use the term in question correctly without giving a theoretical account of the rules for its use. In other cases we may be able to give an explicit formulation of the conditions for the application of the term. If now a certain term x is such that the conditions for its application (as used in the language of science) can be formulated with the help of the terms y, z, etc., we call such a formulation a *reduction statement* for x in terms of y, z, etc., and we call x *reducible* to y, z, etc. There may be several sets of conditions for the application of x; hence x may be reducible to y, z, etc., and also to u, v, etc., and perhaps to other sets. There may even be cases of mutual reducibility, e.g., each term of the set x_1, x_2, etc., is reducible to y_1, y_2, etc.; and, on the other hand, each term of the set y_1, y_2, etc., is reducible to x_1, x_2, etc.

A *definition* is the simplest form of a reduction statement. For the formulation of examples, let us use '$\equiv$' (called the symbol of equivalence) as abbreviation for 'if and only if.' Example of a definition for 'ox': 'x is an $ox \equiv x$ is a quadruped and horned and cloven-footed and ruminant, etc.' This is also a reduction statement because it states the conditions for the application of the term 'ox,' saying that this term can be applied to a thing if and only if that thing is a quadruped and horned, etc. By that definition the term 'ox' is shown to be reducible to—moreover definable by—the set of terms 'quadruped,' 'horned,' etc.

A reduction statement sometimes cannot be formulated in the simple form of a definition, i.e., of an equivalence statement, '. . . . $\equiv$ . . . . ,' but only in the somewhat more complex form 'If . . . . , then: . . . . $\equiv$ . . . . .' Thus a reduction statement is either a simple (i.e., explicit) definition or, so to speak, a conditional definition. (The term 'reduction statement' is generally used in the narrower sense, referring to the second, conditional form.) For instance, the following statement is a reduction statement for the term 'electric charge' (taken here for the sake of simplicity as a nonquantitative term), i.e., for the statement form 'the body x has an electric charge at the time t': 'If a light body y is placed near x at t, then: x has an electric charge at $t \equiv y$ is attracted by x at t.' A general way of procedure which enables us to find out whether or not a certain term can be applied in concrete cases may be called a *method of determination* for the term in question. The method of determination for a quantitative term (e.g., 'temperature') is the method of measurement for that term. Whenever we know an experimental method of determination for a term, we are in a position to formulate a reduction statement for it. To know an experimental method of determination for a term, say 'Q_3.' means to know two things. First, we must know an experimental situation which we have to create, say the state Q_1, e.g., the arrangement of measuring apparatuses and of suitable conditions for their use. Second, we must know the possible experimental result, say Q_2, which, if it occurs, will confirm the presence of the property Q_3. In the simplest case—let us leave aside the more complex cases—Q_2 is also such that its nonoccurrence shows that the thing in question does not have the property Q_3. Then a reduction statement for 'Q_3,' i.e., for the statement form 'the thing (or space-time-point) x is Q_3 (i.e., has the property Q_3) at the time t,' can be formulated in this way: 'If x is Q_1 (i.e., x and the surroundings of x are in the state Q_1) at time t, then: x is Q_3 at $t \equiv x$ is Q_2 at t.' On the basis of this reduction statement, the term 'Q_3' is reducible to 'Q_1,' 'Q_2,' and spatio-temporal terms. Whenever a term 'Q_3' expresses the disposition of a thing to behave in a certain way (Q_2) to certain conditions (Q_1), we have a reduction statement of the form given above. If there is a connection of such a kind between Q_1, Q_2, and Q_3, then in biology and psychology in certain cases the following terminology is applied: 'To the stimulus Q_1 we find the reaction Q_2 as a symptom for Q_3.' But the situation is not essentially different from the analogous one in physics, where we usually do not apply that terminology.

Sometimes we know several methods of determination for a certain term. For example, we can determine the presence of an electric current by observing either the heat produced in the conductor, or the deviation of a magnetic needle, or the quantity of a substance separated from an electrolyte, etc. Thus the term 'electric current' is reducible to each of many sets of other terms. Since not only can an electric current be measured by measuring a temperature but also, conversely, a temperature can be measured by measuring the electric current produced by a thermoelectric element, there is mutual reducibility between the terms of the theory of electricity, on the one hand, and those of the theory of heat, on the other. The same holds for the terms of the theory of electricity and those of the theory of magnetism.

Let us suppose that the persons of a certain group have a certain set of terms in common, either on account of a merely practical agreement about the conditions of their application or with an explicit stipulation of such conditions for a part of the terms. Then a reduction statement reducing a new term to the terms of that original set may be used as a way of introducing the new term into the language of the group. This way of introduction assures conformity as to the use of the new term. If a certain language (e.g., a sublanguage of the language of science, covering a certain branch of science) is such that every term of it is reducible to a certain set of terms, then this language can be constructed on the basis of that set by introducing one new term after the other by reduction statements. In this case we call the basic set of terms a *sufficient reduction basis* for that language.

IV. THE UNITY OF THE LANGUAGE OF SCIENCE

Now we will analyze the logical relations among the terms of different parts of the language of science with respect to reducibility. We have indicated a division of the whole language of science into some parts. Now we may make another division cutting across the first, by distinguishing in a rough way, without any claims to exactness, between those terms which we use on a prescientific level in our everyday language, and for whose application no scientific procedure is necessary, and scientific terms in the narrower sense. That sublanguage which is the common part of this prescientific language and the physical language may be called physical thing-language or briefly *thing-language*. It is this language that we use in speaking about the properties of the observable (inorganic) things surrounding us. Terms like 'hot' and 'cold' may be regarded as belonging to the thing-language, but not 'temperature' because its determination requires the application of a technical instrument; further, 'heavy' and 'light' (but not 'weight'); 'red,' 'blue,' etc.; 'large,' 'small,' 'thick,' 'thin,' etc.

The terms so far mentioned designate what we may call observable properties, i.e., such as can be determined by a direct observation. We will call them *observable thing-predicates*. Besides such terms the thing-language contains other ones, e.g., those expressing the disposition of a thing to a certain behavior under certain conditions, e.g., 'elastic,' 'soluble,' 'flexible,' 'transparent,' 'fragile,' 'plastic,' etc. These terms—they might be called disposition-predicates—are reducible to observable thing-predicates because we can describe the experimental conditions and the reactions characteristic of such disposition-predicates in terms of observable thing-predicates. Example of a reduction statement for 'elastic': 'If the body x is stretched and then released at the time, t, then: x is elastic at the time $t \equiv x$ contracts at t,' where the terms 'stretched,' 'released,' and 'contracting' can be defined by observable thing-predicates. If these predicates are taken as a basis, we can moreover introduce, by iterated application of definition and (conditional) reduction, every other term of the *thing-language*, e.g., designations of substances, e.g., 'stone,' 'water,' 'sugar,' or of processes, e.g., 'rain,' 'fire,' etc. For every term of that language is such that we can apply it either on the basis of direct observation or with the help of an experiment for which we know the conditions and the possible result determining the application of the term in question.

Now we can easily see that every term of the *physical language* is reducible to those of the thing-language and hence finally to observable thing-predicates. On the scientific level, we have the quantitative coefficient of elasticity instead of the qualitative term 'elastic' of the thing-language; we have the quantitative term 'temperature' instead of the qualitative ones 'hot' and 'cold'; and we have all the terms by means of which physicists describe the temporary or permanent states of things or processes. For any such term the physicist knows at least one method of determination. Physicists would not admit into their language any term for which no method of determination by observations were given. The formulation of such a method, i.e., the description of the experimental arrangement to be carried out and of the possible result determining the application of the term in question, is a reduction statement for that term. Sometimes the term will not be directly reduced by the reduction statement to thing-predicates, but first to other scientific terms, and these by their reduction statements again to other scientific terms, etc.; but such a reduction chain must in any case finally lead to predicates of the thing-language and, more-over, to observable thing-predicates because otherwise there would be no way of determining whether or not the physical term in question can be applied in special cases, on the basis of given observation statements.

If we come to *biology* (this term now always understood in the nar-rower sense), we find again the same situation. For any biological term the biologist who introduces or uses it must know empirical criteria for its application. This applies, of course, only to biological terms in the sense explained before, including all terms used in scientific biology proper, but not to certain terms used sometimes in the philosophy of biology—'a whole,' 'entelechy,' etc. It may happen that for the description of the criterion, i.e., the method of determination of a term, other biological terms are needed. In this case the term in question is first reducible to them. But at least indirectly it must be reducible to terms of the thing-language and finally to observable thing-predicates, because the determination of the term in question in a concrete case must finally be based upon observa-tions of concrete things, i.e., upon observation statements formulated in the thing-language.

Let us take as an example the term 'muscle.' Certainly biologists know the conditions for a part of an organism to be a muscle; otherwise the term could not be used in concrete cases. The problem is: Which other terms are needed for the formulation of those conditions? It will be necessary to describe the functions within the organism which are characteristic of muscles, in other words, to formulate certain laws connecting the processes in muscles with those in their environment, or, again in still other words, to describe the reactions to certain stimuli characteristic of muscles. Both the processes in the environment and those in the muscle (in the cus-tomary terminology: stimuli and reactions) must be described in such a way that we can determine them by observations. Hence the term 'muscle,' although not definable in terms of the thing-language, is reducible to them. Similar considerations easily show the reducibility of any other biological term—whether it be a designation of a kind of organism, or of a kind of part of organisms, or of a kind of process in organisms.

The result found so far may be formulated in this way: The terms of the thing-language, and even the narrower class of the observable thing-predicates, supply a sufficient basis for the languages both of physics and of biology. (There are, by the way, many reduction bases for these lan-guages, each of which is much more restricted than the classes mentioned.) Now the question may be raised whether a basis of the kind mentioned is sufficient even for the whole language of science. The affirmative an-swer to this question is sometimes called *physicalism* (because it was first formulated not with respect to the thing-language but to the wider physical language as a sufficient basis). If the thesis of physicalism is ap-plied to biology only, it scarcely meets any serious objections. The situation is somewhat changed, however, when it is applied to psychology and social science (individual and social behavioristics). Since many of the objections raised against it are based on misinterpretations, it is necessary to make clear what the thesis is intended to assert and what not.

The question of the reducibility of the terms of psychology to those of the biological language and thereby to those of the thing-language is closely connected with the problem of the various methods used in psychology. As chief examples of methods used in this field in its present state, the physiological, the behavioristic, and the introspective methods may be considered. The *physiological approach* consists in an investigation of the functions of certain organs in the organism, above all, of the nervous system. Here, the terms used are either those of biology or those so closely related to them that there will scarcely be any doubt with respect to their reducibility to the terms of the biological language and the thing-language. For the *behavioristic approach* different ways are possible. The investigation may be restricted to the external behavior of an organism, i.e., to such movements, sounds, etc., as can be observed by other organisms in the neighborhood of the first. Or processes within the organism may also be taken into account so that this approach overlaps with the physiological one. Or, finally, objects in the environment of the organism, either observed or worked on or produced by it, may also be studied. Now it is easy to see that a term for whose determination a behavioristic method—of one of the kinds mentioned or of a related kind—is known, is reducible to the terms of the biological language, including the thing-language. As we have seen before, the formulation of the method of determination for a term is a reduction statement for that term, either in the form of a simple definition or in the conditional form. By that statement the term is shown to be reducible to the terms applied in describing the method, namely, the experimental arrangement and the characteristic result. Now, conditions and results consist in the behavioristic method either of physiological processes in the organism or of observable processes in the organism and in its environment. Hence they can be described in terms of the biological language. If we have to do with a behavioristic approach in its pure form, i.e., leaving aside physiological investigations, then the description of the conditions and results characteristic for a term can in most cases be given directly in terms of the thing-language. Hence the behavioristic reduction of psychological terms is often simpler than the physiological reduction of the same term.

Let us take as an example the term 'angry.' If for anger we knew a sufficient and necessary criterion to be found by a physiological analysis of the nervous system or other organs, then we could define 'angry' in terms of the biological language. The same holds if we knew such a criterion to be determined by the observation of the overt, external behavior. But a physiological criterion is not yet known. And the peripheral symptoms known are presumably not necessary criteria because it might be that a person of strong self-control is able to suppress these symptoms. If this is the case, the term 'angry' is, at least at the present time, not definable in terms of the biological language. But, nevertheless, it is reducible to such terms. It is sufficient for the formulation of a reduction sentence to know a behavioristic procedure which enables us—if not always, at least under suitable circumstances—to determine whether the organism in question is angry or not. And we know indeed such procedures; otherwise we should never be able to apply the term 'angry' to another person on the basis of our observations of his behavior, as we constantly do in everyday life and in scientific investigation. A reduction of the term 'angry' or similar terms by the formulation of such procedures is indeed less useful than a definition would be, because a definition supplies a complete (i.e., unconditional) criterion for the term in question, while a reduction statement of the conditional form gives only an incomplete one. But a criterion, conditional or not, is all we need for ascertaining reducibility. Thus the result is the following: If for any psychological term we know either a physiological or a behavioristic method of determination, then that term is reducible to those terms of the thing-language.

In psychology, as we find it today, there is, besides the physiological and the behavioristic approach, the so-called *introspective method*. The questions as to its validity, limits, and necessity are still more unclear and in need of further discussion than the analogous questions with respect to the two other methods. Much of what has been said about it, especially by philosophers, may be looked at with some suspicion. But the facts themselves to which the term 'introspection' is meant to refer will scarcely be denied by anybody, e.g., the fact that a person sometimes knows that he is angry without applying any of those procedures which another person would have to apply, i.e., without looking with the help of a physiological instrument at his nervous system or looking at the play of his facial muscles. The problems of the practical reliability and theoretical validity of the introspective method may here be left aside. For the discussion of reducibility an answer to these problems is not needed. It will suffice to show that in every case, no matter whether the introspective method is applicable or not, the behavioristic method can be applied at any rate. But we must be careful in the interpretation of this assertion. It is not meant as saying: 'Every psychological process can be ascertained by the behavioristic method.' Here we have to do not with the single processes themselves (e.g., Peter's anger yesterday morning) but with kinds of processes (e.g., anger). If Robinson Crusoe is angry and then dies before anybody comes to his island, nobody except himself ever knows of this single occurrence of anger. But anger of the same kind, occurring with other persons, may be studied and ascertained by a behavioristic method, if circumstances are favorable. (Analogy: if an electrically charged raindrop falls into the ocean without an observer or suitable recording instrument in the neighborhood, nobody will ever know of that charge. But a charge of the same kind can be found out under suitable circumstances by certain observations.) Further, in order to come to a correct formulation of the thesis, we have to apply it not to the kinds of processes (e.g., anger) but rather to the terms designating such kinds of processes (e.g., 'anger'). The difference might seem trivial but is, in fact, essential. We do not at all enter a discussion about the question whether or not there are kinds of events which can never have any behavioristic symptoms, and hence are knowable only by introspection. We have to do with psychological terms, not with kinds of events. For any such term, say, 'Q,' the psychological language contains a statement form applying that term, e.g., 'The person . . . . is at the time . . . . in the state Q.' Then the utterance by speaking or writing of the statement 'I am now (or: I was yesterday) in the state Q,' is (under suitable circumstances, e.g., as to reliability, etc.) an observable symptom for the state Q. Hence there cannot be a term in the psychological language, taken as an intersubjective language for mutual communication, which designates a kind of state or event without any behavioristic symptom. Therefore, there is a behavioristic method of determination for any term of the psychological language. Hence every such term is reducible to those of the thing-language.

The logical nature of the psychological terms becomes clear by an analogy with those physical terms which are introduced by reduction statements of the conditional form. Terms of both kinds designate a state characterized by the disposition to certain reactions. In both cases the state is not the same as those reactions. Anger is not the same as the movements by which an angry organism reacts to the conditions in his environment, just as the state of being electrically charged is not the same as the process of attracting other bodies. In both cases that state sometimes occurs without these events which are observable from outside; they are consequences of the state according to certain laws and may therefore under suitable circumstances be taken as symptoms for it; but they are not identical with it.

The last field to be dealt with is *social science* (in the wide sense indicated before; also called social behavioristics). Here we need no detailed analysis because it is easy to see that every term of this field is reducible to terms of the other fields. The result of any investigation of a group of men or other organisms can be described in terms of the members, their relations to one another and to their environment. Therefore, the conditions for the application of any term can be formulated in terms of psychology, biology, and physics, including the thing-language. Many terms can even be defined on that basis, and the rest is certainly reducible to it.

It is true that some terms which are used in psychology are such that they designate a certain behavior (or disposition to behavior) within a group of a certain kind or a certain attitude toward a group, e.g., 'desirous of ruling,' 'shy,' and others. It may be that for the definition or reduction of a term of this kind some terms of social science describing the group involved are needed. This shows that there is not a clear-cut line between psychology and social science and that in some cases it is not clear whether a term is better assigned to one or to the other field. But such terms are also certainly reducible to those of the thing-language because every term referring to a group of organisms is reducible to terms referring to individual organisms.

The result of our analysis is that the class of observable thing-predicates is a sufficient reduction basis for the whole of the language of science, including the cognitive part of the everyday language.

V. THE PROBLEM OF THE UNITY OF LAWS

The relations between the terms of the various branches of science have been considered. There remains the task of analyzing the relations between the laws. According to our previous consideration, a biological law contains only terms which are reducible to physical terms. Hence there is a common language to which both the biological and the physical laws belong so that they can be logically compared and connected. We can ask whether or not a certain biological law is compatible with the system of physical laws, and whether or not it is derivable from them. But the answer to these questions cannot be inferred from the reducibility of the terms. At the present state of the development of science, it is certainly not possible to derive the biological laws from the physical ones. Some philosophers believe that such a derivation is forever impossible because of the very nature of the two fields. But the proofs attempted so far for this thesis are certainly insufficient. This question is, it seems, the scientific kernel of the problem of vitalism; some recent discussions of this problem are, however, entangled with rather questionable metaphysical issues. The question of derivability itself is, of course, a very serious scientific problem. But it will scarcely be possible to find a solution for it before many more results of experimental investigation are available than we have today. In the meantime the efforts toward derivation of more and more biological laws from physical laws—in the customary formulation: explanation of more and more processes in organisms with the help of physics and chemistry—will be, as it has been, a very fruitful tendency in biological research.

As we have seen before, the fields of psychology and social science are very closely connected with each other. A clear division of the laws of these fields is perhaps still less possible than a division of the terms. If the laws are classified in some way or other, it will be seen that sometimes a psychological law is derivable from those of social science, and sometimes a law of social science from those of psychology. (An example of the first kind is the explanation of the behavior of adults—e.g., in the theories of A. Adler and Freud—by their position within the family or a larger group during childhood; an example of the second kind is the obvious explanation of an increase of the price of a commodity by the reactions of buyers and sellers in the case of a diminished supply.) It is obvious that, at the present time, laws of psychology and social science cannot be derived from those of biology and physics. On the other hand, no scientific reason is known for the assumption that such a derivation should be in principle and forever impossible.

Thus there is at present *no unity of laws*. The construction of one homogeneous system of laws for the whole of science is an aim for the future development of science. This aim cannot be shown to be unattainable. But we do not, of course, know whether it will ever be reached.

On the other hand, there is a *unity of language* in science, viz., a common reduction basis for the terms of all branches of science, this basis consisting of a very narrow and homogeneous class of terms of the physical thing-language. This unity of terms is indeed less far-reaching and effective than the unity of laws would be, but it is a necessary preliminary condition for the unity of laws. We can endeavor to develop science more and more in the direction of a unified system of laws only because we have already at present a unified language. And, in addition, the fact that we have this unity of language is of the greatest practical importance. The practical use of laws consists in making predictions with their help. The important fact is that very often a prediction cannot be based on our knowledge of only one branch of science. For instance, the construction of automobiles will be influenced by a prediction of the presumable number of sales. This number depends upon the satisfaction of the buyers and the economic situation. Hence we have to combine knowledge about the function of the motor, the effect of gases and vibration on the human organism, the ability of persons to learn a certain technique, their willingness to spend so much money for so much service, the development of the general economic situation, etc. This knowledge concerns particular facts and general laws belonging to all the four branches, partly scientific and partly common-sense knowledge. For very many decisions, both in individual and in social life, we need such a prediction based upon a combined knowledge of concrete facts and general laws belonging to different branches of science. If now the terms of different branches had no logical connection between one another, such as is supplied by the homogeneous reduction basis, but were of fundamentally different character, as some philosophers believe, then it would not be possible to connect singular statements and laws of different fields in such a way as to derive predictions from them. Therefore, the unity of the language of science is the basis for the practical application of theoretical knowledge.

SELECTED BIBLIOGRAPHY

I. LOGICAL ANALYSIS

Carnap, R. *Philosophy and Logical Syntax*, London, 1935. (Elementary.)
——, *Logical Syntax of Language*, London, 1937. (Technical.)

II. REDUCIBILITY

Carnap, R. "Testability and Meaning", *Philosophy of Science*, 3, 1936, and 4, 1937.

III. THE UNITY OF THE LANGUAGE OF SCIENCE; PHYSICALISM

Papers by Neurath and Carnap, *Erkenntnis*, 2, 1932; *ibid.*, 3, 1933. Translation of one of these papers: Carnap, *The Unity of Science*, London, 1934. Concerning psychology: papers by Schlick, Hempel, and Carnap, *Revue de synthèse*, 10, 1935. [The papers by Hempel and Schlick are included in the present collection.]

Realism and the New Way of Words *

WILFRID SELLARS

I

It has been said that a system of philosophy is not refuted, but becomes ignored. This is true. It is equally true (and for the same reason) that a clash of systems in the philosophical drama ends not in victory and defeat, but in a changing of the scene. Put from a somewhat different point of view, the historical development of philosophy is more truly conceived as the periodic formulation of new questions, than as a series of attempted answers to an enduring body of problems. Although the new questions which appear in this process can be regarded, for the most part, as revisions or reformulations of earlier issues, the fact of revision and reformulation is of the essence of the matter, making new questions out of old. Put in these terms, a system dies when the questions it seeks to answer are no longer asked; and only where the questions are the same can there be a genuine clash of answers.

An essentially similar point of view which, however, cuts a bit deeper, argues that in philosophy, as opposed to the factual sciences, the answer to a properly formulated question must, in the nature of the case, be obvious. It suggests that the evolution of philosophical thought is accurately conceived neither as a series of different answers to the same questions, nor as a series of different sets of questions, but rather as the series of approximations by which philosophers move toward the discovery of the very questions they have been trying to answer all the time. This conception of philosophy as a quest of which the goal is the obvious, is, I believe, a sound one. It is the problems and not the answers that are difficult; and a genuine advance is constituted by the replacement of a confused by a less confused question, where the two are in some sense the same.

We have suggested that philosophy as an ongoing enterprise depends for its existence on lack of clarity; that the mere occurrence of philosophical dispute entails that at least one of the parties is tangled in a confused formulation. This thesis is by no means novel, yet many who subscribe to it conceive of philosophical confusion as confusion the removal of which leaves nothing *philosophical* behind unless it be the score for a

* Reprinted, with minor alterations, by kind permission of the editors from *Philosophy and Phenomenological Research*, 8, 1948.

repeat performance, so that philosophy *becomes* and never *is*. I have implicitly rejected this view by speaking of philosophical questions and answers. Yet clarification is the significant element in philosophical activity, however its nature be conceived. In what, then, does philosophical confusion consist? I doubt that it is a proper or unique species. It appears, rather, to be common or garden variety confusion flowering in an unusually fertile field. It is bad reasoning aided and abetted by factual ignorance. It is asking questions which imply answers to prior questions which have not even been raised. It is using terms now in one sense, now in another. In short, it is making mistakes. The factual ignorance which has assisted philosophers in making mistakes has been, and still is, primarily in the field of psychology. The undeveloped state of the science of the higher processes has thrown philosophers on their own resources in an intricate factual field. The absence of a structure of scientific law in which such key terms as 'conscious', 'concept', 'abstracting', 'knowing', 'believing', etc., are firmly held in place, has made it easy to the point of inevitability to pass from one question to another which only appears to be the same. In particular, this lack has tended to result in a failure clearly to distinguish epistemological from psychological issues. While much has been accomplished in the way of securing this distinction, it is still unfinished business. Here is confusion to be clarified.

II

It was long the custom in systematic discussions of epistemology, to ask the man in the street certain questions concerning what, after all, he *knew* (which questions, being a man in the street, he had never asked himself), and from the answers construct the invaluable dialectical foil called Naïve Realism. Thus arrived at, this construction inevitably appeared in the light of a conviction we all share, appeared to be *common sense*, to be something we all wish were true; and the process whereby subsequent examination first raised doubts, then finally pressed it to humiliating collapse tended to take on the character of a tragedy akin to the loss of our childhood faiths. The inevitable stages in the argument which, initiated by this manner of posing the question, dissolved the grim, but comfortingly substantial, world around us in the dialectical acids of the schools left those who stayed to the bitter end convinced, but uneasy. Somehow the magic was gone. The acts of the tragedy (though not always performed in this order) were Naïve Realism, New Realism, Critical Realism, Idealism, Pragmatism and Epistemological Solipsism of the Present Moment.

It has become increasingly clear, in the course of the past decade, that this particular tragedy was based on a mistake; on an asking of the wrong, or better, of a confused question. This suggests immediately, in view of considerations advanced in the first section of this paper, that the curtain is being rung down on this particular cluster of controversies, and that new *dramatis personae* are moving to the center of the stage. This is true; but those considerations also suggest that while the new questions may be clearer, they will none the less be in essence the same, and that consequently the new play will be the old, cut and adapted to modern dress. The empirical and the formal, the psychological and the epistemological will be more clearly distinguished, yet the competing points of view will be found capable of translation into the new frame of reference, if only to be curtly dismissed. In the remainder of this paper I propose to indicate how the realism issue becomes transformed when translated into the new way of words.

III

A Claim of Language. One of the most striking features of the language we use, from the standpoint of epistemological analysis, is the fact that it enables us to speak not only about this or that individual occurrence in space and time, but also about *some* individuals and about *all* individuals. Thus, it makes sense to say that while 'All swans are white' does not entail 'There are swans', and consequently is not in the technical sense an existential proposition, it does none the less talk about *everything* that *is* and about *nothing* that *is not* and says of *each* item that either it is white or else it is not a swan. It has not always, however, been realized that this train of thought leads directly to the conclusion that our language claims somehow to contain a designation for every element in every state of affairs, past, present and future; that, in other words, it claims to mirror the world by a complete and systematic one-to-one correspondence of designations with individuals. If it is obvious that our language does not *explicitly* contain such designations (and it would hardly be illuminating to say that it contains them *implicitly*), it is equally clear that our language behaves as though it contained them. We shall begin our epistemological examination of language by considering the nature and status of general propositions. But first we shall introduce a methodological device that will be used throughout this paper as an aid to the formulation of epistemological issues.

Epistemology Writ Large: The Language of Omniscience. Philosophers have on occasion found it useful to stand back and essay a God-like vision of the universe; to attempt to see things as they would be seen by an omniscient being. Translated into the new way of words, this endeavor becomes the attempt to envisage the language of omniscience. A consideration of the larger writing may assist us in our argument as it did Socrates in the *Republic*. To be of value, however, the omniscient being whose language we have in mind must be no transcendent Deity with vaguely specified though omnivorous cognitive powers, but rather one who shares, apart from his omniscience, our human lot through being immersed in time, and limited to our characteristic ways of confronting the world. The notion of such a being will be used as a device for suggesting statements to be clarified. We shall begin with no other characterization of omniscience than that offered by common sense. It is not a question of using a clear notion of omniscience and the language of omniscience to clarify a confused notion of human cognition and language. It is rather a matter of writing the latter confusion large so that it may more easily be clarified.

The feature of the language of an omniscient being with which we shall primarily be concerned in this paper is the fact that it permits him to formulate a body of completely unpacked or logically simple sentences which together constitute the story of the universe in which he lives. In the previous section we permitted ourselves to be puzzled by the fact that it makes sense to say that our language enables us to *speak about everything* though it does not enable us to *list each thing*. Since it is involved in the notion of the language of omniscience that it is able to do both, an examination of the status of general propositions in this language should prove fruitful.

Omniscience and the Universal Proposition. When our hypothetical omniscient being (we shall call him, for convenience, Jones) makes the statement 'All A's are B', he makes no claim which he cannot back up with an explicit use of language. Thus he can also say:

> (1) 'i_1 is B or not-A and i_2 is B or not-A . . . and i_n is B or not-A . . . .'

where the dots serve only to indicate the unreproducible magnitude of the statement Jones would actually make. Such a device would play no rôle in the Jonesean utterance. But can we say that (1) even as formulated by Jones would be equivalent to 'All A's are B'? Would he not have to add a further statement,

> (2) 'i_1, i_2, . . . i_n, . . . are all the individuals'

where the dots, again, would not appear in the Jonesean formulation? But (2) as it stands is misleading. Individuality is not a quality, or, to put it more technically, in the language in which (1) and (2) are formulated, the term 'individual' has the status of a reflection of the syntactical predicate 'individual constant of the Jonesean language.' Thus (2) must be understood as the reflection ("quasi-syntactical" expression) of something like

> (2') ' 'i_1,' 'i_2,' . . . 'i_n,' . . . are all the individual constants of the (Jonesean) language.'

This step brings with it a considerable clarification, for it is clear that the question as to what individual constants a language contains is a purely linguistic question which as such involves no reference to the extra-linguistic. Its truth rests on what we shall take to be an analytic truth, namely,

(2″) 'An individual constant of the (Jonesean) language is either 'i_1' or 'i_2' . . . or 'i_n' or . . .'

Thus we see that doubts concerning the adequacy of a given conjunction as a translation of a sentence beginning with 'all' in the Jonesean language are resolvable by appeal to the battery of individual constants included in the resources of that language. We are now in a position to give our problem a more accurate formulation:

Granted that in the syntactical dimension the core of "all-ness" in the language of omniscience is to be found in the battery of individual constants which make up one segment of the resources of the language, *what makes the Jonesean language with its battery adequate to Jones' world so that as an omniscient being he uses it?* Or, to put it somewhat differently, what is the non-syntactical core of the reach of the language of an omniscient being?

A Pragmatic Step. If the question were so phrased as to read, "What criterion enables Jones to select a language which contains a just adequate supply of individual terms?" we should be tempted to reply by formulating a thesis to the effect that the world is directly present to the Jonesean mind, and that consequently he can compare his language with the world. Not only, however, would such a notion be out of keeping with the restrictions we have imposed on our omniscient being; it could not in any case begin to give the explanation demanded of it. Even if Jones could confront all the individual items in his language with items directly present to his mind, it would not follow that this set of terms was adequate to the 'totality of existence', for no *collection* of objects of awareness could give the required assurance of totality. As a last resort, we might claim that the items directly present to the Jonesean mind form a system one of the characteristics of which is that it is *incompatible with the existence of anything more*. There may be some sense to the notion of such a system, but as thus formulated it makes the mistake which underlies the ontological argument. Properly formulated (as will be brought out later) it is as much a "quasi-linguistic" concept as that of *individual*. We are thus forced to the conclusion that if it makes sense to speak of a one-to-one correspondence of the individual constants of the Jonesean language with the constituents of his world, this correspondence cannot be ascribed to a direct comparing of language with world.

Now to say that a battery of individual constants is adequate to the world, is to say that each constant *means* an item in the world, and each item in the world is *meant* by an individual constant of the language. Thus we can at least say that the concept of adequacy must be clarified in terms of a meta-language involving semantic resources (for semantics gives us a logic of *meaning*). Furthermore, in spite of the failure of the above attempts, this clarification must involve some relation of the language to Jones who uses it, and whose omniscience it embodies. In this latter respect, it is clear that our account must involve a *pragmatic* element, for the term "pragmatic" in current semiotics refers to language *as used*.

Language and Language Schema. If the situation stands so with respect to the concept of the language of omniscience, how stands it with us? We have said that our language *claims*, as far as its reach is concerned, to be an omniscient language. We are now in a position to reformulate this idea. If by 'language' is meant a symbolic system in which all individual constants and predicates are explicitly listed without the use of such devices as '. . . .' or 'and', a system, that is to say, in which the expressions which are substitutable for variables are explicitly listed, then it is clear that we do not speak a language, but rather the schema of a language. Only an omniscient being could effectively use such a language. As a matter of fact, to say that a being effectively uses such a language seems to be at least part of what is meant by calling him omniscient. The symbolic structure we employ resembles a language (in the sense above defined) reasonably well as far as predicates are concerned, but is almost completely schematic as far as individual constants are concerned. We are obliged to make use of general propositions in talking about the world. We rarely, if ever, make a statement which when clarified is not, at least in part, general in form. *But general propositions as we use them are not the full-blooded general propositions of a language proper.* The variables in the latter are genuine (even if bound) variables. The language contains individual and predicate constants which are the domains of these variables. The symbolic structure we use contains *schemata* of general propositions. These we use as though we spoke a complete language proper to which they belonged. *They serve as pragmatic devices which enable us to get along somewhat as though we spoke a language proper.*

We can sum up our line of thought as follows:

The adequacy in reach of even an omniscient language is to be pragmatically construed. The language of a non-omniscient being is therefore doubly pragmatic. It enables him to get along to some extent as though he spoke the adequate language of an omniscient being. *These two uses of the term 'pragmatic' need not have the same sense. Indeed, we shall see that they do not, for the former sense turns out to be a purely formal one belonging to pure pragmatics; the latter, on the other hand, is empirical or factual, belonging to empirical pragmatics.*

IV

The Meaning of 'Meaning': Psychologism. It has until recently been a characteristic assumption of philosophers of both nominalistic and, in the medieval sense, realistic persuasions, that *meaning* in epistemological contexts is a psychological fact involving self, sign and *designatum*. Perhaps the most explicit expression of this notion is to be found in Russell's *Problems of Philosophy*. He writes, "We must attach some meaning to the words we use, if we are to speak significantly and not utter mere noise; and the meaning we attach to our words must be something with which we are acquainted" (p. 91). It needs but a moment's reflection to realize that this conception of the meaning of symbols leads directly to Platonism.

A nominalist who commits himself to this account of meaning is committing himself to nonsense. For if the meaning of a symbol must always be something with which someone is or can be acquainted on the occasion of a significant employment of that symbol, then either there are subsistent essences and propositions with which we can be acquainted, or else the meanings of symbols are restricted to *sensa* and *introspecta*, so that indeed symbols must be radically ambiguous, meaning different data on each occasion of their use.[1] But the latter (nominalistic) alternative not only reduces the scope of what can be meant to an extent which makes it equivalent to a denial of meaning by limiting meaning, it would appear, to exactly what does not need to be meant; it actually makes even this limited scope of meaning impossible, for even sentences about *sensa* and *introspecta* involve universal terms, the meaning of which clearly transcends the hard data of the present moment.

It has become the fashion to accuse nominalism of this type of psychologism. The charge is a sound one *if correctly interpreted*. If, however, the charge is taken to mean that these philosophers limit what can be meant to psychological facts, then a consequence of nominalistic psychologism is confused with the psychologistic blunder itself. For the essence of the latter consists *not* in any assertion as to what can be meant, *but in taking meaning to be a psychological fact*.[2] To be guilty of it is to suppose that the term 'means' in such sentences as " 'A' means B" stands for a psychological fact involving the symbol 'A' and the item B, whether the psychological fact be analysed in terms of *Schau*, acquaintance or just plain experience. Psychologism underlies both Platonism and Humian nominalism, not to mention the conceptualistic attempt at compromise.[3]

[1] I leave out of consideration the conceptualistic approach which substitutes for subsistent essences a special class of mental item called 'concepts' in which *abstracta* have 'objective' or 'intentional' being, and for propositions a class of mental phenomena called 'judgments' which have more complex intentional objects.

[2] The appearance of extreme paradox presented by this statement can be removed by drawing a distinction, implicit in our discussion, between two uses of the term 'meaning', (1) that which occurs in distinctively philosophical (epistemological) contexts, (2) that which occurs in psychological statements concerning symbol behavior. Our contention can be summarized by saying that the epistemological sense turns out to be purely formal, and sharply to be distinguished from the empirical or psychological sense, though it is, in a sense that is difficult to analyse, a "reconstruction" of it. Once this is seen, the latter loses its metaphysical aura, and becomes a less mysterious subject for empirical analysis. An equally important gain in the opposite direction is the elimination of one of the most persistent sources of confusion in epistemology.

[3] Thus under the broader heading of *psychologism* as the confusion of epistemology with psychology, we can distinguish two sub-forms according as epistemology or empirical psychology predominate in the confusion. If the former, epistemological content appears in the guise of psychological acts and objects *sui generis* (*Wesensschau*, universals as apprehendable objects, intentional acts, intentional objects, etc.). These are ranged alongside the facts of empirical psychology, which persist in the confusion. This first sub-form can be called *epistemologism* (Plato, Aristotle, Kant). On the other hand, if empirical psychology dominates, we have *psychologism* in the narrower sense attacked by Husserl (who was himself guilty of epistemologism). Here the episte-

The essentially *new* feature of the New Way of Words is that it does not commit this mistake. Epistemologism leads to *ontological realism* with respect to classes and universals. Psychologism in the narrower sense leads to the absurdities of *logical nominalism*. The New Nominalism avoids both, and defends instead *logical or epistemological realism* with respect to universals and classes. As we shall see, the New Way of Words does justice to the Platonic insight, while avoiding its supposed factual implications. (See pp. 444 ff. and footnote 14 below.)

Behavior, Norm and the Semantic Meta-Language. The psychologistic blunder with respect to "means" is related to another fundamental error, that, namely, of confusing between (1) language as a descriptive category for which symbols are empirical classes to which certain events belong (and hence are symbol-events) by virtue of performing an empirical function, with (2) language as an epistemological category for which the relation of type to token is not that of empirical class to member. We shall develop and explain this contrast in the course of this paper. *For the moment* it will help clarify the epistemological distinction between symbol-types and symbol-tokens, if we think of the former as norms or standards, and the latter as events which satisfy them. We can therefore, *for the moment* at least, contrast the above two senses of 'language' as the descriptive and the normative respectively. Making use of this distinction, we argue that 'meaning' or, better, 'designation' is a term belonging to language *about* languages in the second sense. Its primary employment is therefore in connection with linguistic expressions as norms, and consequently cannot concern a psychological relation of language expressions to objects of acquaintance (even essences). It is only symbol-events which could enter into such a psychological transaction. If this is the case, it is hard to see what kind of a factual relation 'designates' could be. The New Nominalism takes 'means' or 'designates' to be a purely formal term, that is to say, a term which as little stands for a feature of the world as 'implies' or 'and'. It has nothing to do with psychological acts, intuitions, or, indeed, with experience of any kind. It refers to no psychological act, intuition or transaction of any sort.

If this is the case, then the *limitations of meaning* can no more be settled by an "appeal to experience," than can the limitations of (mathematical) *addition* or *logical deducibility*. To say this, however, is not to say that experience imposes no limitations on the meaning of empirically meaningful language, so that we have magically been saved from a solipsistic account of such language. It is merely to say that if epistemology has anything to say about the relation of *meaning* to *experience*, then the term 'experience' as used by the epistemologist must belong to the same frame as 'meaning' and 'implication.' 'Experience' in this

mological (which has less survival power) tends to be reduced to a descriptive study of *how we think*. Epistemologism has the virtue of preserving philosophical content, though at the expense of constructing a fictitious psychology. Psychologism in the narrower sense lacks merit as philosophy, although the philosopher and psychologist can join hands in approving its avoidance of pseudo-psychology.

use must be contrasted with 'experience' as a term of empirical psychology, just as we have already contrasted 'language' as an epistemological term with 'language' as an expression in socio-psychologico-historical linguistics. Our discussion will lead us to the conception of a type of meta-language in which a family of expressions among which are 'experience' and 'meaningful' supplement customary semantical and syntactical predicates in such a way that the theory of such meta-languages is the pure, *a priori*, in short non-empirical, theory of empirically meaningful languages.

V

The Use of Language: Background to Pragmatics. If the language of our omniscient being permits the formulation of a world-story which, in a sense to be clarified, constitutes knowledge of the world in which he lives, the language also permits the formulation of sentences which are incompatible with sentences included in the story, and indeed, *it would seem*, of alternative world-stories. Thus we can hardly say that one of these bodies of sentences constitutes knowledge on the part of Omniscient Jones, unless we can also say that his selection of this set of sentences is in some sense *justified*. Now the problem we are attempting to formulate does not belong to empirical psychology. We are not concerned with the psychology of belief. *Our goal is a pragmatics which avoids psychologism as rigorously as does semantics as we have conceived it.* Until, however, we can make our problem stand out, we must be content with a blurring of distinctions, and wander for a time between pure pragmatics and psychology.

Before we ask concerning the *justification* of the selection of a set of sentences by Jones as the story of his world, let us seek to understand what such selection involves. In the first place, this selection would seem to involve that tokens of the sentences of this world-story occur in the immediate sense-experience of Jones. But while this would constitute a *sine qua non* of such selection, it would hardly seem to be a sufficient condition; for while such tokening might conceivably constitute Jones' selection of a story of *a* world, the fact that the world is *his* world would not have been clarified. Let us take another look at the Jonesean world-story. It occurs to us that, since it speaks about everything, it must mention Jones *who uses it*. That is to say, it must include sentences which constitute the biography of Omniscient Jones, and, which is more important, sentences which constitute the sense-biography [4] of Jones. Combining this train of thought with the above, we have the notion that for the world-story which Jones selects to be the story of *his* world, Jones' immediate experience must include tokens of sentences which constitute the sense-biography of Jones. In other words, Jones' immediate experience must include items which are tokens of sentences which *designate* the contents of that immediate experience. Tersely put, *tokens of (Jones-) sense-*

---

[4] The phrase 'sense-biography' will be used as short for 'immediate-sense-experience-biography'.

biographical sentences must be co-experienced with the sense-data which these sentences mean or designate. Thus, if i_n is a Jonesean sensation of green, the world-story includes the sentence 'i_n is co-experienced with a case of the sound *eye-sub-en-iz-grēn*,' where the case of *eye-sub-en-iz-grēn* is a token of the sentence 'i_n is (a sensation of) green.' We must say, then, that in one aspect these tokens are *included in* Jones' immediate experience, while in another aspect they are *about* Jones' immediate experience.

It is clear that since 'type', 'token' and 'designates' are meta-linguistic terms, what we have been saying about the relation of Jones to the Jonesean world-story *cannot be said in the language in which the story itself is formulated.* The world-story cannot characterize any feature of the world it is about as a token of a type. This means that insofar as Jones himself "recognizes" that the story is the story of his world, the sentences in which this recognition is "formulated" belong at a higher linguistic level than the sentences which describe his world. This higher level in the epistemological analysis of Jonesean cognition will occupy our attention later on when we shall be concerned with the notion of demonstratives. For the time being we shall meta-talk about Jones, ignoring the fact that Jones must meta-talk about himself.

Meaning, Meaningfulness and the Pragmatic. Let us review briefly the course of the argument. Apart from the introductory comments, it has consisted in the following steps:

(1) A consideration of the use of general propositions by common sense led us to the notion that our language behaves as though it were an ideal language which contained a designation (involving a coördinate system) for every constituent in every state of affairs, past, present and future; as though, in other words, it contained a map which represented in complete detail the history of the world, and mapped nothing not contained in that history. Though it was obvious that our language is not a language in this ideal sense, we concluded that such a language would be our language writ large, and that an investigation of the way in which epistemological predicates geared in with it would throw light on the significance of "normative" statements relating to cognition. We thereupon introduced the figure of Omniscient Jones who has succeeded in formulating a body of sentences constituting the complete story of the universe in which he lives, a body of sentences worthy of the term 'knowledge'. In examining the notion that his coördinate system contains an adequate and no more than adequate number of individual constants, we concluded that such adequacy is not to be explained in terms of a direct comparison of language with the world (naïve realism). We tentatively concluded that it is a pragmatic feature of the language in a sense to be clarified. (2) A preliminary discussion of meaning found us adopting the notion that the term 'meaning' as used in such statements as " 'a' means b" is properly to be understood as a purely formal term in a language whose business it is to be about language, as it is the business of the Jonesean language to be about his world. To say that 'means' is a formal term in such a language is to say that 'means' or 'designates' is one of the bones of the skeleton of the language, enabling it to contain a logic of meaning and truth, just as logical words enable a language to contain a logic of implication. *Meaning* in this sense is no more to be found in the world than is a referent for 'or'. (3) This leads to the conclusion that whether or not a language is *used*, there corresponds

to it a meta-language which contains (formally) true meaning-statements about the expressions of the language. In this sense, then, the expressions of any constructible language designate or mean. Consequently, the difference between an applied and a non-applied language has nothing to do with the *meanings* of its expressions. (4) On the other hand, it is obvious that a language that is not applied is, in a sense to be clarified, *empty*. At the present stage in our argument we are considering the possibility that the opposite of empty is *meaningful*, and that a language is meaningful (as opposed to *has meaning*—in the semantic sense) by virtue of being *applied*. We are talking about meaningfulness in terms of the language used by Omniscient Jones, and are suggesting that to say that such a language is applied is to say that *a world-story formulable in it is applied*. (5) We are therefore looking for a pure theory of the application of a language; for a non-empirical theory of the relation of a meaningful language to experience. This we must find if epistemology is to be something more than the empirical psychology of how we use language. Pure semantics, today, studies meaning in abstraction from the being used of a language. In it, therefore, neither the realism nor the solipsism issue can be formulated. Students of pure semantics turn the study of the use of language over to empirical linguistics. There also neither the realism nor the solipsism issue can be formulated. On the other hand, pure pragmatics *is* concerned with the relation of language to experience. It is here that these issues can be formulated and solved. But this is getting ahead of our story.

VI

Verification and Confirmation. Let us return to the analysis of the idea that Jones knows his world through the application of a world story. We had arrived at the notion that the application by Jones of the world-story as a whole involves that tokens of the (Jones) sense-biographical sentences are co-experienced with the (Jones) sense-data which these sentences designate or mean. Thus while all the sentences are *ex hypothesi* tokened in the immediate experience of Jones, only sense-biographical sentences have tokens which *confront* their *designata*. To this account, however, the objection naturally arises that according to it only the sense-biographical sentences, for which this confrontation obtains, are *applied*, as opposed to merely being *tokened*, whereas we have been purporting to give an account of the application of the world-story as a whole. The challenge, thus, is as follows: Can we say that for a sentence system as a whole to be *applied* is for it to be *tokened as a whole* in the immediate experience of a user, and for a sub-set of the sentences to be *sense-biographical sentences*, that is to say, *sentences tokens of which confront their designata?* Let us call sense-biographical sentences "confronting sentences". The objection, then, can also be put in the form of a question. What is the connection between the confronting sentences and the non-confronting sentences belonging to the world-story which enables it to be said that they belong together to *one* sentence *system?*

Let us be quite clear that the mere fact that a group of sentences illustrate a common set of *formation* rules does not suffice to make them one system in the sense that is relevant when speaking of a group of sentences as applied. Unless they have some further relation to one another, the sentences are like the windowless monads of Leibnitz. We are thus forced to the conclusion that we can answer 'yes' to the first question only if we can specify a way in which sentences can constitute a system which is more than a heap of which the only unity is the fact that they conform to the same syntactic specifications. For if the world-story we are considering were such a heap, the fact that the *Jones-biographical* sentences were *confronting* sentences would be of exactly no significance for the *remaining* sentences of the 'system', and we should be forced to admit that even though 'meaning' does not mean confrontation with a datum, the only expressions that are *meaningful* are in point of fact those which have tokens which do confront data, because these are the only sentences which are *applied* [5] as opposed to merely tokened. Should this be the case, we should have defended ourselves against the contention that the nature of *meaning* forces the new way of words into a nonsensical solipsism, only to fall into a solipsistic account of *meaningful* language.

Let us now introduce two terms which will be of great assistance in clarifying our problem. Let us rebaptize the sense-biographical sentences which we have called "confronting sentences" by the phrase "sentences verified (by Jones)", and let us call the tokens of these sentences which are co-experienced with the states of affairs designated by the verified type sentences, "verifying tokens". *A verified sentence is a sentence, a token of which is co-experienced with its designatum.*[6] Let us also characterize each sentence of a world-story about a world which contains an omniscient knower of that world, that is to say, which contains a sub-set of sentences verified by that omniscient knower (in the case of our example, Omniscient Jones) as a "sentence confirmed (by Jones)." The story as a whole as the conjunction of these sentences would also be confirmed (by Jones). Our problem as we posed it above can therefore be rephrased as follows:

In order for a world-story to contain sentences which are *confirmed* but not *verified,* the atomic sentences which constitute the story must have a unity over and above that of satisfying the syntactic requirements (formation rules) of the

[5] The frequently encountered locution which speaks of the "application" of concepts to the given is surely a mistake. The following is a loose formulation of some threads which can be disentangled: (1) The confusion of a token of a sentence "$\phi(o)$" —"object o is of kind ϕ"—on the occasion of the presentation p, with a token of the sentence "$\phi(p)$". The appropriate sentence involving "p" would be something like "p is a presentation of o, and o is of kind ϕ." (2) The confusion of the relevant token of "$\phi(o)$" with an utterance of "$\phi!$" on the occasion of o, that is to say, a confusion of tokens of subject-predicate sentences with utterances of nouns and adjectives in the presence of states of affairs. But whatever the difference between an utterance of the kind "Fire(o)" and an utterance of the kind "Fire!" from the standpoint of descriptive pragmatics, there is none from the standpoint of epistemological analysis. The important thing is to realize that particulars as well as universals belong to the "realm of the conceptual", that it is *sentences* and not *predicates* which are, in any genuinely epistemological sense, "applied."

[6] It might seem more natural to say that a verified sentence is one whose *meaning* is found to be realized in directly experienced fact. This approach, however, is permissible only to the platonist for whom it makes sense to speak of apprehending, finding, intuiting, grasping meanings. See "Epistemology and the New Way of Words" (ENWW), *The Journal of Philosophy,* Vol. 44, no. 24, 1947, especially pp. 648 ff.

language. The status of being confirmed but not verified requires a criterion of togetherness in one sentence-structure; *conformation rules* as well as *formation rules*.

But have we not implicitly specified such a principle in describing the sentence-system in terms of which we have set out our problem, as a *world*-story? As the history of a *universe*? Would not the principle be one to the effect that in order for a group of sentences to constitute a system capable of being confirmed, every individual constant must participate in *relational* as well as *non-relational* sentences; and, indeed, that every individual constant must participate in either an atomic-relational or a relational-product sentence with every other individual constant in the sentence-system? Do spatial and temporal relations suffice to constitute such a structure? In terms of the specific problem we are considering, can we say that in order for the world story to be *confirmed* (by Jones), the *remainder* of the sentences must cohere with the *verified* (by Jones) segment to make up *a whole which is about a spatio-temporal system in which every item has its place?* We shall, of course, see that this suggestion is inadequate, but that the concept of such a structure is essential to our argument.

Verification and Time. We must now take into account a most important fact which we have hitherto kept out of the argument. Not only is the Jonesean world-story *about* a temporal world; its application can only be its application *at a time*. Verified sentences fall into sets which are about momentary slices in the Jonesean flow of experience. Each slice contains the verifying tokens for the corresponding set of verified sentences.

If we speak of such a set of verifying tokens as a *verification*, we can say that both *confirmed* and *verified* are relative concepts, relative, that is to say, to *a* verification. Consequently, in relation to a given verification, the greater part not only of the world-story as a whole, *but also of the Jonesean sense-biography*, has the status of the merely confirmed.

Let us comment briefly on the relation of the world-story and its confirmation to time. As world-story it can characterize its universe of discourse as a serial order by means of a predicate designating a transitive asymmetrical relation, *before*. By the use of this predicate, each event mentioned in the story is characterized as earlier than, simultaneous with or later than, each other event.[7] Each of these events would have corresponding to it three classes of events, those earlier than it, those simultaneous with it, and those later than it. Each set of three classes would constitute candidates for the positions of Past, Present and Future, respectively. But the world-story as such could not *elect* such a set to these positions any more than it can contain demonstratives, and for the same reason.

[7] Complexities in the account of time made necessary by relativity theory are not relevant to our problem, and will be ignored.

To speak of the universe of discourse of a story as dividing into a past, a present and a future, is to speak (and detailed analysis must be postponed) of the story *in relation to a verification.* Consequently, the distinction between past, present and future relates not to the *meaning* of a world-story, but to its *meaningfulness;* for, as we have proposed to show, it is the latter and not the former that is tied up with the confirmation of a sentence-structure. If the universe of discourse of a world-story as confirmed includes items which are *before* the verified items and items which are *after* the verified items, then it necessarily consists of a past, a present and a future. To put it bluntly, statements about the past mean the past, just as statements about the present mean the present and statements about the future mean the future, *just because these distinctions are irrelevant to meaning.* But this has been denied in a curious way in recent philosophy: I refer to Ayer and Lewis [8] on the meaning of statements "ostensibly about the past".

The Relation of the Confirmed to the Verified. The discussion of the relation of verification to time in the preceding paragraphs leads us to reformulate our problem. We have been asking: Granted that there is such a thing as the confirmation of sentences that are not verified, what is the relation between the verified sentences and the confirmed but not verified sentences such that the verification of the verified sentences make a difference to those which are merely confirmed? In terms of our illustrative material we were asking: What is the relation between the verified sentences and the merely confirmed sentences of the Jonesean world-story in virtue of which the latter can be said to be confirmed? We are now led to ask:

[8] A. J. Ayer, *Language, Truth and Logic;* C. I. Lewis, *Mind and the World Order.* The above was written in the summer of 1946 before Professor Lewis' important Carus lectures were available. There he *suggests* an analysis of statements about the past with which I am in essential agreement. As I would like to interpret him (but see Stace's acute comments in his review of Lewis in *Mind,* 57, 1948, especially p. 80), he now distinguishes between the *semantic reference* of historical statements to the past, and the *necessary equipollence* which these statements must have to statements about future experiences if they are to be *empirically significant.* His new account recognizes that this necessary equipollence must be given a far more subtle analysis than the "translatability of statements *ostensibly* about the past into statements *genuinely* about the future" which I have taken, perhaps unjustly, to be the crux of his earlier account. If I have misinterpreted that position, my plea is that in it *(semantic) reference to the past* was so overshadowed by *logical equivalence to the future* that it could scarcely be seen—particularly by one who failed to notice that Lewis' harsh words about *transcendent reference* concealed a warm friendship for what only wanted a name to become the *semantic dimension of meaning.*
But while Lewis hints at such an account, he does not give it; nor does he explicate unambiguously his conception of the relation of objective statements to terminating judgments. Here also he havers between an identification of the *semantic reference* of an objective statement with its *sense meaning* (a thesis which corresponds to the complete translatability approach to statements about the past mentioned above) and the conception that an objective statement must be *equipollent* with a set of sense meanings in order to have experiential significance. His stress on real connections is in the right direction, but, unfortunately, he *tacitly* presupposes that real connections are limited to connections between phenomenal given-nesses which fall within the same specious or epistemological present.

What is the relation between a verified moment-slice of the Jonesean sense-biography and the remainder of the world-story *including the other segments of the Jonesean sense-biography, in virtue of which the latter can be said to be confirmed?*

At this point in our argument we seem to be confronted with a dilemma. *On the one hand,* if we consider all the world stories formulable with the individual constants and predicates of the Jonesean language, which stories include a given momentary sense-biographical slice, the verification of that slice would seem equally to confirm, and hence equally not to confirm, all these stories. *To say otherwise would surely be to claim that the slice requires one specific context of sentences: but are not the sentences that make up a world-story logically independent of one another? On the other hand,* unless the verification of the moment-slice *picks out* for confirmation *one* of the infinite number of formulable world-story contexts, there is no such thing as confirmation. This clash or antinomy boils down to the following:

(A) *A confirmed sentence-system must be one in which a sub-set of sentences (a sense-biographical slice) requires all the others;* and (B) *No factual sentence requires another factual sentence that is not logically contained in it.*

VII

The Syntax of Temporal Predicates. It will be remembered that in our first attempt at characterizing the type of system formed by the sentences making up the world-story confirmed by Jones, we suggested that the unity of the system might be constituted by the story's being about a coherent spatio-temporal structure. This suggestion looked promising, but an examination of the world-story as time structure has led to the above impasse. Perhaps, however, from this impasse we can gain a clue as to how our analysis should proceed. We have spoken of the individual constants of the world-story as having subscripts indicating that they belong to a coördinate system. They do so as constituting the field of the relational predicate 'before'. In other words, the story involves a set of sentences illustrated by 'i_7 is before i_8'. Now the term 'before' is the relational term it is because of its syntax. This syntax involves the familiar postulates of serial order. In these terms we can formulate our problem as follows:

Unless the syntax of the term 'before' is geared in with the factual predicates of the story in such a way that 'i_n' and 'i_{n+m}' can belong to the story only if the predicates other than 'before' conjoined in it with these individual constants also conform to certain order requirements, *then a given biographical slice can form a world-story with any set of sentences so long as it has the proper background of sentences involving the predicate 'before', necessary in order for it to constitute a story at all, and confirmability flies out the window.*

Meaning and Syntax. We have arrived above at the notion that the predicates of a language in which a confirmed world-story can be formulated must stand in certain "order-relations" to one another. This is a vague concept, and would be of very little assistance were it not for the fact that it dovetails with certain considerations we advanced some time ago. We argued [in Section IV] above that 'means' or 'designates' is a non-factual term. This can be elaborated into the notion that semantic sentences are non-factual sentences which are true or false in a purely formal sense, that is to say, are decidable on purely formal grounds. Thus, consider the question: In virtue of what are two different predicates 'ϕ' and 'θ' different? We might be tempted to say either (1) because they are empirically different marks, or (2) because they have different meanings. The first answer is obviously inadequate. The second is more satisfying. But once we have drawn a sharp distinction between *meaning* as a concept of empirical psychology, and *meaning* or *designation* as a concept of epistemological semantics, we see that though the second answer is true, it does not clarify. The question asked above can no longer be characterized as a psychological side-issue, *but must be answered in terms appropriate to the conception of 'means' or 'designates' as a purely formal concept.* The conclusion at which we are arriving is that from the standpoint of epistemological analysis, the predicates of a language are differentiated from one another in terms of the formal rôles they play in the language. Using the term 'syntax' in a broader sense than is current, we could say "different syntax, different predicate; same syntax, same predicate". We shall prefer to say that predicates are differentiated only by the conformation rules which specify their combining properties. The concept of the combining properties of predicates (and it must be remembered that in this paper we are concerned only with primitive predicates) concerns the relation of predicates to individual constants in the following way. It involves (1) *the concept of a "skeletal" relational predicate (there may be more than one, provided they are syntactically related) which signifies the fundamental type of order in which the individuals to which the language can refer must stand;* [9] and (2) the concept of restrictions on the non-relational predicates which can be associated with given individual constants where the restrictions are a function of (a) the predicates, (b) the (skeletal) relational sentences in which these individual constants are making an appearance. These restrictions constitute the conformation rules for the predicates of the language. *We have here a coherence theory of meaning characterized in purely syntactical terms.* Rather, we have here the germ of such a theory, the working out of which must be reserved for another occasion. *It is in terms of such conformation rules that predicate families are formally specified ("determinates under common determinables") and different predicate families are distinguished and related.*

[9] These skeletal relations are, to use Hume's phrase, "relations of matter of fact" in the world to which the language applies. Putting the matter crudely, and with the aid of Hume's terminology, we can say that "relations of ideas" can only be 'defined' by reference to "relations of matter of fact." See also footnote 13 below.

The implication of such an approach to *meaning* for the concept of a *natural law* will be touched on later in the paper.

The Pragmatic Meta-language. The next step in the line of thought we have developed in this paper is to see that 'verified', 'confirmed' and 'meaningful' are to be understood as predicates belonging in a type of meta-language the central concept of which is that of a confirmed world-story. As a matter of fact, meta-languages of this type alone are meta-*languages* in the complete sense of the term, for they alone deal with languages *as languages*, that is to say, as *meaningful* symbols. Syntactics and semantics as epistemological rather than empirical disciplines are abstractions from pure pragmatics, and are misunderstood in a way which leads directly to psychologism when their fragmentary character is overlooked. It is with some hesitation that I speak of these meta-languages as pragmatic, for they have nothing to do with language as expressive or persuasive, or with such other concepts of empirical psychology as have come to be characterized as the subject-matter of a science of pragmatics. Pure pragmatics or, *which is the same thing*, epistemology, is a formal rather than a factual area. In addition to the concepts of pure syntactics and semantics, pure pragmatics is concerned with other concepts which are *normative* as opposed to the factual concepts of psychology, as 'true' is normative as opposed to 'believed', or 'valid' is normative (again, remember that our use of the term "normative" is tentative) as opposed to 'inferred'. These other concepts round off a system of concepts which undercuts the dispute between Rationalist and Empiricist. Psychologism is to be as carefully avoided in the treatment of specifically pragmatic concepts, as in the partial areas of semantics (Plato, Hume), and syntactics (J. S. Mill).

In addition to the resources of syntactics and semantics, a pragmatic meta-language involves the concepts of *symbol-type* and *symbol-token*. These presuppose the concept of designation. Thus, 'token' is a meta-linguistic predicate, and is used properly when it is said that the state of affairs designated by one expression in a language is a token of another (perhaps the same) expression in the language. The formal significance of the concept of token is brought out by the following: If 'p' designates p, and p is a token of 'q', then all the metalinguistic predicates which apply to 'q' apply also to p. In other words, we have here a grammar in accordance with which metalinguistic predicates can be associated with certain expressions belonging on the "right hand side of designation sentences". We shall consider the concept of *token* in more detail at a later stage in our argument.

Finally, a pragmatic meta-language requires its object language to contain a predicate designating a reflexive, symmetrical and transitive relation, R, which, whatever its *factual* rôle, plays an additional formal rôle as the *coex* relation of the pragmatic system (cf. ENWW, p. 654). 'Coex' appears in expressions of the form 'p coex q'. The *factual* correlate would be 'aRb';

(sentence) 'p' being true of *a* and 'q' of *b*. These resources enable the following definitions:

The meaning base of a language is a world-story formulated in that language. A world-story can be semantically characterized as designating a world consisting of a connected system of atomic states of affairs which conform to a set of natural laws (the status of which will be explained in a moment).

Languages come in families. The languages of a family have primitive descriptive predicates and skeletal relational predicates in common, but not individual constants. The predicates of a language family are differentiated from one another by conformation rules. These latter specify certain formal implications which hold in all world-stories which are meaning-bases of languages in the family. Hence they specify the natural laws of the worlds designated by these stories.

It is a necessary condition of an empirically meaningful language that every universal designated by a primitive descriptive predicate of the language either (1) be exemplified in the worlds of the language only by states of affairs which belong to the domain of *coex*, or (2) function in a law with such universals.

A confirmed world-story is a story which contains a sub-structure of sentences, (*a*) which can be built into only this complete story in view of the conformation rules (natural laws) of the language, (*b*) the *designata* of which sub-structure constitute a set of items mutually related by the relation *coex*, and (*c*) which sub-structure consists of sentences *verified in the story*.

A sentence 'p' will be said to be a sentence verified in story S, if *p* (the *designatum* of 'p' in the world of S) stands in the coex relation to a state of affairs which is a token of 'p'. This token of 'p' will be said to be the *verifying token* of 'p'. Each sub-structure of verified sentences as characterized in the preceding paragraph will be called a *verification base* of S.

A set of conformation rules which defines a class of languages at least one member of which has a meaning base which permits of pragmatic characterization as a confirmed world-story, will be said to constitute an *empirical language form*. It will be remembered that the conformation rules of a language determine the meanings of its predicates. Thus, an empirical language form defines a class of languages involving the same predicates. However, while the languages of a family have their predicates in common, they do not have individual constants in common. The individual constants of a language are formally determinate only with respect to that single world-story which is the meaning-base of the language.[10] Now, not all the languages associated with a given empirical language form will have a meaning-base consisting of a *confirmed* world-story

---

[10] I have expanded this point as far as individual constants are concerned in "Epistemology and the New Way of Words," *The Journal of Philosophy*, Vol. 44, no. 24, pp. 655 ff.

The conclusion at which we have arrived in the above paragraph can be summed up by saying that the world designated by the meaning-base of a language is the 'actual world' of that language. Needless to say, while the world-story which is the meaning-base of a language occupies a privileged position with respect to that language, the latter permits the formulation of false statements about its 'actual world.' Consequently, Carnap's distinction (*Meaning and Necessity*, pp. 8 ff.) between 'possible states of the universe' (expressed by false state descriptions), and 'the actual state of the universe' (expressed by the true state description) *is relative to a language*. The world designated by the meaning-base of any language is the *fundamentum* of a set of state descriptions, and is 'the actual state of the universe (of that language)' in relation to which one of the state descriptions (the meaning-base) is true.

(i.e., be correlated with a world which is completely 'known' by 'minds' contained in that world). Thus, while any language of the family will have predicates which appear in a confirmed world-story, only those languages whose meaning-base is itself a confirmed world-story will have individual constants appearing in a confirmed world-story. Since we are explicating the linguistic implications of omniscience, we shall be concerned only with languages of the latter type. Thus, we shall define an *empirical language* to be a language whose meaning-base is a confirmed world-story. The study of languages which are empirical only in the weaker sense that they belong to a family of languages which includes at least one empirical language in the stronger sense we have just defined, must be deferred to a later occasion.

Any atomic sentence in an empirical language L will be said to be a *confirmable sentence of L*. A confirmable sentence of L which belongs to the story S which is the *meaning base* of L, will be said to be *confirmed in S*, and will be called a *confirmed sentence of L*. Similarly, a sentence verified in story S will be called a *verified sentence of L*.[11]

It is a direct implication of our argument that the predicate '(factually) true sentence of L' is decidable on purely formal grounds. (It must be constantly born in mind that we are discussing epistemological issues in the frame of reference of "perfect languages" and omniscience. The implication of our discussion for the significance of epistemological predicates in relation to "imperfect" languages will be drawn toward the conclusion of the paper.) With respect to language L resting on story S which is its meaning base, it is decidable that $\phi(i_n)$ is the case rather than $\theta(i_n)$.[12] The concept of factual truth is a semiotic concept appropriate to a certain type of calculus, namely empirical languages. The notion of an empirical language is itself a purely formal notion. To suppose that it makes sense to speak of THE set of factually true sentences, is to cast aside painfully acquired insights, and to return to the metaphysics of Meinong and the New Realists. Semantic truth is not "absolute truth". To say this is not to say that truth is relative to psychological facts whether needs, convictions or satisfactions. It is, however, relative to appropriately constituted calculi; that is, as long as an expression in a calculus of a certain kind has the ap-

---

[11] If we asked a classical rationalist to verbalize about the confirmation of the Jonesean story through the verification of a segment of the story, the answer would be instructive. As I have since formulated it in "Epistemology and the New Way of Words" (see note 6 above) . . . "He appeals to an *a priori* principle of supplementation, the principle of sufficient reason, which is bound up with the existence of a realm of universals so related to one another that they constitute a system which can be viewed in one light as a system of necessary connections, and in another as a system of compossibilities. (It is this system which underlies the concept of the laws of nature.) Thus in answer to our question the rationalist might be expected to say, 'Omniscient Jones justifies his selection of a group of sentences as those which are true of his world and constitute its story, by reference to the fact that this group includes a sub-set of verified sentences the meanings of which are propositions known to require supplementation by reference to the principle of sufficient reason, and which, given the structure of the domain of universals meant by the predicates of the language, can be supplemented in only one way to make a complete world-story.'" For the rationalistic account of verification, see note 6 above.

[12] Compare ENWW, pp. 658–659.

propriate characteristics, it is properly characterized as a factually true sentence of the calculus.

The semantic analysis of factual truth, as well as the semantic analysis of factual meaning is incomplete as long as it fails to do justice to the claims of *coherence*. Not that coherence is the *definition* of truth. The point is rather that the Idealistic conception of coherence has its contribution to make to the theory of meaning, confirmation, and truth.

The final abandonment of Naïve Realism comes with the realization that the right-hand side of designation sentences together with the predicate 'designates' and the semi-quotes on the left-hand side are all alike formal devices belonging to the grammar of epistemological predicates; that is to say, their function is the purely formal one of hooking up with the rules relating to the assignment of such predicates as 'verified sentence of L', 'true sentence of L', 'meaningful predicate of L' (see below) and many derivative epistemological predicates that would have to be introduced in a complete discussion. This means that "talking about the *designata* of sentences" is an essential ingredient in "characterizing these sentences in terms of epistemological predicates". If we introduce the term 'world' as a collective term for the designata of a world story, then it is a purely formal truth that every story in every empirical language designates a world.

The pure theory of empirical languages as formally defined systems which are about worlds in which they are used, has no place for THE world; but only for the world designated by the story which is the meaning base of a language. A given set of conformation rules defines a family of empirical languages, or, which is the same thing, a family of possible worlds which have the same laws. An understanding of the completely non-factual character of epistemological statements rests on the insight that not even the predicates 'verified' and 'confirmed' have an intrinsic tie with any single world, with "the REAL world". They are purely formal predicates and no properly constructed world-story stands in a privileged position with respect to them. This principle of indifference could be discarded only if something akin to an ontological argument could be formulated in the pure theory of empirical languages; if it could be shown, for example, that only one set of conformation rules is possible which enables a story to be constructed in the language form of which they are the rules; and if only one story could be constructed in that language form.[13]

[13] We are now in a position to point out an important sense in which the connections of meaning specified by conformation rules are truth-functional in character. "Surely," it might be objected, "matters of meaning can hardly depend on what is the case!" Yet from the standpoint of Pure Semantics the meanings of the expressions of a language *do* depend on what is the case, though not in "*the* actual world" but rather (1) in the family of worlds which is the family of the language form to which the language in question belongs, as far as its predicates are concerned, and (2) in that world of this family which is *the world of the language in question*, for its individual constants.

Put in this context, the formal characterization of the primitive one-place predicates of a language involves the following: (*a*) the specification of one or more basic relations, (*b*) the specification of a set of worlds consisting of all possible relational arrays of atomic states of affairs exemplifying the qualitative universals designated by these

A comment is relevant at this point concerning the term 'existence' which is beginning to cause trouble again. The syntactical dimension of 'exists' has been clarified. This clarification is exemplified in the translation of 'Lions exist' into 'Something is a lion'. There is, however, a further usage of 'exists' which is a more restricted one, since it is used appropriately only in connection with factual expressions, whereas the syntactical sense is not so restricted. I am referring to the usage in which the term 'exists' is associated with either (1) empirical class terms, as in the sentence '(the class) Lion exists' (as opposed to 'Lions exist'), or (2) logically proper names, as in the sentence 'i_n exists' where 'i_n' is a logically proper name. Let us introduce the root pragmatic sense of 'exists' as follows:

Let us say that the primitive factual expressions (predicates and individual constants) of an empirical language L are (empirically) *meaningful* expressions of L. We shall then say that the class ϕ exists in the world designated by the meaning base, S, of L, if 'ϕ' designates ϕ and 'ϕ' is a meaningful expression of L; similarly, that i_n exists in the world designated by S, if 'i_n' designates i_n and 'i_n' is a meaningful expression of L. In the case of primitive classes and individuals, the corresponding expressions must appear in S in order to be meaningful, and indeed to belong to L at all. The existence of complex classes and individuals is defined in terms of the existence of primitive classes and individuals.

Since existence in this sense is a "quasi-pragmatic" concept corresponding to 'meaningful,' to say that universals or classes exist is not to lump them together with lions. The sense in which lions exist corresponds rather with '(factually) true.' Thus one can admit that classes and individuals exist without swallowing a two-story world.[14] Note that the pragmatic concept of existence applies only to the designata of the factual expressions of the object-language. It does not make sense to say that verification exists, or that truth or entailment exists, in this pragmatic sense. That verification, truth, entailment, and, in general, formal "facts" or systems *do not exist* in either this "quasi-pragmatic" sense or the (closely related) sense which correlates with '(empirically) true' is the final clarification and destruction of the rationalism-empiricism issue.

---

predicates, subject only to the condition that, (c), certain formal implications (synthetic in the kantian sense) involving these predicates and relations are true of all these worlds, such that, (d), each predicate can be distinguished from the others in terms of the rôle it plays in these formal implications. The specifying of such a set of formal implications is exactly what is accomplished by a set of conformation rules. For a more complete discussion see my article, "Concepts as Involving Laws and Inconceivable Without Them," in *Philosophy of Science*, October, 1948.

[14] The solution of the problem of universals thus consists exactly in showing that the following statements are all true: (1) "There are universals." (2) "Some mental events *mean* universals." (3) "It is nonsense to speak of any psychological relationship between mental events and universals." The solution involves, as we have seen, *first* a making explicit of the ambiguities of the term 'existence'; *second* a distinction between "meaning" as a term belonging to the framework of epistemological or logical analysis, and "meaning" as a descriptive term in empirical psychology relating to habits of response to and manipulation of linguistic symbols. The classical conception of mind as apprehending universals and propositions is based on a confusion of these two frames of reference. To deny that universals exist *when speaking in the logical frame*, is as mistaken as to assert that universals exist when speaking in the framework of the psychological description of thought. We must, and can, avoid both *logical nominalism* and *ontological realism*.

No Predicaments. The pragmatic meta-language we have been considering characterizes the meaning base, S, of its object language as confirmed in relation to many verification bases, those, namely, which concern successive momentary experiences on the part of Jones. That a pragmatic meta-language should be thus neutral with respect to successive Jones-experiences does not startle. Can it be similarly neutral as between Jones and his neighbor Smith? The principle is exactly the same. Demonstratives do not belong in the object language. They are not to be confused with proper names—e.g., 'i_8', 'i_9'—either as types (which is obvious) or as tokens. They belong, rather, to the pragmatic meta-language, and, indeed, are to be construed in terms of (certain) *tokens* of expressions of this meta-language. The trivial fact that *tokens* are localized in a world entails no provincialism on the part of language *types*. Indeed, the concept of such provincialism is self-refuting.

Type and Token Again. In introducing the meta-linguistic predicates 'type' and 'token', we pointed out that it would be a mistake to conceive of type as classes of tokens. The distinction between type and token being traceable to the difference between the left and right hand side of designation sentences, there is a difference of semantic level incompatible with such a conception. On the other hand, while a type expression is not a class of tokens, the tokens of a given type expression are specified in terms of one or more empirical classes. It is essential for the discussion of the mind-body problem below to realize that empirical difference of symbols relates in epistemological contexts to language only as token. One and the same language as type may have two or more sets of tokens.[15] (Thus, from the epistemological standpoint, English and German as empirically meaningful languages constitute two sets of token-classes for the same type expressions.) The identity of a language as type is not an empirical identity, but rather a formal distinctness bound up with its formation and conformation rules. Same formal rules, same language as type; though it may be represented in its world by many empirically different sets of token classes which bear its meaning.

All our argument up to date is the unpacking of the notion that meaningful language is language about a world in which it is used. This means that in the idea which defines the what-it-is to be a meaningful language, it is an analytic truth that linguistic tokens conform to the rules of the language. If we look at the matter from the opposite side, we may say that to characterize certain items in a world as true, verified, meaningful, etc., is to talk in a pragmatic meta-language about designata of sentences in a story being tokens of other sentences in the story.[16] Now we do not speak

[15] Since writing the above it has been called to my attention that Professor D. Rynin, in the essay which accompanies his edition of Johnson's *Treatise on Language*, makes a similar distinction. See also ENWW, pp. 653 f.

[16] Consider an item in the world designated by a world-story, where the item is a token of a sentence which designates another item in that world. Thus (1) the first item *qua* token designates the second item. Now (2) consider the relation of the first

a language proper. It is because of this that there is a sting in the pragmatic concept of meaningful language. *It is this which leads us to confuse the necessary formal harmony between type and token with factual relationships of utterances to standards or norms.* For it is the whole pragmatic mode of speech with its (among others) 'type', 'token', 'verified', 'true', 'world-story', and, to sum up, 'meaningful language', that shames our language behavior, and consequently carries on the philosopher's traditional task of "criticism". Behind the therapeutic activity of the modern Socrates lies the medicine kit of a more or less fully developed pure theory of empirically meaningful languages. The task of philosophy today is to determine the specifications of such kits, and make them generally available.

Pure Pragmatics and the Uniformity of Nature. The above account of pure pragmatics and pragmatic meta-languages is a tentative account of an intricate and highly technical area. It would be foolish for me to pretend that I have done more than grope in the right direction. Before we turn to comment on the specific problem of Realism, let us sum up our results to date by pointing out an historical parallel. Kant argued that conformity to the causal principle (the temporal *schema* of the principle of sufficient reason) is a necessary condition of the possibility of temporal experience. We argue that conformity of its expressions to conformation rules built upon the skeletal predicate 'before' (the temporal form of the coherence theory of meaning) is a necessary condition of the possibility of a meaningful temporal language. *Put in the quasi-pragmatic mode of speech,* this amounts to saying that a necessary condition of the meaningfulness of a temporal language, is that the temporal order of the events occurring in the world it is about, be reflected in a necessary and systematic coherence of the characteristics exemplified by these events. Other parallels to Kant might be drawn. We note only that the truth of Kant's conception of Space and Time as *pure* manifolds is contained in the pragmatic conception of skeletal relations in terms of which the primitive one-place predicates of a language are distinguished, and hence, in a sense, defined. This latter also underlies the insight contained in definitions of causality in terms of a space-time indifference of the laws of nature.

First Thoughts on Realism. We must now examine another aspect of the Jonesean world-story in terms of which we have been formulating epistemological issues. We have contrasted not only a slice of Jones' sense-

---

qua item in the world to the second item. (Thus, consider the relation of p to aRb where 'p' designates p, 'aRb' designates aRb and p tokens 'aRb'). In considering this relationship, we are still operating in the formal mode of speech. We see that p must be a complex fact, consisting of, say, q, r and s, where q tokens 'a', r tokens 'R' and s tokens 'b'. In this respect, p as fact in the world must *map* aRb. The ineffable mapping of which Wittgenstein speaks is thus capable of characterization in pure pragmatics, for it is a confusion of *token-designation* as in (1) and the mapping characterized in (2).

It might be pointed out here that the *epistemological* concept of *objective reference*, is that of *psychological events* in perception as *tokens of sentences about physical objects.*

biography with his sense-biography as a whole, but also the latter with sentences which do not belong to the Jonesean, or indeed to any other sense-biography belonging to the story. We have spoken as though physical event sentences belong to such an idealization of the sentence structures we use, in exactly the same way as do sense-biographical sentences. If asked to justify this assumption, our answer would probably be that a human sense-biography is not by itself coherent, in that causal considerations inevitably take us beyond it. In schematic metalinguistic statements we speak of the laws of psycho-physics, implying that it makes sense to speak of a language proper the conformation rules of which tie together predicates appearing in the verification base of the story with predicates which do not. Two questions arise: (1) Does this make sense? (2) What justification can be offered for saying that our language is to be understood in terms of such a structure?

As to the first question, the answer is surely "yes". The concept of an empirically meaningful language rests on that of a verification base, but by no means presupposes that every sentence of the story which is its meaning base is to be found in that verification base. That the Jonesean world-story and the language in which it is formulated are, as we have characterized them, *realistic*, is clear. It is essential to note, however, that this realistic character is conceived of as a consequence of specific conformation rules, and that if it is possible for an empirically meaningful language to be realistic, it also makes sense to speak of non-realistic empirically meaningful languages. If it is a theorem in pure pragmatics that a meaningful language must be defined in terms of conformation rules, the only requirement that the conformation rules of a given language must fulfil is that they be sufficient to permit the definition in that language of a confirmed world-story. The difference between 'realistic' and 'non-realistic' languages is to be defined in terms of differences in the formal properties of different sets of conformation rules. Thus it seems possible to conceive of stories of the following different types:

1. Stories which consist entirely of verified sentences.
2. Stories which include some sentences which are confirmed but not verified. These can be divided in turn into two types:
   a. Stories all the predicates of which appear in the verification basis of the story.
   b. Stories some of the predicates of which appear only in sentences which are confirmed but not verified.

If we introduce the term 'datum predicate' for predicates which appear in the verification base of a story; and 'non-datum predicate' for those that do not, then the three possibilities listed above become: I. All sentences verified sentences, all predicates datum predicates; IIa. Some merely confirmed sentences, all predicates datum predicates; IIb. Some merely confirmed sentences, some non-datum predicates. As far as I can see, I. would be what is meant by a non-realistic story. II*a* is a realistic story of the type proposed by Neutral Monism. II*b* is that proposed by common or garden variety realism.

What concerns us here is that epistemology as the pure theory of languages can develop the formal properties of languages with different conformation rules; can compare realistic with non-realistic languages; but as a purely formal discipline cannot choose THE conformation rules or THE language. It is a mistake to look for a formal (epistemological) justification of "Realism" or "Idealism", etc.

If, on the other hand, we turn from epistemological to factual statements, we make use of *language* as a factual (psychological) category. In this context a language is a set of causally related events and habits, and the distinction between language and meta-language a factual distinction between habits of different levels, the latter being, in *a causal sense* built upon the former. It is a task of empirical psychology to characterize the factors leading to the adoption and abandonment of language habits. Further, "formal" (here used as a *factual* predicate) meta-languages might be characterized, tentatively, by empirical psychology as habits relating to the "clarification" or "unpacking" of linguistic phenomena. From the empirical standpoint, the linguistic behavior of an epistemologist is evaluated in terms of the clarification it brings, by doing more adequately what is done by metalinguistic activity at the common-sense level. This suggests that the only way to recommend a "non-realistic epistemology" of a certain sort is to give a formal account of a language which combines the following features: (*a*) its conformation rules require a confirmed world-story to include no atomic sentence not appearing in the verification base of the story (type I above), and (*b*) the language is such that from its conformation rules via introduced defined terms one can derive rules which would be *recognized by one observing the epistemologist as echoing the language habits of scientists*. It is something along these lines that the conventional realist is asking for when he demands that the idealist or positivist "come across" with the "sense-datum language" to which he is always referring.[17]

[17] We have been insisting that epistemological predicates, whether they appear in the mouth of the philosopher or the common sense man, have the same formal status as logical predicates in the narrower sense. (I should not object to the term 'transcendental logic' in place of 'pure pragmatics'). We shall see in Section VIII below that from the formal or epistemological standpoint a "here-now" sentence is such only as a token of a pragmatic meta-sentence, and as such *presupposes* a confirmed world-story. Thus the idea that the term 'protocol sentence' is a factual one belonging to the language of psychology, rests on a confusion between *psychological indubitability* and the *formal status of verified sentences in an empirically meaningful language*.

From the standpoint of pure pragmatics, the meaningfulness of expressions involving variables depends on their relation to a complete world-story. This applies also to Russellian descriptions. Furthermore, a world-story as a whole is logically prior to its parts. "How can it be that in the formal mode of speech we can speak of objects (languages-proper, world-stories) which transcend humanly possible experience?"

Sense-Data Again. That human sense-biographies are incomplete, and would require supplementation in order to yield the story of the world in which we live is hardly a matter for debate. Yet what would be the nature of this supplementation? If one answers, "physical event sentences", one is likely to meet the contention that sentences about physical events make sense only as translatable into sense-biographical sentences.[18] Let us introduce the term *'verificatum'* as a means of referring to the *designatum* of a verified sentence in a world-story. Could it seriously be proposed that human sense-biographies require completion by sentences about physical events, where the latter are conceived to be translatable into sentences about *verificata?* Hardly, for then physical event sentences would not perform the work of *supplementing* the sense-biographies which are *ex hypothesi* incomplete. *What must be meant is that the physical event sentences are translatable into a set of alternative sense-biographies, only one of which consists of verified sentences,* that is to say, designates *verificata.* This won't work. The incompleteness with which the argument began was a *causal* incompleteness and (1) *possibilia* are not causes; (2) the problem of incompleteness would break out for each of the alternative sense-biographies. I suspect that in addition to the semantic psychologism which underlies the demand for the translatability of physical event sentences into sentences about actual or possible sense-data, there is an additional confusion which adds to its plausibility. This is the confusion between physical *object* sentences and physical *event* sentences. Physical object sentences themselves involve a reference to sets of *possibilia* [19] and if these *possibilia* are confused with possible sensa (a confusion which involves the mistake of taking *actual*

The question is a confused one. It must be clarified by a distinction between *factual* statements about the utterance limitations of formal scientists, and formal sentences about meta-linguistic tokens in a constituted world. See Section VIII below.

[18] In "Epistemology and the New Way of Words" I point out (p. 656, note 20) that "(the) conception that . . . a set of verified sentences can formally entail and be entailed by a complete world-story . . . without the story being translatable into—or 'reducible to'—the set of verified sentences, is what distinguishes my position from positivism." The use of the term 'entail' in this passage obviously rests on our analysis of causal necessity in terms of logical necessity.

[19] Object- or thing-sentences are clearly more complicated than event-sentences. Thus they involve a special class of predicates, namely *dispositional predicates.* These are to be understood in terms of the concept (which they help define) of *alternative* event sequences which involve (1) the same functional correlation of non-dispositional predicates (laws) and (2) the same *things.* As for (2) it is clear that a language which includes dispositional predicates must also include a special class of individual constants (said to designate *things* or *substances*) which combine with these predicates to constitute sentences. Since the syntax of these individual constants will not admit of their combining directly with spatio-temporal predicates, a relational predicate 'is an event happening to' must also be introduced. The syntax of substance terms, dispositional predicates, event-terms and event predicates would define the meaning of such expressions as "would have happened to the same thing if . . ." It would also clarify such terms as 'change', 'interaction', etc. For an excellent account of the perplexities which arise when one forgets that sentences about substances are derived expressions in a language which is about a *single* world of *states of affairs,* see the selection from Broad's *Examination of McTaggart's Philosophy* below, pp. 472 ff.; also note 10 above.

sensa to be external physical events—see next paragraph), the phenomenal-ist position gains an unjustified appearance of dovetailing with common usage. It is clear, however, that it is physical *event* sentences and not physi-cal *thing* sentences which the phenomenalist must translate into sentences about possible sensa.

As for the notion that the predicates of physical-object sentences in a world-story must be definable in terms of sense-predicates, the following comment is sufficient. The pragmatic meta-language of L distinguishes predicates of L by means of conformation rules; thus *predicate of L* and *law of S* are correlative notions, as are *quality manifested in W* and *natural necessity in W* (*Law of W*, where 'law' does not refer to a linguis-tic expression)—where W is the world meant by S. *It is nonsense to speak of the same qualities obeying two different sets of laws in different contexts. To say that physical events are complexes of sense qualities, is to say that physical laws are analysable into psychological laws.* It is per-haps more plausible to say that sense qualities are complexes of physical events. If so, Neutral Monism is plausible only as physicalism. These are issues that cannot be settled by a mere appeal to epistemological concepts. The usual argument rests on the psychologistic blunder of supposing that only predicates appearing sometimes in verified sentences can be meaningful. But psychological meaning must not be confused with either designation or meaningfulness. A third sense of 'sense-datum language' is bound up with the contention that the verification base of a language can-not be formulated in physicalistic terms. This question is discussed below in the section on the mind-body problem in the new way of words.

VIII

The Pragmatics of 'Now'. We noted above (p. 437) that ". . . to speak of the universe of discourse of a story as dividing into a past, a present and a future, is to speak . . . of the story in relation to a verification," and that "consequently, the distinction between past, present and future re-lates not to the *meaning* of a world story, but to its *meaningfulness*." In terms of the arguments which followed, this means that temporal distinc-tions are bound up with the specifically pragmatic concepts of verifica-tion and confirmation. Indeed, as we shall see, *the distinctively temporal predicates belong in a pragmatic metalanguage.* Since the applicability of pragmatic predicates to the expressions of a language presupposes that the language is "about a coherent world," and since the coherence of a tem-poral world is "causality", we are in a position to de-psychologize Kant's argument and show that *the use of distinctly temporal predicates logically presupposes the framework of a causally ordered world.* Furthermore, the following discussion lays the foundation for a general theory of egocen-tric expressions and demonstratives.

That the language of common sense involves a pragmatic stratum is clear from its use of epistemological predicates. The radical pervasiveness of this stratum is easily overlooked in the absence of an analysis of distinctively temporal utterances in the framework of the pure theory of languages. In this connection we must abandon the assumption that the immediate experience of Omniscience Jones need only token object-language sentences in order to be a model adequate to the clarification of all epistemological issues. In doing so, however, we shall raise questions that take us beyond the scope of the present paper.

It will have been noticed by the student of McTaggart that the world designated by the Jonesean world-story constitutes, as we have characterized it above (pp. 436 ff.), a *B-series*. That is to say, it is a series of items which are the field of the relation *earlier than* or *before*. What he calls an *A-series*, namely a division of the items into a past, a present and a future, has been stated by us to be bound up with a confirmation of the story in relation to a given set of the verified sentences of the story (those which designate a momentary set of co-experiences). Our analysis needs further refinements.

McTaggart, speaking as a naïve realist with respect to the events which the object-language is about, puts our claim that the A-predicates ('past', 'present', and 'future') are bound up with the pragmatic metalanguage into ontological terms when he says that an A-series is a matter of *appearance* rather than *reality*. He argues that the relation *earlier than* is a temporal relation only by virtue of its connection with the A-characteristics; but that it cannot be defined in terms of them for as a transitive, asymmetrical relation it underlies the distribution and redistribution of the A-characteristics. It is as such a non-temporal relation, and gains the appearance of being a temporal relation through the appearance which is presentness. The constituents of reality as related by this non-temporal relation, which as such should not be called 'earlier than', make up what he calls the *C-series*. Our distinction between world-story sentences and pragmatic meta-sentences corresponds to his distinction between reality and appearance. The world designated by a temporal world-story contains a skeletal relation which corresponds to his non-temporal C-relation in that its complete character as *temporal* transcends its object-language status. To call it 'earlier than' or 'before' is to view it in another context.

Statements making a particular assignment of A-predicates are interpreted by McTaggart as *factual* statements which, however, are about *apparent*, as opposed to *real*, facts. Our claim is that an utterance "Now (. . . .)" is to be interpreted as a token of a pragmatic meta-sentence. But this is just a beginning, for the utterance, if valid, must be simultaneous with the state of affairs (. . . .), and, if meta-linguistic, must involve the sentence designating the state of affairs (. . . .). *What we must actually do is reconstruct the notion of a world containing tokens of pragmatic meta-sentences* to the effect that certain items are *verificata*—a *verificatum* being defined as the *designatum* of a verified sentence—where the pragmatic tokens and *verificata* are not only co-experienced, but the pragmatic tokens *say* they are co-experienced. This we do as follows:

Consider the sentence 'p' which belongs to a set of verified sentences N about a momentary set of co-experiences C. '*Verificatum(p)*' is a type sentence in the pragmatic meta-language. Consider an experience *r*, belonging to C, which plays the rôle of a token of the pragmatic meta-sentence '*r* coex *p* · *verificatum(p)*'. This token is the reconstruction of an utterance "Ecce(p)", and provides the key to the understanding of all derived "ego"-centric expressions. (This revision of my earlier account was stimulated by reflection on tantalizing § 50 of Reichenbach's *Elements of Symbolic Logic*.)

Two remarks are relevant: (1) The above analysis clearly makes it necessary to distinguish sharply between "here-now" statements and what we have called "verifying tokens". (2) The above analysis involves the notion of the constitution of *empirical-language-cum-world* in a meta-meta-language, and suggests of a hierarchy of such constitutions.[20]

Apart from such an analysis as the above, the distinction between time merely as serial order, and time as involving the contrast between past, present and future simply cannot be made; for any attempt to clarify this contrast solely in terms of relative position in a linear series cannot bring out the 'ecce!' element involved in genuine temporal distinctions. *On the other hand, our account does not involve the vicious regress found by McTaggart*, since temporal distinctions do not apply to the pragmatic *as pragmatic*. "Now (verified ('*p*'))" is nonsense. Only the names of empirical language sentences make sense with pragmatic predicates.

IX

The Mind-Body Problem in the New Way of Words. Since we have been led to the conclusion that in the type of world-story relevant to a clarification of our employment of epistemological predicates, there belong physical event sentences as well as sense-biographical sentences, it is clear that the meeting place of these two sets of sentences in such a structure requires analysis. The problem as to the coherence of these two sets of sentences must be distinguished from the psychologistic pseudo-problem of "perceptual epistemology".

As containing the above two types of sentences, the Jonesean world-story *apparently* will contain the following two sets of sentences: (1) the set of verified sentences constituting the sense-biography of Jones; (2) the set of physical event sentences constituting the biography of the sensory centers of the Jonesean brain. It is in terms of these two sets of sentences that the hook-up of *verified sense-biographical sentences* with *confirmed physical event sentences* must be analysed.

It is frequently claimed that psychological advances are pointing toward

---

[20] For an elaboration of this point see the concluding pages of my "Pure Pragmatics and Epistemology" in the July, 1947, issue of *Philosophy of Science*.

the truth-value equivalence of mentalistic sentences with sentences in the language of an, as yet, ideal neuro-physiological psychology. What would be the implications of such a claim for the structure of the ideal world-story we are envisaging? One's first line of thought might be that it points towards a world-story which contains, in connection with each sentient being described in it, two isomorphic sub-sets of sentences, (a) a mentalistic sense-history, and (b) a selection from a physicalistic brain history. Once started on this line of thought, one would be troubled by the question, "How is *identity* to be distinguished from *parallelism?*" But to initiate this train of thought presupposes that one has given an affirmative answer to a prior question, namely, "Can a world-story contain such isomorphic sub-sets *and still have that coherence which makes it confirmed?*" In an older parlance, the corresponding question was, "Is parallelism compatible with the (self-evident) principle of sufficient reason?" If the question as we have formulated it is answered in the negative, as it must be, then we might be led to say that to the extent that psychology "points toward the truth-value equivalence of mentalistic sentences with sentences in the language of an as yet ideal neuro-physiological psychology," it is pointing toward the truth value equivalence of *two world stories,* one of which is in completely physicalistic terms, whereas the other contains a sub-set of mentalistic sentences in place of what in the first are selections from brain biographies. Reflection shows, however, that *formally* the "mentalistic language" would be indistinguishable from a section of the physicalistic language. Furthermore, they are *ex hypothesi* about the same world. The proper interpretation of this situation would be to say that in the sense in which the mentalistic "language" and the segment of the physicalistic "language" were *two* they are to be understood as different *token classes* of the *same* type language. A genuine difference of the "mentalistic" and "physicalistic" expressions must be traced to a difference in the conformation rules relating to the predicates of these expressions; in other words, *same laws, same qualities; different laws, different qualities.* (See pp. 438 ff., *Meaning and Syntax,* and 445 ff. *Type and Token Again.*)

If the expectation of such a "truth value equivalence" is doomed to disappointment, then some form of dualism is the alternative to the above approach. Such dualism would take the form either of minds and bodies as *interacting things,*[21] or of different kinds of events taking place in the *same* thing (the emergence form of the identity approach). May I express my (inherited?) predilection for the latter approach, while insisting that

---

[21] If we leave out of account those arguments which rest on the epistemologistic fallacy, and which seem to be invalid even if one grants the fruit—intentional acts, awareness of propositions, intuitions of square roots, etc., etc.—of this fallacy, the only reasonable basis for accepting a dualism of mind and body as two interacting things would be a general acceptance by scientists—the Psychical Research Society?—of the separate existence of mental events.

emergence has nothing to do with indeterminism or Bergsonian *elan?* Emergence is one form taken by a negative answer to the question: "Could a world which includes minds be described with the same primitive predicates (and laws) as a mindless universe?" Needless to say, the dates at which emergent qualities occur has nothing to do with the case. The history of the universe could be as Aristotle conceived it.

X

Ideal Language and Language Schema. Our aim in the present paper has been to explore the group grammar of epistemological predicates, and particularly to bring out the relation of the concepts of verification, confirmation and meaningfulness to the concepts of semantic analysis as practiced by Carnap and Tarski. In attempting to make explicit this grammar, we have made use of the Wittgensteinian device of speaking in terms of a perfect language; that is to say, the language of an omniscient being. We have written the grammar of epistemological predicates large in order better to see it. We pointed out that after a discussion conducted in this framework, the problem next in line would be that of drawing the implications of this discussion for the grammar of these predicates in connection with "imperfect languages". It is now my aim to indicate that the difference between "perfect" and "imperfect" languages cannot be drawn in epistemological contexts, that is to say, is not an epistemological distinction.

But before we elaborate on the above contention, let us point out that the epistemological predicates with which we have been concerned are those which are primary, and apply for the most part to atomic sentences belonging to a world-story, or to the individual constants or primitive predicates appearing in these sentences. But it is clear that derivative pragmatic predicates can be defined in terms of these fundamental predicates. 'Confirmed,' as we have used this term, applies to atomic sentences in a world-story, and entails 'true'. Now, a predicate 'confirmed-to-degree-n' can be introduced in terms of the primary syntactical, semantical and pragmatic predicates which has neither of these limitations. Similarly, a family of predicates can be introduced which rests on the predicate 'meaningful' as we have defined it. All these defined pragmatic predicates will (1) *presuppose* the notion of a complete world-story in a language with given conformation rules; (2) be such that their applicability is (in principle) determinable on purely formal grounds. The application of such a predicate to an expression implies that the expression belongs to a formal system defined in such a way that the sentence making the application is either analytic or self-contradictory. This is what we mean when we say that the use of epistemological predicates involves presuppositions. Was Bosanquet so far wrong when he suggested that "Reality" is the subject of all judgments? We make the concept of *reality* a purely formal one, and say that each empirical language speaks about its own "Reality" or world.

Since our discussion of epistemological predicates has been in terms of what we called (pp. 429 ff.) languages proper as opposed to language *schemata*, we must end with a review of this distinction. The first thing to note is that it is one which breaks out at all linguistic levels. We can say that a pragmatic meta-schema claims to be a pragmatic meta-language proper, just as we have said that a language schema claims to be a language proper. Now it is clear from this very formulation that the whole distinction between the schematic and the proper is a factual-psychological rather than a formal-epistemological distinction.[22] It relates to the psychology of formal *manipulations*, and can no more be formulated within formal science itself then can the concept of *mistake*. If this is the case, then our factual inability to construct complete world-stories no more entails an inability to give a formal account of a complete world-story, or of a language proper, than our inability to construct an infinite series entails an inability to give a formal account of infinite, or, indeed, of particular infinite series. Our everyday use of epistemological predicates is formally or epistemologically sensible even though we cannot turn it into petty cash. Furthermore, the *psychological* contrast between language schema and language proper must not be mixed with *formal* distinctions between different formal predicates. Thus, the difference between 'confirmed' and 'confirmed-to-degree-n' must not be confused with a difference between "confirmed" as appearing in a meta-language, and "confirmed" as appear-

---

[22] Cf. "Pure Pragmatics and Epistemology," pp. 195–197, also notes 10–13. The fact that the distinction between language proper and language schema is a factual-psychological one also throws light on the "puzzle" of the fruitfulness of deduction. When as logicians we characterize an argument as *valid*, we are "reconstructing" it as a token of an expression in a language in the formal sense of the term. We *take it* (to use a metaphor) as a token of an expression in a language which is *posited* as a complete and exhaustive structure in which everything that is formally involved in the language is "given." On the other hand, when we characterize an argument as *fruitful*, we are making empirical statements about a series of linguistic events in the psychological sense of "language".

The higher mental processes *as empirical facts* can be described without reference to the categories of pure semiotics. This is the proper task of a psychology of "knowing," "believing," etc. The puzzles which lead to epistemologism arise when we confuse this task with the formal reconstruction of "knowings," "believings," etc. as tokens of linguistic expressions in the formal sense of "language." Our sense of human dignity focuses our attention on empirical description when we are concerned with Fido's belief that he has a bone. In the case of Smith's belief that he has a penny, we are prone to confuse.

It must be emphasized that over and against the formal theory of languages, there is the empirical theory of languages which includes empirical concepts relating to "formal" language behavior. (Put a psychologist to watching a mathematician.) We must admit that just as there is a formal distinction between the "empirical" and the "formal," so there is an *empirical* distinction between the "empirical" and the "formal" aspects of language as an empirical category. See also H. Feigl, "Operationism and Scientific Method," *Psychological Review*, 1945, included in this volume, pp. 498–508 below, especially p. 500.

ing in a meta-schema. Confusions of this kind give comfort to psychologism in pragmatics, and stimulate attempts to connect meaningfulness in a primary sense with probability.

According to our argument, it is a tautology to say that a meaningful language is about a causal world. The predicates of a meaningful language are such only by virtue of the conformation rules which differentiate them.[23] In these statements, the expression "language" appears as a formal predicate. On the other hand, as we have seen, the expression "language" also functions as a factual predicate relating to behavioral habits. This ambiguity of significance brings with it the danger of confusing the *psychological* factors leading to the discarding of one set of *habits* in favor of another with *formal* considerations of *probability*, *evidence* and *truth*. In speaking formally we "posit" a subject-matter which is *complete* within the scope of its presuppositions in that it doesn't make sense to say that the domain of this subject-matter is *incomplete*. On the other hand, the behavior which posits this domain is legitimately characterized as schematic. The English language as an anthropological fact may grow and change with the times. But the formal positing of a linguistic structure which clarifies (rationally reconstructs) the English language at a given time is the positing of a *complete* language (indeed, reflection would show, a *class of complete languages*).

Conclusion. This paper represents a meeting of extremes. The echoes of Leibnitz, Hume and Kant are no less obvious than those of Wittgenstein, Carnap and Tarski. But as a matter of historical justice long due, I like to think that we have reformulated in our own way a familiar type of Idealistic argument. It has been said that human *experience* can only be understood as a fragment of an ideally coherent *experience*. Our claim is that our empirical *language* can only be understood as an incoherent and fragmentary schema of an ideally coherent *language*. The Idealism, but not the wisdom, disappears with the dropping of the term 'experience'. Formally, all languages and worlds are on an equal footing. This is indeed a principle of indifference. On the other hand, a reconstruction of the pragmatics of common sense and the scientific outlook points to conformation rules requiring a story to contain sentences which are confirmed but not verified. In this sense the ideal of our language is a realistic language; and this is the place of Realism in the New Way of Words.

---

[23] The conformation rules of an empirically meaningful language determine the *necessary* elements in the structure of the world in which it is used. Here is the key to the concept of *causal law* and the *causal modalities*. A study of the requirements which conformation rules must fulfil in order to permit the construction of a confirmed world-story in the language of which they are the rules, as well as of the different properties of different sets of such rules, is the primary task of Pure Pragmatics.

VII

PROBLEMS OF DESCRIPTION AND
EXPLANATION IN THE EMPIRICAL SCIENCES

The Function of General Laws in History *

CARL G. HEMPEL

1. It is a rather widely held opinion that history, in contradistinction to the so-called physical sciences, is concerned with the description of particular events of the past rather than with the search for general laws which might govern those events. As a characterization of the type of problem in which some historians are mainly interested, this view probably can not be denied; as a statement of the theoretical function of general laws in scientific historical research, it is certainly unacceptable. The following considerations are an attempt to substantiate this point by showing in some detail that general laws have quite analogous functions in history and in the natural sciences, that they form an indispensable instrument of historical research, and that they even constitute the common basis of various procedures which are often considered as characteristic of the social in contradistinction to the natural sciences.

By a general law, we shall here understand a statement of universal conditional form which is capable of being confirmed or disconfirmed by suitable empirical findings. The term "law" suggests the idea that the statement in question is actually well confirmed by the relevant evidence available; as this qualification is, in many cases, irrelevant for our purpose, we shall frequently use the term "hypothesis of universal form" or briefly "universal hypothesis" instead of "general law," and state the condition of satisfactory confirmation separately, if necessary. In the context of this paper, a universal hypothesis may be assumed to assert a regularity of the following type: In every case where an event of a specified kind C occurs at a certain place and time, an event of a specified kind E will occur at a place and time which is related in a specified manner to the place and time of the occurrence of the first event. (The symbols "C" and "E" have been chosen to suggest the terms "cause" and "effect," which are often, though by no means always, applied to events related by a law of the above kind.)

2.1 The main function of general laws in the natural sciences is to connect events in patterns which are usually referred to as *explanation* and *prediction*.

The explanation of the occurrence of an event of some specific kind E at a certain place and time consists, as it is usually expressed, in indicating

* Reprinted by kind permission of the author and the editors from *The Journal of Philosophy*, 39, 1942.

the causes or determining factors of E. Now the assertion that a set of events—say, of the kinds C_1, C_2, . . . , C_n—have caused the event to be explained, amounts to the statement that, according to certain general laws, a set of events of the kinds mentioned is regularly accompanied by an event of kind E. Thus, the scientific explanation of the event in question consists of

(1) a set of statements asserting the occurrence of certain events C_1, . . . C_n at certain times and places,
(2) a set of universal hypotheses, such that
   (a) the statements of both groups are reasonably well confirmed by empirical evidence,
   (b) from the two groups of statements the sentence asserting the occurrence of event E can be logically deduced.

In a physical explanation, group (1) would describe the initial and boundary conditions for the occurrence of the final event; generally, we shall say that group (1) states the *determining conditions* for the event to be explained, while group (2) contains the general laws on which the explanation is based; they imply the statement that whenever events of the kind described in the first group occur, an event of the kind to be explained will take place.

Illustration: Let the event to be explained consist in the cracking of an automobile radiator during a cold night. The sentences of group (1) may state the following initial and boundary conditions: The car was left in the street all night. Its radiator, which consists of iron, was completely filled with water, and the lid was screwed on tightly. The temperature during the night dropped from 39° F. in the evening to 25° F. in the morning; the air pressure was normal. The bursting pressure of the radiator material is so and so much.—Group (2) would contain empirical laws such as the following: Below 32° F., under normal atmospheric pressure, water freezes. Below 39.2° F., the pressure of a mass of water increases with decreasing temperature, if the volume remains constant or decreases; when the water freezes, the pressure again increases. Finally, this group would have to include a quantitative law concerning the change of pressure of water as a function of its temperature and volume.

From statements of these two kinds, the conclusion that the radiator cracked during the night can be deduced by logical reasoning; an explanation of the considered event has been established.

2.2 It is important to bear in mind that the symbols "E," "C," "C_1," "C_2," etc., which were used above, stand for kinds or properties of events, not for what is sometimes called individual events. For the object of description and explanation in every branch of empirical science is always the occurrence of an event of a certain *kind* (such as a drop in temperature by 14° F., an eclipse of the moon, a cell-division, an earthquake, an increase in employment, a political assassination) at a given place and time, or in a given empirical object (such as the radiator of a certain car, the planetary system, a specified historical personality, etc.) at a certain time.

What is sometimes called the complete description of an individual event (such as the earthquake of San Francisco in 1906 or the assassination of Julius Caesar) would require a statement of all the properties exhibited by the spatial region or the individual object involved, for the period of time occupied by the event in question. Such a task can never be completely accomplished.

A fortiori, it is impossible to explain an individual event in the sense of accounting for *all* its characteristics by means of universal hypotheses, although the explanation of what happened at a specified place and time may gradually be made more and more specific and comprehensive.

But there is no difference, in this respect, between history and the natural sciences: both can give an account of their subject-matter only in terms of general concepts, and history can "grasp the unique individuality" of its objects of study no more and no less than can physics or chemistry.

3. The following points result more or less directly from the above study of scientific explanation and are of special importance for the questions here to be discussed.

3.1 A set of events can be said to have caused the event to be explained only if general laws can be indicated which connect "causes" and "effect" in the manner characterized above.

3.2 No matter whether the cause-effect terminology is used or not, a scientific explanation has been achieved only if empirical laws of the kind mentioned under (2) in 2.1 have been applied.[1]

3.3 The use of universal empirical hypotheses as explanatory principles distinguishes genuine from pseudo-explanation, such as, say, the attempt to account for certain features of organic behavior by reference to an entelechy, for whose functioning no laws are offered, or the explanation of the achievements of a given person in terms of his "mission in history," his "predestined fate," or similar notions. Accounts of this type are based on metaphors rather than laws; they convey pictorial and emotional appeals instead of insight into factual connections; they substitute vague analogies and intuitive "plausibility" for deduction from testable statements and are therefore unacceptable as scientific explanations.

Any explanation of scientific character is amenable to objective checks; these include

    (*a*) an empirical test of the sentences which state the determining conditions;

[1] Maurice Mandelbaum, in his generally very clarifying analysis of relevance and causation in history (*The Problem of Historical Knowledge*, New York, 1938, Chs. 7, 8) seems to hold that there is a difference between the "causal analysis" or "causal explanation" of an event and the establishment of scientific laws governing it in the sense stated above. He argues that "scientific laws can only be formulated on the basis of causal analysis," but that "they are not substitutes for full causal explanations" (*loc. cit.*, p. 238). For the reasons outlined above, this distinction does not appear to be justified: every "causal explanation" is an "explanation by scientific laws"; for in no other way than by reference to empirical laws can the assertion of a causal connection between certain events be scientifically substantiated.

(*b*) an empirical test of the universal hypotheses on which the explanation rests;

(*c*) an investigation of whether the explanation is logically conclusive in the sense that the sentence describing the event to be explained follows from the statements of groups (1) and (2).

4. The function of general laws in *scientific prediction* can now be stated very briefly. Quite generally, prediction in empirical science consists in deriving a statement about a certain future event (for example, the relative position of the planets to the sun, at a future date) from (1) statements describing certain known (past or present) conditions (for example, the positions and momenta of the planets at a past or present moment), and (2) suitable general laws (for example, the laws of celestial mechanics). Thus, the logical structure of a scientific prediction is the same as that of a scientific explanation, which has been described in 2.1. In particular, prediction no less than explanation throughout empirical science involves reference to universal empirical hypotheses.

The customary distinction between explanation and prediction rests mainly on a pragmatical difference between the two: While in the case of an explanation, the final event is known to have happened, and its determining conditions have to be sought, the situation is reversed in the case of a prediction: here, the initial conditions are given, and their "effect"—which, in the typical case, has not yet taken place—is to be determined.

In view of the structural equality of explanation and prediction, it may be said that an explanation as characterized in 2.1 is not complete unless it might as well have functioned as a prediction: If the final event can be derived from the initial conditions and universal hypotheses stated in the explanation, then it might as well have been predicted, before it actually happened, on the basis of a knowledge of the initial conditions and the general laws. Thus, e.g., those initial conditions and general laws which the astronomer would adduce in explanation of a certain eclipse of the sun are such that they might also have served as a sufficient basis for a forecast of the eclipse before it took place.

However, only rarely, if ever, are explanations stated so completely as to exhibit this predictive character (which the test referred to under (*c*) in 3.3 would serve to reveal). Quite commonly, the explanation offered for the occurrence of an event is incomplete. Thus, we may hear the explanation that a barn burnt down "because" a burning cigarette was dropped in the hay, or that a certain political movement has spectacular success "because" it takes advantage of widespread racial prejudices. Similarly, in the case of the broken radiator, the customary way of formulating an explanation would be restricted to pointing out that the car was left in the cold, and the radiator was filled with water.—In explanatory statements like these, the general laws which confer upon the stated conditions the character of "causes" or "determining factors" are completely omitted (sometimes, perhaps, as a "matter of course"), and, furthermore, the enumeration of the determining conditions of group (1) is incomplete; this is illustrated by the preceding examples, but even by the earlier analysis of the broken-radiator case: as a closer examination would reveal, even that much more detailed statement of determining conditions and universal hypotheses would require amplification in order to serve as a sufficient basis for the deduction of the conclusion that the radiator broke during the night.

In some instances, the incompleteness of a given explanation may be considered as inessential. Thus, e.g., we may feel that the explanation referred to in the last example could be made complete if we so desired; for we have reasons to assume that we know the kind of determining conditions and of general laws which are relevant in this context.

Very frequently, however, we encounter "explanations" whose incompleteness can not simply be dismissed as inessential. The methodological consequences of this situation will be discussed later (especially in 5.3 and 5.4).

5.1 The preceding considerations apply to *explanation in history* as well as in any other branch of empirical science. Historical explanation, too, aims at showing that the event in question was not "a matter of chance," but was to be expected in view of certain antecedent or simultaneous conditions. The expectation referred to is not prophecy or divination, but rational scientific anticipation which rests on the assumption of general laws.

If this view is correct, it would seem strange that while most historians do suggest explanations of historical events, many of them deny the possibility of resorting to any general laws in history. It is, however, possible to account for this situation by a closer study of explanation in history, as may become clear in the course of the following analysis.

5.2 In some cases, the universal hypotheses underlying a historical explanation are rather explicitly stated, as is illustrated by the italicized passages in the following attempt to explain the tendency of government agencies to perpetuate themselves and to expand [italics the author's]:

As the activities of the government are enlarged, more people develop a vested interest in the continuation and expansion of governmental functions. *People who have jobs do not like to lose them; those who are habituated to certain skills do not welcome change; those who have become accustomed to the exercise of a certain kind of power do not like to relinquish their control*—if anything, *they want to develop greater power and correspondingly greater prestige.* . . . Thus, government offices and bureaus, once created, in turn institute drives, not only to fortify themselves against assault, but to enlarge the scope of their operations.[2]

[2] Donald W. McConnell, *Economic Behavior*, New York, 1939; pp. 894-895.

Most explanations offered in history or sociology, however, fail to include an explicit statement of the general regularities they presuppose; and there seem to be at least two reasons which account for this:

First, the universal hypotheses in question frequently relate to individual or social psychology, which somehow is supposed to be familiar to everybody through his everyday experience; thus, they are tacitly taken for granted. This is a situation quite similar to that characterized in 4.

Second, it would often be very difficult to formulate the underlying assumptions explicitly with sufficient precision and at the same time in such a way that they are in agreement with all the relevant empirical evidence available. It is highly instructive, in examining the adequacy of a suggested explanation, to attempt a reconstruction of the universal hypotheses on which it rests. Particularly, such terms as "hence," "therefore," "consequently," "because," "naturally," "obviously," etc., are often indicative of the tacit presupposition of some general law: they are used to tie up the initial conditions with the event to be explained; but that the latter was "naturally" to be expected as "a consequence" of the stated conditions follows only if suitable general laws are presupposed. Consider, for example, the statement that the Dust Bowl farmers migrate to California "because" continual drought and sandstorms render their existence increasingly precarious, and because California seems to them to offer so much better living conditions. This explanation rests on some such universal hypothesis as that populations will tend to migrate to regions which offer better living conditions. But it would obviously be difficult accurately to state this hypothesis in the form of a general law which is reasonably well confirmed by all the relevant evidence available. Similarly, if a particular revolution is explained by reference to the growing discontent, on the part of a large part of the population, with certain prevailing conditions, it is clear that a general regularity is assumed in this explanation, but we are hardly in a position to state just what extent and what specific form the discontent has to assume, and what the environmental conditions have to be, to bring about a revolution. Analogous remarks apply to all historical explanations in terms of class struggle, economic or geographic conditions, vested interests of certain groups, tendency to conspicuous consumption, etc.: All of them rest on the assumption of universal hypotheses [3] which connect certain characteristics of individual or group life with others; but in many cases, the content of the hypotheses which are tacitly assumed in a given explanation can be reconstructed only quite approximately.

5.3 It might be argued that the phenomena covered by the type of ex-

---

[3] What is sometimes, misleadingly, called an explanation by means of a certain *concept* is, in empirical science, actually an explanation in terms of *universal hypotheses* containing that concept. "Explanations" involving concepts which do not function in empirically testable hypotheses—such as "entelechy" in biology, "historic destination of a race" or "self-unfolding of absolute reason" in history—are mere metaphors without cognitive content.

planation just mentioned are of a statistical character, and that therefore only probability hypotheses need to be assumed in their explanation, so that the question as to the "underlying general laws" would be based on a false premise. And indeed, it seems possible and justifiable to construe certain explanations offered in history as based on the assumption of probability hypotheses rather than of general "deterministic" laws, i.e., laws in the form of universal conditions. This claim may be extended to many of the explanations offered in other fields of empirical science as well. Thus, e.g., if Tommy comes down with the measles two weeks after his brother, and if he has not been in the company of other persons having the measles, we accept the explanation that he caught the disease from his brother. Now, there is a general hypothesis underlying this explanation; but it can hardly be said to be a general law to the effect that any person who has not had the measles before will get them without fail if he stays in the company of somebody else who has the measles; that a contagion will occur can be asserted only with a high probability.

Many an explanation offered in history seems to admit of an analysis of this kind: if fully and explicitly formulated, it would state certain initial conditions, and certain probability hypotheses,[4] such that the occurrence of the event to be explained is made highly probable by the initial conditions in view of the probability hypotheses. But no matter whether explanations in history be construed as "causal" or as "probabilistic" in character, it remains true that in general the initial conditions and especially the universal hypotheses involved are not clearly indicated, and can not unambiguously be supplemented. (In the case of probability hypotheses, for example, the probability values involved will at best be known quite roughly.)

5.4 What the explanatory analyses of historical events offer is, then, in most cases not an explanation in one of the meanings developed above, but something that might be called an *explanation sketch*. Such a sketch consists of a more or less vague indication of the laws and initial conditions considered as relevant, and it needs "filling out" in order to turn into a full-fledged explanation. This filling-out requires further empirical research, for which the sketch suggests the direction. (Explanation sketches are common also outside of history; many explanations in psychoanalysis, for instance, illustrate this point.)

Obviously, an explanation sketch does not admit of an empirical test to the same extent as does a complete explanation; and yet, there is a difference between a scientifically acceptable explanation sketch and a pseudo-

---

[4] E. Zilsel, in a very stimulating paper on "Physics and the Problem of Historico-Sociological Laws" (*Philosophy of Science*, Vol. 8, 1941, pp. 567–579), suggests that all specifically historical laws are of a statistical character similar to that of the "macro-laws" in physics. The above remarks, however, are not restricted to specifically historical laws since explanation in history rests to a large extent on non-historical laws (cf. section 8 of this paper).

explanation (or a pseudo-explanation sketch). A scientifically acceptable explanation sketch needs to be filled out by more specific statements; but it points into the direction where these statements are to be found; and concrete research may tend to confirm or to infirm those indications; i.e., it may show that the kind of initial conditions suggested are actually relevant; or it may reveal that factors of a quite different nature have to be taken into account in order to arrive at a satisfactory explanation.—The filling-out process required by an explanation sketch will, in general, assume the form of a gradually increasing precision of the formulations involved; but at any stage of this process, those formulations will have some empirical import: it will be possible to indicate, at least roughly, what kind of evidence would be relevant in testing them, and what findings would tend to confirm them. In the case of non-empirical explanations or explanation sketches, on the other hand—say, by reference to the historical destination of a certain race, or to a principle of historical justice—the use of empirically meaningless terms makes it impossible even roughly to indicate the type of investigation that would have a bearing upon those formulations, and that might lead to evidence either confirming or infirming the suggested explanation.

5.5 In trying to appraise the soundness of a given explanation, one will first have to attempt to reconstruct as completely as possible the argument constituting the explanation or the explanation sketch. In particular, it is important to realize what the underlying explaining hypotheses are, and to judge of their scope and empirical foundation. A resuscitation of the assumptions buried under the gravestones "hence," "therefore," "because," and the like will often reveal that the explanation offered is poorly founded or downright unacceptable. In many cases, this procedure will bring to light the fallacy of claiming that a large number of details of an event have been explained when, even on a very liberal interpretation, only some broad characteristics of it have been accounted for. Thus, for example, the geographic or economic conditions under which a group lives may account for certain general features of, say, its art or its moral codes; but to grant this does not mean that the artistic achievements of the group or its system of morals has thus been explained in detail; for this would imply that from a description of the prevalent geographic or economic conditions alone, a detailed account of certain aspects of the cultural life of the group can be deduced by means of specifiable general laws.

A related error consists in singling out one of several important groups of factors which would have to be stated in the initial conditions, and then claiming that the phenomenon in question is "determined" by and thus can be explained in terms of that one group of factors.

Occasionally, the adherents of some particular school of explanation or interpretation in history will adduce, as evidence in favor of their approach, a successful historical prediction which was made by a representative of their school. But though the predictive success of a theory is certainly relevant evidence of its soundness, it is important to make sure that the successful prediction is in fact obtainable by means of the theory in question. It happens sometimes that the prediction is actually an ingenious guess which may have been influenced by the theoretical outlook of its author, but which can not be arrived at by means of his theory alone. Thus, an adherent of a quite metaphysical "theory" of history may have a sound feeling for historical developments and may be able to make correct predictions, which he will even couch in the terminology of his theory, though they could not have been attained by means of it. To guard against such pseudo-confirming cases would be one of the functions of test (c) in 3.3.

6. We have tried to show that in history no less than in any other branch of empirical inquiry, scientific explanation can be achieved only by means of suitable general hypotheses, or by theories, which are bodies of systematically related hypotheses. This thesis is clearly in contrast with the familiar view that genuine explanation in history is obtained by a method which characteristically distinguishes the social from the natural sciences, namely, *the method of empathetic understanding:* The historian, we are told, imagines himself in the place of the persons involved in the events which he wants to explain; he tries to realize as completely as possible the circumstances under which they acted, and the motives which influenced their actions; and by this imaginary self-identification with his heroes, he arrives at an understanding and thus at an adequate explanation of the events with which he is concerned.

This method of empathy is, no doubt, frequently applied by laymen and by experts in history. But it does not in itself constitute an explanation; it rather is essentially a heuristic device; its function is to suggest certain psychological hypotheses which might serve as explanatory principles in the case under consideration. Stated in crude terms, the idea underlying this function is the following: The historian tries to realize how he himself would act under the given conditions, and under the particular motivations of his heroes; he tentatively generalizes his findings into a general rule and uses the latter as an explanatory principle in accounting for the actions of the persons involved. Now, this procedure may sometimes prove heuristically helpful; but its use does not guarantee the soundness of the historical explanation to which it leads. The latter rather depends upon the factual correctness of the empirical generalizations which the method of understanding may have suggested.

Nor is the use of this method indispensable for historical explanation. A historian may, for example, be incapable of feeling himself into the rôle of a paranoiac historic personality, and yet he may well be able to explain certain of his actions; notably by reference to the principles of abnormal psychology. Thus, whether the historian is or is not in a position to identify himself with his historical hero, is irrelevant for the correctness of his explanation; what counts, is the soundness of the general hypotheses involved, no matter whether they were suggested by empathy or by a strictly behavioristic procedure. Much of the appeal of the "method of understanding" seems to be due to the fact that it tends to present the phenomena in question as somehow "plausible" or "natural" to us; [5] this is often done by means of attractively worded metaphors. But the kind of "understanding" thus conveyed must clearly be separated from scientific understanding. In history as anywhere else in empirical science, the explanation of a phenomenon consists in subsuming it under general empirical laws; and the criterion of its soundness is not whether it appeals to our imagination, whether it is presented in suggestive analogies, or is otherwise made to appear plausible—all this may occur in pseudo-explanations as well—but exclusively whether it rests on empirically well confirmed assumptions concerning initial conditions and general laws.

7.1 So far, we have discussed the importance of general laws for explanation and prediction, and for so-called understanding in history. Let us now survey more briefly some other procedures of historical research which involve the assumption of universal hypotheses.

Closely related to explanation and understanding is the so-called *interpretation of historical phenomena* in terms of some particular approach or theory. The interpretations which are actually offered in history consist either in subsuming the phenomena in question under a scientific explanation or explanation sketch; or in an attempt to subsume them under some general idea which is not amenable to any empirical test. In the former case, interpretation clearly is explanation by means of universal hypotheses; in the latter, it amounts to a pseudo-explanation which may have emotive appeal and evoke vivid pictorial associations, but which does not further our theoretical understanding of the phenomena under consideration.

7.2 Analogous remarks apply to the procedure of ascertaining the *"meaning"* of given historical events; its scientific import consists in determining what other events are relevantly connected with the event in question, be it as "causes," or as "effects"; and the statement of the relevant connections assumes, again, the form of explanations or explanation sketches which involve universal hypotheses; this will be seen more clearly in the subsequent section.

7.3 In the historical explanation of some social institutions great emphasis is laid upon an analysis of the *development* of the institution up to the stage under consideration. Critics of this approach have objected that a mere description of this kind is not a genuine explanation. This argument may be given a slightly different aspect in terms of the preceding reflections: A description of the development of an institution is obviously not

---

[5] For a criticism of this kind of plausibility, cf. Zilsel, *loc. cit.*, pp. 577–578, and sections 7 and 8 in the same author's "Problems of Empiricism," in *International Encyclopedia of Unified Science*, Vol. II, 8.

simply a statement of *all* the events which temporally preceded it; only those events are meant to be included which are *"relevant"* to the formation of that institution. And whether an event is relevant to that development is not a question of the value attitude of the historian, but an objective question depending upon what is sometimes called a causal analysis of the rise of that institution.[6] Now, the causal analysis of an event consists in establishing an explanation for it, and since this requires reference to general hypotheses, so do assumptions about relevance, and, consequently, so does the adequate analysis of the historical development of an institution.

7.4 Similarly, the use of the notions of *determination* and of *dependence* in the empirical sciences, including history, involves reference to general laws.[7] Thus, e.g., we may say that the pressure of a gas depends upon its temperature and volume, or that temperature and volume determine the pressure, in virtue of Boyle's law. But unless the underlying laws are stated explicitly, the assertion of a relation of dependence or of determination between certain magnitudes or characteristics amounts at best to claiming that they are connected by some unspecified empirical law; and that is a very meager assertion indeed: If, for example, we know only that there is some empirical law connecting two metrical magnitudes (such as length and temperature of a metal bar), we can not even be sure that a change of one of the two will be accompanied by a change of the other (for the law may connect the same value of the "dependent" or "determined" magnitude with different values of the other), but only that with any specific value of one of the variables, there will always be associated one and the same value of the other; and this is obviously much less than most authors mean to assert when they speak of determination or dependence in historical analysis.

Therefore, the sweeping assertion that economic (or geographic, or any other kind of) conditions "determine" the development and change of all other aspects of human society, has explanatory value only in so far as it can be substantiated by explicit laws which state just what kind of change in human culture will regularly follow upon specific changes in the eco-

[6] See the detailed and clear exposition of this point in M. Mandelbaum's book; *loc. cit.*, chs. 6–8.

[7] According to Mandelbaum, history, in contradistinction to the physical sciences, consists "not in the formulation of laws of which the particular case is an instance, but in the description of the events in their actual determining relationships to each other; in seeing events as the products and producers of change" (*loc. cit.*, pp. 13–14). This is essentially a view whose untenability has been pointed out already by Hume; it is the belief that a careful examination of two specific events alone, without any reference to similar cases and to general regularities, can reveal that one of the events produces or determines the other. This thesis does not only run counter to the scientific meaning of the concept of determination which clearly rests on that of general law, but it even fails to provide any objective criteria which would be indicative of the intended relationship of determination or production. Thus, to speak of empirical determination independently of any reference to general laws means to use a metaphor without cognitive content.

nomic (geographic, etc.) conditions. Only the establishment of concrete laws can fill the general thesis with scientific content, make it amenable to empirical tests, and confer upon it an explanatory function. The elaboration of such laws with as much precision as possible seems clearly to be the direction in which progress in scientific explanation and understanding has to be sought.

8. The considerations developed in this paper are entirely neutral with respect to the problem of *"specifically historical laws"*: neither do they presuppose a particular way of distinguishing historical from sociological and other laws, nor do they imply or deny the assumption that empirical laws can be found which are historical in some specific sense, and which are well confirmed by empirical evidence.

But it may be worth mentioning here that those universal hypotheses to which historians explicitly or tacitly refer in offering explanations, predictions, interpretations, judgments of relevance, etc., are taken from *various* fields of scientific research, in so far as they are not pre-scientific generalizations of everyday experiences. Many of the universal hypotheses underlying historical explanation, for instance, would commonly be classified as psychological, economical, sociological, and partly perhaps as historical laws; in addition, historical research has frequently to resort to general laws established in physics, chemistry, and biology. Thus, e.g., the explanation of the defeat of an army by reference to lack of food, adverse weather conditions, disease, and the like, is based on a—usually tacit—assumption of such laws. The use of tree rings in dating events in history rests on the application of certain biological regularities. Various methods of testing the authenticity of documents, paintings, coins, etc., make use of physical and chemical theories.

The last two examples illustrate another point which is relevant in this context: Even if a historian should propose to restrict his research to a *"pure description"* of the past, without any attempt at offering explanations, statements about relevance and determination, etc., he would continually have to make use of general laws. For the object of his studies would be the past—forever inaccessible to his direct examination. He would have to establish his knowledge by indirect methods: by the use of universal hypotheses which connect his present data with those past events. This fact has been obscured partly because some of the regularities involved are so familiar that they are not considered worth mentioning at all; and partly because of the habit of relegating the various hypotheses and theories which are used to ascertain knowledge about past events, to the "auxiliary sciences" of history. Quite probably, some of the historians who tend to minimize, if not to deny, the importance of general laws for history, are actuated by the feeling that only "genuinely historical laws" would be of interest for history. But once it is realized that the discovery of historical laws (in some specified sense of this very vague notion) would not make history methodologically autonomous and independent of the other branches of scientific research, it would seem that the problem of the existence of historical laws ought to lose some of its weight.

The remarks made in this section are but special illustrations of two broader principles of the theory of science: first, the separation of "pure description" and "hypothetical generalization and theory-construction" in empirical science is unwarranted; in the building of scientific knowledge the two are inseparably linked. And, second, it is similarly unwarranted and futile to attempt the demarcation of sharp boundary lines between the different fields of scientific research, and an autonomous development of each of the fields. The necessity, in historical inquiry, to make extensive use of universal hypotheses of which at least the overwhelming majority come from fields of research traditionally distinguished from history is just one of the aspects of what may be called the methodological unity of empirical science.

The "Nature" of a Continuant *

C. D. BROAD

. . . The distinction between the nature of a thing and its various situations; between the situation in which it *was* placed at a certain moment and others in which it *might have been* placed instead at that moment; and between how it *actually did* behave and how it *would have* behaved if its situation had been different; is continually drawn in ordinary life and in science. It must correspond to something real, even if it distorts the facts which it claims to express. Philosophy certainly cannot afford to ignore it completely, as McTaggart does. Now this seems to be the most appropriate place at which to treat this question. I will therefore end this chapter with a few remarks on the subject. I may say that the best treatment of it with which I am acquainted is to be found in Lotze's *Metaphysik*, though I should hesitate to recommend Lotze's writings to a reader who was pressed for time or in search of thrills.

The Popular-Scientific View. I will begin by trying to state explicitly certain things which we all tacitly presuppose in science and common life when we use the concepts of Cause and Substance.

We all distinguish between a thing and its actual history, i.e., the actual series of states or events of which this thing is supposed to have been the common subject. This distinction is closely bound up with another, which we all draw, viz., the distinction between a thing, with its inner nature and its states, on the one hand, and the external circumstances in which it happens from time to time to be placed, on the other. The external circumstances consist of the standing of this thing in certain relations at certain times to other things which are not parts of itself. We assume that the very same thing, which in fact was in certain external circumstances and in fact had a certain history, *might* have been in dissimilar circumstances and *would* then have had a dissimilar history.

At this point the intimate connexion between the notions of Substance and Cause, which led Johnson to say that they are not two categories but two factors in a single more concrete category, becomes plain. We ascribe to a thing a certain inner nature, and we hold that its history is determined jointly by its inner nature and its external circumstances. Given the inner

* Excerpted and reprinted by kind permission of the author and the publisher from *Examination of McTaggart's Philosophy*, Vol. I, pp. 264-278. University of Cambridge Press, 1933.

nature and the actual circumstances, it is assumed, the actual history *could not* have been dissimilar to what it in fact was. And, given the same inner nature and assignably dissimilar circumstances, it is assumed, the history *would necessarily* have been dissimilar in certain assignable respects from the actual history. Thus a Thing is conceived as a store of powers or dispositions. Some of these may not be manifesting themselves at a given moment, though they may have done so in the past and may do so again in the future. Some may never yet have manifested themselves. And those which are manifesting themselves in a certain way would have done so in an assignably dissimilar way if the external circumstances had been different. A bit of arsenic, for example, is always poisonous, but it may not now be poisoning anyone. The earth is moving round the sun in a certain way, and it would have been moving in a certain different way if the sun had been twice as massive as it is. And so on.

We must now go into further detail about powers or dispositions.

(i) We can divide them into generic, specific, and singular. All bits of matter resist attempts to change their state of motion or of rest. Thus inertia is a *generic* dispositional property of matter. Similarly, retentiveness and the power of association are probably generic dispositional properties of mind. Then there are certain dispositions which belong to all samples of gold (e.g., to melt at a certain temperature at normal pressure) and do not belong to any other kind of matter. These are *specific* dispositional properties of gold. It is probably a specific dispositional property of *human* minds to be capable of seeing formal relations, to desire to do "what is right and reasonable, as such", and so on. Lastly, it may well be that a certain individual *A*, and no other, has the capacity to fall in love with a certain individual *B*. This would be an example of a *singular* power or disposition.

(ii) We must next notice that dispositions fall into a hierarchy. A bit of iron which has been put inside a helix in which an electric current circulates acquires the power to attract iron-filings. A bit of copper, placed in similar circumstances, does not. Under certain other circumstances, e.g., if it be sharply hit or heated to a certain temperature, the bit of iron will lose the magnetic property. If we call the magnetic property a "first-order disposition", the power to acquire this property when placed in a helix round which a current is circulating may be called a "second-order disposition" specific to iron. For it is a disposition to acquire the first-order disposition under certain circumstances, and it is common and peculiar to bits of iron. Similarly, the power to lose the magnetic property when heated or sharply hit will be a second-order disposition of iron. A disposition of the second order is, in general, a disposition to acquire or to lose, under assigned conditions, a disposition of the first order. In the same way we could define dispositions of the third or higher order. The power of learning to talk is a mental disposition of at least the second order, for it is a power to acquire a power of doing something. One of the peculiarities of minds in general, and of human minds in particular, is that they start with very few first-order powers, but rather with powers to acquire powers.

In this connexion it is important to distinguish between two cases, viz., the reversible and the irreversible. In the first case a power can be gained and lost and gained again repeatedly by appropriate changes in the external circumstances. A bit of iron can be magnetised, and demagnetised, and remagnetised, repeatedly. In the second case the substance has not the power to regain a certain power which it has lost, or to lose a certain power which it has gained. If you injure a man's brain in certain ways, his mind will lose certain powers, and there is no known way of restoring these powers to his mind.

Now presumably this hierarchy of powers cannot continue indefinitely upwards in the case of any substance. It would seem that any substance must have some powers which are not the joint products of its other powers of higher order and the special external circumstances in which it has been placed. Such powers may be called the "Supreme Dispositions" of the substance in question. So far as we know, retentiveness is a supreme disposition of minds, and electric charge is a supreme disposition of electrons.

A substance can change in respect of its external circumstances, its states, and its lower-order dispositions. Could it change in respect of its supreme dispositions? If such a change were to take place, it would, by definition, be not completely determined by causes. For, if it were so determined, it would have to be determined jointly by some disposition of the substance and by the circumstances in which the substance was placed. But, if this were so, the disposition which has changed would *not* be supreme, since the disposition which determines the change of it would, by definition, be of a higher order than it. Thus there seem to be three logically possible alternatives. Either (*a*) a substance has no supreme dispositions, and the hierarchy of its dispositions goes upwards without end; or (*b*) it has supreme dispositions, and these cannot change; or (*c*) it has supreme dispositions, and these can change, but the changes of them are not completely determined by causes. I think that, in ordinary life and in science, we tacitly reject the first and the third alternatives and accept the second.

(iii) We must next consider the distinction between "Simple" and "Compound" substances, so far as it is relevant to the subject of dispositions. Some substances are certainly composed of other substances interrelated in some fairly intimate and specific way. It is practically certain that even the smallest bit of matter which we can perceive and on which we can operate is of immense complexity. Now a complex substance will always have some dispositions which do not belong to the substances which are its constituents. Thus water boils, under normal pressure, at 100° C., whilst neither oxygen nor hydrogen, of which it is composed, has this property. Let us call properties which belong to a compound substance as a whole, and not to any of its constituents "Collective Properties". It is, of course, plain that, if there be simple substances, they can have no collective properties.

Now it is theoretically possible that there should be collective properties of two different kinds, which I will call "Reducible" and "Emergent". A collective disposition is *reducible* if the presence of this property in a compound substance is logically entailed by the dispositions which its constituents manifest in *other* circumstances and the special relations in which they stand to each other in *this* substance. All the characteristic properties of a clock, for example, are reducible, since they are entailed by the properties which brass, steel, etc., manifest in other circumstances, and by the special forms into which these materials are shaped and the special relations in which they are set to constitute a clock. But it is possible that there may be collective dispositions which are not, in this sense, reducible. Common salt, for example, is certainly a complex substance composed of sodium and chlorine; but nothing that is known of the behaviour of sodium in other circumstances, and of the behaviour of chlorine in other circumstances, and of the mutual relations of the two elements in salt, entails that this combination of them will have the characteristic "salty" taste. By an "emergent" disposition I mean a collective disposition which is not reducible, in the sense defined and illustrated above. Whether there be any such properties, or whether it be merely our present imperfect knowledge which makes it seem as if there were, is a question of detail into which we need not enter here and now. It is enough to say that it is plainly *possible* that some collective dispositional properties should be emergent; though it is the natural and proper ambition of scientists to show, with regard to as many collective properties as possible, that they are really reducible even though they have seemed to be emergent.

Modern physics does not differ from mediaeval physics in having dispensed with dispositions or "faculties". Its advantage, in this connexion, over mediaeval physics consists in the following closely connected points. (*a*) It has shown that there is very strong reason to believe that many substances, which seem to be simple and homogeneous (e.g., water, salt, etc.), are in fact complex and heterogeneous; being composed of simpler substances, which can occur singly or in other combinations, interrelated in a certain characteristic way. This makes the properties of such substances to be certainly collective, and therefore possibly reducible. (*b*) It has shown that these simpler substances are of a very few kinds, and that the immense variety of kinds of material substance is due to differences in the number, spatial relations, and motions of substances of these few kinds. (*c*) It can often plausibly derive many very different dispositions of a compound substance from a single hypothesis about its components, their arrangements, and their motions; and can predict from this hypothesis further dispositional properties, which had not hitherto been suspected but are found to be present on further investigation. (*d*) Until lately physical science enjoyed what I can only describe as an extraordinary bit of luck, which, like that which made England so prosperous in the nineteenth century, is now deserting it. Experimenting with samples of matter which are enormously complex, it found certain laws governing their effects on each other in the way of starting, modifying and stopping each other's motions. It boldly and unthinkingly assumed that these laws would apply also to the imperceptible components of these immensely complex perceptible substances. To a most amazing extent this draft on the unknown was honoured by Nature. But we have now exhausted our overdraft; and we have to realise that, beyond a certain point, concepts and laws derived from observing extremely complex substances do not apply to their simpler and imperceptible components. The only surprising thing is that we should all have been so surprised when this at last happened.

Poor dear Psychology, of course, has never got far beyond the stage of mediaeval physics, except in its statistical developments, where the labours of the mathematicians have enabled it to spin out the correlation of trivialities into endless refinements. For the rest it is only too obvious that, up to the present, a great deal of Psychology consists mainly of muddle, twaddle, and quacksalving, trying to impose itself as science by the elaborateness of its technical terminology and the confidence of its assertions.

It is now time to consider the connexion or want of connexion between the various pairs of opposites which I have distinguished, viz., supreme and lower-order dispositions, reducible and emergent properties, and simple and compound substances. At any given stage of scientific knowledge certain substances are taken as simple, and their properties are therefore taken as non-collective and so irreducible. At one time the atoms of the various chemical elements were supposed to be in this position; now the electrons and protons have ousted them. The ideal would presumably be to have one and only one ultimate kind of substance, but it is not self-evident that this ideal must be realised in nature. On the other hand, I think that we do tacitly assume that there must be simple substances, and that all other substances must be built out of these; though we do not assume, with regard to any kind of substance which is at a given time the simplest known, that *it* is in fact simple.

It is plain that all the dispositions of any simple substance would have to be accepted as so many independent brute facts about it, and must be incapable of any kind of explanation. To this extent there is an analogy between the dispositional properties of a simple substance and the emergent properties, if there be any, of a compound substance. But there is an important difference. Although the emergent properties of a compound substance could not be explained, in the sense of being *inferred* from the properties which its constituents have manifested in other combinations and from their special interrelations in this substance, yet they are *subject to laws*. There will be the law that *any* substance composed of such constituents so related to each other will have such and such an emergent property. The peculiarity of these laws is that they are ultimate, and cannot be inferred from anything else. The laws are brute facts, but there *are* the laws. But the dispositions of a simple substance could not be subject to laws even of this kind. Since a simple substance has no components and no structure, there cannot even be an ultimate and non-deducible law connecting the properties of such a substance with each other by connecting them all with its structure and components.

On the other hand, it is not necessary that all the properties of a simple substance should be supreme, in the sense in which I defined the term "supreme properties". There is no reason why a simple substance should not have a certain property p under certain circumstances, which changes into the property p' under certain other circumstances. If so, neither p nor p' would be supreme properties in my sense, for the property of losing p and gaining p' under certain circumstances would be a property of higher order than p and p' themselves. Let us take an example. So far as I know, my mind is a simple substance. It has gained the power of repeating the multiplication table. Under certain conditions it would lose this power. Therefore this power is not a supreme property of my mind, though the power of learning and forgetting may be so.

It remains to remind ourselves of a remark which was made in Section 1·21 of Chap. VII of the present work. We know what we mean by the generation or the destruction of a compound substance. It is generated when certain simpler substances come into certain characteristic determinate relations to each other; it lasts so long as they remain in the same, or approximately the same, mutual relations; and it is destroyed when they cease to stand in these relations to each other. These are processes which are subject to ordinary causal laws, with which science can deal. But the generation or destruction of a simple substance seems to be something quite unintelligible to the human mind; it falls altogether outside the ordinary notions of change and causation. It does not, of course, follow that it could not happen. Nor does it follow that we could not discover and state the circumstances under which it does happen, if it does.

The fact is that we are again faced with three alternatives, as we were in the case of supreme properties. Either (*a*) there are no simple substances; or (*b*) there are simple substances, and they are all eternal or sempiternal; or (*c*) there are simple substances which are generated and annihilated, but their generation and annihilation are unique processes which involve a unique kind of "causation". I think that common-sense, if pressed, would reject the first alternative as impossible and the third as intellectually humiliating, but would feel rather uncomfortable if one were to be so ungentlemanly as to say openly that this commits it to accepting the second.

It is now possible to explain what common-sense and science understand by the "inner nature" of a substance. They mean primarily the collection of all its supreme dispositional properties. If the substance in question be, so far as we know, simple, there is an end of the matter for the present. If, on the other hand, we have reason to believe that it is complex, there is more to be said. Many of its supreme dispositional properties may be inferable from the natures of its components and the mutual relations in which they stand within the compound substance. In such cases it would probably be said that the "inner nature" is the property of being composed of components of such and such natures interrelated in such and such ways, together with any supreme dispositional properties which are emergent, i.e., not inferable from the former property.

Now I think that science and common-sense would regard the following three propositions as self-evident. (i) Every substance has a set of supreme dispositional properties, each of finite order. This is little more than asserting that every substance has a definite inner nature. (ii) No substance can change in respect of any of its supreme dispositional properties. This again is largely a matter of definition, viz., the definition of "continuing to be the same substance". If a case arose which seemed to conflict with the present principle, we should say that what had happened was that "one substance had been annihilated and another substance of a different kind had been generated in its place". (iii) Any substance whose inner nature had differed in any respect from that which S in fact has would necessarily have been a different substance from S. It does seem clearly nonsensical to say that what is in fact a bit of gold might instead have been a bit of silver or a potato or a kangaroo; whilst it does not seem clearly nonsensical to say of *this* bit of gold, which is in fact now on my table, that it might instead have been on the floor.

Critical Discussion of the Above View. I think that the last sub-section contains a reasonably clear and accurate account of the meaning which we attach in ordinary life and science to the phrase "the nature of a substance", and of the propositions which we believe about the natures of substances. It remains to consider briefly whether it is internally coherent.

I have already given my reasons for doubting, in company with McTaggart, whether the sentence "This, which in fact stood in the relation R to that at t, might instead have then stood to that in the relation S" has any meaning if "this" and "that" be used as pure proper names. But we are almost certainly not acquainted with the substances about which we profess to be making such statements, and so our "this" and "that" are not functioning as proper names. It may be, then, that such statements, when properly interpreted, have a good meaning. There is, however, another difficulty in taking such statements literally, which we have not yet considered. Our objection to taking these statements literally was quite independent of questions about *causation;* our objection was that, in such statements, modal predicates were ascribed to subjects which are not capable of modality. We have now to consider the bearing of the doctrine of universal causal determination upon the legitimacy of such suppositions.

Suppose that we are considering a material thing, and saying of it that *it* might have been in different circumstances from those in which it in fact was, and that *it* would then have had an assignably dissimilar history from that which it in fact had. And suppose we want this statement to be taken literally. The most important circumstances of a material thing are its relationships of contact, separation, etc., to other material things. Now is it possible for anyone who accepts the laws of mechanics to say literally that the very same thing which was in fact in contact at a certain moment with certain other things might instead have stood in different spatial relations to the very same things at that moment? The position of anything at any moment is supposed to be completely determined by its previous position and velocity, and its previous spatial relations to other things, and the natures and previous states of itself and other things. No doubt we can say consistently that this thing *would have been* now in such and such a different spatial position *if* it had previously stood in such and such different spatial relations to other things. But this merely pushes the question of the legitimacy of this kind of supposition further and further back in time. And, in the end, we seem unable to give any clear meaning to the supposition that this very thing might now have been differently related to the same things, unless we think of this thing as being created and suddenly put into the pre-existing system of nature at a certain time and place. No doubt, if this very same thing could have been "launched into existence" in a different time or place from that in which it in fact was, it would now be in different spatial relations to the same things. But is there really any sense in this supposition? Can we really think of substances being shot into the course of nature at certain places and dates? And, if we can, what sense is there in saying that the very same substance, which in fact began its career at a certain time and place, might instead have begun at a different time and place? Would not a substance which had started to exist at a different time and place from this one have necessarily been a different substance from this one? The problem is certainly no easier in the case of mental substances. I have sometimes caught myself wondering what I should have been like if my father had not married my mother but had married some other woman. But I always ended by thinking that the question was meaningless.

We may sum up the position as follows. The popular-scientific view of the world ostensibly combines the following four propositions. (i) That any substance might have been in different circumstances at a given moment from the circumstances in which it in fact then was. (ii) That the circumstances of any substance at any moment are completely determined by its nature, the natures of the other substances in the universe, and the previous internal states and external circumstances of it and of them. (iii) That the natures of substances cannot change, and that it is nonsensical to suppose that a substance which in fact has one nature might instead have had a dissimilar nature. (iv) That the "coming to be" and the "passing away" of simple substances is unintelligible and can play no part in science, whilst the "coming to be" and the "passing away" of compound substances is completely determined as to time, place, and the nature of the substance concerned, by previous events. My criticism is that, even if there were no logical objection to the first supposition by itself, when taken literally, it cannot be taken literally and consistently combined with the other three. Nor is this criticism merely captious. Any mathematical physicist who troubles to think what he is doing must often be puzzled to know what he really means when he talks of "the most probable initial state of a gas", or when, in applying the Principle of Least Action, he compares the various "possible paths" (all but one of which are physically *impossible*) by which a system "might" pass from one actual state to another.

It seems plain then, on several grounds, that the common statement that a certain thing might have been situated otherwise than it was, and would then have behaved otherwise than it did, cannot be interpreted literally. And, if we consider the kind of evidence on which such statements are founded, we can see what interpretation should probably be put upon them. My evidence for saying that *this* might have been in an assignably different situation, and that *it* would then have behaved in an assignably different way, is always of the following kind. I have observed *this* at *various* times in various situations, and noted its behaviour. I have observed *other things*, which closely resembled this, at various times and in various situations, and have noted *their* behaviour. Each observed determinate situation s, and the corresponding determinate behaviour b, are found to fall under a certain general formula $B = f(S)$ connecting the determinables B and S. It is assumed that this formula is characteristic of substances of a certain kind; and that, if at *any* time any substance of this kind were put into a situation which was *any* determinate form of S, its determinate behaviour would be that form of B which is obtained by substituting the given determinate form of S in the formula $B = f(S)$. I believe that the statement that *this* very thing might have been in an assignably different situation from that in which it actually was, and that *it* would then have behaved in an assignably different way from that in which it actually did, is intelligible and consistent with other parts of the popular-scientific view *only* if it be taken as an abbreviation of the above statement about *any* thing of a given *kind*.

Now, if this view be accepted, an important consequence follows. Unless the nature of *this* thing remains constant throughout its history, and unless there are *other* things exactly similar in nature to this, any attempt to say what *this* would have done if its circumstances had been different becomes entirely meaningless. For, if taken literally, such statements are meaningless in themselves and inconsistent with the other parts of the popular-scientific view. And, when interpreted in the only way that seems to make them intelligible and consistent, the interpretation presupposes constancy of nature in individuals and the existence of natural kinds.

Suppose, for example, that, after merely looking at a certain bit of matter, or performing a single simple experiment on it, such as determining its specific gravity, I say "This would dissolve if it were put into *aqua regia*, and would not dissolve if it were put into nitric acid". What exactly do I mean? I believe, from experiments on other bits of matter which looked like this and had the same specific gravity, that these are sufficient signs of the compresence of a whole group of dispositional properties, of which being soluble in *aqua regia* but not in nitric acid is one. I therefore assume that this disposition is present in this bit of matter. I further assume that, if it is now present, it has been and will be so. From this it follows deductively that, if this bit of matter ever was immersed in *aqua regia* it then dissolved; that, if it ever was immersed in nitric acid, it then did not dissolve; that, if it ever shall be immersed in *aqua regia* it will then dissolve; and that, if it ever shall be immersed in nitric acid, it then will not dissolve. The doubtful parts of my belief are (*a*) whether the characteristics which I take to be trustworthy signs of the presence of this dispositional property really are so, and (*b*) whether this dispositional property really is supreme, or whether it may not be a disposition of lower order, like the solidity of water between certain limits of temperature, and therefore susceptible of change. To conclude: When I say that this, which in fact is immersed in nitric acid and is not dissolving, might instead have been immersed in *aqua regia* and would then have been dissolving, I doubt whether any more is meant than a short summary of facts and beliefs of the kind which have been stated earlier in this paragraph. And I do not think that there is anything further that I can usefully say on this topic at present.

The Contrary-to-Fact Conditional * [1]

RODERICK M. CHISHOLM

I

A significant part of our knowledge is usually expressed in subjunctive and "contrary-to-fact" conditional statements. We seem to have knowledge of what *might* have happened, of what *would* happen if certain conditions were realized, of what tendencies, faculties, or potentialities an object *could* manifest in suitable environments. And this, most of us would be inclined to say, is valid and significant, even though the possible events to which it seems to pertain may never become actual. The type of statement in which this knowledge is usually formulated, however, appears to have been by-passed by contemporary logic; for the theories of generality, implication, and "statement composition", as they have been developed in recent years, seem to concern only indicative statements and to make no adequate provision for what we usually express in the subjunctive. Our problem here is to determine whether there is any other means of expressing this important counter-factual information. As we shall see, the philosophical problems which this question involves are fundamental to metaphysics, epistemology, and the general philosophy of science.

Many contrary-to-fact conditionals are not expressed in the subjunctive mood and many conditionals which are expressed in this mood are not actually contrary-to-fact, but in the present discussion we may use the labels "subjunctive conditional" and "contrary-to-fact conditional" interchangeably. Neither term is adequate, but each has been used in recent literature. The essential characteristics of this important type of statement will be more clearly delineated as we proceed.

There is a variety of types of situation where the use of the contrary-to-fact conditional appears to be the most natural means of expressing what we claim to know. First of all, of course, there are those occasions where we assert a conditional statement, knowing or believing its antecedent to be false. I may contend, for example, that had we followed a different policy toward Germany in the 1920's, the second World War would not have occurred. If this contention is correct, it must be considered, along with

* Reprinted, with slight alterations, by kind permission of the author and the editor from *Mind*, 55, 1946.
[1] I am much indebted to W. V. Quine, with whom I have discussed this question at length. He should not be held responsible, however, for any of my remarks.

all other true and relevant opinions, in any reasonable discussion of contemporary policy. In general, it may be said that adequate understanding of science and history requires the ability to consider the consequences of hypotheses known to be contrary-to-fact. In the study of anatomy, for instance, it would be difficult to assess the importance of an organ or function unless we were able to conceive what would happen if that organ or function did not exist. In physics it is necessary to be able to conceive of states of affairs which, in all likelihood, will never become actual. Thus Galileo, as is well known, founded his dynamics upon the conception of a body moving without the influence of any external force. Examples of this sort may be readily multiplied.[2]

Equally important, from the point of view of knowledge, are those subjunctive conditionals which we assert, not knowing whether the antecedents are true or false. C. I. Lewis has emphasized that it is only by means of such conditionals that we can adequately express the reasons behind our precautionary activity; it is essential for a being who is active that "there should be 'If—then—' propositions whose truth or falsity is independent of the truth or falsity of the condition stated in their antecedent clauses".[3] I try to avoid falling through the ice because I believe that if I were to fall I should get wet. Since I believe the conditional to be true, I endeavour to prevent the realization of the conditions mentioned in the antecedent. Bradley's "All trespassers will be prosecuted" is a further example: what this intends to convey is that if anyone were to trespass he would be prosecuted—and the message is usually posted conspicuously in order to insure that it remain contrary-to-fact.

Still another use of this type of conditional is what has been called its "deliberative use".[4] When we prepare for a crucial experiment, we review the situation and consider what would happen if our hypothesis were true and what would happen if it were false. The subjunctive conditional is essential to the expression of these deliberations. In defending a hypothesis, I may employ a subjunctive conditional even though I believe the antecedent to be true; I may say, "If this were so, that would be so; but, as you see, this *is* so. . . ." It is said that detectives talk in this manner. Whenever we modify our conditional assertions "for the sake of argument", withholding commitment concerning the truth or falsity of their antecedents, we find ourselves falling into the subjunctive.[5] Similarly, in order to falsify a theory or reduce it to absurdity, we must be able to consider its conse-

[2] Cf. ch. V, "Facts and Ideals", *An Essay on Man*, by Ernst Cassirer; M. R. Cohen, *Reason and Nature*, p. 69; C. G. Hempel, "Studies in the Logic of Confirmation", *Mind*, 54, esp. p. 16.

[3] C. I. Lewis, *Mind and the World Order*, p. 142; cf. pp. 140–142, 182–183. Cf. the same author's "Meaning and Action", *Journal of Philosophy*, 36, 1939. Cf. F. H. Bradley, *Logic*, Part I, ch. II.

[4] Roderick Firth, *Sense-Data and the Principle of Reduction*, Ph.D. Thesis, Harvard University Library, 1943, ch. VII.

[5] *Ibid.*

quences in a conditional, the component truth-values of which we deliberately ignore and which, therefore, we should normally express in the subjunctive.[6]

This type of conditional is implicit in the use of what Broad and Carnap have called "dispositional adjectives" or "disposition terms"—terms such as "malleable", "fragile", "soluble" and so on—which are used when we want to refer to the dispositions or potentialities of a thing.[7] Broad has pointed out that "whenever we conjoin a dispositional adjective to a substantive we are expressing in a categorical form a hypothetical proposition of the following kind. 'If this *were* in a certain state, and *were* in certain relations to certain other things of certain specified kinds, then certain events of a specific kind *would* happen either in it or in one of these other things' ".[8] To say that a thing is fragile, for instance, is to say that if certain conditions were realized it would break. To say that an acorn is potentially an oak is to say at least that, under certain conditions which may or may not become actual, it would grow into an oak. This potentiality increases with the likelihood of the conditions being realized. To say that an individual is predisposed toward psychoneurosis is to say that under certain conditions he would become neurotic and possibly also that under those conditions a normal individual would not become neurotic. This notion of "disposition" is central to the ancient philosophical questions concerning possibility and potentiality.

There are many other important philosophical theories whose central tenets depend upon the admissibility of what is formulated in the contrary-to-fact conditional. Four instances may be cited from contemporary philosophy. (1) The phenomenalist maintains that, apart from those sense-data which are objects of actual experience, the ultimate constituents of the universe are what H. H. Price has called "hypothetical sense-impressions", sense-data which *would* become actual if certain other sense-data *were* to become actual. Indeed, Price notes that "the phrase 'hypothetical sense-impression', in fact, is just an abbreviation for a hypothetical *statement* of the form: if so and so were the case, such and such a sort of sense-impression would exist".[9] (2) The essence of pragmatism, as well as of "realism", according to C. S. Peirce, is to make "the ultimate import of what you please to consist in conceived conditional resolutions, or their substance".[10] These conditional resolutions are formulated in subjunctive conditionals which state what the "real generals" of the universe "*would* or might (not actually

---

[6] Cf. Bertrand Russell, *Introduction to Mathematical Philosophy*, p. 161.

[7] C. D. Broad, *Examination of McTaggart's Philosophy*, Vol. I, pp. 148 ff.; R. Carnap, "Testability and Meaning", *Philosophy of Science*, 3, 1936, pp. 419–471, and 4, 1937, pp. 1–40.

[8] *Op. cit.* p. 149. Italics mine.

[9] H. H. Price, *Hume's Theory of the External World*, p. 179. Cf. A. J. Ayer, *Language, Truth and Logic*, pp. 75 ff., esp. p. 78; *The Foundations of Empirical Knowledge*, ch. V.

[10] C. S. Peirce, *Collected Papers*, 5. 453.

will) come to in the concrete".[11] (3) Much of contemporary analytic philosophy seems also to involve these conditionals, although somewhat less explicitly. The subject-matter of this philosophy comprises statements or sentences, so that a philosophical assertion may be a statement such as "The scientist compares his hypothesis with the protocol statements". Inasmuch as many, if not most, of the statements thus mentioned, are never actually uttered, discussion of them seems to presuppose an implicit use of the sub-junctive (concerning what the scientist *would* state if he *were* to formulate his observations, etc.). Thus Carnap tells us that, implied in his notion of "protocol statement", is "a simplification of actual scientific procedure *as if* all experiences, perceptions, . . . etc., . . . *were* first recorded in writing as 'protocol' to provide the raw material for a subsequent organization".[12] (4) Finally it is significant to note the extent to which those logicians who have not explicitly sanctioned the use of such conditionals are apparently unable to avoid falling into that mode of speech in the formulation of crucial points in the logic of science.[13]

It is clear, then, that the subjunctive or contrary-to-fact conditional seems to be required for the formulation of important assertions which are constantly made in philosophy, science, and ordinary discourse. Although there is extreme difficulty involved in analysing the meaning of these asser-tions, we are not thereby justified in dismissing counter-factual questions as "pseudo-problems" or in concluding that the contrary-to-fact condi-tional does not say anything.[14] We may agree with Broad that the distinc-tion between what will be and what would be must in some sense "cor-

---

[11] *Ibid.* 6. 485. Peirce's italics. Cf. 5. 526, 5. 517, 3. 526 ff.

[12] R. Carnap, *The Unity of Science*, p. 43. My italics.

[13] Instances may be drawn from the writings of the logicians referred to thus far who fit in this category. Carnap, "Testability and Meaning": "If we knew what it *would* be for a given sentence to be found true then we *would* know what its meaning is. . . . We call it [a sentence] *confirmable* if we know under what conditions the sentence *would* be confirmed. . . . A sentence may be confirmable without being testable; e.g., if we know that our observation of such and such a course of events *would* confirm the sentence, and such and such a different course *would* confirm its negation without knowing how to set up either this or that observation" (pp. 420–421). Carnap takes "observable" and "realizable" as basic descriptive terms in his theory of empiricism (p. 454). Like "confirmable" and "testable" these are disposition terms and thus may be said to furnish abbreviations for subjunctive conditionals.

Hempel, *op. cit.*, p. 109; "The concept of the development of a hypothesis H, for a finite class of individuals, C, can be defined [as] what H *would* assert if there existed exclusively those objects which are elements of C". Cf. also pp. 2, 25.

Russell, *Inquiry into Meaning and Truth*, pp. 278–279. An "unexperienced percept" is what "*would* verify 'ϕa' if we could assert 'ϕa'. But we cannot assert it. . . ." Cf. also pp. 250, 281, 320, 350.

The italics in the above quotations are mine.

[14] Cf. E. Mach, *Die Mechanik in ihrer Entwickelung*, 1st ed., p. 216. Mach held that it is always invalid to argue on the basis of an assertion about what-would-have-happened-if. It is of historical interest to note Russell's early repudiation of Mach's view in *The Principles of Mathematics*, pp. 492–493. A recent dismissal of counter-factual questions as "pseudo-problems" occurs in a review by Robert Eisler of *The Philosophy of Bertrand Russell*, *Hibbert Journal*, 43, p. 283.

respond to something real" and that philosophy cannot afford to ignore it.[15] In the present paper, I shall try to make some progress toward clarifying and solving this problem.

II

Our problem is to render a subjunctive conditional of the form, "(x) (y) if x were ϕ and y were ψ, y would be χ", into an indicative statement which will say the same thing. Some subjunctive conditionals are simpler, e.g., they may be of the form, "(x) if x were ϕ, x would be ψ", or "if a were ϕ, a would be ψ" (where "a" represents a proper name); and some are more complex. But we shall find that the problem is the same in principle, whatever the complexity of the conditional. Like Russell in his theory of descriptions, we want to find a new way of saying something—in this case, in order to assure ourselves that we *can* restate what we ordinarily express in subjunctive conditionals. The problem is epistemological and metaphysical, as well as logical and linguistic; we want to know what it is, if anything, that we have to assume about the universe if we are to claim validity for our counter-factual knowledge.

There appears to be no problem connected with those subjunctive conditionals which are logically true (e.g., "If wishes were horses, wishes would be horses") or those which are analytic (e.g., "If that animal were a quadruped, it would have four legs"). Hence, in what follows, all reference to subjunctive or contrary-to-fact conditionals should be understood to intend only those which are not analytic or logically true. Similarly, any reference to statements or to specific types of statement should be understood to intend only *indicative* non-counter-factual statements, unless qualification is made. At the present stage of the discussion we shall leave undecided the question whether statements name (or, in any sense, refer to) propositions.

The simplest methods of translating these conditionals are clearly inadequate. Consider this example: "If the vase were dropped to the floor, it would break". Is an adequate translation yielded by replacing the 'were' and 'would' by 'is' and 'will' and interpreting the statement as a truth-functional material conditional? If it is a material conditional, there can be no doubt of its truth, for (let us assume) the vase will never have been dropped to the floor. Such conditionals are true when their antecedents are false. This becomes more evident when we transform the conditional into an alternation, which is another means of expressing the same thing: "Either the vase will not be dropped on the floor or it will break". On similar grounds, this material conditional is also true: "If the vase is dropped on the floor, it will grow into an oak". But this conditional, we may agree, is not relevant in any discussion concerning the care of the vase. A material conditional seldom affords a ground for action unless one can assert the cor-

[15] *Op. cit.* Vol. I, p. 264.

responding subjunctive. In the present instance, the corresponding subjunctive, "If the vase were dropped on the floor, it would grow into an oak", is (according to all evidence) false. A subjunctive conditional cannot be transformed into a simple alternation and it may be false when its antecedent is false and may be false when its consequent is true. Therefore, since the subjunctive conditional may be true when the corresponding material conditional is not, and vice versa, we may conclude that the subjunctive cannot be thus simply rendered. As Lewis has put it, we want to be able to infer the consequent *hypothetically* from the antecedent; but, knowing merely that the antecedent of a material conditional is false (or that its consequent is true) and hence that the conditional is true, we cannot say that the consequent *would* be true if the antecedent *were* true.[16] A subjunctive conditional is one such that we can know that the antecedent in some sense implies the consequent without knowing the truth-values of either.

A similar objection may be made to the simple translation of a universal subjunctive statement. Consider: "(x) if x were a vase and were dropped to the floor, x would break". Interpreted as an indicative universal conditional (or "formal implication"), it would be true merely if no vases were ever dropped to the floor, for what such a statement really says is: "(x) either x is not a vase which is dropped to the floor or x breaks". On similar grounds we may assert, "(x) if x is a vase and is dropped to the floor, x bounces to the ceiling". In cases such as these, the universal statements may be said to be only trivially or vacuously true and, although admissible in logic, of little interest either in science or in ordinary discourse. The inadequacy of these types of statement is most apparent in science when we wish to make a universal statement which we believe to be without existential import—for instance, a statement about the behaviour of bodies which are freely falling, or are at absolute zero, or in a perfect vacuum.

Carnap has proposed a rather involved method of dealing with "disposition predicates" which might appear to be relevant to our problem.[17] He does not note that they involve an implicit use of the subjunctive (i.e., that they may be regarded as abbreviations of subjunctive conditionals), but he admits that apparently they cannot be defined by the usual techniques. Despairing of defining them, he offers another method of "introducing" them, viz., the use of "reduction sentences", which, he admits, can at best yield "a partial determination only".[18] Whatever its merits, however, this method is of little aid to us in our present problem.

A reduction sentence for the property Q_3 (e.g., soluble in water) is a statement that the conjunction in any object of two other properties—the "experimental situation" Q_1 (being placed in water at time t) and the "experi-

[16] C. I. Lewis and C. H. Langford, *Symbolic Logic*, p. 261.
[17] "Testability and Meaning", pp. 440 ff. Cf. "Logical Foundations of the Unity of Science", *Encyclopedia of Unified Science*, Vol. I, No. 1, pp. 50 ff.
[18] "Testability and Meaning", p. 449.

mental result" Q_2 (dissolving in water at time t)—is a sufficient condition for the predication of the disposition term "Q_3", provided that the conjunction of Q_1 and Q_2 occurs at least once. In the simplest cases, the situation is such that the non-occurrence of Q_2 indicates that the thing in question does not have the property Q_3. A reduction sentence for any disposition term, then, is a sentence stating a *sufficient* condition for the application of that term, but it gives us a rule for applying the term only in those cases in which the sufficient condition (Q_1 and Q_2 in our illustration) is realized. We may state more and more sufficient conditions, but "a region of indeterminateness" will always remain—i.e., those cases where none of the sufficient conditions ever obtain. Thus Carnap admits that "if a body b consists of such a substance that for no body of this substance has the test condition—in the above example: 'being placed in water'—ever been fulfilled, then neither the predicate nor its negation can be attributed to b".[19] We are compelled to say that, in this "region of indeterminateness" where neither the predicate nor its negation may be applied, the disposition term has "no meaning".[20] In other words, instead of saying that our rare body b either is or is not soluble, we must say that it is *meaningless* to call it soluble (or insoluble). Even if this were consonant with actual practice, which seems at least doubtful, this conclusion would hardly be satisfactory. This is particularly evident in view of the fact that the statements "Body b is placed in water at time t" and "Body b dissolves at time t" (which would be the components of a reduction sentence pertaining to body b) are themselves perfectly meaningful.[21] Carnap's method, therefore, does not solve our problem, nor does it seem to be a completely satisfactory means of dealing with disposition terms.[22]

In *The Examination of McTaggart's Philosophy*, Broad proposed the view that a subjunctive conditional about what a particular entity might have been, or could be, should "be taken as an abbreviation" for a "statement about *any* thing of a given *kind*". A statement about the disposition of an individual then becomes a statement which says, among other things, "that, if at *any* time any substance of this kind were put into a situation which was any determinate form of S, its determinate behaviour would be . . ." etc., etc.[23] This view does not contribute toward the solution of

19 *Ibid*. p. 445.

20 *Ibid*. p. 449.

21 Cf. Firth, *op. cit.* ch. VII. Firth's discussion, to which I am indebted, contains a penetrating analysis of Carnap's theory and its relation to the general problem of the contrary-to-fact conditional.

22 Carnap does not discuss what would be the consequences for the philosophy of empiricism if this method were to be applied to the terms, "observable" and "realizable", which are the two basic terms of his "empirical methodology". ("Testability and Meaning", p. 454.) Applied to the former term, it might conceivably lend new support to the doctrine that to be is to be perceived.

23 Vol. I, p. 276. [The quoted passage occurs in the excerpt from *The Examination of McTaggart's Philosophy* included in this volume. See above, p. 480.]

our problem, however, since it merely reduces subjunctives about individuals to subjunctives about classes. Similarly, we may dismiss C. L. Stevenson's brief treatment of dispositions in *Ethics and Language* (pp. 46 ff.), since his account admittedly presupposes the notions of "cause" and "law". At the present stage of our discussion, these notions would, of course, be question-begging.

Apparently, then, if we are to succeed in analysing disposition terms, we must make explicit the subjunctive conditionals which they involve (e.g., "If body *b* were placed in water at time *t*, it would dissolve at time *t*") and then consider these as instances of our more general problem. Similarly, it is likely that satisfactory analyses of the notions of "law" and "physical necessity" must await a solution of the problem of the subjunctive.

III

Let us now consider in detail the difficulties which are involved in the attempt to eliminate the contrary-to-fact conditional. We may proceed on the basis of certain suggestions made by F. P. Ramsey in his posthumous paper, "General Propositions and Causality".[24] Let us assume that my belief in the conditional, "If you were to see the play, you would not enjoy it", constitutes my principal reason for suggesting that you do not go. The situation may be described in this manner: I feel that you would be ill-advised in going, because I have (or believe I have) information which is such that from it and the hypothesis that you do see the play, I can derive the conclusion that you won't enjoy it. And if you should question my advice, our difference would most probably be with respect to this alleged information. Ramsey stated the essence of the matter: "In general we can say with Mill that 'If p then q' means that q is inferrible from p, that is, of course, from p together with certain facts and laws not stated but in some way indicated by the context. This means $p \supset q$ follows from these facts and laws. . . . If two people are arguing about 'If p will q?' and are both in doubt as to p, they are adding p hypothetically to their stock of knowledge and arguing on that basis about q".[25] What is the nature of the connection on the basis of which we derive q? We shall go astray if we confine ourselves to a search for the "connection" which must hold *between* p and q. This is confirmed by the fact that we affirm many subjunctive conditionals in order to show that there is *no* relevant connection between antecedent and consequent; e.g., "Even if you were to sleep all morning, you would still be tired". What, then, is the nature of the "connection" which is involved and between what entities does it obtain?

W. V. Quine has suggested that possibly some "strong relation of state-

---

[24] Included in *Foundations of Mathematics*, pp. 237–257.

[25] *Ibid.*, pp. 247, 248. Cf. A. Tarski, *Introduction to Logic*, p. 24; W. V. Quine, *Elementary Logic*, p. 24.

ments" such as logical implication or entailment could be used when we want to formulate what is expressed in a subjunctive conditional.[26] An entailment, which may be interpreted as saying something *about* statements, does not involve the paradoxes of "vacuous truth" which we have considered in the cases of the material and universal conditionals and material and formal implication. Now it is obvious that the antecedents of most subjunctive conditionals do not logically entail the consequents, for in most cases (as in our example) there is no *contradiction* involved in denying one and affirming the other. We have, in fact, restricted ourselves in this discussion to a consideration of those subjunctive conditionals which are not analytic or logically true. But let us consider this along with the previous suggestion and look in another place for this "strong relation of statements". C. I. Lewis has pointed out that, when an inference is made in ordinary discourse, even though a material conditional may be involved ,we are using an entailment of the form "p and $p \supset q$ logically imply q".[27] Let us consider, then, whether a subjunctive or contrary-to-fact conditional can be reformulated as an entailment stating that the consequent is entailed (logically implied) by the antecedent taken in conjunction with a previous stock of knowledge.

Consider this conditional, C: "If Holbrook were elected, the price of wheat would rise." Is this another way of saying that the indicative statement "Holbrook is elected" (which we may call 'H') in conjunction with certain previous information entails "The price of wheat will rise" (W)? First of all, it is necessary to revise the reference to "previous information", since the meaning of the conditional should not be confused with the particular grounds upon which it happens to be asserted. You and I may have quite different "stocks of knowledge" and affirm C on extremely divergent grounds, but when each of us does affirm C, we are, it must be assumed, saying exactly the same thing. The "something additional" which each of us adjoins to H in order to deduce W need not be a statement expressing any particular item in either of our stores of knowledge, nor indeed need it express any knowledge at all. When we assert a subjunctive conditional, we are saying something more general. In the present instances, we are saying that there is *some* true statement which, taken with H, entails W. If, knowing nothing about politics and economics, I none-the-less presume to conjecture that prices would rise if Holbrook were elected, I am conjecturing that there is some true statement, I know not what, which, in conjunction with H, entails W. If I knew *what* the true statement is, I could be said to have an *explanation* for the situation which C describes, but, obviously, I do not need to know such an explanation in order to know the *meaning* of C. It is quite possible that the statement may refer in part to some future events concerning which I shall never know anything.

[26] *Mathematical Logic*, p. 29.
[27] Cf. C. I. Lewis and C. H. Langford, *Symbolic Logic*, pp. 242-246.

May we conclude, then, that our conditional may be reformulated: "There is a statement p such that p and H entail W and p is true"? This may appear to be the most promising way of dealing with the problem; unfortunately, however, there are possible values of p which would trivialize our complex statement and render it inadequate as a translation of the original subjunctive. In order to preclude such trivialization it is necessary to place exceedingly complex restrictions upon p. And, what is worse, it appears to be impossible to state all the restrictions that are needed.

Suppose, for instance, that p included a statement which is vacuously true. If Holbrook will never have been elected to office, then the universal conditional "(x) if x is a public office and Holbrook is elected to x, the price of wheat will rise" is vacuously true and its inclusion as a part of p would make our translation inadequate. That this is so becomes evident if we reflect that the universal conditional, "(x) if x is a public office and Holbrook is elected to x, this year's wheat will turn to gold", is also vacuously true. Our formula, as it now stands, would require that, on the basis of this triviality, we assert the subjunctive conditional, "If Holbrook were elected, this year's wheat would turn to gold", which, we may assume, is absurd.

It is necessary to modify the formula in order to insure that it contain no "vacuous truths", i.e., in order to insure that it contain no universal conditional whose antecedent determines an empty class and no material conditional (or material implication) which is asserted merely on the ground that its antecedent is false (or its consequent true). Every universal conditional included in p must have "existential import", that is, every universal conditional must have conjoined with it a statement asserting that there are members of the class determined by the antecedent. Even this is not enough, however.

Suppose, for instance, we desired to translate our earlier example, "If you were to see the play you would not enjoy it", according to the formula thus restricted. Trivialization is still possible. Let p be "(x) [$x =$ you $: \supset : x$ saw the play $. \supset . x$ did not enjoy the play], there exists an x such that $x =$ you". This will be a true statement if the vacuous material conditional corresponding to the original subjunctive conditional is true (and, of course, whenever we can assert the subjunctive, we can also assert the corresponding indicative). The translated subjunctive will then become equivalent to the material conditional. To preclude this type of difficulty, we must add a further provision to our formula. Let us say: p includes no universal conditional whose consequent includes any two functions which are logically equivalent to "x sees the play" and to "x does not enjoy the play": i.e., any consequent must exclude either functions logically equivalent to "x sees the play" or functions logically equivalent to "x does not enjoy the play".[28]

[28] If we understand the term "entailment" in the very strict sense of logical implication, this provision will take care of our difficulty, but if, as is often the case, the term is construed in a wider sense, further modification is necessary. I.e., if we so construe

There are more qualifications to be made. To preclude trivialisation in those cases where the consequent of the subjunctive conditional happens to be true, we should add that the indicative version of the consequent does not entail p. And some types of subjunctive conditional must be reformulated before the formula can be applied. E.g., "Even if you were to sleep all morning you would still be tired". This type of statement is what one gets by negating the consequent of an ordinary subjunctive conditional and then denying the whole thing: "It is false that if you were to sleep all morning you would not be tired". The "even if" conditionals must be reduced to this form; hence they would read: "It is false that there is a true statement p . . . etc.".[29] (If we reformulate the even-if conditionals in the manner suggested, we may then say correctly that the problem of the subjunctive conditionals concerns the *connection* which obtains between antecedent and consequent.) With all these qualifications, however, we still cannot make the formula sufficiently restrictive.

For one thing, the above restrictions as they stand are really not sufficient to exclude the types of case for which they were designed. F. L. Will, in a discussion of an earlier version of this paper, has pointed out that, with a little ingenuity, these restrictions may be evaded and, in consequence, that, in order to deal with the cases hitherto considered, our formula must be one of extraordinary complexity.[30] The reader is referred to Will's paper for details. What is even more serious, however, is that there is another type of case which, so far as I can see, will break any indicative formula we may devise, whatever its complexity.

Suppose that one afternoon two men, quite independently of each other (as we should ordinarily say), were to sit on the same park bench, that they were alone there, and that, as it happened, each of them was Irish. We could then say: "(x) if x is on . . . park bench at . . . time, x is Irish". Our formula is such that, if we were to apply it to this case, we could infer: "If Ivan were to be on . . . park bench at . . . time, Ivan would be Irish". But this conclusion would hardly be warranted. (It would be warranted, if we were to interpret the subjunctive conditional as saying "If Ivan were *identical* with any one on the bench . . . ", but this, as we shall see, is not what we should ordinarily intend it to say.) Again, consider a small community where each of the lawyers happens to have three children. We may

---

it that "x sees the play" and "x witnesses the play" may be said to entail each other (on the ground that, although they are not logically equivalent in the strict sense, they are *synonymous*), the latter phrase may be substituted for the former and the translation trivialized as before. Hence, if we use "entailment" in the wider sense, we should substitute "synonymous" for "logically equivalent" in the provision. For a discussion of these terms, see W. V. Quine, *O Sentido da Nova Lógica*, pp. 148–152.

[29] These "even if" subjunctives are usually employed either (*a*) when we have affirmed the consequent and desire to stress its inevitability, or (*b*) as appendages to other subjunctive conditionals (*e.g.*, "If you should work like that all night you would be tired and even if you were to sleep all morning you would still be tired").

[30] F. L. Will, "The Contrary-to-Fact Conditional," *Mind*, 56, pp. 236–249.

say: "(*x*) if *x* is a lawyer in . . . community in 1946, *x* has three children". But we should not want to say of Jones, whom we know not to be a lawyer there, that if he *were* to have practised there he too would have had three children. The difficulty is that our universal conditionals about the park bench and the lawyers describe what are, in some sense, "accidents" or "coincidences". How are we to distinguish such "accidental" conditionals, of which examples are easily multiplied,[31] from statements such as "all men are mortal", "All wolves are ferocious", etc., which describe "non-accidental" connections? This is the crux of the whole problem. Our formula must exclude these "accidental" universal conditionals; but the only means we have of distinguishing these is to note that, unlike the "non-accidental" ones, they do not warrant the inference of certain contrary-to-fact conditionals. That is to say, in the case of the park bench we should hesitate to infer "If *a* were on the park bench, *a* would be Irish"; but in the case of the wolves we should not hesitate to infer "If *a* were a wolf, *a* would be ferocious". (These considerations will become more obvious when we consider, below, the question of the formulation of contrary-to-fact conditionals.)

It is plain that the statements which formulate "natural laws" are a subclass of the non-accidental universal conditionals. One cannot say, as most philosophers and logicians now incline to do, that a natural law is merely what is expressed in a synthetic universal conditional. We must find the differentia so that we can exclude the "accidental" conditionals. The alternatives are: (1) supply the qualifications which our formula lacks or in other manner, reduce the subjunctive to the indicative; (2) accept the subjunctive as describing some kind of irreducible connection and thus reject, or alter radically, the extensional logic which most contemporary logicians have tried to apply to the philosophical problems of science. The problem is not an easy one; indeed, we may be justified in asserting that it constitutes *the* basic problem in the logic of science.

IV

There are three further considerations which will enable us to see more clearly what is involved in this problem.

1. A contrary-to-fact conditional, when formulated in the customary manner, may give rise to misunderstanding if considered outside the context of its utterance. Given a conditional with an antecedent of the form "if *x* were *y*" one may ask whether the supposition is that *x* is changed to accommodate itself to *y* or *y* is changed to accommodate itself to *x*. I might say, for instance, "If Apollo were a man, he would be mortal", to which the reply could be made, "No: if Apollo were a man, at least one man would

---

[31] Cf. C. H. Langford, review, *Journal of Symbolic Logic*, 6, 1941, pp. 67 f. Langford provides here a very clear statement of the present problem. Along with C. I. Lewis, he has been one of the few logicians to recognise explicitly the importance for the logic of science of the subjunctive conditional.

be immortal". The possibility of this type of misunderstanding is most apparent where the antecedent of the conditional designates some equivalence relation (e.g., "if x were identical with y", "if x were in the same place as y") or some relation of comparison (e.g., "x is greater than y"). But theoretically it might occur in connection with the interpretation of any antecedent.

Let us refer to "If Apollo were a man, he would be mortal" as a and to "If Apollo were a man, at least one man would be immortal" as b. Knowing Apollo to be immortal and all men to be mortal, should we assert a or b? [32] The answer depends upon whether we are supposing our beliefs about Apollo, or our beliefs about men, to be contrary-to-fact. (If we were supposing *neither* to be contrary-to-fact, the antecedent would be, not merely false, but contradictory; if we were supposing *both* to be contrary-to-fact, we could assert neither a nor b.) Ordinarily the context of inquiry determines which supposition is being made. But in a language which was logically adequate, the antecedents of these conditionals would be so formulated that such misunderstanding and ambiguity would not arise. [33] Thus one who had asserted a instead of b would have said something like, "If Apollo were different from what we have believed him to be and had instead the attributes which all men possess, then he would be mortal". And one who had asserted b would have said something like, "If the class of men were wider than what we have believed it to be and included Apollo, then some men would be immortal". In the first case, Apollo's status is in question and one is supposing certain commonly accepted statements about him to be false, and in the second case, it is not Apollo, but it is the class of men, which is in question. The advantage of thus formulating the antecedents of these conditionals, so that the wording leaves no doubt concerning which is the object of hypothesis and which is assumed to remain "as is", is further evident when we consider the extent to which the usual canons of inference may be applied to subjunctive conditionals when the object of hypothesis is left ambiguous. [34]

[32] It was evidently difficulties of this sort which led Broad to question whether subjunctive conditionals about individuals were meaningful if taken literally. (*Op. cit.*, Vol. I, pp. 273-278 [pp. 478 ff. in this collection].)

[33] In their customary formulation, the antecedents of subjunctive conditionals are, to a certain extent, analogous to "He is a thief", "I am hot", "Your dog is here", etc., which statements, when considered in isolation, are incomplete and may be true or not, depending upon which of the many possible interpretations of "I", "He", "here", etc. are selected. Like the subjunctive conditionals, these statements are such that when uttered in ordinary discourse, the context of their occurrence determines the interpretation, but in a logically adequate language they would receive a more satisfactory formulation.

[34] There seems to be a convention implicit in ordinary discourse according to which the antecedent is always so formulated that the subject-term designates the entity which we are supposing to be different or are considering hypothetically. When one says, "If Paoli were the same size as New York . . .", it is more natural to conclude "Paoli would be larger than it is" than "New York would be smaller". The latter conclusion would be drawn from the converse of our antecedent.

Let us assume, for the moment, the view held by Wittgenstein, Ramsey, and others, according to which, "For all x, fx" is held to be equivalent to the logical product of the values of "fx" (i.e., to the conjunction of fx_1, fx_2, fx_3, etc.) and "There exists an x such that fx" is held to be equivalent to their logical sum (i.e., to the alternation, either fx_1, or fx_2, or fx_3, etc.). This view, whatever its limitations as an ultimate ontology, has the advantage that it makes clear the manner in which valid inferences can be made connecting particular instances with the general rules under which they fall.[35] Suppose, now, we are considering "If Apollo were a man, Apollo would be mortal". The statement p in our translation may be assumed to be "All men are mortal and there are men". Let us assume that Socrates, Plato, and Aristotle are all the men there are; p then becomes "Socrates, Plato, and Aristotle are men and are mortal". But this statement, taken in conjunction with "Apollo is a man", does not entail "Apollo is mortal". Hence one might contend that use of the contrary-to-fact conditional necessitates the preservation of an "element of generality" in our universal statements, so that "all men" will refer to more than the particular men who will have existed.[36] And it might be concluded, therefore, that the contrary-to-fact conditional, even granted the adequacy of our formula for translation, presents unique problems in the theory of inference, for we do not encounter such difficulties in connection with "If Socrates is a man, Socrates is mortal".

As in the previous instance, however, the apparent difficulty is explained by the fact that the antecedents of subjunctive conditionals are usually formulated inadequately. The difficulty vanishes if we formulate them in the manner proposed above. If, instead of "If Apollo were a man", we say something like "If Apollo were different from what we have believed him to be and had instead the attributes which all men possess", the problematic inference is seen to be valid, even though statements about all men refer only to Socrates, Plato and Aristotle. Hence, by formulating the antecedents of subjunctive conditionals unambiguously, we cut the ground from under the two objections which might otherwise be made to the use of this type of statement.

2. It is very important to note that, wherever we have a "non-accidental" non-vacuous universal conditional, we can always supply an "accidental" one which will cover the same instances. Suppose, for instance, (i) "(x) if x drinks from that well, x is poisoned" is such a conditional. And suppose that, of those who have thus been poisoned, one was born in place p at time t, another in p' at t', etc. We can assert the "accidental" conditional: (ii) "(x) if x is born in p at t, or in p' at t', etc., x is poisoned". It is quite plain that (ii) is accidental and (i) is not, for, given (i) we could infer "If a were

---

[35] Cf. Ramsey, *op. cit.*, pp. 153-154.
[36] What this reference to an "element of generality" means, of course, is not altogether clear, but, as we shall see, it is the sort of thing which we must countenance if we are to regard the subjunctive as irreducible.

to drink from that well a would be poisoned"; but, given (ii), we cannot infer "If a had been born in p at t, a would have been poisoned". Whether a universal conditional is to appear "accidental" or not thus depends upon how one has *described* the entities which fulfil the component clauses.[37] This suggests that the terms of "non-accidental" connections are the *properties* of things. And if we cannot get rid of the subjunctive by any other means, we can define it in terms of these "connections". To say "(x) if x were ϕ, x would be ψ", would then be to say "ϕ and ψ are *connected*". *Connection* becomes an irreducible ontological category and a source of embarrassment for empiricism. It was this doctrine that C. S. Peirce was defending with his concept of "thirdness".

It is really not clear, of course, what we are trying to convey when we assert that "connection" or "thirdness" is an ultimate ontological category, if we mean to do more than state the problem. And it still may be that the ontology of logical atomism is correct, that, being creatures having a need to rationalise, we have invented these notions of what-might-have-been and what-might-but-won't-be, and that they have no objective significance. But apparently we can't say all the things we want to say in our more serious moments unless we employ them.

3. Any formula, of the sort which was described in section III above, must presuppose a satisfactory solution to the problem of the designata of statements. Application of our formula for translation must involve in every case a reference to a *statement* and, in many, if not in the majority, of cases, a reference to a statement which has never been uttered, written down, or even conceived. What is the status of a statement which will never have been made? Is it a merely *possible* statement, one which *might* or *could* be made? It might be assumed that, if we attempt to dispense with entities designated by statements, as is sometimes done in logic,[38] we must employ the contrary-to-fact conditional in discussing the statements which have not been made. In this event, we should find ourselves using the contrary-to-fact conditional in the very application of the formula which was designed to eliminate it. If we were to revise our formula so that it would mention facts or states of affairs where it now mentions statements, we should then have to countenance the existence of entities which are merely possible but

[37] These considerations are unquestionably connected with the distinction, recently noted by Nelson Goodman, between "projectible" and "non-projectible" predicates and with the fact that degree of confirmation "varies widely with the way the given evidence is described". ("A Query on Confirmation", *The Journal of Philosophy*, 43, pp. 382–385.) The distinction between "accidental" and "non-accidental" universal statements is fundamental to the theory of confirmation. These considerations also suggest the possibility of an alternative formula for eliminating the subjunctive, referring to classes or properties but not to statements. The "class method", however, seems to involve many more difficulties than does the "statement method" and it breaks down at an earlier point.

[38] Cf. W. V. Quine, "Ontological Remarks on the Propositional Calculus", *Mind*, 43, 1934, pp. 472–476; *Mathematical Logic*, p. 32.

not actual states of affairs. In this case, instead of defining the merely possible in terms of the subjunctive (as what *would* happen if . . .), we should be following the reverse course, which would have been easy enough at the outset, although not particularly clarifying. If we are to admit the types of case which give rise to these difficulties, there are apparently only two alternatives left to us. The first is to assume that there exist entities which function as designata of sentences; these may be objectives, propositions, etc. This assumption, of course, is very often made on other grounds. If we adopt this course, we may substitute for the reference to *statements* in our formula a reference to *propositions* (or whatever entity we had chosen). But if we are deterred by "the obscurity of these alleged entities", we may attempt to extend the term "statement" beyond its normal usage in order to insure that there be an actual entity to answer for every conceivable statement. But how should we describe the semantical properties of these "statements" (which they must have if they are to be statements at all) except by saying that they *would* designate or *would* denote such-and-such things if some interpreter *were* to take account of them? These difficult questions, however, are beyond the scope of the present paper.

Operationism and Scientific Method [*]

HERBERT FEIGL

1. WHAT IS OPERATIONISM?

'Operationism' is a new name for certain fairly generally recognized aspects of scientific method. It is indeed no more than a refined and modernized emphasis upon the requirements that scientific concepts must meet if they are to be meaningful and fruitful. Descriptions, laws, hypotheses, and theories may be critically examined on the basis of such criteria applied to the concepts they contain. In the perspective of the history of science and the history of philosophy, operationism represents a recent formulation of some of the essential features of the experimental method and of empiricism generally, accentuated in the direction of pragmatism and instrumentalism (Peirce, James, and Dewey). Bridgman's formulations of the criteria of empirical meaning, though probably quite original with him, have much in common especially with C. S. Peirce's in "How to Make Our Ideas Clear" (first published in 1878). There are two questions with which we are (or at least *should* be) concerned in any cognitive enterprise: '*What do we mean by the words or symbols we use?*' and '*How do we know that what we assert in these terms is true (or confirmed to some degree)?*' The characteristically pragmatic turn becomes manifest when these two questions are scrutinized in the light of two further questions: 'What do we *do* in order to find out whether a term is legitimately applicable?' and: 'What are the *fruits by which we shall know* whether the introduction of a term is scientifically useful?' The first of these two latter questions stresses the element of active intervention in measurement and experiment. The second intends to remind us that concepts are scientifically worthwhile only if they help in the task of prediction (and, possibly, practical control). The essence of the operationist emphasis may thus be seen in the formulation of criteria of scientific meaningfulness and fruitfulness for concepts and of criteria of validity for factual statements. While these criteria were implicitly respected in much of the scientific work of recent centuries (and even occasionally to some degree explicitly formulated), the trend of our age toward a fuller awareness of and critical reflection upon the underlying presuppositions and guiding principles of our thinking and doing has, among

[*] Reprinted, with slight alterations, by the kind permission of the American Psychological Association and the editors from *The Psychological Review*, 52, 1945.

other results, promoted a more penetrating analysis of scientific method. The particular interest in operationism may be understood as arising from the need (1) of purifying scientific method by the elimination of pre-scientific and non-scientific (e.g., metaphysical) elements and (2) of understanding more clearly the meaning of the highly complex concepts employed in the more abstract and constructive levels of modern scientific theories. Such critical awareness is especially valuable when one needs to examine science where it is in the making. The numerous approaches in recent psychological theory are most certainly a case in point.

2. THE NATURE AND PURPOSE OF DEFINITIONS, OPERATIONAL OR OTHERWISE

Clarification or analysis of meaning is pursued by *definition*. Definition, i.e., specification or delimitation of the meaning of a term or symbol, may be considered a statement of the *rule concerning the use* of a term or symbol. In practice the need for definition arises only when (*a*) we are not sure what a given term or symbol means, if it means anything at all (obscurity); (*b*) where there is a plurality of meanings (ambiguity)—to be removed by multiple definition; (*c*) when the term or symbol in question is used so vaguely that a definition giving it greater precision is demanded; (*d*) when the term or symbol, though defined clearly, unambiguously, and precisely in some respects, is to be given a place in a wider context and thereby enriched in meaning. This wider context may be a system of symbols only (such as we find in a pure calculus) or it may include symbols with empirical reference —in this latter case the definition may be 'co-ordinating', i.e., relating a symbol of an abstract system to terms which through previous definition already possess empirical reference; (*e*) finally, definition is needed whenever a situation in research calls for the coining of a new term as an abbreviatory convenience for more complex aggregations of terms either already in use or logico-mathematically so aggregated for the first time. This latter condition arises particularly in the context of the discovery of new elements or relationships in the subject-matter of research.

Definition as here conceived is *nominal* (i.e. definition of *terms* or *symbols*). So-called *real* definitions (of *things, properties*, etc.) reveal themselves either as empirical descriptions with all terms understood (by previous nominal definition) or as characterizations of things for the sake of identification. Since in this latter alternative, identification occurs through labelling of things on the basis of observational test, it is tantamount to *nominal* definition of the label. Just how precisely, completely or directly operational definitions enable us to identify objects is a matter of great methodological importance, but also surely a matter of degree.

To demand definition of *every* term used in a piece of scientific discourse would not only be unduly pedantic (beside being incapable of practical fulfilment and thus utopian) but also quite unnecessary. The adult and sane use of common language is on the whole sufficiently definite to permit intersubjective communication and intelligibility as regards terms representing things and their observable properties. Doubt as to meaningfulness or as to precise meaning arises usually only regarding higher-order constructs and/or terms of fairly clear subjective meaning but lacking sufficient determination for successful intersubjective testability. Doubts of this second sort are rare in physics but plentiful in psychology. Doubts of the first sort may arise in any science which organizes its subject-matter by means of constructs above the level of observable-property predicates.

Aside from these practical considerations, it is obvious also from a logical or epistemological point of view that there can never be an occasion for an unlimited regress in definition. A series of definitional steps may be long, but it will terminate with definientia which are linked to something outside the realm of terms and symbols—namely, items of direct observation. As to whether this last step in the definition of any empirical concept is to be considered itself a kind of definition is a mere question of terminology. It is rather fashionable nowadays to speak of '*ostensive definitions*'. Psychologists in particular should not have much trouble with this: our use of language is after all a product of learning and we learn the intra-linguistic relations of words to each other as well as the extra-linguistic application of *some* words to items of experience. What from the viewpoint of logical analysis appears as a rule for the use of symbols represents itself as a habit (or rule-regulated pattern) of symbolic (i.e., verbal) behavior to the psychologist. An ostensive definition, then, may be considered either as a designation rule formulated in a semantical metalanguage or as a piece of practical drill in the learning of the 'right use' of words. Quite generally, an exact logical analysis of the meaning of scientific terms requires the use of the apparatus of syntax and semantics. The corresponding psychological analysis can be carried out in the object language of (preferably a behavioristic) psychology, where words in use are described as physical events, e.g., of emission of sounds, and are thus included in a general study of the behavior of human organisms. These two ways of studying definitions, and the uses of language generally, supplement each other very well, are entirely compatible, and fulfill, each in its way, important functions. The logical analysis examines given uses of language in the light of critical standards, such as consistency, non-circularity, sufficiency, etc. The psychological study is essentially a description and causal analysis of verbal behavior. Each can be made to reflect the other on any level of investigation. The psychologist in his study of definitional behavior uses, at least implicitly, definitions himself—and thus provides subject-matter for logical appraisal. And the logician in appraising definitions (or in any other syntactical or semantical pursuit) is, after all, *behaving* in specifiable ways and thus furnishes material for the psychologist.

If all definitions amount to rules delimiting the use of terms or symbols, aren't *all* definitions operational in character? This is indeed a purely terminological question. But terminology is a significant weapon in the strategy of scientific enlightenment. It is my personal conviction that the battle-cry of operationism can have its intended beneficial effects only if the meaning of 'operational' is confined in its application to the definition of *empirical* concepts. The problems of concept formation in pure logic and pure mathematics are of a very distinct character, and rash transference, by analogy with the empirical sciences, of restrictive meaning conditions is, to say the least, of highly dubious value. When we demand operational definability for the terms of the factual sciences, we may (and must!) indeed include purely calculational operations—but these operations, called variously "mental", "paper-and-pencil", or better "logico-mathematical", should be applied to root-terms which have *empirical* reference. Without this restriction the term 'operational' would become synonymous with, say, 'functional', implying that any definition that is worth its salt must specify the functions that the term to be defined is to fulfill. Such 'functional' definitions could be given for the terms of pure mathematics on the one side but, on the other hand, also for terms used in the most transcendent speculations of theology and metaphysics. As Bridgman has repeatedly stated, the original impetus toward his operational analysis in physics came from a consideration of Einstein's procedure in the theory of relativity. Einstein had realized that certain terms, like 'absolute length', 'absolute duration', 'absolute simultaneity' in Newtonian physics were devoid of empirical meaning because no observational or experimental procedures were or could be specified for their application. The operational criterion here serves to distinguish physics from metaphysics. It will seem obvious to many psychologists that, for example, Freud's 'death instinct', though possibly of some emotive or literary value, is devoid of factual, scientific meaning. To put it briefly, if crudely, operational analysis is to enable us to decide whether a given term, in the way it is used, has a 'cash value', i.e., factual reference. If it does have factual reference, operational analysis is to show us precisely *what* that factual reference is, in terms, ultimately, of the data of direct observation.

3. POSSIBLE AND IMPOSSIBLE OPERATIONS. THE LIMITS OF SCIENTIFIC MEANINGFULNESS

The velocity of a uniformly moving vehicle may be determined by means of a yardstick and a stopwatch. The I.Q. of a person may be determined by the Binet-Stanford testing procedure. In both cases a simple arithmetical division (s/t; mental age/chronological age) yields the final result. In the case of more complex concepts or higher-order constructs, the mathematical operations by means of which these constructs are defined are correspondingly more complicated. The factual reference of scientific concepts in physics or psychology, however, depends not so much upon the purely mathematical operations but rather upon the observational and manipulatory (mensurational, experimental) operations. These establish the link between the empirical (or descriptive) terms of our scientific language and the data of experience. Again, it is a merely terminological question as to whether simple acts of perceptual discrimination and identification by themselves should be labeled 'operations'. Such acts are certainly involved in the terminal ostensive steps of any definition of factual terms. Most of the cases in which definitions are called for, present situations of greater complexity. Thus the question concerning the *possibility* of operations practically always amounts to asking whether certain measuring or testing procedures referred to in the definition of a term can be carried out. But 'possible' and 'can be' are notoriously ambiguous words. We must distinguish between (a) logical ('in principle'), (b) empirical (natural), and (c) practical (technical) possibility. Since the limits of practical possibility are relative and, as a matter of fact, receding with every advance in the techniques of observation and experiment, no scientist restricts factual meaningfulness to testability within the bounds of the technical facilities of the moment. Bigger and better microscopes, telescopes, electroencephalographic instruments, etc., are obvious reminders. Of course, there is always an element of risk involved if definitions of terms hinge upon operations that are technically not feasible at the moment. It is like issuing or accepting a promissory note. But, if the operations are compatible with well-established natural laws, merely practical impossibility of the testing procedure does not deprive the term in question of its scientific meaningfulness. All we may have to wonder about is the fruitfulness of concepts whose definition necessitates reference to operations too far removed from technical feasibility at the time. Concepts of atomic structure were very far beyond practical testability only forty years ago. Concepts regarding the nature of cerebral memory traces are in the promissory-note stage today. Scientific research as an ongoing process involves a continuous scale of degrees of technical testability. Only considerations of a very practical and inductive sort enable the scientist to draw a line between operationally satisfactorily and unsatisfactorily defined terms. Much more serious is the limitation of empirical (or natural) testability. A testing procedure that is incompatible with well-established natural laws will never define a scientifically acceptable concept. For example: the very well confirmed laws of quantum mechanics exclude operations which would enable simultaneous determination of the speed and the location of electrons. Therefore it is now generally agreed that some of the customary concepts of classical mechanics as applied to electrons are not false but scientifically meaningless. Absolutely or downright meaningless (i.e., devoid of factual reference) are terms whose definition would involve contradictions with any testing procedure. Vitalistic conceptions of 'entelechies', for example, belong in this last category (of by definition unconfirmable ideas).

4. IS OPERATIONISM COMPATIBLE WITH SCIENTIFIC THEORIZING?

Operationism has occasionally hypertrophied into a radically anti-theoretical attitude. Ever since Galileo replaced the question "Why?" by the question "How?" and since Newton pronounced his (much misunderstood) *"Hypotheses non fingo"* postivistic scientists have been inclined to restrict their endeavors to pure description and correlation. *Explanation* is considered a metaphysical misfit. Mach and Ostwald rejected the atomic theory in physics and chemistry. Some outstanding psychologists of our day still reject as non-operational the psycho-analytic theory of the unconscious; others consider neuro-physiological hypotheses when used as explanations for behavior as so much metaphysical verbiage. If the student of the history and the methodology of science be permitted to mediate in this quarrel, he would say that, as so often, the truth lies somewhere in the region of the golden mean. The issue is closely connected with the one discussed in the preceding section. The positivists are objecting to the use of terms (and theories employing such terms) which are only very tenuously and indirectly connected with the evidence technically accessible at the moment. They are, temperamentally, perhaps because of a general fear of the intangible, extremely wary and reluctant in accepting promissory notes. But their lack in confidence is more than made up by the enthusiasm of the theorists. And, just as in other matters involving guesswork, it is hard to tell whose attitude will prove more fruitful in a given case. In physics the atomists won out over the positivists. The ether-theorists lost. In psychology it is perhaps still too early to tell, but it looks as if substantial components of psycho-analysis as well as of neuro-physiological behavior-theory were to stay with us and to be developed more extensively. The case of psycho-analysis is particularly favorable if some of its outright mythological and metaphysical features are dismissed and the remainder translated into behavioristic terms. Such systems as those of Hull, Tolman and Skinner are generally quite in keeping with the narrower operational criterion of meaning. Relatively few references are made to operations of a purely hypothetical sort. The essential point worth noting is that even in these highly positivistic approaches *explanation* does have a legitimate place. On the basis of only indirectly confirmed theoretical assumptions (not only of experimental laws) more specific descriptions of phenomena are logically deduced. The difference between these approaches and the theories condemned as speculative seems to this impartial observer one of degree. W. Köhler, in his *Dynamics in Psychology*, may be said to issue a great number of promissory notes. But who can tell how soon they may be backed by independent verifications coming from neuro-physiology? His critique of C. C. Pratt's conception of scientific explanation and the function of theories seems perfectly adequate. All one can say in favor of the conservative side is that the knowledge of empirical laws concerning behavior in terms of macro-concepts is still far from being complete and that a long and fruitful period of investigations on this level of analysis will yield significant results—which will in any case be required in order to test neuro-physiological 'micro'-theories.

5. THE CONVERGENCE OF OPERATIONS AND THE MEANING OF THEORETICAL CONSTRUCTS

If the linear expansion of a mercury column in a glass tube of even width furnishes the basis of an operational definition of 'temperature', then the question whether mercury expands in linear proportion to temperature (so defined) must be answered with "yes" as a matter of logical necessity or tautology. Analogous considerations apply to similar questions regarding psychological concepts (such as I.Q., habit strength, excitatory potential, etc.) operationally defined by standard testing procedures. Out-and-out operationists have often resorted to such easy and dogmatic quips as: "Intelligence is what intelligence tests test";—"temperature is what thermometers measure". Statements of this sort may be intended to intimidate inquirers of a somewhat mystical or metaphysical bent. But they do not even begin to give an adequate account of the meaning of concept formation in the sciences. Quantitative concepts of the type just mentioned are usually the product of long labors of adjustment by repeated redefinition. Thermometers or intelligence tests did not arise in an historical vacuum. They were devised in a context of problems that arose out of a background of previous qualitative and semi-quantitative knowledge. Problems of description and prediction led to a search for suitably precise, objective, and fruitful concepts. The concepts thus designed, in their logico-mathematical (functional) relations with other concepts, were to represent *empirical laws*, i.e., relationships between the various measurable (or at least testable) variables (or factors). In the light of these considerations it makes perfectly good sense to ask whether a mercury thermometer measures temperatures adequately. There are empirical laws, such as the First Law of Thermodynamics which relates temperature to mechanical energy. If we wish to give this law its most universal and simple form, we are forced to consider thermometer readings of *any* sort merely as an approximation which is to be corrected or replaced by the Kelvin scale. Similar but usually more complex considerations apply to psychological magnitudes.

Empirical laws enable us to define the same concept by different operational routes. The fact that length may be defined by the yard-stick as well as by the triangulation techniques is a consequence of the empirical laws of (applied) geometry according to which hard and solid bodies as well as light rays exhibit (in terrestrial experiments with a high degree of accuracy) Euclidean relationships. Nevertheless, Bridgman's warning to the effect that different operational routes define *different* concepts is not unjustified: The convergence of operational results is to be taken for granted only until further notice, i.e., until evidence to the contrary emerges. But until then, as a policy of typically inductive procedure and with all the provisos just made, it is one of the most helpful devices of scientific method to *identify* the concepts corresponding to results of convergent operational routes. This becomes especially clear when we consider the role of scientific theories.

A *theory* may be regarded as a set of assumptions from which empirical laws are derivable by logico-mathematical deduction. From physical theory we can deduce the electrolytic, magnetic, and thermal effect of electric currents. From a theory of learning we can deduce regularities of the emission or omission of responses. Through the unifying procedure of theoretical explanation we 'understand' what on the level of empirical law is a mere brute fact of functional dependency or correlation. Such 'understanding' is, of course, bought at the price of assumptions which are under the jurisdiction of confirming or disconfirming evidence. Deduction merely explicates what is implicit in the premises. The theoretical constructs therefore contain in compressed form the empirical concepts which can be extracted by explicit definition.

Theories and the constructs which constitute them may significantly, even if not too sharply, be grouped in two classes. In physics it is customary to distinguish phenomenological from atomistic theories. Neither characterization is terminologically fortunate. We shall here call them quite neutrally 'theories of the first kind' and 'theories of the second kind' and distinguish them by illustrations. Chemistry with its concepts of elements, compounds, compounding weights, affinities, etc., is a theory of the first kind. So is classical thermodynamics with its concepts of energy, thermodynamic potential, and entropy. Atomic theory and statistical thermodynamics are theories of the second kind. In psychology such theories as those of Hull, Tolman, Skinner, and Lewin are of the first kind. Neurophysiological theories such as those advanced by Sherrington, Adrian, and Köhler are of the second kind. The constructs of the theories of the first kind are homogeneous with the operationally defined terms in the empirical laws of the given fields. The constructs of the theories of the second kind are in this respect heterogeneous: Atomic structure, which explains chemical properties and reactions, is a construct mainly derived from spectroscopy. Concepts of nerve-currents and their patterns are distinctly physiological. If these physiological concepts are ever to furnish an explanation of behavior, they would have to be 'identified' with constructs of pure behavior theory. As a matter of program, but not of actual achievement, this is anticipated in Hull's system. What remains to be shown is the actual convergence of operational routes for both types of constructs. On the physiological side this is still in the promissory stage and may remain there generally still for a long time. This means that the operations for the definitions of constructs in theories of behavior of the second kind are largely hypothetical (i.e., at present technically impossible). It will not do to consider them sufficiently defined by the molar behavior route any more than it would do to consider atomic structure sufficiently defined by operations available to chemists at Dalton's time. Yet, as pointed out before, these are matters of degree. The prototype of an operational definition such as we can advance for directly measurable magnitudes should not mislead us into banishing all concepts which do not come up to this high level of methodological aspiration. Even in physics we have to define many concepts (not only highly indirectly but) sometimes only very partially. Before any theory of X-rays was developed, X-rays were simply "what you got when cathode rays impinged upon metal surfaces"; and "that which produced photographic images of a certain kind". Only as we advance in discovery and technique such very sketchy definitions are supplemented by fuller qualitative, quantitative, and far-flung relational characteristics. Operationism wisely understood and applied must take account and render account of the level of precision, completeness, and fruitfulness reached at the given stage of concept formation.

By way of an appendix to this section I should like to analyze by means of a simple schema the 'economic' function of concept construction. If we as yet have not reached the level of theory, we often prepare a place for theoretical constructs through the introduction of operationally defined empirical terms. The term 'electric current' had a sufficiently definite meaning already before the Maxwell electromagnetic theory or the electron theories had arisen. There were numerous different conditions which were said to produce an electric current, and numerous types of effects which were said to be caused by the current. The current itself seemed to many an intangible mystery. Similarly, there are many ways of acquiring a habit. And there are many ways in which this habit manifests itself. But what *is* the habit? These foolish questions disappear if one adopts the operationist outlook. The constructs ('electric current'; 'habit') are introduced in order to save statements. If there are m causal conditions and n possible effects we would need mn statements in order to formulate all possible observable relations. If, however, we introduce our auxiliary concepts the number of statements required shrinks to $m + n$. For large numbers m and n the conceptual economy is accordingly quite considerable. Since the established scientific procedures keep all constructs in principle open for additional definitional routes, m and n are never limited in a dogmatic manner. This feature in an enlightened operationism prevents the typical ultra-positivistic (I would call it 'negativistic') fallacy according to which things (particularly those inferred entities designated by constructs) 'are simply what they are known as' or 'are nothing but fictions introduced in order to speak more conveniently about certain sets of data'. Things are, rather, what they are known *and* know*able* as; and the sets of data are in principle capable of unlimited extensions in various (sometimes even surprising) directions. Once the empirical constructs (i.e., these auxiliary concepts) are linked to each other, either through empirical discovery or by deduction from theoretical assumptions of further functional relations between them, a whole network of variously connected concepts arises and the scientific discipline in question has attained a high degree of maturity.

Operational definitions then, or the concepts which they define, may be classified into various sorts: Purely qualitative; semi-quantitative ('comparative' or 'topological'—such as the hardness scale; or introspective concepts of 'more' or 'less'); fully quantitative or metrical (e.g., temperature; loudness); causal-genetic concepts (e.g., habit); theoretical constructs (e.g., electric fields; excitatory potential). It depends entirely upon the level of research attained which of these forms or which of their possible combinations may be applied. Concept formation in psychology, and particularly in psychiatry, is on the whole still in a relatively unfinished stage. The situation is here similar to the one in medicine where the definition of diseases is at first primarily in terms of symptoms, later in terms of more reliable causal-genetic data and, perhaps, finally in terms of a micro-account of the physiological type.

6. THE CRITERION OF INTERSUBJECTIVITY AND THE OPERATION-ISTIC JUSTIFICATION OF BEHAVIORISM

Since science is, as one might say, by definition, a social enterprise, it must insist upon operations which are repeatable not only by one observer but in principle performable by any properly equipped observer. A statement is scientifically meaningful only if it is intersubjectively testable. Subjective peculiarities, subjective differences can, of course, become the subject-matter of scientific study—if—as in the psychology of individual differences—we can verify them in a perfectly objective manner. Private, immediate experience as such is only the raw material, not the real subject-matter of science. One's own immediate experience, the actual-lived-through stream of data, may therefore be conceived as the epistemological basis of all concept formation and theoretical construction in the empirical sciences. In that sense it is not a construct but that small foothold in reality that any observer must have in order to get at all started in his business of exploring the world of things and organisms surrounding him. If one wishes to convert this narrow realm of directly given experience into subject-matter for description one is limited to a purely phenomenological approach of the introspective type. The scientific value of such a study is very insignificant as long as it remains unrelated to a study of extra-dermal and intra-dermal stimuli (physical and physiological processes) or to behavior responses. If, however, one does so relate the phenomenally given to these processes inferred (or constructed conceptually), it can itself be conceptualized as overt or potential behavior (or, by way of promissory hypothetical anticipation, as cerebral processes). That is precisely what happens in the "psychology of the other one", where one constructs on the basis of one's own data the other one's 'experience'.[1] And here again we have the choice of various conceptual systems or languages for description: mentalistic, behavioral, or—ultimately—physiological. In this sense then, we may say that 'the other one's experiences' (or better: the concepts describing it) are constructs. In this sense, also, and in this sense only, con-

---

[1] Operations which would enable one to 'inspect' the other one's private experience are by definition, i.e., logically, impossible. What would happen if nervous systems were connected is a matter of conjecture; but certainly the logical impossibility of *having* the other one's experience will thereby not be removed.

cepts referring to one's own experience are constructs. They designate processes which at least to a very small extent fall within the scope of direct phenomenal acquaintance.

Much as the epistemologist or phenomenologist may wish to clarify and formulate the meaning of 'experience' along these lines, there is the alternative of a strictly physicalistic or behavioristic approach right from the start. From the point of view of the methodology of science this is preferable, since it eliminates with one stroke the pitfalls of the traditional metaphysical pseudo-problems of solipsism, the mind-body puzzle, etc. If only intersubjective operations are admitted, one's own experience is in every respect on a par with that of the other one. Introspection itself is then described as a response to previous responses ('early retrospection'). The only asymmetry that remains is that an individual person is able to predict some (but by no means all) of his own behavior better than another observer could. But that is a matter of degree. Many of the intra-dermal and particularly the cerebral conditions are not as yet technically as directly accessible to outside observers as they are (however vaguely and diffusely) to the individual subject himself.

CONCLUSION

Operationism is not a system of philosophy. It is not a technique for the formation of concepts or theories. It will not by itself produce scientific results. Those are brought about by the labor and ingenuity of the researchers. Operationism is, rather, a set of regulative or critical standards. In the light of these critical standards the meaningfulness and fruitfulness of scientific concepts may be appraised. It seems that the outstanding requirements which operationism has quite justifiably stressed may be formulated as follows: Concepts which are to be of value to the factual sciences must be definable by operations which are (1) logically consistent; (2) sufficiently definite (if possible, quantitatively precise); (3) empirically rooted, i.e., by procedural and, finally, ostensive links with the observable; (4) naturally and, preferably, technically possible; (5) intersubjective and repeatable; (6) aimed at the creation of concepts which will function in laws or theories of greater predictiveness.

The degree to which these ideals are approximated varies from one science to another. But it would seem that all of these criteria are applicable not only to a well-developed and systematized science such as physics but also to a science still largely in the making such as psychology.

Note: The epochmaking article by C. S. Peirce: "How to Make Our Ideas Clear", appeared first in the *Popular Science Monthly*, Jan. 1878; reprinted in: *Collected Papers*, Vol. V; also in *The Philosophy of Peirce* (ed. Buchler). For the relations of operationism to modern positivism see my paper: "Logical Empiricism" in *Twentieth Century Philosophy*, ed. Runes [and included as the introductory selection in the present volume]. The logic of empirical constructs is discussed in some technical detail by R. Carnap in "Testability and Meaning", *Philosophy of Science*, 1936 and 1937. For a sketch of the same, more elementary, and applied to psychological concepts see: S. Koch: "The Logical Character of the Motivation Concept", *The Psychological Review*, 48, 1941. The operational criteria of measurement are very clearly formulated in: G. Bergmann and K. W. Spence: "The Logic of Psychophysical Measurement", *The Psychological Review*, 57, 1944. A very penetrating analysis of the epistemological problems of psychology has been given by H. Reichenbach in *Experience and Prediction*, §§ 26, 27, 28.

Some Remarks on the Meaning of Scientific Explanation *

HERBERT FEIGL

Some positivistic and operationistic definitions of "scientific explanation" have all too narrowly stressed: (1) that there is no fundamental difference between *description* and *explanation;* (2) that all scientific explanation is *circular* or *tautological;* (3) that in explanation we *reduce the unfamiliar to the familiar.* I would urge that there is something basically wrong, or in any case something very misleading, in all three contentions. A modern logical empiricism may retain the valuable anti-metaphysical tendency in the older point of view while at the same time giving a methodologically more adequate reconstruction of the explanatory process as actually employed in the various sciences. It is agreed that scientific explanation differs sharply from the pseudo-explanations of the animistic, theological or metaphysical types in that the explanatory premises of legitimate science must be capable of test, and must not be superfluous (i.e., not redundant in the light of the principle of parsimony). The significance of the premises and verbalisms of pseudo-explanations is usually purely emotive, i.e., pictorial and emotional. It is also agreed that all legitimate explanation is never absolute but *relative,* in the following two regards: (*a*) any given explanation proceeds from premises which, although possibly capable of further explanation, are *assumed* or *taken for granted* in the given case. It is only at the price, and in the light, of such assumptions that we can account for the explicanda; (*b*) the explanatory premises, as regards their validity, are relative to the confirming evidence, and therefore subject to revision.

My terminological suggestion thus amounts to the definition of "explanation" as the inductive-deductive or (on higher levels) hypothetico-deductive derivation of the more specific (ultimately descriptive) propositions from more general assumptions (laws, hypotheses, theoretical postulates) in conjunction with other descriptive propositions (and often together with definitions). "Explanation" is thus taken primarily as a *procedure of inference* (just like the closely related "prediction"), with the

* Reprinted, with slight alterations, by kind permission of the American Psychological Association and the editors, from *The Psychological Review,* 52, 1948.

only admissible alternative of the more substantival use that calls the required *set of premises* in those deductions "the explanation" of the facts to be explained (as formulated in the conclusions).

The "necessity" which is bestowed upon the facts by their explanation is the *logical necessity* of the *implication* underlying the inference from assumptions to conclusions. Neither the premises nor the conclusions in explanatory inferences of the empirical sciences are logically necessary in and by themselves. Only in a purely mathematical proof, such as we find in arithmetic or algebra, premises as well as conclusions may in themselves be logically necessary (analytic).

It is very helpful to restrict the meaning of "description" to singular statements representing fully specific facts, events or situations. Such descriptions may appear as the conclusions of explanatory, i.e., deductive inferences. Some of the premises of these inferences must then be scientific laws or theoretical assumptions. Since laws and theoretical assumptions are (or at least contain) generalized statements (i.e., unlimited universal propositions) they are not here classified as descriptions. They are the premises of explanatory or predictive (deductive) inferences and thus are themselves essentially of inductive validity. Sometimes these laws or assumptions may be more familiar than the conclusions. The whole trend of mechanistic explanation manifests this tendency toward familiarization. But since, even in physics, this mechanistic trend found its very definite limitations, and since, particularly in the scientific achievements of the last eighty years, the trend has often been reversed, we may say that very frequently the well-known, long familiar facts have been explained by principles only much more recently discovered and lacking the tang of familiarity. (Among dozens of examples bearing out this point I will only mention the electromagnetic explanations of the familiar properties of light; the quantum-mechanical explanations of chemical processes; or the neuro-physiological explanations of sensory or reflex phenomena.) That which matters is thus not the familiarity but the *generality* of the explanatory premises.

Since generality is a matter of degree, or rather of level, it is useful to distinguish levels of explanation. The empirical (i.e., experimental, or else, statistical) laws which function as premises in the deductive derivation of strictly descriptive conclusions may in turn become the conclusions of a super-ordinated deductive derivation from higher theoretical assumptions. In principle this process could repeat indefinitely but in practice it is usually found to stop at a second or third level. There is neither a danger of nor a need for an infinite regress. The top level at any given stage of theoretical research (in the ideal case) simply covers all relevant and available descriptive data; and there is no need for climbing higher on the tower of constructs if all the data one cares to see are within sight.

It seems convenient to represent the levels of explanation along the lines of the following scheme (read from bottom up!):

Theories, 2nd order	Still more penetrating interpretation (still higher constructs).
Theories, 1st order	Sets of assumptions using higher-order constructs (results of abstraction and inference). (Deeper interpretation of the facts as rendered on the Empirical Law-level.)
Empirical Laws	Functional relationships between relatively directly observable (or measurable) magnitudes.
Description	Simple account of individual facts or events (data) as more or less immediately observable.

In actual scientific practice the distinctions, as well as the number, of levels are neither quite as sharp or fixed as suggested here. The scheme is offered merely as a suggestion toward a first orientation. The question "why" (in the sense of a demand for explanation) is answered by deduction either from empirical laws or from theories. Deduction from empirical laws may be styled "low-grade" explanation. It merely puts the fact to be explained into a class of facts characterized by the same empirical law. Thus the explanation for the fact, e.g., that there is a mirror image of a bridge in a river is achieved by subsuming this fact under the law of reflection in geometrical optics. This law is simply the common denominator of all the various phenomena in which light-reflection is the essential feature. A "higher-grade" explanation we find in the Maxwell-electromagnetic wave theory, which serves as a basis for deduction for a variety of optical phenomena: reflection as well as refraction, diffraction, interference, dispersion, polarization, etc., etc. It is on this theoretical level (the "row of genius" as I like to call it) that we gain a "real insight into the nature of things" (as metaphysicians call it). What we give on this level are interpretations concerning the *structure* of light, of matter, of electricity, etc. The constructs of this theoretical level usually concern the micro-structure of the observed macro-phenomena, i.e., they involve existential assumptions (atom, electron, photon-hypotheses) or constructs of the abstract mathematical order (energy, entropy, tensors, probability functions, etc.). No wonder that the "Aha-experience" is much stronger for these deductions from theories than for the much simpler deductions from empirical laws.

Once the theoretical concepts are properly introduced they can be used also for purposes of description on the lowest level—e.g., Einstein can describe the physical state of a given volume of space in terms of 14 highly theoretically defined magnitudes. Similarly Tolman or Hull can *describe* the behavior of an organism in terms of the intervening variables of their respective systems.

The question regarding circularity may be resolved by defining what is usually called an "ad hoc" explanation. Now, an "ad hoc" explanation is deceptive because it has only the external form of a "real explanation". It is "ad hoc" in that it explains *only* the fact which it was to explain (i.e., for the sake of which it was introduced). It may be either purely verbal, e.g., "Birds build nests because they have nest-building instincts". Or it may be unscientific in that it assumes entities which don't manifest themselves in any other way (explanation of Gravitation by Lesage: particle-radiation, etc.) or it may be down-right metaphysical, if the explanatory hypotheses are in principle incapable of test (such as the assumptions of entelechies, vital forces in vitalistic and animistic biology and psychology). Of course, everything depends on how the explanatory phrases are interpreted; the use of the word "instinct" can be quite legitimate (and more than purely verbal) if, e.g., it is meant in the sense of an empirical regularity in the behavior of a species. *Then* it is a "low-grade" explanation, possibly preparing the way for a "higher-grade" theoretical explanation (say on the basis of a physiological theory of heredity, maturation, etc.). Similarly, explanations of rapidity of learning on the basis of "intelligence" are not purely verbal (or "ad hoc") but *low-grade* explanation on the basis of empirical laws. That is, as long as the "intelligence-quotient" refers to various types of capacities, various types of learning-activities, it enables us to relate the ones to the others *via* the common factor, "I.Q."

In some cases the reproach of "circularity" is made against "low-grade explanation" *if* it pretends to be "high-grade". But it seems there is no absolutely sharp line between the two—because sets of empirical laws sometimes function very much like theoretical assumptions of the higher construct type.

More fundamentally and logically speaking, the contention of circularity or tautologicality in scientific explanation is right in one interpretation but definitely wrong in another: It is right if it stresses the analytic (i.e., strictly logical, sometimes called "tautological") character of the deductive inference leading from premises to conclusion in any explanatory argument. In a more precisely definable sense it can be said that the conclusion is "contained" in the conjunction of the premises. The charge of circularity or of *petitio principii* is justified only if either the conclusion appears literally as one of the premises or if the truth of one of the premises is proved by appeal to the conclusion. The customary procedure of the hypothetico-deductive method in the empirical sciences is perfectly capable of avoiding both sources of circularity. The (psychological) novelty, sometimes amounting to surprise (Eureka!), in the more advanced and worthwhile instances of scientific explanation shows that the conclusion was not one of the premises. And the truth of the explanatory assumptions is always only suggested (i.e., confirmed to some degree) but never fully proved by evidence which is distinct from the facts to be explained. Newton's law of gravitation together with his laws of mechanics were already highly confirmed by the facts of planetary motion, by the orbits of satellites, comets, and many other items of evidence, when Leverrier and Adams used those laws as explanatory premises, together with the existential hypothesis regarding the orbit of another up to then not observed planet, in order to explain the irregularities of Uranus' motion. True, by a "tautological" (better: deductive) transformation the conclusion (concerning Uranus' path) was derived from premises (laws of mechanics, law of gravitation, etc.) but the major premise says infinitely more than the conclusion and it is therefore not possible to deduce the premises from the conclusion. Pratt [1] overlooks the inductive leap, the leap from "this" to "all" in explanatory generalizations. By declining to differentiate sharply between explanation and description Pratt views generalizations as descriptions. "Description" thereby loses its ordinarily precise meaning and the distinction between fact on the one hand and law or theory on the other, is in danger of being blurred or even obliterated.

Moreover, the hypothesis of the existence of a further planet (after its telescopic discovery called "Neptune") was suggested by the analogy with the facts regarding the then known planets. The inductive probability of this existential hypothesis therefore (at the time of Leverrier and Adams) did not rest exclusively on the "ad hoc" or circular procedure described by Pratt but had an independent foundation, no matter how weak or strong, in the already established body of astronomical knowledge. Similarly in psychology: However vague and uncertain Freud's original hypotheses regarding the repressed or unconscious parts of the mind may have been, they were *not* circular in the sense of "ad hoc". He was guided by analogies of the conscious and pre-conscious and was able to unify through his hypothesis a great number of previously unrelated facts, such as certain types of forgetting, slips and lapses, dreams, hysterical and neurotic symptoms, etc. A methodologically similar situation prevails also in psychophysiology.

To summarize: A scientific explanation is free from objectionable circularity or "ad hoc" character if it helps connect hitherto unconnected specific facts ("low-grade" explanation) or laws ("high-grade" explanation). While the deductive part of the hypothetico-deductive procedure may be said to be "tautological" or analytic (in the sense in which the classical syllogism is valid only if a denial of the conclusion strictly implies a denial of at least one of the premises): but it is not *circular* (in the sense that the conclusion is logically equivalent with one of the premises or that the conclusion itself is the sole basis of the inductive probability of the hypothetical premise).

[1] C. C. Pratt, *The Logic of Modern Psychology*, The Macmillan Co., New York, 1939, pp. 147 ff.

Causality in Everyday Life and in Recent Science *

MORITZ SCHLICK

I

There is an old rule, formulated long ago in scholastic philosophy, that warns us against confusing the "post hoc" and the "propter hoc." This means that from the fact that an event E happened after another event C we must not infer that E happened "because of" C. In other words, the rule maintains that the meaning of the proposition "E follows C" is entirely different from the meaning of the proposition "E is the effect of the cause C." But what *is* the difference between the two meanings? This question, it seems to me, is the philosophical problem of Causality.

I call it philosophical, because it is a question of meaning only, not of truth. It deals with the signification of the word "propter" or "because of"; we have to know what these words signify in order to understand the mere meaning of the principle of causality; the question whether this principle (if we can discover any meaning in it) is true or false would be a scientific problem, i.e., it could be decided only by observation and experience.

Our rule seems to presuppose that we are already acquainted with the signification of the words *post* and *propter*, for if we were not, there would be no possibility of ever applying the rule to any particular case. At best it would yield us an information of an entirely negative nature: it would tell us that the causal relation is *not* merely the relation of temporal succession, but something more; yet it would not give the slightest hint as to the positive essence of the causal relation.

Now there is no doubt that we do apply the rule continually and that it is a perfectly good and sound rule which people ought to follow even much more frequently than they do. If we take a certain medicine and get well after it, it would be very rash to assert that the medicine was the *cause* of our getting well. Or if we try to discover the causes of the depression, we know we are looking for much more than merely for events which *preceded* the depression. It is evident, therefore, that we actually are in possession of some kind of criterion which enables us to distinguish

* Reprinted by kind permission of Mrs. Schlick and the editors from University of California *Publications in Philosophy*, 15, 1932.

between events that merely follow each other and events that cause each other; for we do make this distinction every day, and we make it with a sufficient accuracy to have nearly all our behavior guided by it.

We simply have to observe how this distinction is actually made in order to find out the meaning of the concept of causality as it is used in our daily experience. This simple proceeding will surely not be difficult, and yet it is the general method—and I am convinced the only method—of philosophy: it discovers the meaning of propositions by finding out just how they are verified, i.e., how their truth or falsity is tested.

This is what I propose to do with propositions in which the concept of causality is used. I shall certainly not propose any "theory of causality"; I believe there can be no such thing. There are no theories and hypotheses in philosophy; hypotheses are the material out of which the sciences are constructed, and I believe that philosophy is something different from the sciences.

How, then, do we verify the statement that the taking of some medicine was not only the antecedent but also the *cause* of the recovery of the patient?

At a first glance there seem to be two different ways of such a verification (remember, we do not ask how it *should* be done, but how it is really done in practice):

1. We try the medicine many times and perhaps on many different patients. If we find that in every single case a person suffering from a particular complaint is cured, we shall say: the recovery after the use of the medicine was not a mere *chance*, but was *caused* by it. In other words: if the event E *always* occurs after the event C has occurred before, if C never occurs without being followed by E, then we do not hesitate to call C the cause and E the effect. It is important to notice that we do this whether we are able to "explain" the cure or not; there are cases in which we just know that a medicine is good without knowing how it works.

This is a fact; and I should like to express it, as it has often been expressed by thinkers of the positivist school, by saying that the difference between a mere temporal sequence and a causal sequence is the regularity, the uniformity of the latter. If C is *regularly* followed by E, then C is the cause of E; if E only "happens" to follow C now and then, the sequence is called a mere chance. And since (as we just saw) the observation of the regularity was, in this case, the *only* thing that was done, it was necessarily the *only* reason for speaking of cause and effect, it was the *sufficient* reason. The word cause, as used in everyday life, implies *nothing but* regularity of sequence, because *nothing else* is used to verify the propositions in which it occurs.

I am sure the reader must feel very much disappointed to have me repeat these old "positivistic" statements which have been discussed and, some believe, refuted so many times. I appeal to his patience and hope he will presently see the import of these remarks for the higher aspects of the problem of causality as they are presented by recent science.

Metaphysicians will, of course, find fault with our representation of the facts. Although they will admit, I think, that in the above example the verification consisted entirely in the observation of uniformity and nothing else, they will probably maintain that even the most unprejudiced observer never thinks that the regularity of sequence constitutes the whole of causality, but regards it only as a sign or as the consequence of something else, of some "real connection" or some peculiar "intimacy" between cause and effect, or by whatever name he may call the unobservable "tie" which he believes to be present in causation.

I do not deny that this may be so, but I answer: we are not concerned with what any observer thinks or says; our investigation of meaning is concerned only with what he *does* and can show us. Speaking, thinking, believing implies interpretation; we must not discuss interpretations or the results of philosophical analysis, we have to do with verification only, which is always an act or an activity. With regard to meaning we have to be pragmatists, whatever we may be with regard to the conception of truth. If the existence of that mysterious "tie" is verified *only* by the observation of regular sequence, then this regularity will be all the meaning the word "tie" actually has, and no thinking, believing, or speaking can add anything to it.

Perhaps the best known objection against the identification of causality and regularity is the remark that nothing is more regular than the succession of day and night, and yet we do not call the one the cause of the other. But this is simply accounted for by the fact that "day" and "night" are really not names for "events" at all in the sense in which this word is used in science. And as soon as we analyze day and night into the series of natural events for which these names stand, we find that the sequence of those events must be regarded as a very good example of "causal connection."

The real difficulties involved in the notion of uniformity are of a different nature and much more serious. We said that E was called the effect of a cause C, if in many cases it was observed to follow C each time without exception. Should we not ask: *how many* times? A physician who has tried a medicine in six cases and has seen the patient get better six times may feel pretty confident that his remedy was the cause of the recovery of his patients (provided, of course, that in his former experience they did not get well without the medicine), but undoubtedly it is possible that in all future cases the remedy will fail to have the desired result; and then we shall say: those first six times were nothing but a chance, the word "chance" meaning simply the negation of causality. If instead of six times the experiment were repeated successfully a hundred times, surely everybody would believe in the beneficial effect of the medicine; nevertheless it must be admitted that the future may bring exceptions and destroy the regularity. A hundred will be considered better than six, but evidently *no* number will be considered absolutely satisfactory; for if in one single case only C were not followed by E, one would feel no longer justified to call C the cause of E, and for all we know such a crucial case might always occur in the future.

So this is the state of affairs: the proposition "C is the cause of E" seemed to mean nothing but "C is always followed by E"; but this latter proposition can unfortunately never be verified on account of the unfortunate "always" it contains. Verification would be possible only if a finite number is substituted for "always," but no finite number is satisfactory, because it does not exclude the possibility of exceptions.

This difficulty has been pointed out about as many times as the problem of induction has been discussed, and the conclusion has usually been that causality cannot be explained as meaning simply uniformity, but that it must mean something else. Perhaps so. But we must insist: it *can* mean something else only if there is a way of verifying causal judgments different from the one we have described. What shall we do if no such way is discovered?

We can do nothing but stick to the facts with absolute frankness. Since the meaning of a proposition lies entirely in its verification, it will have meaning only *in so far* as it is verified.[1] And if the verification is never considered complete and final, if we never declare a certain C to be the cause of a certain E without reserving the right of revocation (and this, it is important to notice, not on account of any incorrect observation or similar "mistake"), then we shall have to admit that we simply have no clear concept of causality. Where there is no definite verification, there can be no definite meaning. The function of the word "cause" will be vague. A sentence containing this word may serve a very good purpose in the practice of everyday life as well as of science, but it will have no theoretical meaning.

There is a very curious way in which the difficulty hidden in the word "always" is sometimes apparently overcome. It consists in saying: if it cannot be verified that E *always* follows C, it can also never be falsified, for the cases in which it does not seem to be the case can be explained as mere appearances, and so our belief in the causal relation between C and E can never be proved to be false. A physician, for instance, who has had complete success with a cure in ninety-nine cases but finds it to fail in the hundredth case, will by no means give up his belief that his treatment has been the "cause" of the ninety-nine recoveries, but will explain that in the negative case there must have been a circumstance which intervened and prevented the effect. And we shall very likely accept this explanation as very natural, just as we would not blame a medicine for not making a

---

[1] [Editor's note: This seems to be a slip. Schlick must have intended to say "verifiable".]

patient well, if five minutes after taking it he were killed by an automobile accident. Theoretically, and in a very crude symbolism, we might say that in the negative case the cause is not any more C at all, but C + C', where C' is the intervening circumstance, and C + C' does *not* have the effect E, which C alone would have had. This statement must, of course, be capable of being verified by really observing C'; if we were to admit unobservable C's we could consider *any* event to be the cause of any other event by merely assuming the existence of convenient C's, and then surely our judgments about causal relations would lose all meaning. There are certain philosophers, those who advocate the doctrine of "conventionalism," who believe that this is really the nature of all our causal judgments; in their opinion all these judgments—which would include all laws of nature—have no real meaning, they do not say anything about the world, but only indicate the way in which we select, or even arbitrarily invent, events in order to make them fit into a preconceived scheme, which we have decided to use as our most convenient means of describing nature. Among famous scientists the astronomer A. S. Eddington may be mentioned as holding similar views.

We must note here that the interpretation of negative cases by means of disturbing influences—intervening C's—does *not* offer any criterion of causality other than uniformity of sequence; on the contrary, it saves causality only by substituting a hidden regularity for an apparent irregularity.

The regularity may at first be hidden, but it must be discoverable, if we are not to fall into the snares of conventionalism; that is, we must be able to find a C' such that C and C' together will always be followed by an E' which is different from E. And if there should be cases in which C + C' is not followed by E', we have to find a new event C'', and so on. Evidently it would be a great advantage and would help to elucidate special cases of causality, if there were a way of making sure that no further C's could possibly intervene. There would be no hope of doing this, if *any* event in the world could eventually play the rôle of the C' for which we are looking. But if these events were restricted in a certain way so that it would be possible to examine *all* of them, then we would know that no other disturbing element could come into question, and verification would become more satisfactory.

Now it has usually been assumed by science that the possible causes were indeed very definitely restricted. In looking for the cause of a given event E it was thought that we could exclude all events happening *long before* E, and all events happening *at a great distance* from E (events occurring *after* E had, of course, been already ruled out by pre-scientific thinking). Assuming these conditions in their most rigorous and consistent form one arrived at the idea that no event could be regarded as the proper cause of E unless it occurred in the immediate spatial and temporal vicinity of E.

So the causal relation between two events C and E was thought to imply their contiguity in space and time. Action-at-a-distance (temporal as well as spatial distance) was considered impossible. If this were so, one would have to look for the causes of any event only in its immediate neighborhood, there would indeed be no time and no room for any other event to interfere. It is irrelevant that this view was supported by *a priori* arguments such as "an event can act only at the place where it occurs, and nowhere else"; nevertheless such arguments show that one believed one could *understand* the causal relation better if there was contiguity; if cause and effect were separated from each other, their relation appeared to be more mysterious. This brings us to the consideration of the second way in which the existence of a causal relation seems to be established (the first one being observation of uniformity of sequence).

2. Supposing there were a case in which we believed we really and completely "understood" the working of a certain treatment or medicine in the human body: in such a case we should not have to wait for any repetition of the sequence treatment-recovery in order to assert a causal relation between these two events; we could assert it even before it occurred a single time, because our "understanding" of this particular causation would imply our conviction that the first event would entail the second one, or, as it is often put, C would *necessarily* be followed by E. If a surgeon amputates a man's leg, he will know beforehand that the man will be one-legged afterwards. Nobody thinks that we must wait for a long series of experiences in order to know that amputation results in the loss of a limb. We feel we "understand" the whole process and therefore know its result without having experienced it.

So there seems to be a second way of verifying a causal judgment independent of observation of regularity: it consists in simply pointing to the "understanding" of the particular causal relation. And those who believe in this second way will immediately add that it is the only real way, the only legitimate method, and that our first criterion—uniformity of occurrence—was nothing but an untrustworthy symptom, which might be good enough for an empiristic scientist, but could never satisfy the philosopher.

But let us examine what exactly is meant by "understanding" as the word is used here.

It is usually supposed to be a matter of "pure reason." Now, the only sense I can find for this term is the purely logical, which would mean the same as the purely deductive, the merely analytical. And there is indeed a purely logical element in the case we have just been examining. That amputation of a leg causes a man to be one-legged is an identical inference; it is, like all logical inferences, a mere tautology. But it is easy to see, unfortunately, that this has nothing to do with causation. The causal connection is hidden in the word "amputation." We usually believe we understand this connection, because we think we comprehend the process, say, of a saw cutting through a bone: the hard particles of the steel are in immediate contact with the soft particles of the bone, and the latter some-how must give way to the former. Here again we have contiguity in space and time, which appears to flatter our imagination, but apart from that we have again nothing but a sequence of events which we have often observed to happen in a similar way and which we therefore expect to happen again. For aught we know we might some day come across a bone that would resist any saw and that no human power would be able to cut in two.

So we see that, at least in our example, we were led to think we under-stood or comprehended the causal nexus: partly by a misinterpretation of the way in which logical inference entered into our thought, and partly by analyzing the causal process into a spatial and temporal continuity of events. This means that our second criterion is really only a hidden application of the first one; it is not different, and consequently not any better.

The examination of any other example leads to the same result. What, for instance, is the difference between a case in which we *understand* that a certain medicine must have a certain effect, and another case in which we just know by experience that it does have that effect? It is evidently this: in the second case we observe only two events, the application of the drug and, after a reasonable lapse of time, the recovery of the patient; in the first case we know how the gap between cause and effect is filled by an unbroken chain of events which are contiguous in space and time. The drug, e.g., is injected into the veins, we know it comes into immediate contact with the blood particles, we know that these will then undergo a certain chemical change, they will travel through the body, they will come into contact with a certain organ, this organ will be changed in a particular way, and so on. In this way we infer that in the end the patient *must* be healed, *if* all the other events follow each other in the way we have assumed. And how do we know that they do follow each other so? All we know is that in former experiences in the laboratory this has always been the regular course of things.

From all this we must draw the negative conclusion that it is impossible—at least in so far as the judgments of everyday life and of qualitative science are concerned—to find any meaning for the word causation, except that it implies regularity of sequence. And this is rather vague, because there is no rule as to how many instances have to be observed in order to justify our speaking of regularity.

But the two chief things we can learn from the foregoing considerations seem to me to be these:

1. The "understanding" of a causal relation is not a process of logical reasoning; what is called causal necessity is absolutely different from logical necessity (which is nothing but identity). But at the same time we see why former philosophers so frequently made the mistake of confusing the two

and believing that the effect could be logically inferred from the cause. The only serious philosopher of our present time who still believes that there must be some kind of identity of cause and effect and therefore believes the relation between them to be in some way rational or logical, is (so far as I know) E. Meyerson. He tries to prove this historically by analyzing the statements of famous philosophers and scientists; but the psychological explanation of his view lies in the fact that he started as a chemist, who is used to thinking in terms of identical substances, whereas the physicist, who goes more deeply into the explanation of nature, has to think in terms of events.

2. We learn that the causal relation between two separate events is actually explained or understood when we can conceive the two as being connected by a chain of intermediate events. If some of these are still separated, we have to look for new events between them, and so on, until all the gaps are filled out and the chain has become perfectly continuous in space and time. But evidently *we can go no further*, and it would be nonsense to expect more of us. If we look for the causal link that links two events together, we cannot find anything but another event (or perhaps several). Whatever can be observed and shown in the causal chain will be the links, but it would be nonsense to look for the linkage.

This shows that we are perfectly right when we think of cause and effect as *connected* by a causal chain, but that we are perfectly wrong when we think that this chain could consist of anything but events, that it could be a kind of mysterious tie called "causality." The conception of such a "tie," which is really not a concept but a mere word, is due to a faulty process of thinking that is very common in the history of philosophy: the continuation of a thought beyond its logical limit; we transcend the region in which a word makes sense and necessarily find ourselves in the region of nonsense. After the scientist has successfully filled up all the gaps in his causal chains by continually interpolating new events, the philosopher wants to go on with this pleasant game after all the gaps are filled. So he invents a kind of glue and assures us that in reality it is only his glue that holds the events together at all. But we can never find the glue; there is no room for it, as the world is already completely filled by events which leave no chinks between them. Even in our times there are some philosophers who say that we directly experience causation, e.g., in the act of volition, or even in the feeling of muscular effort. But whatever such feelings of willing or of effort may be, they are certainly events in the world; they can be glued to other events, but they cannot be the glue.

All this has of course been seen very clearly by Hume when he said that it was impossible to discover any "impression" for the idea of causal nexus. Only we can express this even more strongly by saying that we are already committing a kind of nonsense when we try to *look* for such an impression. At this point we find complete agreement between Hume and Kant. Kant applauded Hume for seeing that when we speak of causation we cannot possibly mean a sort of tie which connects the events or establishes a kind of intimacy between them, and he conceived causality as something entirely different, namely as a Principle of Order. He believed that the human mind imposed a certain order on the events of its experience, and that causality was one of the principles according to which this was done. And according to him, the human mind did this because it could not help doing it; the Principle was simply part of its metaphysical nature.

Although we must of course reject the latter part of Kant's view, we can most heartily consent to his opinion that if causality is anything at all it can be nothing but a Principle of Order.

II

It is the object of science to discover Order in the world. This is done by finding and formulating Laws of Nature. So there must be a relationship between causality and the laws of nature, and it is easy to see what it is. The principle of causality seems to assert that every definite cause will have a definite effect, and a law of nature tells us, what will be the particular event that belongs to a given cause as its effect. So the principle of causality itself is not a law but can be regarded as the statement that all events in nature are subject to laws. And this must not be interpreted as if a law of nature were something imposed upon reality, compelling nature to behave in a certain way, just as a civic law would force a certain behavior upon the citizens. Laws of nature do not *pre*scribe a certain order *to* the world, but simply *de*scribe the order *of* the world; they do not command what must happen, but simply formulate what does happen. The "necessity" which we attribute to them must not be misunderstood as a kind of compulsion (this term would imply the possibility of "obedience" and "disobedience"), but it means only that there is *no exception* to the laws, that they hold in *all* cases.

From what I said a moment ago we might expect all laws of nature to have the form: "the cause so-and-so has the effect so-and-so"; but if we look at the actual formulations in science we do not find a single law of this form, wherever the expression is perfectly precise, as is the case in theoretical physics. What we do find there is always a mathematical equation. The vague notions of cause and effect have been replaced by the more precise concept of mathematical function. Cause and effect are both names for events, and one of the reasons why it seems impossible to use them with the necessary scientific precision lies in the fact that it is impossible to *isolate* events. If I drop my pencil on the table, this would be considered as one event in everyday language; but think of the innumerable facts it involves: the motions of all the molecules of my fingers, of the table, of the surrounding air! It would be hopeless to give a complete description of such an "event," and still more impossible to find its complete *cause;* we know that, for instance, the position of the moon would somehow enter into the cause, as the presence of the moon contributes to the gravitational field in which the pencil is falling.

So science does not speak of causes and effects, but of functional relations between measurable quantities; it starts with measurement of quantities rather than with description of occurrences. And it seems to be the essence of every law of nature that it states the way in which the values of some quantities measured at certain places and times depend on the values of some other quantities measured at certain other places and times.

This introduction of mathematical functions is an enormous advantage, but we must not believe that all our difficulties in interpreting causality can be overcome by simply abandoning the use of the terms cause and effect.

In the first place it must be remembered that the scientific conception of nature as a system of functional relations is a sort of idealized scheme which acquires physical meaning only by being applied or attached to reality; it is referred to reality only by observation, of course; and every observation is an observation of an event (such as the change of color of a liquid in a chemical experiment or the motion of the mercury in a thermometer), which will be regarded as isolated and as causally connected with other events (e.g., certain manipulations of the observer). In this way the old concepts which have been eliminated from the system of science seem to reappear when we examine the actual experiences on which science is based. It is true that a careful analysis would show that this is not a very serious predicament in itself, and it is also true that the difficulties connected with the isolation of events can be minimized by careful experimental arrangements; but the recent development of physics has shown that there is a definite limit to this isolation, and the consequences of this fact *are* serious.

In the second place, we must not rejoice too much in the replacement of the concept of causality by the concept of law, before we are quite sure that we know exactly what we mean by the word *law.* Is it really a satisfactory explanation to say (as we did a little while ago) that a law of nature is a function between measured quantities? I think it is not sufficient. In order to show this let us consider a special form of law which corresponds to the ideas of classical physics (but our arguments would remain true in a more general case).

Let us suppose that there is no "action-at-a-distance," so that the occurrence of any event at a given point of space and at a given time would depend only on what happened immediately before and in the immediate vicinity of that point. The laws describing such a kind of dependence would be expressed by differential equations. Now consider a physical system within a closed surface, the happenings in which were completely governed by these laws: then it seemed possible for classical physics to give a perfectly precise expression of the Principle of Causality for such a system. It used to be given by the following statement: "The state of the system (i.e., the totality of the events within our surface) at any time t is completely determined by its state at some other time t_o and by all the events which happen *on* the closed boundary during the whole time-interval t—t_o." (If *nothing* were happening at the boundary—i.e., if we had a completely isolated system—or if there were no boundary—which would be the case if our system were the whole universe, as Laplace considered it in his famous formula—then the same statement could be made more simple by saying that the state of the system at *any* particular time determines its states at *all* other times.) This is, of course, a formulation of determinism.

We must analyze very carefully what can be meant by this statement. The clue must evidently be found in the word "determine," which is used here. The word indicates a certain relation between two states of the system: one which determines and one which is determined. This is, of course, nothing but our *causal* relation, and we see that the word determination has taken the place of the word causation. This does not seem to be a great advantage; but let us see how the scientist uses the word determination—then we shall find out what he *means* by it. When he says that the state E at the time t is determined by the state C at the time t_o, he means that his differential equations (his Laws) enable him to *calculate* E, if C and the boundary conditions are known to him. Determination therefore means Possibility of Calculation, *and nothing else.*

It does *not* mean that C in some magic way *produces* E. And yet we can now understand how the idea of production comes in and what justification can be given for it. "To produce" literally means to bring forth; and in a very definite sense the calculation does "bring out" if not E, at least the complete description of E, i.e., the values of all the physical quantities which are characteristic of E. From the logical point of view a mathematical computation is a process of analysis which can bring out only what is already contained in the presuppositions; and in fact, the description of the initial state C (and of the boundary conditions) together with the Laws do logically contain the description of all the succeeding states E, in the same sense in which all the terms of a series may be said to be contained in the law of the series together with its first term.

Here again it might seem as if the causal relation were in some way reduced to a sort of logical inherence of the effect in the cause, and as if a logical interpretation of "production" were found; but a moment's thought shows the futility of such an interpretation. For calculation can only show what will occur *if* certain laws are valid, but it can never show that they *are* valid. In other words: the logical equivalence does not hold between cause and effect, or in fact between anything in reality, but it holds only between the two propositions: (1) State C has been observed and certain states E will follow; and (2) State C has been observed and certain laws L are valid. The meaning of these two propositions is identical (if the proper substitutions are made for E and L), and the calculation is nothing but the analytic method of transforming one into the other. Mathematical analysis teaches us how to express a sequence of events by means of a Law, *if* there is a certain order in nature; the principle of causality asserts that there *is* order in nature. These are two entirely different and independent things. Logical necessity and "production" belong to calculus, causality belongs to real nature.

We see again that laws of nature must not be thought of as supernatural powers forcing nature into a certain behavior and thereby "producing" the effects of given causes, but simply as abbreviated expressions of the order in which events do follow each other.

Before we return to our result that determination means nothing but possibility of calculation, and before we analyze the sense in which the word "possibility" is to be understood here, let us remark in passing how an old purely philosophical problem can be disposed of by a simple application of our result; I mean the problem of "logical determinism." This "problem" deals with the relationship between logical principles and reality. Aristotle believed (and there are even modern logicians who follow him in this) that the Principle of the Excluded Middle could not be applied to *future* events unless we assume the truth of Determinism. For let us suppose that our universe were indeterministic; then the proposition "The United States of Europe will be founded in the year 1950" could be neither true nor false today. For it would be true only if the occurrence of that event were already determined today; and it would be false only if the non-occurrence of the event were determined today. Both cases are in contradiction with our presupposition of indeterminism; therefore either determinism is true, or the Principle of the Excluded Middle is not valid for propositions concerning the future.

From our point of view we can easily see why this argument is wrong. It rests on the false assumption that the word "determined" denotes a property of events in themselves, while it really means nothing but "calculable" (which is the same as "capable of being predicted"). Indeterminism does *not* assert that the proposition "the event E will take place in 1950" is not true or false today, but it asserts only that the truth or falsity of that proposition cannot be *inferred* (predicted) from present and past events. It says only that there is no *law* which will enable us to calculate the future if the present is known. Indeterminism, in other words, asserts that there are no means of *knowing* now whether a proposition about the future is true or false—it can be verified only in the future; but this in no way contradicts the Principle of the Excluded Middle, which says that the proposition *is* either true or false. So our interpretation of causal determination allows us to see that the logical principles are really independent of matter or fact (such as the truth of determinism or indeterminism in the world), as of course they must be, since they are nothing but rules of symbolism and do not make any statements whatever about the world.

Before we go on, just one remark about another "philosophical problem," the question of "teleology" or "finality" as opposed to causality. Several philosophical writers have tried to give a meaning to these terms by saying that by teleology is meant the determination of a present event by future events; and they believe that there are certain cases in nature, especially in the realm of animate beings, where the determination goes in the direction from future to past, while in the case of causality (which they believe to prevail in inanimate nature) it goes the other way. Regardless of other arguments that may be brought forward against such a view, we can see immediately that it is untenable. After we have learned from science what the word *determination* really stands for, we know that this distinction between teleological and causal determination breaks down. For if a later event E is determined by an earlier event C, then E can be calculated from C by means of certain mathematical functions; but if this is possible, then these very same functions will always enable us to calculate C when E is known (excepting very special cases of many-valued functions which are of no practical significance), and so we shall have to say that C is also determined by E. So causality and teleology would not be different at all; it makes no difference whether we say "the past determines the future" or "the future determines the past." It is really a great advantage of scientific language, which speaks in terms of functions rather than in terms of causes, that it treats the causal relation as symmetrical, while in everyday life it is usually thought to be asymmetrical. This has long been acknowledged, and the attempts of some writers, like H. Reichenbach, to introduce an asymmetry into the scientific expression of causal relations seem to me to have failed.

We now return to our analysis of the concept of determination. We found it to mean "possibility of calculation"; and from what we have seen thus far it seems that possibility of calculation implied nothing but the existence of some mathematical functions which connect the values of the quantities that describe different states of a physical system at different times. But here we strike a serious difficulty. It is this: whatever the succeeding states of a physical system may be—after we have observed them it is *always* possible to find functions connecting them in such a way that if one of those states is given, all the rest of them can be computed by means of those functions. The mathematician assures us that he has no difficulty in constructing analytical functions which with any desired degree of approximation will represent any succeeding states of the system, however chaotic it may be. This proves that we cannot identify Law with functional relations; for if *any* sequence of events can be described by functions, then the possibility of such a description cannot be used to distinguish an orderly or causal sequence from a chaotic or non-causal one. The principle of causality would always be true: whatever happened, it would be a mere tautology which says nothing about nature.

We conclude that "possibility of calculation" cannot simply mean possibility of description by functions; something more is needed. It is usually thought that what is needed is some kind of specification of the functions, so that laws of nature must be defined by functions possessing some special property.

The first property which presents itself here is *simplicity*. Many writers hold that the difference between a causal chain of events and a non-causal one is this, that the former can be described by simple function, the latter only by complicated ones. I do not doubt for a moment that all the laws we know, and probably even all the laws we shall ever know, do comply with this criterion, which I usually call the aesthetic criterion, because simplicity seems to be an aesthetic rather than a scientific concept. Nevertheless, it is entirely unsatisfactory from the logical point of view, and this for two reasons. The first one is that we cannot give a strict definition that will enable us to distinguish between simple and complicated functions; I suppose the latter ones are those that can be handled successfully only by a very skilful mathematician—but evidently no such definition could have the necessary objectivity and clarity. The second reason is that we can easily imagine circumstances in which nobody would refuse to regard even the most complicated function as a perfectly good law of nature. This would be the case if all the predictions made by the complicated formula were found to be true, and no simpler function of equal efficiency could be discovered. For these reasons the logician must dismiss the criterion of simplicity as inadequate.

Another criterion of causality that might be chosen consists in postulating that the functional relations describing the flow of events must not contain the space and time coordinates in an explicit form. This sounds rather technical, but it is nothing but the mathematical formulation of the principle: Same cause, same effect. It means that if under certain circumstances at a particular place and time a certain sequence of events is observed, then a similar sequence of events will be observed if similar circumstances occur at some other place and some other time. This postulate has been adopted by such a great authority as Maxwell, and it may perhaps be regarded as a special form of the simplicity principle, as the absence of explicit space and time values could be considered as a particular kind of simplicity of the functions. The postulate is fulfilled if space and time enter only as the independent variables of differential equations, and this is true in our present-day physics.

Now again I certainly expect that all laws of nature will actually conform to Maxwell's criterion just as well as to the general criterion of simplicity (if they did not it would mean that we should have to change our views concerning the nature of space and time considerably)—none the less it remains theoretically possible that a future physics might have to introduce formulae which contain space and time in an explicit form, so that the same cause would never have the same effect, but the effect would also depend, in a definite way, e.g., on the date, and would be different tomorrow, or next month, or next year.

However improbable this may seem to be—the philosopher has to take into account all possibilities, no matter how remote they are; he must never tie himself down to the particular state of science at this time, which is always only one of many possible states; his realm is the field of possibilities, because it is the realm of all meaningful propositions. In our case he must ask himself: would we regard the universe as non-causal or chaotic, if it did not conform to Maxwell's criterion? And the answer is: by no means! If we knew formulae which we could use just as successfully for the description of that strange universe as we use our present scientific formulae to describe the actual world, we should have to say that both worlds were completely orderly. This brings us to the essential point, at last: we have to see how the formulae are actually *used*.

Instead of inventing definitions of *law*, which always prove more or less artificial, we must direct our attention to the way in which the scientist really tests a formula in each particular case and tries to verify whether or not it represents the law for which he is looking. He first constructs a function by connecting all the observed data, and he will certainly try to construct it so that it obeys Maxwell's criterion as well as that of simplicity—but he is not content with this. His success in finding a function of this nature is not a sufficient, and not even a necessary, reason for him to be convinced that the Law is found. He will proceed to apply it to *new* data, which have not been used for the construction of his formula. If observation shows that the function fits the new data he will triumph and believe that it expresses the real law. He will *believe* it; he will never be absolutely sure, because new data may come up in the future which will not fit into the formula. But, of course, his faith will grow with the number of verifications. The mathematician can always construct an analytic formula that will cover all the observed data, but he can never guarantee that it will also fit future data which he does not know yet and which nature will furnish after having been asked to do so by the skilful experiments and observations of the scientist.

Now at last we know what is meant by the "possibility of calculation" which we found to be the essence of causality or "determination." It does not mean possibility of finding a function with particular mathematical properties, but it means possibility of *applying* a function with *any* properties to such data (or "events" or "states of a physical system") as have not been used for its construction. The technical term for this procedure is "extrapolation," and so we can now say that in science causality stands for possibility of extrapolation. From the way in which we introduce the term "possibility" it is clear that it implies correspondence with observation or (which is saying the same thing) with reality: when we say that it is possible to extrapolate from a physical formula we mean that the extrapolated values will correspond to the values which are really observed. This process of computing values which are confirmed by future experience is usually called *prediction*, and so we may say quite simply: a Law is a formula which allows us to make true predictions.

The criterion of causality is successful prediction. That is all we can say. It is not much more than what we said in the beginning, after analyzing causality in everyday life, where we ended by speaking of regularity of sequences. Regularity of occurrence in the ordinary sense is just a particular case in which the method of prediction is especially easy to grasp. Our former difficulty in understanding causality was that we were unable to say when a causal judgment should be considered definitely verified, and therefore could give no definite meaning to it. This difficulty has not been overcome by our analysis of scientific law. Even in science there is no way of ever establishing a law as absolutely valid and thereby proving the existence of causation in any particular case. We can never be sure that *all* predictions from a law will come true. Although in practice a small number of successful predictions will suffice to cause a very strong belief in a law, and sometimes even one single verification will be regarded as sufficient: from the strictly logical point of view all our formulae will always remain hypotheses, theoretically it will always remain possible to say that the verifications were just "chance."

There is no room to discuss the logical consequences of this situation [2] and we must turn to the most recent development of science in order to see whether it agrees with the results of our analysis. Does it support the view that the *only* criterion, and therefore the only meaning, of causality is successful prediction?

It is gratifying to state that the recent discussions of causality in connection with the quantum theory afford a very striking confirmation of our view. As is well known, the quantum theory in its present form asserts that a strictly deterministic description of nature is impossible; in other words, that physics has to abandon the Principle of Causality.

What does physics mean when it thus denies causality? In order to find this out we need only examine the specific reasons which are given for this denial.

If causality were defined by simplicity of mathematical functions, as was done by the aesthetic criterion, then its denial would mean that it is impossible to describe nature by simple functions. Does science assert this?

[2] This is done in the author's article "Die Kausalität in der gegenwärtigen Physik", published in *Die Naturwissenschaften*, 1931, Heft 7 [also published in *besammelte Aupaetze*], where a more complete analysis of the whole problem is given.

Does it despair of causality because the formulae it has to use are too complicated? Certainly not! Therefore its rejection of determinism is not guided by the aesthetic criterion.

If causality were essentially defined by Maxwell's criterion, i.e., by the principle that the describing functions must not contain space and time coördinates in an explicit form (which, as we saw it, is equivalent to the rule "same cause, same effect"), then denial of determinism would mean: it is impossible to describe nature by equations in which space and time do not occur explicitly. And is this the great revelation made by the quantum theory? By no means! Therefore violation of Maxwell's criterion is not the reason why determinism is rejected.

What *is* the real reason? None other but that it is found impossible to *predict* phenomena with perfect accuracy. Within certain well-defined limits it is impossible to construct functions that can be used for extrapolation. This is the essential consequence of Heisenberg's famous Uncertainty Principle, and it proves that the physicist in his actual proceeding has adopted just that view of causality which we have been advocating.

It is true that the formulation given by most physicists seems to be a little different. They usually insist on the impossibility, not of prediction of future states, but of complete description of the present state of a physical system. But an easy analysis shows that this must be interpreted as involving incapacity of extrapolation. For the sake of simplicity we may assume that a description of a system would be complete if it included the positions of all the electric particles composing the system at the present moment, and the velocities of all these particles at the same moment. But what is "velocity"? What does it mean in actual experience when we assert that a certain particle moves with a certain velocity? It means nothing but that the particle which at one moment has been observed at a definite particular place will, after a definite short interval of time, be observed at another definite place. Thus assigning a certain velocity to a particle at a given moment means predicting its position at a given future moment. Theoretically, the Principle of Indeterminacy does not make it impossible to observe two succeeding positions of a particle in a short interval of time and assign to it a velocity equal to the ratio of the distance and the time interval, but in this way we have described only the *past* behavior of the particle—or, I should rather say, its *observed* behavior. As soon as we try to use this value of velocity for an extrapolation in order to get a future position of the particle, the Uncertainty Principle steps in to tell us that our attempt is in vain; our value of velocity is no good for such a prediction, our own observation will have changed the velocity in an unknown way, therefore the particle will probably not be found in the predicted place, and there is no possibility of knowing where it could be found.

In this way the concept of velocity is connected with prediction, and only because there is no predictability here, does the ordinary procedure of science (which is implied by the words Law and Causation) become inapplicable.

Perhaps it is not unnecessary to remind the reader that these consequences of the Uncertainty Principle become practically serious only when we are concerned with very small particles whose position we try to describe with unlimited accuracy. If we are content to determine the position with a certain approximation we shall be able to predict future positions with a probability the exact amount of which is stated by Heisenberg's formula. And if we have to do with larger particles, such as molecules for instance, not to speak of rifle bullets or billiard balls, the approximation and the probability reach such enormous amounts that the certainty of our predictions becomes incomparably greater than the accuracy of our most perfect observations.

This is very fortunate from the practical point of view, for it means that for all ordinary purposes of science and everyday life the deterministic attitude not only remains justified but is the only one compatible with our knowledge of nature. If it were otherwise, if Planck's constant h, which in a way measures the uncertainty of our predictions, were more than 10^{30} times greater than it actually is, then the Principle of Indeterminacy would make our lives very difficult, because hardly anything could ever be planned ahead. If human beings could exist at all in a world of so much disorder, they would have to give up many pursuits, such as medicine, engineering, and they would have to give up morality. For there can be no morals without responsibility, and there could be no responsibility if human actions were simply random events in the world. (Lack of determination means pure chance, randomness; the alternative "either determination or chance" is a logical one, there is no escape from it, no third possibility.) A serious amount of indeterminism would be nothing to rejoice about, it would mean fatal disorder. Such considerations make us wonder why metaphysicians so often thought it necessary to defend indeterminism for ethical or religious reasons; they have been misled by a strange confusion concerning the terms necessity and law, freedom and determinism. But we are not concerned with this here.

The situation is a little different in the case of those philosophical writers and philosophizing scientists who have derived great satisfaction from the recent development of science because the indeterminism to which it leads is a *physical* indeterminism. They rejoice in the incomplete determination of nature by physical laws because it seems to leave room for Mind in the universe. If there are little gaps in physical causation, why should they not be filled by the activity of mental factors, such as thoughts or feelings, which would in this way have some influence on the course of events?

If this view were logically sound it would mean that the happenings in the physical world which modern physics leaves partly indetermined could be made deterministic again by the introduction of mental events (either partly, if only some of the gaps were supposed to be filled, or wholly, if mental factors were believed to be at work everywhere). Reduced to sober scientific language this would mean that the psychologist could make exact predictions in cases where the physicist must fail; if, e.g., the laws of physics could not tell him where a certain electron was going, he would still be able to predict the future position of this electron by consulting certain psychological laws.

I admit that there might be some intellectual satisfaction in this restoration, or partial restoration, of determinism; but I fail to see why the metaphysician should welcome it as satisfying his deepest desires. It is only through some secret additions and misinterpretations that this view could seem so valuable to him. But in reality I am convinced that the whole view is logically unsound. To regard physical and mental events as two different entities which between themselves determine the course of the universe in the described manner seems to me to be a particularly shallow and crude attempt to deal with the so-called Psycho-physical Problem, and to rest on a very naïve and uncritical use of the terms "physical" and "mental." A view that succeeds in finding a place for Mind in the universe only with the utmost difficulty and only after physics has discovered the principle of indeterminacy—such a view, I am sure, must be based on an analysis of the term "mind" which is fundamentally wrong. The true analysis of the terms "physical" and "mental" (with which we are not concerned here) will show that they cannot be used in this dualistic way without severe violation of the rules of philosophical grammar, and that the understanding of the real meaning of these terms has nothing to do with any particular theory of physics and is quite independent of any present doctrines and of the progress of science.

No metaphysical conclusion can be drawn from the discoveries of recent science—as indeed such conclusions cannot be drawn from *anything*. Science, as the pursuit of truth, can and must stimulate philosophy, as the pursuit of meaning, but one of these can never be the explanation of the other.

We found that recent science confirmed the view that causality must be understood as meaning "possibility of extrapolation," because we found that this was exactly the sense in which the word is used in quantum physics. But, of course, our view and our analysis in no way presuppose the truth of the present state of quantum physics. If future science should abandon the principle of indeterminacy and should return to a deterministic interpretation of nature, our result would not be affected. For determinism could be restored only by showing that the laws of nature did not set any finite limit to the accuracy of our predictions. This would mean that we should have no more reason definitely to lose confidence in the applicability of our extrapolations, and it would presuppose just that view of causality which I have been trying to explain here.

Mechanical and Teleological Causation *

C. A. MACE

The term "conation" has been employed by psychologists not only with reference to a certain type of experience, but also with reference to a certain type of process, viz., what is described as a conative process. Those who attach importance to the concept of conation do in general hold that a conative process is invariably associated with conative experience, but if this is so it must, I think, be defended on empirical grounds; the one does not entail the other. That this is so becomes clearer if it be agreed that what psychologists commonly mean by a conative process is identical with what philosophers more usually describe as a teleological process. The latter term belongs to a philosophical tradition, the former to a psychological tradition.

At first sight it might appear that a conative or teleological process might be defined in the manner in which Dr. Broad defines a teleological system.[1] That is, we might define it as any process which brings into existence, or terminates in, a "teleological system," or more generally in a "teleological state of affairs." The latter would be defined by the two requirements specified by Dr. Broad, viz., (i) the state of affairs must have the characteristics which might have been expected if it had been arranged by some intelligent being to fulfil a purpose he had in mind, and (ii) further examination reveals additional features in this state of affairs in accord with this hypothesis. Such a definition does not, of course, imply that the state of affairs does in fact realize an actual purpose, but that it has certain features which would be present in a state of affairs which did in fact realize a purpose.

A definition of this kind, however, is difficult to apply without letting in cases which one wishes to exclude. Given a meteorological system involving a distribution of rainfall which encourages certain plants and tends to destroy others, this system would have precisely the features which might be expected if it had been designed by a being who preferred the existence of the former to that of the latter. And if there be any class of plants which are, in fact, favoured by the distribution of rainfall in the world and another class that is adversely affected, there is no doubt that further investigation would reveal facts which accord with the hypothesis.

* Excerpted and reprinted with the kind permission of the author and the editors of the *Proceedings of the Aristotelian Society* from the article with the above title in *Aristotelian Society, Supplementary Volume* 14, for 1935.

[1] *The Mind and its Place in Nature*, p. 82.

The difficulty, in general terms, is that given *any* state of affairs or *any* system it is possible to conceive *some* purpose with which the existence of that system or state of affairs would accord. Even a completely chaotic world—one that precluded the possibility of a scientific account of its structure—would conform to the conditions, since this kind of world would admirably fulfil the purpose of a creator who wished to bewilder his creatures and to check the growth of an immoderate intellectual conceit. Are there not, by the way, theologians who hold that this is in fact the case?

Perhaps the difficulty could be met by the specification of further conditions, but I prefer not to define a teleological process by reference to a teleological system, but to define the system by reference to the process. Thus we might say that a teleological system is one that is constructed by a teleological process (usually also *for use in* a teleological process). Whether organisms are covered by this definition as well as artificial machines requires special discussion, but they, too, can be defined by reference to such processes, and in a manner which indicates their important differences from artificial machines. An organism is a system some of the activities of which are teleological processes, whilst the activities of a machine never are. This, of course, puts the whole burden on the definition of a teleological process. This type of process is, I think, to be defined by reference to its *form*.

Consider a sequence of actions of the kind which has been very persistently studied by psychologists who have concerned themselves with animal behaviour. The case of Thorndike's cat is a classical example. A hungry cat is placed within a cage from which it can escape by clawing in a suitable manner at a ring suspended in the cage and connected with the latch of the door. The cat engages in a variety of apparently random movements of locomotion, clawing and biting at the bars of the cage and so forth until, in the course of these movements, it happens, more or less by chance, to perform the operation which effects its release. If the cat is returned to the cage this procedure is repeated. But with continued repetitions of the situation it is found that there is a progressive decrease in the time required for the cat to effect its escape. This is due to the fact that movements which, in fact, do not contribute to its release, recur less frequently and movements which do contribute to release occur with increasing frequency or earlier in the series. This general tendency has been observed in an immense variety of cases, and in this manner even complicated chains of action may be learned.

In a sequence of this kind there are three features of interest:

(i) It is evoked by a negative condition E' and is such that the introduction of a contrasting condition, E, at any time in the sequence would terminate the process in question.

(ii) It is such that (so far as E may be present in varying degrees) any action which increases the degree of E tends to be continued or repeated, whilst any action which decreases the degree of E tends to be discontinued.

(iii) It is such that with repetition of the process constituent actions which favour E tend to be stabilized whilst actions which are adverse to E tend to be eliminated, with the result that the process as a whole approximates to a form in which it consists of a set of component actions performed in a certain order which (a) performed in that order are sufficient to produce E and (b) are such that the omission of any action would prevent the occurrence of E.

Any train of actions conforming to this description would, I think, be commonly described as a conative or teleological process. The definition makes no claim to economy or elegance, and some qualifications and amendments might be necessary to cover special cases, but I trust that it is sufficiently near the mark to indicate the sort of process with which I am concerned. Certain observations may serve to correct some of the defects in its description.

In the first place, I think it would be generally agreed that the definition really does apply to something, and that what it applies to is a train of activity of a peculiar and distinctive kind.

Secondly, and this is a point I wish to emphasize, the definition does not directly entail the presence of consciousness. It is theoretically possible that a purely physical process might conform to the description.

Nevertheless, I am tempted to believe that this, in point of fact, is the kind of process which Prof. Stout [2] in his discussion of active tendencies chiefly has in mind. At least, if I am permitted to interpret his statements as referring to a process of this kind, I find so much more in his doctrine which I can understand and with which I can agree.

Prof. Stout speaks of an active tendency as finding expression in a process which exhibits a characteristic unity, and of this as a kind of unity which varies in degree. He suggests that a tendency of this kind does not admit of analysis in terms of anything that could be expressed solely in hypothetical statements. In our awareness of it we apprehend its intrinsic nature in a manner which is similar to our awareness of colours and sounds. We apprehend in it, further, something which is akin in nature to our own experience of striving. These statements so far as they apply to the kind of active tendency exhibited by a conative tendency, as I have defined it, are all statements with which I feel strongly inclined to agree.

My difficulty with Prof. Stout's references to the unity of processes expressive of active tendencies is that such processes seem to me to have more than one kind of unity. They have the kind of unity which is expressed by saying that they do not consist of "loose and separate events," but there is a different and further kind of unity implied in speaking of the

[2] *Aristotelian Society, Supplementary Volume* 14, 1935, pp. 46 ff.; see also G. F. Stout, *Mind and Matter.*

peculiar unity exhibited by an active tendency "in its development in the direction of its own fulfilment." This kind of unity, in part at least, consists in that which I have endeavoured to define as characteristic of processes initiated by an E' and terminated by an E. This unity certainly varies in degree, and its several degrees are represented by the successive forms assumed in the transition from the initial relatively random form to the final more systematic form of the process.

Moreover, whilst such processes can be defined in a manner which does not entail the presence of mind, it is, I am prepared to believe, highly probable that they occur only where mind is operative. I confess I do not see at all clearly how this can be established, but I am fairly satisfied that the presence of the form in question in any process constitutes the principal criterion on the basis of which we do, in fact, attribute experiences to the lower animals and to persons other than ourselves. One fact to which I attach significance is that both in the final and in the initial forms of the process, when the behaviour in question is our own, we find a curiously detailed correspondence between the features observed in the behaviour itself and certain features in the experience as introspectively cognized. To E there corresponds an object of appetition, and to E' an object of aversion, and in the final form of the process the successive actions constitute an e_1, e_2, e_3 . . . etc., of which it could be said that they are precisely the means which an intelligent being might select in order to obtain what he desired. It is in this sense that we may say that even an instinctive behaviour cycle is carried through *as if* it were the expression of a design. And although the prior history of this cycle shows that it has not in fact been designed, this prior history does encourage us to believe that it is at all stages of its development the expression of (short range) pre-cognition and desire. It shares a similarity of form with various kinds of conative experience less developed than the explicit volitional act.

Let it be granted, then, that some arguments can be adduced in support of the hypothesis that mind is present whenever a chain of activity is observed which assumes a teleological form; what would follow? This would afford an extremely important consideration in any attempt to ascertain the range of incidence of mind in Nature, and would almost certainly commit us to the admission of its operation in many places where biologists, at least, are extremely loth to ascribe it. And, for my own part, I am quite prepared to believe that on this issue Prof. Stout is right.

This admission commits me to a substantial measure of agreement with his thesis, but two substantial differences remain:

(i) I do not find the required criterion present in the behaviour of stretched bows and of springs which are tending to unbend. If the plain man is tempted on the basis of his own motor experiences to ascribe conation to the counter-forces with which he has to deal he is, I think, able to correct this first impression by the patent absence in the behaviour of material things of the most important features of teleological form. The unity of an active tendency, it has been agreed, varies in degree; but the range of variation, I would suggest, is completely covered within the limits provided by the commonly accepted phenomena of life. The limits of life are the limits of teleological form.

(ii) It would follow that the facts with which Prof. Stout is concerned can be invoked in explanation of causal process only in the special case in which a causal sequence assumes the teleological form. It throws no light on causality in general. On the contrary, some simpler notion of causality is already presupposed in the very definition of teleological form. A teleological sequence is a more or less economical arrangement of causes in a manner which secures the realization of an end.

I propose to devote the final section of this paper to a brief discussion of what I take to be the relation between these two types of processes—the merely mechanical and the teleological.

I have already suggested that a causal sequence assumes what may fairly be described as a teleological character whenever a sequence of events occurs which satisfies certain conditions, viz.: (i) that for the sequence in question there is a possible state of affairs, E, such that its introduction at any stage terminates the process; (ii) that phases which promote E are repeated or continued whilst those that are adverse to E are discontinued; (iii) that with repetition the process approximates to a form in which every phase is relevant to the production of E. In this final state the process as a whole has a character which is often (though, I think, very misleadingly) expressed by saying that the end determines the means. All that can properly be meant by this statement is that had the E been other than what it was, the sequence e_1, e_2, e_3, &c., would have been different. This, I think, no one would wish to question.

It will, perhaps, sufficiently elucidate the view I wish to defend if I conclude with two observations as to the relations between mechanical and teleological causal process in the senses in which these terms have been employed.

In the first place, it is obvious that on this view mechanical and teleological causation are not to be conceived as alternative or opposed processes. On the contrary, to assert that a process exhibits teleological causation *entails* that the end in question and each of the intervening phases of the process are mechanically determined. In the contemplation of vital and mental processes there are, then, two complementary types of "explanation." We can "explain" it in teleological terms. These are not, in such a case, opposed explanations, but two distinct senses of the word "explain." Of this, perhaps a crude example may suffice. A train runs regularly from London to Edinburgh. The fact can be explained, and completely explained, in the relevant sense of "explain" by reference to the structure and mode of action of locomotives and the disposition of lines and points on the way. But precisely the same fact is "explained" by the consideration that people frequently wish to travel from one place to the other. Although it is common and, in general, legitimate to express the teleological explanation in terms of conscious desires, it is equally possible and frequently important to express the explanation in behaviouristic terms. The definition of a teleological process here adopted was expressly designed with this intention.

There is, moreover, in principle no overwhelming difficulty in accounting for the fact that "mechanical" sequences admit of organization in teleological form. On this point I suspect that there is no divergence between the opinion here expressed and the doctrines of Prof. Stout. I believe that he also would hold that the mechanist is right in holding that it must be possible to give a "mechanical" account of vital processes and wrong only in supposing that it is not possible and desirable *also* to give a teleological account of these processes.

This leads to my second observation. Although I wish to hold that whenever we can give a teleological explanation of a process we must also be able to give a mechanistic explanation, I do not see any reason to suppose that the converse is true. I admit that it is possible that every mechanical causal sequence is either some part of a larger sequence which is characterized by teleological form or is part of a sequence which in the course of its repetition tends, in the way characteristic of the kind of processes I have considered, to approximate to the final teleological form. Possibly this is part of the doctrine which Prof. Stout wishes to maintain. If so, I cannot see any way in which this belief can be refuted, but, for my own part, I see no reason to suppose that it is true.

Explanation, Mechanism, and Teleology *

C. J. DUCASSE

In a recent article in this Journal (Vol. XXI, No. 25), Dr. E. R. Guthrie considers Purpose and Mechanism as categories of explanation in psychology, his general conclusion being that teleological explanation is not so intrinsically despicable, after all, as it is often thought to be. The present writer is in thorough agreement with that conclusion, but it seems to him that Dr. Guthrie's distinction between mechanism and teleology is much too loose to be satisfactory, and that he classes as explanations many things which have no title to that name. It is obviously highly desirable to define explanation, purposiveness, and explanation in terms of purpose with precision, for otherwise clear and firm conclusions can not possibly be reached. The present paper attempts such definitions briefly.

First, with regard to the logical nature of Explanation. Dr. Guthrie characterizes explanation as the "assigning a fact or an event to a category of some sort." Thus, "the apple falls . . . because every pair of physical objects will, under similar circumstances, approach each other. The dog seeks food because all living creatures do this." And he quite rightly, although I believe with undue resignation, points out that these cases are, logically, exactly parallel to the classical horrible example, according to which the fact that a man who has taken opium, sleeps, is "explained" by saying that men who have taken opium always do. But the correct conclusion to be drawn from this parallelism is, I submit, that since admittedly nothing whatever is explained in the latter case, neither is anything explained at all in the former, and therefore that explanation can not be defined as the "assigning the event to be explained to a class of similar events."

Explanation essentially consists in the offering of a hypothesis of fact, standing to the fact to be explained as case of antecedent to case of consequent of some already known law of connection (laws of bare conjunction statistically obtained, will not do). Thus, the hypothesis that the tree was shaken *does* explain the fact that an apple fell, under the general rule, already experimentally ascertained, that when an apple tree is shaken, ripe apples fall. We may, of course, go on and ask for an explanation of the *other* fact

* Reprinted by kind permission of the author and the editors from *The Journal of Philosophy*, 23, 1926.

that they always fall then. And one can doubtless be given, but it will consist, once more, in the mention of something from which, under some already known law, the fact that apples do fall then, follows. Charles Peirce,[1] with great insight, pointed out something which seems never to have been adequately noticed before, and to have been largely forgotten since, namely that inferences are not of two sorts only, but *of three sorts:* From Rule and Case to Result (Deduction), from Case and Result to Rule (Induction), *and from Rule and Result to Case.* Peirce very unfortunately called this third sort of inference "Hypothesis," while hypothesis in fact means the making of *any sort* of a conjecture. The word which exactly designates this third sort of inference in common usage, from which there is no occasion to depart, is *Diagnosis,* or inference from Circumstantial Evidence. Now, when the Rule under which a diagnosis is made is a law of *connection* (causal or logical), the diagnosis *explains* the observed fact from which it started. But (and Peirce did not perceive this) when the Rule is a law of bare *conjunction,* a merely statistical uniformity, the diagnosis *does not explain.* Thus, from the observation that an animal has cloven hoofs one frames, diagnostically, the hypothesis that it ruminates, under the statistical law that all ruminants have cloven hoofs. But that diagnosis, whether correct or not, *does not* in the least *explain* the cloven hoofs; it *merely predicts them* under the law.

My second point concerns certain cases referred to by Dr. Guthrie as cases of purposiveness, which, it seems to me, have no *a priori* title to that name, e.g., in particular those which he borrows from Haldane—"physiological states of equilibrium whose disturbance causes their own reëstablishment." One can not help wondering why the predictions on the basis of known normal causal sequences mentioned by Dr. Guthrie in the last paragraph on p. 676 are referred to by him as predictions "in terms of purpose." The only excuse for it would seem to be the perfectly gratuitous labeling of the effect an "end result." When the water level in a tank equipped with a ball float is lowered by the withdrawal of water, that disturbance causes the ball to fall and to open the intake pipe, and thus the disturbance itself causes the reëstablishment of the original water level.[2] The process is automatic, but none the less purely mechanical, for automatism is one thing and purposiveness another. And the fact that, in the similar case of the maintenance of the proportion of blood salts to blood volume, we do not know the mechanism, does not warrant the conclusion that purpose is involved, but only the conclusion that we do not know what the explanation is (which the details of the mechanism would constitute). Prediction is one thing, and explanation of the predictability another thing.

---

[1] *Popular Science Monthly,* Aug., 1878, "Deduction, Induction and Hypothesis". *Johns Hopkins Studies in Logic,* "A Theory of Probable Inference".

[2] Stevenson Smith, "Regulation in Behavior", *The Journal of Philosophy,* 11, pp. 320–326.

Moreover, it is not strictly correct to say, as Haldane apparently does, that the maintenance of the proportion is predictable. What can be said is, that either somehow the proportion will be maintained, or else the animal will sicken or die—which, as Dr. Guthrie notes, many have done. Of course, that an animal is *now* healthy, enables us to infer (predict) that, in spite of the ingestion of water, the proportion was somehow maintained— also, obviously, that somehow he escaped his enemies, etc.—but *not* that these various necessary conditions of life and health were provided by some intelligence *purposing* that it should live and be healthy. Again, that the soldiers in a hospital ward were all wounded in "non-vital organs" was not, as a pious man thought, evidence of the purpose and mercy of God— unless perhaps none of the soldiers shot were to be found in the graveyard! The phenomenon of maintenance of an equilibrium, whether physical or physiological, is, like every other phenomenon, dependent upon the joint presence of various conditions, but is not on that account any more purposive than the rest. If we label it an "end" or "end result," rather than an "effect," it is only because *we* then *import* into it our own interest in it and our desire that it occur, but not because we *find* a purpose objectively and intrinsically present in it as a necessary part of its description. In all cases of this sort, what we have as the law under which we infer, is a law of the type "Only if X, Y," instead of one of the type "If X, Y," i.e., a law informing us of that in the *absence* of which Y *does not* occur, instead of one informing us of that in the *presence* of which Y *does* occur. And obviously, when the law is of the "Only if X, Y" type, prediction is from the truth of the consequent to that of the antecedent, or from the falsity of the antecedent to that of the consequent.

But, in such cases, how about *explanation?* It is here, truly, that the methodological Devil puts forth his strongest and most subtle temptation, against which nothing but the most careful analysis will avail. The situation is this: Explanation, as we have seen, consists in the supposition of something that would have been *sufficient to* the existence of the observed fact under a given known law. This being so, *no explanation is possible under a law of the "Only if X, Y" type* (e.g., Only if moisture is present will a plant live); for since the observed fact is here X (e.g., moisture is present), the factuality of X could under this type of law be explained, if at all, only by the hypothesis of the factuality of Y (e.g., that the plant will live). But the relation of Y to X under a law of this type is *not* "sufficient to," but the very different one of *"contingent upon."* Therefore the hypothesis that Y will be a fact cannot explain the factuality of X. How, indeed, could a fact that has not yet occurred explain, i.e., be a possible cause of, a fact that has already occurred? And it is here that the teleological temptation comes in: Obviously, whispers the Devil, only if an intelligence aware of the contingency of the second upon the first, and desiring the occurrence of the second, is thereby moved to bring about the first!

That is, in truth, a hypothesis explanatory of the occurrence of X, and it is a teleological one. And I do not mean to say that such an explanation is not, in some cases, a perfectly good and proper one and the only correct one. My only concern is to point out that *it is even then not what was asked for*, i.e., it is not an explanation of the occurrence of X under the law that "Only if X occurs, does Y occur." It is an explanation of X under *another* law, viz., the law that "If an agent believes that Y is contingent upon X and desires Y, then that agent is likely to do X"; and this is still a law of the "If" type, which is the only type under which explanations are possible. It is also, of course, the only sort of explanation of X in which the dependence of Y on X enters, although it enters in it *not as something true*, but only *as something believed*. But then we may well ask, if all that is wanted is an explanation of X, why insist on dragging Y into it at any cost? Why not, in the absence of evidence of the existence of an agent and his purpose, frame an explanation of X under some other law known, e.g., under the law that "If W, X" by the hypothesis that W occurred? The teleological explanation is certainly not forced on us *a priori* by the situation. It must compete with possible mechanical explanations, e.g., an evolutionary one, and the choice between them is to be made on precisely the usual grounds of choice between rival explanations, viz., relative antecedent probability, relative simplicity, etc.

The analysis of the distinction between purpose and mechanism has already been adumbrated in the above. To be able properly to speak of an act (or event) as purposive, it is neither necessary nor sufficient that the act be such that unless it occurs some specified result will not occur. What is essential, on the other hand, is that the following elements be present, or be supposed, by the speaker, to be present:

1. *Belief* by the performer of the act in a law (of either type), e.g., that If X occurs, Y occurs.

2. *Desire* by the performer that Y shall occur.

3. *Causation by that desire and that belief jointly*, of the performance of X.

It follows from this definition of purposiveness that only the acts of entities capable of belief and desire, are capable of being purposive, and therefore that the occurrences of "inanimate nature" can not be spoken of as purposive without contradiction, unless belief and desire be injected into nature, e.g., as often has been done, by viewing its occurrences as acts of God. And the disrepute into which teleological explanations have fallen is doubtless due to their having been so frequently thus put forth in cases where the existence of the agent appealed to and of his beliefs and desires, was not already known, but invented outright and purely *ad hoc*,—this obviously constituting explanation of the *ignotum, per ignotius*. But when antecedent evidence for their existence is present (e.g., when the hypothetical agent is a human being), a teleological explanation is methodologically quite respectable, although, like any other, it may in a given case not happen to be the correct one.

It is interesting and quite important to note that it makes no essential difference to the definition of a purposive act given above, whether the words "belief" and "desire" which occur in it, be interpreted in terms of consciousness, or purely in terms of neurons and nerve currents. The essential point is, that unless it be *true* that belief and desire (no matter in what terms described), are present, there is no purposiveness. If belief and desire are given a description in terms of purely neural mechanisms, then what we have to say is that unless *just these particular types of neural mechanisms* are involved, the act performed can not be spoken of as purposive, while if they are involved it must be so spoken of. And there is usually little dispute between the behaviorists and their opponents as to whether, in any given case, belief and desire *are* present; the dispute is as to how they shall be described. By way of illustration, we may take two examples used by Dr. Stevenson Smith (*loc. cit.*, p. 324) as cases of what he calls "positive regulation." When a squirrel stores away food, I take it that neither behaviorists nor their opponents would assert that the squirrel *believes* that if he stores nuts he will not starve next winter, nor that he, at the time, *desires* not to starve next winter. Then, if that is not asserted, the squirrel's act may be "positive regulation," but it is *not a purposive act*. On the other hand, when a prospector digs for gold, behaviorists and their opponents alike would grant that he *believes* that if he digs he will probably find gold, and that he *desires* to find some. If both these things are granted, then the prospector's act may be "positive regulation," but *it is a purposive act* all the same.

So much for the definition of purposive acts. Now an *explanation* of a fact, e.g., the fall of an apple, can be said to be teleological, or in terms of purpose, when the hypothetical cause offered as explanation (e.g., that a boy shook the tree) is regarded not as a "blind" occurrence, but as a "purposive" act, i.e., as being the *effect* in an agent of his *desire* for the fact (the fall of the apple) and of his *belief* that the act (shaking the tree) would cause the fact. Obviously that is sometimes the exact history of the occurrence of the fall of an apple, and in every such case none but a teleological explanation will be correct, and therefore no other can ever replace it. This remains so, as already stated, even if "belief" and "desire" are themselves capable of being described as special kinds of mechanisms. Mechanism and teleology are therefore not logically incompatible.

VIII

PROBLEMS OF THEORETICAL ETHICS

Some of the Main Problems of Ethics *

C. D. BROAD

Ethics, in the sense in which that word is used by philosophers, may be described as the theoretical treatment of moral phenomena. I use the phrase "moral phenomena" to cover all those facts and only those in describing which we have to use such words as "ought," "right and wrong," "good and evil," or any others which are merely verbal translations of these.

Moral phenomena fall into three distinct, though closely interconnected groups, viz., Moral Judgment, Moral Emotion, and Moral Volition. Suppose that I know or believe that I *ought* to keep a promise, though it might be more convenient to break it; that it is *wrong* to inflict useless pain on an innocent person, though it might be pleasant to score off him in public; that love is a *good* emotion and jealousy an *evil* one; and so on. These bits of knowledge or belief are instances of Moral Judgments. Suppose that I believe myself to have behaved wrongly on a certain occasion and that I feel *remorse* or *self-disapproval*, as distinct from mere fear of punishment or embarrassment at being found out, on that account. These feelings will be instances of Moral Emotion. Suppose, finally, that I have to decide between two alternative courses of action, one of which I believe to be *right*, and the other of which is pleasanter in itself or more attractive in its probable consequences. In so far as I am influenced in my decision by the thought that one of them is *right* and that the others would be wrong, and by the desire to do what is right as such, this is an instance of Moral Volition.

ANALYSIS OF MORAL JUDGMENTS

The first and most fundamental problem of Ethics is about the nature of Moral Judgments and the concepts "ought," "right," "good," etc., which are the most characteristic elements in them. Suppose I assert, deliberately and reflectively and not merely talking like a parrot, that *A* on a certain occasion ought not to have broken a promise which he had made to *B*. Then, *prima facie*, the following things seem to be true: (1) That in uttering this sentence, which I will call a "moral sentence in the indicative mood," I am asserting an *opinion* (correct or incorrect) which I hold, and am not merely expressing an emotion which I feel. (2) That the opinion which I

* Reprinted by kind permission of the author and the editors from *Philosophy*, 21, 1946.

am asserting is not merely about my own feelings or wishes or beliefs. In saying that *A* ought to have kept his promise to *B*, I seem to be asserting about *A* and *B* and their relationship something which is no more about me and my attitude towards them than if I had asserted that *A* is *B's* second cousin. (3) That what I assert about *A's* breach of his promise to *B*, viz., that it was *wrong* and *ought not* to have happened, is something unique and peculiar, though perfectly familiar and intelligible to everyone. It cannot be expressed by any form of words which does not contain the words "right" or "ought" or some others which are obviously mere verbal translations of them.

Now all these *prima facie* appearances have been questioned on more or less plausible grounds by competent moral philosophers, and this has led to some of the most fundamental discussions in Ethics. I will now say something of the various alternative views which have been held on these points.

1. *The Interjectional Analysis.* The most radically sceptical view is that what appear to be moral judgments are not really *judgments*, i.e., assertions of knowledge or opinion, at all; but are merely expressions of a certain kind of *emotion*. It is alleged that, when a person utters such a sentence as, "This is wrong," or "That is evil," he is really only expressing a certain kind of anti-emotion towards this or that. It is true that he uses a form of sentence which inevitably suggests that he is asserting an opinion and not merely expressing an emotion. For the sentence is of the same grammatical form as if he had said "This is triangular," which is certainly an assertion of opinion. But, it is alleged, the grammatical form is misleading in the case of moral sentences in the indicative.

I propose to call this theory the *Interjectional Analysis*. On this view there are no moral judgments; there are only what might be called "ostensible moral judgments." Moral sentences in the indicative mood are really interjections, like "Hurrah!" or "Blast!", masquerading as assertions of opinion.

2. *The Autobiographical Analysis.* Suppose we reject the Interjectional Analysis. Suppose we hold that, when a person utters a moral sentence in the indicative, he really is making a moral judgment. Then the next most sceptical view is that what he is asserting is simply that he feels a certain kind of emotion, *pro* or *anti*, towards the subject which he pronounces to be right or wrong, good or evil. I shall call this the *Autobiographical Analysis.*

It must be noticed that it could take two different forms. (*a*) It might be held that, when I judge that so-and-so is right, what I am asserting is simply that I here and now am feeling towards so-and-so a certain kind of pro-emotion. If so, my judgment is analogous to "This butter tastes nice" uttered by a person while eating that butter. (*b*) It might be held that what I am asserting is that I have a *disposition* to feel this kind of pro-emotion towards such persons or acts or situations as so-and-so. If so, my judgment is analogous to "I like butter." A person might truly say that he likes butter even if, on the occasion when he said so, he found the taste of butter repulsive because, e.g., he was feeling bilious. I shall call these two forms of the Autobiographical Analysis respectively the *Occurrent* and the *Dispositional* form.

It might be thought that there is no difference between the Interjectional Analysis and the Occurrent Form of the Autobiographical Analysis. This would be a mistake. There is a difference between merely expressing an emotion by means of an exclamation, e.g., ejaculating "Damn!" when one is annoyed at losing one's collar-stud, and asserting that one is feeling such and such an emotion towards such and such an object, e.g., saying, "I am annoyed at finding that I have lost my collar-stud." An animal, e.g., can express an emotion of anger by snarling, but it cannot make the judgment which a man would express by saying, "I am angry with so-and-so." On the Interjectional Analysis to utter a moral sentence in the indicative is like expressing a feeling of annoyance with so-and-so by exclaiming, "Damn you!"; on the Occurrent Form of the Autobiographical Analysis it is like stating that one is feeling annoyed with so-and-so.

3. *The Statistical Analysis.* Suppose next that both forms of the Autobiographical Analysis are rejected also. It is still possible to suggest an analysis in terms of pro-emotion and anti-emotion. The suggestion would be that, when I judge that so-and-so is right, what I am asserting is that all or most men, or all or most members of some more restricted class, e.g., Englishmen or Etonians, have a disposition to feel a certain kind of pro-emotion towards persons or acts or situations like so-and-so. On this view moral judgments may be compared to such a judgment as "Jazz music is popular." This might be truly asserted by a person even if he were himself indifferent to jazz music or heartily disliked it. I shall call this the *Statistical Analysis.*

Before going further I want to make two remarks about the three alternative kinds of analysis which I have been describing. (*a*) All three of them are stated in terms of certain emotions which a person may feel towards himself or towards another person or towards an action or a relationship. They may therefore all be described as *Emotional-Reaction Theories.* (*b*) The Interjectional Analysis and the two forms of Autobiographical Analysis agree with each other and differ from the Statistical Analysis in the following respect. The former may be described as *intra-subjective.* For, according to them, when a person utters a moral sentence in the indicative, what he is doing is either to express an emotion which *he* is feeling or to make an assertion to the effect that *he* is feeling a certain emotion or has a disposition to feel it. The Statistical Analysis, on the other hand, may be described as *trans-subjective.* For, according to it, when a person utters such a sentence he is asserting something about a whole class of persons which may or may not happen to include himself.

4. *The Objective Analysis.* Finally, let us suppose that all forms of Emotional Reaction Theory are rejected. Then we must hold that a person who makes a moral judgment is ascribing to its subject a certain property which would belong to it even if no one had ever contemplated it or felt any kind of emotion towards it. On this view *A's* judgment that *B's* act of telling a lie on a certain occasion was wrong is comparable, in this respect at any rate, to a person's judgment that the weather in Cambridge on a certain day was rainy. He may indeed have been *influenced* by his emotions to make this assertion; but what he asserts is not *about* the emotions of himself or anyone else towards the weather in Cambridge on that day. Let us call this the *Objective Analysis* of moral judgments.

NATURALISTIC V. NON-NATURALISTIC THEORIES

The question of analysis brings us to another question which is closely connected with it. Are moral predicates, such as *right, ought* and *good*, unique and peculiar; or can they be completely analysed and defined in terms of non-moral predicates? Theories which answer this question in the affirmative are called *naturalistic;* those which answer it in the negative are called *non-naturalistic.* The following would be typical examples of naturalistic theories. "*Better* conduct means conduct that comes later in the course of evolution and is more complex and unified than earlier conduct of the same kind." "*Right* action means action which tends to promote the stability and increase the complexity of society." "To say that a person *ought* to do so-and-so means that, if he does not, he will be punished either in this life by his fellow-men or in the next by God."

It should be noticed that, if any form of the Emotional Reaction analysis be true, the question is answered automatically in favour of naturalism. Ethics becomes a branch of psychology. Nevertheless, there would remain a somewhat similar question even for those theories. It would take the following form. "Is the emotion which we express, or assert ourselves to feel or to have a disposition to feel, or which we assert that most members of a certain class have a disposition to feel, when we utter a moral sentence in the indicative an emotion of a quite unique kind? Or is it just a combination of emotions, e.g. fear, love, hope, etc., each of which can occur in non-moral contexts?"

If the Objective Analysis be correct, the question of Naturalism *v.* Non-naturalism remains quite open, and special arguments are needed to answer it.

The importance of the question is this. If non-naturalism be true, Ethics is an autonomous science with an irreducibly peculiar subject-matter, though it will still have very intimate connexions with certain other sciences, such as psychology, sociology, etc. But, if Naturalism be true, Ethics is not an autonomous science; it is a department or an application of one or more of the natural or the historical sciences. Now the reduction of a plurality to a unity is a source of intellectual satisfaction, and therefore philosophers have a strong motive for trying to produce a workable naturalistic theory.

RIGHT-MAKING AND GOOD-MAKING CHARACTERISTICS

We pass now to another very important problem. It may be introduced as follows. If a person says of anything that it is right or that it is wrong, it is always sensible to ask, "Why? What *makes* it right or *makes* it wrong, as the case may be?" The sort of answers that one expects to such questions are: "Because it will relieve pain," "Because it is a breach of promise," and so on. Similar remarks apply, *mutatis mutandis*, to good and evil. If anything is said to be good or to be evil, it is always sensible to ask what makes it so. The sort of answers which one expects to get are: "Because it is an act of courage," "Because it is a feeling of pleasure at another man's misfortune," and so on.

We may generalize this as follows. Moral characteristics are always dependent upon certain other characteristics which can be described in purely neutral non-moral terms. Let us call those non-moral characteristics whose presence in anything confers rightness or wrongness on it *right-making* and *wrong-making* characteristics. And let us define *good-making* and *bad-making* characteristics in a similar way.

We will begin with right-making and wrong-making characteristics. On the face of it there is a whole mass of these. E.g., being a breach of promise, being a deliberately misleading answer to a question, being an intentional infliction of needless pain, and dozens more, are characteristics which may plausibly be said to make an act wrong.

Now an extremely important question is whether we can discover any kind of systematic unity among all these various right-making and wrong-making characteristics. Can we reduce them to a few fundamental ones? Can we perhaps reduce them all to a single fundamental one? Moral philosophers have naturally tried their hardest to do this, since it would plainly be tidier and more satisfactory to the intellect if it could be done.

When we reflect on this problem we notice the following fact. At first one is inclined to say that *every* lie is as such wrong, that *every* breach of promise is as such wrong, and so on. But one soon finds that there are cases where this is not plausible; e.g., is it certain that a lie told to an invalid or a breach of promise to a child is wrong when the results of telling the truth or keeping the promise would be extremely bad for him? Again, there are cases where any possible action will, e.g., be either a lie or a breach of promise. Suppose, e.g., that *A* has told me a secret on my promise not to reveal it, and that *B* afterwards asks me a question which I can neither answer truly nor refuse to answer at all without revealing the secret. Then whatever I may do in response to *B's* question will be either a breach of my promise to *A* or a lie told to *B*. But we are not prepared to say that whatever I do in such a situation will be wrong. On the contrary, we should hold that in some cases it would be my duty to tell the truth to *B* and thus break my promise to *A* whilst in others it would be my duty to keep my promise to *A* and thus deceive *B*.

For such reasons it is necessary to modify our notion of right-*making* and wrong-*making* characteristics and to talk instead of right-*tending* and wrong-*tending* characteristics. An intentionally deceptive answer to a question *tends* as such to be wrong, and so too does a breach of promise. If an act were nothing but an answer to a question, it would be right if true and wrong if false. If an act were nothing but the keeping or the breaking of a promise, it would be right if it were the former and wrong if it were the latter. But, if an act is *both* a true answer to a question and a breach of a promise, we can say only that it *tends* to be right in the former respect and *tends* to be wrong in the latter. The right act in such circumstances will be the one that makes the best compromise between the various moral claims on the agent, after allowing due weight to the relative urgency of each claim. We might compare the claims which arise from various right-tending and wrong-tending characteristics to forces of various magnitudes and directions acting on a body at the same time. And we might compare what I will call the *resultantly right course of action* to the course which a body would pursue under the joint action of such forces. Looking at the situation from the point of view of the agent, we can say that each right-tending and wrong-tending characteristic imposes on him a *component obligation* of a certain degree of urgency; and that his *resultant obligation* is to make the best compromise that he can between his various component obligations.

When we consider the various right-tending and wrong-tending characteristics we find that they can be divided into two great groups, which I will call *teleological* and ostensibly *non-teleological*.

1. One characteristic which tends to make an act right is that it will produce at least as good consequences as any alternative open to the agent in the circumstances. And one which tends to make it wrong is that it will produce less good or more evil consequences than some other act open to the agent. We can sum this up by saying that the property of being *optimific* is a very important right-tending characteristic. I call it *teleological* because it refers to the goodness of the ends or consequences which the act brings about.

2. Now there are also many characteristics which are certainly right-tending or wrong-tending but are not *prima facie* reducible to the property of being optimific. No doubt truth-telling and promise-keeping do in the end and on the whole lead to better consequences than lying and breach of promise. But most people do not feel that this is the reason why truth-telling and promise-keeping tend to be right. They feel that the mere fact of being asked a question or having made a promise imposes on one an urgent component obligation to answer truly or to perform what one has

promised, quite independently of whether the consequences will be good or bad. I therefore call these right-tending and wrong-tending characteristics *ostensibly non-teleological*.

We have already seen that various ostensibly non-teleological right-making characteristics may lead to conflicting component obligations. It is also true that the ostensibly non-teleological obligation to tell the truth, e.g., may conflict with the teleological obligation to produce as much good and as little evil as possible. Consider, e.g., the following as a case. A commanding officer knows that one of his subordinates, who has been killed, has displayed disgraceful cowardice. No one else knows this or will ever do so unless the officer divulges it. The dead man's mother asks the officer leading questions about the circumstances of her son's death. If he tells the truth the mother will be made miserable for life and no one will be a penny the better. If he tells a suitable lie the mother will be a penny better. If he tells a suitable lie the mother will retain her ideals and be made happy and no one will be a penny the worse. Here there seems to be a plain conflict between the teleological obligation to produce as much good and as little evil as possible and the ostensibly non-teleological obligation to answer questions truly.

Ostensibly non-teleological obligations can be subdivided into two groups, which I will call *non-distributive* and *distributive*. Truth-telling is an example of the former. Distributive obligations are concerned with the right distribution of benefits and disadvantages. Suppose that I am the sole executor and trustee under the will of a certain rich man. He has made two wills. In the first he has distributed his property more or less equally among a number of needy and deserving persons and institutions. In the second he has left the whole of it to a worthless rich relative. I am the only person now alive who knows that the second will has been made, and I could safely destroy it and carry out the provisions of the first. It is obvious that by doing this I should produce more good and less evil than by divulging the second will. Nevertheless I am under an extremely urgent ostensibly non-teleological obligation to distribute the property in accordance with the testator's second will, whilst my purely teleological obligation would be to distribute it in accordance with the first.

Now much the most important attempt which has been made to reduce all the many and various right-tending characteristics to a single one is the theory called *Utilitarianism*. According to this one's only ultimate obligation is teleological; the only ultimate reason why an act is right is that it is optimific, and the only ultimate reason why any act is wrong is that it would produce less good or more evil consequences than some other act open to the agent in the circumstances. All ostensibly non-teleological obligations, whether distributive or non-distributive, are secondary and derivative from the one teleological obligation to act optimifically. The only reason why there is a component obligation to keep promises, to answer questions truly, and so on, is that on the whole such action will secure the best consequences in frequently recurring kinds of situation, such as having made a promise, being asked a question, etc. Suppose that a situation should occur in which, when all the remote, secondary, and collateral consequences as well as the immediate ones have been taken into account, the result of telling a lie or breaking a promise would be better than that of telling the truth or keeping the promise. Then it will be right to lie or to break one's promise, and wrong to tell the truth or keep faith.

It is plain that, if Utilitarianism can be made to cover the facts without distorting them, it has several advantages. (1) It gives us the intellectual satisfaction of reducing a litter of disconnected grounds of obligation to a single one. (2) To many people it does seem difficult to believe on reflexion that it can *ever* be right to do what will have worse consequences when one could have done something else which would have better consequences. (3) Utilitarianism gives a plausible explanation for the various degrees of urgency of the various ostensibly non-teleological component obligations; and it provides, in theory at any rate, a rule for compounding such obligations when several of them co-exist and conflict with each other.

I will now say something about *good*-tending and *bad*-tending characteristics. The general principles are the same as in the case of right-tending and wrong-tending ones. It is plain that *prima facie* there are a number of different characteristics which tend to make a person or an experience or an action good, and a number which tend to make it bad. Now several of these may be present together in a single subject; and the question whether it is resultantly good or resultantly bad, and, if so, to what degree, will depend on the nature and the proportion of its various good-tending and bad-tending characteristics.

Here again there is naturally a strong desire among philosophers to try to reduce the litter of various good-tending characteristics to a single good-making one. The best known effort in this direction is the theory known as *Ethical Hedonism*. This theory involves the following propositions. (1) Nothing is either good or bad in the primary sense except actual experiences. (2) The only characteristic of an experience which makes it good is its pleasantness, and the only one which makes it bad is its unpleasantness. (3) The degree of goodness of a pleasant experience depends jointly on its duration and on the degree of its pleasantness. According to this theory anything other than an experience which is called "good" is so called in a secondary and derivative sense, viz. in so far as it contributes or tends to contribute to the occurrence of pleasant experiences and the non-occurrence of unpleasant ones.

If both Utilitarianism and Ethical Hedonism could be accepted, we should have introduced the greatest possible unity into the region of moral phenomena. Unfortunately each of them seems to be too simple to cover the facts without distorting them.

Before leaving this part of the subject I will make two remarks connecting it with the topic of Analysis which I discussed earlier.

1. Suppose that a person has persuaded himself that there is one and only one right-making characteristic, e.g., that of being optimific, or one and only one good-making characteristic, e.g., pleasantness. Then he is very liable to make the following mistake. He is apt to think that he has proved that "right" *means* optimific or that "good" *means* pleasant, i.e., that he has provided an analysis of rightness or of goodness, as the case may be. All that he has really shown in the first case, e.g., is that, if the words "right" and "optimific" are names of two different characteristics, then these two mutually involve each other. That is quite different from showing that the two words are really names for the same characteristic, and that what is meant by "optimific" is the analysis of what is meant by "right." The distinction can be made quite clear by a simple non-ethical example. To be an equilateral triangle means to be a plane figure bounded by three equal straight lines. To be an equiangular triangle means to be a plane figure with three angles, all of which are equal. Evidently these are two different characteristics. But they mutually involve each other; for any figure which has either property necessarily has both. It seems not unlikely that many people who have thought that they have given a naturalistic analysis of moral judgments have made this mistake; and that really they have done no more than to produce reasons for thinking that there is one and only one right-making or good-making characteristic, and have then proceeded to identify rightness or goodness with this.

2. In discussing right-tending and good-tending characteristics I have spoken in terms of the Objective Analysis of moral judgments. It is important to notice that the same problem exists in a slightly modified form if we accept the Emotional-Reaction Analysis. In that case what we have called a "right-tending" or a "good-tending" characteristic will be one which tends to call forth the peculiar emotion in its *pro*-form. What we have called "conflicts of component obligations" will depend on the fact that the same act may have features which call forth the *pro*-emotion and others which call forth the *anti*-emotion. What we have called "resultant obligation" will be connected with one's total emotional reaction to an object which has some features that tend to call forth the *pro*-emotion and others which tend to call forth the *anti*-emotion.

INTENTION AND RIGHTNESS

When a person performs a deliberate action he does so in view of his knowledge and beliefs about the present situation and with certain expectations about the consequences which will ensue. These two factors are closely connected; for his expectations about the consequences are in part determined by his knowledge or beliefs about the present situation. I shall say that an act is *intentional* in respect of (1) all those features and only those which the agent knows or believes to be present in the initial situation, and (2) all those consequences and only those which he expects to follow. Now a person's information on both these matters will always be incomplete and it may be in part mistaken. No man can foresee the very remote consequences of an action; and anyone may be mistaken about some of its immediate consequences, either through miscalculation or through inadequate or inaccurate information about present circumstances. Suppose, e.g., that a person receives a letter purporting to come from his old nurse and that he is moved to send her a postal money-order in the belief that she is in want and with the expectation that it will enable her to buy comforts. It may be that in fact the nurse has died, that the letter has been written in her name by a dishonest relative, and that the money will be spent by him on drink. What this man intended to do was to bring relief to his old nurse; what he in fact did was to enable a dishonest stranger to get drunk.

Now, if we consider the agent's intention in this example, we are inclined to say that he acted rightly. But, if we consider the actual facts of the situation and the consequences, we are inclined to say that he acted wrongly and that the right action would have been to refuse to send money and to have reported the matter to the police. Thus we are faced with the problem of the relation between intention and rightness or wrongness.

This question may be approached in the following way. Any act which can be called "right" or "wrong" can be viewed from two standpoints, viz., that of the agent who does it and that of the patient who is affected by it. In general these will be different persons, though there are special cases in which the agent and the patient are the same person at an earlier and a later stage of his life. Now in considering whether an act is right or wrong we must view it, so to speak, from both ends, i.e., in relation to the patient and in relation to the agent. In relation to the patient an act is right if and only if it fulfils his claims on the agent, or, as we say, "gives the patient his rights in the matter concerned." From this standpoint the agent's intention is irrelevant. In relation to the agent an act is right if and only if it is done with the intention of fulfilling the patient's claim and giving him his rights in the matter. From this standpoint anything in the actual consequences which is outside or contrary to the agent's intention is irrelevant.

I propose to call any act which in fact fulfils the claims of the patient upon the agent *materially right*, regardless of whether the agent intended it to have this consequence or not. I propose to call any act which was intended by the agent to bring about the fulfilment of the patient's claims *formally right*, regardless of whether it does in fact have that result or not. A *perfectly right* act in a given situation would be one that was both formally and materially right. It would be an act which was intended by the agent to give to the patient his rights and which did in fact do so. Owing to incomplete or incorrect information on the part of the agent, or to defects in his powers of inference, it may happen that an act which is formally right is materially wrong, or that one which is formally indifferent or wrong is materially right. It should be noticed that the notion of material rightness is, in a certain sense, more fundamental than that of formal rightness. For what is formally right for the agent to do is to try to secure to the patient what is materially right for him to have done to him.

There remains, however, a further serious complication to be considered. So far I have supposed that the agent makes no *ethical* mistakes. I have supposed only that he may have incomplete or inaccurate information about *matters of fact* and may make mistaken inferences on such matters from his information. I have assumed that he knows what ought to happen to the patient if his factual information were adequate and accurate. But of course the agent *may* be ignorant or mistaken about *ethical* matters too.

Suppose, e.g., that a person is brought up in a community in which it is held to be a duty to carry on a family vendetta, and that he accepts that opinion. Let us assume, for the sake of argument, that it is mistaken, and that it is wrong to kill a member of another family simply because one of his ancestors killed one of one's own family. Suppose that this person is in a situation in which he can either kill a certain member of the family or let him escape. Whichever alternative he chooses we are inclined to say that he acts wrongly. If he kills the patient, he intentionally does to him what he believes ought to be done to him, but this is in fact what ought not to be done to him. If he lets the patient escape, he intentionally does to him what he believes ought not to be done to him, but this is in fact what ought to be done to him.

It is plain that we are here concerned with yet another sense of "right" and "wrong". I propose to call it *subjective* rightness and wrongness. An act is subjectively right if and only if the effects which the agent expected it to have on the patient are those which he believed that the patient is entitled to have produced in him.

The relations between the various senses of "right" which I have distinguished may be summarized as follows. (1) A person could be sure of doing a *perfectly right* act only if both his relevant factual and his relevant ethical beliefs were complete and correct and if he had made no mistakes in his inferences. It is therefore plain that, if a person ever does a perfectly right act, it is largely a matter of luck that he does so. (2) A person could be sure of doing a *formally right* act, even if his factual information were incomplete or inaccurate and he made mistakes in his inferences, provided that the effects which he *thinks* his act would have upon the patient are such as the latter *really would* be entitled to if his nature and situation were as the agent *believes* them to be. Therefore when an agent's relevant ethical information is incomplete or incorrect it is a matter of luck if he performs a formally right act. (3) A person could be sure of doing a *subjectively right* act, no matter how inadequate or inaccurate his factual and his ethical beliefs might be or how mistaken he may be in his inferences provided only that the effects which he *thinks* his act will have on the patient are such as he *thinks* that the latter would be entitled to if his nature and situation were as the agent *believes* them to be. It is therefore plain that a person who is ignorant, stupid, and misinformed about facts, who is incapable of drawing reasonable inferences, and who is insensitive or crazy in his opinions about what is materially right and wrong, may perform acts that are subjectively right. So it is not surprising that such acts may inflict the most terrible wrongs on those whom they affect.

The problems which we have been discussing arise because we fail to distinguish these three senses of "right" and "wrong," and use these words in a vague way to include them all, sometimes having one meaning predominantly before our minds and sometimes another.

MOTIVES AND THEIR ETHICAL FUNCTION

Among the characteristics which an agent believes an action to have, and among the consequences which he expects to follow from it, some will attract him towards doing it, some will repel him from doing it, and others will leave him indifferent. Suppose, e.g., that a person contemplates throwing a bomb at a ruler in a public procession. He may expect that the effects will include the death of the ruler, the death or injury of a number of innocent bystanders, and the breakage of a number of windows in the neighbourhood. The first part of the expected consequences may attract him, the second may repel him, and the third may leave him indifferent. A person's total motive *in* doing a certain action consists of all that he believes about the action itself and all that he expects about its consequences, which either attracts him towards or repels him from doing it. The former constitutes his total motive *for* doing it, and the latter his total motive *against* doing it. If, in fact, he does it, he does it *because of* his motives for doing it and *in spite of* his motives against doing it. Suppose, e.g., that the anarchist in my example is in general a humane man and that he decides to throw the bomb at the ruler. Then his motive for doing so is the attractive belief that it will kill the ruler; his motive agaisnt doing so is the repellent belief that it will kill or injure innocent bystanders; and he acts because of the former and in spite of the latter motive.

It is plain that there are two aspects to any motive, viz., a cognitive and a conative-emotional aspect. The cognitive aspect of a motive is the fact that it is a *belief* about the nature of the action or an *expectation* about its consequences. The conative aspect is the fact that the agent has a certain disposition to be *attracted or repelled* which is excited by this belief.

When we know what was a person's intention in doing an action and what consequences in fact followed from it, we are in a position to judge whether it was subjectively right, or formally right, or perfectly right, without needing to know anything about his motives in doing the action. But it is quite obvious that a man's motives in doing an action have a very important bearing on *some* kind of moral judgment which we make either on the agent or on the action. This fact is indicated in ordinary speech by such phrases as, "He did the right thing from the wrong motive."

Suppose, e.g., that a man performs an act which is intended to secure the just punishment of a criminal. He will forsee that the criminal will suffer directly and his family and friends indirectly, so this must be included as part of his intention. Now it may be that the belief that the law will be vindicated, that other men will be deterred from committing similar crimes, and that the criminal may be reformed, is an attracting one; that the belief that the criminal and his family will suffer is a repelling one; and that the agent acts because of the former and in spite of the latter. If so, we should be inclined to say, not only that his action was right, but also that his motives in doing it were good. But it may be that the belief that the law would be vindicated, other men deterred, and the criminal perhaps reformed, exercised no attraction on the agent. He had, perhaps, had a quarrel with the criminal or was jealous of him; and what attracted him was his belief that the criminal and his family would suffer. If so, the action would still be right in any of the senses which we have considered, but we should certainly say that the agent's motive in doing it was bad.

I have no doubt that the words "right" and "wrong" have, in addition to the ambiguities which we have already cleared up, the further ambiguity that they are sometimes used to include a reference to this agent's motives and sometimes used without such a reference. I think that it is on the whole more convenient explicitly to exclude reference to motives from our description of right and wrong action. One important reason for drawing the line at this point is the following. A person can choose which of several alternative possible actions he will do. But he cannot, in the same sense, choose which of several alternative motives shall attract him towards or repel him from doing a certain action. Now the predicates "right" and "wrong" are commonly understood to be confined to that which is directly dependent on a person's volition, in the sense in which his actions are so and his motives in acting are not.

SPECIFICALLY MORAL MOTIVATION AND EMOTION

It seems, *prima facie*, that human beings have a great many different desires, and that these cannot all be reduced to a single head. Naturally attempts have been made to do this. The most celebrated of them is the theory called *Psychological Hedonism*. This asserts that the only ultimate objects of desire for any person are to get and to prolong pleasant experiences and to avoid and cut short unpleasant ones. It is now generally admitted by competent authorities that this theory cannot be maintained, and that such plausibility as it has depends upon certain verbal ambiguities.

Now, *prima facie*, there appears to be among our other desires and aversions one which is specifically moral. It seems that, if one believes that a certain course of action would be *right*, that belief stirs a certain conative disposition in one and is a motive for doing it. If, on the other hand, one believes that an action would be *wrong*, that belief stirs the same conative disposition and is a motive against doing it. These desires and aversions are often opposed to very strong non-moral desires and aversions, and they feel very peculiar in comparison with the latter whether they happen to oppose them or to reinforce them. For this reason they are commonly marked out by the name *Feelings of Obligation*, and some philosophers have thought it inappropriate to classify them as desires and aversions. For my part I see no objection to classifying them in this way, provided that one does not lose sight of their peculiarities. Therefore I propose to describe this peculiar kind of desire and aversion as the *Desire to do what is Right as such*.

Now the following questions arise at this point. (1) Is there really a desire to do what is right as such, or is the opinion that there is mistaken? Is it the case that, whenever a person thinks that he is attracted towards a course of action by the belief that it would be right or repelled from it by the belief that it would be wrong, he is really being attracted or repelled, *not* by these beliefs, but by beliefs about certain *non-moral* features of the act or of its consequences? (2) Supposing that there is a desire to do what is right as such, is it ever *sufficient* to determine one's actions, or does it always need to be supported by some non-moral motive, such as desire for praise or fear of punishment? (3) Supposing that this desire exists and is sufficient to determine one's action *in the absence* of opposing motives, is it ever sufficient by itself to *overcome* opposing motives when they are present? Or must it in such cases always be reinforced by some non-moral motive? (4) Supposing that Question 3 is answered in the affirmative, is there any sense, and if so what, in which we can say that the desire to do what is right as such *always could have* overcome *all* opposing motives, even when it did not in fact do so? (5) Is it essential for the validity of moral judgments that Question 4 should be answered in the affirmative? And, if an affirmative answer is relevant to the validity of some but not all moral judgments, which are those to which it is relevant?

It will be seen that Questions 4 and 5 bring us to the problem of Free-Will *v.* Determinism and its bearing on morality.

As regards Question 1 it is important to notice and to avoid the following very common fallacy. Suppose it could be shown that what we take to be the desire to do what is right as such has developed, either in the history of each individual or in that of the human race, on regular principles out of desires which were all purely non-moral. (More or less plausible attempts to show this have been made, e.g., by certain psychoanalysts, on the one hand, and by certain sociologists, on the other.) It would be a fallacy to conclude that what we take to be the desire to do what is right as such is not what it appears to be, but is really just one or a combination of purely non-moral desires. An account of the stages out of which something developed in a regular way is one thing, and an analysis of it as it is when fully developed is another. But it is very common to confuse the two and to imagine that one has shown that the end-term of such a process just consists of the earlier terms in a disguised form.

This fallacy is often made plausible by the use of question-begging epithets for describing the earlier phases in such a process of development. Thus, e.g., some psychoanalysts describe an emotion which is supposed to occur in babies at the pre-moral stage by the name "feeling of *guilt*." Now the phrase "feeling of guilt," if taken literally, means an emotion which a person feels towards himself in respect of his belief that he has done something *morally wrong*. It is therefore quite meaningless to suggest that anyone who has not already got the notion of right and wrong can literally have a feeling of guilt. The phrase "feeling of guilt" must therefore be used in some unexplained metaphorical sense. But the use of it to describe the pre-moral stages illegitimately helps the suggestion that the end-term contains nothing that was not present in the earlier phases.

This brings us to the general notion of specifically moral emotion. By this I mean emotions which appear *prima facie* to be felt towards persons or actions in respect of certain *moral* characteristics which they are believed to have. Such emotions may be either reflexive or non-reflexive. The former are felt by a person towards himself or his own actions, e.g., feelings of guilt, of remorse, of self-approval, etc. The latter are felt towards another person or his actions, e.g., feelings of moral approval or disapproval felt by one person for the acts of another.

The only remark that I wish to make here about them is that their apparent existence presents a considerable difficulty to any form of the Emotional Attitude analysis of moral judgments. According to such analyses, to be right or to be wrong consists in being the object of moral approval or disapproval, as the case may be, to some person or class of persons. But, *prima facie*, an action becomes the object of a feeling of moral approval or disapproval to a person only in so far as he already believes it to be right or to be wrong, as the case may be. There is certainly the appearance of a vicious circle here, and it remains to be seen whether supporters of the Emotional Attitude type of analysis can show that this appearance of circularity is delusive.

EPISTEMOLOGICAL QUESTIONS

The last set of problems which I wish to mention can be stated as follows. How do we come to have ideas of specifically moral terms, such as *right, ought, morally good*, and so on? And how do we come to know or believe propositions connecting non-moral characteristics, such as truth-telling or promise-breaking with moral characteristics such as rightness or wrongness? These may be described as epistemological questions. It is plain

psychological, methinks!

that the answers to them will be closely bound up with the answers to the question how moral judgments should be analysed.

Suppose, e.g., that the Interjectional Analysis were correct. Then there are no moral judgments and therefore no moral predicates. The first question would then have to be transformed into the following. How do we come to make the mistake of thinking that we are ascribing to subjects predicates of a peculiar kind when in fact we are merely expressing certain emotions towards objects? The second question would have to be transformed somewhat as follows. Is it just an ultimate fact about human nature that most people tend to feel a certain kind of emotion when they contemplate, e.g., an act of promise-breaking; or is this explicable by general psychological principles and the particular influences to which most people are subjected in early childhood?

Suppose, next, that the Interjectional Analysis is false, but that it were true that moral concepts, such as *right* and *ought*, are definable in terms of certain kinds of pro-emotion and anti-emotion. Then the origin of such concepts would presumably be like that of our concepts of other psychological terms. We should feel these pro-emotions and anti-emotions on certain occasions, we should introspect them and compare and contrast them with other experiences which we have and introspect, and then by a process of abstraction, we should form the idea of their characteristic emotional quality. Then, finally, we should define "right" and "ought" in terms of emotions which have this quality. Moral concepts would in fact be empirical in origin.

Now, if this kind of analysis of moral judgments were correct, what we have called "right-tending" and "wrong-tending" characteristics would be those characteristics which tend to evoke pro-emotions or anti-emotions of a certain specific kind towards persons or actions which are believed to possess them. So the second question would reduce to the following. How do we come to know or to believe that such and such non-moral characteristics of persons or actions tend to evoke in those who believe them to be present such a pro-emotion or anti-emotion? Presumably the answer would be that we derive such beliefs by generalizing from our experience. We observe that a belief that an act has a certain non-moral characteristic, e.g., that it is an intentionally misleading answer to a question, is regularly accompanied by an anti-emotion of a specific kind towards the act in question. And we base upon this an inductive generalization. Such beliefs would in fact be empirical and inductive in origin.

Even if all forms of the Emotional Attitude Analysis were rejected and some form of the Objective Analysis were accepted, it would still be reasonable to hold that both moral concepts and moral judgments are of empirical origin, provided only that a *naturalistic* form of the Objective Analysis is adopted. But, if we feel obliged to accept a *non-naturalistic* theory of moral judgments and concepts, the case is altered.

Let us define an "empirical concept" as the concept of a characteristic which is either (a) manifested to us in sensation or introspection, or (b) is definable in terms of such characteristics together with the notions of Cause or Substance or both. (The concepts of sensible redness and of anger, e.g., come under the first heading; those of physical redness and irascibility, e.g., come under the second.) If we adopt this definition, it seems certain that the concepts of moral characteristics, such as *right, ought, and morally good,* cannot be empirical unless those characteristics are naturalistic. Therefore anyone who accepts a non-naturalistic account of moral characteristics is almost certainly committed to the proposition that moral concepts are non-empirical. Now many philosophers accept, either as self-evident or as a postulate, the principle that all concepts are empirical. If one is quite sure of this epistemological principle, one will have to reject the non-naturalistic account of moral characteristics, no matter how plausible it may seem on other grounds. If one is quite sure of the non-naturalistic account of moral characteristics, one will have to reject this epistemological principle, no matter how self-evident it may seem or how useful it may be as a postulate. If, on the other hand, one is not quite sure of either, the conflict will tend to diminish one's confidence in both.

Again, it seems plain that, if *right* and *good* are non-naturalistic characteristics, the propositions connecting them with right-tending or good-tending non-moral characteristics, such as promise-keeping or tendency to promote happiness must be *synthetic.* Now to many people it seems that such propositions as "Any act of promise-keeping tends as such to be right" are *necessary* and *self-evident* like the axioms of pure mathematics. But it is also a very widely accepted epistemological principle that there can be no synthetic necessary propositions. There are, according to this principle, synthetic propositions and there are necessary propositions; but the former are all contingent and empirical, and the latter are all analytic. Now a person who holds that moral characteristics are non-naturalistic seems committed to holding that such propositions as "Any act of promise-keeping tends as such to be right" are either (a) contingent empirical generalizations, or (b) synthetic necessary propositions. The former alternative conflicts with the *prima facie* appearance that these propositions are self-evident and necessary; the latter conflicts with the epistemological principle that all necessary propositions are analytic. Thus he must either reject the principle or try to show how it is that such propositions appear to be necessary and self-evident although they are in fact contingent and empirical.

I have now completed my account of what seems to me to be the main problems of Ethics. I have confined myself to stating alternatives and indicating the connexions and disconnexions between them. This is not very exciting, but I think it is a necessary preliminary to anything more positive.

Review of Julian S. Huxley's
Evolutionary Ethics *

C. D. BROAD

This little book contains the *Romanes Lectures*,[1] delivered in the Sheldonian Theatre on 11th June, 1943, together with 13 pages of notes.

The contents may be divided into the following five main sections. (1) A theory of the development of conscience in the individual from infancy. (2) An account of the chief features of evolution in general. (3) An account of the evolution of moral codes and of their correlation with different stages in the evolution of societies. (4) An attempt to show that objective moral standards can be based on a study of the characteristic features of evolutionary change. (5) A statement of the chief peculiarities of a code of morality based on a study of evolution.

I propose first to state the various parts of the theory as fairly as I can, and then to make some comments and criticisms.

(1) *Development of Conscience in the Individual.* The theory which Prof. Huxley puts forward is based on the speculations of certain psychoanalysts. So far as I can understand it, it may be stated as follows.

At about the second year of its post-natal life a baby begins to draw a distinction between itself and the outer world. At this stage the focal point of the latter for the baby is its mother or any other person, such as its nurse, who has constant charge of it. This individual is recognized by the baby as another *person*, and it views her under two aspects, viz. (i) as a source of satisfaction, peace, and security, and (ii) as an authority who has and exercises the power to thwart certain of its impulses. The baby's cognition of its mother under the former aspect is toned with affection; its cognition of her under the latter is toned with hostility.

Hostile emotion towards the mother, and the associated hostile wishes and actions, become the objects of a new kind of emotion in the baby. To this second-order and reflexive emotion Prof. Huxley gives the name 'feeling of guilt'. Emotions, wishes, and tendencies towards action which are the objects of guilty emotion tend to be either relegated to the background of consciousness or wholly repressed into the unconscious. There

* Reprinted with the kind permission of the reviewer and the editors of *Mind*, from *Mind* 53, 1944.
[1] Oxford University Press, 1943; also contained in *Touchstones for Ethics*, Harpers, 1947.

they continue to exist and to be the objects of guilty emotion, and thence they continually seek an outlet. Generally they can find one only in disguised forms; but from time to time they emerge more or less openly in the form of rage and violence against the mother.

The process described above is useful to human beings for the following reason. Young children are faced with many kinds of conflict to which other young creatures are not exposed. Owing to their lack of experience they cannot solve them rationally. Now it would be highly detrimental to the development of the individual if the conflicting impulses merely inhibited each other and led to a complete deadlock, or if they just alternated with each other on equal terms leading to endless vacillation. The attachment of a feeling of guilt to some and not to others of the conflicting impulses, and the consequent fairly complete suppression or repression of the former, ensures that these two disadvantages will be avoided.

After the capacity to feel guilty emotion has once been brought into activity over the conflict between love and hate of one's mother that kind of emotion can be directed to one term in *any* conflict of impulses, and it will then lead to the same kind of results in the way of suppression or repression. This, however, is subject to one limitation. Such an extension of the guilty emotion from a person's hostility towards his mother to certain of his other impulses will take place only when the latter are viewed by him in relation to some person or institution for which he feels love or respect. This latter feeling may be either unmixed or blended with other emotions into some complex sentiment, such as awe, patriotism, self-respect, etc.

Prof. Huxley envisages another way of dealing with conflicting impulses, which becomes available to an individual only when he has acquired adequate experience. This is described as solving such conflicts 'rationally'. It is not clear to me what Prof. Huxley considers this process to be, or how he supposes it to be connected with the 'proto-ethical mechanism' which he has been describing. Does this mechanism merely set the stage and prepare certain of the conditions without which no *persistent* action of any kind, and therefore no deliberately planned action, can take place? Or is there some more detailed connexion between the proto-ethical mechanism and the deliberate subordination and co-ordination of impulses in pursuance of a course of action inspired by moral ideals and limited by moral principles?

(1.1) *Healthy and Unhealthy Development of Conscience*. The processes which have been described above may go on in a 'healthy' way or may be subject to various 'unhealthy' aberrations. In the former case, we are told, 'the feeling of rightness reflects, though in an embryonic form, a morality which is objectively right'. It can then be 'developed by reason and aspiration into a conscience which is indispensable as a moral guide'. In the latter case, however, the patient will develop a conscience which is described as 'distorted and unrealistic'. He may also develop (what is not the same thing) 'distorted and unrealistic' beliefs about the nature of Conscience. It is not clear to me whether these two very different pathological results are held by Prof. Huxley to be invariable concomitants.

(1.11) *Healthy Development.* About the 'realistic' conscience which develops when the process goes on healthily we are given the following information. It is 'normal' and 'healthy' to feel *some* degree of guilty emotion towards one's hatred of those 'whom we must at all costs love'. In particular it is said to be 'perfectly realistic to feel *some* guilt at hating one's beloved mother'.

A distinction is drawn between 'internal' and 'external' realism. The former consists in not feeling excessive guilt and in not compensating for it in certain pathological ways to be described later. It seems to be identified (p. 23) with a satisfactory adjustment between the individual's conscience and the moral standards current in the society in which he lives. But these standards may themselves be 'unrealistic'; and in that case the individual's conscience, if adjusted to them, will lack *external* realism. The latter is said to be relative to (i) the general state of knowledge and belief in a given society at a given time, and (ii) to its 'intellectual and moral climate, and the quality of the human beings who live in it'. Since both these factors gradually change, a set of moral standards which have been externally realistic may, unless they change concomitantly, become unrealistic.

(1.12) *Unhealthy Forms of Development.* The following are said to be typical unhealthy ways of development from the infantile proto-ethical stage:

(i) Instead of, or in addition to, the baby feeling guilty emotions towards its hostility to its mother, it may feel such emotions towards those of its impulses by checking which its mother incurred its hostility. In that case those impulses may be repressed instead of, or in addition to, its feelings of hostility towards its mother.

(ii) The repressed guilt-laden hatred, originally felt towards the mother for checking a certain impulse, may be extended or diverted to that impulse itself. If both the first and the second of the unhealthy developments should take place in an individual, he will feel towards certain of his impulses both a transferred emotion of *guilt* and a transferred emotion of *hatred* which will itself be the object of a guilty feeling.

(iii) Whilst it is 'normal and healthy' and 'perfectly realistic' to feel *some* degree of guilt towards one's hatred of those whom 'one must at all costs love', the degree of guilt felt may be too great. It is then described by Prof. Huxley as 'an excessive load which does not correspond with any reality'. This may lead to a sense of unworthiness and self-hatred which Prof. Huxley describes as 'quite irrational'.

(iv) It is alleged that when the degree of guilt felt is excessive the following further distortions are liable to ensue. (*a*) Suppose that the inordinate feeling of guilt has arisen through being afflicted with a fussy or domineering parent. Then the patient will be apt to model his dealings with himself on his parent's dealings with him, and thus to develop a finicky and over-severe conscience. (*b*) Another alternative, which may be either combined with or substituted for the first, is to model one's idea of God on one's early experiences of one's parents. God is then liable to be regarded as a fussy and domineering person, of irresistible power and superhuman knowledge, mainly occupied in forbidding one to do what one would like to do. God will then be hated, but the hatred will be the object of a strong guilty feeling and will be largely repressed. (*c*) A person may get rid of an excessive load of guilt by thinking of himself as the innocent victim of unfortunate circumstances, of wicked and hostile individuals, or of an oppressive society.

(v) When a person's conscience has developed, whether healthily or unhealthily, he will find himself condemning some of his impulses and approving others of them. Now he may not be able to face the fact that he has certain strong impulses of which he strongly disapproves. He may then come to ignore their presence in himself and to imagine them to be present to a marked degree in certain other individuals or classes. His disapproval of such impulses, which prevents him from acknowledging their presence in himself, is then turned upon these other persons, who thus act as scapegoats or whipping-boys. He may then feel it to be his duty to loose upon them, for their supposed moral defects, those impulses of cruelty and aggression in himself which he would otherwise have disapproved and kept in check.

(1.2) *Inferences from the Above Theory of Conscience.* From the psycho-analytic theory of the development of conscience in the individual as he grows up, Prof. Huxley draws the following conclusions:

(i) There are no innate moral principles or concepts. What is innate in a child is the tendency to love its mother in respect of most of her dealings with it and to hate her in respect of those of her acts which check its impulses; the tendency to feel guilty about this hostility and not about this love, and to repress or suppress the former and not the latter; and the tendency to extend the feeling of guilt to one member of other pairs of conflicting impulses. The kinds of action which eventually come to be regarded as right or wrong depend wholly on the individual's environment and are very largely determined by the influence of his mother. Even the general capacity to develop a conscience of some kind or other will not be fulfilled if the circumstances are unfavourable. It is asserted, e.g., that persons who have had no mother or mother-substitute between the ages of one and three years from birth fail to develop a moral sense of any kind.

(ii) The psycho-analytic theory is alleged to provide an explanation for what Prof. Huxley calls the 'absolute, categorical, and other-worldly quality' of moral obligation. He asserts that this quality becomes attached to moral obligation through the following causes. (*a*) The fact that thoughts, emotions, and wishes to which the feeling of guilt is attached tend to be repressed into the unconscious, and do not merely take turns on an equal footing with their opposites in occupying consciousness or issuing in overt action. (*b*) The fact that the occasion on which guilt is first felt is that on which the infant discovers with a shock that there is a world outside himself which is not amenable to his wishes. It is alleged that a baby is originally in a state of 'magic solipsism', and that what first awakens it from this is the intrusion of the external world in the form of its mother demanding control over its primitive impulses.

(2) *General Account of Evolution.* The main points in Prof. Huxley's general account of evolution may be summarised as follows:

(i) It is a process of change which is 'creative' in two senses. (*a*) New and more complex levels of organisation are successively reached. (*b*) New possibilities for further development are opened up.

(ii) The growth in complexity of organisation is in general gradual, but there are occasional sudden and rapid changes to new and more comprehensive types of organisation. After any such critical point there are new emergent qualities and new methods of further evolution. The two most important critical points known to us are (*a*) the change from inorganic to living matter, and (*b*) the change from pre-human to human life. After each such turning-point the *area* of further evolution tends to be restricted to those creatures which have taken the new turning and their descendants, but the *tempo* of evolution among them tends to be greatly accelerated.

(iii) Living beings are highly complex and unified material systems with the power to produce offspring which predominantly resemble their parents but have variations which may themselves be handed on. At their highest levels living organisms have a very considerable degree of self-regulation, they become to a large extent independent of variations in their environment, and they acquire appreciable powers of controlling it. At this end of the biological scale the presence of a mind something like the human mind is apparent for the first time.

(iv) At the level of life a new method of evolution emerges, viz., natural selection between competing variants. This greatly accelerates the process, and it is still further hastened by the development of bi-sexual reproduction with Mendelian recombination of genes.

(v) Purely organic evolution merges into evolution which is social and is to some extent deliberately controlled. This becomes possible when speech and conceptual thinking have developed. Then and not till then the results of experience become transmissible, tradition becomes cumulative, and deliberate training becomes possible. This leads to a new type of organisation, viz., that of a self-perpetuating society of conscious individuals, and it becomes possible to take deliberate control of further evolution.

(vi) A line of evolution may be said to be 'progressive' so long as there remains a capacity to reach a higher level of organisation along that line which will not itself cut out the possibility of still further advance. In organic evolution this requires all-round flexibility as opposed to one-sided specialisation. The latter leads to a blind alley, and thereafter only minor variations are possible. Prof. Huxley says that all the main lines of purely organic evolution seem to have ended in such blind alleys a very long time ago. The field of further evolution on earth has now been restricted to one species, viz., man; and in them it is social and thought-determined, not blindly biological. But the possible tempo has been enormously increased.

(vii) Prof. Huxley asserts that, after the level of social and thought-determined evolution has been reached, two important new features emerge: (*a*) Many of the experiences which now become available for the first time have 'intrinsic value'; and (*b*) it becomes possible to 'introduce faith, courage, love of truth, goodness—moral purpose—into evolution'. (I am not at all sure what Prof. Huxley understands or wishes his readers to understand by either of these statements.)

(3) *Evolution of the Moral Codes of Societies.* The moral standards prevalent in various societies and at various stages of a single society are roughly correlated with the stage reached by the society in its evolution. But Prof. Huxley mentions, and tries to account for, certain exceptions to this general rule. He says that careful study of a number of primitive communities has shown that there is no close correlation between, e.g., the degree of competitiveness or of co-operation enjoined by the moral code of such a community and the prevalence of competition or co-operation in the life of it. Similar facts, he says, have been observed about peaceableness and aggressiveness. It appears that peaceableness may be morally approved in a community which is predominantly aggressive, and aggressiveness in one that is predominantly peaceable.

He tells us that a more detailed study of such facts discloses that all such societies are primitive, small, culturally isolated, and on the same general level of social evolution. Now it is found that small and isolated species of fairly simple plants or animals are liable to develop and propagate variations which are not specially adapted to their circumstances and their mode of life. The reason alleged is that, in the absence of severe competition, random variations have a fair chance of surviving even when they are not useful.

Suppose, however, that we confine our comparisons to communities which are either (i) at quite different levels of culture, or (ii) highly advanced but on very different lines of development. Then, he says, we shall find that there is a high positive association between those types of character and action which are morally approved in a community and those which are favourably relevant to its chief functions.

Prof. Huxley distinguishes the following main levels:

(i) *Pre-agricultural Societies.* Here morality is chiefly concerned with the propitiation of supposed super-natural beings, the harnessing of supposed magical forces, and the solidarity of the group. The principal subjects of moral approval and disapproval are acts and sentiments connected with totem and taboo, and the acts which are approved or disapproved are viewed mainly in the light of their supposed magical efficacy.

(ii) *Early Civilised Societies.* Here the chief subjects of moral approval or disapproval are those which are concerned with class-domination and the rivalries of groups. Moral codes tend to be regarded as expressions of the will of God, and morality is closely connected with religion.

(iii) *Later Civilised Societies.* The most important development here is the appearance for the first time of a set of moral principles which are supposed not to be restricted in their application to the members of a certain community as a whole or to those of a certain group within it, but are held to apply to every human being as such. Prof. Huxley asserts that the first known appearance of such a universalistic moral code was in about 500 B.C. Such a code has generally been thought of as fixed for all time and independent of local and temporal variations in circumstances. Prof. Huxley thinks that this attitude has been fostered by the uncritical use of certain abstract nouns, such as *The Good*, which are really nothing but 'convenient pigeon-holes for a variety of qualities which have *nothing in common but a certain emotive quality*' (my italics). He also considers that the belief in the immutability of the principles of universalistic morality has been but-tressed by regarding them as expressions of the immutable will of God.

In all advanced societies there have been several more or less distinct moral codes which partly conflict and partly support each other. Among these Prof. Huxley enumerates the following: (*a*) An official code imposed by a ruling class to ensure the stability of their own position; (*b*) the work-ing code of the ordinary citizen; (*c*) the codes of certain oppressed classes or minorities, seeking consolation or revolutionary change; (*d*) a code con-cerned with securing personal salvation as an escape from inner conflict or outer violence and misery; (*e*) the code of an 'impossible perfection'; and (*f*) what he calls 'the true ethics of disciplined and developed goodness and sainthood'. Prof. Huxley alleges that there is nothing common and peculiar to all these except that they are concerned with 'the labels of rightness and wrongness'.

(4) *Evolution as a Clue to an Objective Moral Standard.* Prof. Huxley says that we are left with the following problem: 'How can we be sure that the objects to which our moral sense affixes the labels of felt right-ness and wrongness are *in fact* right and wrong?' So far we have been told only of the adaptation of particular moral codes to particular kinds of society. Is there any criterion for judging whether the labels 'right' and 'wrong' are *correctly* attached? Again, have we any right to say that one adaptation or one society is *better than* another? He asserts that a study of the course of evolution provides answers to such questions and enables us to discover 'independent ethical standards' in three different but intercon-

nected regions, viz., nature as a whole, human society, and the human individual.

So far as I can see, Prof. Huxley bases his moral code on certain ultimate judgments of value. I will collect at this point his main statements on this topic.

(i) Men find that some of the possibilities which are realisable at the human level of evolution 'have value in and for themselves'.

(ii) Among these they assign a higher value to those which are either (*a*) 'more intrinsically or permanently satisfying', or (*b*) 'involve a greater degree of perfection'.

(iii) Those evolutionary trends which are likely to lead to such intrinsically valuable possibilities being realised are judged to be 'the most desirable direction of evolution'.

(iv) It is said to be evident 'on evolutionary grounds' that the individual is 'higher than the state or the social organism'. Again, we are told that 'the rightly developed individual is, and will continue to be, the highest product of evolution'. It is explained that the phrase 'rightly developed', in this context, is to cover both (*a*) the full all-round development of a person's powers, and (*b*) the one-sided development of any special capacity in which he is capable of excelling. Prof. Huxley realises that there may be a conflict between developing a certain talent to the utmost and performing one's ordinary duties towards one's family, colleagues, country, etc. He does not explicitly mention, what is equally obvious, that there may be a conflict between all-round self-development and the cultivation of a particular talent to the highest degree of which it is capable.

The ground which is given for holding that an individual is higher than any social group is that the 'possibilites which are of value for their own sake . . . are not experienced by society as a unit'.

(v) In a group of individuals it is desirable that there should be the maximum of variety that is compatible with the unity of the group as a whole. 'It is not uniformity which our evolutionary analysis shows to be right', says Prof. Huxley, 'but the maximum of variety-in-unity'.

Prof. Huxley's main pronouncements about what is *right* may be summarised as follows:

(i) The most fundamental proposition seems to be that it is right to 'aim at whatever will promote the increasingly full realisation of increasingly high values'.

(ii) There is also a principle of equality. It is right that there should be universal equality of opportunity for development. This is said to follow from the fact that 'the right development of an individual is an evolutionary end in itself'. But there appears to be an independent argument for it which would make it a derivative principle, viz., that equality of opportunity leads to the maximum of variety.

(iii) It is right (*a*) to realise new possibilities in evolution, especially those which are intrinsically valuable; (*b*) to respect human individuality and to encourage its further development; and (*c*) to construct such a social organisation as will best subserve (*a*) and (*b*).

From these principles Prof. Huxley draws the conclusion that the right course at any moment will be a compromise between one which would wholly sacrifice future possibilities of further development to the fullest realisation of existing possibilities and one which would wholly sacrifice the latter to the former. Social organisation should be designed to encourage change in desirable directions, but at any moment there will be an optimum rate of change in those directions.

(5) *Special Features of Evolutionary Ethics.* Prof. Huxley realises that a good many more or less educated persons in England and the United States and the Dominions might be prepared to assent, with minor qualifications, to most of what he has said about the sort of things which have value and the sort of actions which are right. But they might be inclined to ask: Is not this just the ethics of 'Christianised Liberalism'? What has the appeal to evolution done for us?

There would seem to be two different questions here. (i) Has the appeal to evolution provided any reason, which was not already available, for accepting the judgments of value and of obligation enumerated above? (ii) Does it provide us with any new or modified judgments of value or of obligation?

To the first question Prof. Huxley answers that the study of evolution has provided an *inductive basis* for what had already been guessed by religious moralists, viz., a universalistic morality based on the ultimate and intrinsic value of human personality.

In considering the second question Prof. Huxley enumerates what he takes to be the main points of likeness and the main points of unlikeness between the evolutionary moral code and that of 'Christianised Liberalism'. He says that the only likenesses are the following: (i) That both codes are in principle *universalistic*. I take this to mean that each requires that any two persons shall be treated alike unless it can be shown, to the satisfaction of an unbiassed third party, that there are such differences between themselves or their circumstances that better results on the whole are likely to follow from treating them differently. (ii) That both take the value of the *individual* to be primary and paramount. (iii) The two codes will further resemble each other in any principles which follow from (i) or (ii) or the conjunction of both of them.

The main differences between the two systems of morality are said to be the following: (i) The moral standards or criteria of 'Christianised Liberalism' are accepted on authority or on the grounds of an alleged revelation, and are therefore fixed once and for all. Those of the evolutionist can be modified and developed. (ii) The moral standards of the evolutionary system are 'dynamic', whilst those of its rival are 'static'. This seems to mean that the moral code of 'Christianised Liberalism' takes the nature of human individuals and human societies to be now fixed and henceforth susceptible only of minor fluctuations, and legislates only for the relations of such individuals in such societies. The moral code of the evolutionist is concerned, not only with this, but also with the rights and wrongs of *processes of change* which carry individuals and societies from one stage of evolution to another.

From these primary differences Prof. Huxley claims to derive the following secondary ones. The evolutionist will lay more stress than the 'Christianised Liberal' on (i) the obligation to plan for *social change;* (ii) the value of *knowledge* as a means to controlling future evolution; (iii) the value of *art*, both as introducing new possibilities of intrinsically valuable experience and as providing the chief means by which emotional, as distinct from intellectual, experiences may be shared; and (iv) certain kinds of *personal religion* as opening the way to attaining certain kinds of 'satisfying experience and desirable being'. On the other hand, we are told, the evolutionary code condemns practices aimed at securing salvation in a supernatural other life, in so far as these may retard or oppose 'right social change'.

(6) *Comments and Criticisms.* I hope that the above is a fair and a reasonably complete synopsis of the main points in Prof. Huxley's theory. I shall now proceed to make some comments and criticisms upon it.

(6.1) *Development of Conscience in the Individual.* I will begin with one general remark. Of all branches of empirical psychology that which is concerned with what goes on in the minds of babies must, from the nature of the case, be one of the most precarious. Babies, whilst they remain such, cannot tell us what their experiences are; and all statements made by grown persons about their own infantile experiences on the basis of ostensible memory are certainly inadequate and probably distorted. The whole of this part of psychology therefore is, and will always remain, a mere mass of speculations about infantile mental processes, put forward to explain certain features in the lives of grown persons and incapable in principle of any independent check or verification. Such speculations are of the weakest kind known to science.

The next general remark that I would make is this. The connexion between the psycho-analytic and the evolutionary part of Prof. Huxley's theory is by no means clear. The former is concerned entirely with conation and emotion, the latter professes to supply a criterion for judging what is really right and really wrong, i.e., it is concerned with cognition. How are the two inter-related? I will try now to clear this up.

There is evidently a close positive association between what a person calls 'right' and what he feels morally obliged to do and guilty in omitting to do, and between what he calls 'wrong' and what he feels morally obliged to avoid and guilty in doing. A person tends to feel *guilty* (as distinct from merely apprehensive, embarrassed, disgusted, etc.) when and only when he knows himself to be acting or wishing or feeling, or believes himself to have acted or wished or felt, in a way which he would call '*morally wrong*'. Conversely, a person tends to call an act or wish or feeling of his 'morally wrong' only if his contemporary awareness or his subsequent memory of it is qualified by a feeling of *guilt* (as distinct from one of mere apprehension, embarrassment, disgust, etc.).

Now, it might be held that when a person calls an act or experience of his 'wrong' he is either (*a*) merely expressing his feeling of guilt, as a person who is angry might express that feeling by exclaiming 'Blast!'; or (*b*) merely stating the fact that he is feeling guilty, as a person might state that he is feeling angry by uttering the sentence, 'I am angry'. I will call these two alternatives respectively the *Interjectional* and the *Autobiographical* analysis of what a person is doing when he calls one of his own acts or experiences 'wrong'.

It is quite clear that Prof. Huxley could not consistently accept either of these analyses. For, in the first place, he asks: 'How can we be sure that the objects to which our moral sense affixes the labels of felt rightness and wrongness are *in fact* right and wrong?'; and he claims that a study of the course of evolution provides an answer to such questions. Plainly the question would be meaningless and the answer ridiculous if, when a person calls one of his actions 'right' or 'wrong', he is only expressing a certain emotion towards it or is only stating that he is feeling such an emotion towards it. On the first alternative the speaker is not expressing an opinion at all, and so there can be no question of his being correct or incorrect in calling the action 'right' or 'wrong'. On the second alternative he is making an autobiographical statement about his own present feeling towards the action. Such a statement is hardly likely to be false unless he is deliberately lying; and, if it can reasonably be questioned, it is plain that a study of the course of evolution is completely irrelevant to testing its truth or falsehood.

Secondly, Prof. Huxley evidently holds that the emotion of guilt is *appropriate* to some kinds of action or experience and inappropriate to others, and that it may be felt in an *ordinate* or an inordinate degree towards those objects to which it is appropriate to feel it. For he says that guilt is an appropriate emotion for a person to feel towards his hatred of his 'beloved mother', and more generally towards his hatred of those whom 'he must at all costs love'. And he tells us that, whilst it is 'perfectly realistic to feel *some* degree of guilt at hating one's beloved mother', it is possible to feel a degree of guilt which is 'excessive', which 'does not correspond to any reality', and which is 'quite irrational'. From this I conclude that he holds that it is appropriate to feel guilt towards those, and only those, of one's actions and experiences which are 'in fact' wrong; and that there is some proper proportion between the degree of wrongness and the degree of guilt felt.

It seems certain then that Prof. Huxley must hold that, when a person utters the sentence, 'So-and-so is wrong', he is not just expressing an emotion but is making a judgment; and that in this judgment he is ascribing to so-and-so a predicate which has no special reference to his present feelings towards so-and-so.

I suppose, therefore, that the connexion between the psycho-analytic and the evolutionary part of the lecture must be this. The former claims to explain how a person comes to attach feelings of guilt of such and such degrees to such and such of his actions, desires, and feelings; and to show what function this attachment of guilt performs in his general development. The conclusion of it is that a feeling of guilt may become attached to anything, wrong or right or indifferent, and that its intensity need bear no proportion to the degree of wrongness of the actions or experiences to which it becomes attached. A person will be inclined to believe that those and only those of his actions and experiences to which he has attached a feeling of guilt are wrong, and to believe that the degree of wrongness of each is measured by the intensity of the guilty feeling which he has attached to it. But in believing an action or experience of his to be right or wrong he is ascribing to it a certain predicate which has no special reference to his feelings towards it. Whether or not it has this predicate, and the degree to which it has it if it has it at all, are questions which can be decided only by criteria which are elicited in the evolutionary part of the lecture by a study of the course of evolution.

If this account of Prof. Huxley's theory as a whole be correct, we must notice that one important question concerning the development of conscience is ignored by it. How does the individual acquire the notions of right and wrong? According to the evolutionary part of the theory when a person calls one of his actions or experiences 'right' or 'wrong' he is not just talking about his own emotions. He is ascribing to that action or experience (whether correctly or incorrectly) a predicate whose presence or absence can be tested by an objective evolutionary test. If so, he must have an *idea of* that predicate; and nothing that has been said in the psychoanalytic part of the theory about the emotion of guilt and its gradual transference from hatred of the mother to other acts and experiences takes us a step towards explaining the origin of that idea. It is obvious that no theory which is entirely in terms of a person's emotions will explain how he comes to attach to the words 'right' and 'wrong' a meaning which is not definable in terms of his emotions.

It is no reproach to a theory that it does not explain everything; but it is very important that it should not be thought to explain more than it does. Therefore I shall state explicitly what seem to me to be two presuppositions of the present theory. (i) It presupposes that the notions of right and wrong are either innate or are acquired by the individual in some way which it does not explain. (ii) It presupposes that a person has a tendency (*a*) to ascribe wrongness to those and only those of his actions and experiences towards which he feels an emotion of guilt, and (*b*) to ascribe to an act or experience a degree of wrongness which is measured by the intensity of the guilty emotion which he feels towards it.

I think that the theory can be illustrated by means of an analogy with the emotion of fear. The theory maintains that the native and primary object of a person's guilty emotion is his hostility to his mother. We are told by psychologists that the native and primary object of fear in infants is sudden loud noises. The guilty emotion may be extended or diverted from a person's hostility towards his mother to any of his other acts or experiences, right, wrong, or indifferent. Similarly, fear may be extended or diverted to almost any object, whether dangerous, harmless, or beneficial. Therefore the fact that a person feels guilty about X and not about Y, though it will certainly tend to make him *believe* that X is wrong and that Y is not, is no guarantee that these beliefs are correct. And the fact that he feels more guilty about X than about Z, though it will certainly tend to make him *believe* that X is more wrong than Z, is no guarantee that this is true. Similarly, a person may be frightened of X and not of Y, and may be more frightened of X than of Z. This will certainly tend to make him think that X is dangerous and that Y is not, and that X is more dangerous than Z. But it may in fact be the case that Y is dangerous and X is not, or that Z is more dangerous than X. It might be held to be 'reasonable' that a person should feel fear only towards what is really dangerous, and that the intensity of his fear should be proportionate to the real degree of danger. Similarly, it is in some sense 'reasonable' that a person should feel guilt only towards those of his acts and experiences which are really wrong, and that the intensity of his guilty feeling should be proportionate to the real degree of their wrongness.

Perhaps this notion of 'reasonableness' or 'appropriateness' might be analysed somewhat further on the following lines. Prof. Huxley might say that the emotion which the average baby feels towards the average mother in respect of the vast majority of her dealings with it is *love*. It is only in respect of a special class of occasional acts, viz., those which check certain of its impulses, that the average baby feels hatred and hostility towards the average mother. Therefore love is the 'normal' emotion for a baby to feel towards its mother, in the sense that it is the emotion which is habitually felt. Hatred towards its mother is 'abnormal', in the sense that it is opposite in kind to the emotion which is normally felt by it towards the same object and that it is felt only on certain isolated special occasions.

Prof. Huxley might add that love, and the actions which spring from it, are more conducive to the harmonious development of the individual and the stability of society than are hate and the actions which spring from it. A human being is at first wholly dependent on its mother; throughout a long childhood he remains predominantly dependent on her and on others; and throughout his whole life he will be largely dependent on the good-will of his fellows. He will not receive such support for long, and he will be incapable of benefiting from it, unless he is on the whole docile, co-operative, and friendly. Now, unless certain of his impulses are checked at an early age, and unless he largely represses his instinctive reactions of hostility against those who check them, he will become an object of disgust and enmity to those with whom he has to live. To say that a guilty feeling is 'appropriate' to a person's hostility towards his mother and 'inappropriate' to his love for her might mean that (*a*) it tends to repress anything to which it is attached, and (*b*) the repression of the former is, whilst that of the latter is not, conducive to the harmonious development of the individual and the stability of society.

Finally, Prof. Huxley might give the following account of the distinction between a 'reasonable' and an 'unreasonable' degree of guilty feeling. He might compare the feeling of guilt to a medicine which tastes nasty and has various collateral ill-effects on general health. The feeling is unpleasant in itself and depressing and cramping in its effects. It will be too weak if it is not strong enough to repress the hostility to the mother. But, if it is present in more than the minimal degree needed for that and similar purposes, it will hamper rather than forward the all-round development of the individual and his adjustment to society. So the 'right' or 'reasonable' degree of guilty feeling is the smallest dose that suffices for the function which Prof. Huxley ascribes to it.

I will end this part of my comments with the following observations. Any theory which claims to trace the development of conscience in the individual is faced with at least two questions: (i) How does the individual acquire the *notions* of moral rightness and wrongness, goodness and badness, etc.? (ii) How does he come to *apply* these notions to the particular objects to which he does eventually apply them, i.e., to count such and such actions as right, such and such others as wrong, and so on? I have tried to show that the psycho-analytic theory supplies no answer to the first question. So far as it goes, moral rightness and wrongness, goodness and badness, might be simple, unanalysable characteristics, and the disposition to form concepts of them might be innate in the human mind. In that case the only answer that could be given to the first question would be to describe the conditions which are severally necessary and jointly sufficient to stimulate this innate disposition into activity and cause the individual actually to think of these characteristics. But, even on this supposition, there might be no innate *moral principles* and even no innate *moral biases*. A person might be equally ready to attach the notion of right or wrong, good or evil, to anything; and the particular ways in which he did in fact come to apply them might be wholly determined by the conditions to which he was subjected in early childhood.

Now, as we have seen, Prof. Huxley does hold, on the basis of the psycho-analytic theory, that there are no innate moral principles. For, if I have interpreted him correctly, he holds that an individual's earliest judgments of right and wrong are completely determined by and moulded upon his feelings of guilt, and that the extension of his feelings of guilt from his hatred of his mother to any other of his acts or experiences is entirely de-termined by the influences which are brought to bear on him in early childhood. Prof. Huxley does not explicitly consider the possibility of what I have called 'innate moral bias'. By this I mean the possibility that the human mind may be so constituted that attempts to make a person feel guilty about certain kinds of act or experience might 'go against the grain' and seldom be wholly successful, whilst attempts to make him feel thus about certain other kinds of act or experience might 'go with the grain'. There is some *prima facie* evidence for this, but I do not know whether it would survive critical investigation.

I think that Prof. Huxley's conclusions about how an individual comes to have the beliefs which he does have about what is right and what is wrong might be compared in certain respects to the known facts about the development of intelligible speech as a person grows up. The power to speak is not innate in human beings; but the power to acquire that power may fairly be said to be innate, since the vast majority of men do learn to speak whilst no other creatures can be taught to do so. Nevertheless, a child will not acquire the power to speak unless it is surrounded by other persons who talk to it, listen to it, and train it. Again, the particular language which a child will first talk if it ever learns to speak at all depends entirely on the particular way in which it is conditioned by those who train it in its early years. Of course other languages may be learned deliberately in later life; but, if so, they will probably be spoken with the 'accent' of the language which was first acquired spontaneously in infancy.

On Prof. Huxley's theory the contents of different moral codes might be compared to different languages, or perhaps more profitably to the characteristic grammatical structures of different groups of languages, e.g., Indo-European, Semitic, Chinese, etc. In this connexion it is worth re-marking that the grammatical rules which a person follows correctly but unwittingly in speaking his native tongue may be of extreme subtlety, as becomes apparent when they are formulated by grammarians and have to be learned and applied deliberately by a foreigner. There is obviously some analogy to this in the highly complex rules of totem and taboo which anthropologists laboriously elicit from the practices of certain primitive communities.

(6.2) *The Notions of 'Internal' and 'External Realism'*. So far as I can see, the essential points here are the following: A person's conscience is internally realistic if (i) he feels guilty about those and only those of his acts and experiences which are *commonly believed* to be wrong in the society in which he has to live, and (ii) if the intensity of the guilty emotion which he feels towards any act or experience is roughly proportionate to the degree of wrongness which is *commonly ascribed* in that society to acts or experiences of that kind. Thus internal realism is necessary and sufficient to ensure a satisfactory adjustment between an individual's conscience and the moral code prevalent in the society in which he lives.

Now, whether an act of a certain kind is really right or wrong will largely depend on the nature of the effects which acts of that kind are likely to produce either severally or collectively. And these effects in turn will depend, not only on the nature of the act, but also on the circumstances, both material and mental, in which it is done.

Suppose, now, that a person judges a certain act to be *right*. Then it may be that, *if* it would have the effects which he believes that it would have, it *would* be right. In that case I shall say that his judgment is 'ethically reasonable', even if he is mistaken about the effects that it will have. On the other hand, it may be that, if it would have the effects which he believes it would have, it *would not* be right but would be indifferent or wrong. Then I shall say that his judgment that it is right is 'ethically unreasonable', even if he is correct in his beliefs about the effects of the action. If he is correct in his judgment about the circumstances in which an act is done and the effects which it will have, I shall say that he is 'factually correct'; if not, I shall say that he is 'factually incorrect'. It is plain then that, if a person makes the judgment, 'So-and-so is right', there are four possibilities, viz., (i) that he is being ethically reasonable and factually correct, or (ii) ethically reasonable but factually incorrect, or (iii) ethically unreasonable but factually correct, or (iv) ethically unreasonable and factually incorrect. Similar remarks apply, *mutatis mutandis*, if a person makes the judgment, 'So-and-so is wrong'.

Now, there is no doubt that what Prof. Huxley calls 'external realism' is closely connected with what I have called 'ethical reasonableness'. If a person makes a moral judgment which is ethically reasonable I shall describe it as 'realistic relative to his factual information', no matter whether that information is adequate, correct or incorrect. If, in addition, his relevant factual information is adequate and correct, I shall describe his moral judgment as 'absolutely realistic'.

It is evident that the moral code of a society might not be realistic even in relation to the factual information which is common in that society. It may never have been so. And, even if at some time in the past it was realistic in relation to the relevant factual information then available, it may have ossified at that stage, whilst the relevant factual information available has since been extended and corrected. I have no doubt that a great deal in the current moral code about sexual matters is unrealistic, from the one cause or the other, in relation to the relevant factual information at present available.

Even if the moral code of a society were completely realistic relative to the factual information which is common in that society at a given time, it might not be absolutely realistic; for that information might be either inadequate or inaccurate. And, even if it were absolutely realistic at a certain time, there is no guarantee that it would remain so. For conditions might change, and similar acts performed in widely different conditions might have consequences which were good in one set of conditions and bad in the other.

Obviously the ideal position for an individual is that he should live in a society whose moral code is absolutely realistic, and that his conscience should be fully adjusted to it. But neither of those conditions will ever be completely fulfilled. Suppose that one had to train a child who one knew would be obliged to live in a society whose moral code was largely unrealistic. Then one would have to compromise between the two evils of giving him a conscience adjusted to the society in which he is to live and therefore largely unrealistic, or a conscience which is highly realistic and therefore largely out of adjustment to the society in which he is to live. This is by no means a merely academic problem for an intelligent and well-intentioned parent or teacher who has to compromise as best he can between producing contented philistines or embittered prigs.

(6.3) *Objective Rightness and Wrongness*. Prof. Huxley's theory of the nature of rightness is a particular form of a very ancient and familiar doctrine, viz., Utilitarianism. For it takes intrinsic value as the primary notion in ethics, and it makes the definition or the criterion of the rightness of an act to be its tendency to produce or to conserve or to increase what is intrinsically valuable. There is, so far as I can see, no special connexion between this account of rightness and the theory of evolution. Utilitarianism was put forward, elaborated, criticised, and defended long before the theory of evolution was thought of, and all the best arguments for it are quite independent of that theory and of the facts on which it is based.

In my opinion the only relevance of the facts of evolution to Utilitarianism is the following. The most serious rival to Utilitarianism is what I will call 'Intuitionism'. This is the theory that the rightness or wrongness of certain kinds of act, e.g., promise-keeping, lying, etc., depends, not on their tendency to produce consequences which are good or bad, as the case may be, but on their intrinsic nature as acts. E.g., this theory holds that the non-ethical characteristic of being an act of promise-keeping necessarily involves the ethical characteristic of being right, and that the non-ethical characteristic of being an act of deliberate deception necessarily involves the ethical characteristic of being wrong, just as the property of being an equilateral triangle necessarily involves that of being an equiangular triangle. Such a theory of the nature of the connexion between rightness or wrongness, on the one hand, and the various right-making or wrong-making characteristics, on the other, is generally combined with the *epistemological* theory that such connexions are immediately obvious to careful inspection, i.e., that they not only *are* intrinsically necessary but also can be *seen* to be so by any rational being who reflects on the terms. Now anything that tended to weaken this theory would *pro tanto* strengthen Utilitarianism which is its most formidable rival. I suspect that the only relevance of the psycho-analytic account of the development of conscience to the Utilitarian part of Prof. Huxley's theory is that, if it were true, it would cut away the grounds for the rival doctrine of Intuitionism. On the psycho-analytic theory it would be very improbable that a person really does see any necessary connexion between the nature of certain acts, such as promise-keeping or lying, and their rightness or wrongness; and there would be a psychological explanation of the fact that many people are inclined to think that they do so. But, for reasons which I have given, I consider that the evidence for this theory of conscience is too weak to make it a strong weapon against Intuitionism.

Prof. Huxley enunciates the general principle of Utilitarianism in the formula that it is right to 'aim at whatever will promote the increasingly full realisation of increasingly high values'. But, as Bentham saw, and as Sidgwick insisted, the general principle needs to be supplemented by some principle about *distribution*. For our acts contribute not only to produce good and bad experiences and good or bad individuals, but also to determine *which* individuals shall have good experiences and which shall have bad ones. It will be remembered that Bentham formulated the distributive principle, 'Everyone to count for one and no-one to count for more than one', whilst Sidgwick enunciates several principles of impartiality in the distribution of goods and evils. Prof. Huxley also has a principle of equality. He says that it is right that there should be universal equality of opportunity for development.

He alleges that this follows from the fact that 'the right development of an individual is an evolutionary end in itself'. I do not see that the addition of the adjective 'evolutionary' to the substantive 'end-in-itself' adds any weight to this argument. I am not sure that the conclusion is true, and I do not see precisely how it follows from the premiss. It is plainly conceivable that circumstances might exist in which if equal opportunities were given to all members of a society none of them could develop very far; whilst, if the opportunities given were distributed most bountifully among those who had the greatest innate capacity, much greater aggregate development would result. It is certainly not obvious to me that, in such circumstances, opportunities for development ought to be distributed equally. And I should like to see the steps by which it is supposed to follow from the premiss that the right development of an individual is an end in itself. I suspect that some additional premisses would be needed, and that they would not be particularly plausible if they were brought into the light.

Whether the argument in support of the principle of equality of opportunity from the premiss that an individual is an end-in-itself be valid or invalid, it is not a Utilitarian argument. But Prof. Huxley does also support the principle on Utilitarian grounds. He says that equality of opportunity leads to maximum variety, and he holds that a group of inter-related individuals is in the best state possible when there is in it a 'maximum of variety-in-unity'. It seems to me quite uncertain whether equality of opportunity for development would necessarily lead to the maximum variety possible with a given amount of resources. If the available resources were small, there could be only very slight development for anyone if the opportunities were equal, and this would seem to involve a fairly uniform low level of attainment. If the same resources were distributed unequally, e.g., if they were used to enrich a small class of aristocrats with a taste for being patrons of art and learning and sport, it is quite likely that far greater variety would result.

(6.4) *Intrinsic Values.* Utilitarianism, which is a theory about the nature and criteria of *rightness and wrongness*, does not logically entail any particular theory about *intrinsic goodness and badness*. But it presupposes some view or other on this latter subject. So we must now consider Prof. Huxley's opinions about intrinsic value.

In Section 4 above I have collected all that I could find of Prof. Huxley's views on this topic. I will begin by remarking that there are three main questions which may be asked about intrinsic value. (i) What is the right analysis of statements of the form 'So-and-so is intrinsically good (or bad)'? Do they, as their grammatical form suggests, express judgments in which the speaker ascribes a predicate to a subject? Or is this a delusion, and do they merely express a certain emotion which the person who utters them is feeling? Again, if they do express judgments, what is the nature of the predicate which they ascribe to a subject? Is it simple and unanalysable? If not, how should it be analysed and defined? (ii) If intrinsic value or disvalue be a predicate, of what kinds of subject can it be intelligibly predicated? Or, if the Interjectional Analysis be correct, towards what kinds of object can the emotion be felt which is expressed by sentences which *seem* to ascribe intrinsic value to a subject? (iii) If intrinsic value or disvalue is a predicate, what are the non-ethical characteristics of a subject which make it intrinsically good or bad, as the case may be? Of, if the Interjectional Analysis be correct, what are the non-ethical characteristics of an object which call forth the emotion which is expressed by sentences which *seem* to ascribe intrinsic value to a subject?

(i) I think it is certain that Prof. Huxley holds that such sentences as 'So-and-so is intrinsically good (or bad)' do express judgments in which a predicate is ascribed to a subject, and do not merely express an emotion which the speaker is feeling. But I have no idea whether he thinks that the characteristic denoted by the phrase 'intrinsically good (or bad)' is simple or complex. And I have no idea what he thinks to be the correct analysis of it if it be complex.

(ii) It seems certain that Prof. Huxley holds that intrinsic value can be predicated intelligibly of (a) certain experiences, and (b) human individuals. I am not sure whether he holds that it can also be predicated of (c) certain groups of inter-related human beings.

Some of his statements, if taken literally, seem to imply that he holds (c). He says, e.g., that the individual is 'higher than the state or the social organism'. Now, if such a comparison can be made at all, it implies that both an individual and a society can have intrinsic value. What precisely it means is not clear to me. Does it mean that the value of *any* individual is greater than that of *any* human society? Or does it mean that the value of the *best* individual is greater than that of the *best* society? Whatever it may mean, two reasons are given for it. One is that individuals have experiences, whilst no group of individuals can literally have an experience; and that certain experiences are of very great intrinsic value. The other is that the conclusion is evident 'on evolutionary grounds'.

I find all this very unsatisfactory. Consider the following three questions. (a) Can intrinsic value be predicated intelligibly of certain groups of inter-related individuals? (b) If it can, can the value of such a group and that of an individual be intelligibly compared in respect of magnitude? (c) If so, is the value of any individual, however bad, necessarily greater than that of any group, however good? Or is the value of the best possible individual necessarily greater than that of the best possible group? The mere fact that only an individual can literally have experiences and that certain experiences have very great intrinsic value, does not seem to me to settle any of these questions. And, if there be 'evolutionary grounds' for answering the third question affirmatively in either of its forms, I have failed to discover them in Prof. Huxley's lecture and I am quite unable to imagine for myself what they may be.

(iii) About the non-ethical characteristics whose presence confers intrinsic value on the things which possess them, Prof. Huxley's views seem to be as follows:

(a) He does not explicitly enumerate the characteristics which he thinks confer intrinsic value on *experiences*. He contents himself with mentioning certain experiences which are commonly held to be intrinsically valuable, e.g., certain æsthetic and religious experiences. But he does mention two characteristics which he thinks confer a higher value on an experience the more fully and intensely they are present in it. These are the property of being 'intrinsically or permanently satisfying' and that of 'involving a degree of perfection'.

I do not clearly understand what is meant by 'perfection' in this context.

It seems tautologous, and is certainly not illuminating, to say that the more perfection an experience has the more valuable it will be. The notion of being 'intrinsically or permanently satisfying' also needs a great deal of further analysis and elucidation. The first move would be to attempt to draw and justify a distinction between what 'really would satisfy' a person and what he 'thinks he wants'. At the next move we should have to raise the question whether a stupid or a cruel or a lustful person might not get 'real' satisfaction from experiences which we should hesitate to call intrinsically good. All these questions have been commonplaces of ethical discussion for some two thousand years, and I cannot see that any fresh light has been thrown on them by reference to evolution.

(*b*) Intrinsic value is conferred on an individual by a combination of the fullest all-round development of his powers with the special development of any particular talents in which he is capable of excelling. This, again, is a form of a very ancient and familiar doctrine. It goes back to Plato and was put forward in England in the nineteenth century by moralists of the school of Green and Bradley and Bosanquet under the name of 'self-realisation'. Its strong and weak points have been very fully canvassed, and I do not think that evolution has anything fresh to add to the discussion.

(*c*) If Prof. Huxley does hold that intrinsic value can be significantly ascribed to certain groups of individuals, it is plain that he thinks that what gives intrinsic value to such a group is a combination of individual variety with collective unity.

It is useful in this connection to bear in mind McTaggart's distinction between the value *in* a group and the value *of* a group. I think it is quite possible that, if the distinction were put to him, Prof. Huxley would deny that there is goodness or badness *of* a group, and would say that variety-in-unity is important only as making for maximum goodness *in* a group, i.e., for making it consist to the greatest possible degree of good individuals enjoying good experiences.

(6.5) *The Relevance of Evolution to Ethics.* There are two questions to be discussed, and it is important to be clear about the connexions and disconnexions between them. (i) What bearing, if any, has knowledge of the facts of evolution on the question of what is *intrinsically good or bad?* (ii) What bearing, if any, has it on the question of what is *right or wrong?*

It is important to notice that, even if such knowledge had no bearing at all on the first question, it would almost certainly have a bearing on the second. This would be so even if Utilitarianism were false, but it is more obviously so if it is true. The reason is as follows. On any theory of right and wrong which is worth consideration *one* of our duties, and a very important one, is to produce as much good and as little evil as we can. If Utilitarianism is true, this is our *only* ultimate duty and all our other duties can be derived from it. If Utilitarianism is false, we have other duties not derivable from this which may conflict with and limit it, but it will remain an urgent obligation. Now, in order to decide whether the effects of an action will be good or evil we must first know *what* its effects will be. This is a factual and not an ethical question, and the answer to it depends on the circumstances in which the action is done and the relevant laws of nature. It is plain that knowledge of the laws of evolution may be highly relevant in attempting to foresee the large-scale and long-term consequences of certain types of action. Such knowledge may also suggest possibilities which would not otherwise have been contemplated, and it may rule out as causally impossible certain results at which it might otherwise have seemed reasonable to aim. I do not think that any moralist would deny that evolution has this kind of relevance to the question of what is right or wrong.

If knowledge of the facts of evolution had a bearing on the question of what is intrinsically good or bad, it would have an additional relevance to the question of what is right or wrong. This would be the case on any view of rightness and wrongness which makes beneficence to be one of our duties, and it would be most obvious on the Utilitarian view which makes beneficence to be our only fundamental duty. For, on the present hypothesis, a knowledge of the facts of evolution would help to tell us, not only *what* the effects of certain actions would be, but also whether such and such effects, if they were produced, would be *intrinsically good or bad*. So the question that remains is whether knowledge of the facts of evolution has any bearing on the question of what is intrinsically good or bad.

It is plain that Prof. Huxley thinks that it has an important bearing on this question, but I find it extremely hard to see why he does so. Perhaps I can best bring out the difficulty that I feel in the following way. Take the things which Prof. Huxley considers to be intrinsically good, and imagine him to be confronted with an opponent who doubted or denied of any of them that it was intrinsically good. How precisely would he refute his opponent and support his own opinion by appealing to the facts and laws of evolution? Unless the notion of value is surreptitiously imported into the definition of 'evolution', knowledge of the facts and laws of evolution is simply knowledge of the *de facto* nature and order of sequence of successive phases in various lines of development. In this way we may learn that certain lines of development have stopped short, in the sense that a point has been reached after which the successive phases in this line have shown no further increase of complexity-in-unity. By comparing and contrasting such lines with others which stopped short at a more complex stage or which have not yet done so at all we may be able to infer some of the necessary conditions for continued growth of complexity-in-unity in the successive phases of a line of development. This much could be discovered and understood by an intelligent being who had never had the faintest notion of intrinsic value or disvalue; and this is *all* that a knowledge of the facts and laws of evolution, considered as a part of natural science, amounts to.

If, then, Prof. Huxley is to support his own views about the intrinsic value of so-and-so and to refute those of an opponent by appealing to the facts and laws of evolution, there must be a suppressed premiss in the argument. This premiss must be some such proposition as 'States of affairs which have more complexity-in-unity are as such intrinsically better than those which have less complexity-in-unity', or (what is by no means the same) 'Processes of change in which there is increase of complexity-in-unity in the successive phases are intrinsically better than those in which there is stability or diminution in this respect'. (Prof. Huxley might prefer the latter as more 'dynamic', since it ascribes intrinsic value, not to the separate phases, but to the process of change itself in which they occur.) At any rate he must use *some* 'mixed' premiss, connecting certain *purely factual* characteristics, which are all that a study of evolution can possibly reveal to us, with the *value-characteristics* of intrinsic goodness and badness. I must confess that this seems to me to be so obvious a platitude that I am almost ashamed to insist upon it; but it seems that it is still liable to be ignored.

Now, whatever may be the evidence for such a mixed premiss, it is quite plain that it must be something different from the evidence for the facts and laws of evolution. For the premiss required asserts a connection between certain of those facts and laws and something else, viz., intrinsic value or disvalue, which forms no part of their subject-matter. Therefore, whilst I agree that a knowledge of the facts and laws of evolution might have considerable and increasing relevance to the question whether certain acts would be right or wrong, since it might help us to foresee the large-scale and long-range consequences of such acts, I am unable to see that it has any direct bearing on the question whether certain states of affairs or processes or experiences would be intrinsically good or bad.

The Nature of Ethical Disagreement *

CHARLES L. STEVENSON

When people disagree about the value of something—one saying that it is good or right, and another that it is bad or wrong—by what methods of argument or inquiry can their disagreement be resolved? Can it be resolved by the methods of science, or does it require methods of some other kind, or is it open to no rational solution at all?

The question must be clarified before it can be answered. And the word that is particularly in need of clarification, as we shall see, is the word "disagreement".

Let us begin by noting that "disagreement" has two broad senses: In the first sense it refers to what I shall call "disagreement in belief". This occurs when Mr. A believes *p*, when Mr. B believes *not-p*, or something incompatible with *p*, and when neither is content to let the belief of the other remain unchallenged. Thus doctors may disagree in belief about the causes of an illness; and friends may disagree in belief about the exact date on which they last met.

In the second sense, the word refers to what I shall call "disagreement in attitude". This occurs when Mr. A has a favorable attitude to something, when Mr. B has an unfavorable or less favorable attitude to it, and when neither is content to let the other's attitude remain unchanged. The term "attitude" is here used in much the same sense that R. B. Perry uses "interest"; it designates any psychological disposition of being *for* or *against* something. Hence love and hate are relatively specific kinds of attitudes, as are approval and disapproval, and so on.

This second sense can be illustrated in this way: Two men are planning to have dinner together. One is particularly anxious to eat at a certain restaurant, but the other doesn't like it. Temporarily, then, the men cannot "agree" on where to dine. Their argument may be trivial, and perhaps only half serious; but in any case it represents a disagreement *in attitude*. The men have divergent preferences, and each is trying to redirect the preference of the other.

Further examples are readily found. Mrs. Smith wishes to cultivate only the four hundred; Mr. Smith is loyal to his old poker-playing friends.

* Reprinted by kind permission of the author and the Centro di Metodologia, Milano, Italy.

They accordingly disagree, in attitude, about whom to invite to their party. The progressive mayor wants modern school-buildings and large parks; the older citizens are against these "newfangled" ways; so they disagree on civic policy. These cases differ from the one about the restaurant only in that the clash of attitudes is more serious, and may lead to more vigorous argument.

The difference between the two senses of "disagreement" is essentially this: the first involves an opposition of beliefs, both of which cannot be true, and the second involves an opposition of attitudes, both of which cannot be satisfied.

Let us apply this distinction to a case that will sharpen it. Mr. A believes that most voters will favor a proposed tax, and Mr. B disagrees with him. The disagreement concerns attitudes—those of the voters—but note that A and B are *not* disagreeing in attitude. Their disagreement is *in belief about* attitudes. It is simply a special kind of disagreement in belief, differing from disagreement in belief about head colds only with regard to subject matter. It implies not an opposition of the actual attitudes of the speakers, but only of their beliefs about certain attitudes. Disagreement *in* attitude, on the other hand, implies that the very attitudes of the speakers are opposed. A and B may have opposed beliefs about attitudes without having opposed attitudes, just as they may have opposed beliefs about head colds without having opposed head colds. Hence we must not, from the fact that an argument is concerned with attitudes, infer that it necessarily involves disagreement *in* attitude.

We may now turn more directly to disagreement about values, with particular reference to normative ethics. When people argue about what is good, do they disagree in belief, or do they disagree in attitude? A long tradition of ethical theorists strongly suggest, whether they always intend to or not, that the disagreement is one *in belief*. Naturalistic theorists, for instance, identify an ethical judgment with some sort of scientific statement, and so make normative ethics a branch of science. Now a scientific argument typically exemplifies disagreement in belief, and if an ethical argument is simply a scientific one, then it too exemplifies disagreement in belief. The usual naturalistic theories of ethics that stress attitudes—such as those of Hume, Westermarck, Perry, Richards, and so many others —stress disagreement in belief no less than the rest. They imply, of course, that disagreement about what is good is disagreement *in belief* about attitudes; but we have seen that that is simply one sort of disagreement in belief, and by no means the same as disagreement *in* attitude. Analyses that stress disagreement *in* attitude are extremely rare.

If ethical arguments, as we encounter them in everyday life, involved disagreement in belief exclusively—whether the beliefs were about attitudes or about something else—then I should have no quarrel with the ordinary sort of naturalistic analysis. Normative judgments could be taken as scientific statements, and amenable to the usual scientific proof. But a moment's attention will readily show that disagreement in belief has not the exclusive role that theory has so repeatedly ascribed to it. It must be readily granted that ethical arguments usually involve disagreement in belief; but they *also* involve disagreement in attitude. And the conspicuous role of disagreement in attitude is what we usually take, whether we realize it or not, as the distinguishing feature of ethical arguments. For example:

Suppose that the representative of a union urges that the wage level in a given company ought to be higher—that it is only right that the workers receive more pay. The company representative urges in reply that the workers ought to receive no more than they get. Such an argument clearly represents a disagreement in attitude. The union is *for* higher wages; the company is *against* them, and neither is content to let the other's attitude remain unchanged. *In addition* to this disagreement in attitude, of course, the argument may represent no little disagreement in belief. Perhaps the parties disagree about how much the cost of living has risen, and how much the workers are suffering under the present wage scale. Or perhaps they disagree about the company's earnings, and the extent to which the company could raise wages and still operate at a profit. Like any typical ethical argument, then, this argument involves both disagreement in attitude and disagreement in belief.

It is easy to see, however, that the disagreement in attitude plays a unifying and predominating rôle in the argument. This is so in two ways:

In the first place, disagreement in attitude determines what beliefs are *relevant* to the argument. Suppose that the company affirms that the wage scale of fifty years ago was far lower than it is now. The union will immediately urge that this contention, even though true, is irrelevant. And it is irrelevant simply because information about the wage level of fifty years ago, maintained under totally different circumstances, is not likely to affect the present attitudes of either party. To be relevant, any belief that is introduced into the argument must be one that is likely to lead one side or the other to have a different attitude, and so reconcile disagreement in attitude. Attitudes are often functions of beliefs. We often change our attitudes to something when we change our beliefs about it; just as a child ceases to *want* to touch a live coal when he comes to *believe* that it will burn him. Thus in the present argument, any beliefs that are at all likely to alter attitudes, such as those about the increasing cost of living or the financial state of the company, will be considered by both sides to be relevant to the argument. Agreement in belief on these matters may lead to agreement in attitude toward the wage scale. But beliefs that are likely to alter the attitudes of neither side will be declared irrelevant. They will have no bearing on the disagreement in attitude, with which both parties are primarily concerned.

In the second place, ethical argument usually terminates when disagreement in attitude terminates, even though a certain amount of disagreement in belief remains. Suppose, for instance, that the company and the union continue to disagree in belief about the increasing cost of living, but that the company, even so, ends by favoring the higher wage scale. The union will then be content to end the argument, and will cease to press its point about living costs. It may bring up that point again, in some future argument of the same sort, or in urging the righteousness of its victory to the newspaper columnists; but for the moment the fact that the company has agreed in attitude is sufficient to terminate the argument. On the other hand: suppose that both parties agreed on all beliefs that were introduced into the argument, but even so continued to disagree in attitude. In that case neither party would feel that their dispute had been successfully terminated. They might look for other beliefs that could be introduced into the argument. They might use words to play on each other's emotions. They might agree (in attitude) to submit the case to arbitration, both feeling that a decision, even if strongly adverse to one party or the other, would be preferable to a continued impasse. Or, perhaps, they might abandon hope of settling their dispute by any peaceable means.

In many other cases, of course, men discuss ethical topics without having the strong, uncompromising attitudes that the present example has illustrated. They are often as much concerned with redirecting their own attitudes, in the light of greater knowledge, as with redirecting the attitudes of others. And the attitudes involved are often altruistic, rather than selfish. Yet the above example will serve, so long as that is understood, to suggest the nature of ethical disagreement. Both disagreement in attitude and disagreement in belief are involved, but the former predominates in that (1) it determines what sort of disagreement in belief is relevantly disputed in a given ethical argument, and (2) it determines, by its continued presence or its resolution, whether or not the argument has been settled. We may see further how intimately the two sorts of disagreement are related: since attitudes are often functions of beliefs, an agreement in belief may lead people, as a matter of psychological fact, to agree in attitude.

Having discussed disagreement, we may turn to the broad question that was first mentioned, namely: By what methods or argument or inquiry may disagreement about matters of value be resolved?

It will be obvious that to whatever extent an argument involves disagreement in belief, it is open to the usual methods of the sciences. If these methods are the *only* rational methods for supporting beliefs—as I believe to be so, but cannot now take time to discuss—then scientific methods are the only rational methods for resolving the disagreement in *belief* that arguments about values may include.

But if science is granted an undisputed sway in reconciling beliefs, it does not thereby acquire, without qualification, an undisputed sway in reconciling attitudes. We have seen that arguments about values include disagreement in attitude, no less than disagreement in belief, and that in certain ways the disagreement in attitude predominates. By what methods shall the latter sort of disagreement be resolved?

The methods of science are still available for that purpose, but only in an indirect way. Initially, these methods have only to do with establishing agreement in belief. If they serve further to establish agreement in attitude, that will be due simply to the psychological fact that altered beliefs may cause altered attitudes. Hence scientific methods are conclusive in ending arguments about values only to the extent that their success in obtaining agreement in belief will in turn lead to agreement in attitude.

In other words: the extent to which scientific methods can bring about agreement on values depends on the extent to which a commonly accepted body of scientific beliefs would cause us to have a commonly accepted set of attitudes.

How much is the development of science likely to achieve, then, with regard to values? To what extent *would* common beliefs lead to common attitudes? It is, perhaps, a pardonable enthusiasm to *hope* that science will do everything—to hope that in some rosy future, when all men know the consequences of their acts, they will all have common aspirations, and live peaceably in complete moral accord. But if we speak not from our enthusiastic hopes, but from our present knowledge, the answer must be far less exciting. We usually *do not know*, at the beginning of any argument about values, whether an agreement in belief, scientifically established, will lead to an agreement in attitude or not. It is logically possible, at least, that two men should continue to disagree in attitude even though they had all their beliefs in common, and even though neither had made any logical or inductive error, or omitted any relevant evidence. Differences in temperament, or in early training, or in social status, might make the men retain different attitudes even though both were possessed of the complete scientific truth. Whether this logical possibility is an empirical likelihood I shall not presume to say; but it is unquestionably a possibility that must not be left out of account.

To say that science can always settle arguments about value, we have seen, is to make this assumption: Agreement in attitude will always be consequent upon complete agreement in belief, and science can always bring about the latter. Taken as purely heuristic, this assumption has its usefulness. It leads people to discover the discrepancies in their beliefs, and to prolong enlightening argument that *may* lead, as a matter of fact, from commonly accepted beliefs to commonly accepted attitudes. It leads people to reconcile their attitudes in a rational, permanent way, rather than by rhapsody or exhortation. But the assumption is *nothing more*, for present knowledge, than a heuristic maxim. It is wholly without any proper foundation of probability. I conclude, therefore, that scientific methods cannot be guaranteed the definite rôle in the so-called "normative sciences" that they may have in the natural sciences. Apart from a heuristic assumption to the contrary, it is possible that the growth of scientific knowledge may leave many disputes about values permanently unsolved. Should these disputes persist, there are non-rational methods for dealing with them, of course, such as impassioned, moving oratory. But the purely intellectual methods of science, and, indeed, *all* methods of reasoning, may be insufficient to settle disputes about values, even though they may greatly help to do so.

For the same reasons, I conclude that normative ethics is not a branch of any science. It deliberately deals with a type of disagreement that science deliberately avoids. Ethics is not psychology, for instance; for although psychologists may, of course, agree or disagree in belief about attitudes, they need not, as psychologists, be concerned with whether they agree or disagree with one another *in* attitude. Insofar as normative ethics draws from the sciences, in order to change attitudes *via* changing people's beliefs, it *draws* from *all* the sciences; but a moralist's peculiar aim—that of *redirecting* attitudes—is a type of activity, rather than knowledge, and falls within no science. Science may study that activity, and may help indirectly to forward it; but it is not *identical* with that activity.

I have only a moment to explain why the ethical terms, such as "good", "wrong", "ought", and so on, are so habitually used to deal with disagreement in attitude. On account of their repeated occurrence in emotional situations they have acquired a strong emotive meaning. This emotive meaning makes them serviceable in initiating changes in a hearer's attitudes. Sheer emotive impact is not likely, under many circumstances, to change attitudes in any permanent way; but it *begins* a process that can then be supported by other means.

There is no occasion for saying that the meaning of ethical terms is *purely* emotive, like that of "alas" or "hurrah". We have seen that ethical *arguments* include many expressions of *belief;* and the rough rules of ordinary language permit us to say that some of these beliefs are expressed by an ethical judgment itself. But the beliefs so expressed are by no means always the same. Ethical terms are notable for their ambiguity, and opponents in an argument may use them in different senses. Sometimes this leads to artificial issues; but it usually does not. So long as one person says "This is good" with emotive praise, and another says "No, it is bad", with emotive condemnation, a disagreement in attitude is manifest. Whether or not the beliefs that these statements express are logically incompatible may not be discovered until later in the argument; but even if they are actually compatible, disagreement in attitude will be preserved by emotive meaning; and this disagreement, so central to ethics, may lead to an argument that is certainly not artificial in its issues, so long as it is taken for what it is.

The many theorists who have refused to identify ethical statements with scientific ones have much to be said in their favor. They have seen that ethical judgments mold or alter attitudes, rather than describe them, and they have seen that ethical judgments can be guaranteed no definitive scientific support. But one need not, on that account, provide ethics with any extramundane, sui generis *subject matter*. The distinguishing features of an ethical judgment can be preserved by a recognition of emotive meaning and disagreement in attitude, rather than by some non-natural quality —and with far greater intelligibility. If an unique subject matter is *postulated*, as it usually is, to preserve the important distinction between normative ethics and science, it serves no purpose that is not served by the very simple analysis I have here suggested. Unless non-natural qualities can be defended by positive arguments, rather than as an "only resort" from the acknowledged weakness of ordinary forms of naturalism, they would seem nothing more than the invisible shadows cast by emotive meaning.

The Freedom of the Will *

UNIVERSITY OF CALIFORNIA ASSOCIATES

The problem of free will is one of the most ancient of metaphysical questions and it is closely bound up with those philosophical aspects of religion that we have considered in the preceding chapter. Most theologians, together with moralists and jurists, have championed the freedom of the will, while scientists and most philosophers have testified to its bondage. The perennial interest in the problem is motivated by the fact that the assumption of free will is alleged to be inconsistent with certain scientific and philosophical doctrines; the denial of this assumption, with certain doctrines of morality, jurisprudence, and theology. The layman, or "the man in the street," may well wonder why anyone should ever have denied the existence of free will, since the difference between freedom and compulsion appears to him to be a fact that he finds exemplified every day. To his mind, there is no particular problem here; some of his actions are free, while others are compelled or constrained. In order to understand the so-called problem of free will, we have to take into account certain considerations that do not ordinarily occur to him. But before we examine these considerations, which convert free will from a fact into a problem, let us see how the layman himself regards the distinction between freedom and compulsion.

I am free (he would say) when I have the power to abstain from an intended action, when my actions are under my control. I act under compulsion when I am forced to do a thing I had no intention of doing. Freedom, therefore, implies the existence of alternatives, any one of which I could have chosen had I so desired; compulsion implies the removal of one or more of these alternatives. When I am free there are several alternatives, any one of which is as capable of realization as any other. When I act under compulsion I am prevented from realizing one or more of these alternatives. The restriction of alternatives is always effected by means of a command, regulation, ordinance, or law. Where there are no parking laws, for example, I can park my car anywhere along the street and for as long as my fancy pleases. The enactment of parking laws restricts my

* Reprinted by kind permission of The University of California Associates and the publisher from *Knowledge and Society*, copyright 1938 by D. Appleton-Century Company, Inc. New York.

alternatives. The laws inform me that I must not park in certain zones, or that I must not park my car longer than a specified length of time, if I wish to avoid the penalties for violation of an ordinance. Laws, therefore, place constraints on my conduct by threatening me with the penalties that are consequent upon transgression. Even if I have no intention of violating the law, I am still constrained by it, because it prevents me from acting contrary to its provisions. Through my obedience to the law, there is an elimination of some of the alternatives that I am capable of realizing, or might have realized, had I so desired. My conduct is free (so the layman might conclude) only so long as my actions are not determined by a "must."

1. THE PROBLEM OF FREE WILL

Acts of free will do not exist, since every action is determined and hence constrained
Let us first examine the considerations that have been supposed to obliterate the distinction between free and constrained actions. It is alleged that what appear to be acts of free will are in reality instances of constrained action. The argument in support of this allegation is as follows: Every event is determined or necessitated by antecedent events. The acts said to be free are no exception. The belief that at the moment of choice I can act in several alternative ways must be an illusion, since at that moment the antecedent events completely determine my conduct. Thus, every voluntary act is constrained to happen by antecedent causes.

It follows at once that there is no distinction between freedom and compulsion. When I think that I am free and that there are alternatives among which I can choose, I am really the victim of an illusion. Since I am powerless to control the causes of my conduct, I am also powerless to control my conduct, for my conduct is determined by its causes, and these causes necessitate the effect. The possibility of controlling my conduct implies that the causes might have been ineffective—that my behavior could have been different, despite the causes that were present. But a cause that does not produce its effect is not really a cause, and hence the doctrine of free will is incompatible with the doctrine that my conduct has causes. Even when my conduct is not constrained by the dictates of a command, it is always constrained by its causes. They compel my compliance with one alternative to the exclusion of all other alternatives just as effectively as the threats that lend force to a command. The *belief* that my conduct is sometimes free from compulsion can be explained by the fact that I often fail to observe the causes which constrain my conduct. But my conduct is never uncaused and therefore never free.

The denial of free will alleged to be inconsistent with certain doctrines of morality, jurisprudence and theology

The denial of free will is said to be inconsistent with certain doctrines of morality, jurisprudence, and theology. Moralists make a distinction between right and wrong action. They tell us that we *ought* to do what is right, and that we *ought not* to do what is wrong. But, whatever we ought to do we must be able to do, and whatever we ought not to do we must be able to abstain from doing. Moralists cannot require us to perform the impossible. When they say that we ought to do a certain thing they imply that we could do it if we wished. Morality thus presupposes the existence of alternatives, all alike capable of realization. Some of these alternatives may be right and others wrong. Whenever we are confronted by such alternatives, moralists urge us to realize the one that is right. Yet, if every one of my actions is determined by antecedent causes, it follows that, in any given situation, I could not have acted in any other way than I did act. If all my actions are performed under the compulsion of a blind necessity, then it cannot be said that I ought to do a thing which, by supposition, it is impossible for me to do. Actions that I *must* perform are unavoidable, and it is therefore futile to exhort me with an *ought*, when I am forced to comply with a *must*.

Jurists hold that I cannot be held responsible for actions that were performed under compulsion, and that I cannot be justly punished for them. Hence, if all voluntary acts are necessitated by antecedent causes, I cannot be held responsible for my actions, since I have no control over their causes. I am not responsible for actions that I could not help, and it would therefore be unjust to punish me for something over which I had no control. We should not condemn a man who commits fraud, arson, or murder, since no man can help doing what he does do. Instead of "punishing" him by sending him to the penitentiary or the electric chair, we should rather attempt to "cure" him by subjecting him to the action of causes which will modify his behavior in the future so that he will never again commit such acts.

Considerations such as these seem to show that the denial of free will jeopardizes the conceptions on which morality and the administration of justice are based. Morality is impossible unless voluntary acts are exceptions to the principle, that every event is determined by antecedent causes. In order to insure the possibility of morality, therefore, some philosophers have argued as follows: There is no conclusive evidence in favor either of the truth of the principle or its falsity. For aught we know, it may be false. Let us therefore assume it to be false. If it is, then there are events which are not determined by antecedent causes. Of course, even if there are such events, we have no means of *knowing* that voluntary actions are events of this sort. In the absence of knowledge, we can only *postulate* that voluntary actions are exceptions to the rule of universal causation. But the postulate is justified, because it insures the possibility of morality.

Although the freedom of the will is not susceptible of proof, we are justified in assuming free will as a postulate of morality. With this postulate, the validity of the moral "ought" remains unimpaired.

Theology has taken an interest in the problem of free will for two reasons. First, theology shares with morality certain conceptions which become inapplicable to human conduct, or at least lose their force, if the existence of free will is denied. Second, the determination of the attributes of God is dependent on how the problem of free will is decided.

The conceptions which become either inapplicable or nugatory are those of sin, atonement, and repentance. If man has no power to choose between right and wrong the concept of sin ceases to be applicable to his conduct. The characterization of an act as "sinful" implies a moral censure to the effect that the act ought to have been avoided. Similarly, when we exhort a man to atone for his deed we imply that his deed was a manifestation of free will. We cannot ask him to atone for something over which he had no control. Repentance, finally, is a futile gesture, unless freedom is a reality. I feel repentant when I contemplate a deed I wish I had not done—when I am sorry and resolve to do better in the future. This feeling is accompanied by the belief that the deed could have been avoided, had I so desired. But the belief is utterly illusory if freedom is unreal. Not even my future acts will get the benefit of my present mood of repentance unless free will is a reality. If it is not, and if the causes that determined my misdeed are repeated, my misdeed will also be repeated, no matter how repentant I feel now.

The principal problem of theology is to determine the attributes of God. Those that theologians generally regard as essential to the divine nature are "omniscience," "omnipotence," and "goodness." Granting that God is omnipotent, it was in His power either to create man a free agent or not to create him a free agent. Now, some theologians have argued that, if God has created man a free agent, He cannot have complete foreknowledge of his actions, and is therefore not omniscient. The foreknowledge of future events, they have reasoned, presupposes the determination of every event by antecedent events. If man is free, if his actions are not determined by antecedent events, it is impossible to predict the choice he will make between alternative courses of action. To attribute omniscience to God is to assume that man is not a free agent, since every one of his actions must be subject to the compulsion of causes. But if God did not create man a free agent, it follows that God is not good; for God rewards the saint and punishes the sinner. However, rewards and punishments cannot be meted out with justice, as we saw before, unless man is a free agent. If man is not a free agent, the saint's deeds are not to his credit, and the sinner's not to his discredit. The saint simply had the good luck to have his actions determined by propitious causes and does not deserve to be rewarded, since it is God, and not he, who is responsible for the whole causal chain that determines his actions. Likewise, the sinner does not deserve to be punished, since he could not help the misfortune of having had his actions determined by unpropitious causes. God as Creator is responsible for both causal chains, and it is therefore He who deserves to be praised for the deeds of the saint and blamed for those of the sinner. To reward and punish creatures who are not free agents is not consistent with God's goodness. If goodness is a part of the divine nature, it follows that God must have created man a free agent. Hence, God does not possess both the attribute of omniscience and the attribute of goodness. If He possesses the latter, man is a free agent, but in that case He cannot possess the former. If He possesses the former, man is not a free agent, and in that case He cannot possess the latter. We can therefore take our choice: either we can first settle the theological question one way or the other, and thus settle the problem of free will, or else we can first settle the problem of free will one way or the other, and thus settle the theological question.

2. THE CONFUSIONS THAT GENERATE THE PROBLEM

The problem of free will is generated through confusing freedom with indetermination and compulsion with determination

In spite of its antiquity, we find today no substantial agreement as to how the problem of free will can be solved. One begins to suspect that a problem, on which so much intellectual effort has been expended without advancing it towards a solution, has not been properly defined. The layman, it was said, regards the freedom of the will, not as a problem, but as a fact to be verified in everyday experience. We encounter difficulties only as we enter into the considerations we have just been examining. Indeed, it is the latter that have given rise to the problem, because they confound the concept of compulsion (or constraint) with the concept of determination (or causation). The traditional formulation of the problem of free will assumes without question that compulsion, constraint, necessitation, determination, and causation are all synonymous. If the problem is to be solved, this assumption must be challenged. Our task, therefore, is to show that compulsion, constraint, and necessitation are not identical in meaning with determination and causation. If we can do this, we shall have shown, at the same time, that the negative of compulsion, constraint, or necessitation—namely, freedom—is not identical in meaning with the negative of determination or causation—namely, indetermination or chance.

We have to inquire into the meanings of two pairs of concepts: freedom and compulsion, determination and indetermination. Once we have established the meanings of these concepts, we can resolve the so-called problem of the freedom of the will into the following questions: (1) Are voluntary actions free or compelled (constrained, necessitated)? (2) Are voluntary actions determined or undetermined? (3) Does responsibility imply freedom? (4) Does responsibility imply indetermination? (5) Do repentance and remorse imply belief in the existence of free will? (6) Do repentance and remorse imply belief in the indetermination of voluntary acts? The problem of free will is generated by substituting the even-numbered for the corresponding odd-numbered questions, and assuming that these questions are of identical import. Thus, for example, the layman has no difficulty in answering the first question. Some of my actions (he will say) are free, and others are necessitated; I am not always free, and I do not always act under constraint. Those of my actions which are not performed under compulsion are called "voluntary." This being the defined meaning of the term "voluntary," it follows that my voluntary actions are free. The layman who believes that voluntary actions are free might also have ideas about their causation. Perhaps he believes that there is no event that happens without a cause. He will therefore believe that human conduct is never a chance phenomenon, but is always determined by antecedent events. Believing that human conduct is sometimes free and also that human conduct is always determined by antecedent causes, he now falls an easy prey to the arguments that generate the problem of free will. He will be told that he cannot assent to both of these propositions, seeing that freedom is incompatible with determination. If he believes in freedom he must believe that his voluntary decisions are not determined by antecedent events. If, however, he believes in the determination of all events without exception, he must believe that even his voluntary decisions, which appear to him to be free, are in reality necessitated. In all likelihood, our layman will be silenced by this argument; but he will also remain unconvinced.

We shall answer the first question as did the layman: human conduct is sometimes free and sometimes subject to compulsion. When my conduct is free it is called voluntary, and voluntary actions are therefore free by definition. To the second question, we shall be unable to give an unqualified answer. But, subject to the qualifications which are explained below, we shall say that human conduct is determined. The third and fifth questions are both answered in the affirmative. The fourth and sixth questions will be answered in the negative. Responsibility implies determination rather than indetermination. Repentance and remorse imply neither a belief in determination nor a belief in indetermination.

3. THE CONCEPT OF CAUSAL DETERMINATION

There is nothing we need add to what has been said about the distinction between freedom and compulsion. I am free when my conduct is under my own control, and I act under constraint when my conduct is controlled by someone else. My conduct is under my own control when it is determined by my own desires, motives, and intentions, and not under my control when it is determined by the desires, motives and intentions of someone else. It is not under my control even when my own desires and intentions are in agreement with those of another person who seeks to control my conduct; for I might have had desires and intentions which did not agree with his, and I should have then been free only had I been able to seek the realization of my own.

All of this is fairly obvious, and it would have been gratuitous to explain the distinction between freedom and constraint, if these terms had not also been used in an entirely different context, where they have given rise to the problem of the freedom of the will and the many puzzling but fallacious arguments both for and against it. The concepts of freedom and compulsion, as we have just explained their meaning, are applicable only to the conscious actions of organisms. Thus, compulsion always implies the existence of desires in the consciousness of the organism, or at least the possibility of such desires, which, were it free to act in accordance with them, would result in actions that are incompatible with the actions the organism performs under compulsion. It is the crossing of its own desires by the will of some other organism that is experienced as compulsion. The identification of constraint with determination and of freedom with indetermination would be legitimate, therefore, only if determination connoted everything that is connoted by constraint and if indetermination connoted everything that is connoted by freedom. That this is not so we shall now proceed to show.

Determination is predictability by means of law

Suppose I desire to know where a body, which starts from rest, will be after falling vertically downwards for five seconds. In order to solve this problem I have to calculate the distance of the body from its starting point at the end of five seconds. This distance can be determined by means of the formula $s = \frac{1}{2}gt^2$—the well-known formula for falling bodies. This formula connects the temporal interval, during which the body is falling, with the distance it has fallen at the end of the interval. If a body, starting from rest, falls for five seconds, then the vertical distance it has fallen at the end of this interval is obtained, according to the formula, by squaring the time, multiplying the number so obtained by g (the acceleration of gravity whose value is approximately 32 ft. / sec.²), and dividing this product by 2. In five seconds the body will therefore have fallen a distance of 400 feet. If, instead of the distance, we want to calculate the time during which a body falls a specified distance, we solve the formula for t. This process transforms it into $t = \sqrt{\dfrac{2s}{g}}$ Thus if we know that the body has fallen

a distance of 14,400 feet we can calculate the number of seconds it has taken to fall this distance by extracting the square root of the quotient 28,800 ÷ 32. Performing the operations indicated, we find that the body has fallen for 30 seconds. The formula enables us to determine the distance when the time is given and also the time when the distance is given. It can therefore be used for making predictions. The parachute jumper who wants to find out how long he can safely allow his body to fall without pulling the rip cord, relies on this formula. If he jumps from an altitude of 15,000 feet, and if he must pull the rip cord at an altitude of 600 feet in order to descend with safety, he need merely compute the number of seconds in which his body will drop 14,400 feet. The formula enables him to predict that he will be 600 feet above ground at the end of thirty seconds. Having made this prediction, he can confidently entrust his safety to the reliability of his altimeter and his wrist-watch. If he pulls the rip cord promptly at the end of thirty seconds, and if his parachute functions properly, he knows that he will descend without accident in accordance with his prediction.

The formula $s = \frac{1}{2}gt^2$ enables us to predict the future positions occupied by a body falling vertically downwards when its initial position is known. Formulas that make predictions possible are known as *laws*. Thus Kepler's laws enable astronomers to predict the future positions of the planets when their positions at a given instant are known. Similarly, astronomers are able to predict the instants at which solar eclipses will occur, because the laws of planetary and lunar motion enable them to predict the relative positions of earth, sun, and moon at future instants when their relative positions at a given instant are known. Laws alone are insufficient for the making of predictions. Thus the formula $s = \frac{1}{2}gt^2$, the law of falling bodies, connects the distance a body falls from *any* initial position with the time during which it falls. Similarly, the laws of planetary motion connect the position of a planet at any moment with its positions at future moments. The law of falling bodies does not state that a given body is now falling from a specified position P, nor do the laws of planetary motion state that a given planet can now be found in a specified position. These facts can be ascertained only by observation, and have to be ascertained before we can make predictions by means of the laws. Laws are hypothetical propositions. The law of falling bodies not only fails to state that a given body is now falling from the position P; it does not even state that there are falling bodies. Similarly, Kepler's laws convey no information either about the present positions of the planets or about their number, nor do they even assert that there are planets. Laws merely express regularities of connection between physical quantities and properties. If they are interpreted as making assertions about the physical world, their import is hypothetical. Thus, the law of falling bodies may be taken to assert that if a body falls from the position P, then the distance it falls increases as the square of the time. That the body falls from the position P can be ascertained only by observation. But once we have ascertained this fact by observation, we are not dependent on further observation for our knowledge of the future positions of the body. Its future positions can be calculated by means of the law.

We revert now to the concept of determination, since it was for the sake of clarifying its meaning that we undertook to analyze the concept of law. The considerations that generate the problem of free will, we may recall, make no distinction between determination, causation, compulsion, and constraint. Determination and causation are, indeed, identical concepts. "A determines B" and "A causes B" are identical propositions. Thus we say, indifferently—that is, without intending a difference of meaning— that the increase in the temperature of an iron rod *causes* an increase in its length or that an increase in its temperature *determines* an increase in its length. When we inquire into the meaning of determination (or causation), we must ask ourselves: "Under what circumstances do we regard these statements as being true?" The answer to this question is implied by the results of our analysis of the concept of law. We say that an increase in the temperature of an iron rod determines an increase in its length when the increase in length can be calculated or predicted. And this calculation can be made when we have a law that connects the increase in length with the increase in temperature. Determination therefore means predictability by means of a law. In general, we say that A determines B when B can be calculated or predicted, given A. And B can be predicted, given A, when we have a law that connects the properties of B with those of A. Hence, determination does not mean compulsion. The increase in temperature does not compel the increase in the length of the iron rod. When we say that A compels B we imply that A and B have desires and volitions, and are therefore conscious organisms. The notion of compulsion is obviously inapplicable to the iron rod that is being heated by a flame. The flame does not desire the iron to expand, and the iron neither complies with any such desire nor does it resist any intentions of the flame. Neither the iron nor the flame is conscious, hence they are alike incapable of desire and volition.

4. LAWS OF NATURE AND HUMAN LAWS

The confusion between determination and compulsion seems to be explained by the fact that we speak of the determination of B by A whenever A and B are connected by a law. The laws of nature, it might be said, hold without exception; they cannot be transgressed. Hence, when A and B are connected by a law, the happening of B is necessitated whenever A has happened. The iron rod cannot avoid expanding when it is being heated, because its failure to do so would involve the violation of one of nature's laws. The law prescribes what the iron must do whenever its temperature is increased.

This sort of argument is undoubtedly encouraged by the view, once widely held and not yet entirely obsolete, that the laws of nature are divine enactments. According to this view, God governs nature as a ruler governs a state, by means of laws. Everything that happens is subject to the control and regulation of His laws. He keeps the planets in their courses by forcing them to follow prescribed orbits, and He compels the iron rod to expand whenever it is subjected to the influence of heat. Human laws are sometimes transgressed. The laws of nature are absolutely binding; they cannot be transgressed.

Human laws are prescriptions; natural laws are descriptions
We have only to state the assumptions of this argument in order to expose the fallacy on which it rests. The argument assumes that human and natural laws have something in common, namely, the fact that they are both prescriptions. Human laws—that is, moral or judicial laws—regulate and control the behavior of human beings; natural laws regulate and control the behavior of nature. Human laws prescribe certain modes of action and prohibit others; natural laws prescribe the manner in which natural processes are to take place. Human laws differ from natural laws solely in the fact that the former are sometimes violated, while the latter are never violated. The argument assumes that human and natural laws are different species of the same genus. It is this assumption that constitutes the fallacy. For human laws are rules of conduct, constraining conduct by the threat of penalties for violation of the rules. They prescribe the things one ought to do and prohibit the things one ought not to do. In short, they are imperatives. But natural laws are not imperatives and they have nothing in common with human laws except the name. To attribute to the former the functions that belong only to the latter is like the fallacy of attributing to the stocks that are sold on stock exchanges the properties of the stocks that grow in gardens. Natural laws do not prescribe the happenings that ought to take place; they describe the happenings that do take place. The law of falling bodies describes how bodies actually fall; it does not prescribe or command how they ought to fall. Similarly, the laws of planetary motion describe how the planets actually move; they do not prescribe orbits to the planets. Again, the laws of economics describe how economic processes actually are connected; they are not rules that prescribe how they ought to be connected.

We are, therefore, victims of a confusion of ideas when we say that the planets are forced or compelled by the laws of planetary motion to follow elliptical orbits, or that the manner in which a body falls is constrained or necessitated by a law. Compulsion, as we have seen, presupposes the existence, or at least the possibility, of desires and intentions, which seek the realization of actions incompatible with the actions performed under compulsion. A planet, not being conscious, could not have the desire to travel on any orbit incompatible with the orbit specified by the laws of planetary motion. Since it has no desires to be crossed, it cannot be forced or compelled to travel on its orbit. But even when the law describes the mechanical behavior of a conscious organism, it exercises no constraint in the proper sense of the word. If I should fall from an airplane and should desire the distance from my starting point to increase as the cube root of the time, my desire would have not the slightest influence on my motion. The distance will increase as the square of the time, whether I desire this to happen or not. Yet it would be incorrect to say that my desires are being crossed, or that my behavior is under constraint, for this implies at least the possibility of resistance or violation. If my resistance were successful, the law of falling bodies would be false. The formula $s = \frac{1}{2}gt^2$ would not describe the behavior of every falling body and would therefore not express a law of nature. If the formula does express a law of nature, then it describes, but does not constrain, even the behavior of a falling man, whatever his desires may be.

Our conclusion remains unaffected in the domain of economic and psychological laws. Although economic laws connect the properties of economic processes, including the activities of human beings, it is not true that they constrain these activities, or that they can be broken by people who do not like them. If, through man's intervention in economic affairs, economic processes are generated that fail to satisfy a given economic "law," we can conclude, not that the "law" has been violated, but only that the alleged law is false. In view of the fallibility of induction, we must always reckon with the contingency that what is taken to be a law, according to a scientific hypothesis, may turn out not to be a law after all.

Finally, psychological laws describe the nature of mind; they do not prescribe what the nature of mind ought to be. In particular, the laws of volition are not rules that force me to perform actions which perhaps I should not have performed, had my desires and intentions not been curbed by these laws. They connect my actual wishes and intentions with the circumstances under which they arise, and the nature of my actions with these desires and intentions. I act under compulsion only when I am prevented from realizing the goal I desire or intend. The law that describes the circumstances under which this desire arises does not constrain my action—not even if I should wish to be without this desire. Constraint, to repeat, implies at least the possibility of resistance or of violation.

The difference between a natural and a human law, to sum up, is the difference between a description and a prescription. A description is either true or false; a prescription is neither. A prescription can be obeyed or disobeyed; a description can neither be obeyed nor disobeyed. A prescription is a constraint on action; a description can by its very nature never encounter opposing desires.

5. DETERMINATION VS. INDETERMINATION OF VOLUNTARY ACTS

Now that we have shown that the concepts of determination and indetermination are not identical with the concepts of compulsion and freedom, we return to the questions asked earlier in this chapter. It will be recalled that the problem of free will is generated when questions (2), (4), and (6) are assumed to be identical with questions (1), (3), and

(5). We have already dealt with the questions that were concerned with the freedom and compulsion of voluntary actions. There remain the questions that are concerned with their determination and indetermination.

Classification of voluntary acts

Voluntary acts may be divided into those that are motivated and into those that are not. When it is said that every voluntary act is determined by a motive, the term "motive" is used in the sense of "cause." In order to avoid the initial assumption that every voluntary act is determined, we shall not follow this usage. We shall, instead, use the term in the more familiar sense as the "reason" for the sake of which an act is performed. When, for example, I offer an insult to a person I dislike, I may have been motivated by a desire for revenge. If voluntary actions are determined, then motives in the sense specified determine them only partially at best. The mere presence in my consciousness of a desire for revenge is not enough; various external circumstances are also necessary. If the object of my insult had been three thousand miles away, the motive, however strongly I may have been impelled by it, would have been ineffective. The object of my insult must be within hearing distance and I must be aware of his presence, if my desire is to be realized. The factors that determine my action must therefore include at least the sight of the object in addition to the motive.

For our present purposes, it is unnecessary to enter into the question of the existence of hidden motives. The motives that appear in consciousness are often not the real motives from which we act. If the motive from which we are really acting is reprehensible the mind's censor often refuses to allow this motive to enter consciousness. But since a motive is needed to explain the act, consciousness invents a praiseworthy motive suitable as a reasonable explanation of our action and substitutes it for the real motive. Sometimes we become aware of the deception and discover the hidden motives which impel us to action. When this happens we often refrain from the intended act, namely, whenever we are motivated by the desire not to act from reprehensible motives.

There are many voluntary acts that do not proceed from conscious motives. Can it be said, then, that they proceed from hidden or unconscious motives? If so, it is hard to imagine what they might be. When I am told to choose one of the letters of the word "oblique," and I choose the letter "q," my choice is voluntary, but is certainly not explained by any conscious motive. I had no reason to choose the letter "q" in preference to any other letter. And as for hidden motives, what motive would explain why I chose this rather than some other letter? It will not do to say that my action was motivated by the necessity of having to make some choice among the alternatives. That motive fails to explain the uniqueness of the choice that was made. At best, it only explains the fact that I made a choice. Voluntary acts of this sort are, therefore, unmotivated or arbitrary; they have neither genuine nor fictitious motives.

Voluntary acts may be acts of choice or they may not. If a book review has aroused in me a desire to read *Gone With the Wind*, this desire is the motive for entering a bookstore and buying a copy. I do not here make a choice from among a number of alternatives, for I am not confronted with the problem whether or not to buy *Gone With the Wind* instead of some other book. My desire is not distracted by the contemplation of other alternatives. When there are other alternatives, however, I have to make a choice. Suppose that I have decided to buy one or another of three different books. I want to read the first for pleasure, the second for instruction, and the third to impress my friends and acquaintances. No matter which alternative I choose, my choice will be motivated: I shall select one of the books when one of the reasons has achieved a greater strength than the others. Thus, I may finally regard it as more important to make an impression on my friends and acquaintances than to increase my knowledge or to seek my pleasure. The victorious reason then becomes the motive of my action and initiates the choice I make. We shall not discuss here the question of how one of these reasons becomes transformed into a motive. The occurrence of this transformation, however, is frequently observed. We often do weigh the different reasons in favor of one or the other of a number of alternative courses of action, until one of the reasons wins. This phenomenon is so common that it has received a name. It is known as the conflict of motives. It would be more accurate to speak of the conflict of reasons or of the conflict of possible motives, since a reason is not a motive until it contributes to the initiation of the action. But this does not take place until the reason becomes strong enough to overcome the opposing reasons.

In accordance with the distinctions we have made, voluntary acts may now be divided into four groups. The first division is between acts of choice and acts that do not involve choice. Each of these groups may in turn be divided into motivated and unmotivated acts. When an act of choice is unmotivated our choice is confined to the alternatives, one of which we intend to realize. When it is motivated our choice is, in general, again confined to these alternatives. We never make a choice among the motives themselves unless such a choice is itself motivated.

With the foregoing considerations in mind we can now turn to questions (2), (4), and (6). Question (2) asks: "Are voluntary actions determined or indetermined?" In accordance with our analysis of the concept of determination this question may be restated as follows: "Are voluntary actions predictable or are they unpredictable?" The predictability of voluntary actions presupposes the existence of laws that connect the properties of voluntary actions with the properties of antecedent events. In order to decide question (2) we must therefore answer the question: "Are there such laws?"

Relative and abso-
lute determination
and indetermina-
tion The predictability of an event E is relative to the initial conditions and the laws that connect these initial conditions with the event E. When we know the initial conditions and these laws, we can predict the event. But when there are no laws known to us that connect these initial conditions with events prior to them, we are unable to predict the initial conditions themselves. Hence, when we assert that the initial conditions are also determined, we maintain the existence of these unknown laws. To illustrate: Suppose we observe a rock dislodged by the wind and rolling on a rough stony surface towards the edge of a vertical cliff. From the moment the rock reaches the edge of the cliff we can predict its positions at future moments by means of the law of falling bodies. We may say, therefore, that the falling of the rock is determined. But since there are no laws known to us that connect the position from which the rocks starts its rolling motion with the subsequent positions it occupies between this point and the edge of the cliff, we are unable to predict the moment at which it will reach the edge of the cliff. Hence the further assertion that this event is determined is equivalent to saying that these laws exist. Similarly, we are unable to predict the moment at which the rock will be dislodged by the wind, since there are no laws known to us that connect this event with previous states of the rock, the wind pressure, and an indefinite number of other factors. Hence, once more, the assertion that this event is determined is equivalent to saying that these laws exist.

Our assertion that the future positions of the falling rock are predictable, that there are laws that connect these positions with antecedent events, is therefore ambiguous. For the statement lends itself to the following interpretations: (1) There is a law that connects (a) the positions of the falling rock with (b) its initial position at the edge of the cliff; (2) the law required by (1) exists, and there are laws that connect (b) the position of the rock at the edge of the cliff with (c) its initial position at the moment it is dislodged by the wind; (3) the laws required by (1) and (2) exist, and there are laws that connect (c) the position of the rock at the moment it is dislodged by the wind with (d) the previous states of the rock, wind pressure, etc. Interpretation (1) of our statement is consistent with the view that (b), the initial position at the edge of the cliff, is not determined; interpretation (2) with the view that (c), the initial position of the rock when dislodged, is not determined; and interpretation (3) with the view that (d), the collection of previous states, is not determined. Hence if our statement is to be incompatible with the statement of the indeterminist that (b) and therefore (a) is not determined, we must interpret it in accordance with (2); and if it is to be incompatible with the statement of the indeterminist that (c) and therefore (a) is not determined, we must interpret it in accordance with (3). In general, our statement that (*a*) can be predicted when event E is known is not incompatible with the statement of the indeterminist that (*a*) cannot be predicted because event E cannot be predicted. Our statement will be incompatible with that of the indeterminist only if it is equivalent to the statement that *every* event that is connected with (*a*) by one or more laws is itself connected with antecedent events by laws.

We are now in a position to resolve the ambiguity of the assertion that voluntary actions are determined. When we make the statement that motivated voluntary actions are determined we may intend to maintain one or the other of the following three alternatives:

(i) There are laws that connect (*a*) the action with (*b*) the motive, (*c*) the character and the dispositions of the person who acts, and (*d*) the circumstances under which he is acting.

(ii) The laws required by (i) exist; and there are laws that connect (*b*) the motive with (*c*) the character and the dispositions of the person who acts, and (*d*) the circumstances under which he is acting.

(iii) A. The laws required by (i) exist; and there are laws that connect (*b*), (*c*), and (*d*) with (*e*) the properties of events preceding (*d*).

    B. The laws required by (i) and (ii) exist; and there are laws that connect (*c*) and (*d*) with (*e*) the properties of events preceding (*d*).

When we make the statement that unmotivated voluntary actions are determined we may intend to maintain one or the other of the following two alternatives:

(iv) There are laws that connect (*a*) the action with (*c*) the character and dispositions of the person who acts, and (*d*) the circumstances under which he is acting.

(v) The laws required by (iv) exist; and there are laws that connect (*c*) and (*d*) with (*e*) the properties of events preceding (*d*).

A few explanatory comments will perhaps facilitate the understanding of this exposition of the different ways in which one can understand the propositions that voluntary acts are determined. If we understand this proposition in sense (i) we profess to be able to predict (*a*) when (*b*), (*c*), and (*d*) are known. We have noted that a knowledge of (*b*) alone, the motive of the act, is insufficient for the prediction of voluntary actions. It is also necessary to know (*d*), that the circumstances exist which make it possible to act on this motive. If the proposition be understood in sense (ii) we profess to be able to predict (*b*), the motive, when (*c*) and (*d*) are known, and hence also (*a*) by means of the laws whose existence is asserted in (i). It is obvious that we can predict (*a*) on the knowledge of (*c*) and (*d*) alone, if we are able to predict (*b*). According to (iii. A), we profess to be able to predict (*b*), (*c*), and (*d*), if we know the properties of events preceding (*d*). If there are laws of the kind required by (iii. A), we should be able to predict, for example, from our knowledge of present or past events, (*b*) the motive from which I shall act twenty-four hours from now, (c) my character and my dispositions, and (d) the circumstances which will make it possible for me to act on this motive. After these explanations the remaining alternatives should require no further comments.

An indeterminist could accept (i) and still claim that motivated voluntary actions are not determined, on the ground that there are no laws that permit the prediction of (b) the motive of the action. Our statement that motivated voluntary actions are determined must be understood in sense (ii) if it is to conflict with that of the indeterminist. If, however, the indeterminist should accept the predictability of motives, asserted by (ii), we should have to identify our statement with sense (iii), in order to get a statement that is incompatible with that of the indeterminist. There is no danger that the indeterminist would agree also with interpretation (iii). It is therefore unnecessary to interpret our statement as asserting the existence of laws that permit the prediction of (e) in order to get a proposition that is incompatible with that of the indeterminist.

If the indeterminist agrees with the determinist at all, his agreement is confined to (i) and (ii). As far as the statement that motivated voluntary actions are determined is concerned, it is certain that he disagrees with (iii). He may of course also disagree with formulations (i) and (ii), unless he has been impressed by the evidence in favor of the laws required by (i) and (ii). There is little doubt as to the attitude of the indeterminist regarding either formulation of the statement that unmotivated voluntary actions are predictable. Since he denies (iii), he will certainly also reject (v). And in view of the fact that we do not know the laws required by (iv) any more than we know those required by (v), we may take it for granted that he will also reject formulation (iv) of our statement.

The evidence in favor of the determination of voluntary acts   The indeterminist would have difficulty in supporting his disagreement with (i) and (ii). It must be admitted that we do not know the laws required by (i) and (ii), for otherwise we should be able to predict actions and motives with the same degree of reliability with which astronomers are able to predict eclipses. Our knowledge of the laws of volition is much too fragmentary to make predictions such as these possible. But it is nevertheless a fact that we are sometimes able to predict, with a fair degree of accuracy, what a man will do in a given set of circumstances. We feel almost certain that we can do this when we are acquainted with the man's character and dispositions and when we know his motive. Sometimes, indeed, we are even able to predict the motive from which he will act, when we know only his character, his dispositions, and the circumstances under which he is acting. Hence (i) and (ii) have at least some evidence in their favor. More often, to be sure, our predictions are not verified. However, we regard this as showing, not that indetermination is true of motivated voluntary acts, but only that our knowledge of the laws of volition and of human nature is imperfect. Motivated actions, we have found, do exhibit a considerable amount of regularity, and this fact justifies our presumption that the laws required by (i) and (ii) exist. The reason our predictions occasionally fail is not that these laws do not exist, but that we have an inadequate knowledge of them.

The indeterminist is in a somewhat better position to support his disagreement with (iii), (iv), and (v). For he can at least point out that we do not have even a fragmentary knowledge of the required laws. No one can predict the voluntary actions, whether motivated or unmotivated, that I shall perform during the next hour, or even during the next minute. There are no laws known to us that connect present or past events with my future actions. It must therefore be admitted that there is no evidence for either (iii) or (v). With respect to unmotivated actions, we are unable to predict the one that takes place even when we know the nature of the events that immediately precede the action. No one can predict that I will choose the letter "q" when I am engaged in choosing one of the letters of the word "oblique," no matter how much he knows about my character and my dispositions. Hence, there is likewise no evidence to support (iv). But is the lack of evidence a sufficient ground for denying (iii), (iv), and (v)? There was a time when we did not know the laws of planetary motion and were unable to predict the future positions of the planets. We could hardly have regarded our lack of knowledge as evidence that there were no such laws, or that the motions of the planets were chance occurrences. The fact that we had not as yet discovered them was no reason for inferring, either that they would never be discovered or that there were no such laws to discover. To date, we have failed to discover the laws required by (iii), (iv), and (v), but at some future time they may be discovered as were the laws of planetary motion.

We conclude, then, that the statement, voluntary acts are determined, is a presumption. It has some evidence in its favor when it is interpreted in accordance with (i) and (ii). It has no evidence in its favor when it is interpreted in accordance with one or the other of the remaining alternatives. If we believe it to be true when it is interpreted in accordance with those propositions also, it is only because we believe that the law of causality has no exceptions—that every event is connected with antecedent events by one or more laws. Anyway, the lack of evidence for these propositions is no evidence that they are false, as the indeterminist claims they are.

Free and constrained actions are both instances of determination   The presumption that voluntary acts are determined does not imply that voluntary acts, though apparently free, are in reality not free. Acts of free will are distinguished from compulsory actions, as a matter of fact, on the basis of the kinds of causes that determine them. My acts are free when they are determined by my own desires, intentions, and motives;

and they are constrained when they are determined by the desires, intentions, and motives of another person. It is not only that freedom, as well as compulsion, is compatible with the assumption of determination, but the distinction between them requires this assumption. For the distinction breaks down unless we assume the determination of voluntary action.

This conclusion is supported by the analogous distinction between "free" and "constrained" motion. The motion of a body is said to be "free" when its motion is completely determined by the initial conditions and the forces acting upon the body. It is said to be "constrained" when its motion is determined not only by the initial conditions and the forces acting upon the body, but also by conditions which are not directly expressible in terms of forces. According to these definitions the motions of a falling body, of a thrown body, of a planet, are free; the motion of a body rolling down an inclined plane, the motion of a train, the motion of an automobile, the motion of a pendulum are all constrained, since they are determined not alone by the forces acting on these bodies, but also by the plane, the rails, the road, or the arc of the pendulum. This is exactly analogous to the distinction between free and constrained action. The initial conditions and the forces that determine the free motion of a body correspond to the desires, intentions, and motives that determine my acts of free will. The conditions that are not directly expressible in terms of forces correspond to the desires, intentions, and motives of a person other than myself. When the motion of a body is determined not only by the former, but also by the latter set of conditions, its motion is constrained. And analogously, when my action is determined not only by my own desires, intentions, and motives, but also by the desires, intentions, and motives of another person, my action is constrained.

The distinction between free and constrained motion is a distinction between two kinds of determining causes. Since this distinction is exactly analogous to the distinction between free and constrained action, it follows that determination is destructive of freedom neither in mechanics nor in ethics, jurisprudence, and theology. The fears of moralists, jurists, and theologians are baseless; the determination of the will is not incompatible with its freedom. The freedom of the will, therefore, need not be timidly assumed as a moral postulate; free will is a psychological fact. If moralists complain that ethics requires the concept of "ought" and that "ought" implies "can," while determination supplies us only with an inexorable "must," we reply that they are confusing determination with compulsion. If jurists object that responsibility requires freedom and that determination is compulsion in disguise, we answer that compulsion is neither identical with determination nor implied by it. If theologians preach that the concepts of sin, repentance, atonement, reward and punishment would be nugatory, if voluntary acts were determined, we retort that there could be no sin, that atonement and repentance would be useless, and that the distribution of rewards and punishments would be a futile gesture, unless voluntary acts were determined.

6. FREEDOM AND RESPONSIBILITY

Responsibility
does not imply
indetermination

We can now deal rather briefly with questions (4) and (6). Question (4) asks: "Does responsibility imply indetermination?" Responsibility, we have said before, implies freedom; I am not responsible for acts I am forced to perform. Does it also imply indetermination? That the answer must be in the negative is shown by the following considerations. It will be recalled that punishment is justifiable when, and only when, I am responsible for my actions. But if my voluntary actions were not determined, it would be futile to punish me for them. To punish me for the crime of forgery, for example, would be useless unless the punishment tended to deter me from committing acts of forgery in the future. But if voluntary actions are not determined, my future actions are as unpredictable with the punishment as without it. I shall be just as likely to commit the act of forgery in the future, no matter if I am now punished for the commission of such an act, or the act is ignored, or I receive a reward for it. But if punishment accomplishes nothing, it is hard to see what one can mean by its justification. Responsibility therefore implies determination, rather than indetermination.

Repentance and
remorse do not
imply indeter-
mination

Question (6) asks: "Do repentance and remorse imply belief in the indetermination of voluntary acts?" In accordance with our analysis of the concept of determination, this question may be restated as follows: "When we feel repentant or remorseful, do we believe that there are no laws by means of which the act we repent could have been predicted?" It can be shown very easily that we believe nothing of the sort. Let us first examine our beliefs regarding acts of choice. Before I make a choice among a number of contemplated alternatives, I believe that I can choose any one of them. Both at the time of choice and afterwards, I believe that I could have chosen a different alternative if I had wanted to. Is the earlier belief, at the time of choice, a belief to the effect that there are no laws by means of which my future act can be predicted? Or is it simply the belief that I am free to choose any one of the possible alternatives and that my final choice will not be subject to compulsion? There is no doubt that what I believe in is the freedom and not the indetermination of my choice. Similarly, the later belief, after the choice has been made, is not a belief to the effect that my wanting to choose this rather than that alternative could not have been predicted. It is simply the belief that I was free when I made my choice, that the decision to choose the letter "q" rather than the letter "l" from the word "oblique," for example, was unconstrained, and that any other decision *I had wanted to make* would have been similarly unconstrained.

These conclusions remain unaffected in the special case when motives are present. Before I choose, I believe that I can act on any one of the competing motives. Does this mean anything more than that I believe my choice will be unconstrained? It surely does not mean that I believe my action will not be determined (at least partially) by the victorious motive. Furthermore, at the time of choice and afterwards, I believe that I could have acted on one of the competing motives, and that my action could have been different on that account. This again means no more than that I believe my choice was unconstrained. It is not a belief to the effect either that my choice is not determined by the victorious motive or that the victorious motive is not determined by antecedent events. It is perfectly plain that my choice would have been different had one of the other competing motives been victorious.

Let us turn next to our beliefs regarding voluntary acts that are not acts of choice. Before I act I believe that I can refrain from acting; both at the time of acting and afterwards I believe that I could have refrained from acting, if I had wanted to—these beliefs surely do not claim that I could have wanted to refrain from acting, or that my wanting to act, rather than refrain, was not determined by antecedent events. The presumption is merely that I was free—that I was not acting under compulsion.

These conclusions, too, remain unaffected in the special case when the act is motivated. Before I act, I believe that I can refrain from acting upon the motive. At the time of acting and afterwards I believe that I could have done so. These beliefs claim neither that motives do not determine actions, nor that motives are not determined by antecedent events. It is obvious that I could have refrained from acting or that my action would have been different, if the motive I did act on had been weaker than it was, or if some other motive had been present. These beliefs do not go so far as to maintain that this motive could have been weaker than it was, or that some other motive could have been present. They make only the modest claim that there was no one who compelled me to act as I did.

When the beliefs we have about voluntary actions accompany remorse or repentance they are very intense. We have shown that, in any event, they do not claim the indetermination of voluntary action. Since the greater intensity they have in the instance of remorse and repentance does not affect the claim they do make, we can answer question (6) in the negative.

Solution of the theological problems   It may be of interest to apply the distinction between determination and compulsion and that between indetermination and freedom to the solution of the theological problem we discussed earlier in this chapter. The problem may be stated in the form of four hypothetical propositions. (1) If God is good, then man is a free agent. (2) If man is a free agent, then God is not omniscient. (3) If God is omniscient, then man is not a free agent. (4) If man is not a free agent, then God is not good. From these four propositions theologians have drawn the conclusion that God cannot be at once good and omniscient. This conclusion will not follow if any of these propositions are false. And since (1) is equivalent to (4) and (2) is equivalent to (3) the conclusion will be false if either (1) or (2) should turn out to be false. It is not difficult to show that proposition (1) is true. If man were not a free agent, God would not be justified in meting out rewards and punishments for his actions, as He does, and He would therefore not be good. But proposition (2) is false. The thesis that God is not omniscient is supposed to be a consequence of the hypothesis that man is a free agent. If this thesis can be established at all it can only be established on the hypothesis of the indetermination of man's voluntary actions. Propositions (2) and (3) depend for their plausibility on the confusion between freedom and indetermination. On the supposition that man's voluntary actions are not determined, God would be unable to predict them if, like mundane scientists, He depended upon a knowledge of laws. If He is not so dependent (and there is no reason to suppose that He is), the indetermination of voluntary actions is no hindrance to his foreknowledge. For it follows from the law of excluded middle that in the instance of every one of my actions I either do *A* or I do *non-A*. If God has access to the truth, He can know which one of these alternatives is true. We conclude therefore, theologians to the contrary, that God's goodness is not incompatible with His omniscience.

Determinism and fatalism   It might be useful, finally, to call attention to the common mistake of identifying determinism—the thesis that every event is connected with antecedent events by one or more laws—with fatalism. Fatalism is a doctrine that is primarily concerned with the destiny of man. The doctrine holds that man's destiny is fixed, decided upon, and recorded in the big ledger of fate. Man's will is no match for the decrees of fate. It is futile to take measures for his welfare, his health, and his safety; for man is powerless to escape his fate. Determinism makes no such ominous statements. If we state the doctrine of fatalism in deterministic terms, it presumably holds that a man's voluntary actions are superfluous in determining the circumstances under which his history upon this earth will terminate. Determinism makes no such preposterous claim. Determinism holds instead that all events, not excepting voluntary actions, are connected with preceding as well as with subsequent events by laws. Hence a man's voluntary actions constitute one of the factors in the determination of his future history. In order to predict at the present moment the nature of his eventual demise, it would be necessary to know many more laws than we do know, and it would be necessary to ascertain the state of nature as a whole at this moment. But a complete description of this state would have to include our present resolve to bring this discussion to an end.

SUGGESTED FURTHER READINGS

BOOKS

AYER, A. J., *Language, Truth & Logic,* Oxford Univ. Press, 1936; 2nd ed., Gollancz, London, 1946.
——, *The Foundations of Empirical Knowledge,* The Macmillan Co., N.Y, 1940.
BLACK, M., *The Nature of Mathematics,* Harcourt, Brace and Co., N.Y., 1933.
BLANSHARD, B., *The Nature of Thought,* The Macmillan Co., N.Y., 1940, 2 vols.
BRIDGMAN, P. W., *The Logic of Modern Physics,* The Macmillan Co., N.Y., 1927.
BROAD, C. D., *Perception, Physics and Reality,* Cambridge Univ. Press, 1914.
——, *Scientific Thought,* Harcourt, Brace and Co., N.Y., 1923.
——, *The Mind and Its Place in Nature,* Harcourt, Brace and Co., N.Y., 1929.
——, *Five Types of Ethical Theory,* Harcourt, Brace and Co., N.Y., 1930.
——, *Determinism, Indeterminism, and Libertarianism,* Cambridge Univ Press, 1934.
——, *Examination of McTaggart's Philosophy,* Cambridge Univ. Press, 1934.
BUCHLER, J., *Charles Peirce's Empiricism,* Harcourt, Brace and Cc., N.Y., 1939.
CAMPBELL, N. R., *Physics; The Elements,* Cambridge Univ. Press, 1921.
CARNAP, R., *Der Logische Aufbau der Welt,* Berlin, 1928.
——, *Scheinprobleme in der Philosophie,* Berlin, 1928.
——, *Philosophy and Logical Syntax,* London, 1935.
——, *The Logical Syntax of Language,* Harcourt, Brace and Co., N.Y., 1937.
——, *Introduction to Semantics,* Harvard Univ. Press, 1942.
——, *Meaning and Necessity,* Univ. of Chicago Press, 1947.
——, "The Foundations of Logic and Mathematics", *Int. Encyclopedia of Unified Science,* Vol I, no. 3.
——, *Probability and Induction* (?), Univ. of Chicago Press, forthcoming.
CHURCHMAN, C. WEST, *Theory of Experimental Inference,* The Macmillan Co., 1948.
COHEN, M. R., *Reason and Nature,* Harcourt, Brace and Co., N.Y., 1931.
COLLINGWOOD, R. G., *An Essay on Metaphysics,* Oxford Univ. Press, 1940.
DRAKE, D. & OTHERS, *Essays in Critical Realism,* Peter Smith, N.Y., 1941.
EATON, R. M., *Symbolism and Truth,* Harvard Univ. Press, 1925.
——, *General Logic,* Charles Scribner's Sons, N.Y., 1931.
EINSTEIN, A., *Sidelights of Relativity,* Methuen and Co., London, 1922.
EWING, A. C., *Idealism,* Methuen and Co., London, 1934.
——, *The Meaning of Good,* The Macmillan Co., N.Y., 1947.
FARBER, M., *Foundations of Phenomenology,* Harvard Univ. Press, 1943.
FRANK, P., *Das Kausalgesetz und seine Grenzen,* Springer, Vienna, 1932.
——, *Between Physics and Philosophy,* Harvard Univ. Press, 1941.
——, "Foundations of Physics", *Int. Encyclopedia of Unified Science,* Vol. I, 7, 1947.
FREGE, G., *Die Grundlagen der Arithmetik,* Breslau, 1884.
——, *Die Grundgesetze der Arithmetik,* Vols. I and II, Jena, 1893, 1903.
HAHN, H., *Logik, Mathematik und Naturerkennen,* Vienna, 1925.
JAMES, W., *Pragmatism,* Longmans, Green and Co., N.Y., 1907.
——, *Essays in Radical Empiricism,* Longmans, Green and Co., N.Y., 1912.

JOHNSON, A. B., *Treatise on Language*, edited, with a critical essay, by D. Rynin, Univ. of California Press, 1947.

JOHNSON, W. E., *Logic*, Cambridge Univ. Press, 1924, 3 vols.

JORDAN, Z., *On the Development of Mathematical Logic and of Logical Positivism in Poland*, Oxford Univ. Press, 1946.

KAUFMANN, F., *Methodology of the Social Sciences*, Oxford Univ. Press, 1944.

KNEALE, W. C., *Probability and Induction* (?), Univ. of Chicago Press, forthcoming.

LEWIS, C. I., *Mind and the World Order*, Charles Scribner's Sons, N.Y., 1929.

——, *An Analysis of Knowledge and Valuation*, Open Court Publ., LaSalle, Ill., 1946.

LEWIS, C. I. & LANGFORD, C. H., *Symbolic Logic*, The Century Co., N.Y., 1932.

LOVEJOY, A. O., *The Revolt Against Dualism*, W. W. Norton and Co., N.Y., 1930.

MACH, E., *Contributions to the Analysis of Sensations*, Chicago, 1897.

MANDELBAUM, M., *The Problem of Historical Knowledge*, Liveright, N.Y., 1938.

MISES, R. VON, *Kleines Lehrbuch des Positivismus*, The Hague (Also Univ. of Chicago Press), 1939.

——, *Probability, Statistics and Truth*, The Macmillan Co., N.Y., 1939.

MOORE, G. E., *Philosophical Studies*, Harcourt, Brace and Co., N.Y., 1922.

——, *Principia Ethica*, Cambridge Univ. Press, 1903.

——, *Ethics*, Home University Library, 1912.

MORRIS, C. W., "Foundations of the Theory of Signs", *Int. Encyclopedia of Unified Science*, Vol. I, no. 2.

——, *Signs, Language, and Behavior*, Prentice-Hall, N.Y., 1946.

NICOD, J., *Foundations of Geometry and Induction*, Harcourt, Brace and Co., N.Y., 1930.

OGDEN, C. K. AND RICHARDS, I. A., *The Meaning of Meaning*, 5th ed. Harcourt, Brace and Co., N.Y., 1938.

PAP, A., *Introduction to Philosophical Analysis* (to be published).

——, *The A Priori in Physical Theory*, King's Crown Press, N.Y., 1946.

PEIRCE, C. S., *The Philosophy of*, ed. by J. Buchler, Harcourt, Brace and Co., N.Y., 1940.

——, *Collected Papers*, Harvard Univ. Press, 1931 ff. (ed. by Charles Hartshorne & Paul Weiss).

POINCARÉ, H., *The Foundations of Science*, Science Press, N.Y., 1929.

POPPER, K. R., *Logik der Forschung*, Vienna, 1935.

PRATT, C. C., *The Logic of Modern Psychology*, The Macmillan Co., N.Y., 1939.

——, *The Open Society*, Routledge & Son, London, 1945.

PRICE, H. H., *Perception*, Methuen, London, 1932.

——, *Hume's Theory of the External World*, London, 1940.

QUINE, W. V., *Mathematical Logic*, W. W. Norton and Co., N.Y., 1940.

RAMSEY, F. P., *The Foundations of Mathematics and Other Logical Essays*, Harcourt, Brace and Co., N.Y., 1931.

REICHENBACH, H., *Philosophie der Raum-Zeit-Lehre*, Berlin, 1928.

——, *Wahrsheinlichkeitslehre*, Leyden, 1935.

——, *Experience and Prediction*, Chicago, 1938.

——, *Symbolic Logic*, The Macmillan Co., N.Y., 1947.

ROSS, W. D., *The Foundations of Ethics*, Oxford Univ. Press, 1939.

RUNES, D. (ed.), *Twentieth Century Philosophy*, Philosophical Library, N.Y., 1943.

RUSSELL, B., *The Principles of Mathematics*, 2nd ed., W. W. Norton and Co., N.Y., 1938.

——, *Our Knowledge of the External World*, 2nd ed., W. W. Norton and Co., N.Y., 1929.

——, *Philosophy*, W. W. Norton and Co., N.Y., 1927.

——, *The Analysis of Mind*, London, 1921.

——, *Philosophical Essays*, Longmans, Green and Co., N.Y., 1910.

——, *Problems of Philosophy*, Home Univ. Library, 1912.

——, *An Inquiry into Meaning and Truth*, W. W. Norton and Co., N.Y., 1940.

——, *Mysticism and Logic*, W. W. Norton and Co., N.Y., 1929.

RYLE, G., *Philosophical Arguments*, Oxford Univ. Press, 1945.

RYNIN, D., *See* Johnson, A. B.

SCHAECHTER, J., *Prolegomena zu einer Kritischen Grammatik*, Springer, Vienna, 1938.

SCHILPP, P. (ed.), *The Philosophy of Bertrand Russell*, N.W. Univ. Press, 1944.

——, *The Philosophy of G. E. Moore*, N.W. Univ. Press, 1942.

SCHLICK, M., *Allgemeine Erkenntnislehre*, 2nd ed., Springer, Berlin, 1925.

——, *Gesammelte Aufsaetze*, Vienna, 1938.

——, *Problems of Ethics*, Prentice-Hall, N.Y., 1939.

SHARP, F. C., *Ethics*, The Century Co., N.Y., 1928.

SINGER, E. A., *Mind As Behavior*, Columbus, Ohio, 1924.

STACE, W. T., *Knowledge and Existence*, Oxford Univ. Press, 1932.

STEVENSON, C. L., *Ethics and Language*, Yale Univ. Press, 1944.

TARSKI, A., *Introduction to Logic and to the Methodology of the Deductive Sciences*, Oxford Univ. Press, 1941.

WAISMANN, F., *Einführung in das Mathematische Denken*, Vienna, 1936.

WERKMEISTER, W. H., *The Basis and Structure of Knowledge*, Harper and Bros., N.Y., 1948.

WHITEHEAD, A. N. AND RUSSELL, B., *Principia Mathematica*, 2nd ed., Cambridge, 1925-7, 3 vols.

WILLIAMS, D. C., *The Ground of Induction*, Harvard Univ. Press, 1947.

WITTGENSTEIN, L., *Tractatus Logico-Philosophicus*, Harcourt, Brace and Co., N.Y., 1922.

ARTICLES

The following abbreviations are used in this list:

Arist. Proc. for *Proceedings of the Aristotelian Society*
Arist. Suppl. for *Aristotelian Society, Supplementary Volumes*
Cal. Publ. in Phil. for *University of California Publications in Philosophy*
Erk. for *Erkenntnis*
Int. Jl. of Ethics for *International Journal of Ethics*
Jl. of Phil. for *The Journal of Philosophy*
Jl. of Symb. Log. for *Journal of Symbolic Logic*
Phil. and Phen. Res. for *Philosophy and Phenomenological Research*
Phil. Rev. for *The Philosophical Review*
Phil. of Sci. for *Philosophy of Science*
Psych. Rev. for *The Psychological Review*

ABRAHAM, A., "The Logic of Ethical Intuitionism", *Int. Jl. of Ethics* 44, 1933.

——, "A Note on the Fruitfulness of Deduction", *Phil. of Sci.* 3, 1936.

AJDUKIEWICZ, K., "Das Weltbild und die Begriffsapparatur", *Erk.* 4, 1934.

ALDRICH, V. C.,"Renegade Instances", *Phil. of Sci.* 3, 1936.

AYER, A. J., "Internal Relations", *Arist. Suppl.* 14, 1935.

——, "Does Philosophy Analyse Common Sense?" *Arist. Suppl.* 16, 1937.

————, "Other Minds", *Arist. Suppl.* 20, 1946.

BARRETT, W., "On the Existence of an External World", *Jl. of Phil.* 36, 1939.

BEHMANN, H., "Sind die Mathematischen Urteile Synthetisch?" *Erk.* 4, 1934.

BERGMANN, G., "Outline of an Empiricist Philosophy of Physics", *Amer. Jl. of Physics* 11, 1943.

————, "Psychoanalysis and Experimental Psychology", *Mind* 53, 1944.

————, "Holism, Historicism and Emergence", *Phil. of Sci.* 11, 1944.

————, "Remarks on Realism", *Phil. of Sci.* 13, 1946.

————, "Russell on Particulars", *Phil. Rev.* 56, 1947.

————, "Symposium on Probability", *Phil. and Phen. Res.* 6–7, 1945–46.

————, "Sense Data, Linguistic Conventions and Existence", *Phil. of Sci.* 14, 1947.

————, AND SPENCE, K. W., "The Logic of Psycho-Physical Measurement", *Psych. Rev.* 51, 1944.

BLACK, M., "Relations Between Logical Positivism and the Cambridge School of Analysis", *Jl. of Unified Science*, 1939.

————, "Conventionalism in Geometry", *Phil. of Sci.* 9, 1942.

————, "The Semantic Definition of Truth", *Analysis*, 1948.

BLUMBERG, A. E. AND FEIGL, H., "Logical Positivism", *Jl. of Phil.* 28, 1931.

BOHNERT, H. G., "The Semiotic Status of Commands", *Phil. of Sci.* 12, 1945.

BRAITHWAITE, R. B., "Propositions about Material Objects", *Arist. Proc.* 38, 1937–38.

BROAD, C. D., "Is Space Euclidean?" *Mind* 24, 1915.

————, "Induction and Probability", *Mind* 2, 27–29, 1918–20.

————, "Are There Synthetic *A Priori* Truths?" *Arist. Suppl.* 15, 1936.

————, "Mechanical and Teleological Explanation", *Arist. Suppl.* 14, 1935.

————, "Kant's Theory of Mathematical and Philosophical Reasoning", *Arist. Proc.* 41, 1941–42.

BRITTON, K., "Are Necessary Truths True by Convention?" *Arist. Suppl.* 21, 1947.

BURES, C., "The Concept of Probability", *Phil. of Sci.* 6, 1939.

CARNAP, R., "*Die Alte und die Neue Logik*", *Erk.* 1, 1930.

————, "*Ueber Protokollsaetze*", *Erk.* 3, 1932.

————, "Von der Erkenntnistheorie zur Wissenschaftslogik", *Actes du Congrès International de Philosophie Scientifique*, Paris, 1936.

————, Les Concepts Psychologiques et les Concepts Physiques, sont ils Foncièrement Differents?" *Revue de Synthèse*, 1935.

————, "Testability and Meaning", *Phil. of Sci.* 3–4, 1936–37.

————, "Symposium on Probability", *Phil. and Phen. Res.* 6–7, 1945–46.

————, "Formalwissenschaft und Realwissenschaft", *Erk.* 5, 1935.

————, "Probability as a Guide in Life", *Jl. of Phil.* 44, 1947.

————, "On Inductive Logic", *Phil. of Sci.* 12, 1945.

————, "On the Application of Inductive Logic", *Phil. and Phen. Res.* 8, 1947

CASTELL, A., "Philosophy As Theory of Criticism", *Phil. Rev.* 51, 1942.

CHISHOLM, R., "The Problem of the Speckled Hen", *Mind* 51, 1942.

COLLINGWOOD, R. G., "On the So-called Idea of Causation", *Arist. Proc.* 38, 1937–8.

CREED, ISABEL P., "The Justification of the Habit of Induction", *Jl. of Phil.* 37, 1940.

DALKEY, N., "Symposium on Meaning and Truth", *Phil. and Phen. Res.* 4–5, 1943–44.

DENNES, W. R., "The Appeal to Reason", *Cal. Publ. in Phil.* 21, 1939.

DEWEY, J., "The Existence of the External World as a Logical Problem", *Phil. Rev.* 24, 1915.
———, "How Is Mind To Be Known", *Jl. of Phil.* 39, 1942.
DUCASSE, C. J., "The Attributes of Material Things", *Jl. of Phil.* 31, 1934.
———, "Verification, Verifiability and Meaningfulness", *Jl. of Phil.* 33, 1936.
———, "On the Method of Knowledge in Philosophy", *Cal. Publ. in Phil.* 16, 1940.
———, "Symposium on Meaning and Truth", *Phil. and Phen. Res.* 4–5, 1943–44.
———, "Propositions, Opinions, Sentences and Facts", *Jl. of Phil.* 37, 1940.
EWING, A. C., "A Defense of Causality", *Arist. Proc.* 33, 1932–33.
———, " Meaninglessness", *Mind* 46, 1937.
———, "A Suggested Non-Naturalistic Analysis of Good", *Mind* 48, 1939.
———, "The Linguistic Theory of the *A Priori*", *Arist. Proc.* 40, 1939–40.
———, "The Causal Argument for Physical Objects", *Arist. Suppl.* 19, 1945.
FARRELL, B. A., "An Appraisal of Therapeutic Positivism", *Mind* 55, 1946.
FEIGL, H., "Sense and Nonsense in Scientific Realism", *Actes du Congrès International de Philosophie Scientifique*, Paris, 1936.
FEIGL, H. AND BLUMBERG, A. E., "Logical Positivism", *Jl. of Phil.* 28, 1931.
FINDLAY, J. N., "Morality by Convention", *Mind* 54, 1944.
FRANK, P., "Why Do Scientists and Philosophers So Often Disagree?" *Review of Mod. Physics* 13, 1941.
FRANKENA, W., "The Naturalistic Fallacy", *Mind* 48, 1939.
FREGE, G., "Ueber Begriff und Gegenstand", *Vierteljahrsschrift fuer Wissenschaftliche Philosophie*, 1892.
GOMPERZ, H., "Interpretation", *Erk.* 7, 1938.
———, "Some Simple Thoughts on Freedom and Responsibility", *Philosophy* 12, 1937.
———, "Individual and Collective Responsibility", *Ethics* 50, 1939.
———, "The Meanings of 'Meaning' ", *Phil. of Sci.* 8, 1941.
———, "When Does the End Sanctify the Means?" *Ethics* 54, 1943.
GOODMAN, N., "The Problem of Counterfactual Conditionals", *Jl. of Phil.* 44, 1947.
GRELLING, K., "Identitas Indiscernibilium", *Erk.* 6, 1937.
HALL, E. W., "Metaphysics", in *Twentieth Century Philosophy*, Phil. Library, 1943, ed. by D. Runes.
———, "Stevenson on Disagreement in Attitude", *Ethics* 58, 1947.
HARDIE, C. D., "The Necessity of *A Priori* Propositions", *Arist. Proc.* 39, 1938–39.
HARDIE, W. F. R., "The Paradox of Phenomenalism", *Arist. Proc.* 46, 1945–46.
HAYEK, F. VON, "The Facts of the Social Sciences", *Ethics* 54, 1943.
HEMPEL, C., "Vagueness and Logic", *Phil. of Sci.* 6, 1939.
———, "Studies in the Logic of Confirmation", *Mind* 54, 1945.
———, "The Logical Positivist's Theory of Truth", *Analysis*, 1935.
——— AND OPPENHEIM, P., "Studies in the Logic of Explanation", *Phil. of Sci.* 15, 1948.
HENLE, P., "The Status of Emergence", *Jl. of Phil.* 39, 1942.
———, "On the Certainty of Empirical Statements", *Jl. of Phil.* 44, 1947.
HOBART, R. E., "Free Will As Involving Determinism and Inconceivable Without It", *Mind* 43, 1934.
———, "Hume Without Scepticism", *Mind* 39, 1930.
HOSPERS, J., "On Explanation", *Jl. of Phil.* 43, 1946.
KAPLAN, A., "Are Ethical Judgments Assertions?" *Phil. Rev.* 51, 1942.
———, "Definition and Specification of Meaning", *Jl. of Phil.* 43, 1946.

KAUFMANN, F., "Symposium on Probability", *Phil. and Phen. Res.* 6–7, 1945–46.

KNEALE, W. C., "The Notion of a Substance", *Arist. Proc.* 40, 1939–40.

———, "Truths of Logic", *Arist. Proc.* 46, 1945–46.

———, "Are Necessary Truths True by Convention?" *Arist. Suppl.* 21, 1947.

KOEHLER, W., "Ein Altes Scheinproblem", *Die Naturwissenschaften*, 1929.

LANGFORD, C. H., "The Notion of Analysis in Moore", in *The Philosophy of G. E. Moore*, Northwestern Univ. Press, 1942.

LAZEROWITZ, M., "The Existence of Universals", *Mind* 55, 1946.

LENZEN, V. F., "The Hypothesis of Dualism", *Phil. of Sci.* 6, 1939.

———, "Experience and Convention", *Erk.* 7, 1938.

LEWIS, C. I., "Alternative Logics", *Monist*, 1932.

———, "Symposium on Meaning and Truth", *Phil. and Phen. Res.* 4–5, 1943–44.

LEWY, C., "Why Are the Calculuses of Logic and Mathematics Applicable to Reality?" *Arist. Suppl.* 20, 1946.

LOVEJOY, A. O., "The Meaning of Emergence and Its Modes", *Philosophy* 2, 1927.

MACDONALD, M., "Verification and Understanding", *Arist. Proc.* 34, 1933–34.

———, "The Philosopher's Use of Analogy", *Arist. Proc.* 38, 1937–38.

McGILVARY, E. B., "Freedom and Necessity in Human Affairs", *Int. Jl. of Ethics* 55, 1935.

MALCOLM, N., "The Nature of Entailment", *Mind* 49, 1940.

———, "Are Necessary Propositions Really Verbal?" *Mind* 51, 1942.

———, "Certainty and Empirical Statements", *Mind* 51, 1942.

MARGENAU, H., "Symposium on Probability", *Phil. and Phen. Res.* 6–7, 1945–46.

MARHENKE, P., "McTaggart's Analysis of Time", *Cal. Publ. in Phil.* 17, 1934.

MENGER, K., "The New Logic", *Phil. of Sci.* 4, 1937.

MILLER, D. S., "An Event in Philosophy", *Phil. Rev.* 54, 1945.

———, "Professor Donald Williams versus Hume", *Jl. of Phil.* 44, 1947.

MISES, R. VON, "Symposium on Probability", *Phil. and Phen. Res.* 6–7, 1945–46.

MOORE, G. E., "A Defense of Common Sense", in *Contemporary British Philosophy*, vol. II, ed. by Muirhead, G. Allen & Unwin, London.

MORRIS, C. W., "The Concept of Meaning in Pragmatism and Positivism", *Actès du Congrès International de Philosophie Scientifique*, Paris, 1936.

NAGEL, E., "The Frequency Theory of Probability", *Jl. of Phil.* 30, 1933.

———, "The Meaning of Probability", *Jl. of Amer. Statist. Assn.* 31, 1936.

———, "The Logic of Reduction", *Erk.* 5, 1936.

———, "Impressions and Appraisals of European Philosophy", *Jl. of Phil.* 33, 1936.

———, "Symposium on Meaning and Truth", *Phil. and Phen. Res.* 4–5, 1943–44.

———, "Symposium on Probability", *Phil. and Phen. Res.* 6–7, 1945–46.

NELSON, E. J., "A Defense of Substance", *Phil. Rev.* 56, 1947.

OPPENHEIM, P., *See* Hempel, C.

PAP, A., "The Different Kinds of *A Priori*", *Phil. Rev.* 53, 1944.

———, "The Verifiability of Value Judgments", *Ethics* 56, 1946.

———, "A Semantic Examination of Realism", *Jl. of Phil.* 44, 1947.

PARKER, D. H., "Knowledge by Acquaintance", *Phil. Rev.* 54, 1945.

———, "Knowledge by Description", *Phil. Rev.* 54, 1945.

PAUL, G. A., "Is There a Problem of Sense Data?" *Arist. Soc. Suppl.* 15, 1936.

POPPER, K. R., "What Is Dialectic?" *Mind* 49, 1940.

———, "The Poverty of Historicism", *Economica*, 1943.

———, "Why Are the Calculuses of Logic and Mathematics Applicable to Reality?" *Arist. Suppl.* 20, 1946.

PORTEOUS, A. J. D., "The Idea of Necessary Connection", *Arist. Proc.* 35, 1934–5.

PRICHARD, H. A., "Does Moral Philosophy Rest on a Mistake?" *Mind* 21, 1912.
QUINE, W. V., "Notes on Existence", *Jl. of Phil.* 40, 1943.
———, "Universals", *Jl. of Symb. Log.* 12, 1947.
———, "The Problem of Interpreting Modal Logic", *Jl. of Symb. Log.* 12, 1947.
REICHENBACH, H., "Logistic Empiricism in Germany", *Jl. of Phil.* 33, 1936.
———, "Symposium on Probability", *Phil. and Phen. Res.* 6–7, 1945–46.
REID, J. R., "What Are Definitions?" *Phil. of Sci.* 13, 1946.
ROSSER, B., "An Informal Exposition of Proofs of Gödel's Theorems and Church's Theorem", *Jl. of Symb. Logic* 4, 1939.
RUSSELL, B., "The Philosophy of Logical Atomism", *Monist* 28, 1918.
———, "The Limits of Empiricism", *Arist. Proc.* 36, 1935–36.
———, "On the Relations of Universals and Particulars", *Arist. Proc.* 12, 1911–12.
———, "The Experience of Time", *Monist* 27, 1917.
RYLE, G., "Internal Relations", *Arist. Suppl.* 14, 1935.
———, "Induction and Hypothesis", *Arist. Suppl.* 16, 1937.
———, "Why Are the Calculuses of Logic and Mathematics Applicable to Reality?" *Arist. Suppl.* 20, 1946.
SCHLICK, M., "A New Philosophy of Experience", *College of the Pacific Publ. in Phil.* 1, 1932.
———, "The Future of Philosophy", *College of the Pacific Publ. in Phil.* 1, 1932.
———, "Facts and Propositions", *Analysis*, 1935.
SELLARS, R. W., "The Double Knowledge Approach to the Mind-Body Problem", *Arist. Proc.* 1922.
———, "An Analytic Approach to the Mind-Body Problem", *Phil. Rev.* 48, 1939.
SELLARS, W. S., "Pure Pragmatics and Epistemology", *Phil. of Sci.* 14, 1947.
———, "Epistemology and the New Way of Words", *Jl. of Phil.* 44, 1947.
———, "Concepts as Involving Laws and Inconceivable Without Them", *Phil. of Sci.* 15, 1948.
SHARP, F. C., "Voluntarism and Objectivity in Ethics", *Phil. Rev.* 50, 1941.
SKINNER, B. F., "Symposium on Operationism", *Psych. Rev.* 52, 1945.
SPENCE, K. W., *See* Bergmann, G.
STACE, W. T., "Positivism", *Mind* 54, 1945.
———, "Are All Empirical Statements Hypotheses?" *Jl. of Phil.* 44, 1947 (See also Henle, P., "On the Certainty of Empirical Statements", listed above.)
STEBBING, L. S., "Some Ambiguities in Discussions Concerning Time", in *Philosophy and History*, Oxford Univ. Press, 1936.
STEVENSON, C. L., "The Emotive Meaning of Ethical Terms", *Mind* 46, 1937.
———, "Ethical Judgments and Avoidability", *Mind* 47, 1938.
———, "Some Relations Between Philosophy and the Study of Language", *Analysis*, 1947.
STORER, T., "The Logic of Value Propositions", *Phil. of Sci.* 13, 1946.
STOUT, A. K., "Free Will and Responsibility", *Arist. Proc.* 37, 1936–37.
URBAN, W., "Symposium on Meaning and Truth", *Phil. and Phen. Res.* 4–5, 1943–4.
URMSON, J. O., "Are Necessary Truths True by Convention?" *Arist. Suppl.* 21, 1947.
WAISMANN, F., "Logische Analyse des Wahrscheinlichkeitsbegriffs", *Erk.* 1, 1930.
———, "Ueber den Begriff der Identitaet", *Erk.* 6, 1936.
———, "Ist die Logik eine Deduktive Theorie?" *Erk.* 7, 1938.
———, "Verifiability", *Arist. Suppl.* 19, 1945.

———, "Are There Alternative Logics?" *Arist. Proc.* 46, 1945–46.
WHITE, M. G., "Historical Explanation", *Mind* 52, 1943.
WILL, F., "Is There a Problem of Induction?" *Jl. of Phil.* 39, 1942.
WILLIAMS, D. C., "The Argument for Realism", *Monist*, 1934.
———, "Symposium on Probability", *Phil. and Phen. Res.* 6–7, 1945–46.
WISDOM, J., "Philosophical Perplexity", *Arist. Proc.* 36, 1935.
———, "Metaphysics and Verification", *Mind* 47, 1938.
———, "Other Minds", *Mind* 49–52, 1940–43.
———, "Other Minds", *Arist. Suppl.* 20, 1946.
WITTGENSTEIN, L., "Logical Form", *Arist. Proc.* 1929.